Pichi Pichi Pitch 6

MANGA BY PINK HANAMORI
SCENARIO BY MICHIKO YOKOTE

Translated and adapted by William Flanagan

Lettered by Min Choi

DEL REY

BALLANTINE BOOKS • NEW YORK

A Del Rey Trade Paperback Original

Pichi Pichi Pitch copyright © 2005 by Pink Hanamori, Michiko Yokote, Kodansha Ltd., and We've.

English translation copyright © 2007 by Pink Hanamori, Michiko Yokote, Kodansha Ltd., and We've.

All rights reserved.

Published in the United States by Del Rey Books, an imprint of The Random House Publishing Group, a division of Random House, Inc., New York.

DEL REY is a registered trademark and the Del Rey colophon is a trademark of Random House, Inc.

Publication rights arranged through Kodansha Ltd.

First published in Japan in 2005 by Kodansha Ltd., Tokyo.

ISBN 978-0-345-49201-2

Printed in the United States of America

www.delreymanga.com

9 8 7 6 5 4 3 2 1

Translator/Adaptor—William Flanagan
Lettering—Min Choi
Original cover design—Akiko Omo

Contents

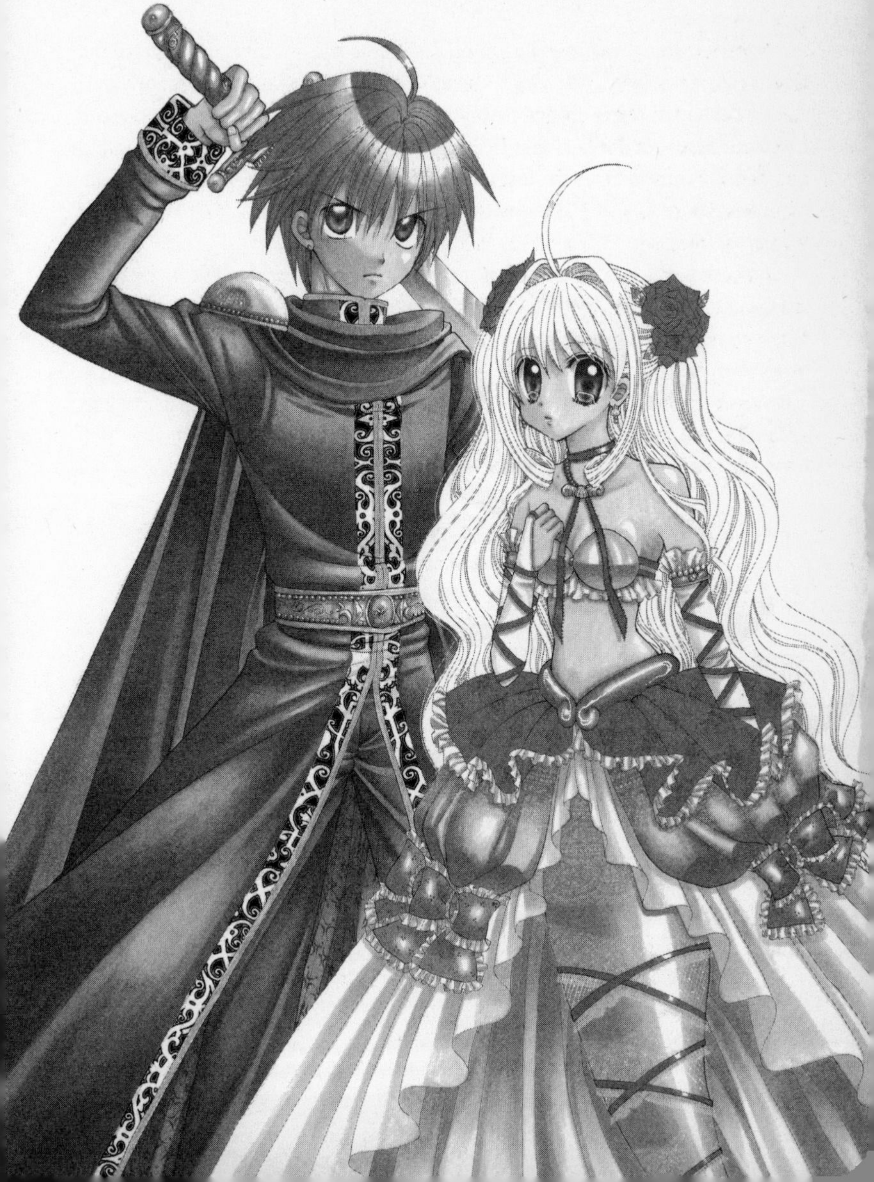

Honorifics Explained

Throughout the Del Rey Manga books, you will find Japanese honorifics left intact in the translations. For those not familiar with how the Japanese use honorifics and, more important, how they differ from American honorifics, we present this brief overview.

Politeness has always been a critical facet of Japanese culture. Ever since the feudal era, when Japan was a highly stratified society, use of honorifics—which can be defined as polite speech that indicates relationship or status—has played an essential role in the Japanese language. When addressing someone in Japanese, an honorific usually takes the form of a suffix attached to one's name (example: "Asuna-san"), or as a title at the end of one's name, or in place of the name itself (example: "Negi-sensei," or simply "Sensei!").

Honorifics can be expressions of respect or endearment. In the context of manga and anime, honorifics give insight into the nature of the relationship between characters. Many English translations leave out these important honorifics, and therefore distort the feel of the original Japanese. Because Japanese honorifics contain nuances that English honorifics lack, it is our policy at Del Rey not to translate them. Here, instead, is a guide to some of the honorifics you may encounter in Del Rey Manga.

-san: This is the most common honorific, and is equivalent to Mr., Miss, Ms., or Mrs. It is the all-purpose honorific and can be used in any situation where politeness is required.

-sama: This is one level higher than "-san" and is used to confer great respect.

-dono: This comes from the word "tono," which means "lord." It is an even higher level than "-sama" and confers utmost respect.

-kun: This suffix is used at the end of boys' names to express familiarity or endearment. It is also sometimes used by men among friends, or when addressing someone younger or of a lower station.

-chan: This is used to express endearment, mostly toward girls. It is also used for little boys, pets, and even among lovers. It gives a sense of childish cuteness.

Bozu: This is an informal way to refer to a boy, similar to the English terms "kid" or "squirt."

Sempai/: This title suggests that the addressee is one's senior in a group
Senpai   or organization. It is most often used in a school setting, where
          underclassmen refer to their upperclassmen as "sempai." It can also be
          used in the workplace, such as when a newer employee addresses an
          employee who has seniority in the company.

Kohai: This is the opposite of "-sempai," and is used toward underclassmen in
          school or newcomers in the workplace. It connotes that the addressee is
          of a lower station.

Sensei: Literally meaning "one who has come before," this title is used for
          teachers, doctors, or masters of any profession or art.

[blank]: This is usually forgotten in these lists, but it is perhaps the most
          significant difference between Japanese and English. The lack of
          honorific means that the speaker has permission to address the person
          in a very intimate way. Usually, only family, spouses, or very close
          friends have this kind of permission. Known as *yobisute,* it can be
          gratifying when someone who has earned the intimacy starts to call one
          by one's name without an honorific. But when that intimacy hasn't been
          earned, it can be very insulting.

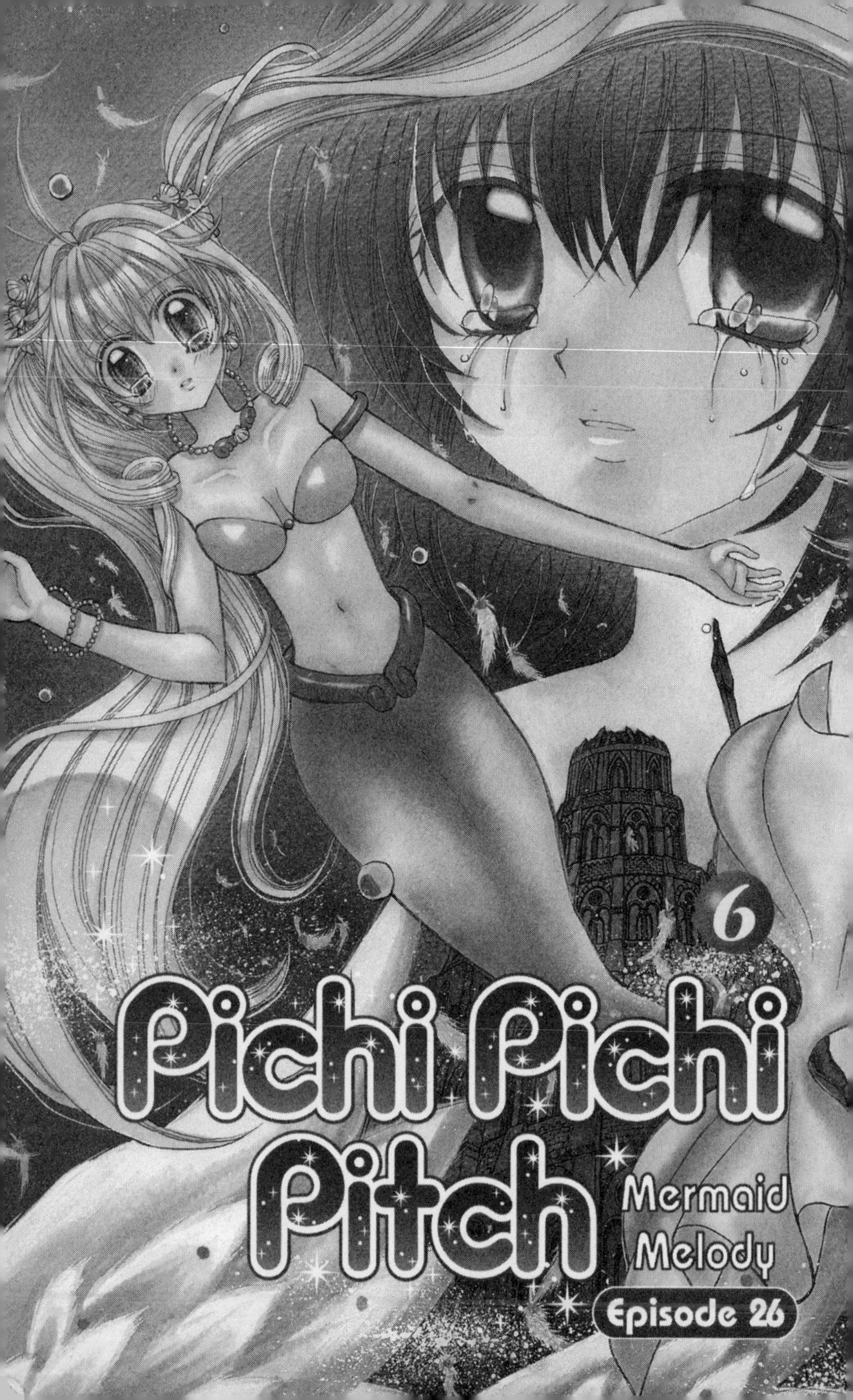
6
Pichi Pichi Pitch
Mermaid Melody
Episode 26

PEARL BATHS ♥

LUCIA'S BATH-WORKER DIARY

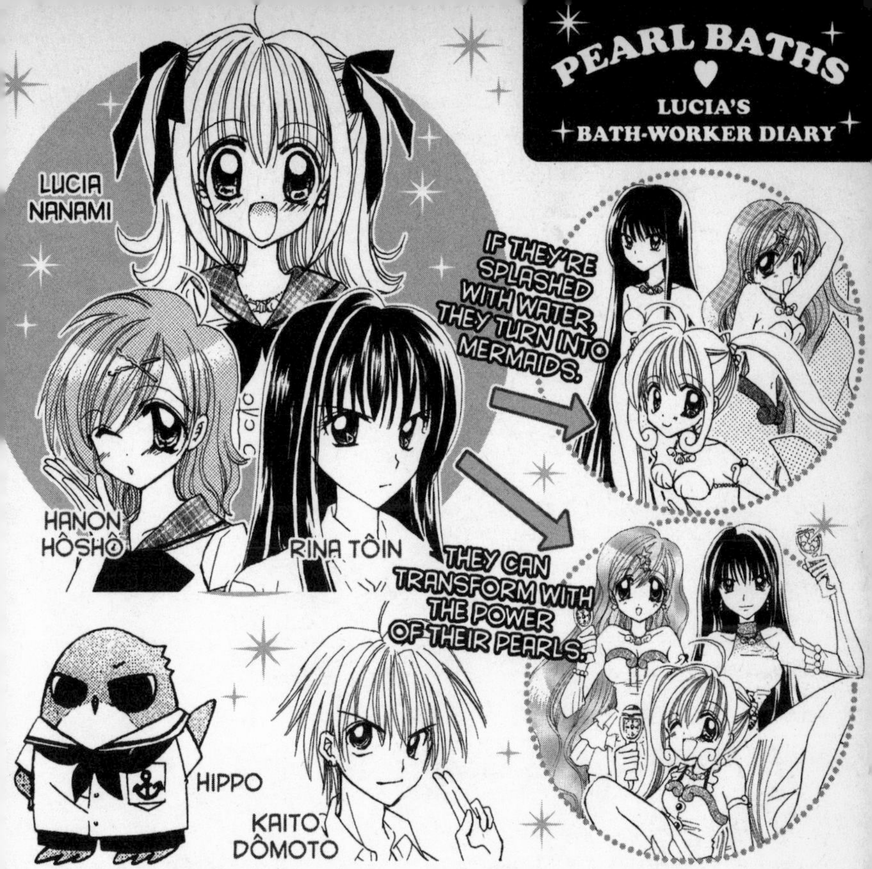
LUCIA NANAMI
IF THEY'RE SPLASHED WITH WATER, THEY TURN INTO MERMAIDS.
THEY CAN TRANSFORM WITH THE POWER OF THEIR PEARLS.
HANON HÔSHÔ
RINA TÔIN
HIPPO
KAITO DÔMOTO

★ LUCIA IS THE PRINCESS OF THE NORTH PACIFIC, ONE OF THE SEVEN MERMAID COUNTRIES. AFTER A TERRIBLE BATTLE WITH GACKTO, KAITO FINALLY REALIZES THAT LUCIA WAS HIS FIRST LOVE, A MERMAID WHO RESCUED HIM YEARS AGO, AND THE TWO BEGIN TO SHARE A ROMANCE. ♡

★ BUT AN ACCIDENT HAPPENED DURING A SURFING COMPETITION, AND KAITO, WHO LOST ALL MEMORY OF LUCIA, BEGAN LIVING WITH THE FAMILY OF HIS RESCUER, MICHAL. AND A NEW ENEMY, MICHEL, HAS STOLEN PIECES OF THE HEART OF THE NEW PRINCESS OF THE INDIAN OCEAN, SEIRA!

★ NOW IN A DESPERATE STRUGGLE, CAN LUCIA'S FEELINGS BRING BACK KAITO'S MEMORY?

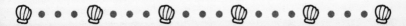

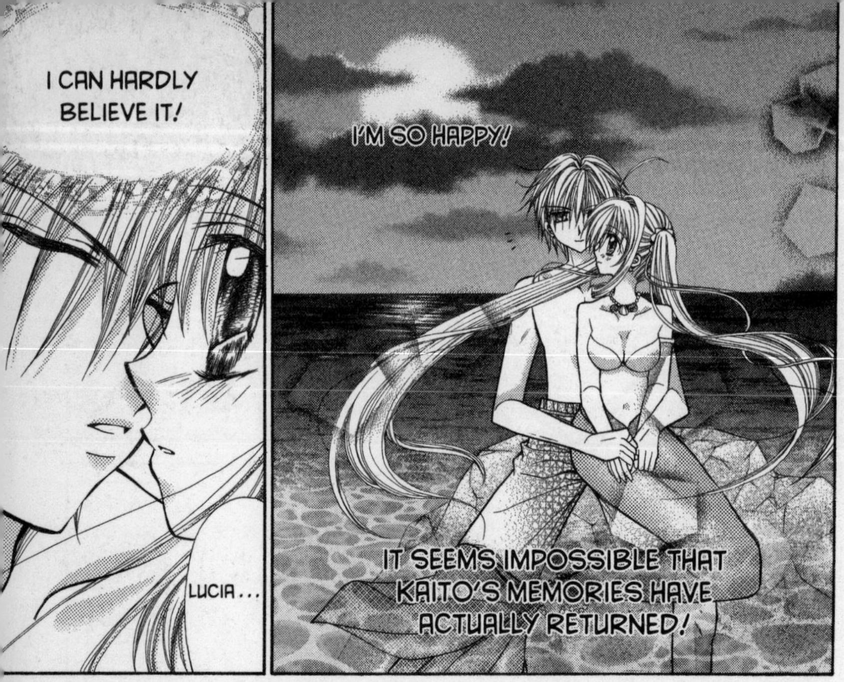
I'M SO HAPPY!
IT SEEMS IMPOSSIBLE THAT KAITO'S MEMORIES HAVE ACTUALLY RETURNED!
I CAN HARDLY BELIEVE IT!
LUCIA...

✱ LIPS ✱ GREETINGS!

HELLO TO THE PEOPLE COMING BACK AFTER SO LONG,
AND TO THOSE READING FOR THE FIRST TIME!
MY NAME IS PINK HANAMORI. BOW.
VOLUME 6 HAS ARRIVED!

<EPISODE 26>
FOR THE SPLASH PAGE, I PAINTED THE HAIR
JUST A LITTLE DIFFERENTLY THAN I USUALLY DO.
I ASKED MY EDITOR, K-SHI ME! TO WRITE
TARÔ-CHAN'S NAME ON THE LETTER.
THE LETTERS FOR HIPPO THAT YOU'LL SEE IN VOLUME
7 ARE WRITTEN BY OUR MASCOT ASSISTANT. I ASKED
THOSE PEOPLE WHO FIT MY IMAGE OF THE CHARACTERS
(TO WRITE THE LETTERS).

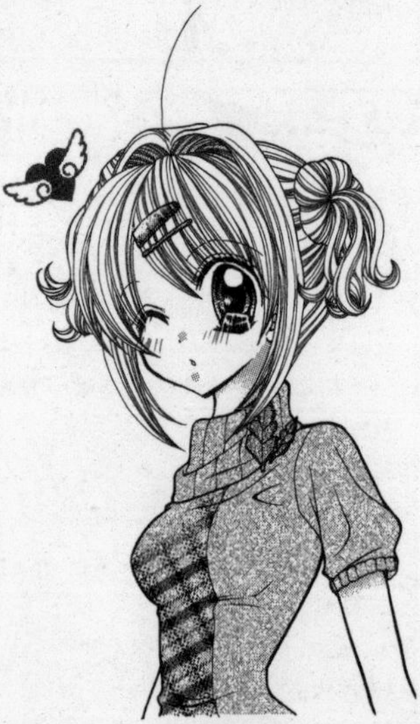

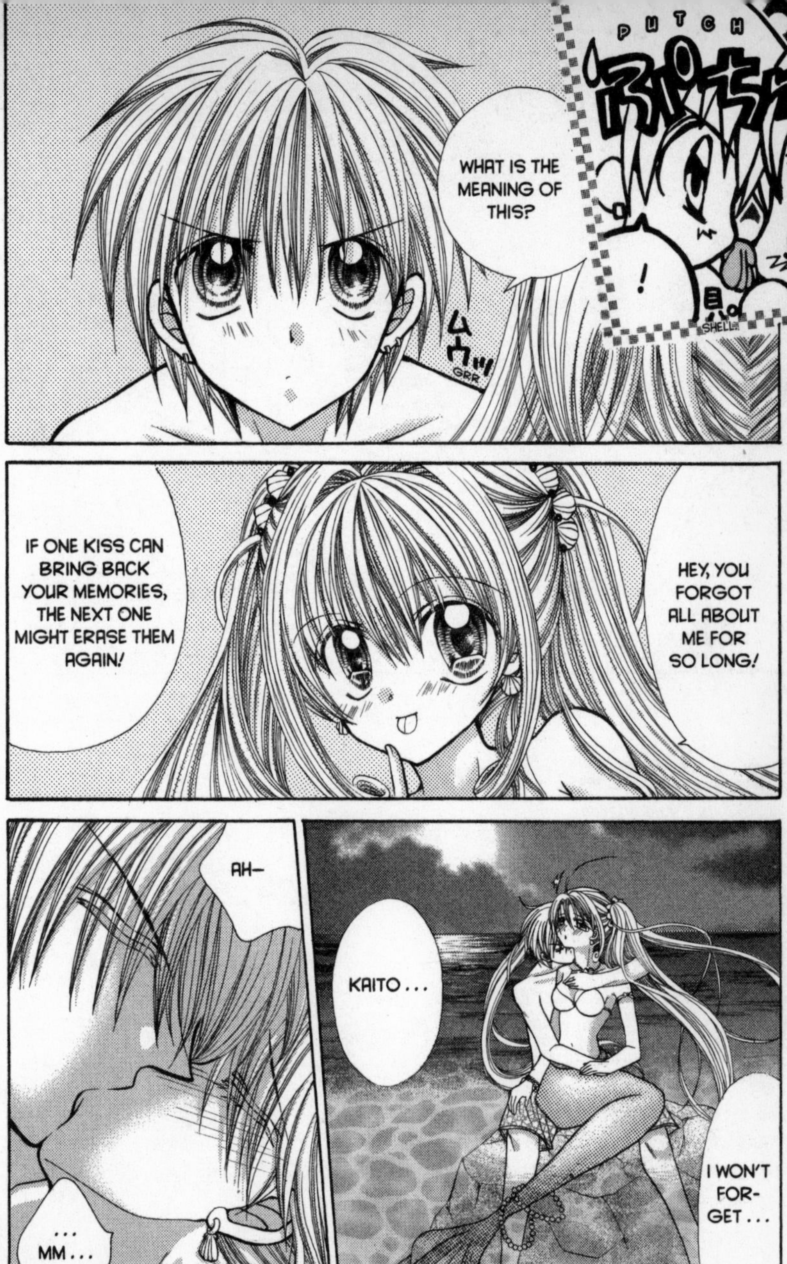
PUTCH
SHELL!
WHAT IS THE MEANING OF THIS?
GRR
HEY, YOU FORGOT ALL ABOUT ME FOR SO LONG!
IF ONE KISS CAN BRING BACK YOUR MEMORIES, THE NEXT ONE MIGHT ERASE THEM AGAIN!
KAITO . . .
I WON'T FOR-GET . . .
AH—
. . . MM . . .

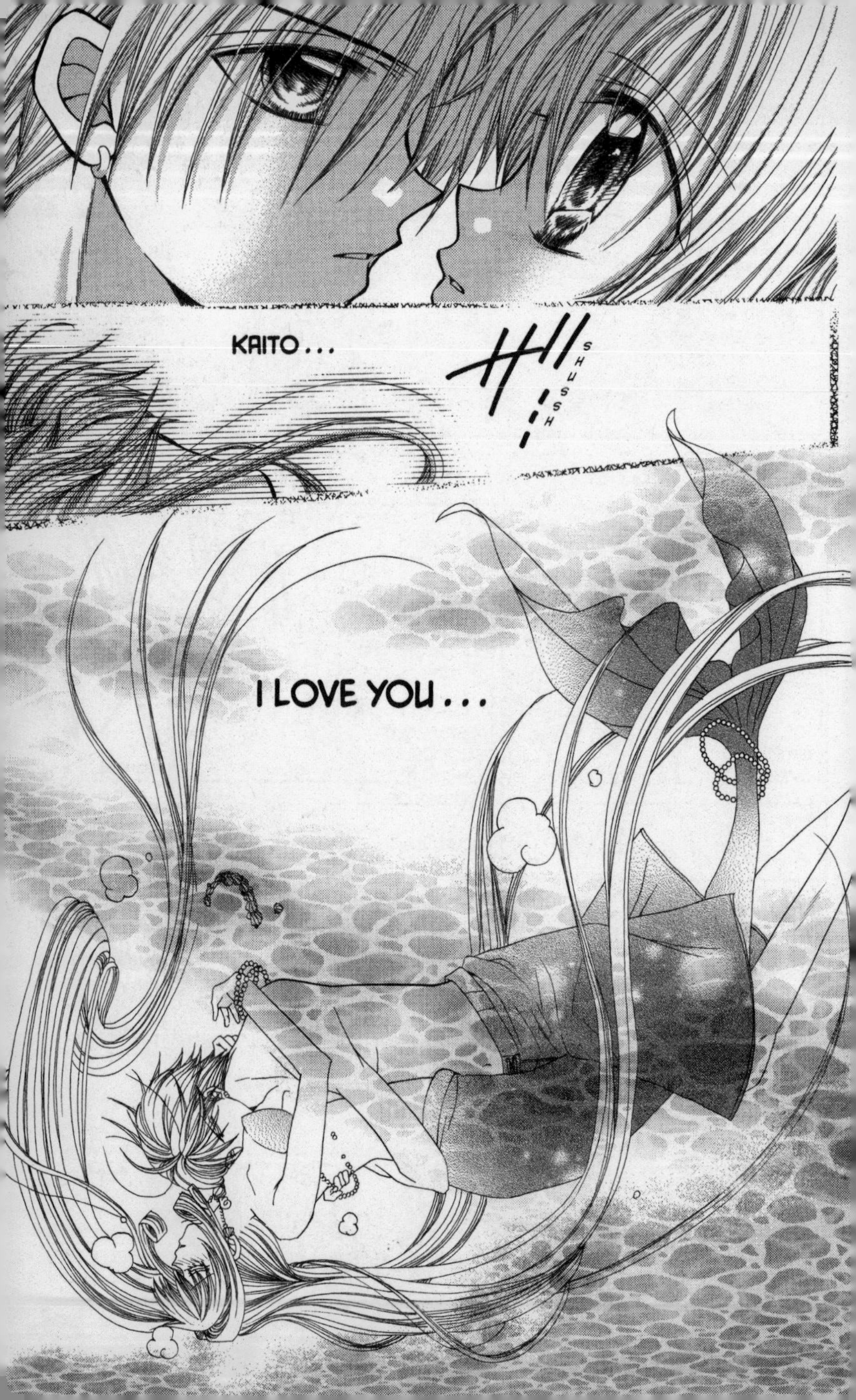
SHUSSH
KAITO...
I LOVE YOU...

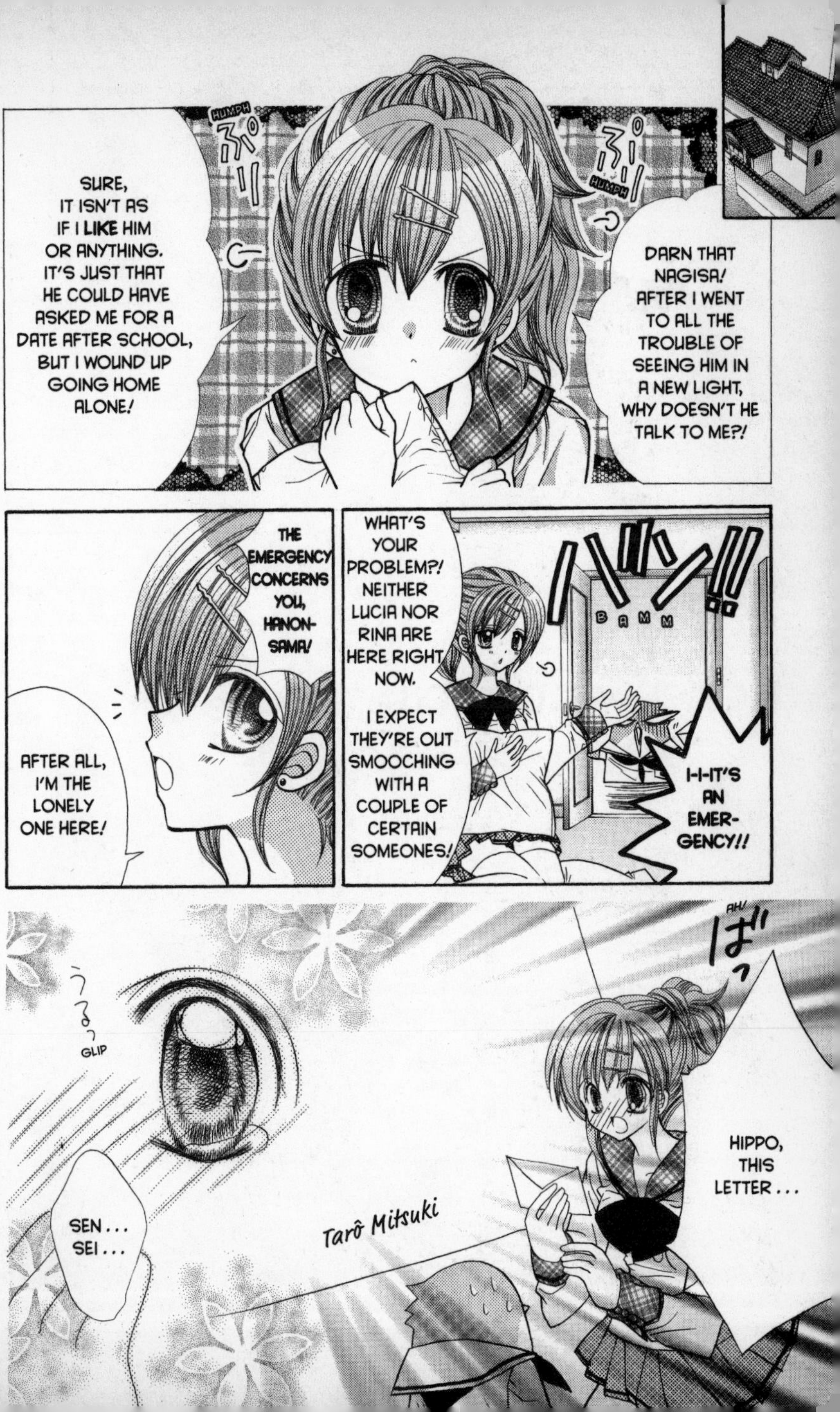

ぷい HUMPH
DARN THAT NAGISA! AFTER I WENT TO ALL THE TROUBLE OF SEEING HIM IN A NEW LIGHT, WHY DOESN'T HE TALK TO ME?!
ぷい HUMPH
SURE, IT ISN'T AS IF I LIKE HIM OR ANYTHING. IT'S JUST THAT HE COULD HAVE ASKED ME FOR A DATE AFTER SCHOOL, BUT I WOUND UP GOING HOME ALONE!
BAMM
I-I-IT'S AN EMERGENCY!!
WHAT'S YOUR PROBLEM?! NEITHER LUCIA NOR RINA ARE HERE RIGHT NOW.
I EXPECT THEY'RE OUT SMOOCHING WITH A COUPLE OF CERTAIN SOMEONES!
THE EMERGENCY CONCERNS YOU, HANON-SAMA!
AFTER ALL, I'M THE LONELY ONE HERE!
ばっ AH!
HIPPO, THIS LETTER...
Tarô Mitsuki
うるっ GLIP
SEN... SEI...

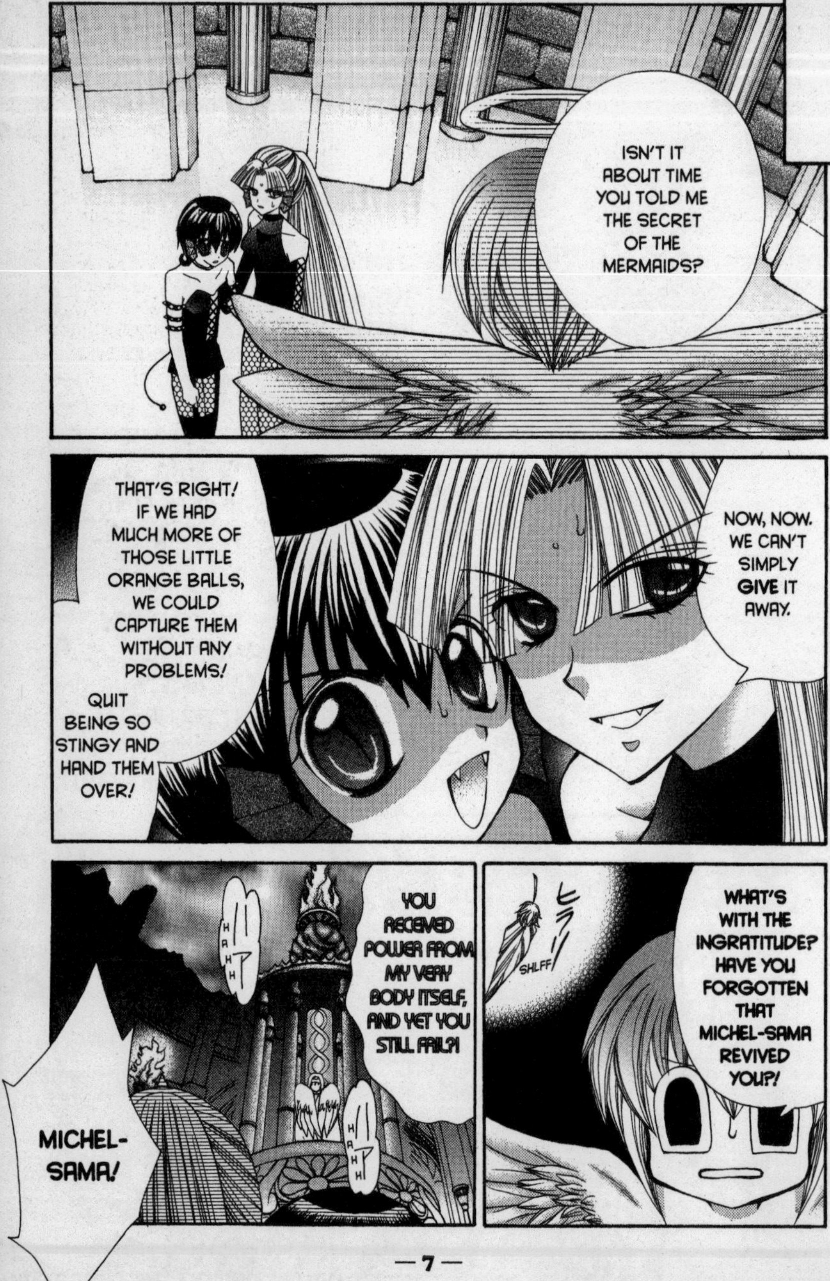
ISN'T IT ABOUT TIME YOU TOLD ME THE SECRET OF THE MERMAIDS?
NOW, NOW. WE CAN'T SIMPLY GIVE IT AWAY.
THAT'S RIGHT! IF WE HAD MUCH MORE OF THOSE LITTLE ORANGE BALLS, WE COULD CAPTURE THEM WITHOUT ANY PROBLEMS!
QUIT BEING SO STINGY AND HAND THEM OVER!
SHLFF
WHAT'S WITH THE INGRATITUDE? HAVE YOU FORGOTTEN THAT MICHEL-SAMA REVIVED YOU?!
YOU RECEIVED POWER FROM MY VERY BODY ITSELF, AND YET YOU STILL FAIL?!
HAHH
HAHH
MICHEL-SAMA!

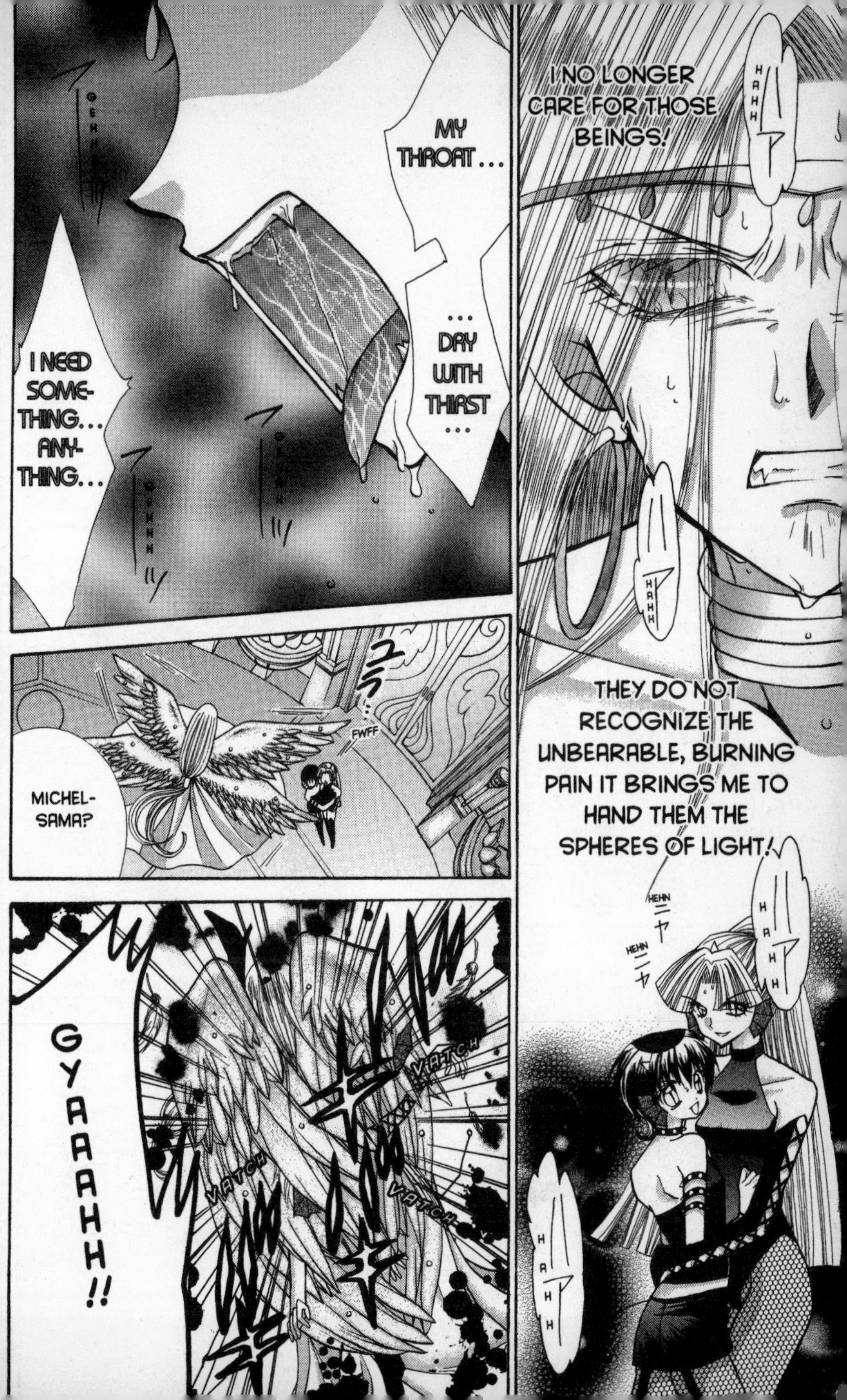
I NO LONGER CARE FOR THOSE BEINGS!
HAHH
THEY DO NOT RECOGNIZE THE UNBEARABLE, BURNING PAIN IT BRINGS ME TO HAND THEM THE SPHERES OF LIGHT!
HAHH
HEHN
HEHN
HAHH
HAHH
MY THROAT...
...DRY WITH THIRST...
I NEED SOMETHING... ANYTHING...
FWFF
MICHEL-SAMA?
GYAAAHH!!
VATCH
VATCH
VATCH

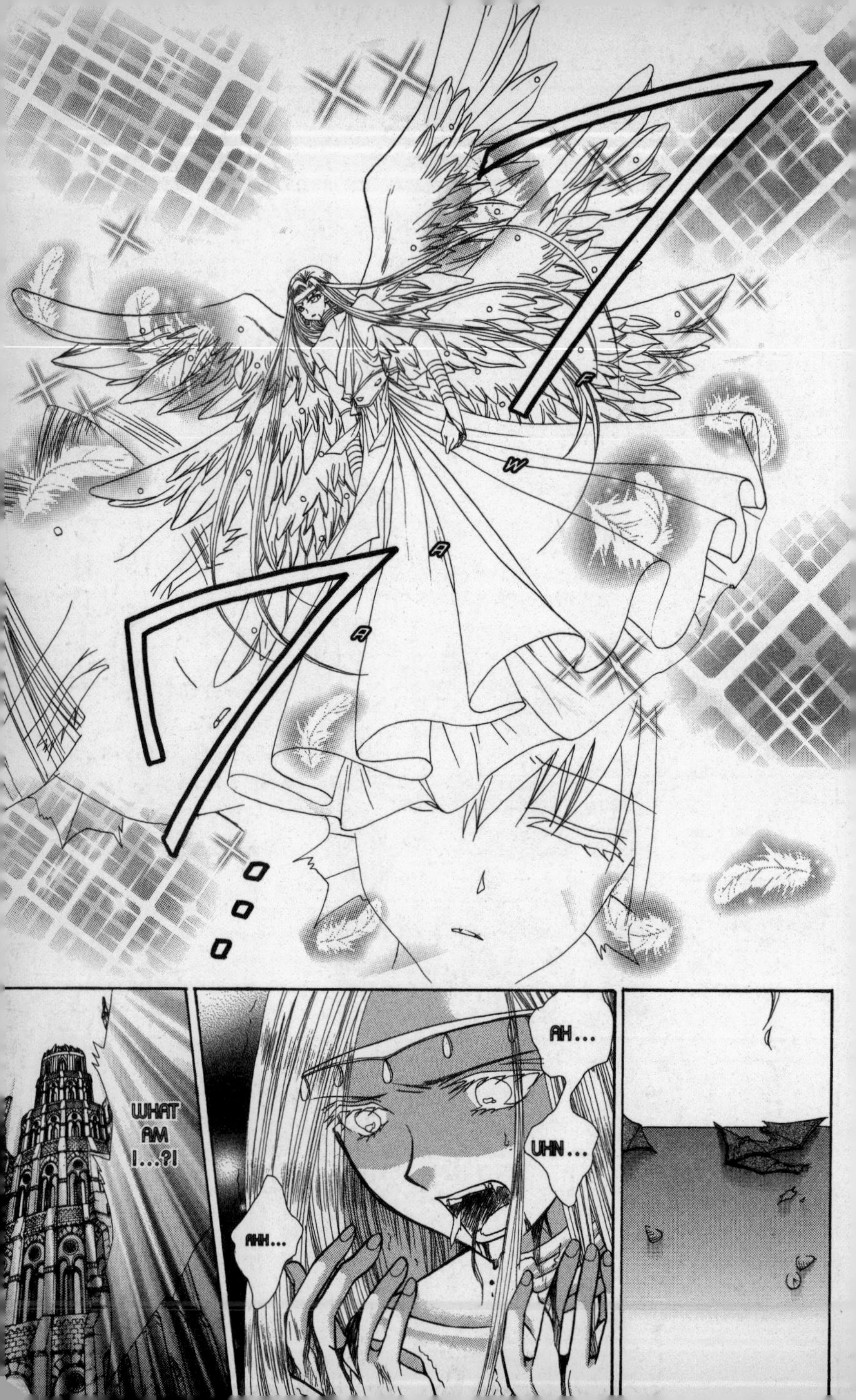
FWAA
AH...
UHN...
AHH...
WHAT AM I...?!

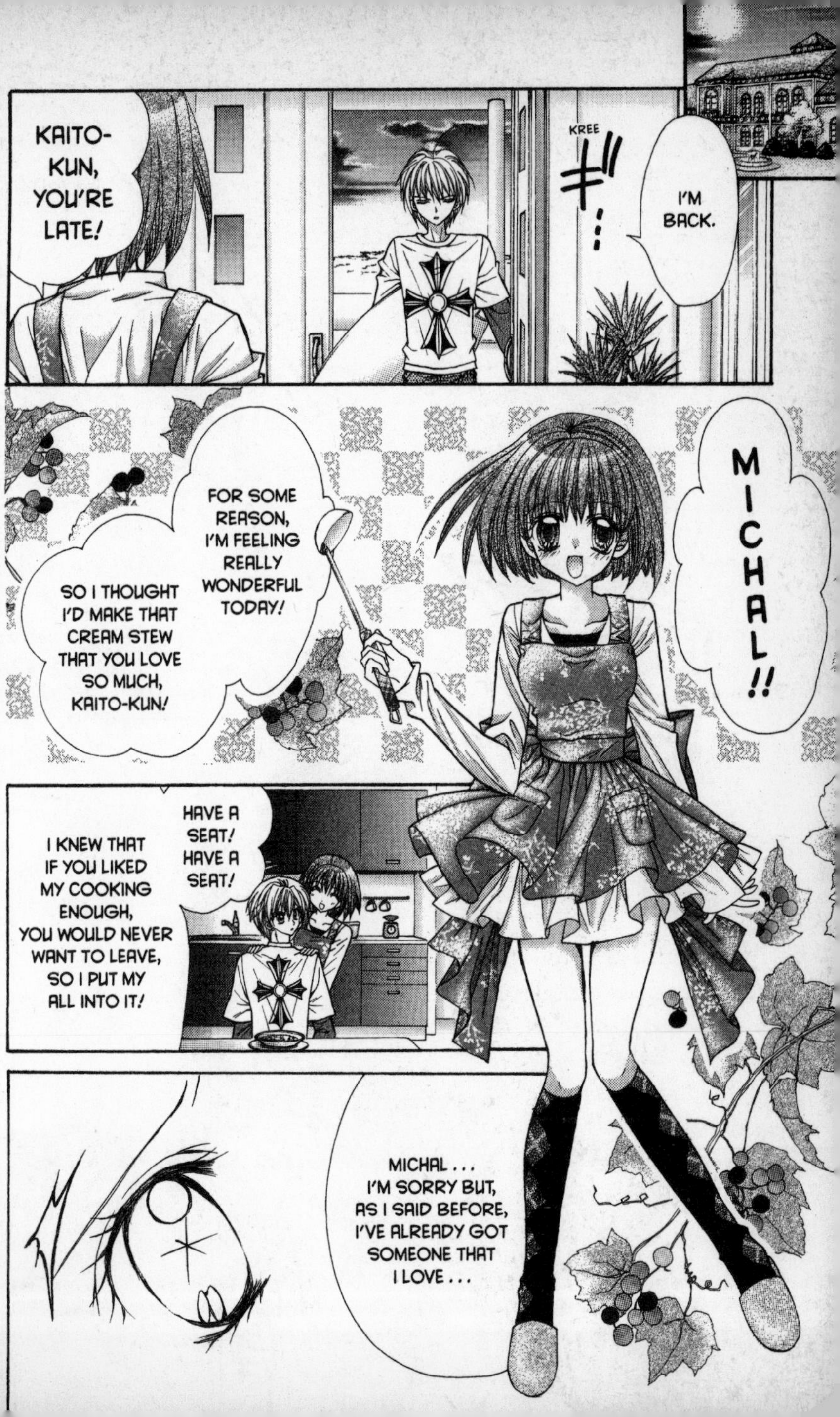
KREE
I'M BACK.
KAITO-KUN, YOU'RE LATE!
MICHAL!!
FOR SOME REASON, I'M FEELING REALLY WONDERFUL TODAY!
SO I THOUGHT I'D MAKE THAT CREAM STEW THAT YOU LOVE SO MUCH, KAITO-KUN!
HAVE A SEAT! HAVE A SEAT!
I KNEW THAT IF YOU LIKED MY COOKING ENOUGH, YOU WOULD NEVER WANT TO LEAVE, SO I PUT MY ALL INTO IT!
MICHAL . . . I'M SORRY BUT, AS I SAID BEFORE, I'VE ALREADY GOT SOMEONE THAT I LOVE . . .

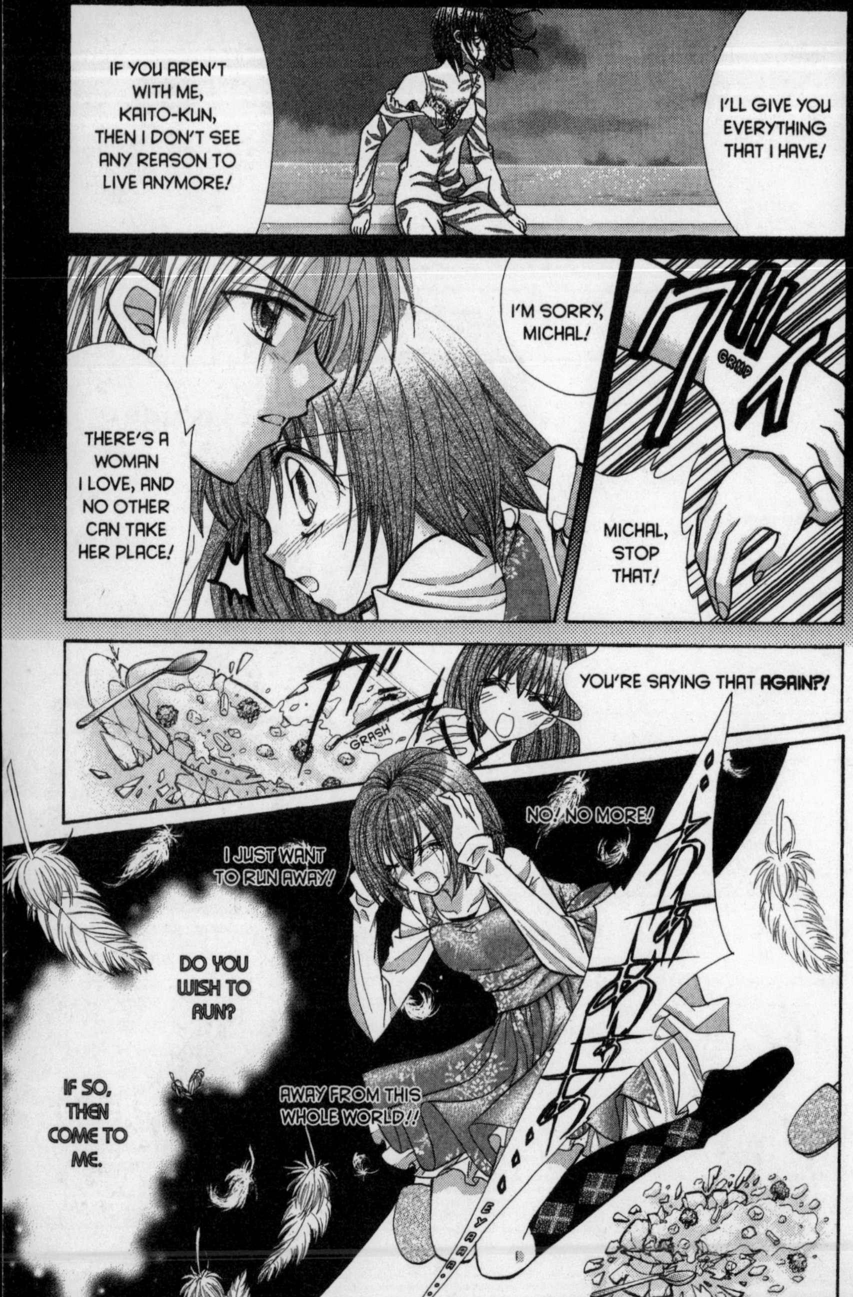
I'LL GIVE YOU EVERYTHING THAT I HAVE!
IF YOU AREN'T WITH ME, KAITO-KUN, THEN I DON'T SEE ANY REASON TO LIVE ANYMORE!
GRMP
MICHAL, STOP THAT!
I'M SORRY, MICHAL!
THERE'S A WOMAN I LOVE, AND NO OTHER CAN TAKE HER PLACE!
YOU'RE SAYING THAT **AGAIN?!**
GRASH
NO! NO MORE!
I JUST WANT TO RUN AWAY!
AWAY FROM THIS WHOLE WORLD!!
DO YOU WISH TO RUN?
IF SO, THEN COME TO ME.

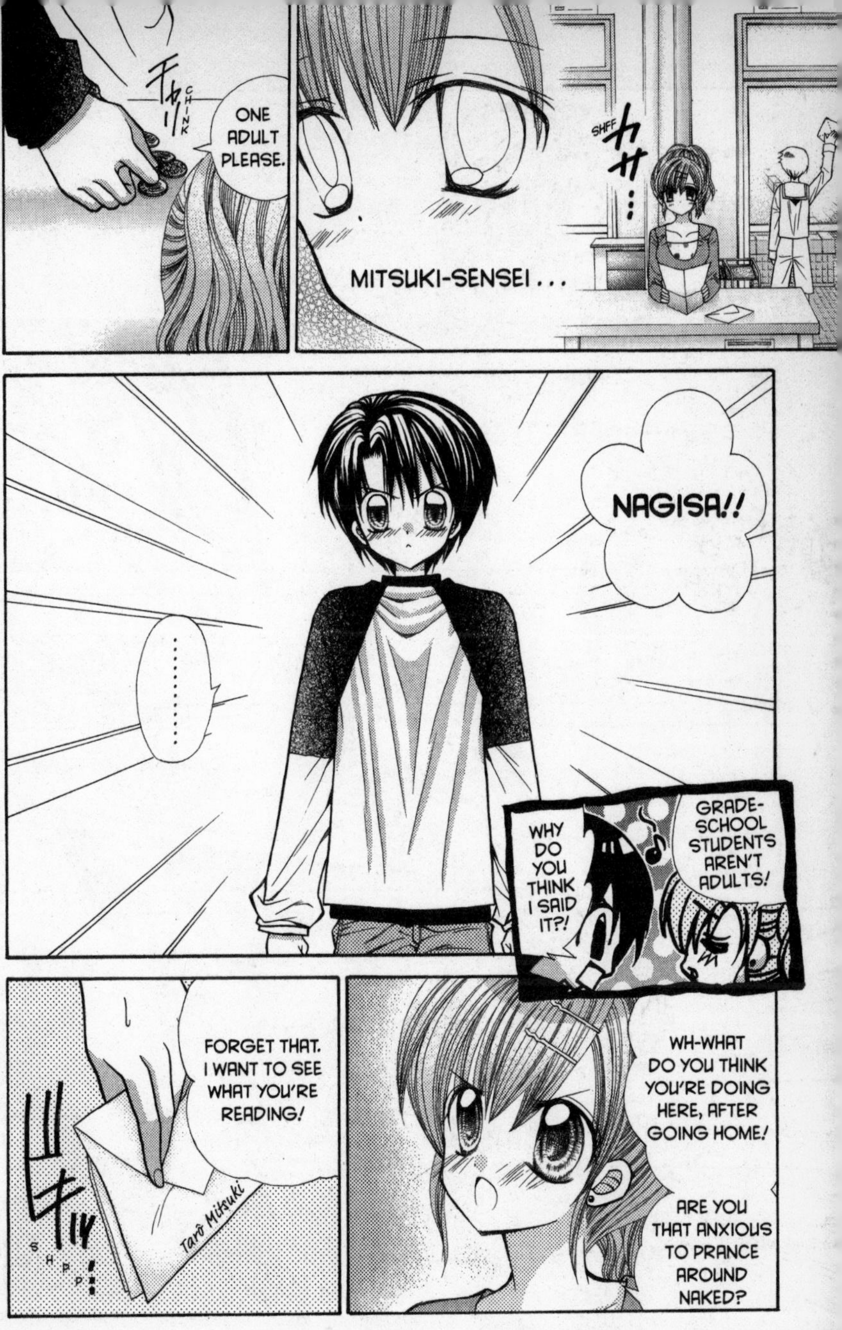
SHFF
MITSUKI-SENSEI . . .
CHINK
ONE ADULT PLEASE.
NAGISA!!
......
GRADE-SCHOOL STUDENTS AREN'T ADULTS!
WHY DO YOU THINK I SAID IT?!
WH-WHAT DO YOU THINK YOU'RE DOING HERE, AFTER GOING HOME!
ARE YOU THAT ANXIOUS TO PRANCE AROUND NAKED?
FORGET THAT. I WANT TO SEE WHAT YOU'RE READING!
Tarô Mitsuki
SHPP

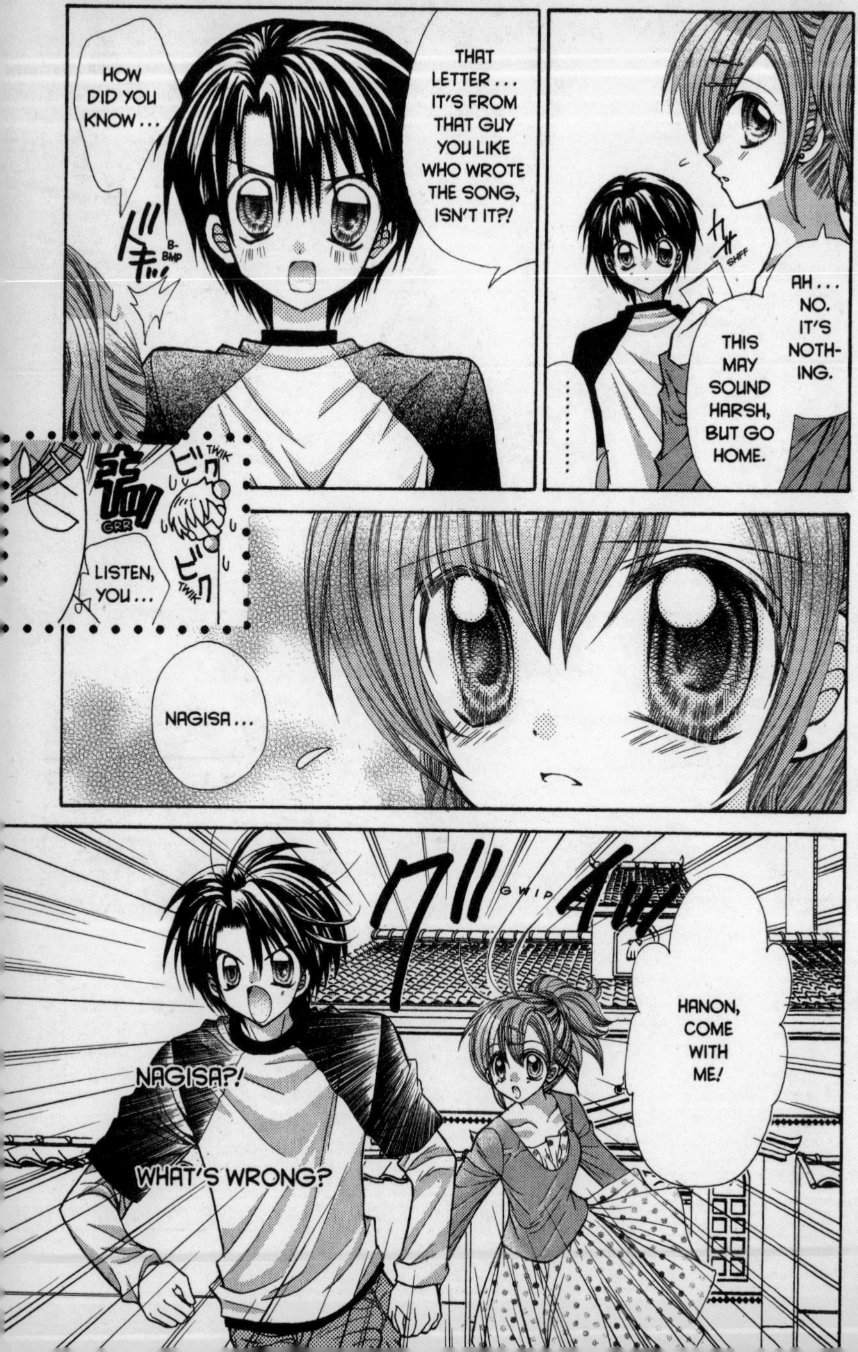

SHFF
AH... NO. IT'S NOTHING.
THIS MAY SOUND HARSH, BUT GO HOME.
THAT LETTER... IT'S FROM THAT GUY YOU LIKE WHO WROTE THE SONG, ISN'T IT?!
HOW DID YOU KNOW...
B-BMP
NAGISA...
TWIK
TWIK
GRR
LISTEN, YOU...
GWIP
HANON, COME WITH ME!
NAGISA?!
WHAT'S WRONG?

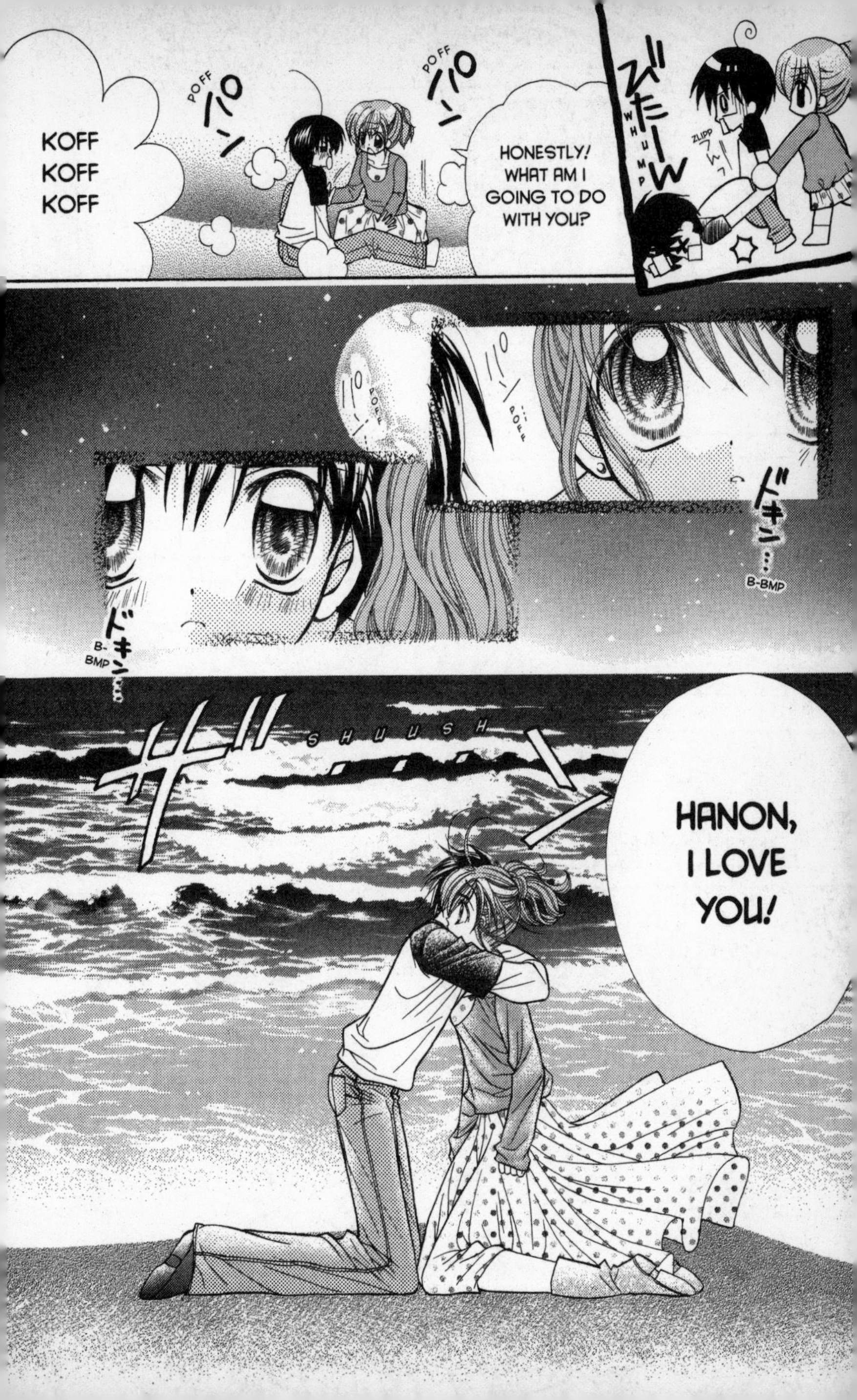

WHUMP
ZLIPP
HONESTLY! WHAT AM I GOING TO DO WITH YOU?
パン POFF
パン POFF
KOFF KOFF KOFF
POFF
POFF
ドキン… B-BMP
ドキン… B-BMP
HANON, I LOVE YOU!
SHUUSH

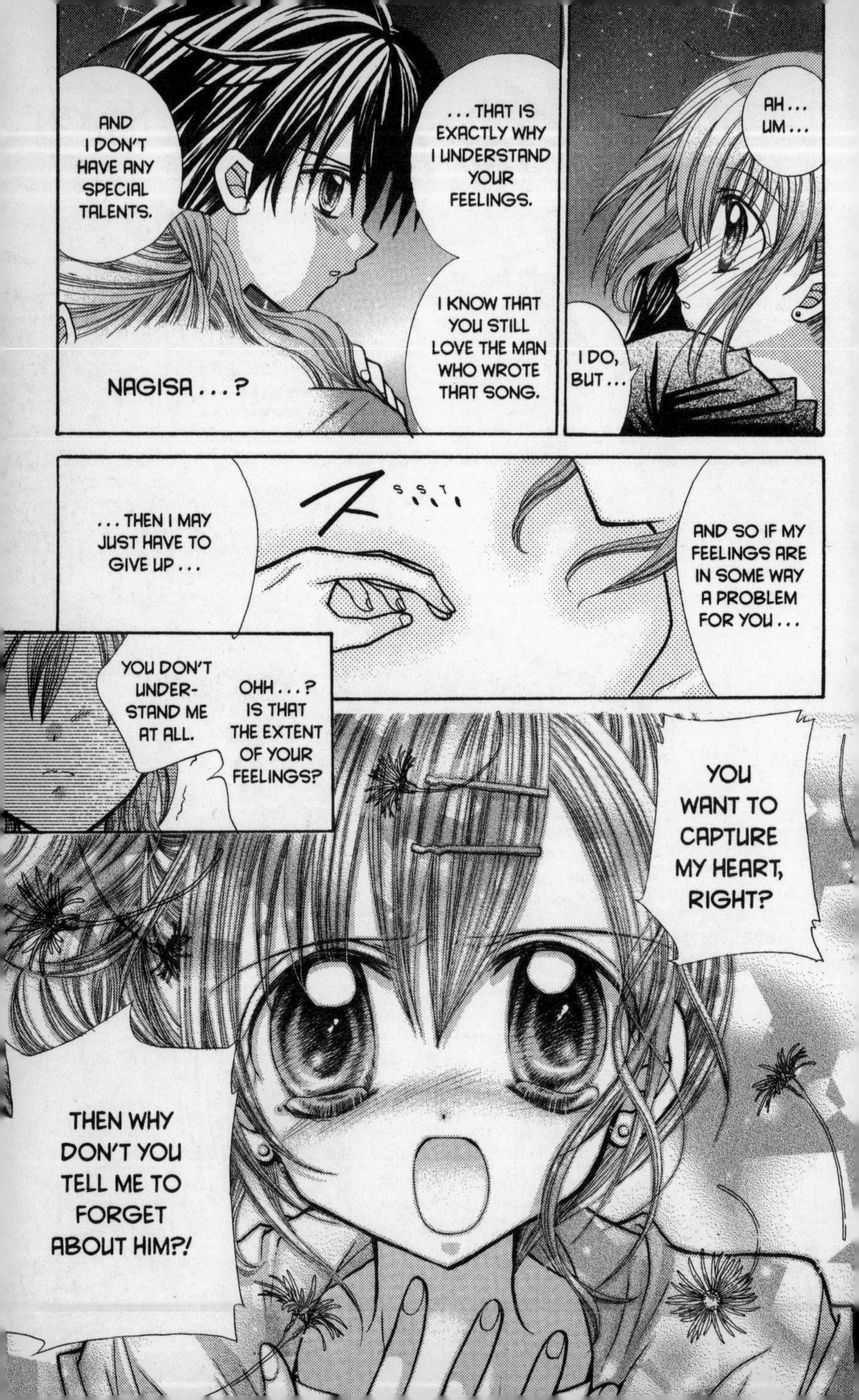

AH... UM...
I DO, BUT...
...THAT IS EXACTLY WHY I UNDERSTAND YOUR FEELINGS.
AND I DON'T HAVE ANY SPECIAL TALENTS.
I KNOW THAT YOU STILL LOVE THE MAN WHO WROTE THAT SONG.
NAGISA...?
AND SO IF MY FEELINGS ARE IN SOME WAY A PROBLEM FOR YOU...
SSST
...THEN I MAY JUST HAVE TO GIVE UP...
OHH...? IS THAT THE EXTENT OF YOUR FEELINGS?
YOU DON'T UNDER-STAND ME AT ALL.
YOU WANT TO CAPTURE MY HEART, RIGHT?
THEN WHY DON'T YOU TELL ME TO FORGET ABOUT HIM?!

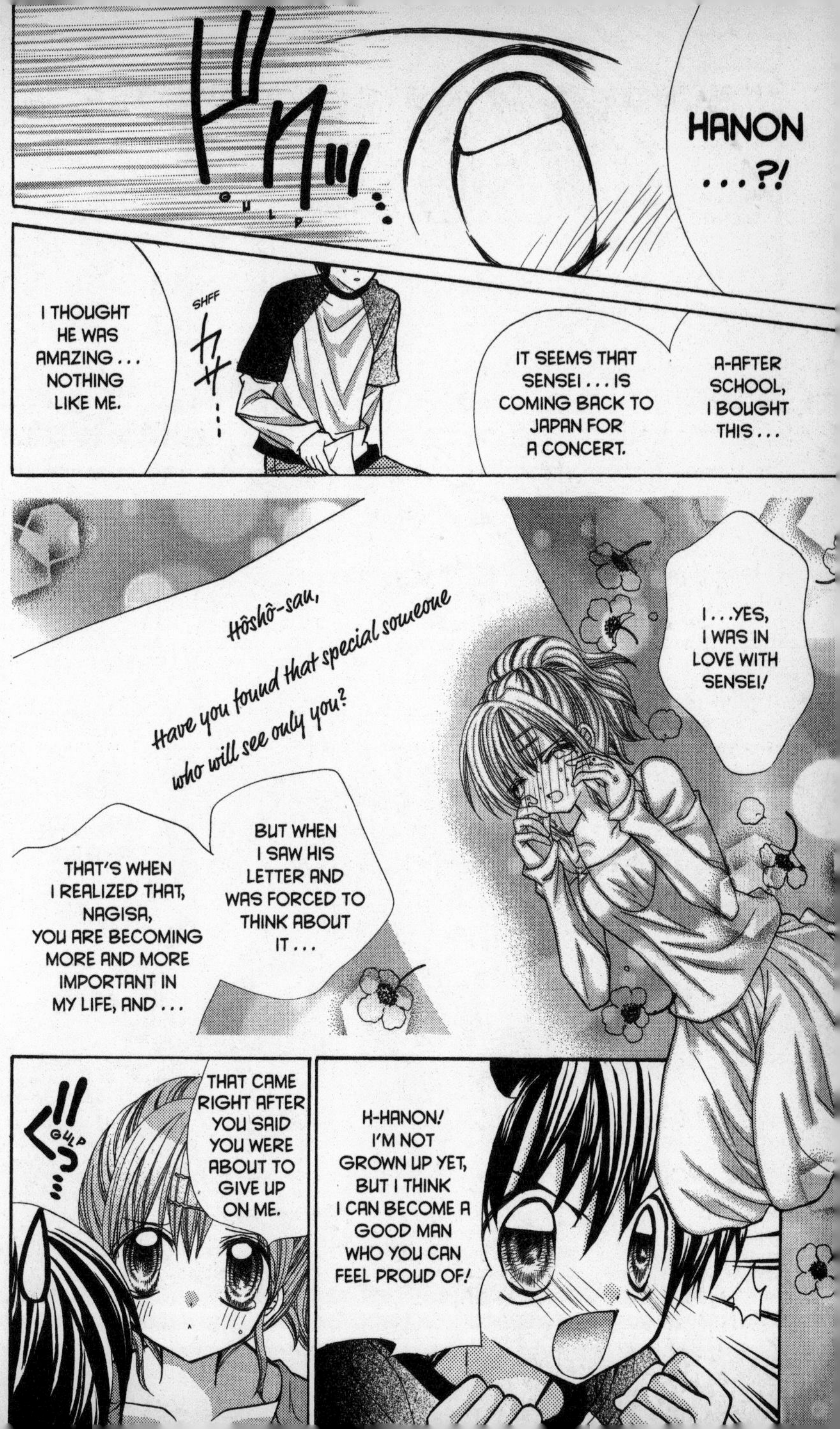
HANON . . . ?!
GULP
A-AFTER SCHOOL, I BOUGHT THIS . . .
IT SEEMS THAT SENSEI . . . IS COMING BACK TO JAPAN FOR A CONCERT.
SHFF
I THOUGHT HE WAS AMAZING . . . NOTHING LIKE ME.
I . . . YES, I WAS IN LOVE WITH SENSEI!
Hôshô-san,
Have you found that special someone who will see only you?
BUT WHEN I SAW HIS LETTER AND WAS FORCED TO THINK ABOUT IT . . .
THAT'S WHEN I REALIZED THAT, NAGISA, YOU ARE BECOMING MORE AND MORE IMPORTANT IN MY LIFE, AND . . .
H-HANON! I'M NOT GROWN UP YET, BUT I THINK I CAN BECOME A GOOD MAN WHO YOU CAN FEEL PROUD OF!
THAT CAME RIGHT AFTER YOU SAID YOU WERE ABOUT TO GIVE UP ON ME.
GULP

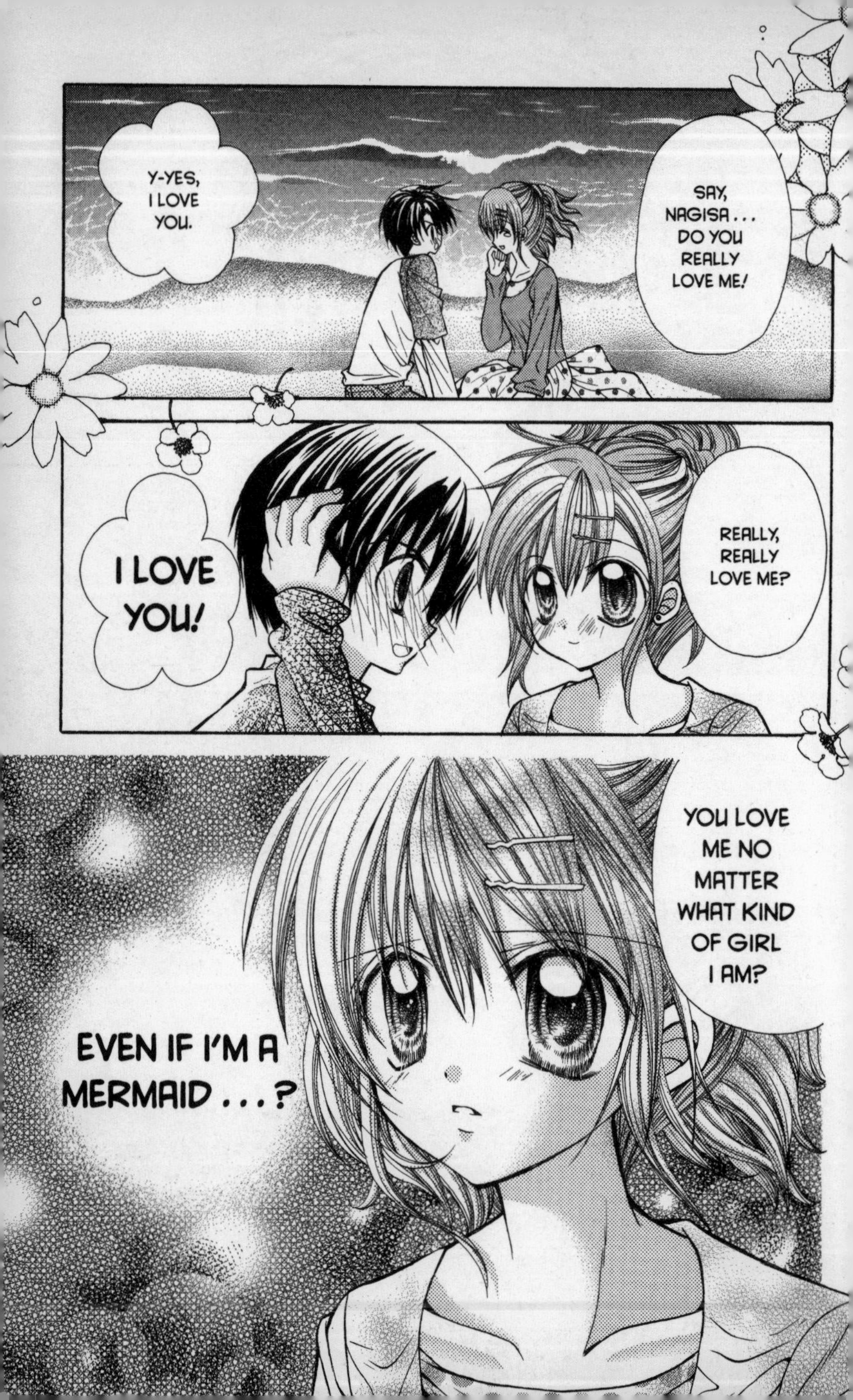
SAY, NAGISA . . . DO YOU REALLY LOVE ME!
Y-YES, I LOVE YOU.
REALLY, REALLY LOVE ME?
I LOVE YOU!
YOU LOVE ME NO MATTER WHAT KIND OF GIRL I AM?
EVEN IF I'M A MERMAID . . . ?

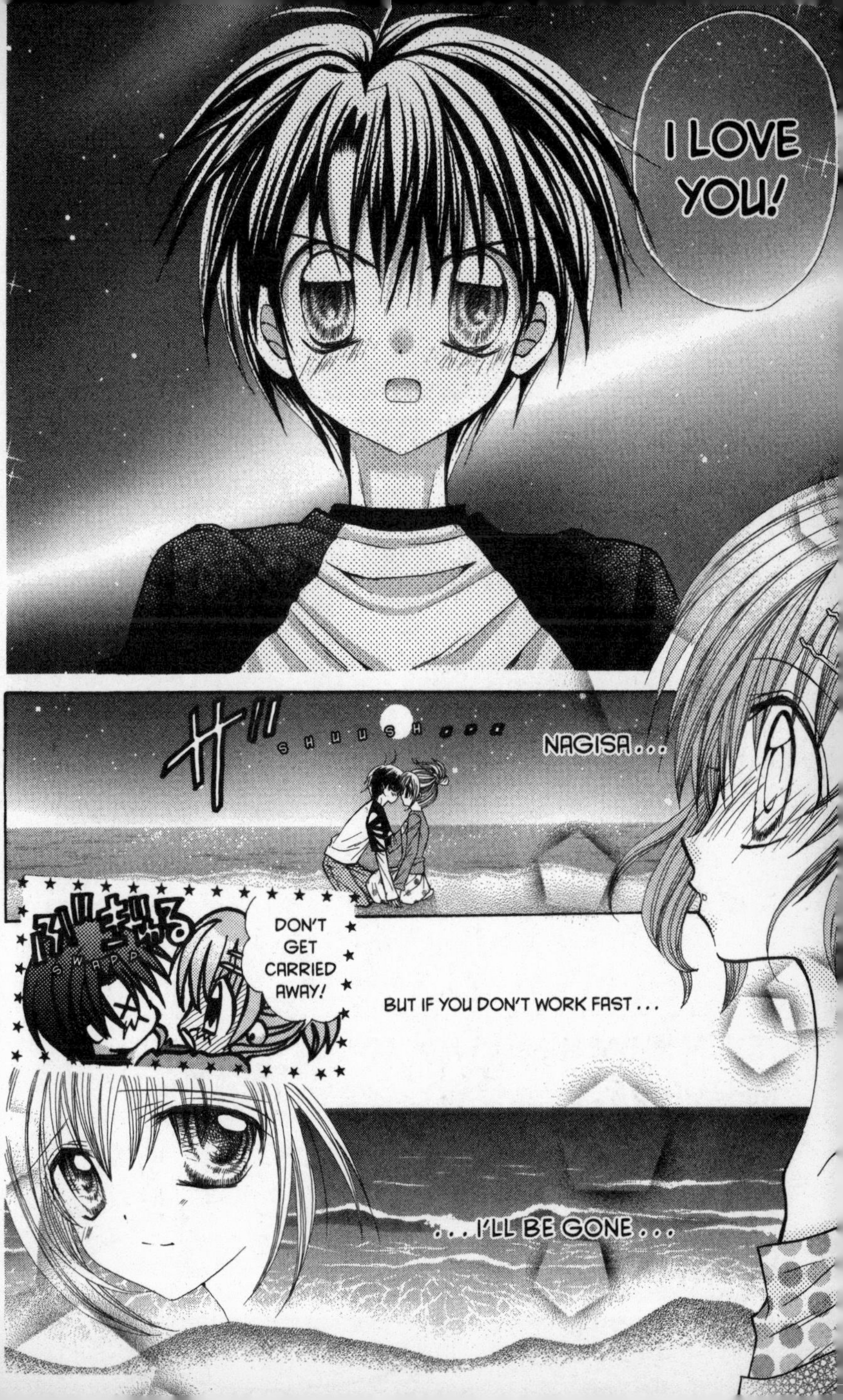
I LOVE YOU!
NAGISA . . .
SHUUSH . . .
SWAPP
DON'T GET CARRIED AWAY!
BUT IF YOU DON'T WORK FAST . . .
. . . I'LL BE GONE . . .

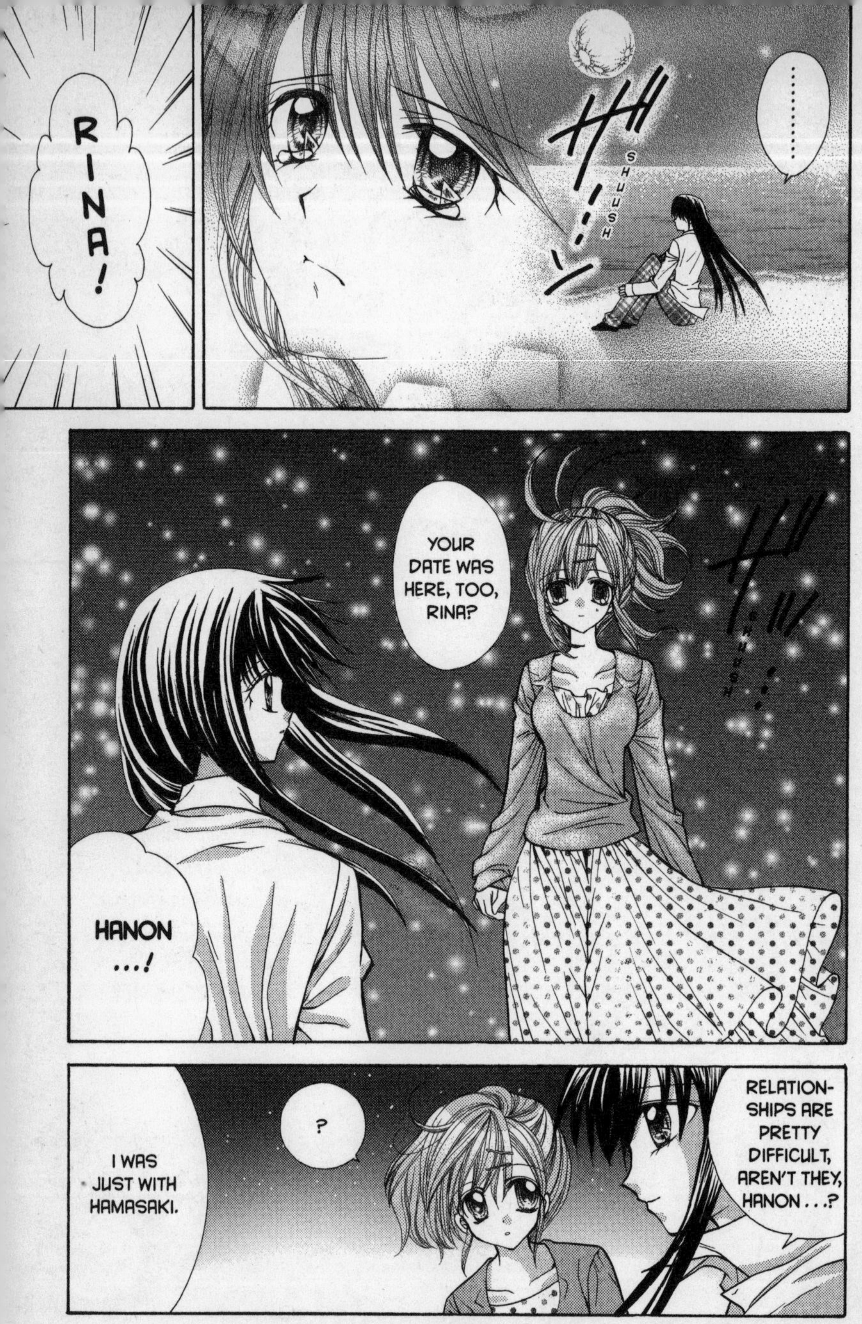
......
SHUUSH
RINA!
SHUUSH
YOUR DATE WAS HERE, TOO, RINA?
HANON ...!
RELATION-SHIPS ARE PRETTY DIFFICULT, AREN'T THEY, HANON . . .?
?
I WAS JUST WITH HAMASAKI.

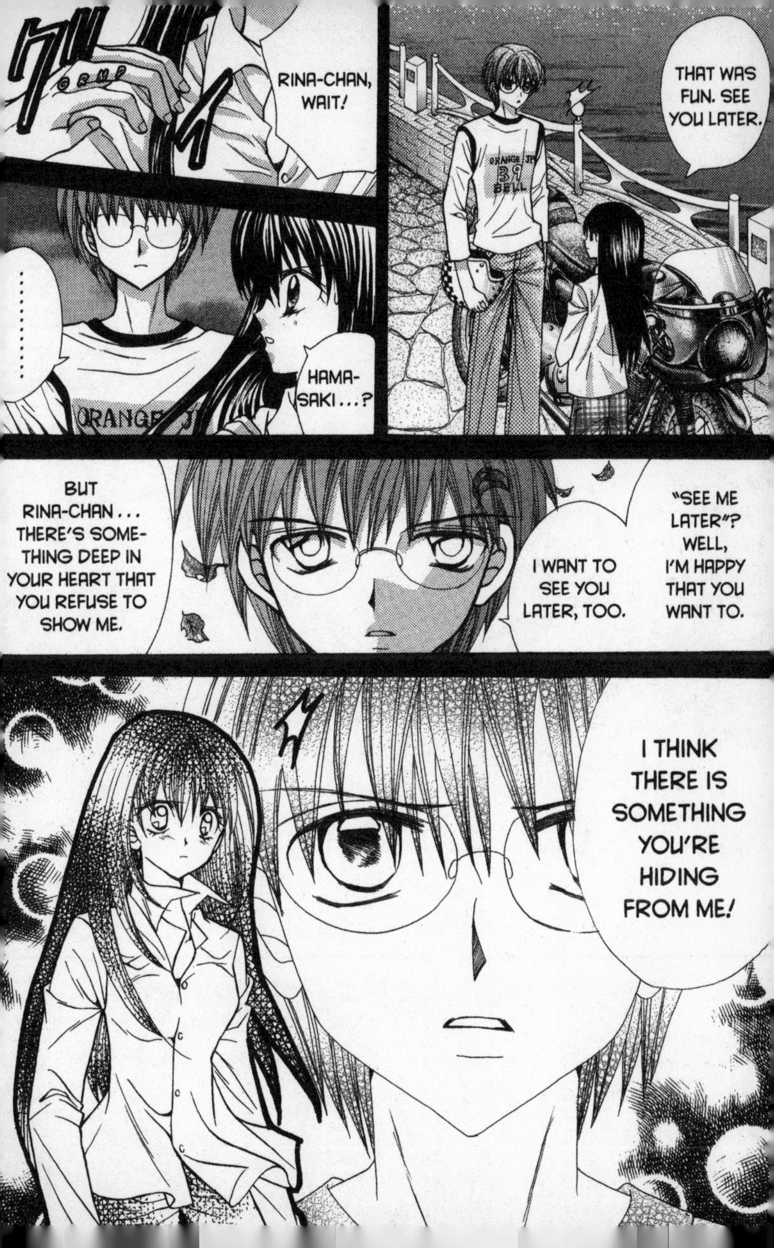
THAT WAS FUN. SEE YOU LATER.
RINA-CHAN, WAIT!
HAMA-SAKI . . . ?
. . . . . .
"SEE ME LATER"? WELL, I'M HAPPY THAT YOU WANT TO.
I WANT TO SEE YOU LATER, TOO.
BUT RINA-CHAN . . . THERE'S SOME-THING DEEP IN YOUR HEART THAT YOU REFUSE TO SHOW ME.
I THINK THERE IS SOMETHING YOU'RE HIDING FROM ME!

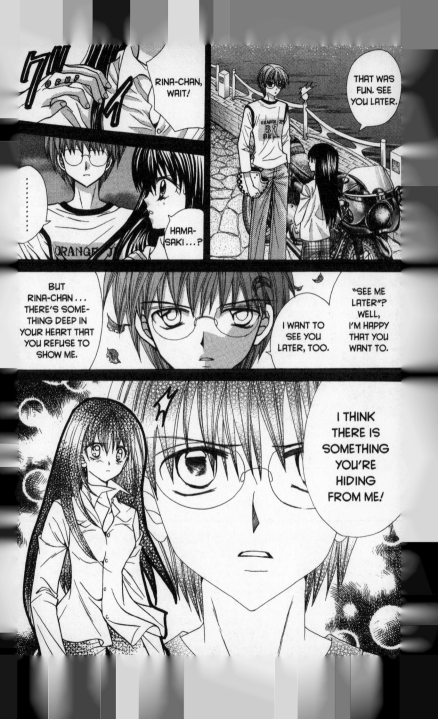

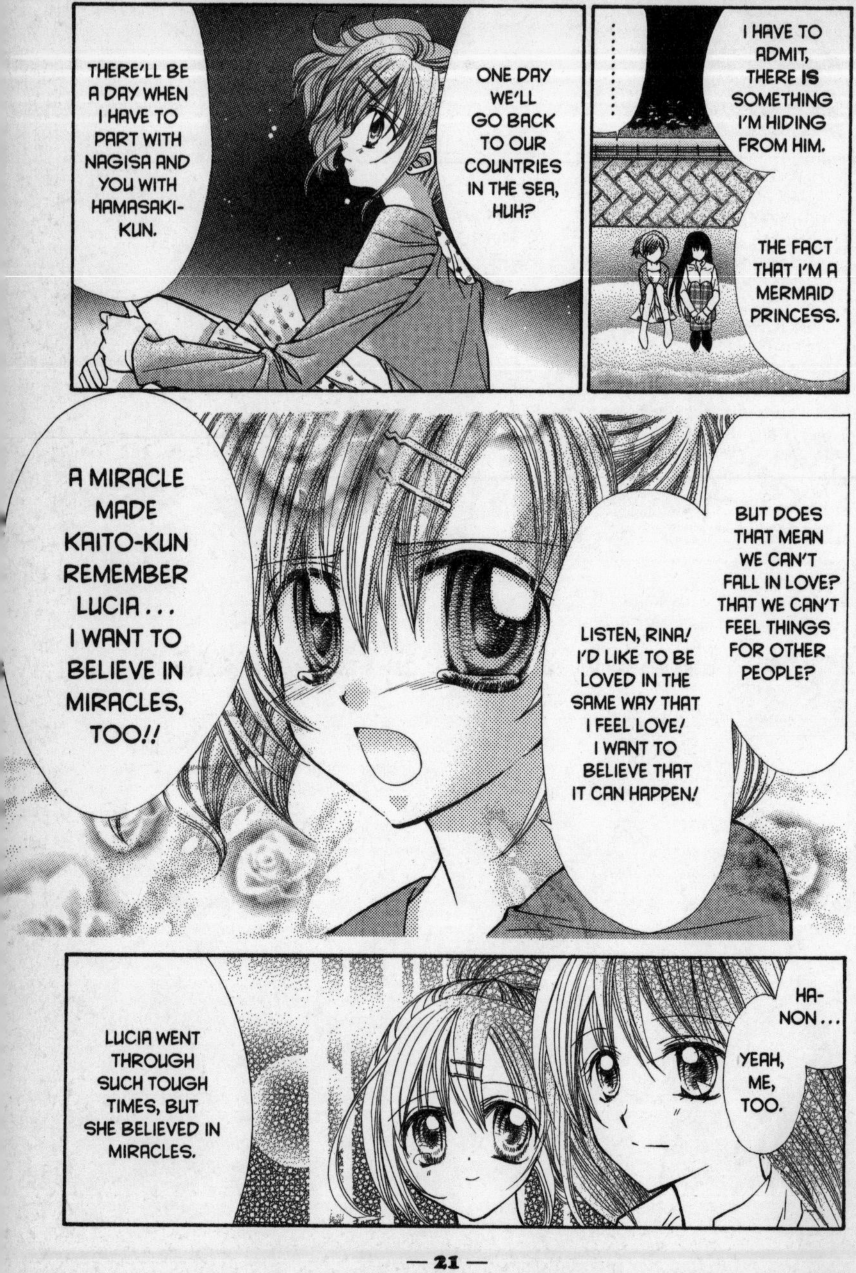
I HAVE TO ADMIT, THERE IS SOMETHING I'M HIDING FROM HIM.
......
THE FACT THAT I'M A MERMAID PRINCESS.
ONE DAY WE'LL GO BACK TO OUR COUNTRIES IN THE SEA, HUH?
THERE'LL BE A DAY WHEN I HAVE TO PART WITH NAGISA AND YOU WITH HAMASAKI-KUN.
BUT DOES THAT MEAN WE CAN'T FALL IN LOVE? THAT WE CAN'T FEEL THINGS FOR OTHER PEOPLE?
LISTEN, RINA! I'D LIKE TO BE LOVED IN THE SAME WAY THAT I FEEL LOVE! I WANT TO BELIEVE THAT IT CAN HAPPEN!
A MIRACLE MADE KAITO-KUN REMEMBER LUCIA . . . I WANT TO BELIEVE IN MIRACLES, TOO!!
HA-NON . . .
YEAH, ME, TOO.
LUCIA WENT THROUGH SUCH TOUGH TIMES, BUT SHE BELIEVED IN MIRACLES.

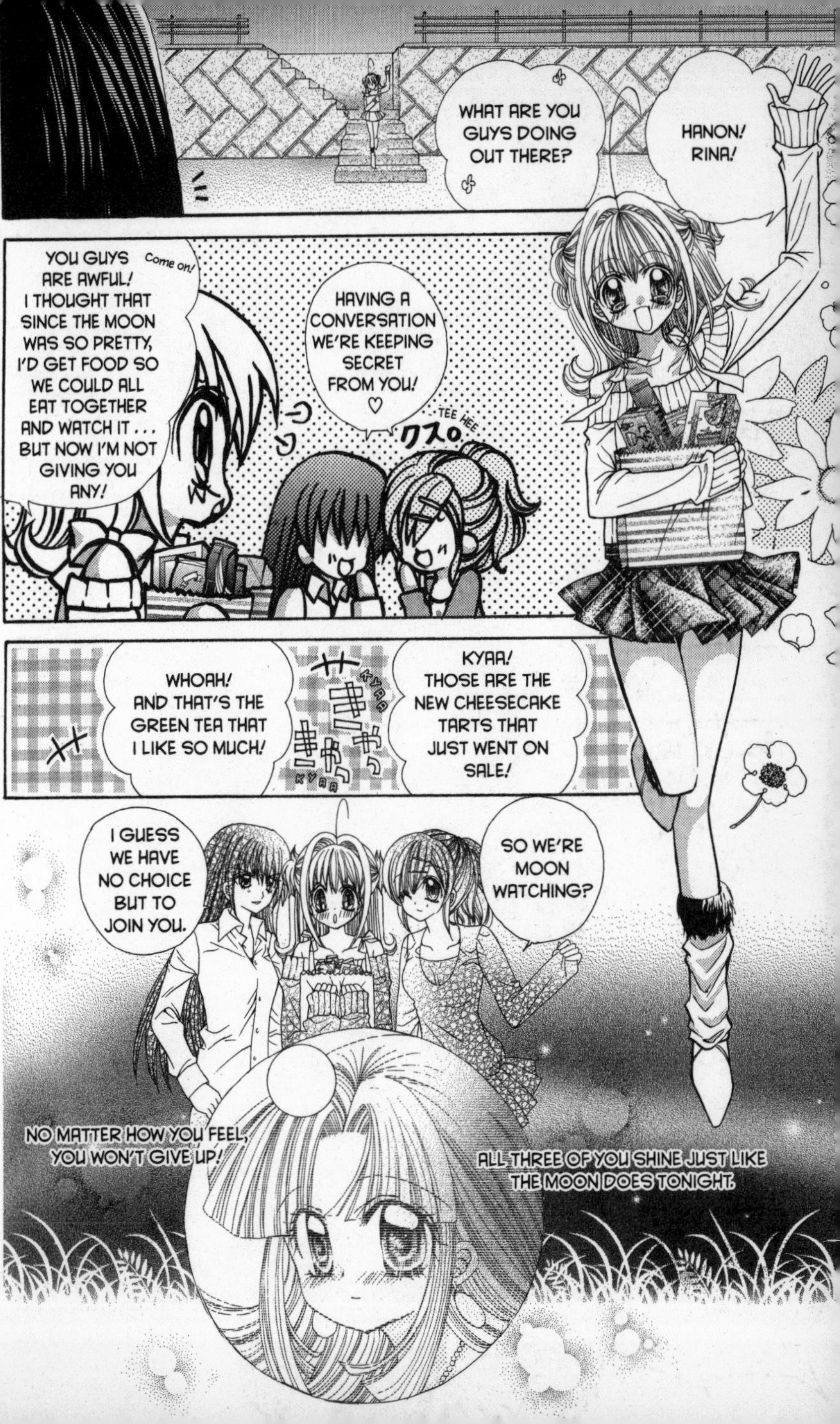
HANON! RINA!
WHAT ARE YOU GUYS DOING OUT THERE?
HAVING A CONVERSATION WE'RE KEEPING SECRET FROM YOU! ♡
TEE HEE
YOU GUYS ARE AWFUL! I THOUGHT THAT SINCE THE MOON WAS SO PRETTY, I'D GET FOOD SO WE COULD ALL EAT TOGETHER AND WATCH IT . . . BUT NOW I'M NOT GIVING YOU ANY!
Come on!
KYAA! THOSE ARE THE NEW CHEESECAKE TARTS THAT JUST WENT ON SALE!
KYAA
KYAA
WHOAH! AND THAT'S THE GREEN TEA THAT I LIKE SO MUCH!
SO WE'RE MOON WATCHING?
I GUESS WE HAVE NO CHOICE BUT TO JOIN YOU.
ALL THREE OF YOU SHINE JUST LIKE THE MOON DOES TONIGHT.
NO MATTER HOW YOU FEEL, YOU WON'T GIVE UP!

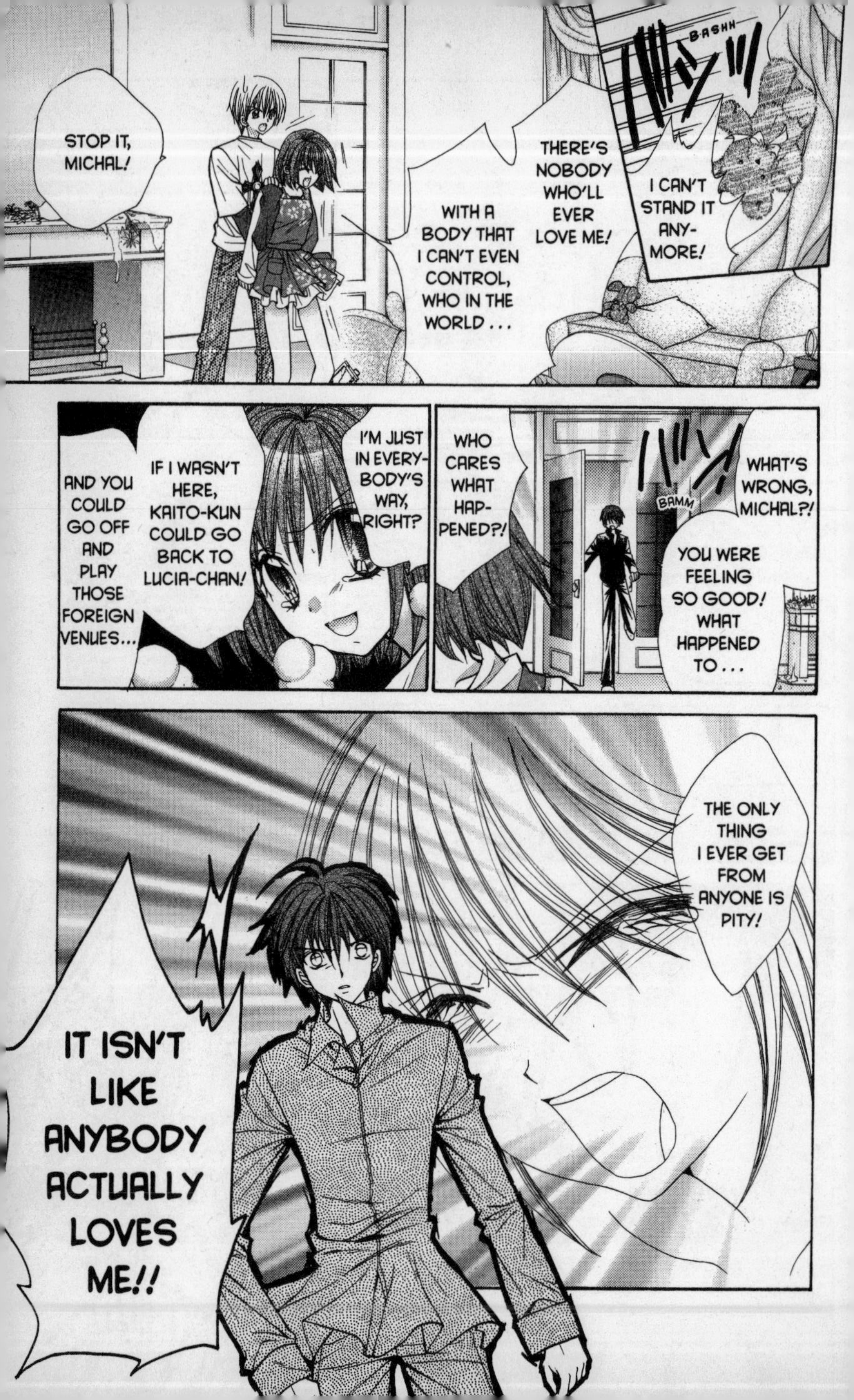
BASHH
I CAN'T STAND IT ANYMORE!
THERE'S NOBODY WHO'LL EVER LOVE ME!
WITH A BODY THAT I CAN'T EVEN CONTROL, WHO IN THE WORLD . . .
STOP IT, MICHAL!
BAMM
WHAT'S WRONG, MICHAL?!
YOU WERE FEELING SO GOOD! WHAT HAPPENED TO . . .
WHO CARES WHAT HAPPENED?!
I'M JUST IN EVERYBODY'S WAY, RIGHT?
IF I WASN'T HERE, KAITO-KUN COULD GO BACK TO LUCIA-CHAN!
AND YOU COULD GO OFF AND PLAY THOSE FOREIGN VENUES...
THE ONLY THING I EVER GET FROM ANYONE IS PITY!
IT ISN'T LIKE ANYBODY ACTUALLY LOVES ME!!

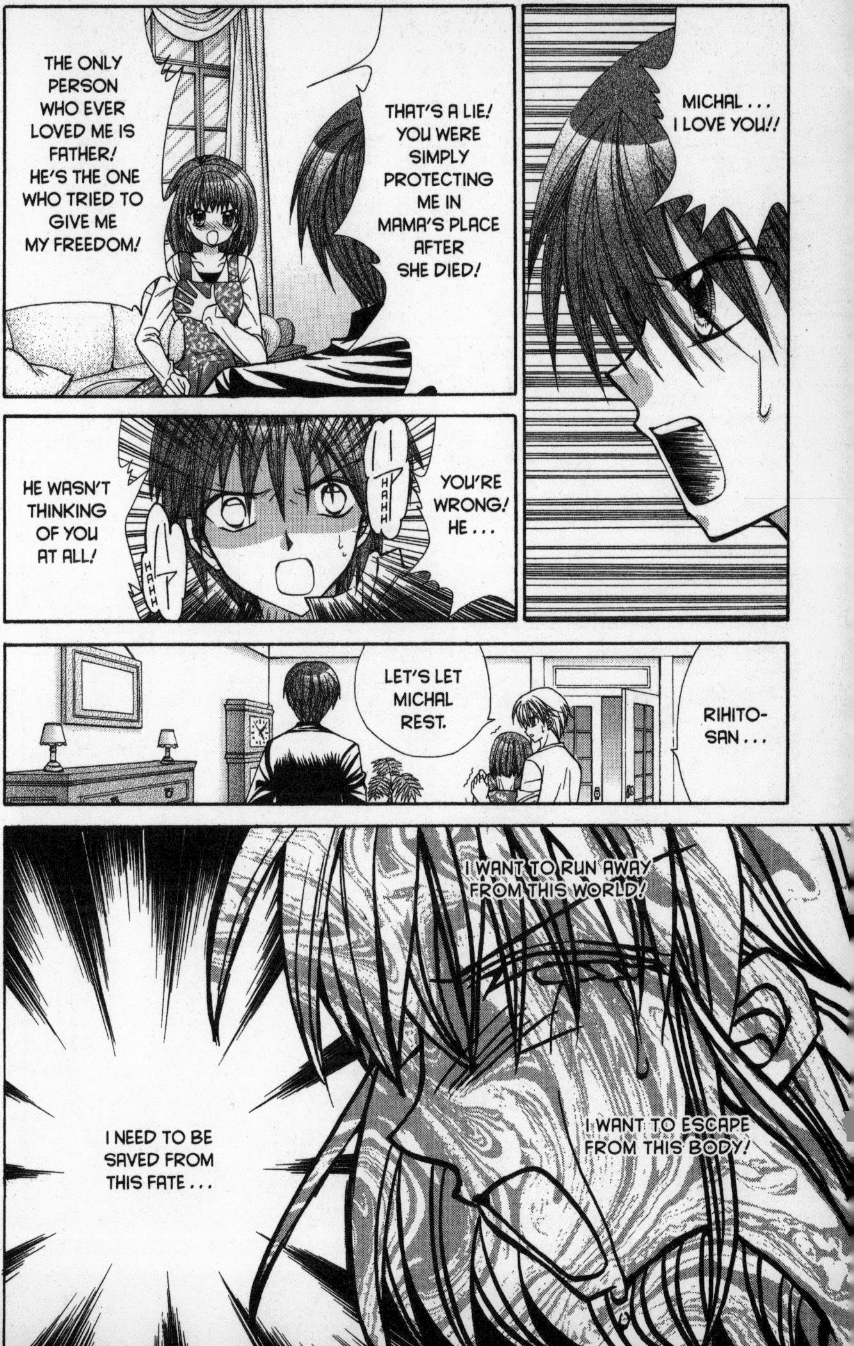
MICHAL . . . I LOVE YOU!!
THAT'S A LIE! YOU WERE SIMPLY PROTECTING ME IN MAMA'S PLACE AFTER SHE DIED!
THE ONLY PERSON WHO EVER LOVED ME IS FATHER! HE'S THE ONE WHO TRIED TO GIVE ME MY FREEDOM!
HAHH
YOU'RE WRONG! HE . . .
HAHH
HE WASN'T THINKING OF YOU AT ALL!
RIHITO-SAN . . .
LET'S LET MICHAL REST.
I WANT TO RUN AWAY FROM THIS WORLD!
I WANT TO ESCAPE FROM THIS BODY!
I NEED TO BE SAVED FROM THIS FATE . . .

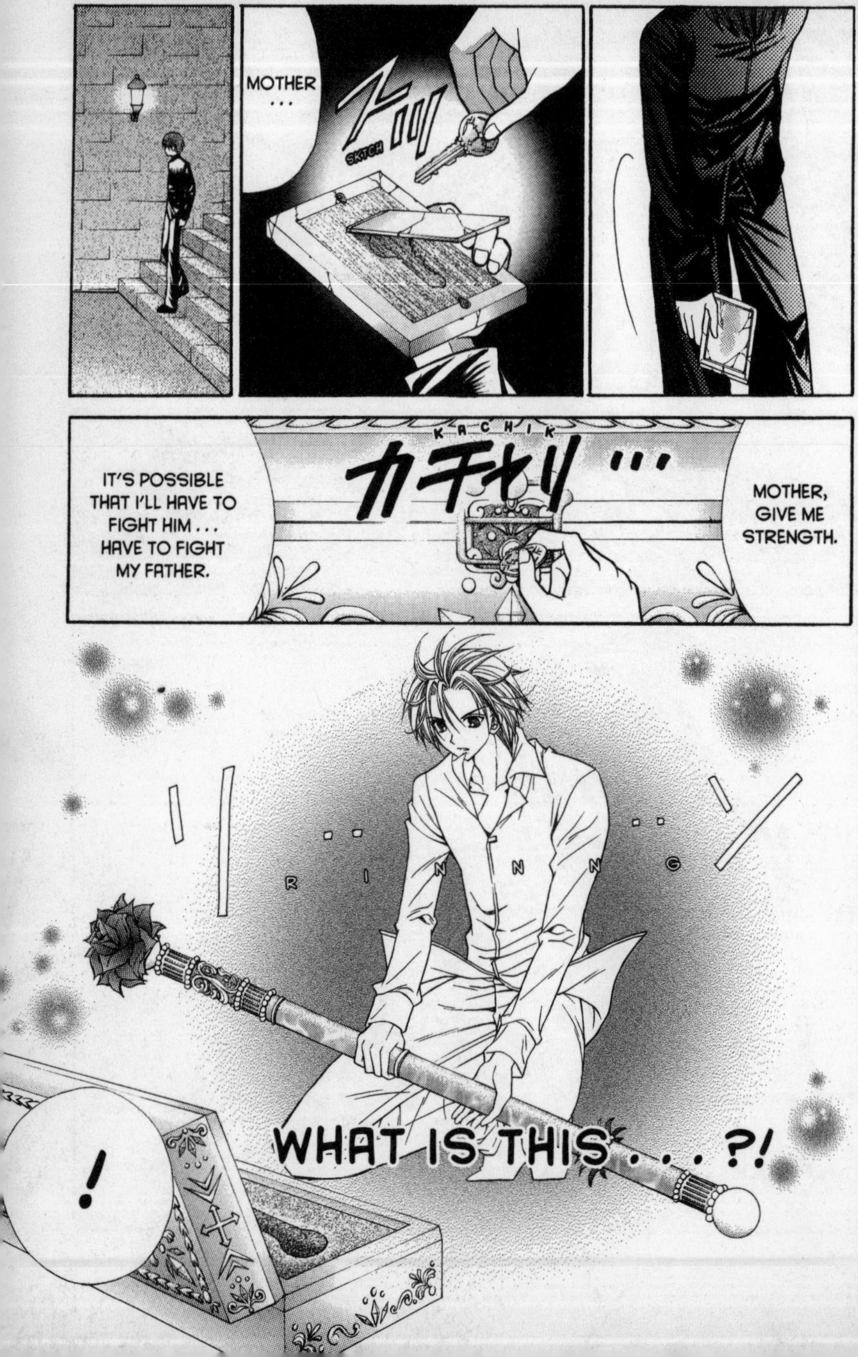
MOTHER . . .
SKTCH
MOTHER, GIVE ME STRENGTH.
KACHIK
カチャリ…
IT'S POSSIBLE THAT I'LL HAVE TO FIGHT HIM . . . HAVE TO FIGHT MY FATHER.
RINNNG
WHAT IS THIS . . . ?!
!

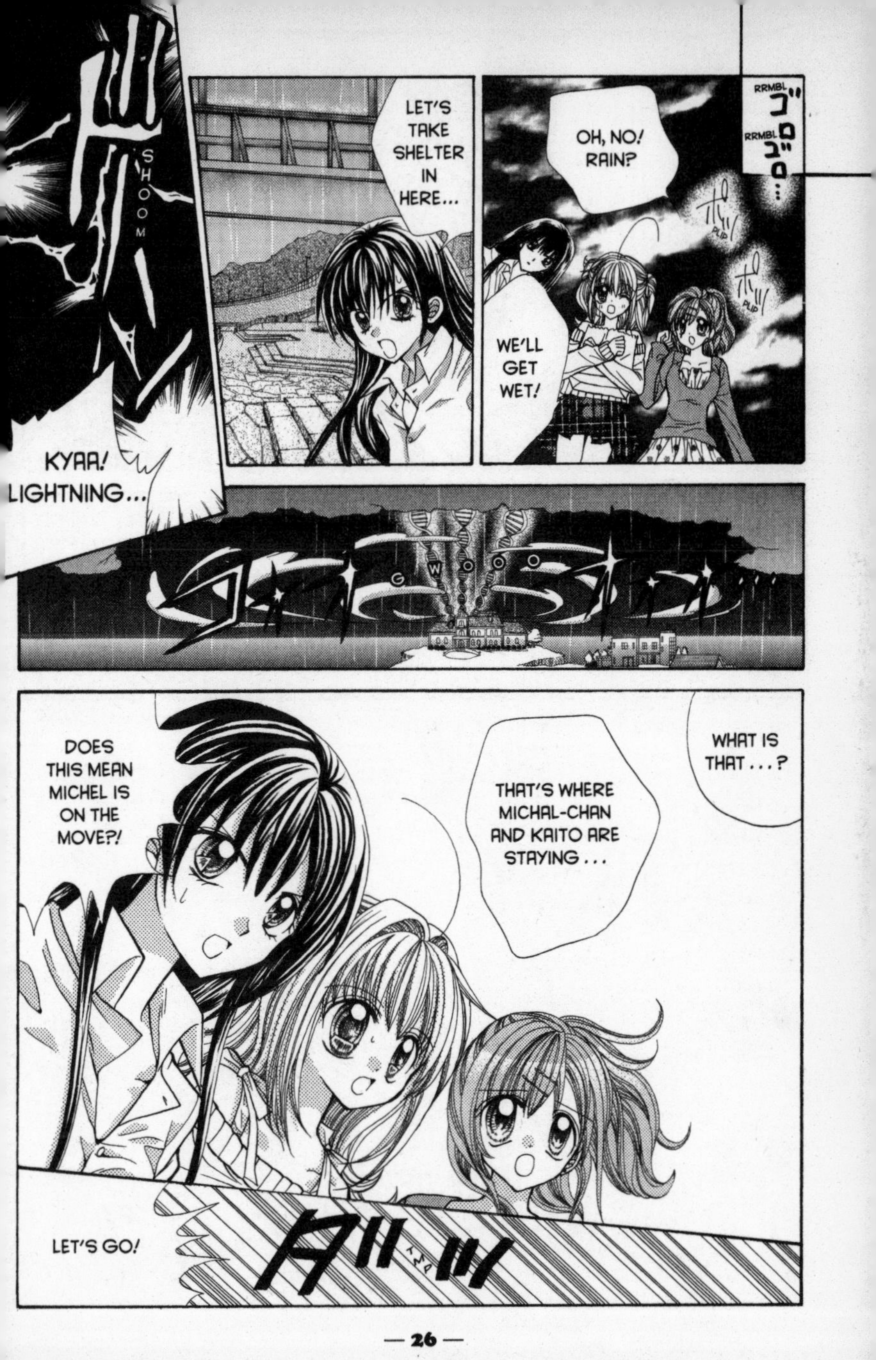
RRMBL RRMBL
ゴロゴロ…
OH, NO! RAIN?
PLIP PLIP
WE'LL GET WET!
LET'S TAKE SHELTER IN HERE...
SHOOM
KYAA! LIGHTNING...
GWOOO
WHAT IS THAT . . . ?
THAT'S WHERE MICHAL-CHAN AND KAITO ARE STAYING . . .
DOES THIS MEAN MICHEL IS ON THE MOVE?!
LET'S GO!

INTRODUCTION TO THE MUSIC

<VOLUME 4>

- LEGEND OF MERMAID
- YUME NO SONO SAKI E (TO THAT DREAM PLACE)

<VOLUME 6>

- TSUBASA O DAITE (EMBRACE THE WINGS)
- KIBÔ KANE-OTO (THE BELL-SOUND OF DESIRE) ~LOVE GOES ON~

(THE CD COMES OUT FROM THE GOOD PEOPLE AT PONY-CANYON.)

PICHI IS A SONG MANGA, SO SONGS WILL OCCASIONALLY BE INCLUDED. THE OTHER CHARACTERS SING, TOO, SO ANYONE WHO IS INTERESTED, PLEASE LISTEN TO THE ALBUMS. THEY'RE ALL REALLY GREAT SONGS!

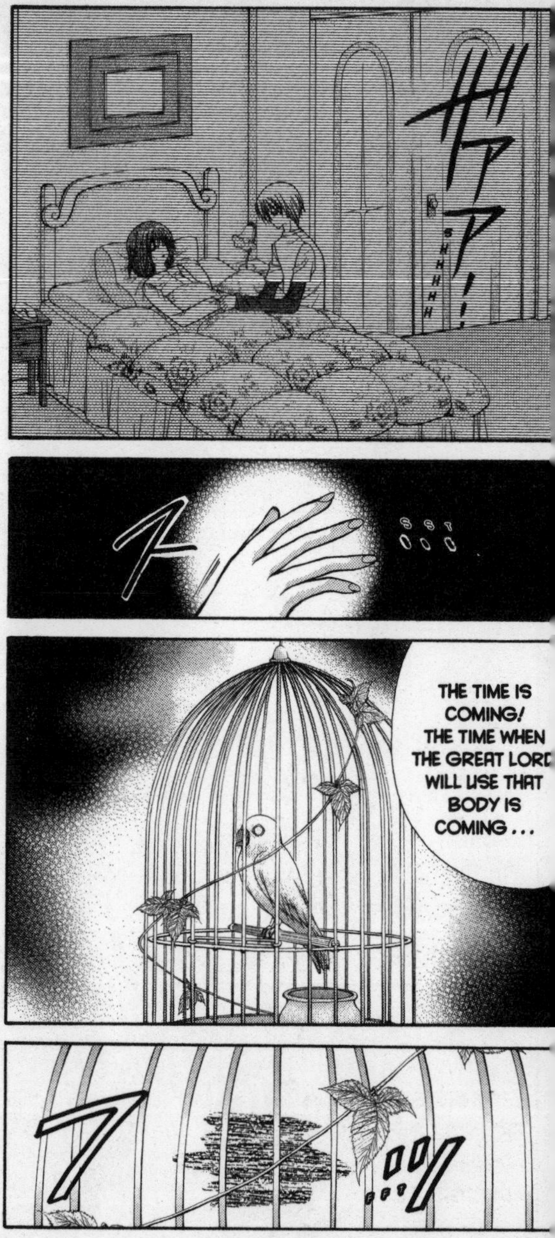
SHHHHH
SST
THE TIME IS COMING! THE TIME WHEN THE GREAT LORD WILL USE THAT BODY IS COMING...
PFT

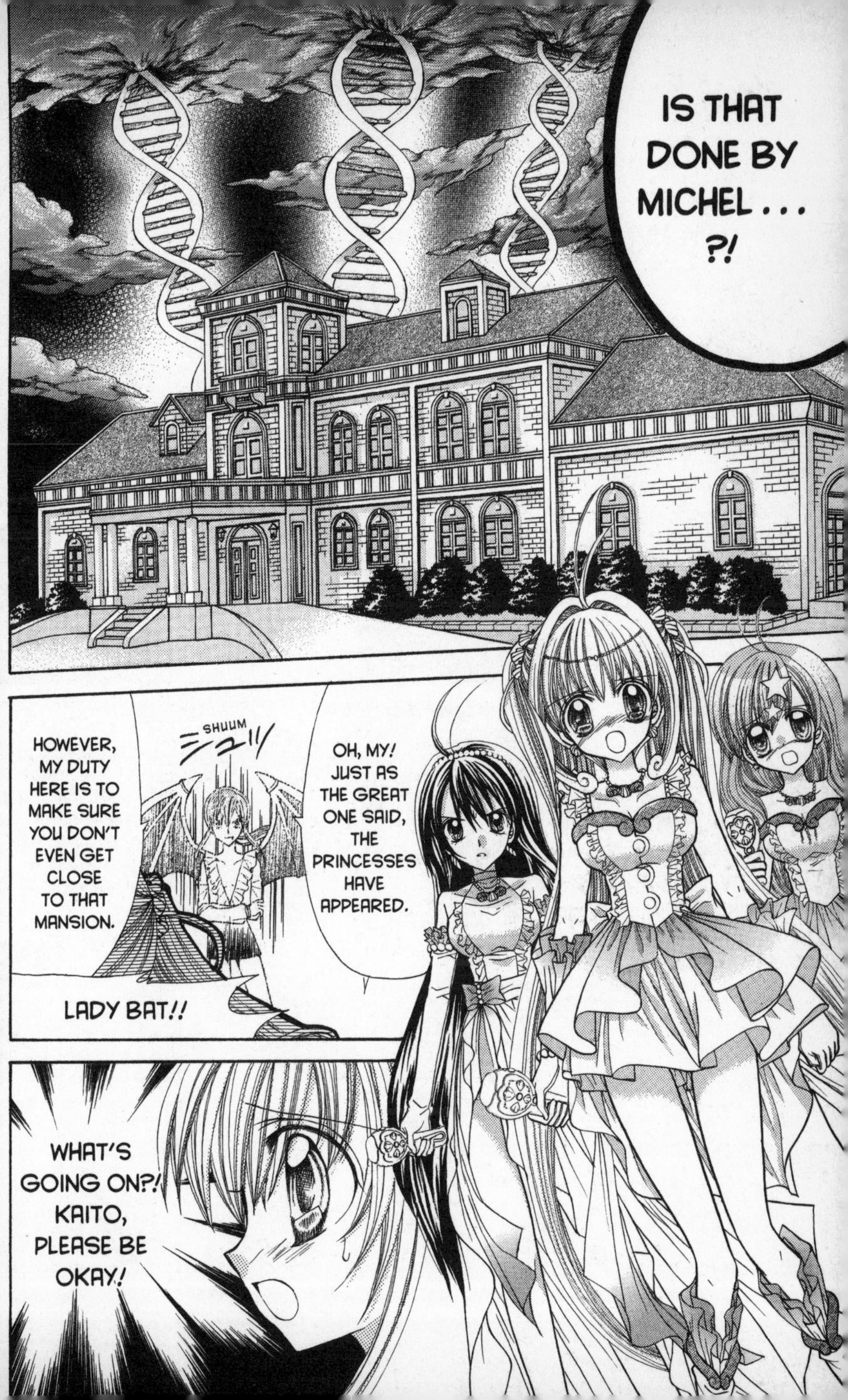
IS THAT DONE BY MICHEL . . . ?!
OH, MY! JUST AS THE GREAT ONE SAID, THE PRINCESSES HAVE APPEARED.
SHUUM
HOWEVER, MY DUTY HERE IS TO MAKE SURE YOU DON'T EVEN GET CLOSE TO THAT MANSION.
LADY BAT!!
WHAT'S GOING ON?! KAITO, PLEASE BE OKAY!

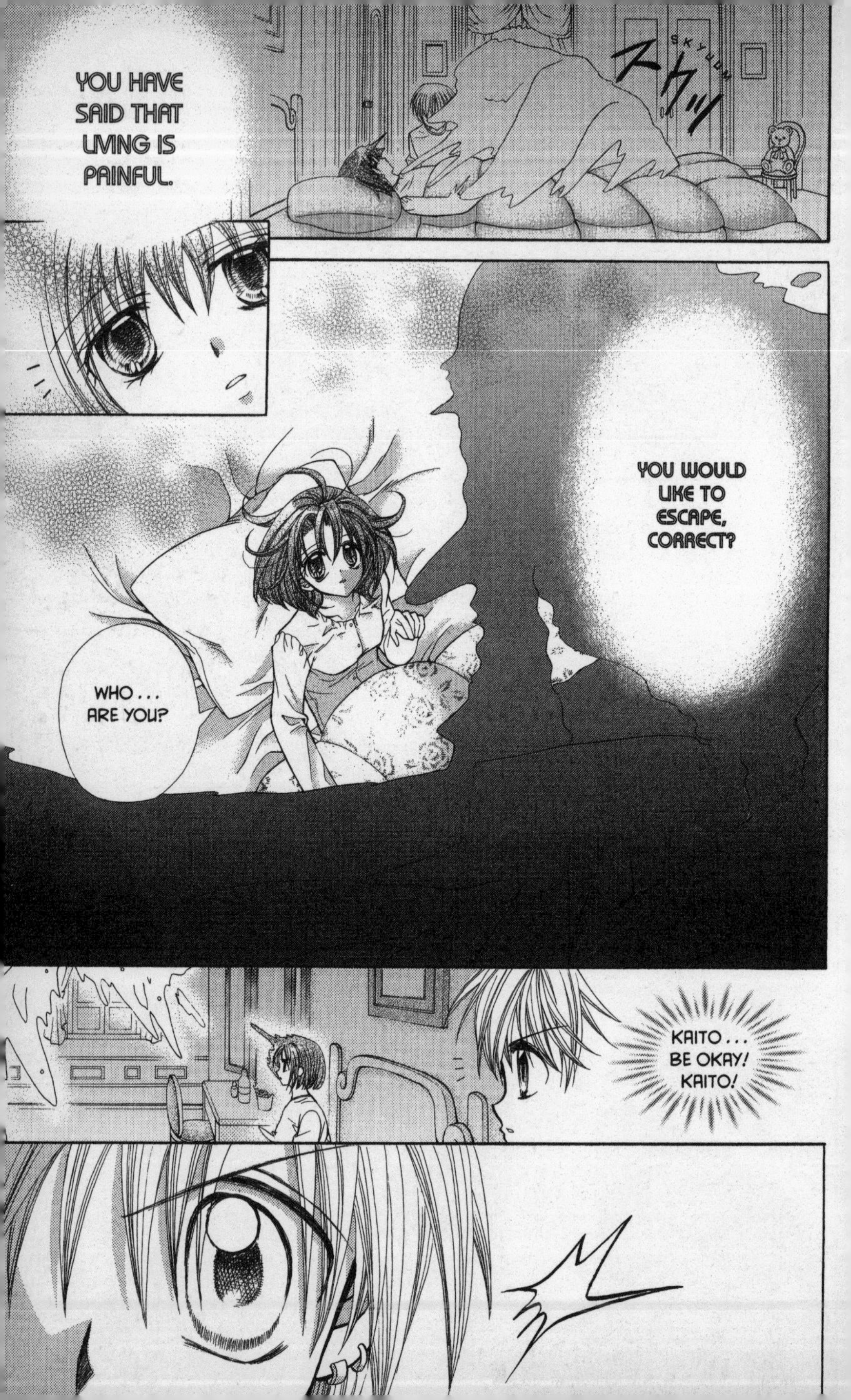
スキュッ
SKYUDN
YOU HAVE SAID THAT LIVING IS PAINFUL.
YOU WOULD LIKE TO ESCAPE, CORRECT?
WHO... ARE YOU?
KAITO... BE OKAY! KAITO!

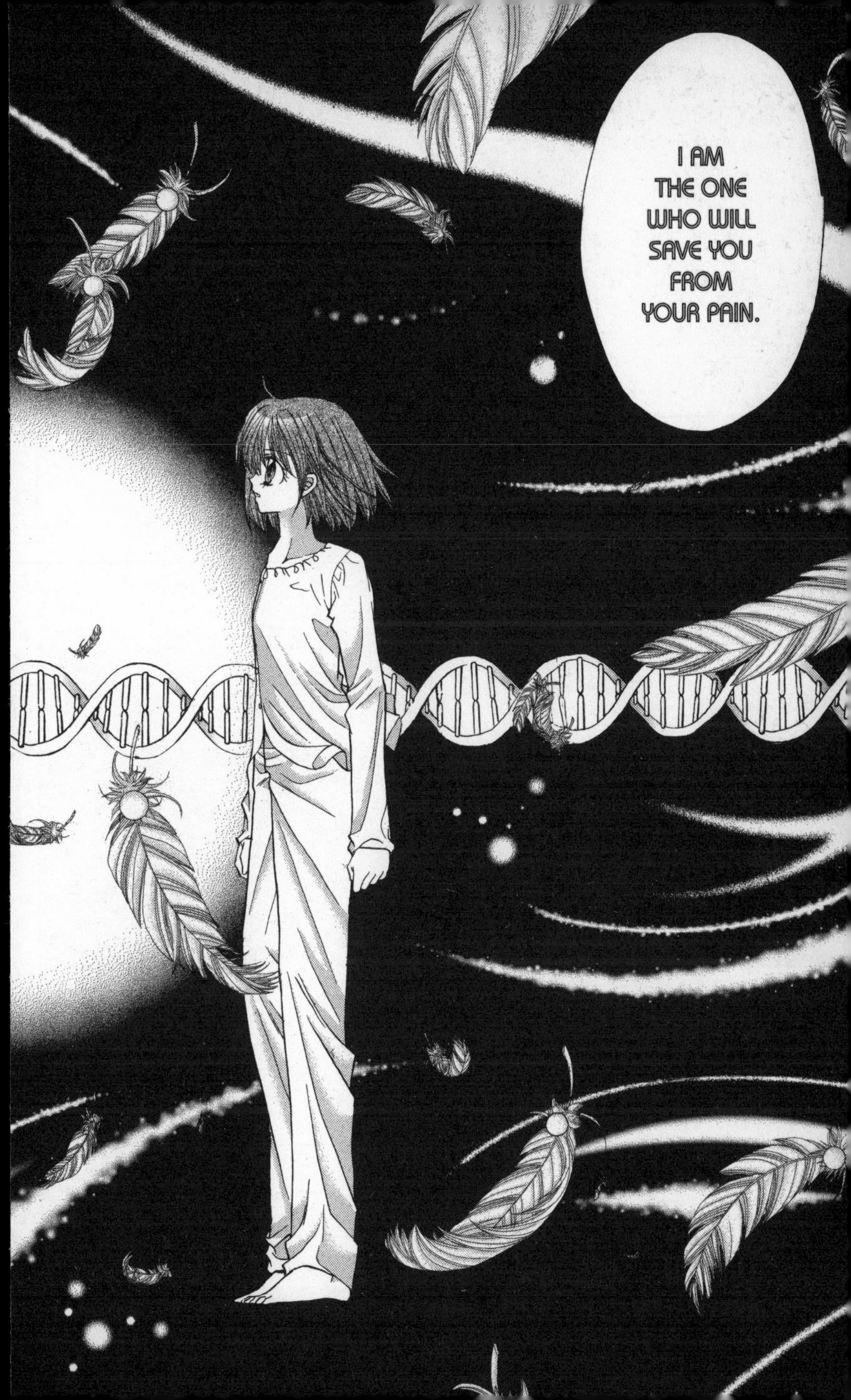
I AM THE ONE WHO WILL SAVE YOU FROM YOUR PAIN.

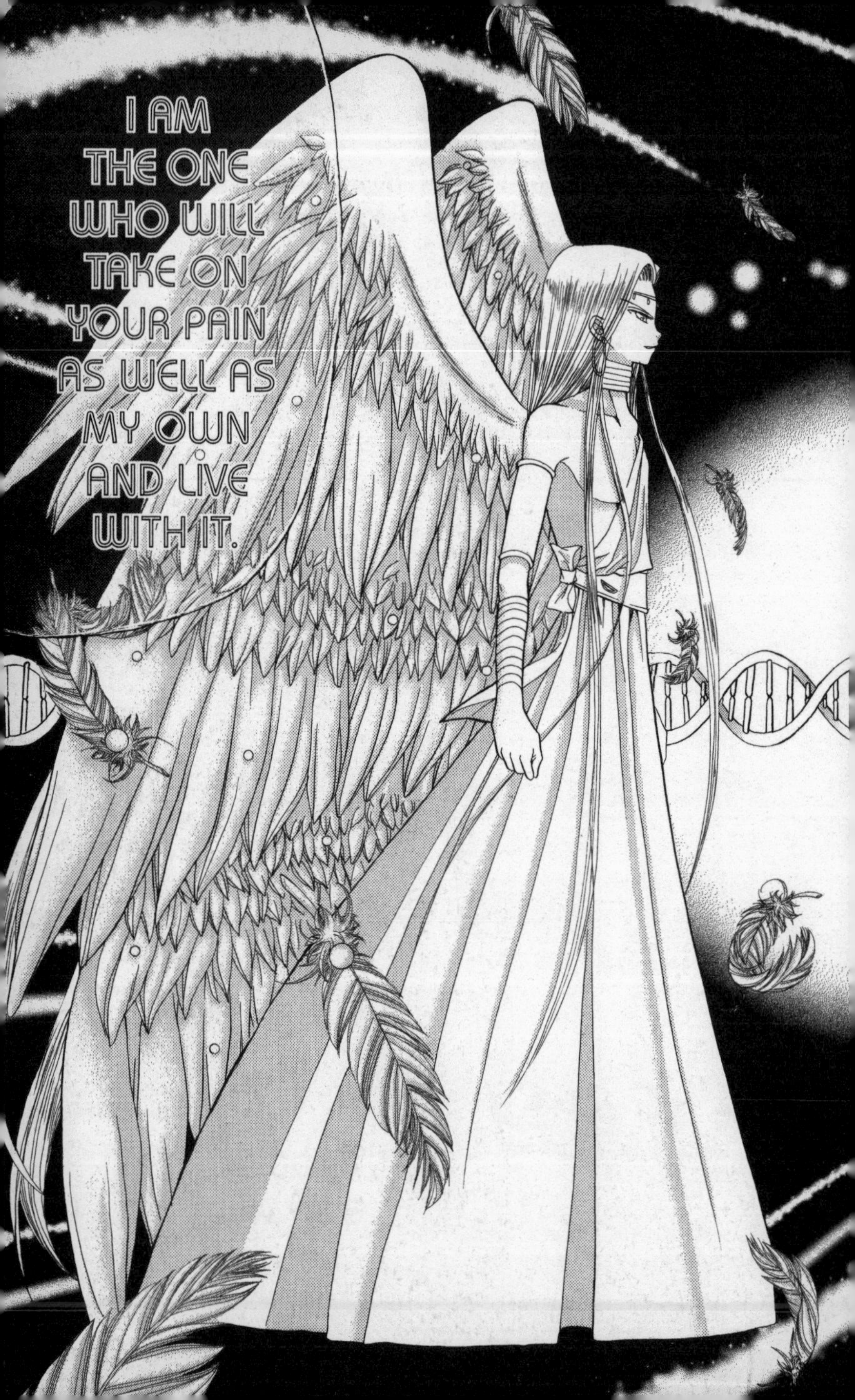
I AM THE ONE WHO WILL TAKE ON YOUR PAIN AS WELL AS MY OWN AND LIVE WITH IT.

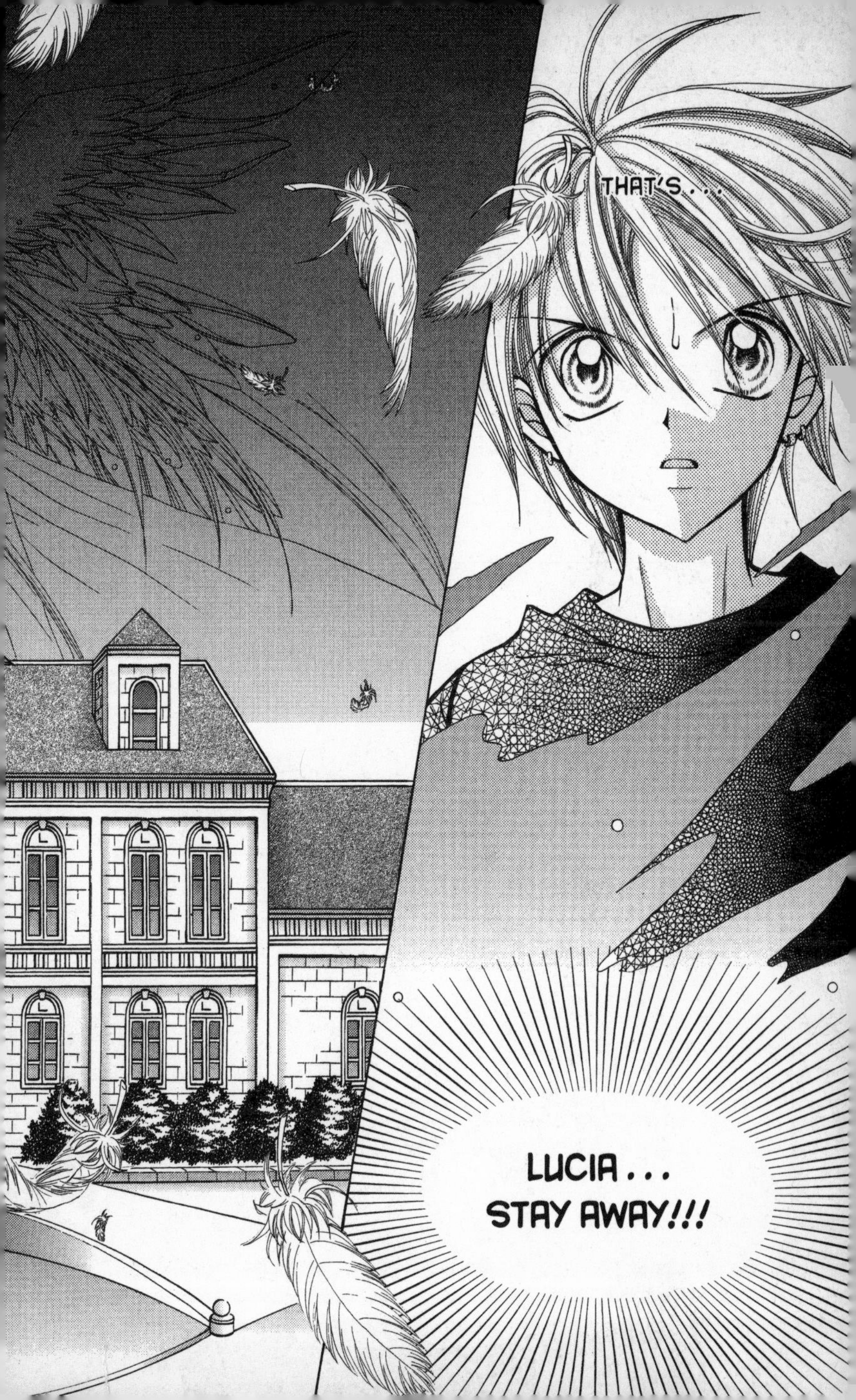
THAT'S...
LUCIA...
STAY AWAY!!!

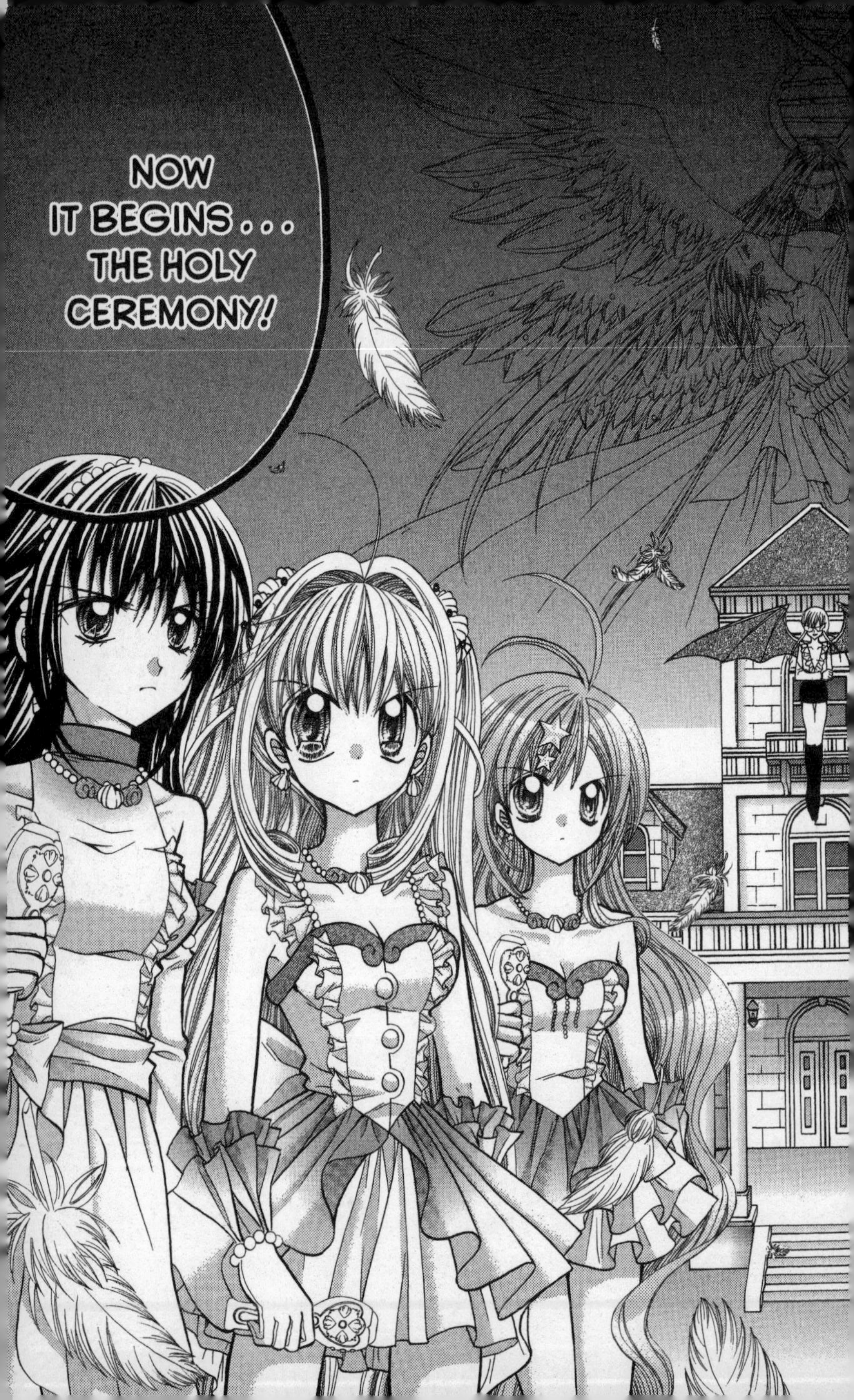
NOW IT BEGINS . . . THE HOLY CEREMONY!

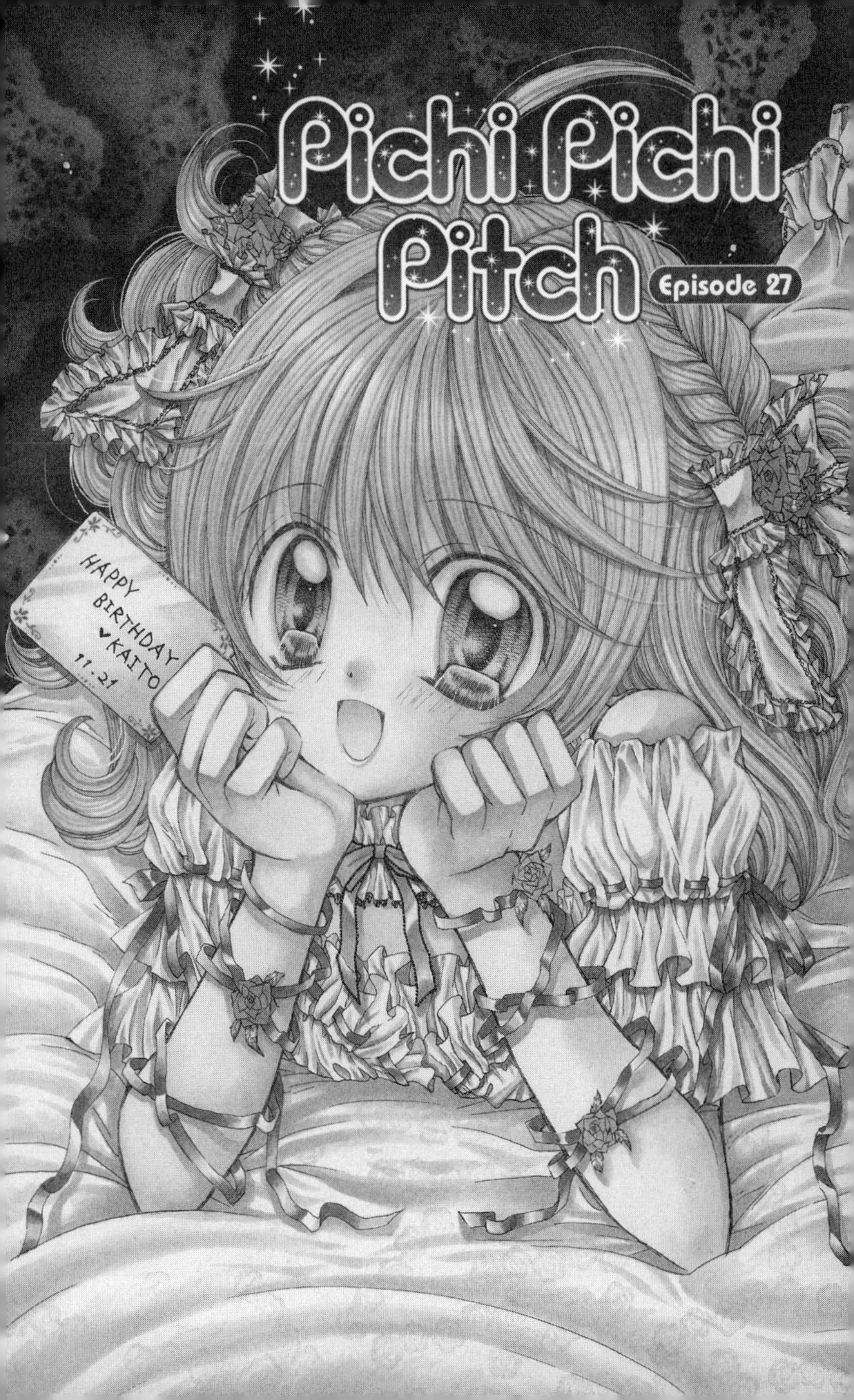
Pichi Pichi Pitch
Episode 27
HAPPY BIRTHDAY ♥KAITO 11.21

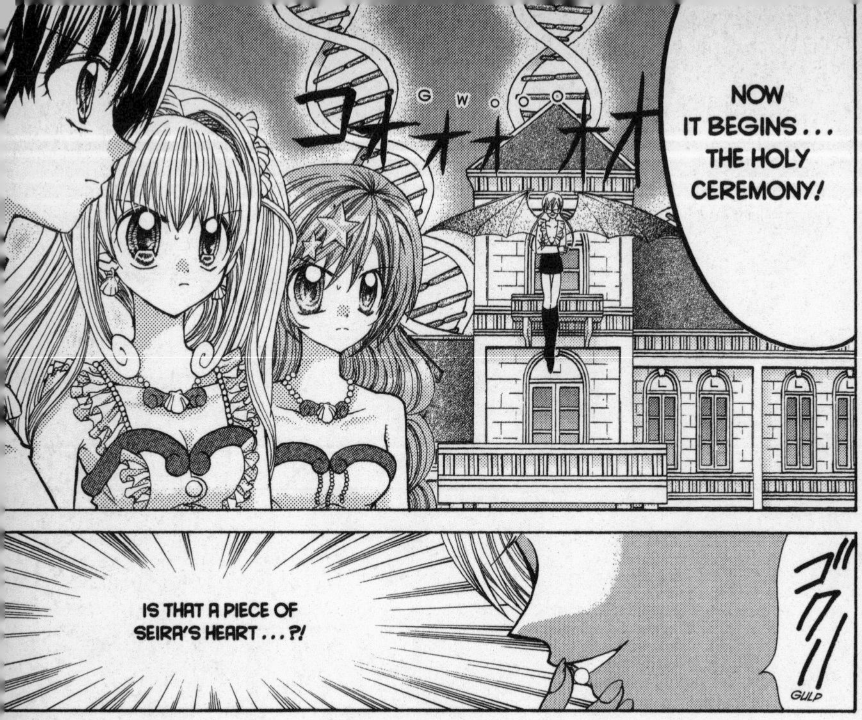
NOW IT BEGINS . . . THE HOLY CEREMONY!
GULP
IS THAT A PIECE OF SEIRA'S HEART . . . ?!

<EPISODE 27>
SPLASH PAGE: I JUST FELT LIKE DRAWING SOMETHING LIGHT AND FLUFFY, AND THIS IS WHAT CAME OUT. I REALLY LIKE IT! FROM ABOUT THIS TIME, I REALLY GOT INTO DRAWING FRILLS. IT WAS ALWAYS DIFFICULT FOR ME BEFORE, SO I SURPRISED MYSELF. (I USUALLY DRAW LIGHT AND FLUFFY, THOUGH.) THIS STORY REVOLVES AROUND THE CHASE INVOLVING MICHEL AND MICHAL. THINGS START TO FALL APART, DON'T THEY? AND TO TELL YOU THE TRUTH, I USED UP ALL OF MY PHYSICAL AND EMOTIONAL STRENGTH DRAWING THIS INSTALLMENT, AND I FELL APART, TOO . . . HA HA HA! I REALLY EMPATHIZED WITH MICHEL. I CAN JOKE ABOUT IT, BUT IT'S HARD TO LAUGH. STILL, LET'S LAUGH ANYWAY. BWA HA HA HA HA! I'M SORRY THAT MY BODY KEPT EVERYONE WAITING. I APOLOGIZE! IT'S JUST MY STRENGTH . . . MY STRENGTH . . . I HAD AN INTRAVENOUS TUBE IN MY LEFT ARM WHILE I WAS DRAWING. THE NURSE GOT THE WRONG SPOT EIGHT TIMES!
↑
THAT WAS PAINFUL!

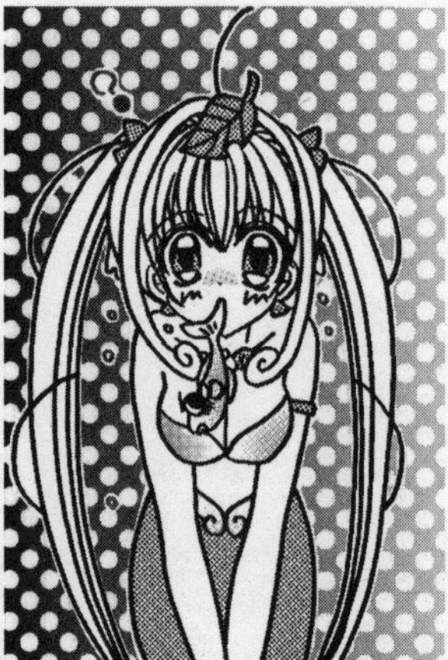

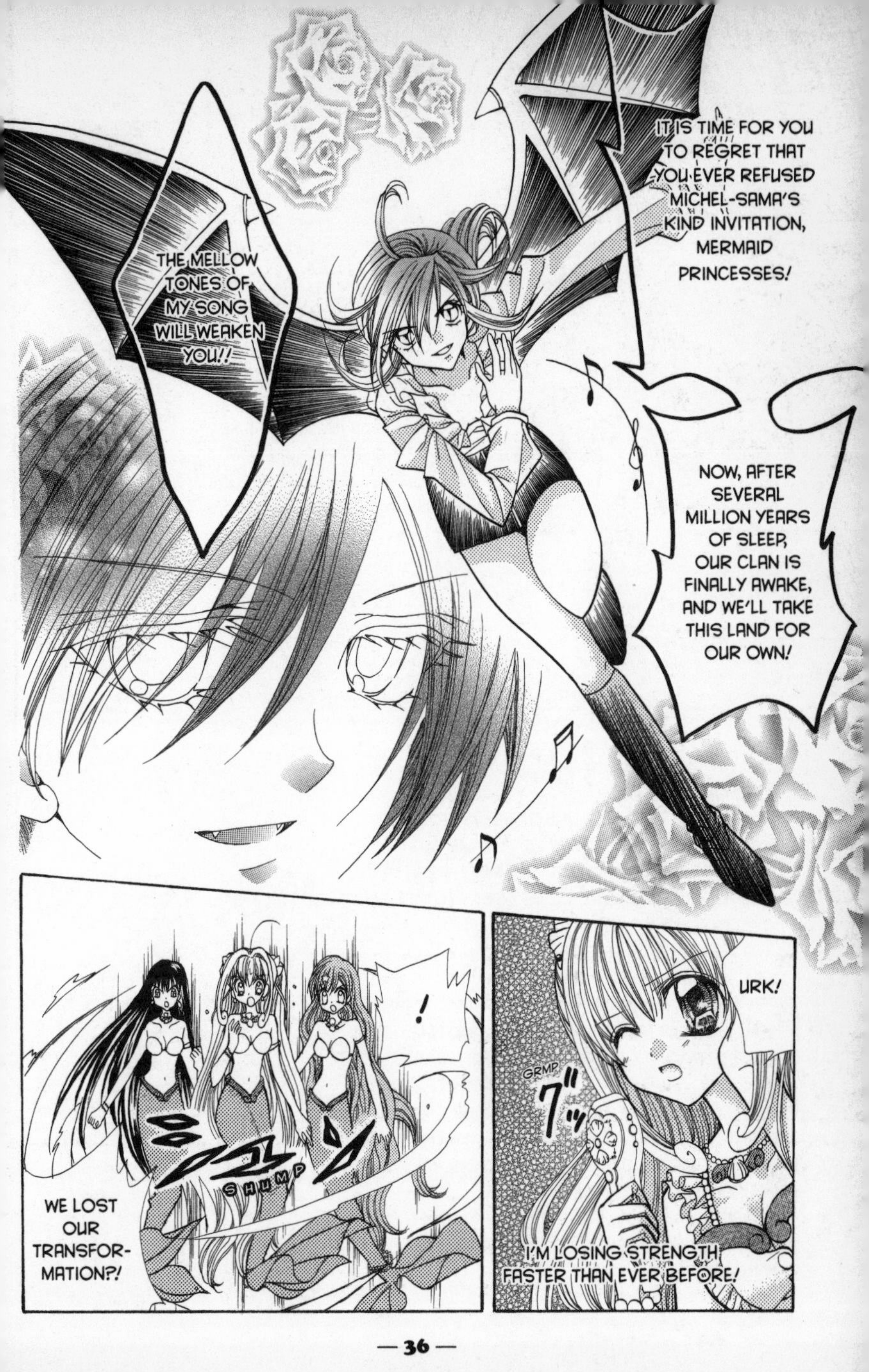
IT IS TIME FOR YOU TO REGRET THAT YOU EVER REFUSED MICHEL-SAMA'S KIND INVITATION, MERMAID PRINCESSES!
NOW, AFTER SEVERAL MILLION YEARS OF SLEEP, OUR CLAN IS FINALLY AWAKE, AND WE'LL TAKE THIS LAND FOR OUR OWN!
THE MELLOW TONES OF MY SONG WILL WEAKEN YOU!!
URK!
GRMP
I'M LOSING STRENGTH FASTER THAN EVER BEFORE!
!
SHUMP
WE LOST OUR TRANSFOR-MATION?!

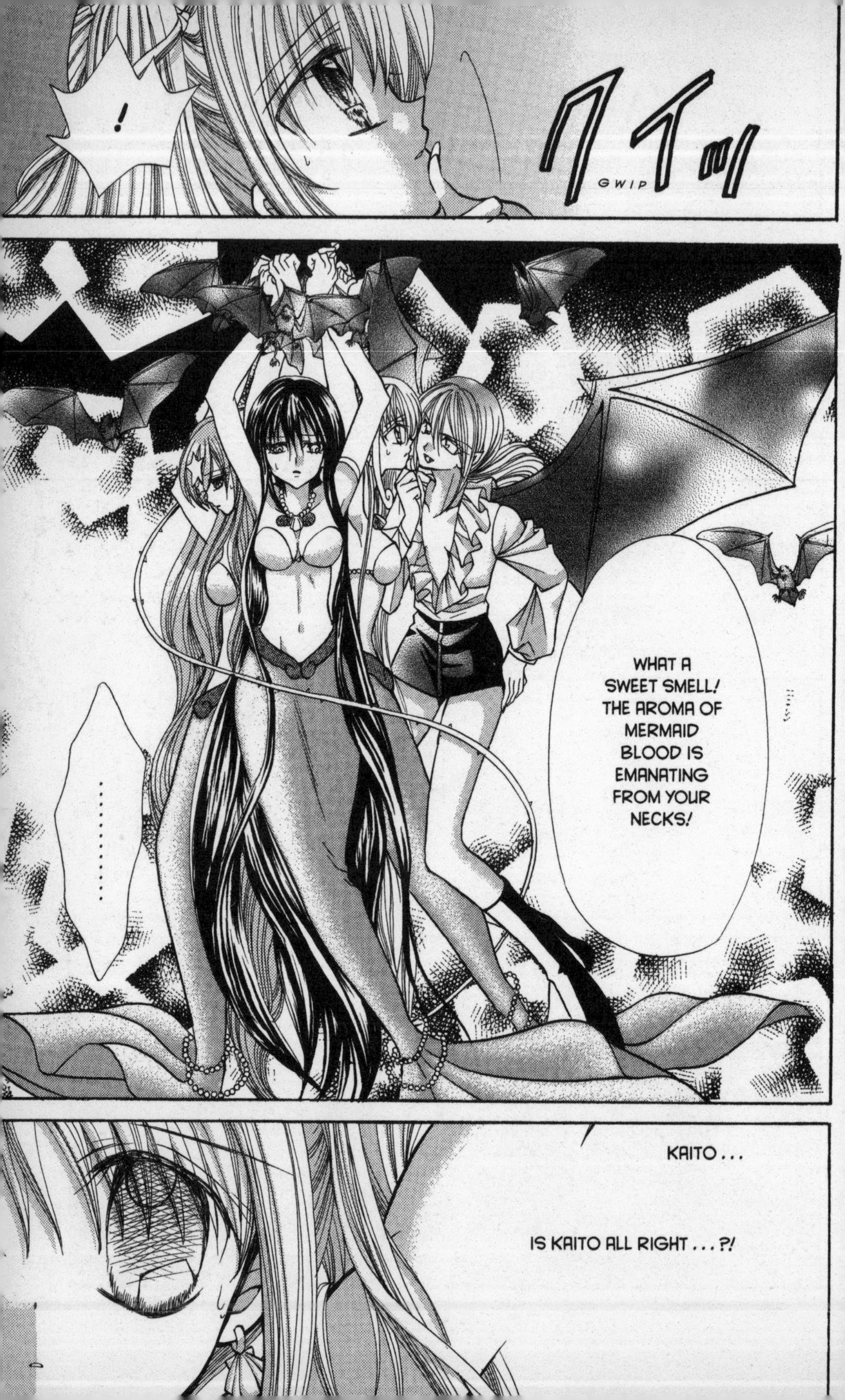
クイッ
GWIP
!
WHAT A SWEET SMELL! THE AROMA OF MERMAID BLOOD IS EMANATING FROM YOUR NECKS!
......
KAITO . . .
IS KAITO ALL RIGHT . . . ?!

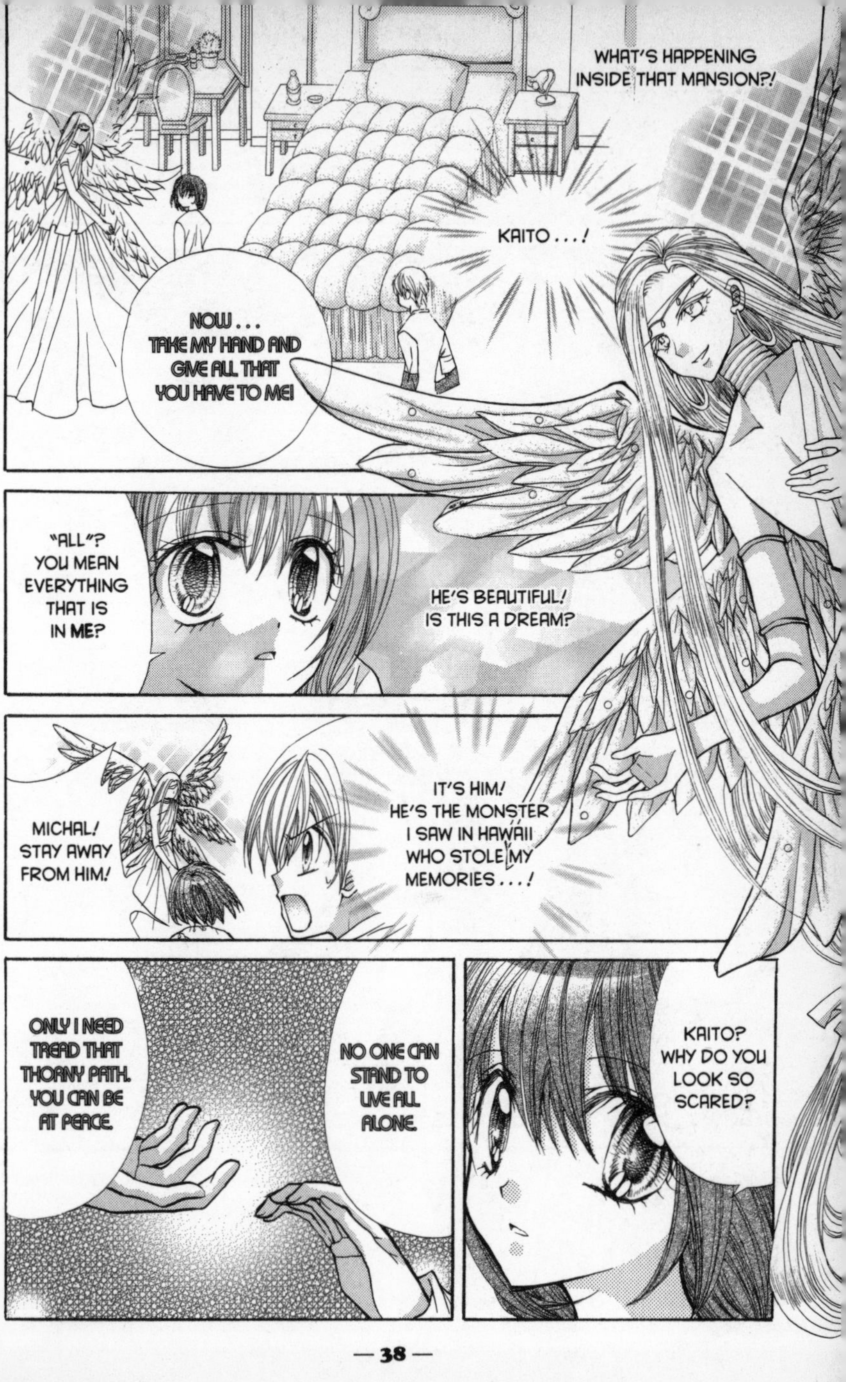
WHAT'S HAPPENING INSIDE THAT MANSION?!
KAITO . . . !
NOW . . . TAKE MY HAND AND GIVE ALL THAT YOU HAVE TO ME!
HE'S BEAUTIFUL! IS THIS A DREAM?
"ALL"? YOU MEAN EVERYTHING THAT IS IN **ME**?
IT'S HIM! HE'S THE MONSTER I SAW IN HAWAII WHO STOLE MY MEMORIES . . . !
MICHAL! STAY AWAY FROM HIM!
KAITO? WHY DO YOU LOOK SO SCARED?
NO ONE CAN STAND TO LIVE ALL ALONE.
ONLY I NEED TREAD THAT THORNY PATH. YOU CAN BE AT PEACE.

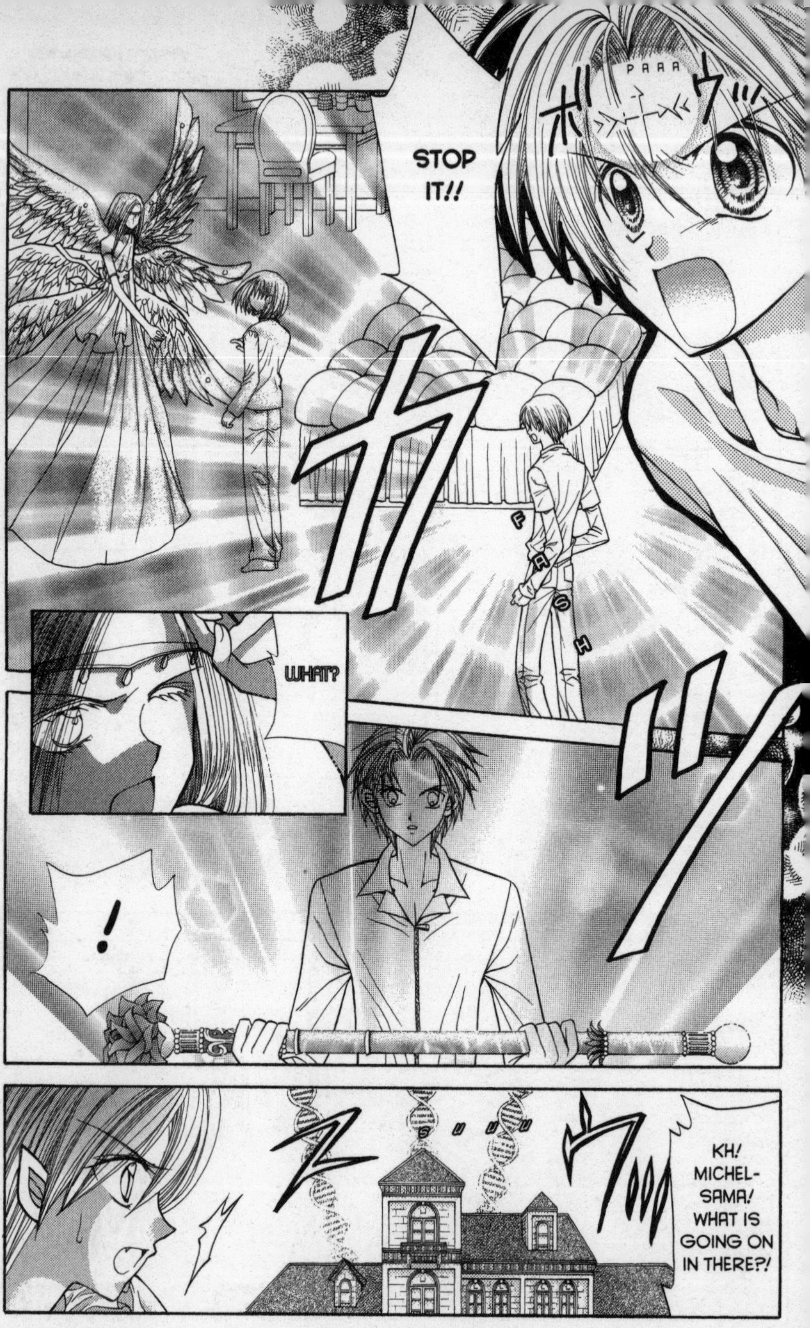
PAAA
STOP IT!!
FASH
WHAT?
!
SUUU
KH! MICHEL-SAMA! WHAT IS GOING ON IN THERE?!

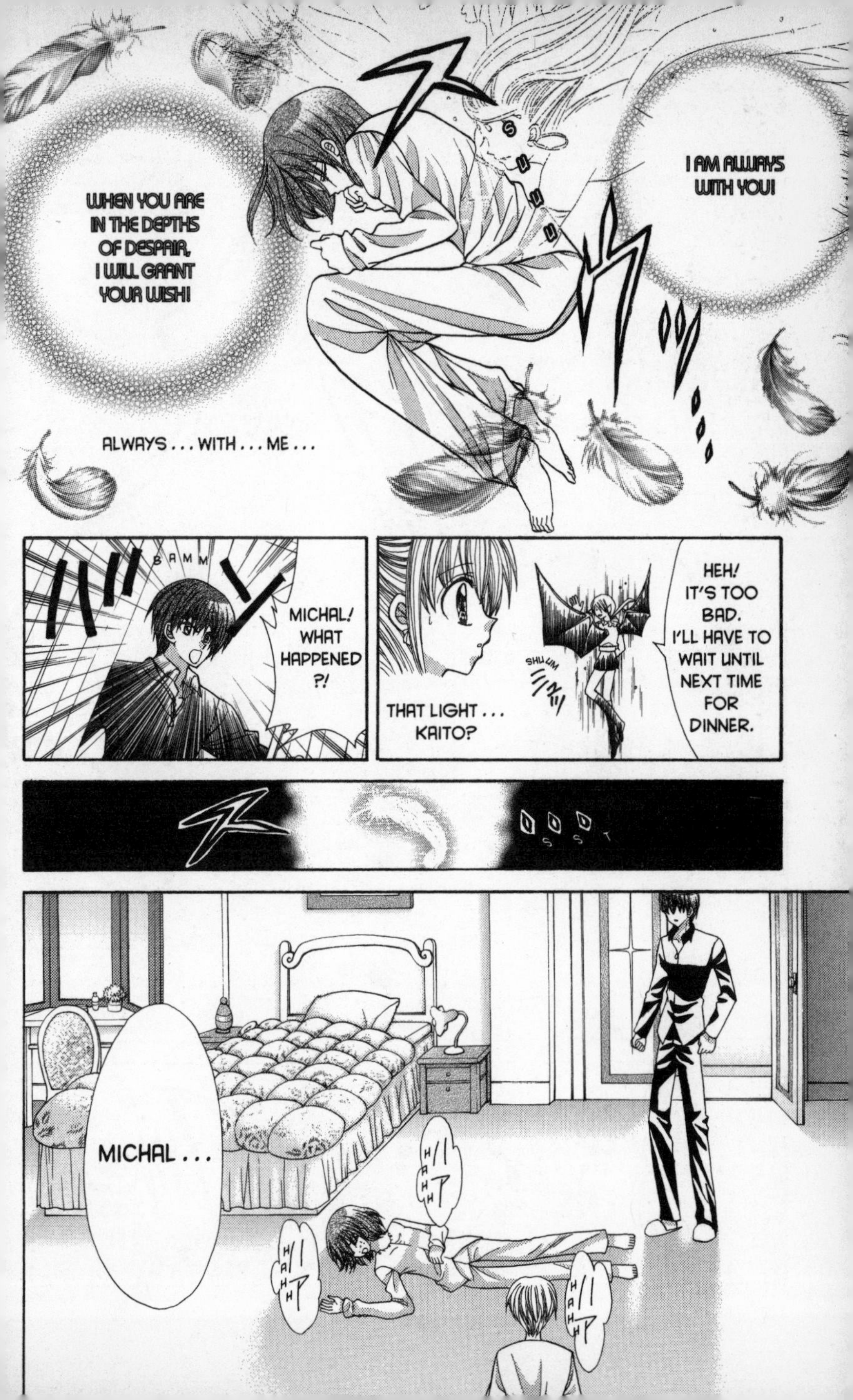
I AM ALWAYS WITH YOU!
WHEN YOU ARE IN THE DEPTHS OF DESPAIR, I WILL GRANT YOUR WISH!
ALWAYS . . . WITH . . . ME . . .
HEH! IT'S TOO BAD. I'LL HAVE TO WAIT UNTIL NEXT TIME FOR DINNER.
SHU UM
THAT LIGHT . . . KAITO?
BAMM
MICHAL! WHAT HAPPENED ?!
MICHAL . . .
HAHH
HAHH
HAHH

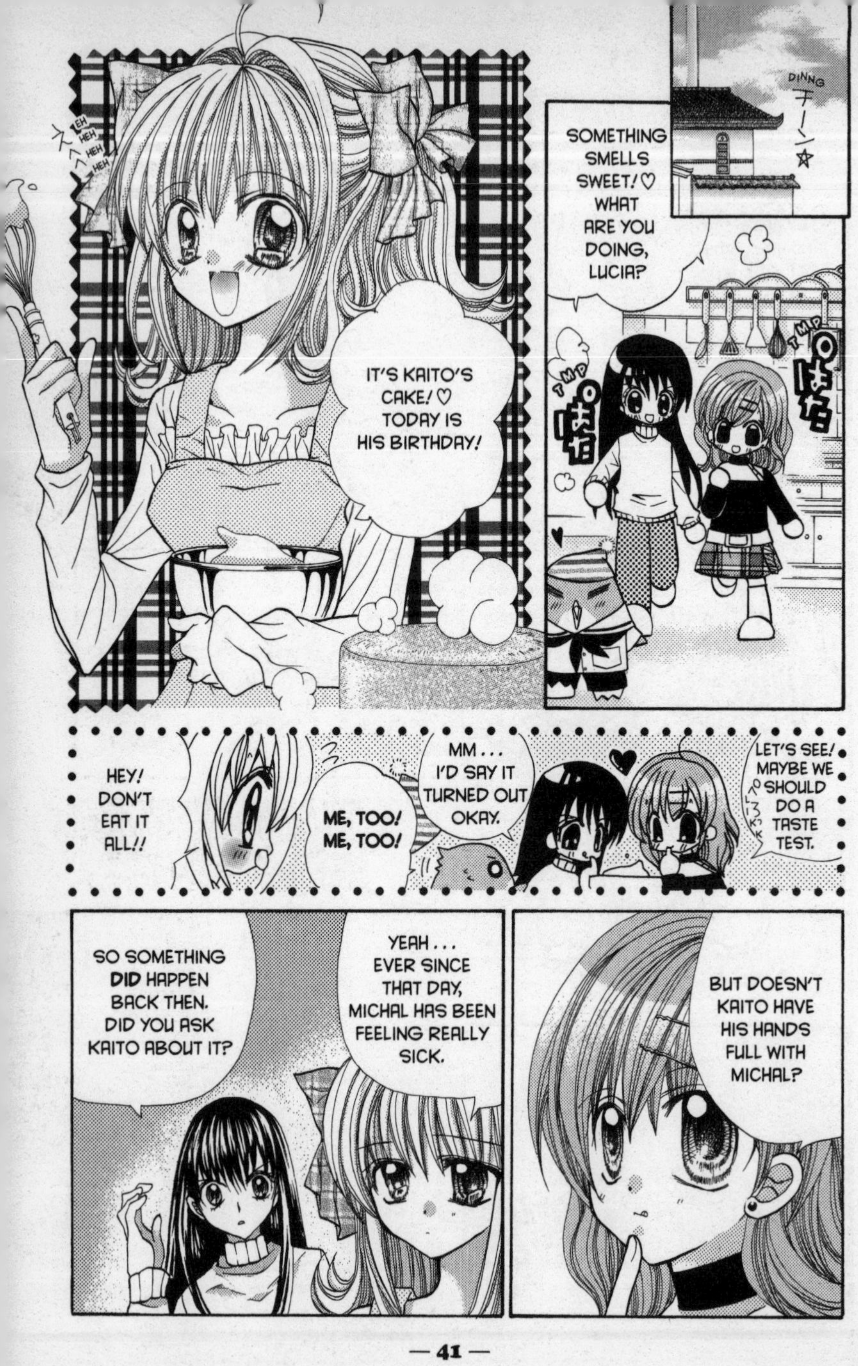
DINNG
チーン☆
SOMETHING SMELLS SWEET! ♡ WHAT ARE YOU DOING, LUCIA?
TMP
TMP
EH HEH HEH HEH
IT'S KAITO'S CAKE! ♡ TODAY IS HIS BIRTHDAY!
LET'S SEE! MAYBE WE SHOULD DO A TASTE TEST.
MM . . . I'D SAY IT TURNED OUT OKAY.
ME, TOO! ME, TOO!
HEY! DON'T EAT IT ALL!!
BUT DOESN'T KAITO HAVE HIS HANDS FULL WITH MICHAL?
YEAH . . . EVER SINCE THAT DAY, MICHAL HAS BEEN FEELING REALLY SICK.
SO SOMETHING DID HAPPEN BACK THEN. DID YOU ASK KAITO ABOUT IT?

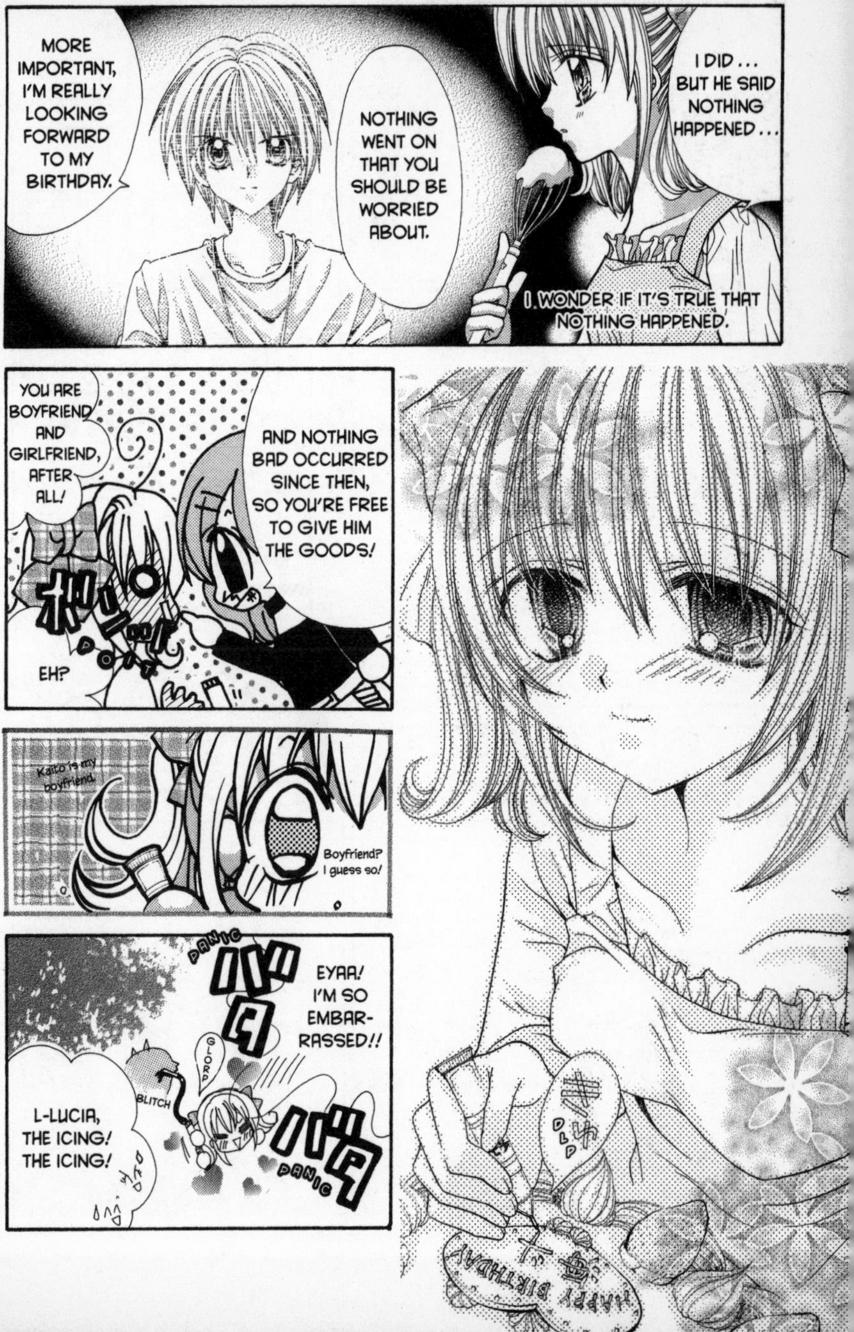
I DID... BUT HE SAID NOTHING HAPPENED...
I WONDER IF IT'S TRUE THAT NOTHING HAPPENED.
NOTHING WENT ON THAT YOU SHOULD BE WORRIED ABOUT.
MORE IMPORTANT, I'M REALLY LOOKING FORWARD TO MY BIRTHDAY.
HAPPY BIRTHDAY
AND NOTHING BAD OCCURRED SINCE THEN, SO YOU'RE FREE TO GIVE HIM THE GOODS!
YOU ARE BOYFRIEND AND GIRLFRIEND, AFTER ALL!
POIT
EH?
Boyfriend? I guess so!
Kaito's my boyfriend.
EYAA! I'M SO EMBARRASSED!!
PANIC
GLORP
BLITCH
L-LUCIA, THE ICING! THE ICING!
PANIC

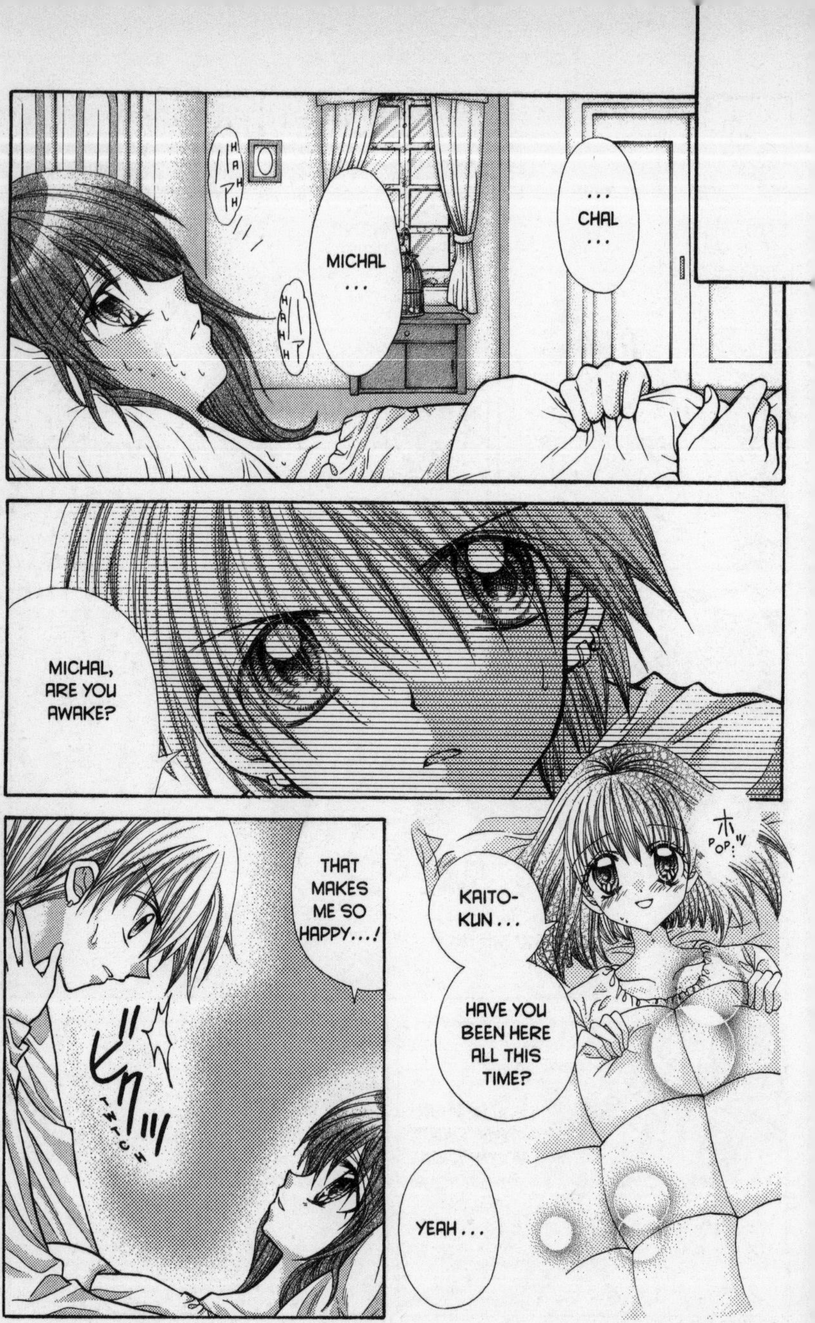
... CHAL ...
MICHAL ...
MICHAL, ARE YOU AWAKE?
POP!
KAITO-KUN ...
HAVE YOU BEEN HERE ALL THIS TIME?
YEAH ...
THAT MAKES ME SO HAPPY...!
TWITCH

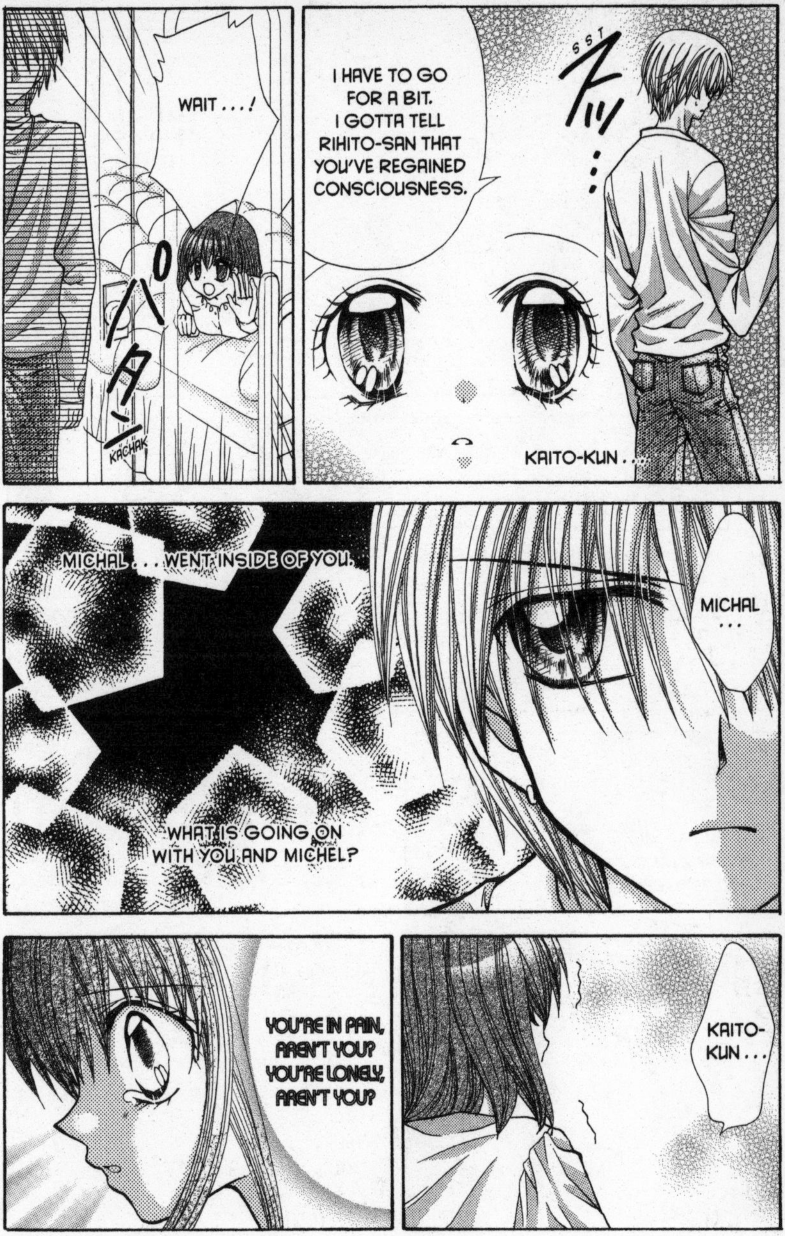
SST
I HAVE TO GO FOR A BIT. I GOTTA TELL RIHITO-SAN THAT YOU'VE REGAINED CONSCIOUSNESS.
KAITO-KUN . . .
WAIT . . . !
KACHAK
MICHAL . . .
MICHAL . . . WENT INSIDE OF YOU.
WHAT IS GOING ON WITH YOU AND MICHEL?
KAITO-KUN . . .
YOU'RE IN PAIN, AREN'T YOU? YOU'RE LONELY, AREN'T YOU?

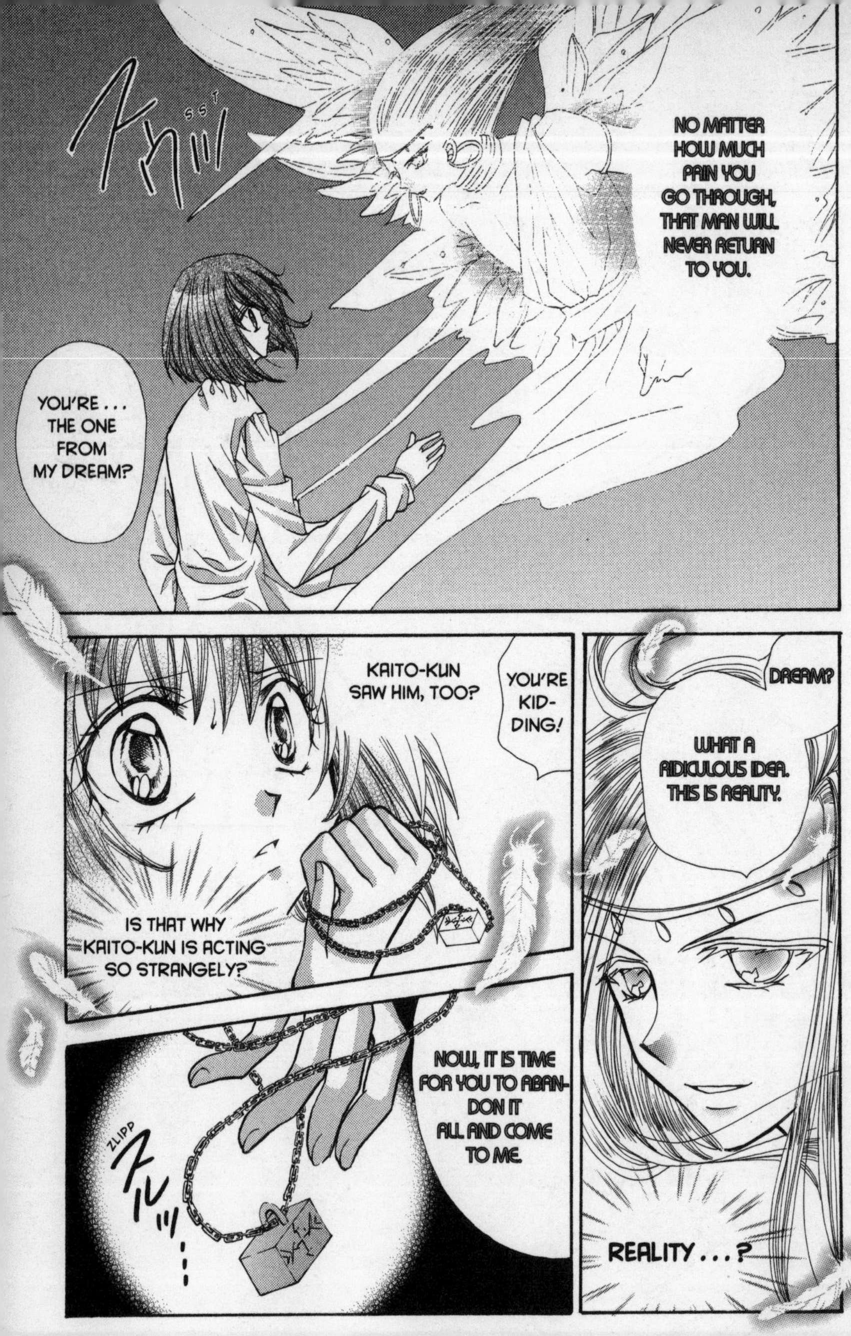
NO MATTER HOW MUCH PAIN YOU GO THROUGH, THAT MAN WILL NEVER RETURN TO YOU.
SST
YOU'RE . . . THE ONE FROM MY DREAM?
DREAM?
WHAT A RIDICULOUS IDEA. THIS IS REALITY.
REALITY . . . ?
YOU'RE KID-DING!
KAITO-KUN SAW HIM, TOO?
IS THAT WHY KAITO-KUN IS ACTING SO STRANGELY?
NOW, IT IS TIME FOR YOU TO ABAN-DON IT ALL AND COME TO ME.
ZLIPP

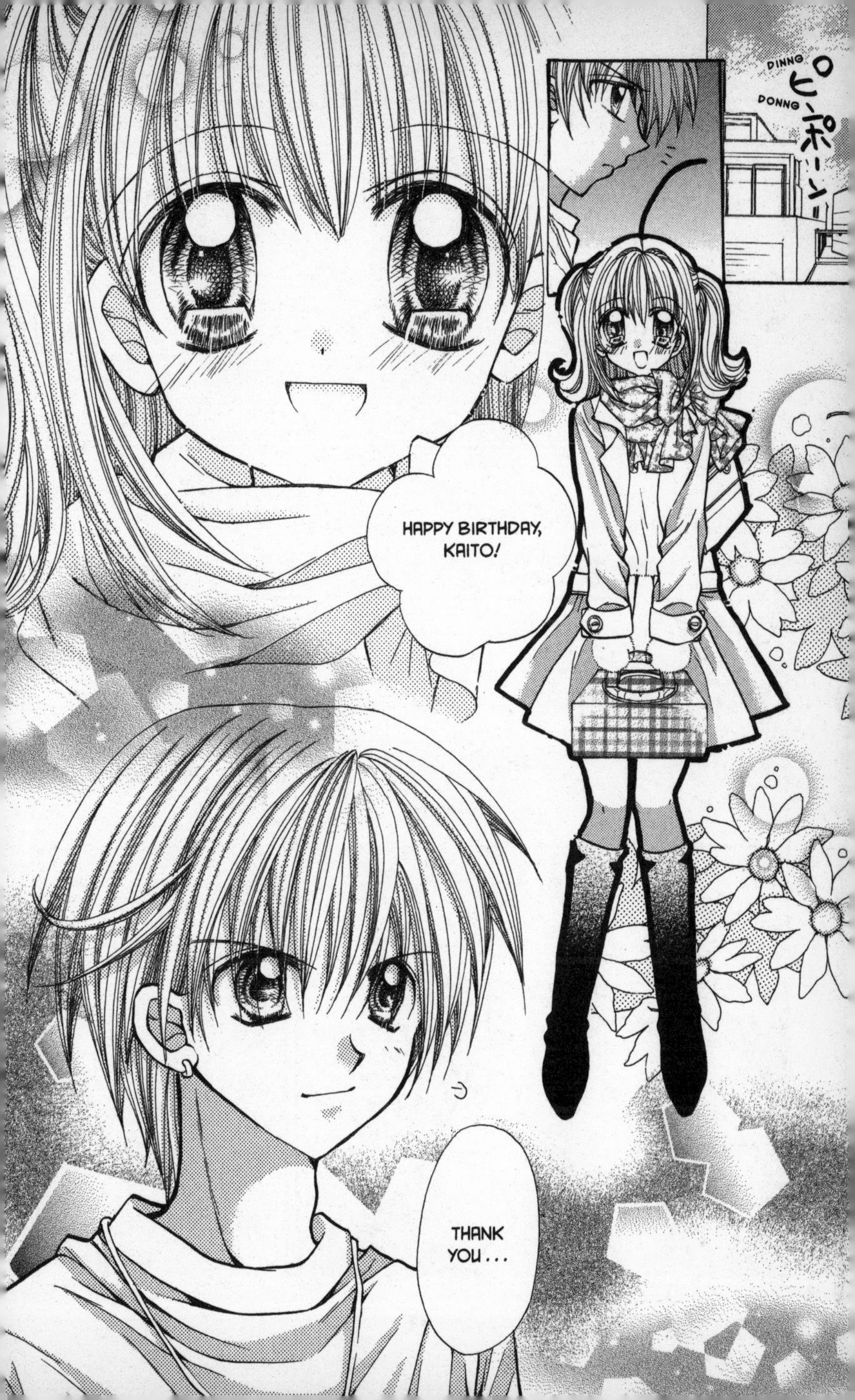
DINNG DONNG
ピンポーン
HAPPY BIRTHDAY, KAITO!
THANK YOU . . .

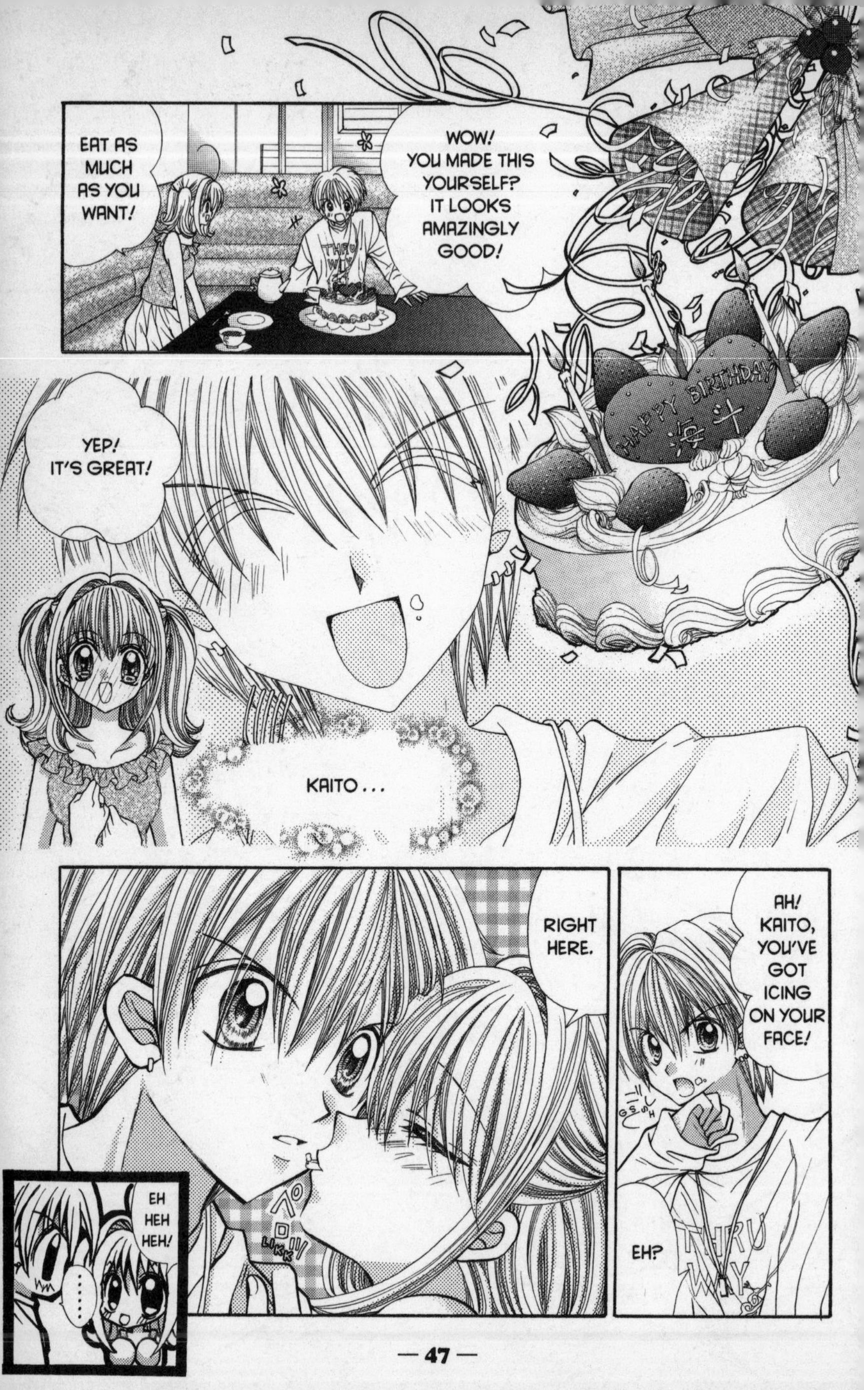

WOW! YOU MADE THIS YOURSELF? IT LOOKS AMAZINGLY GOOD!
EAT AS MUCH AS YOU WANT!
HAPPY BIRTHDAY 海斗
YEP! IT'S GREAT!
KAITO . . .
AH! KAITO, YOU'VE GOT ICING ON YOUR FACE!
EH?
THRU WAY
RIGHT HERE.
EH HEH HEH!
. . . . .

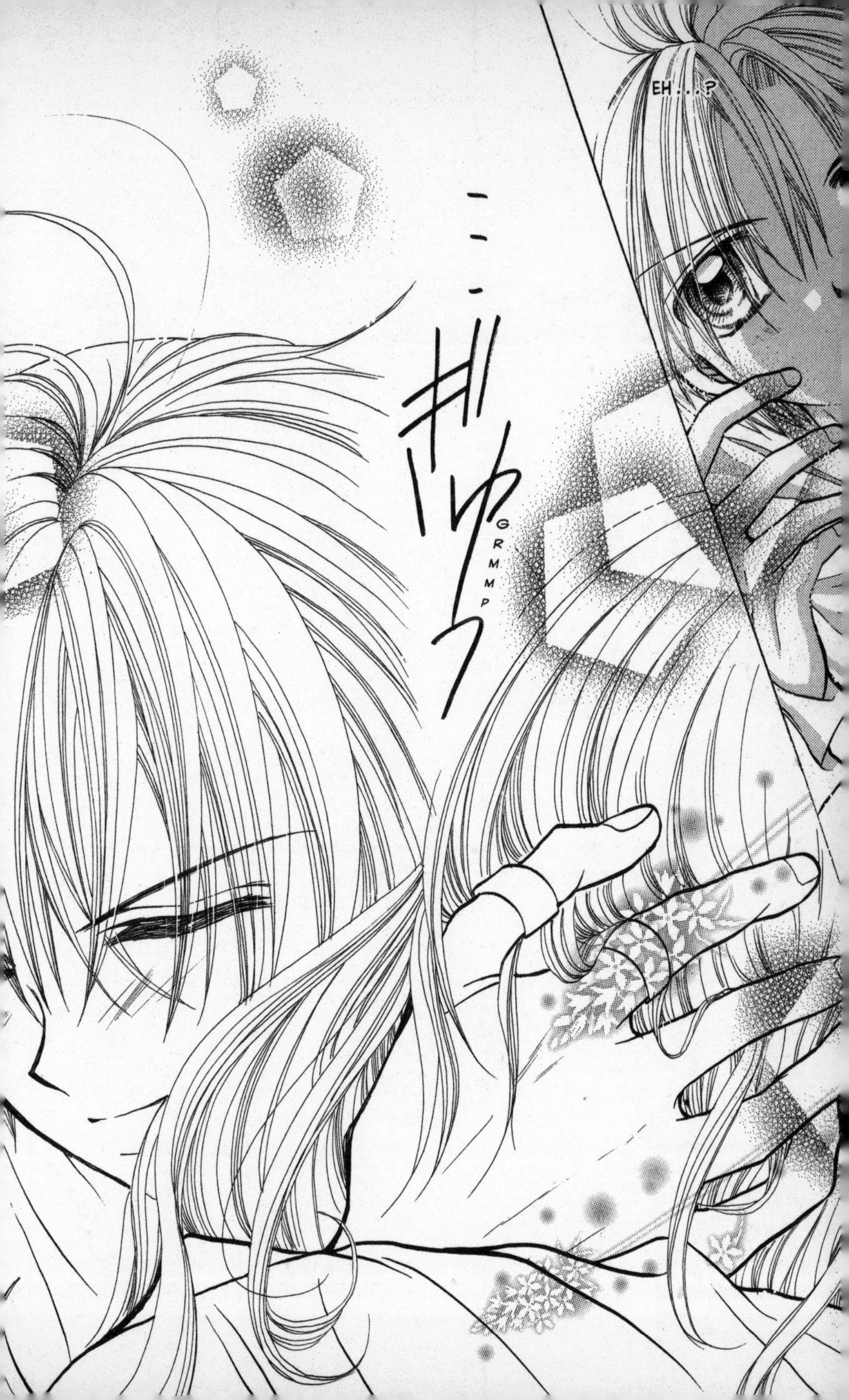
EH...?
ぎゅっ
GRMMP

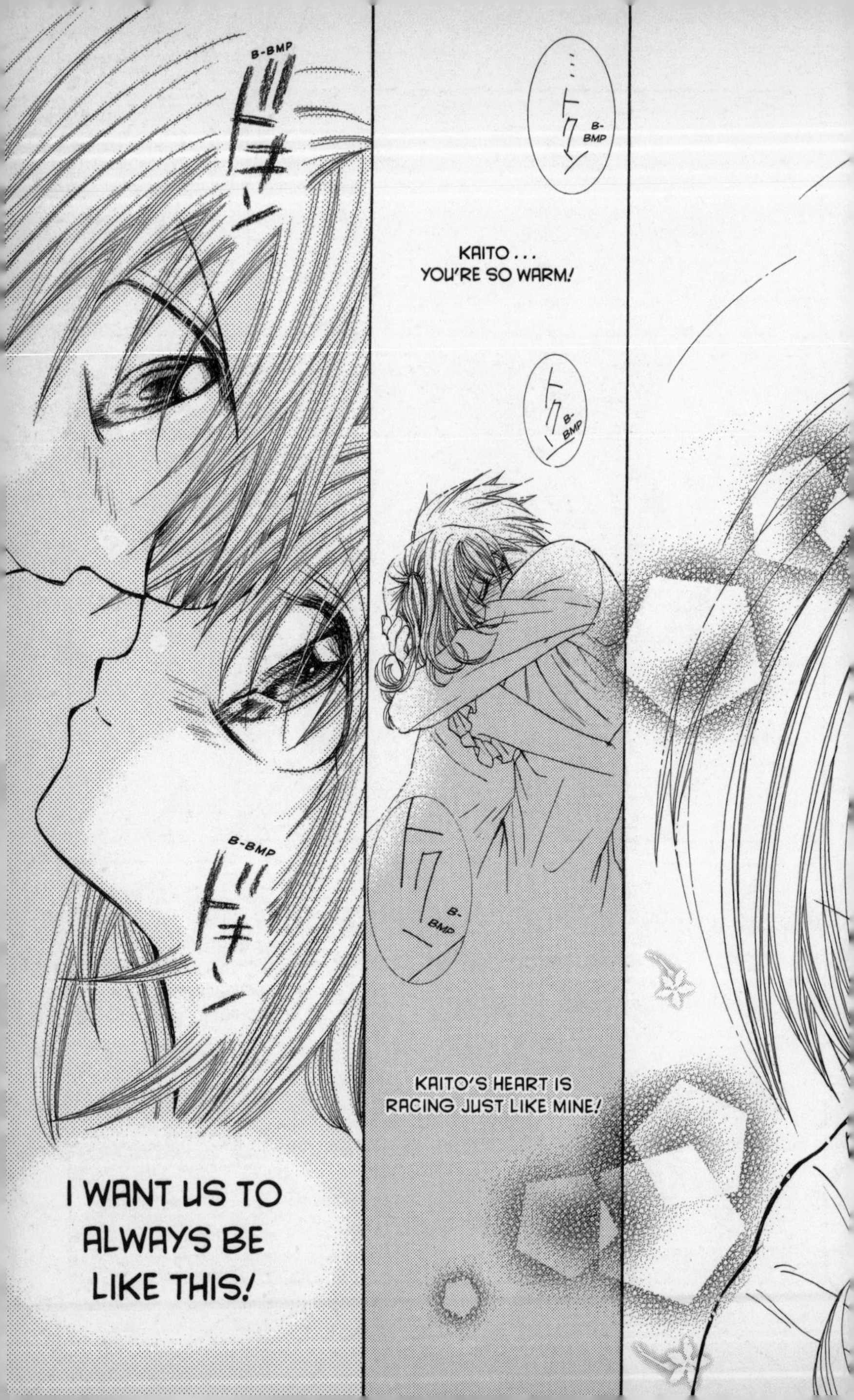
トクン
B-BMP
KAITO . . .
YOU'RE SO WARM!
トクン
B-BMP
トクン
B-BMP
KAITO'S HEART IS RACING JUST LIKE MINE!
B-BMP
ドキン
B-BMP
ドキン
I WANT US TO ALWAYS BE LIKE THIS!

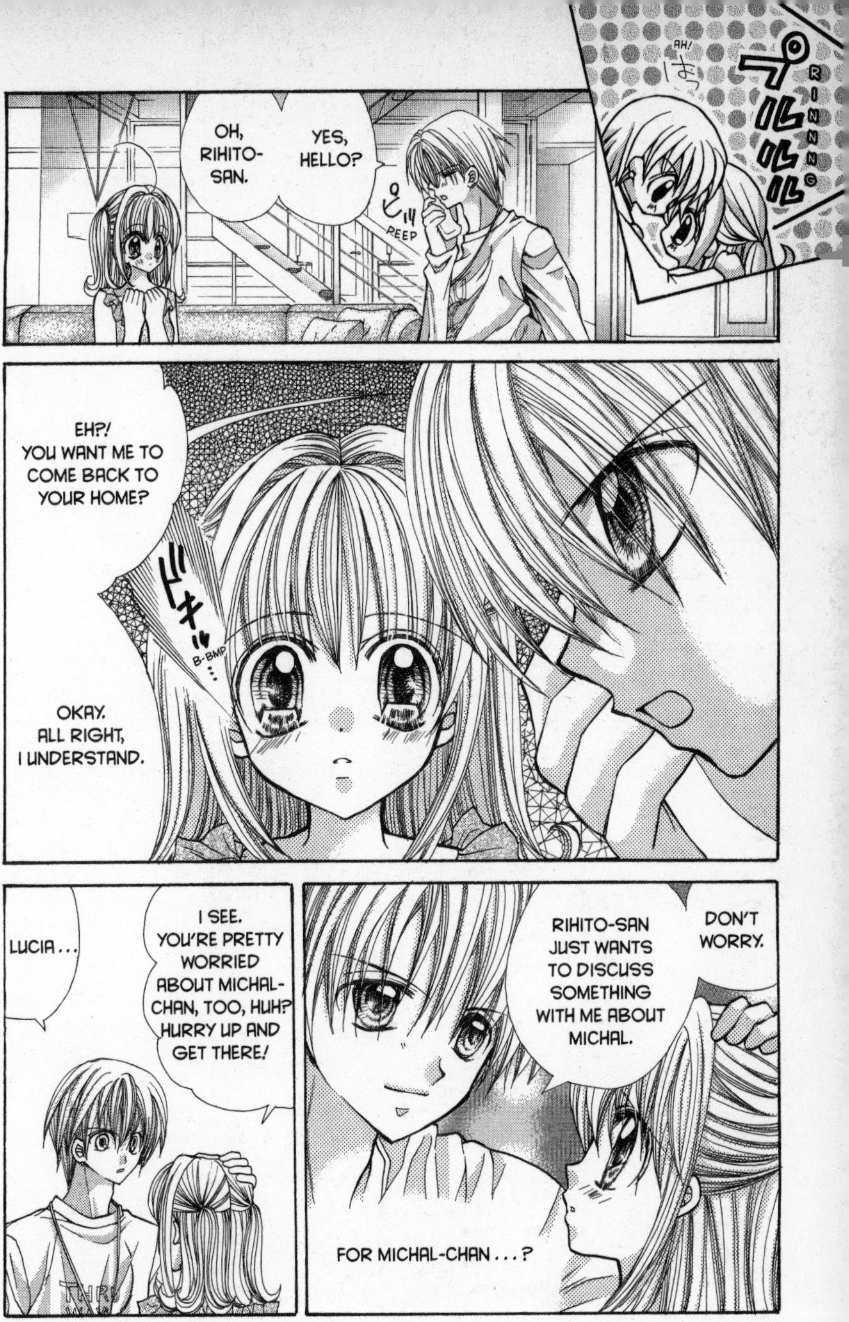

RINNNG
プルルル
AH!
ぽっ
YES, HELLO?
OH, RIHITO-SAN.
ピッ
PEEP
EH?! YOU WANT ME TO COME BACK TO YOUR HOME?
ドキッ
B-BMP
...
OKAY. ALL RIGHT, I UNDERSTAND.
DON'T WORRY.
RIHITO-SAN JUST WANTS TO DISCUSS SOMETHING WITH ME ABOUT MICHAL.
FOR MICHAL-CHAN . . . ?
I SEE. YOU'RE PRETTY WORRIED ABOUT MICHAL-CHAN, TOO, HUH? HURRY UP AND GET THERE!
LUCIA . . .

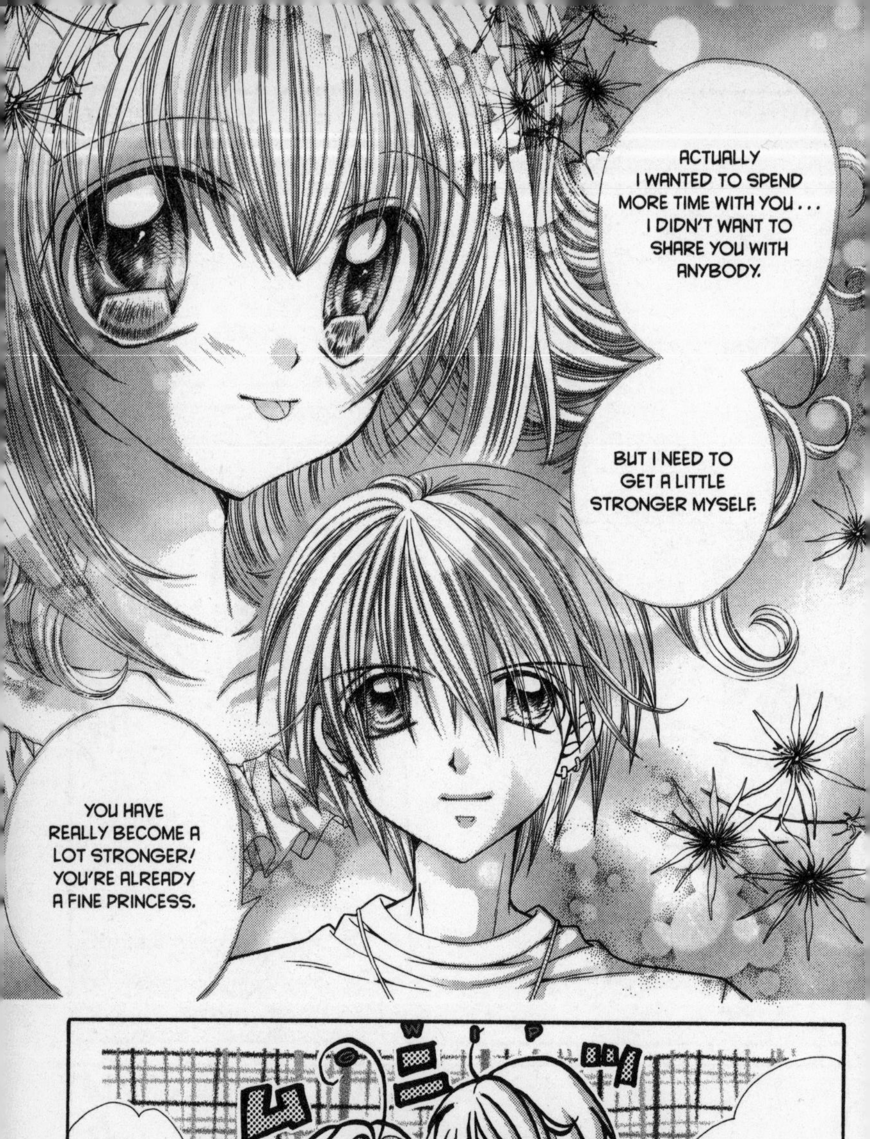
ACTUALLY I WANTED TO SPEND MORE TIME WITH YOU . . . I DIDN'T WANT TO SHARE YOU WITH ANYBODY.
BUT I NEED TO GET A LITTLE STRONGER MYSELF.
YOU HAVE REALLY BECOME A LOT STRONGER! YOU'RE ALREADY A FINE PRINCESS.
YOU WAIT RIGHT HERE!
OH, KAITO! HONESTLY!

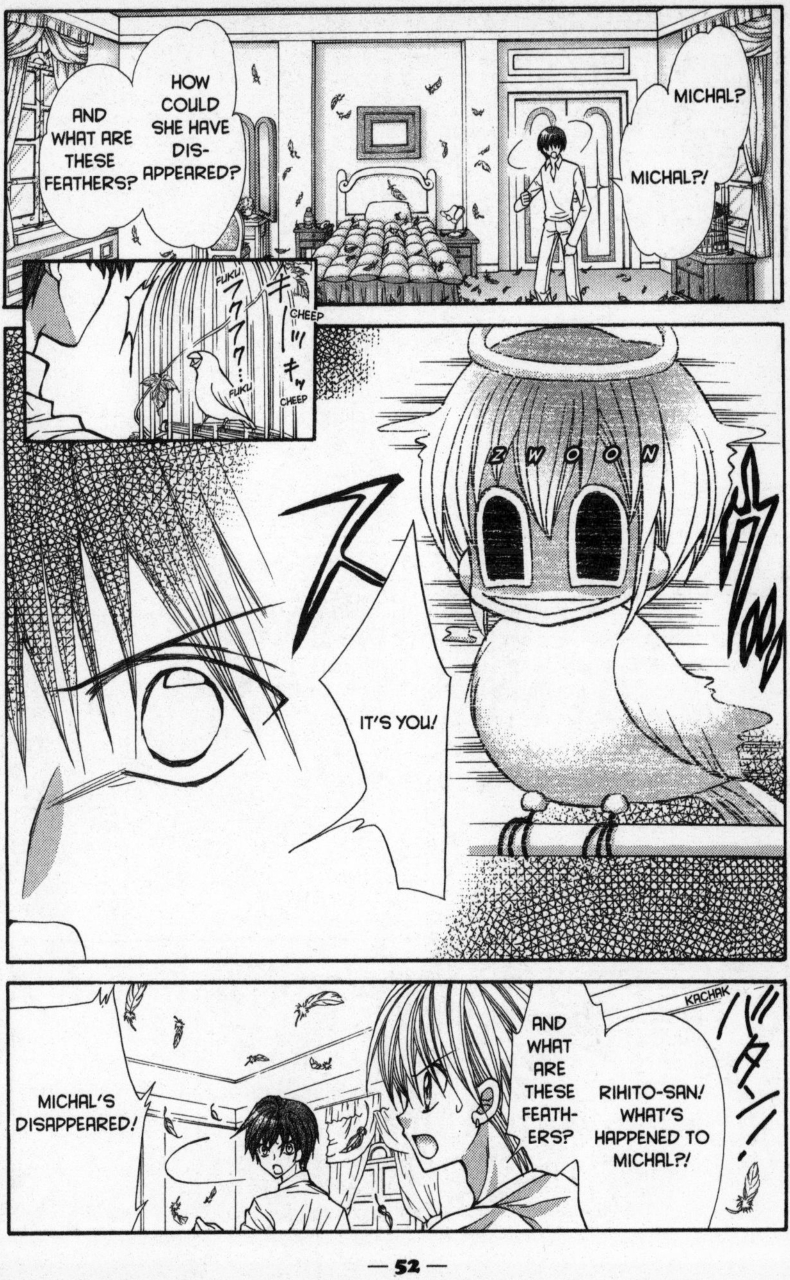
MICHAL?
MICHAL?!
HOW COULD SHE HAVE DIS-APPEARED?
AND WHAT ARE THESE FEATHERS?
FUKU
CHEEP
FUKU
CHEEP
ZWOON
IT'S YOU!
KACHAK
RIHITO-SAN! WHAT'S HAPPENED TO MICHAL?!
AND WHAT ARE THESE FEATH-ERS?
MICHAL'S DISAPPEARED!

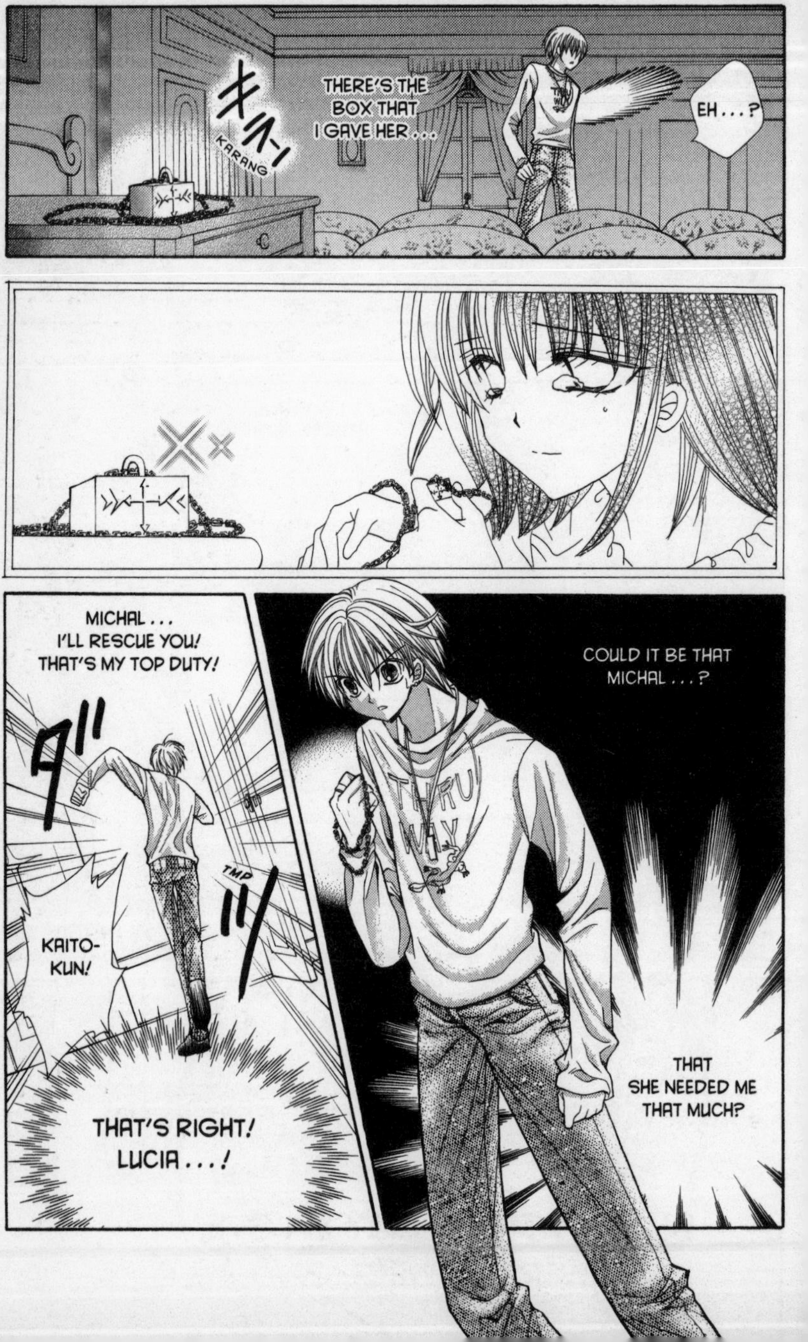
EH . . . ?
THERE'S THE BOX THAT I GAVE HER . . .
KARANG
COULD IT BE THAT MICHAL . . . ?
THAT SHE NEEDED ME THAT MUCH?
MICHAL . . . I'LL RESCUE YOU! THAT'S MY TOP DUTY!
TMP
KAITO-KUN!
THAT'S RIGHT! LUCIA . . . !

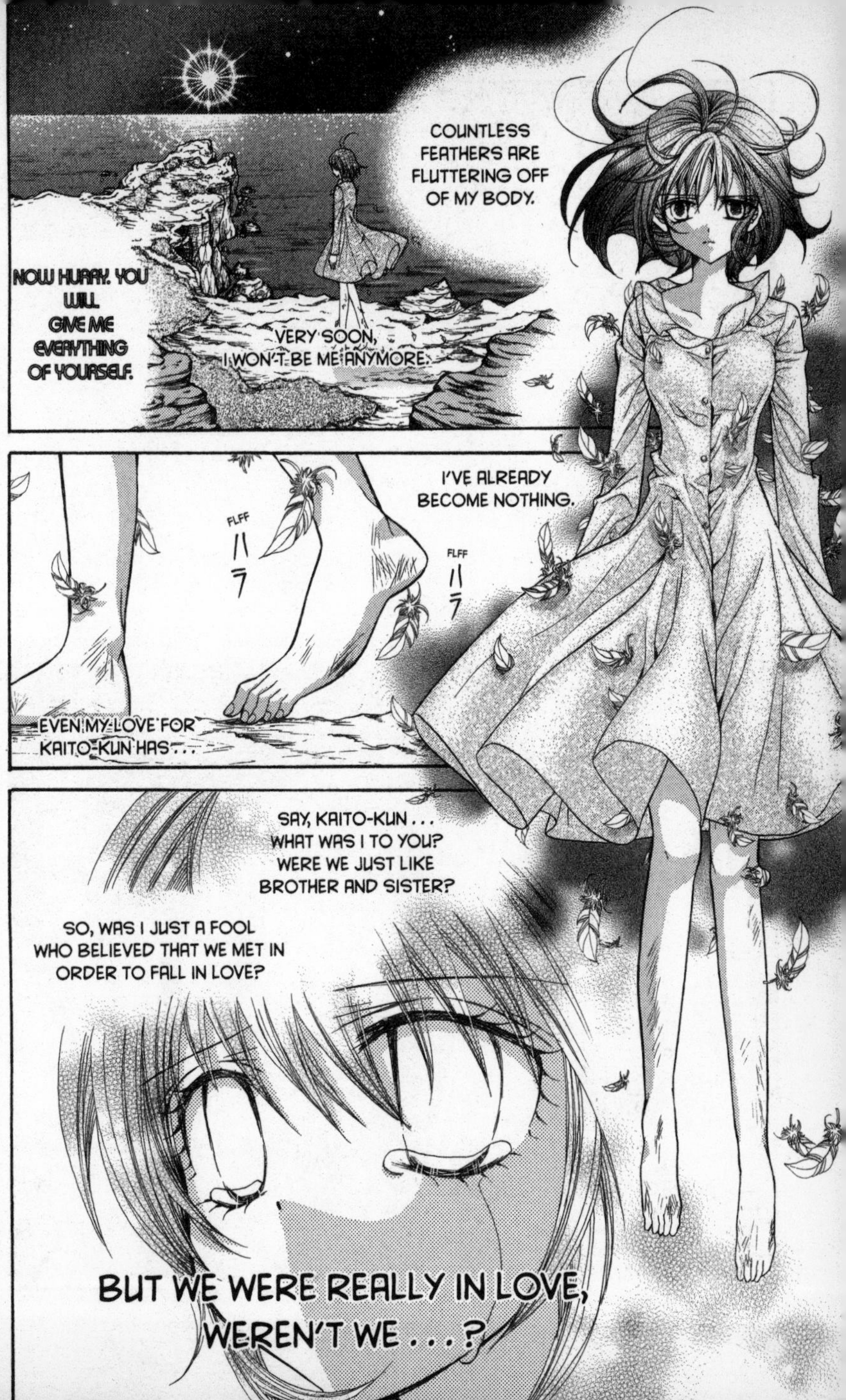
COUNTLESS FEATHERS ARE FLUTTERING OFF OF MY BODY.
VERY SOON, I WON'T BE ME ANYMORE.
NOW HURRY. YOU WILL GIVE ME EVERYTHING OF YOURSELF.
I'VE ALREADY BECOME NOTHING.
FLFF
ハラ
FLFF
ハラ
EVEN MY LOVE FOR KAITO-KUN HAS . . .
SAY, KAITO-KUN . . . WHAT WAS I TO YOU? WERE WE JUST LIKE BROTHER AND SISTER?
SO, WAS I JUST A FOOL WHO BELIEVED THAT WE MET IN ORDER TO FALL IN LOVE?
BUT WE WERE REALLY IN LOVE, WEREN'T WE . . . ?

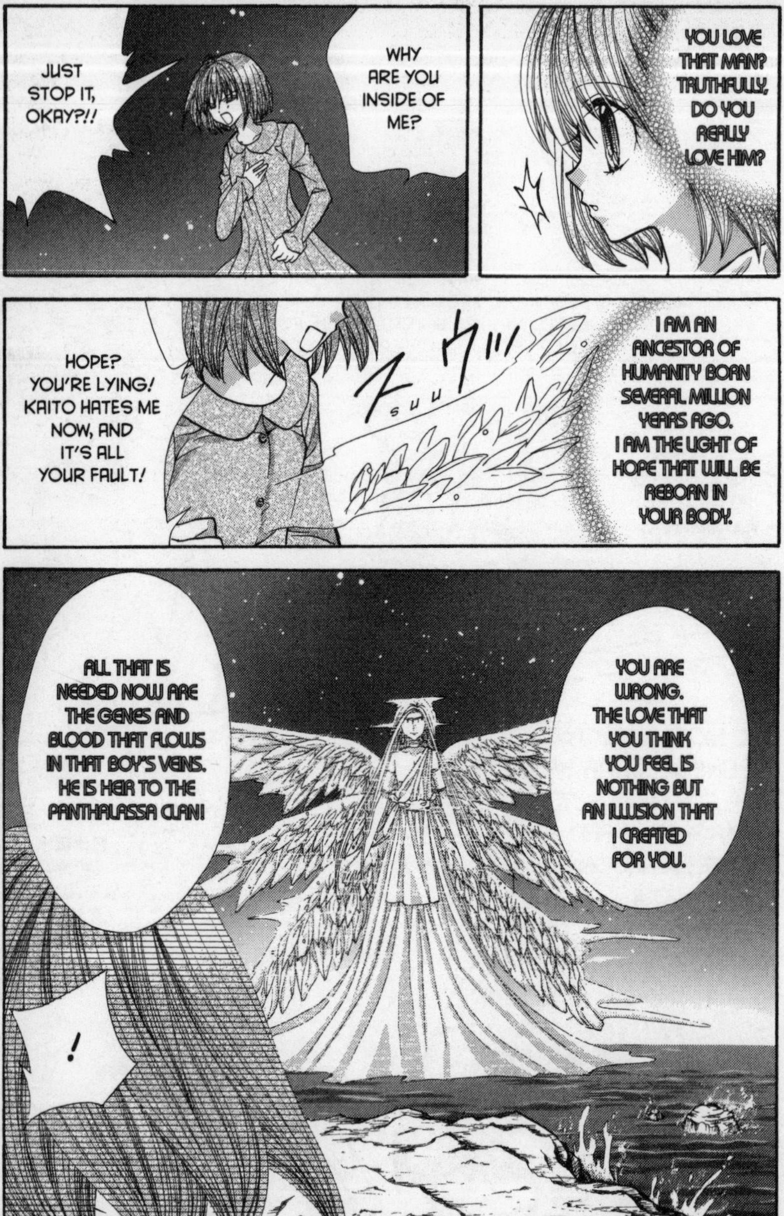
YOU LOVE THAT MAN? TRUTHFULLY, DO YOU REALLY LOVE HIM?
WHY ARE YOU INSIDE OF ME?
JUST STOP IT, OKAY?!!
I AM AN ANCESTOR OF HUMANITY BORN SEVERAL MILLION YEARS AGO. I AM THE LIGHT OF HOPE THAT WILL BE REBORN IN YOUR BODY.
SUU
HOPE? YOU'RE LYING! KAITO HATES ME NOW, AND IT'S ALL YOUR FAULT!
YOU ARE WRONG. THE LOVE THAT YOU THINK YOU FEEL IS NOTHING BUT AN ILLUSION THAT I CREATED FOR YOU.
ALL THAT IS NEEDED NOW ARE THE GENES AND BLOOD THAT FLOWS IN THAT BOY'S VEINS. HE IS HEIR TO THE PANTHALASSA CLAN!
!

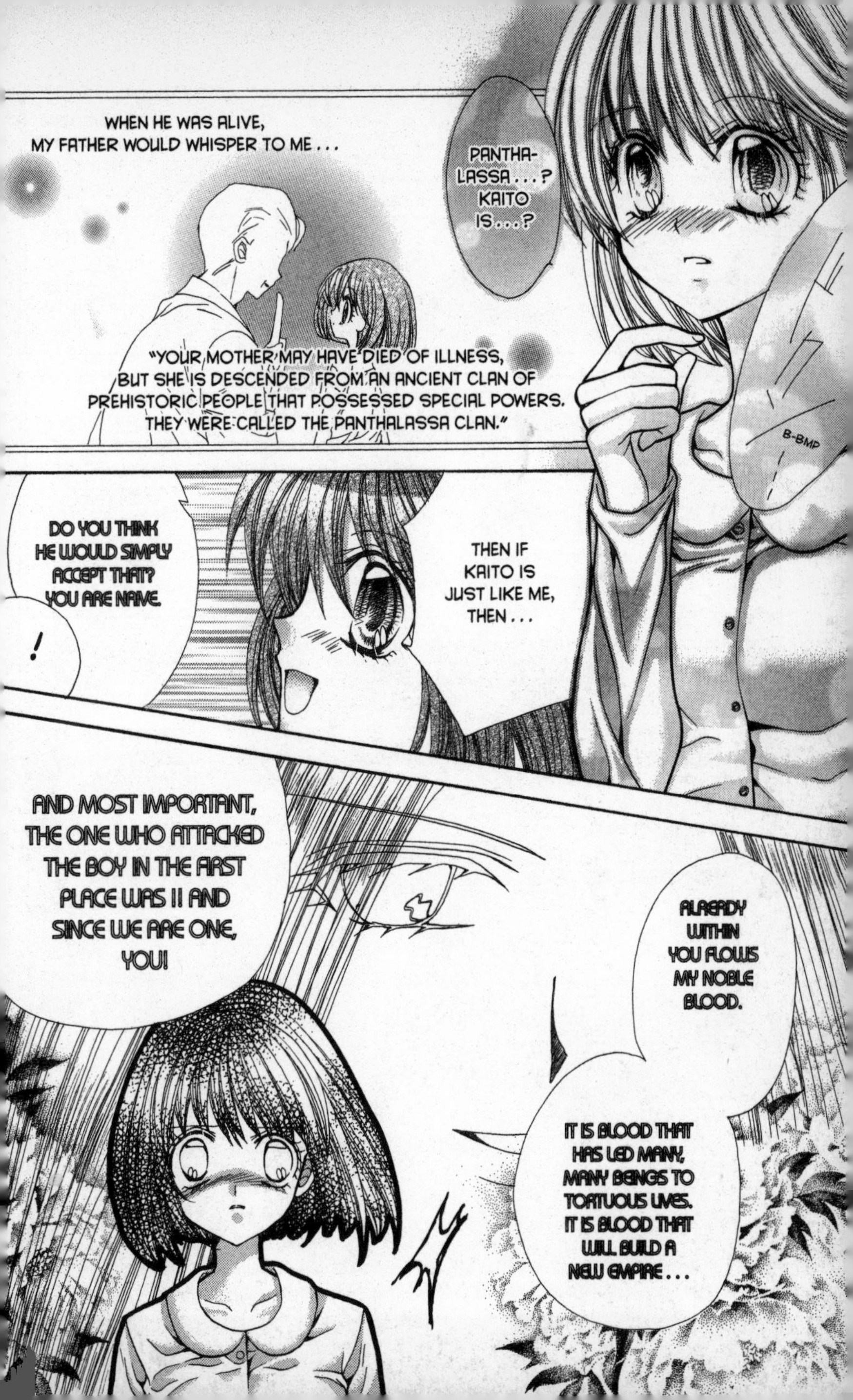
PANTHA-LASSA . . . ? KAITO IS . . . ?
WHEN HE WAS ALIVE, MY FATHER WOULD WHISPER TO ME . . .
"YOUR MOTHER MAY HAVE DIED OF ILLNESS, BUT SHE IS DESCENDED FROM AN ANCIENT CLAN OF PREHISTORIC PEOPLE THAT POSSESSED SPECIAL POWERS. THEY WERE CALLED THE PANTHALASSA CLAN."
B-BMP
THEN IF KAITO IS JUST LIKE ME, THEN . . .
DO YOU THINK HE WOULD SIMPLY ACCEPT THAT? YOU ARE NAIVE.
!
ALREADY WITHIN YOU FLOWS MY NOBLE BLOOD.
AND MOST IMPORTANT, THE ONE WHO ATTACKED THE BOY IN THE FIRST PLACE WAS I! AND SINCE WE ARE ONE, YOU!
IT IS BLOOD THAT HAS LED MANY, MANY BEINGS TO TORTUOUS LIVES. IT IS BLOOD THAT WILL BUILD A NEW EMPIRE . . .

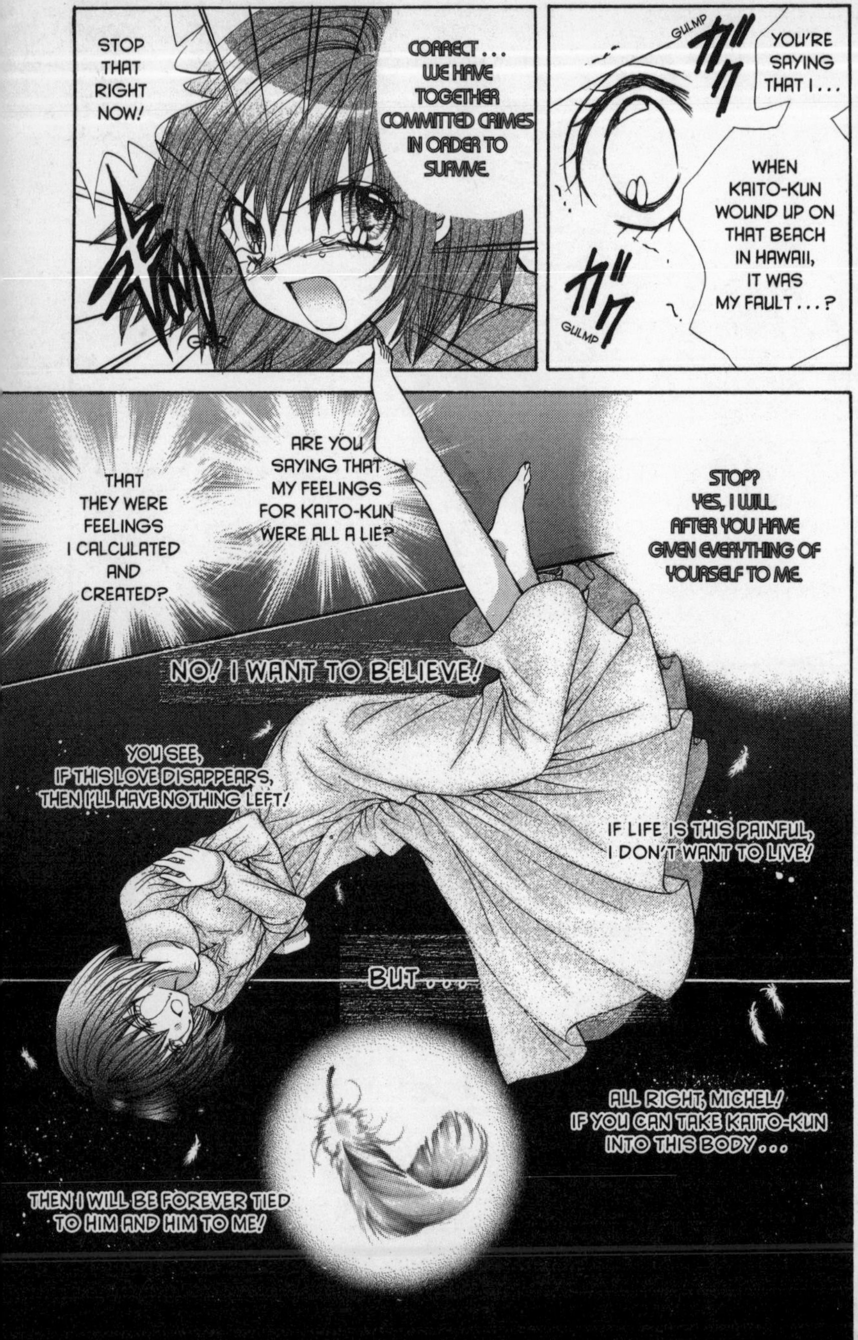
GULMP
YOU'RE SAYING THAT I . . .
WHEN KAITO-KUN WOUND UP ON THAT BEACH IN HAWAII, IT WAS MY FAULT . . . ?
GULMP
CORRECT . . . WE HAVE TOGETHER COMMITTED CRIMES IN ORDER TO SURVIVE.
STOP THAT RIGHT NOW!
STOP? YES, I WILL. AFTER YOU HAVE GIVEN EVERYTHING OF YOURSELF TO ME.
ARE YOU SAYING THAT MY FEELINGS FOR KAITO-KUN WERE ALL A LIE?
THAT THEY WERE FEELINGS I CALCULATED AND CREATED?
NO! I WANT TO BELIEVE!
IF LIFE IS THIS PAINFUL, I DON'T WANT TO LIVE!
YOU SEE, IF THIS LOVE DISAPPEARS, THEN I'LL HAVE NOTHING LEFT!
BUT . . .
ALL RIGHT, MICHEL! IF YOU CAN TAKE KAITO-KUN INTO THIS BODY . . .
THEN I WILL BE FOREVER TIED TO HIM AND HIM TO ME!

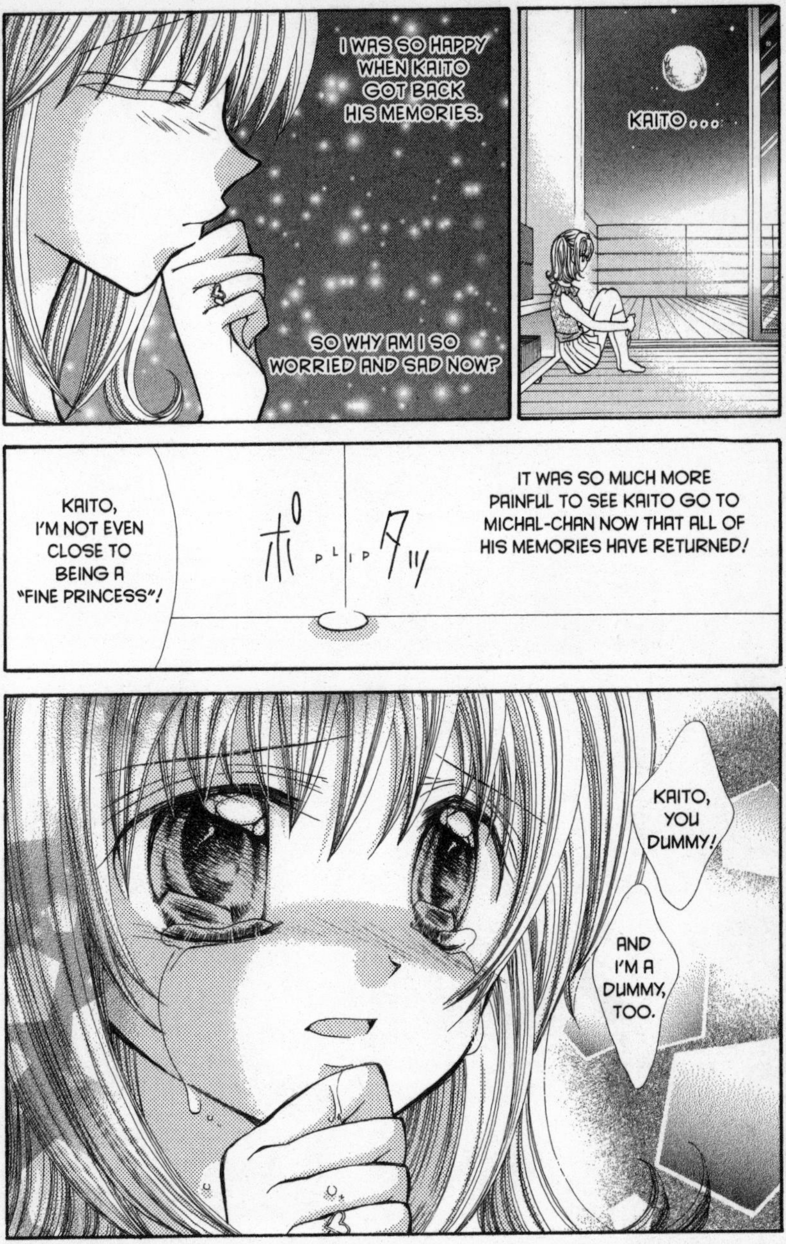
KAITO . . .
I WAS SO HAPPY WHEN KAITO GOT BACK HIS MEMORIES.
SO WHY AM I SO WORRIED AND SAD NOW?
IT WAS SO MUCH MORE PAINFUL TO SEE KAITO GO TO MICHAL-CHAN NOW THAT ALL OF HIS MEMORIES HAVE RETURNED!
ポタッ
PLIP
KAITO, I'M NOT EVEN CLOSE TO BEING A "FINE PRINCESS"!
KAITO, YOU DUMMY!
AND I'M A DUMMY, TOO.

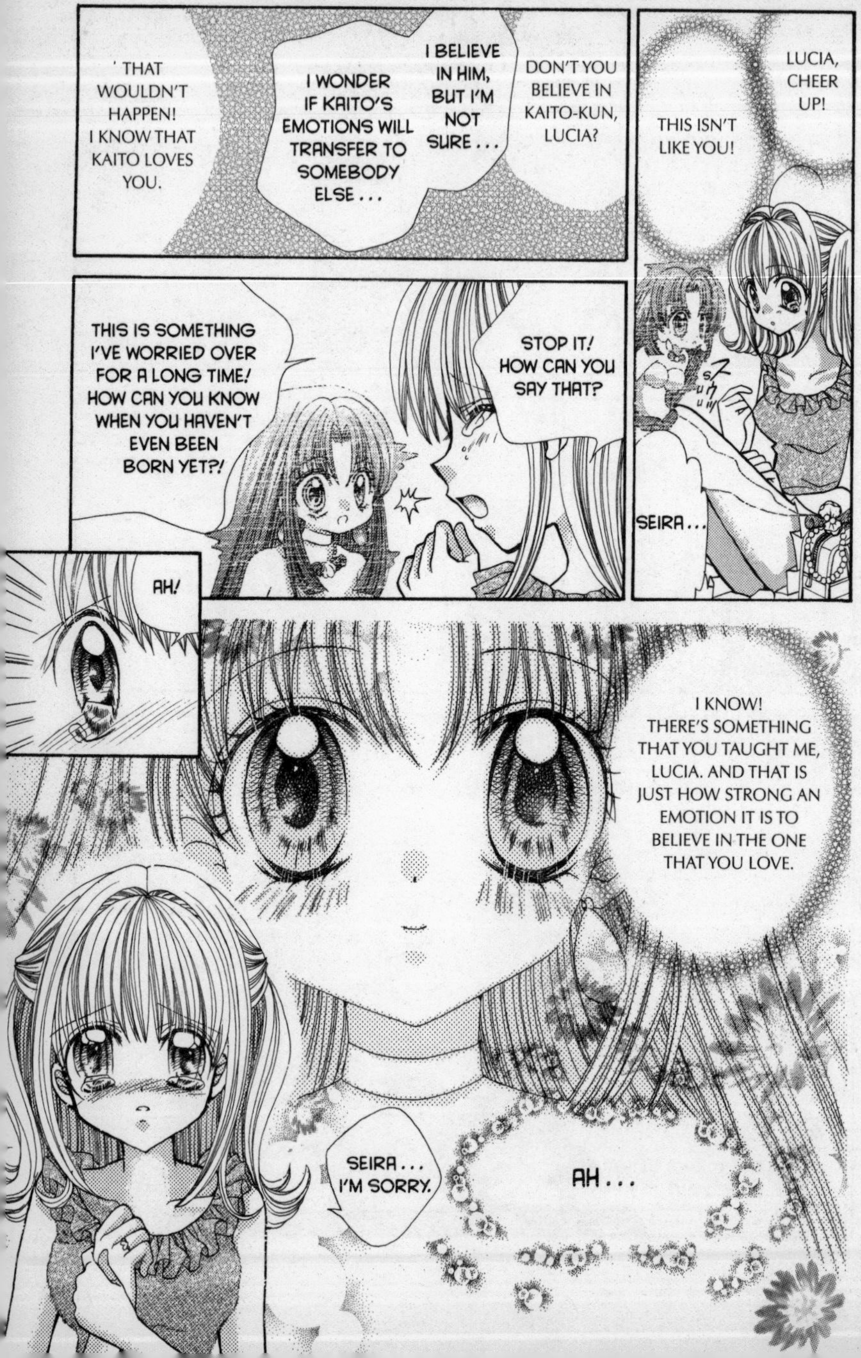
LUCIA, CHEER UP!
THIS ISN'T LIKE YOU!
SEIRA . . .
DON'T YOU BELIEVE IN KAITO-KUN, LUCIA?
I BELIEVE IN HIM, BUT I'M NOT SURE . . .
I WONDER IF KAITO'S EMOTIONS WILL TRANSFER TO SOMEBODY ELSE . . .
' THAT WOULDN'T HAPPEN! I KNOW THAT KAITO LOVES YOU.
STOP IT! HOW CAN YOU SAY THAT?
THIS IS SOMETHING I'VE WORRIED OVER FOR A LONG TIME! HOW CAN YOU KNOW WHEN YOU HAVEN'T EVEN BEEN BORN YET?!
I KNOW! THERE'S SOMETHING THAT YOU TAUGHT ME, LUCIA. AND THAT IS JUST HOW STRONG AN EMOTION IT IS TO BELIEVE IN THE ONE THAT YOU LOVE.
AH!
AH . . .
SEIRA . . . I'M SORRY.

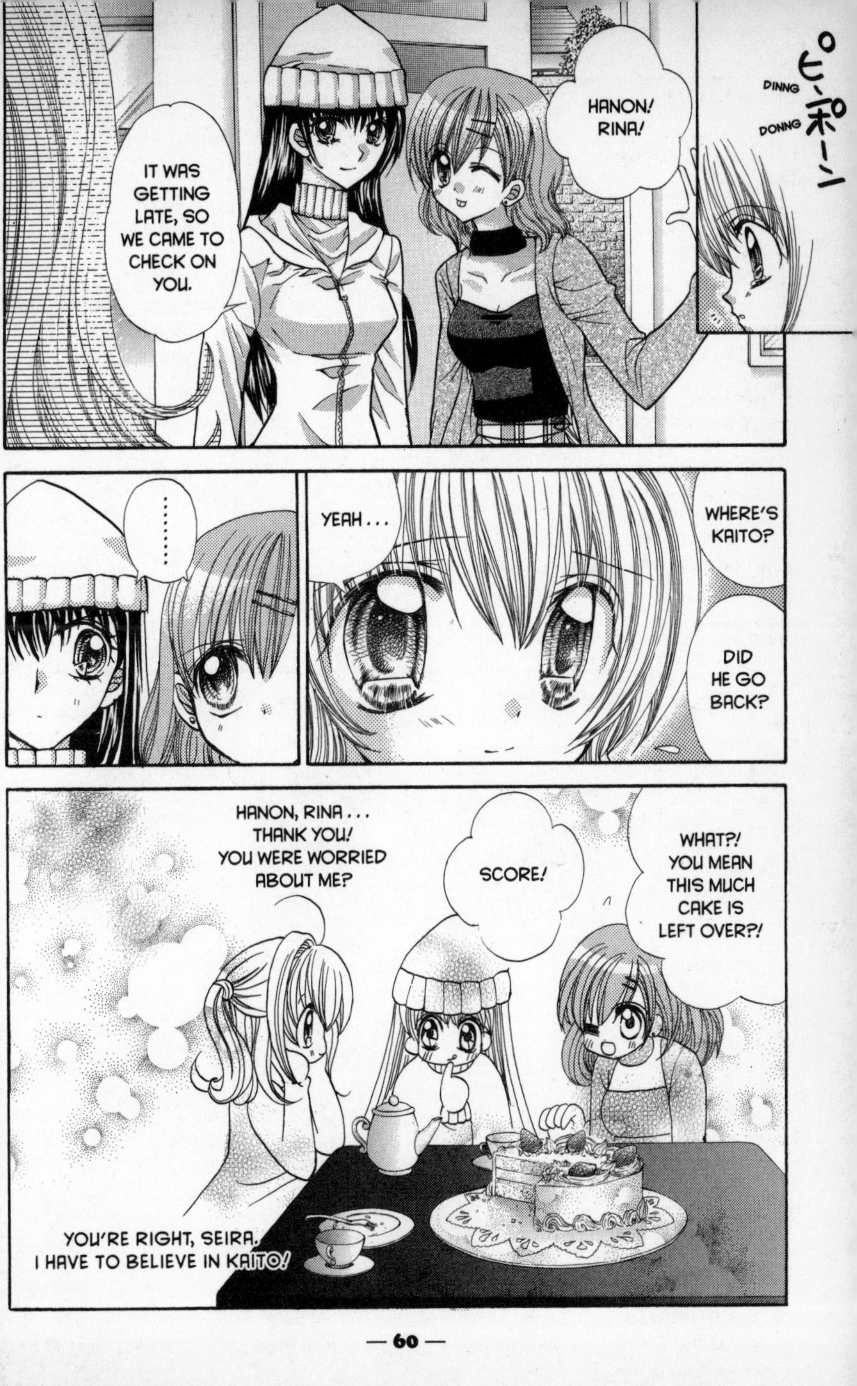
DINNG
DONNG
ピンポーン
HANON! RINA!
IT WAS GETTING LATE, SO WE CAME TO CHECK ON YOU.
WHERE'S KAITO?
DID HE GO BACK?
YEAH . . .
. . . .
WHAT?! YOU MEAN THIS MUCH CAKE IS LEFT OVER?!
SCORE!
HANON, RINA . . . THANK YOU! YOU WERE WORRIED ABOUT ME?
YOU'RE RIGHT, SEIRA. I HAVE TO BELIEVE IN KAITO!

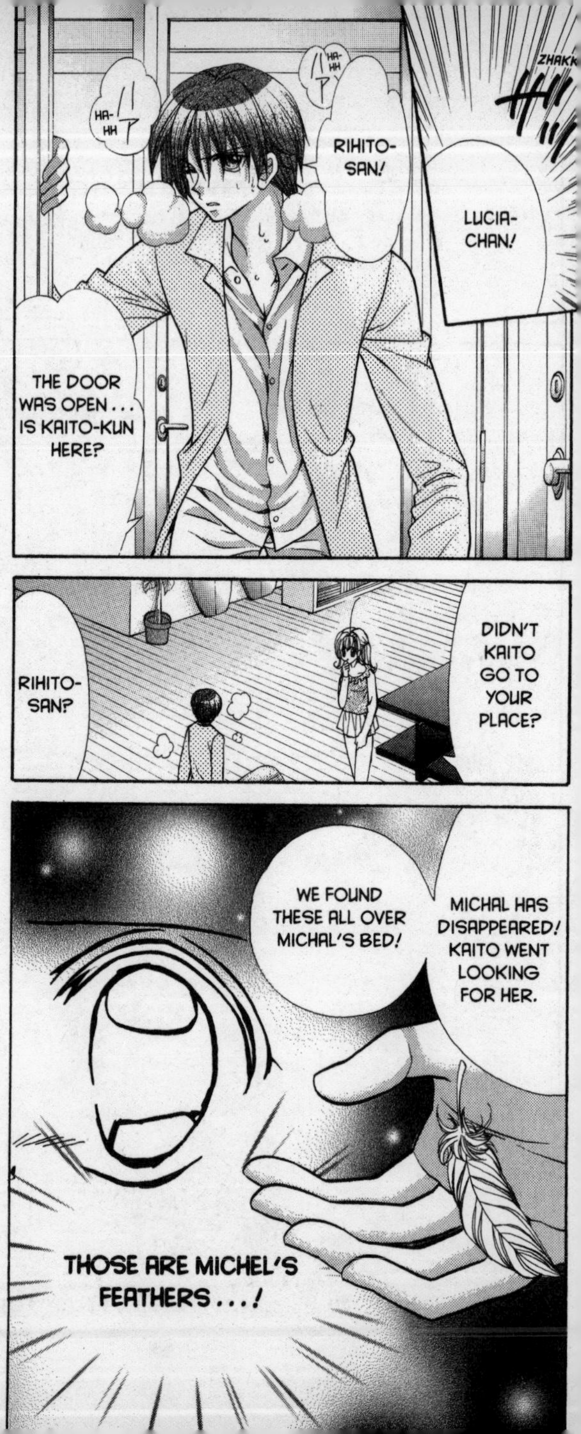
ZHAKK
LUCIA-CHAN!
HA-HH
RIHITO-SAN!
HA-HH
THE DOOR WAS OPEN . . . IS KAITO-KUN HERE?
DIDN'T KAITO GO TO YOUR PLACE?
RIHITO-SAN?
MICHAL HAS DISAPPEARED! KAITO WENT LOOKING FOR HER.
WE FOUND THESE ALL OVER MICHAL'S BED!
THOSE ARE MICHEL'S FEATHERS . . . !

DOGS.

I OWN A POMERANIAN.
POMERS HAVE A CERTAIN MAGIC!
BUT IT'S LIKE THEY LACK IN THE CHARM DEPARTMENT.
POMER . . .
POMER . . . !
AH, POMER . . . !!
VIVA POMER!!!

CALL ME A COMPLETE NUT IF YOU WANT!
I JUST LOVE MY POMER!

POMERRRRRRR--

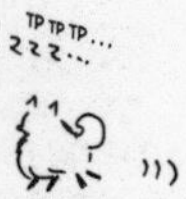
TP TP TP . . .
ZZZ . . .

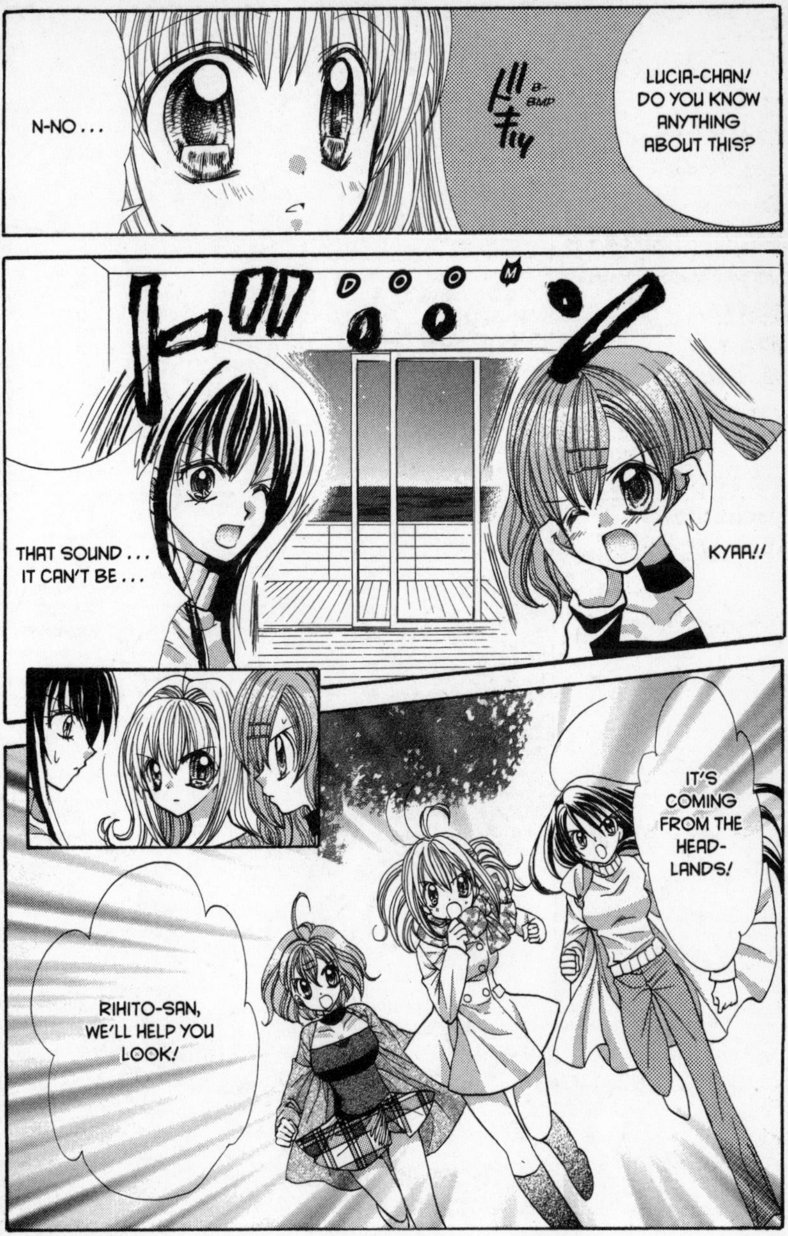
LUCIA-CHAN! DO YOU KNOW ANYTHING ABOUT THIS?
B-BMP
N-NO . . .
DOOOM
KYAA!!
THAT SOUND . . . IT CAN'T BE . . .
IT'S COMING FROM THE HEAD-LANDS!
RIHITO-SAN, WE'LL HELP YOU LOOK!

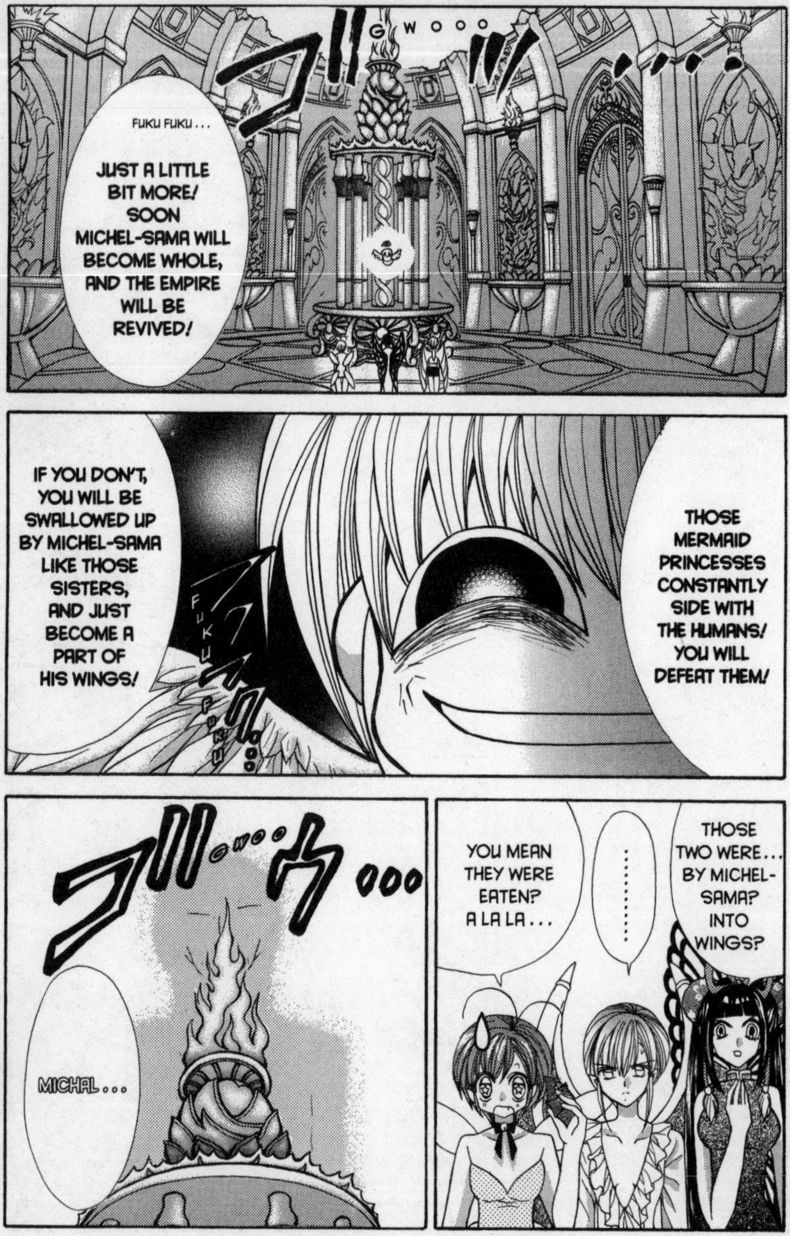
GWOOO
FUKU FUKU . . .
JUST A LITTLE BIT MORE! SOON MICHEL-SAMA WILL BECOME WHOLE, AND THE EMPIRE WILL BE REVIVED!
THOSE MERMAID PRINCESSES CONSTANTLY SIDE WITH THE HUMANS! YOU WILL DEFEAT THEM!
IF YOU DON'T, YOU WILL BE SWALLOWED UP BY MICHEL-SAMA LIKE THOSE SISTERS, AND JUST BECOME A PART OF HIS WINGS!
FUKU FUKU
THOSE TWO WERE . . . BY MICHEL-SAMA? INTO WINGS?
. . . .
YOU MEAN THEY WERE EATEN? A LA LA . . .
GWOO
MICHAL . . .

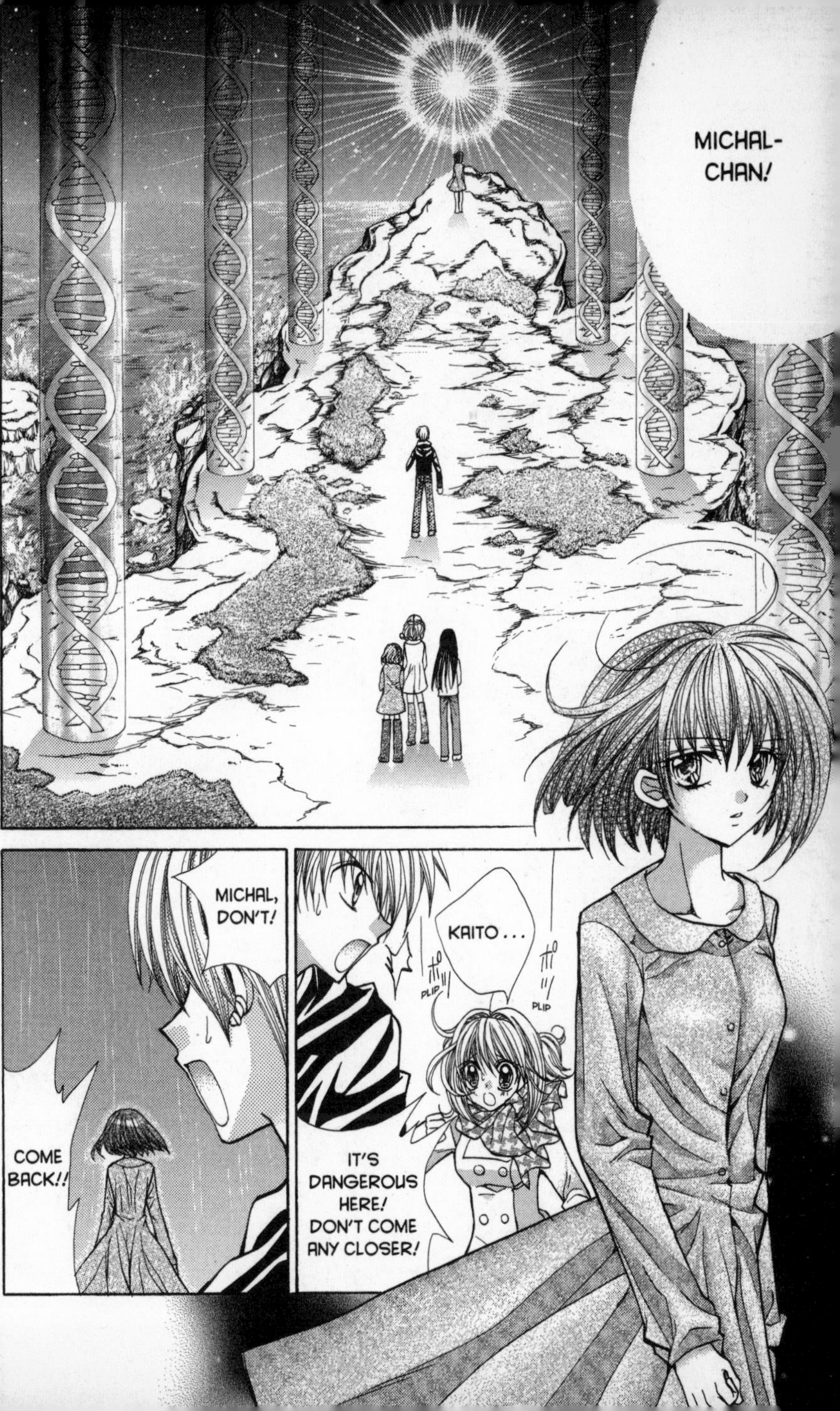
MICHAL-CHAN!
KAITO . . .
PLIP
PLIP
IT'S DANGEROUS HERE! DON'T COME ANY CLOSER!
MICHAL, DON'T!
COME BACK!!

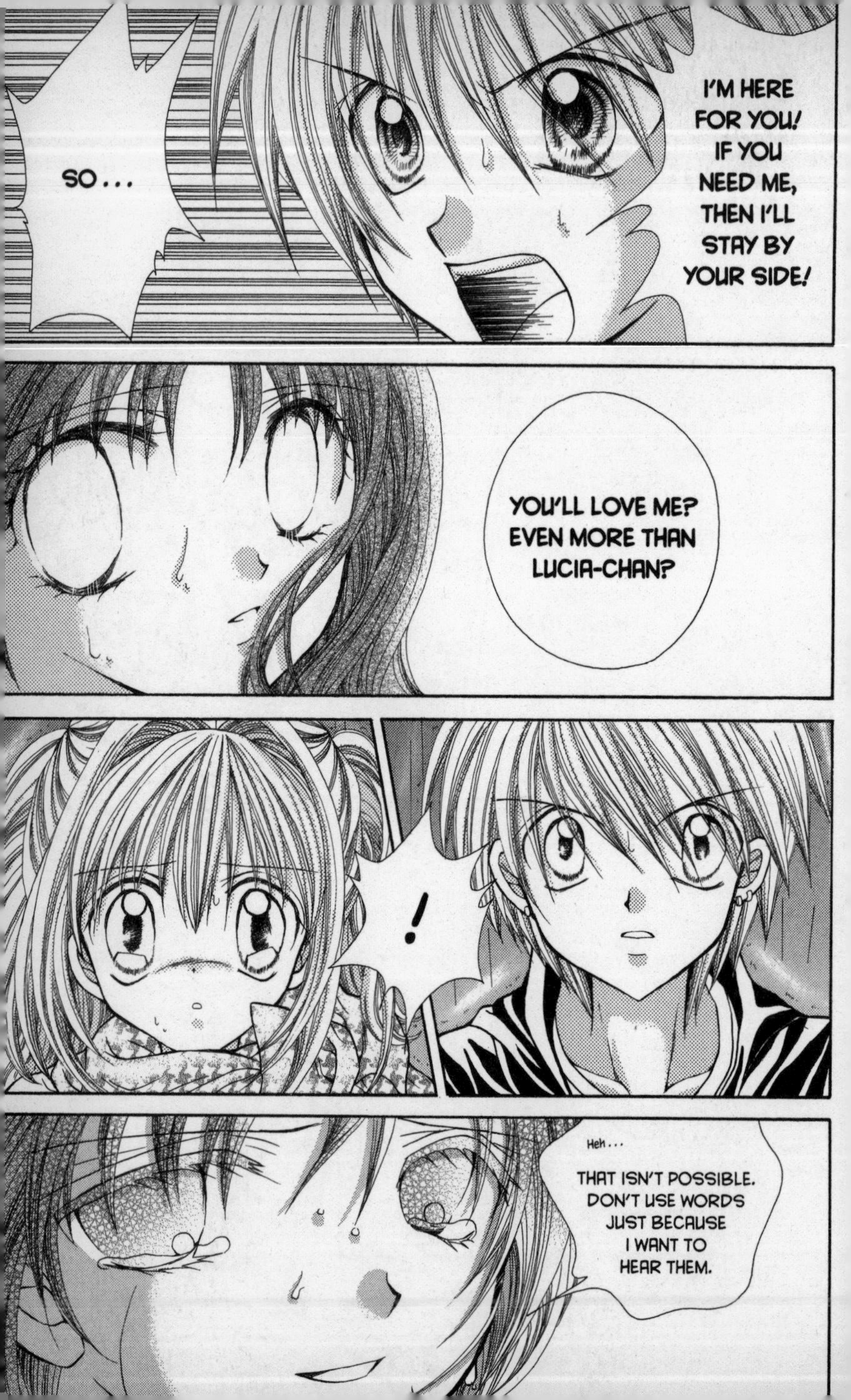
I'M HERE FOR YOU! IF YOU NEED ME, THEN I'LL STAY BY YOUR SIDE!
SO...
YOU'LL LOVE ME? EVEN MORE THAN LUCIA-CHAN?
!
Heh...
THAT ISN'T POSSIBLE. DON'T USE WORDS JUST BECAUSE I WANT TO HEAR THEM.

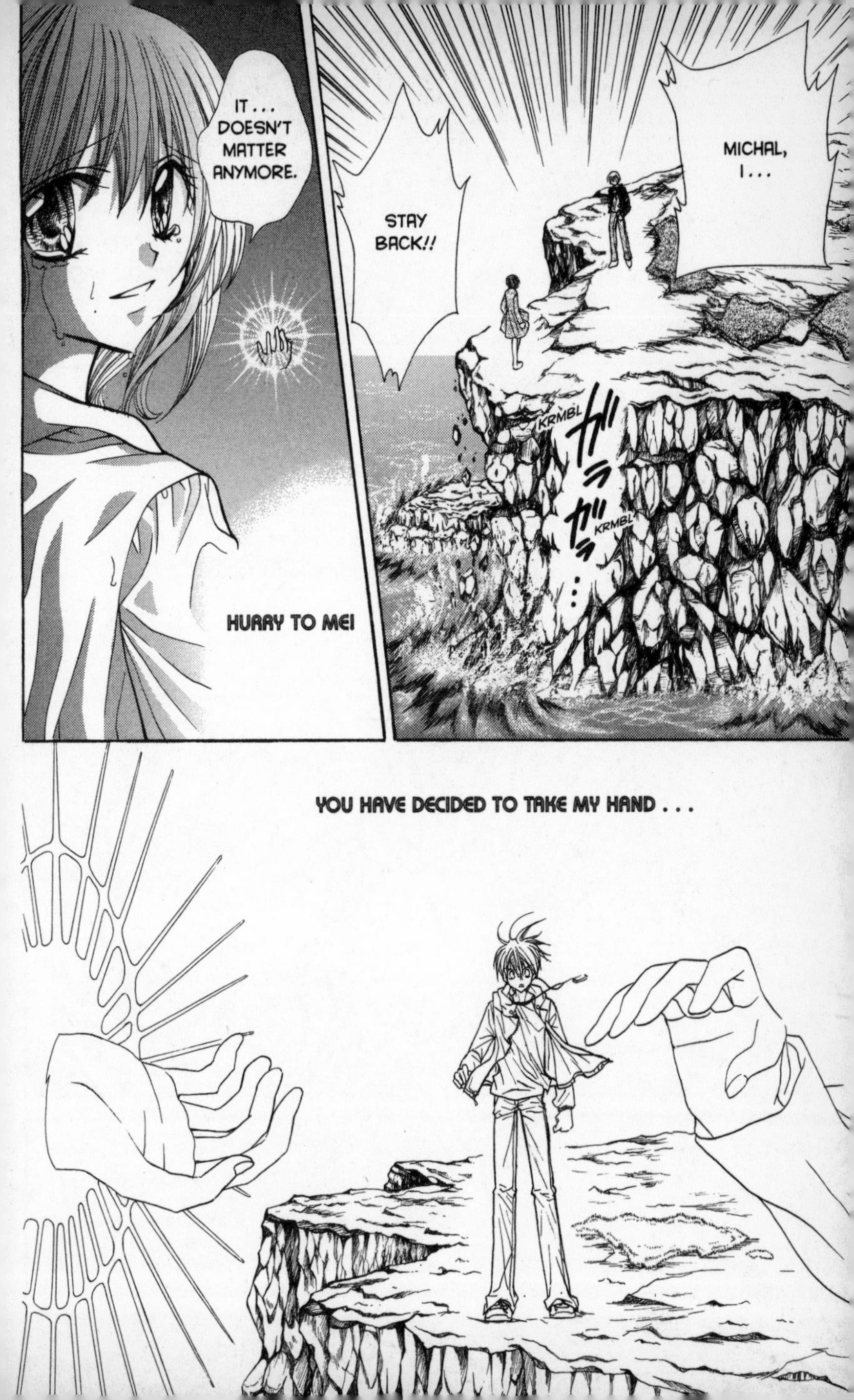
MICHAL, I . . .
STAY BACK!!
KRMBL
KRMBL
IT . . . DOESN'T MATTER ANYMORE.
HURRY TO ME!
YOU HAVE DECIDED TO TAKE MY HAND . . .

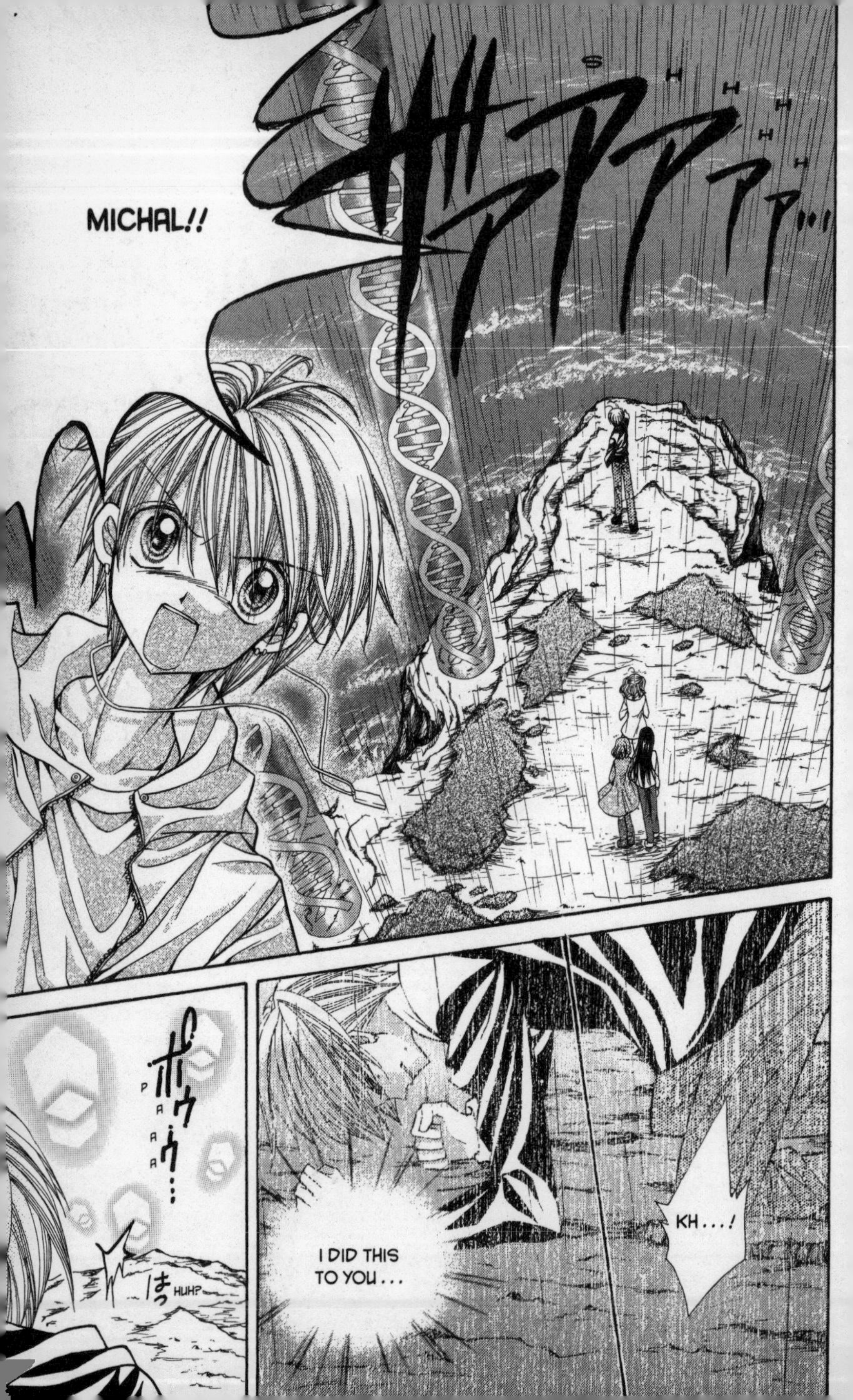
SHHHHH
MICHAL!!
KH...!
I DID THIS TO YOU...
PAAA
はっ HUH?

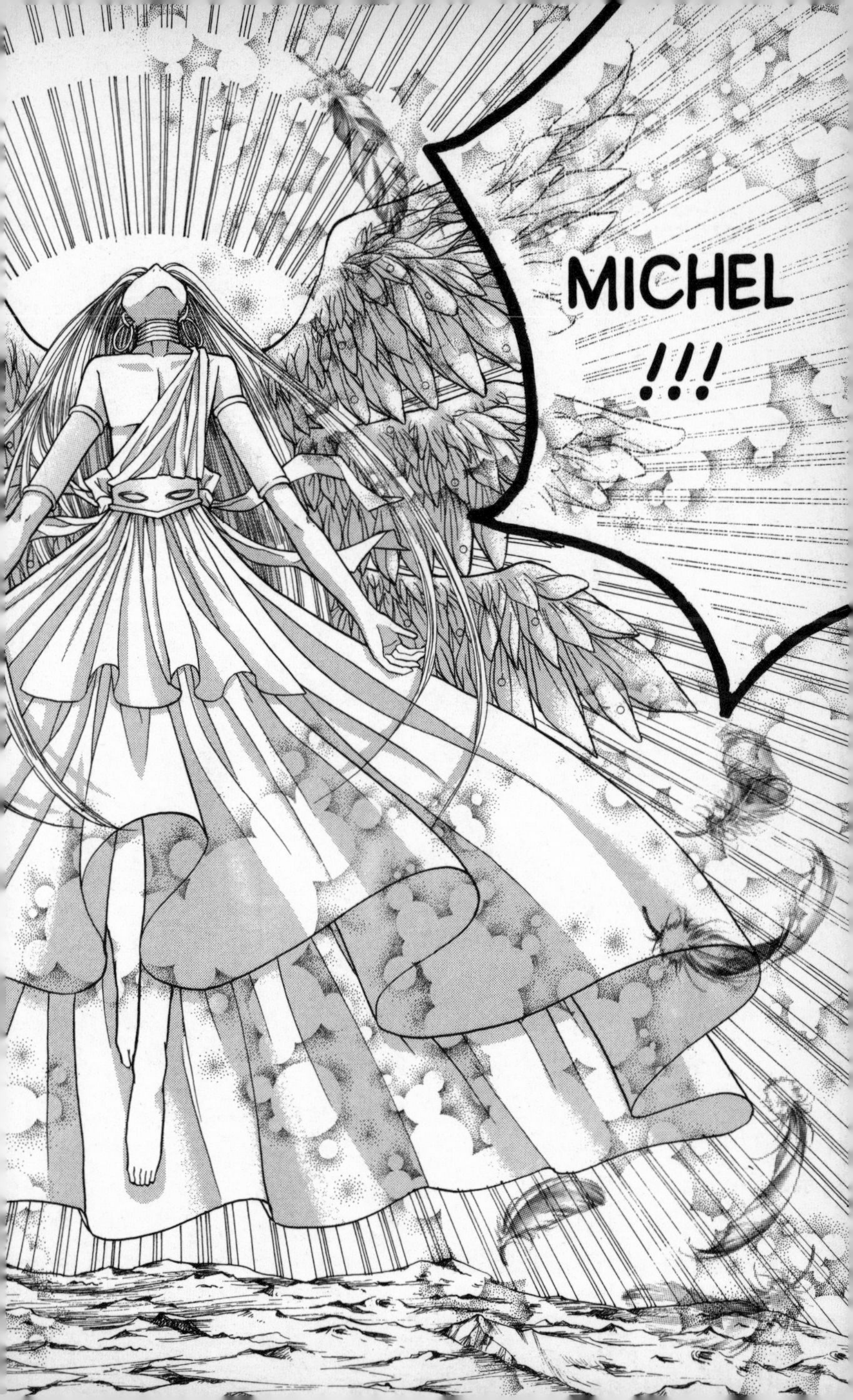
MICHEL
!!!

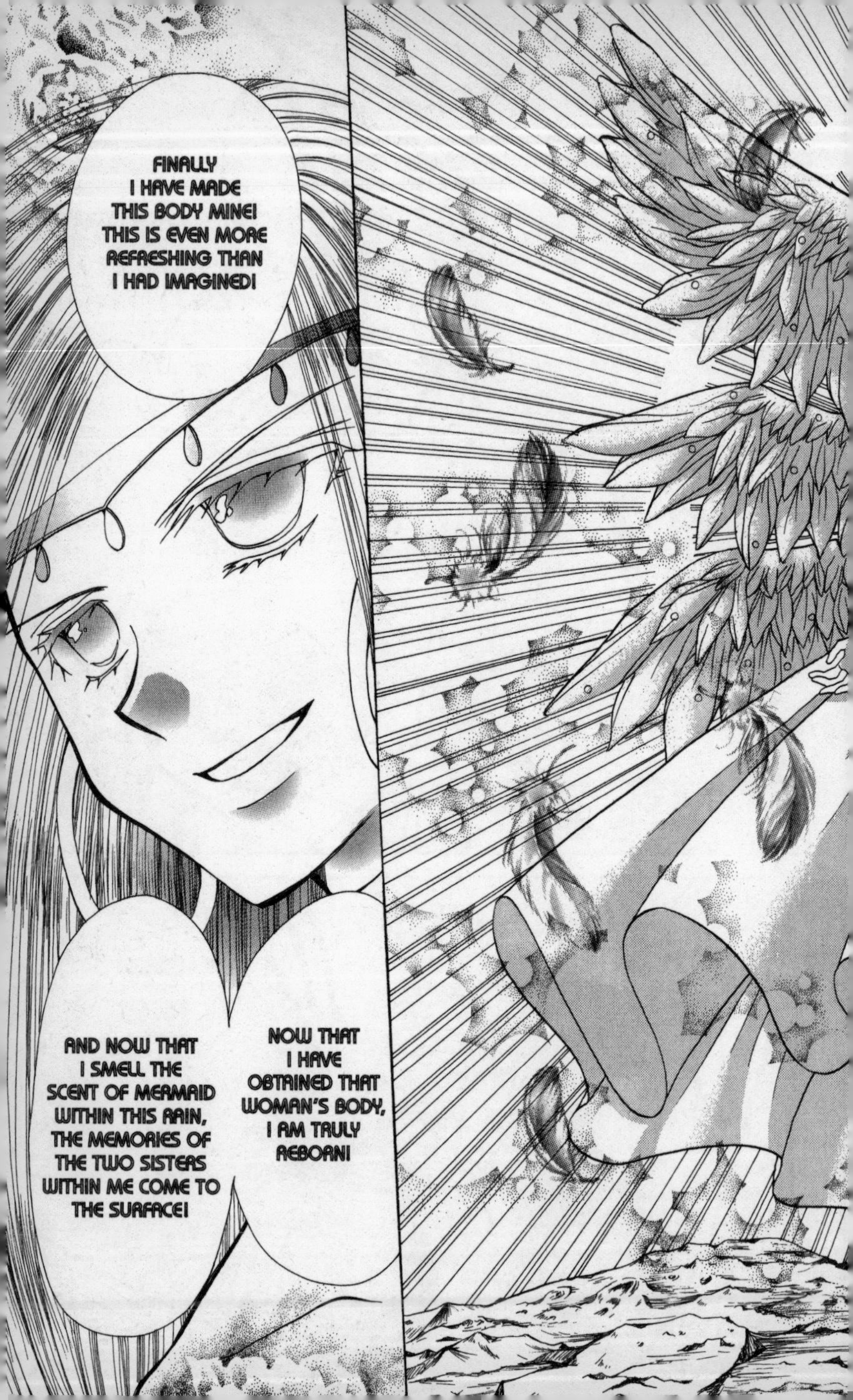
FINALLY I HAVE MADE THIS BODY MINE! THIS IS EVEN MORE REFRESHING THAN I HAD IMAGINED!
NOW THAT I HAVE OBTAINED THAT WOMAN'S BODY, I AM TRULY REBORN!
AND NOW THAT I SMELL THE SCENT OF MERMAID WITHIN THIS RAIN, THE MEMORIES OF THE TWO SISTERS WITHIN ME COME TO THE SURFACE!

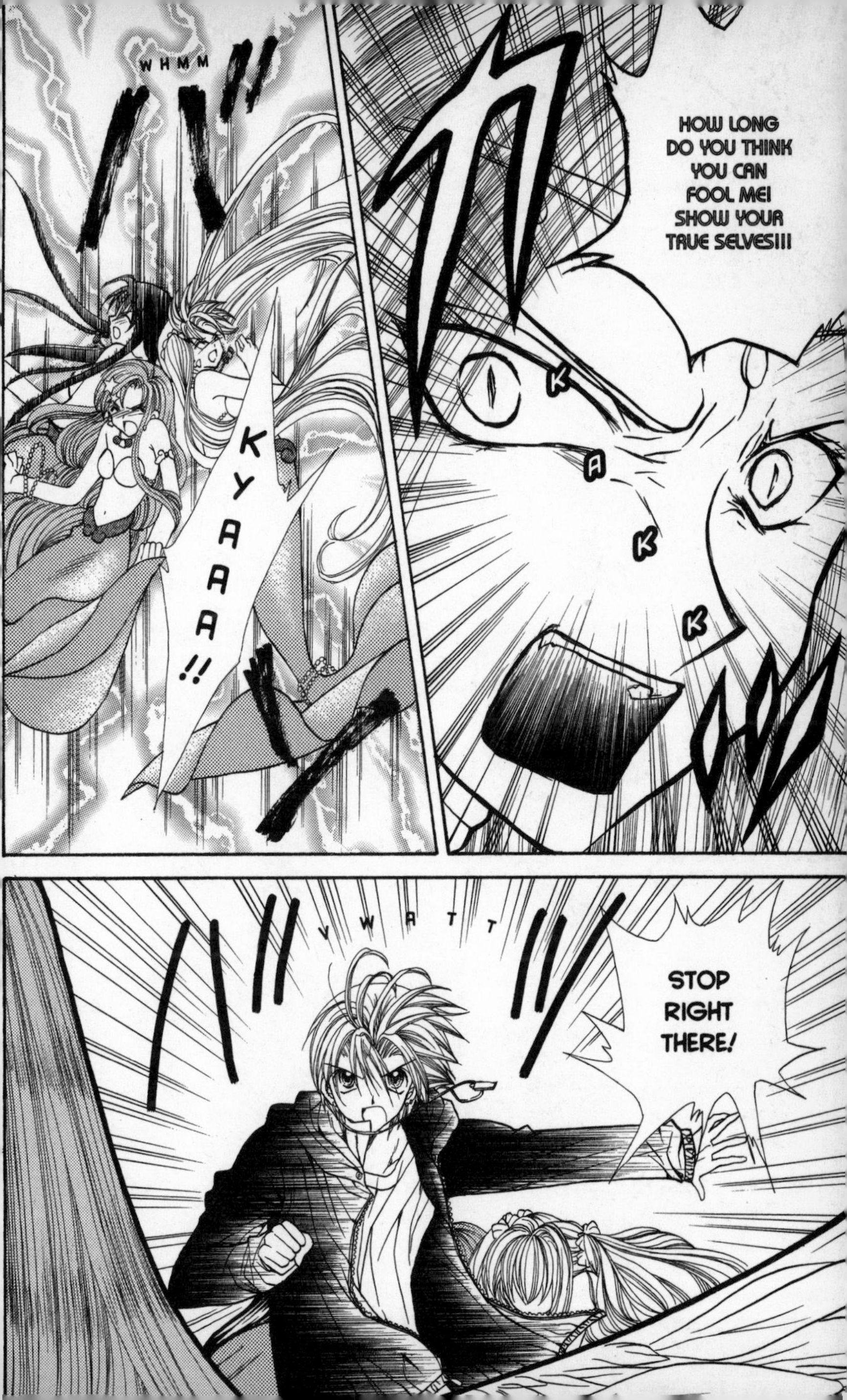
HOW LONG DO YOU THINK YOU CAN FOOL ME! SHOW YOUR TRUE SELVES!!!
KAKKK
WHMM
KYAAAA!!
VWATT
STOP RIGHT THERE!

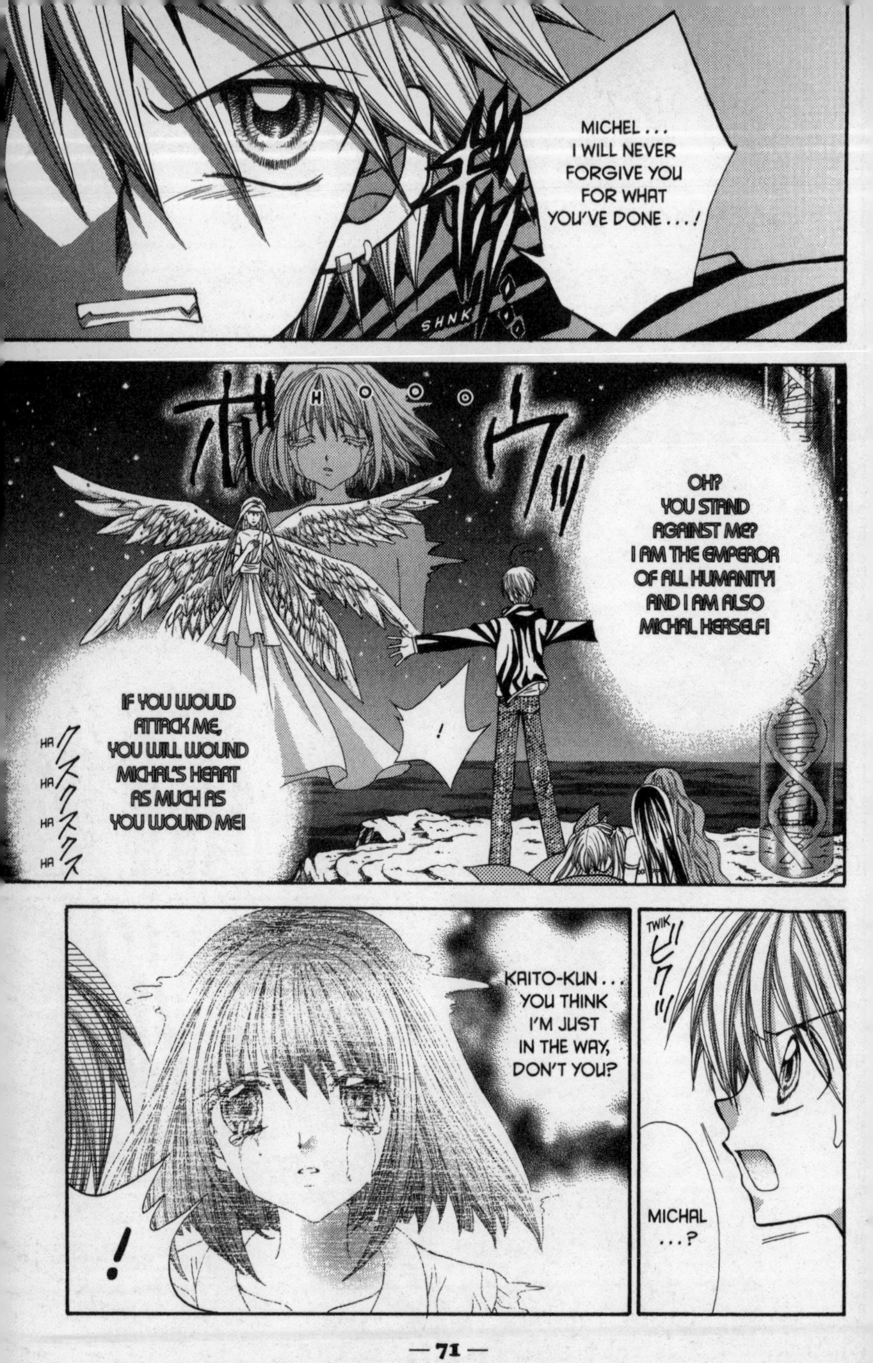
MICHEL . . .
I WILL NEVER
FORGIVE YOU
FOR WHAT
YOU'VE DONE . . . !
SHNK
OH?
YOU STAND
AGAINST ME?
I AM THE EMPEROR
OF ALL HUMANITY!
AND I AM ALSO
MICHAL HERSELF!
!
IF YOU WOULD
ATTACK ME,
YOU WILL WOUND
MICHAL'S HEART
AS MUCH AS
YOU WOUND ME!
HA
HA
HA
HA
TWIK
MICHAL
. . . ?
KAITO-KUN . . .
YOU THINK
I'M JUST
IN THE WAY,
DON'T YOU?
!

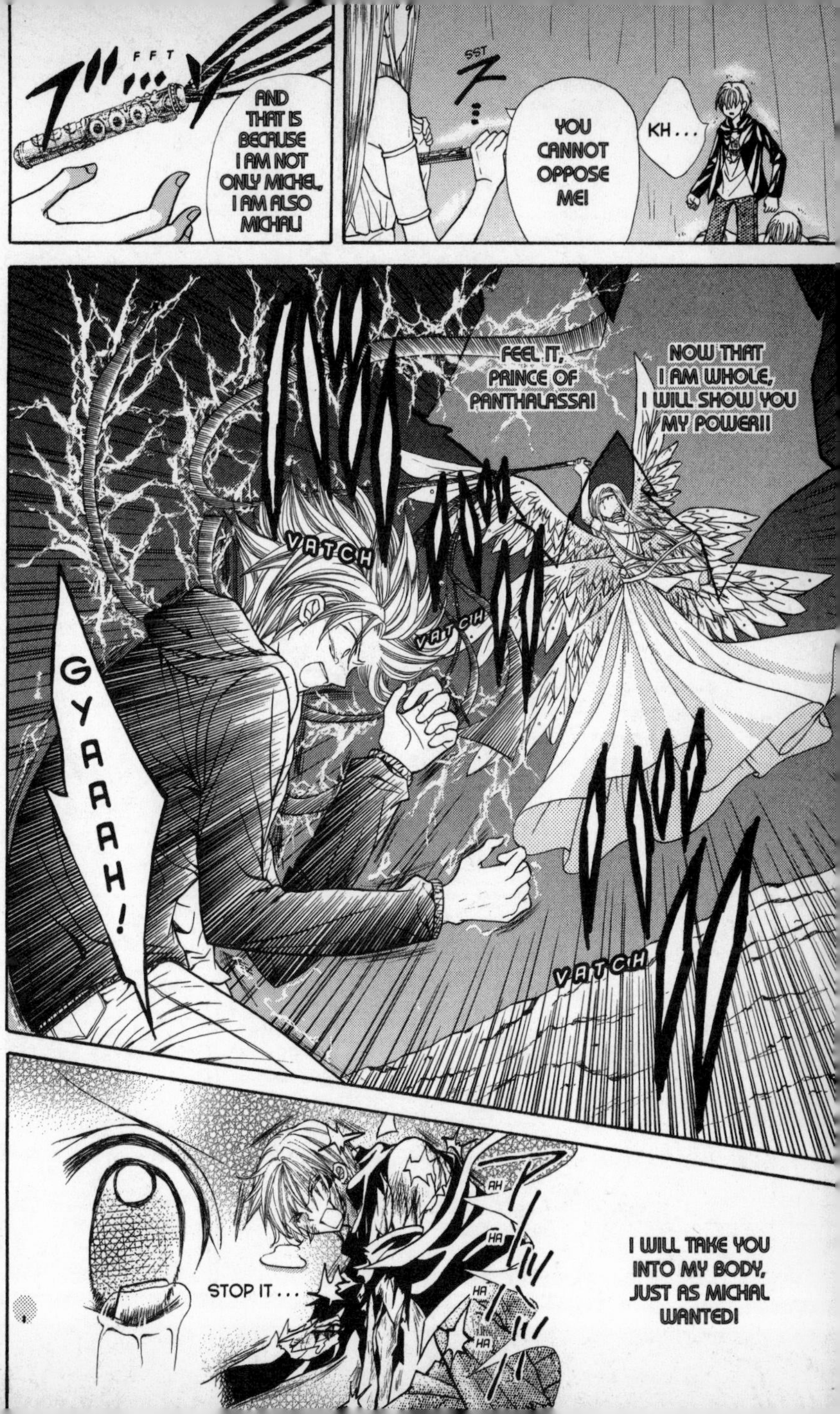
KH . . .
SST
YOU CANNOT OPPOSE ME!
FFT
AND THAT IS BECAUSE I AM NOT ONLY MICHEL, I AM ALSO MICHAL!
NOW THAT I AM WHOLE, I WILL SHOW YOU MY POWER!!
FEEL IT, PRINCE OF PANTHALASSA!
VATCH
VATCH
GYAAAH!
VATCH
I WILL TAKE YOU INTO MY BODY, JUST AS MICHAL WANTED!
AH
HA
HA
HA
STOP IT . . .

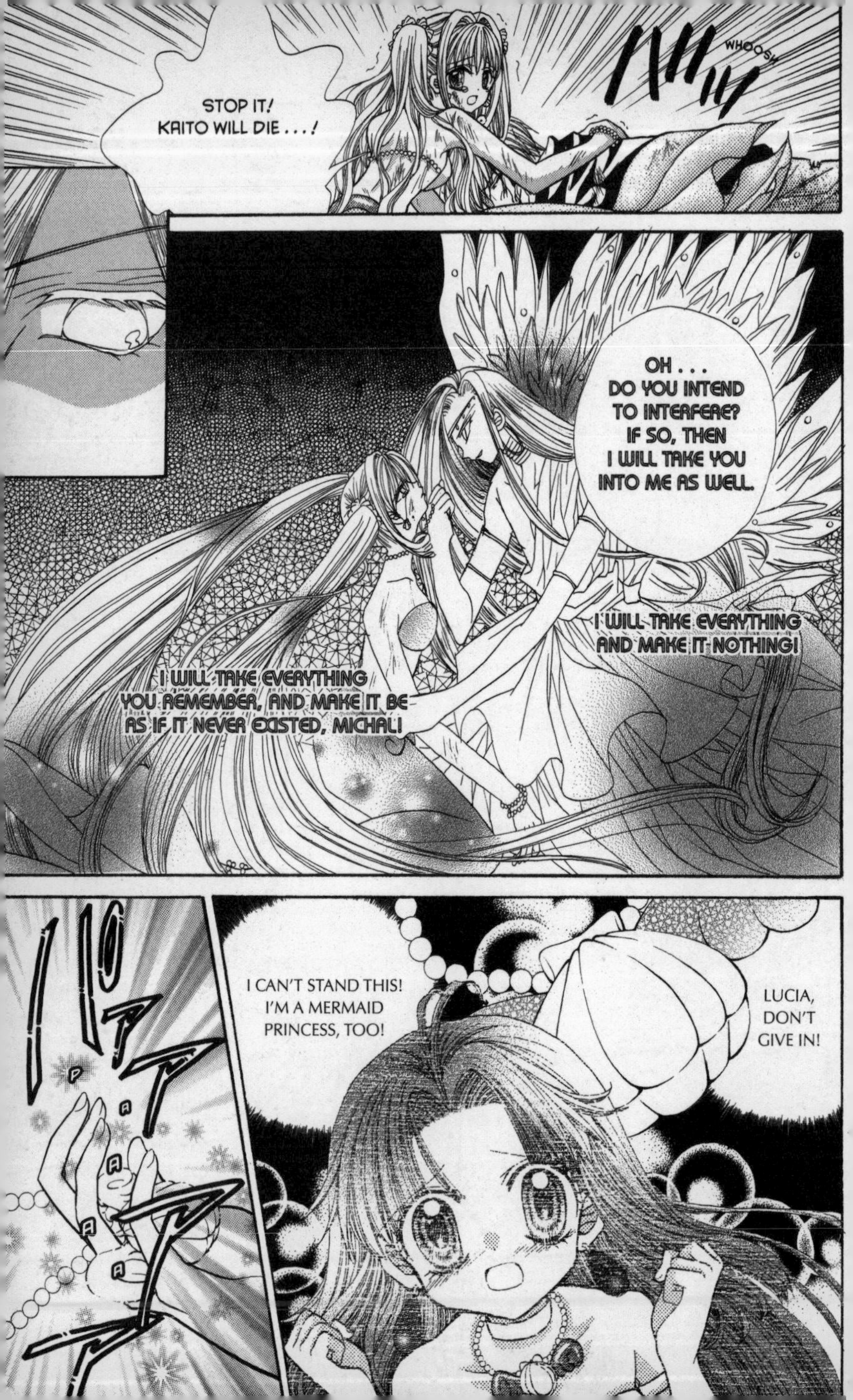
WHOOSH
STOP IT! KAITO WILL DIE . . . !
OH . . . DO YOU INTEND TO INTERFERE? IF SO, THEN I WILL TAKE YOU INTO ME AS WELL.
I WILL TAKE EVERYTHING AND MAKE IT NOTHING!
I WILL TAKE EVERYTHING YOU REMEMBER, AND MAKE IT BE AS IF IT NEVER EXISTED, MICHAL!
LUCIA, DON'T GIVE IN!
I CAN'T STAND THIS! I'M A MERMAID PRINCESS, TOO!

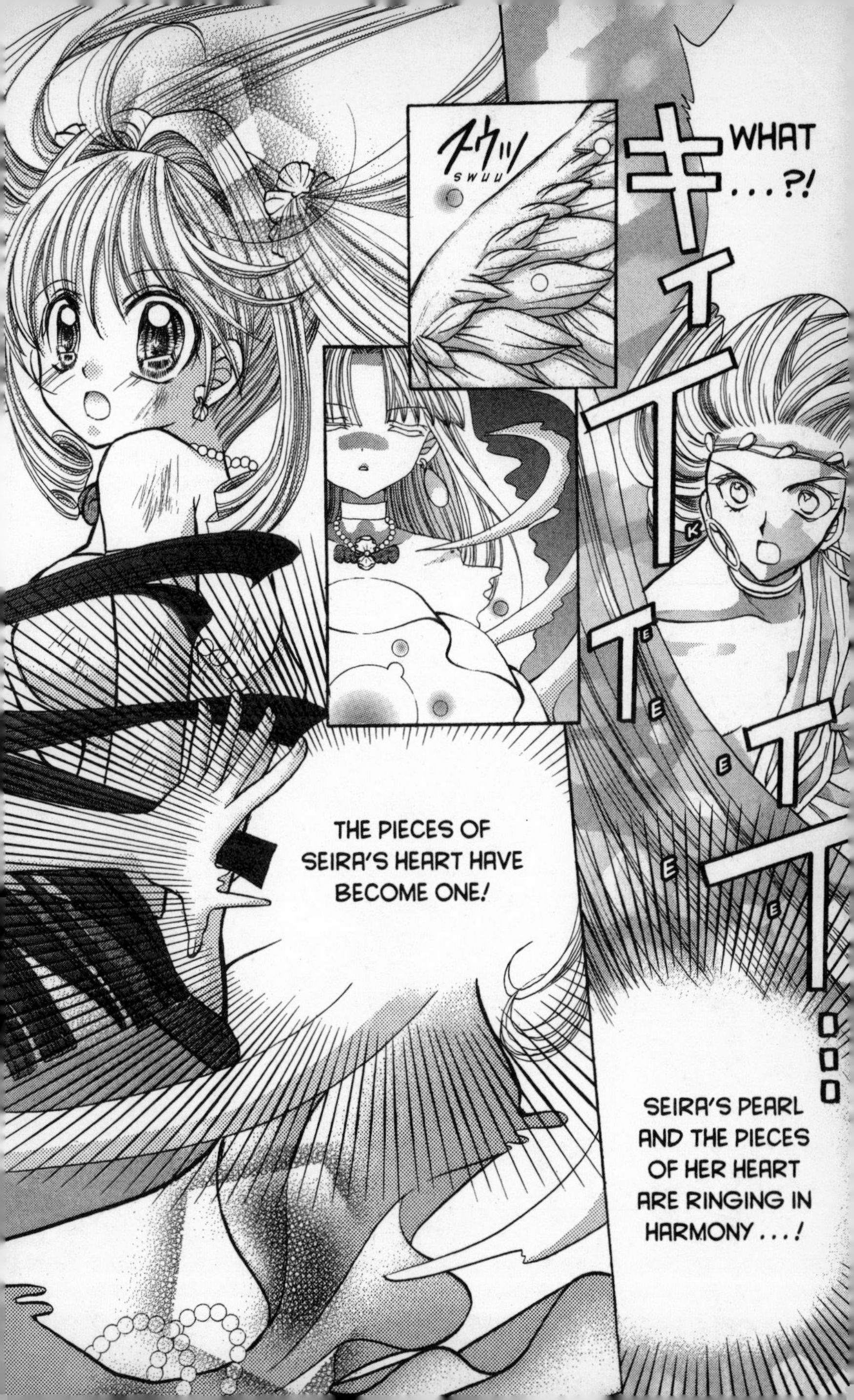
WHAT . . . ?!
SEIRA'S PEARL AND THE PIECES OF HER HEART ARE RINGING IN HARMONY . . . !
スウッ
SWUU
THE PIECES OF SEIRA'S HEART HAVE BECOME ONE!

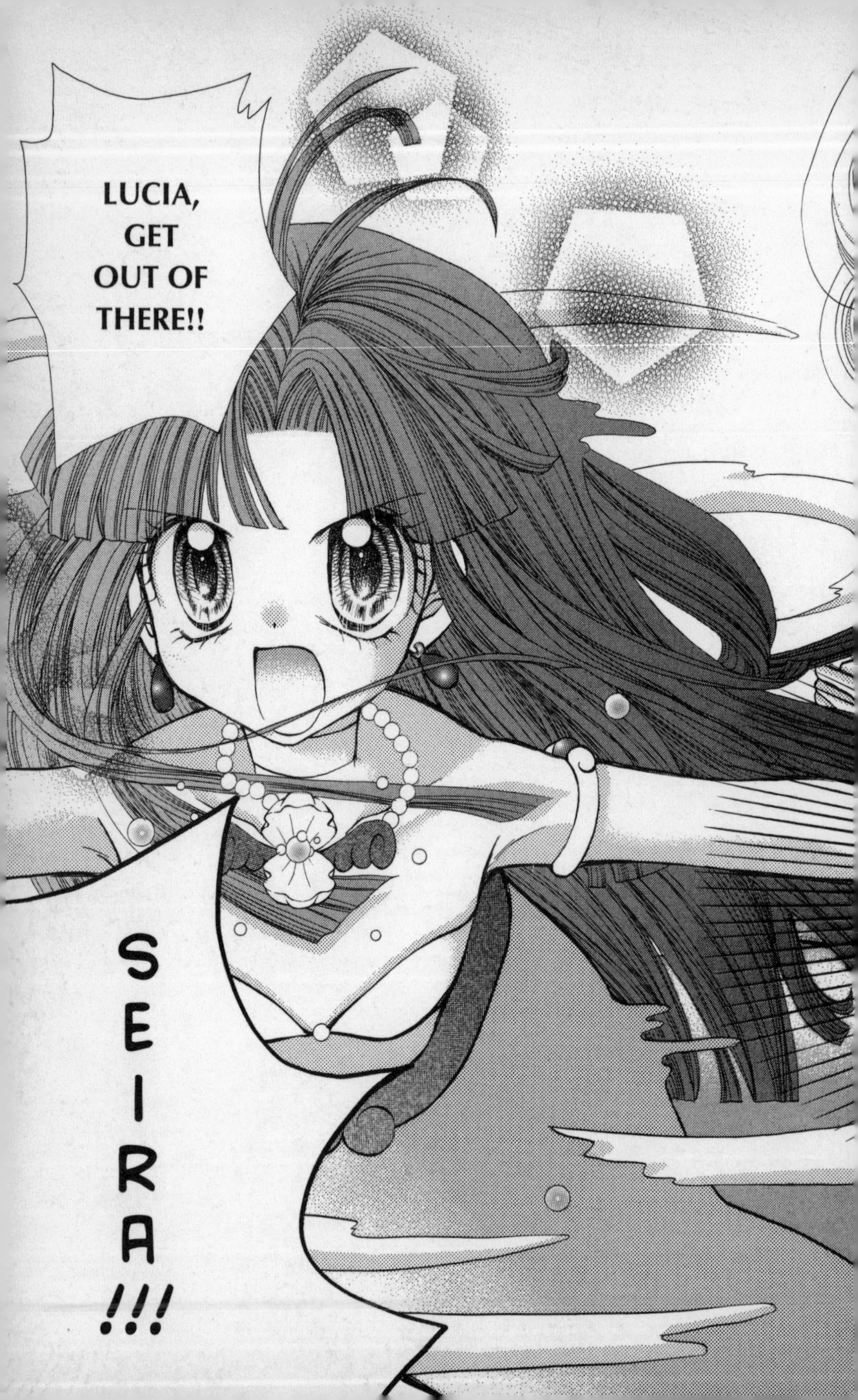
LUCIA, GET OUT OF THERE!!
SEIRA!!!

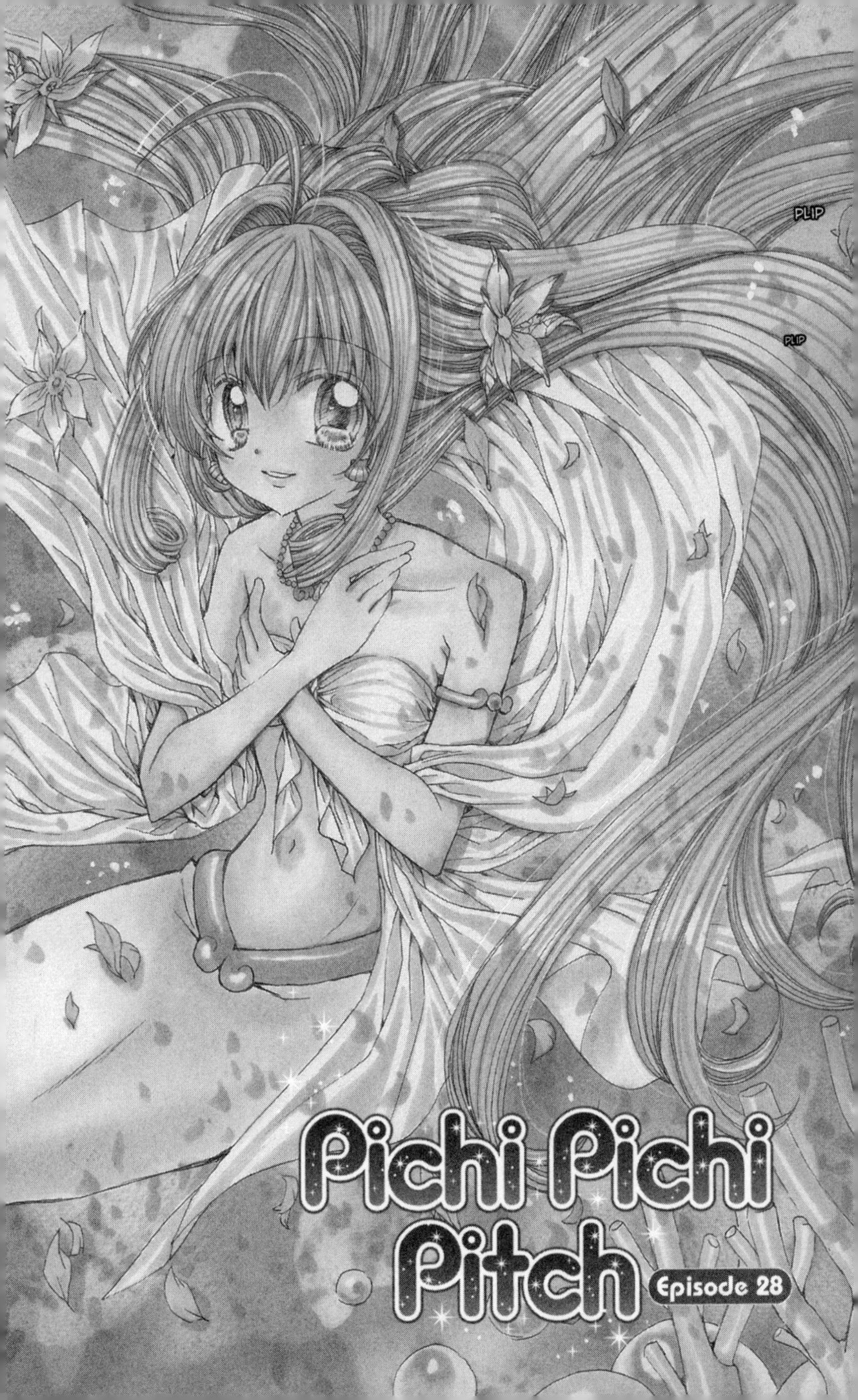
PLIP
PLIP
Pichi Pichi Pitch
Episode 28

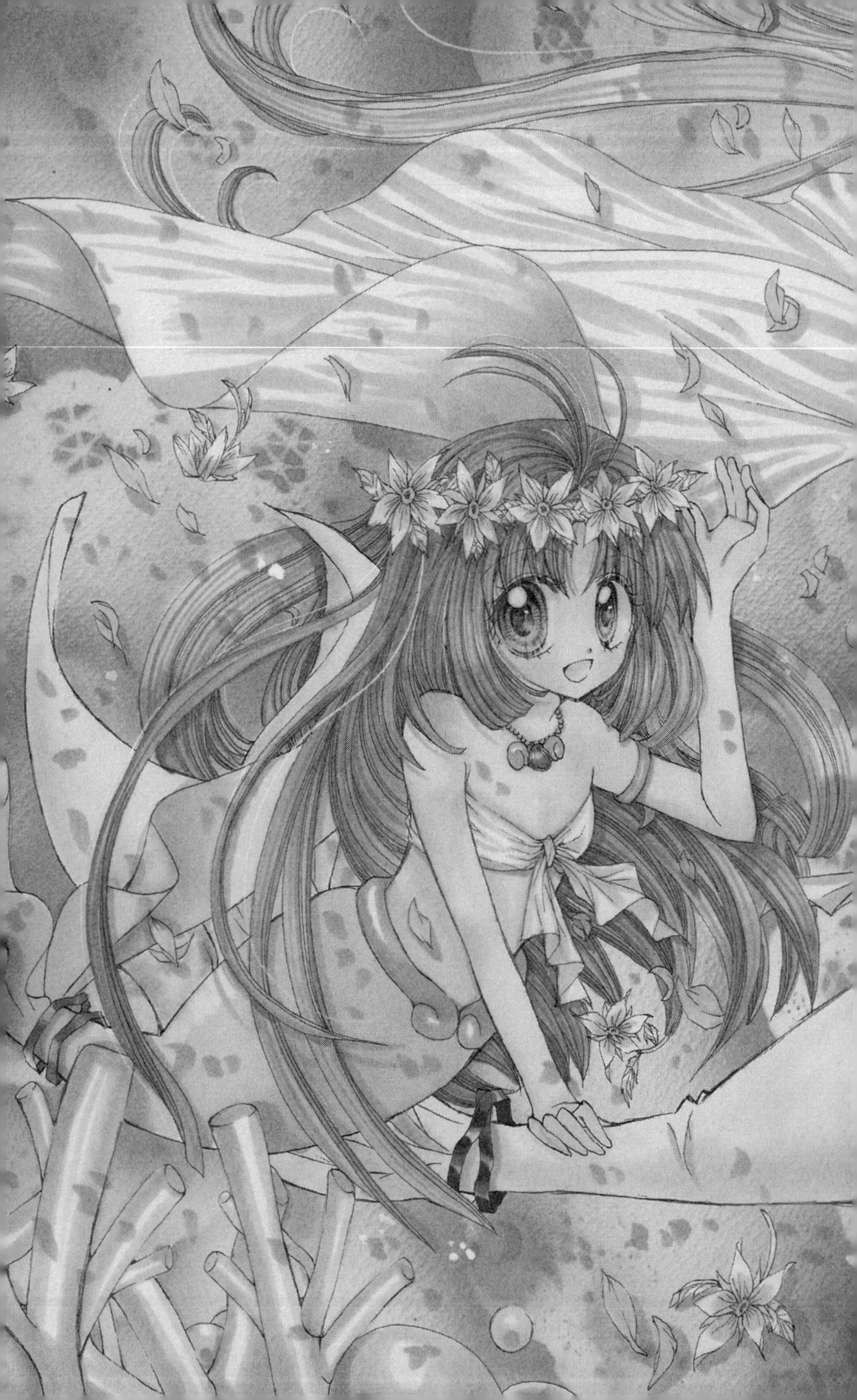

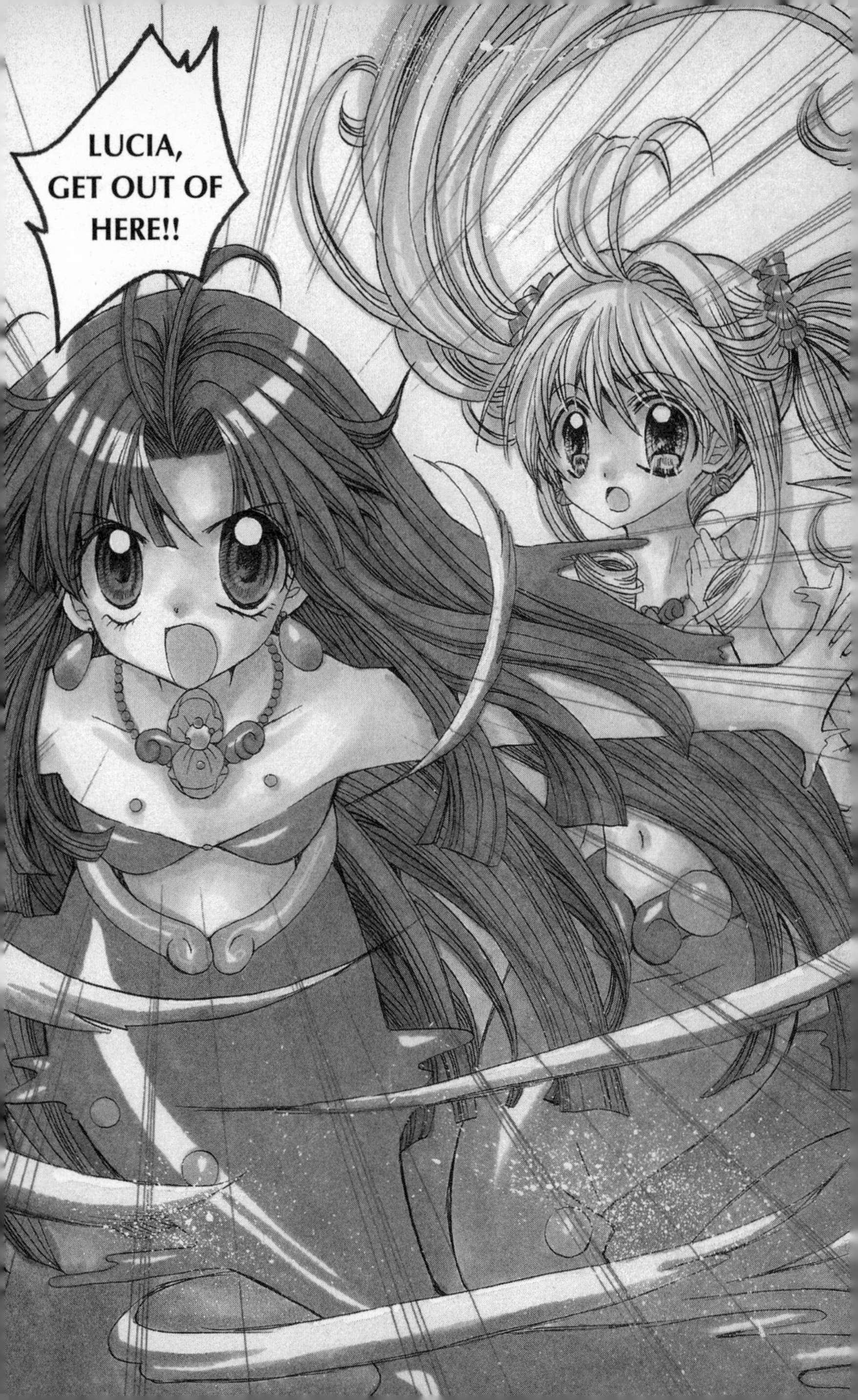
LUCIA, GET OUT OF HERE!!

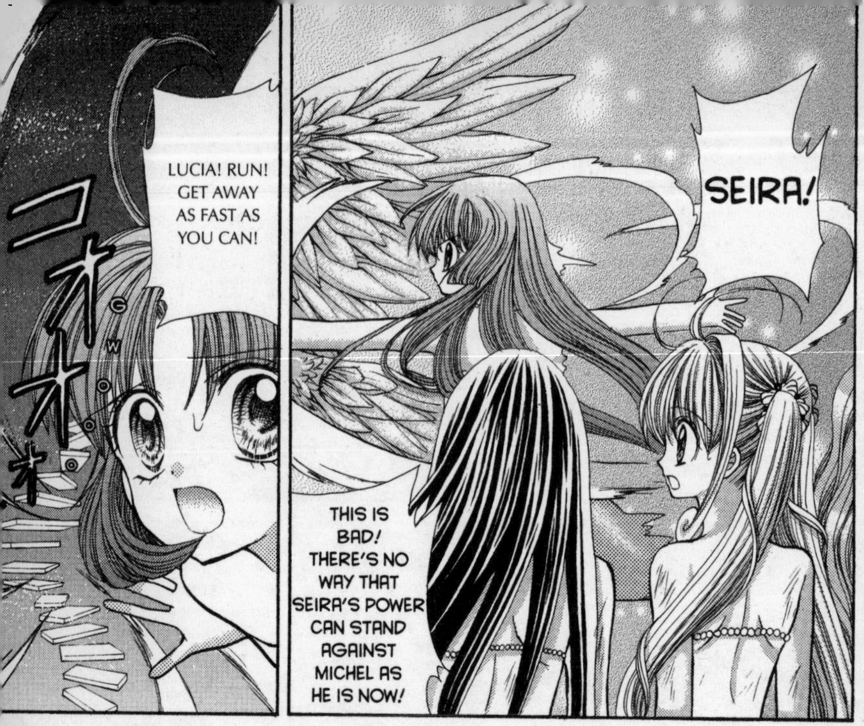
SEIRA!
THIS IS BAD! THERE'S NO WAY THAT SEIRA'S POWER CAN STAND AGAINST MICHEL AS HE IS NOW!
LUCIA! RUN! GET AWAY AS FAST AS YOU CAN!
コオオオ
GWOOOO

<EPISODE 28>
SPLASH PAGE: I TRIED TO PAINT IT WITH A LIGHT, SPRINGLIKE FEEL.
SIXTY-FIVE PAGES IN TWELVE DAYS.
FROM ABOUT VOLUME 4, I'D BEEN DRAWING EVERYTHING WITH A MARU-PEN. BUT FROM VOLUME 6 ON, I WENT BACK TO USING A G-PEN.
(THE G-PEN MAKES THINGS GO FASTER.)
BUT ONCE I WAS USED TO THE MARU-PEN, IT WAS VERY DIFFICULT TO MASTER WHAT PRESSURE TO PUT ON THE G-PEN AGAIN.
(I LOVE THE THICK FORCEFUL LINES YOU CAN MAKE WITH IT THOUGH.)
I LIKED THE SCENES WITH MICHEL PLAYING THE FLUTE AND ALL OF THE YÔKAI WITH WINGS, AND I LOVED THE FINAL TWO PAGES.

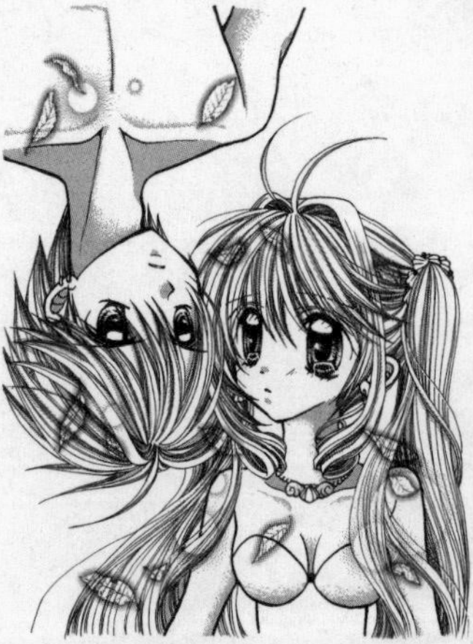

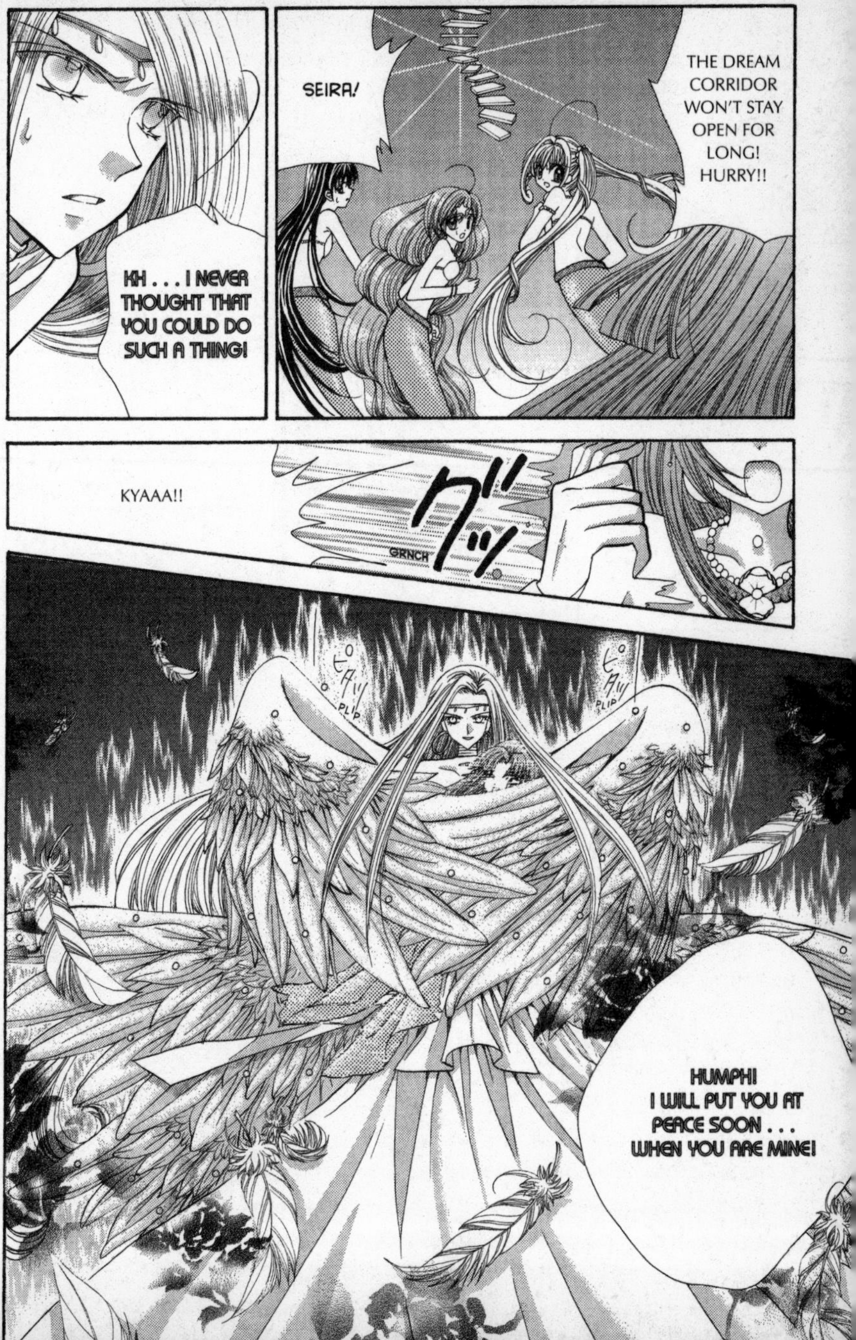
THE DREAM CORRIDOR WON'T STAY OPEN FOR LONG! HURRY!!
SEIRA!
KH . . . I NEVER THOUGHT THAT YOU COULD DO SUCH A THING!
ヴッ
GRNCH
KYAAA!!
ピタッ
PLIP
ピタッ
PLIP
HUMPH! I WILL PUT YOU AT PEACE SOON . . . WHEN YOU ARE MINE!

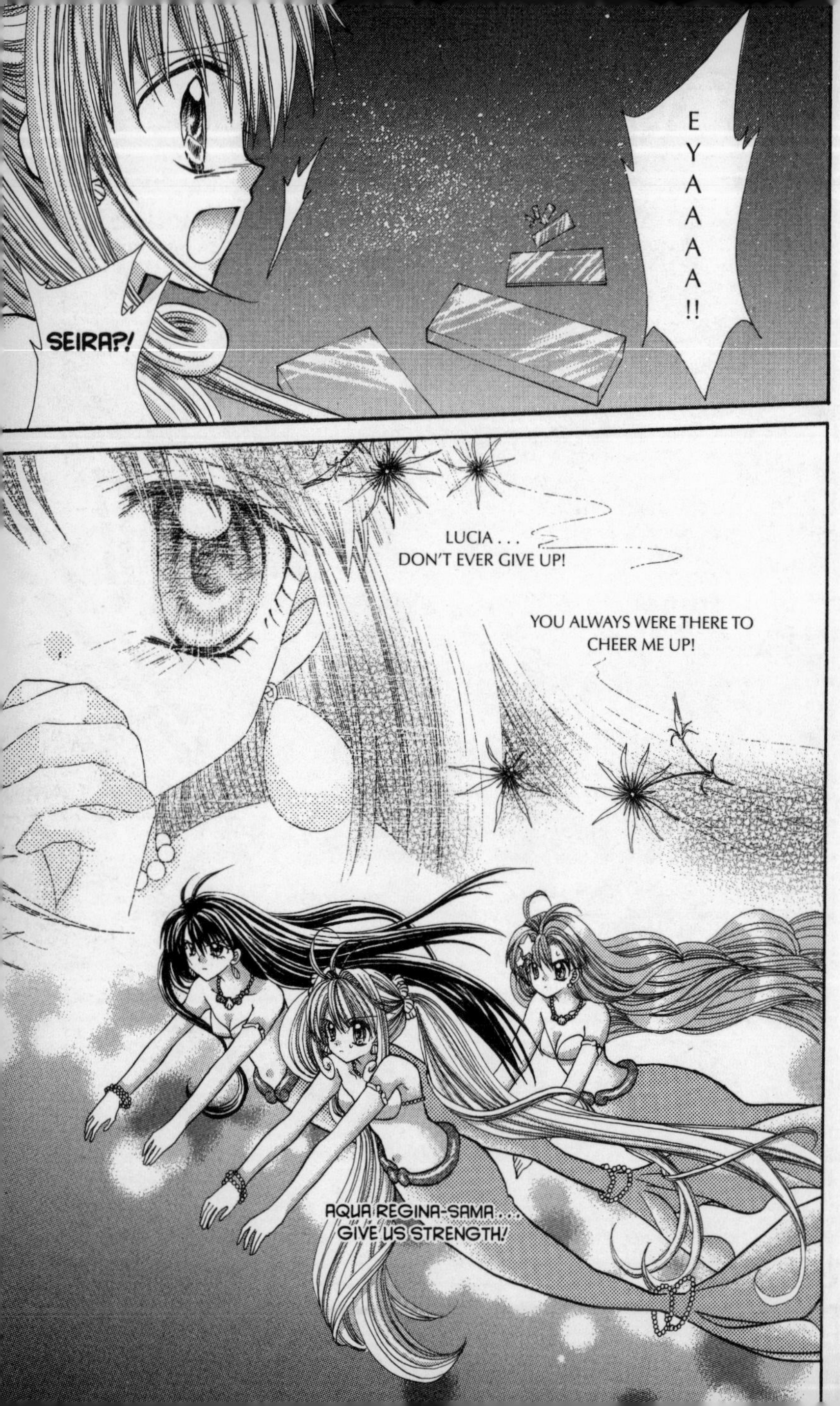
EYAAAAA!!
SEIRA?!
LUCIA . . . DON'T EVER GIVE UP!
YOU ALWAYS WERE THERE TO CHEER ME UP!
AQUA REGINA-SAMA . . . GIVE US STRENGTH!

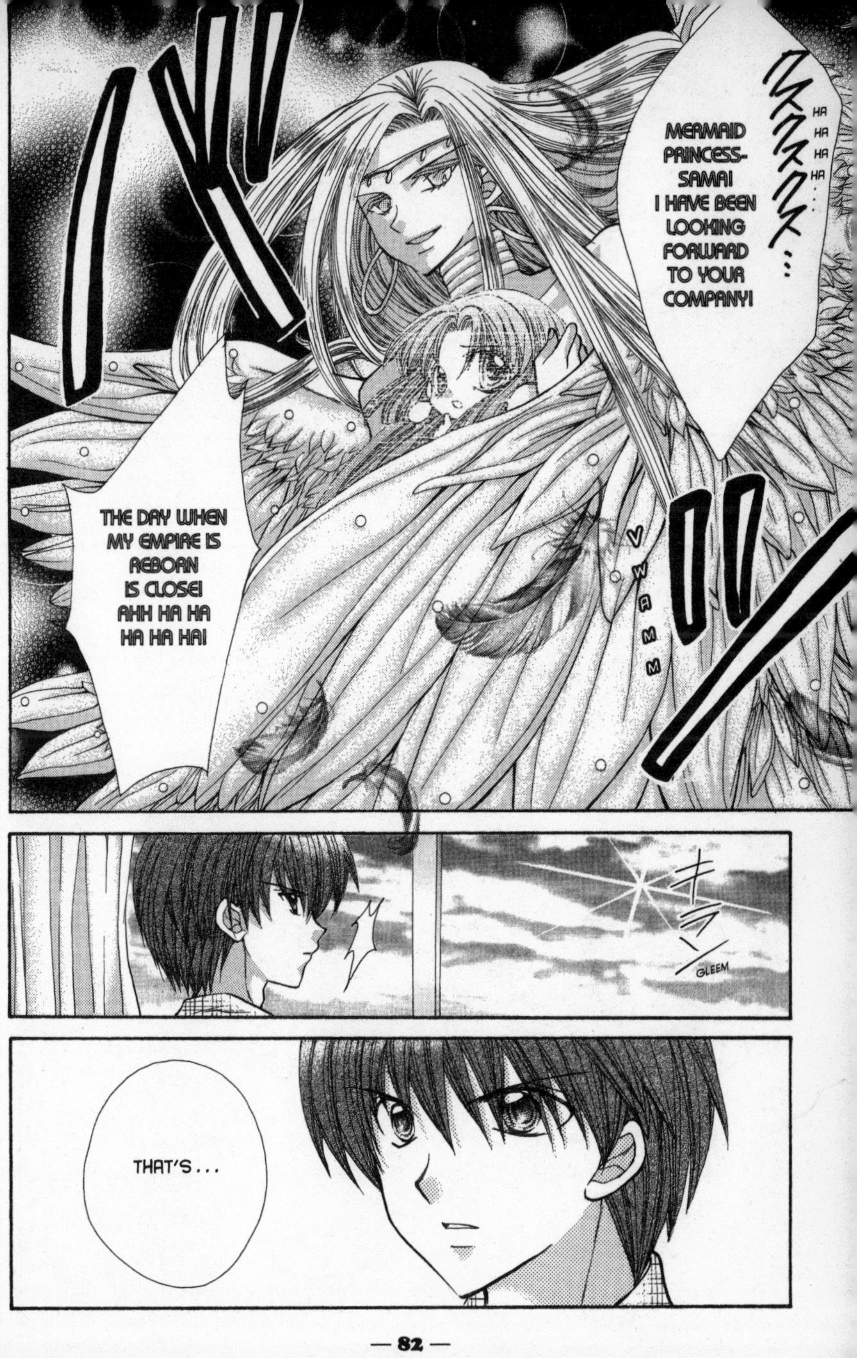

MERMAID PRINCESS-SAMA! I HAVE BEEN LOOKING FORWARD TO YOUR COMPANY!
クスクスクス…
HA HA HA HA...
THE DAY WHEN MY EMPIRE IS REBORN IS CLOSE! AHH HA HA HA HA HA!
VWAMM
キラン
GLEEM
THAT'S...

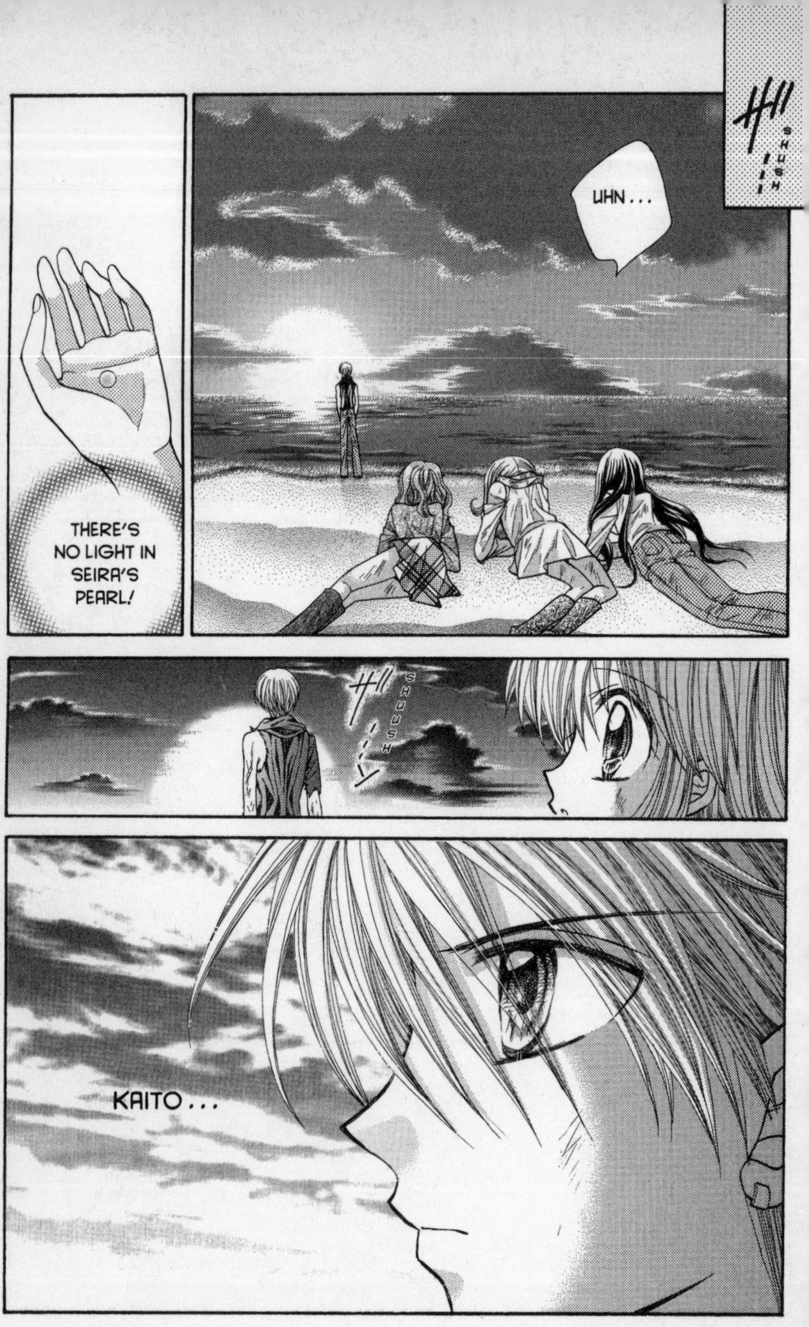
SHUSH
UHN...
THERE'S NO LIGHT IN SEIRA'S PEARL!
SHUUSH
KAITO...

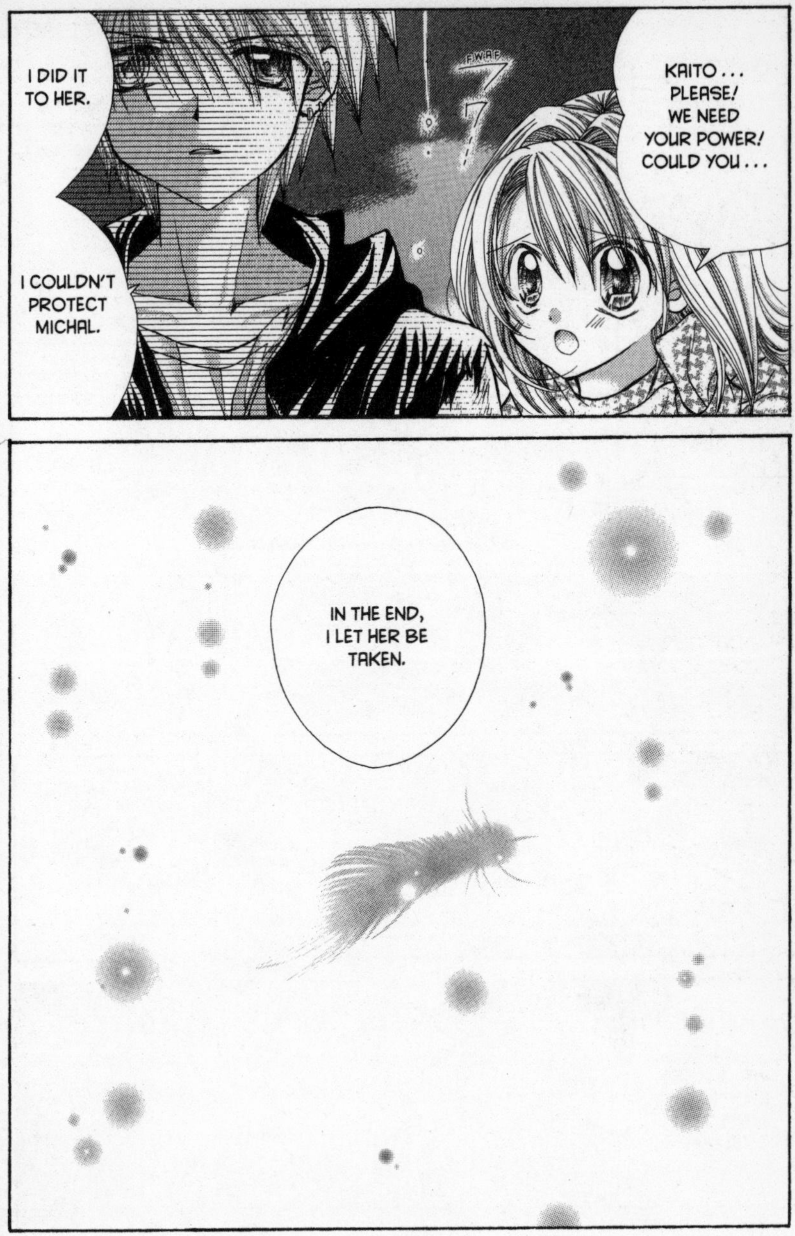
KAITO . . . PLEASE! WE NEED YOUR POWER! COULD YOU . . .
FWAF
I DID IT TO HER.
I COULDN'T PROTECT MICHAL.
IN THE END, I LET HER BE TAKEN.

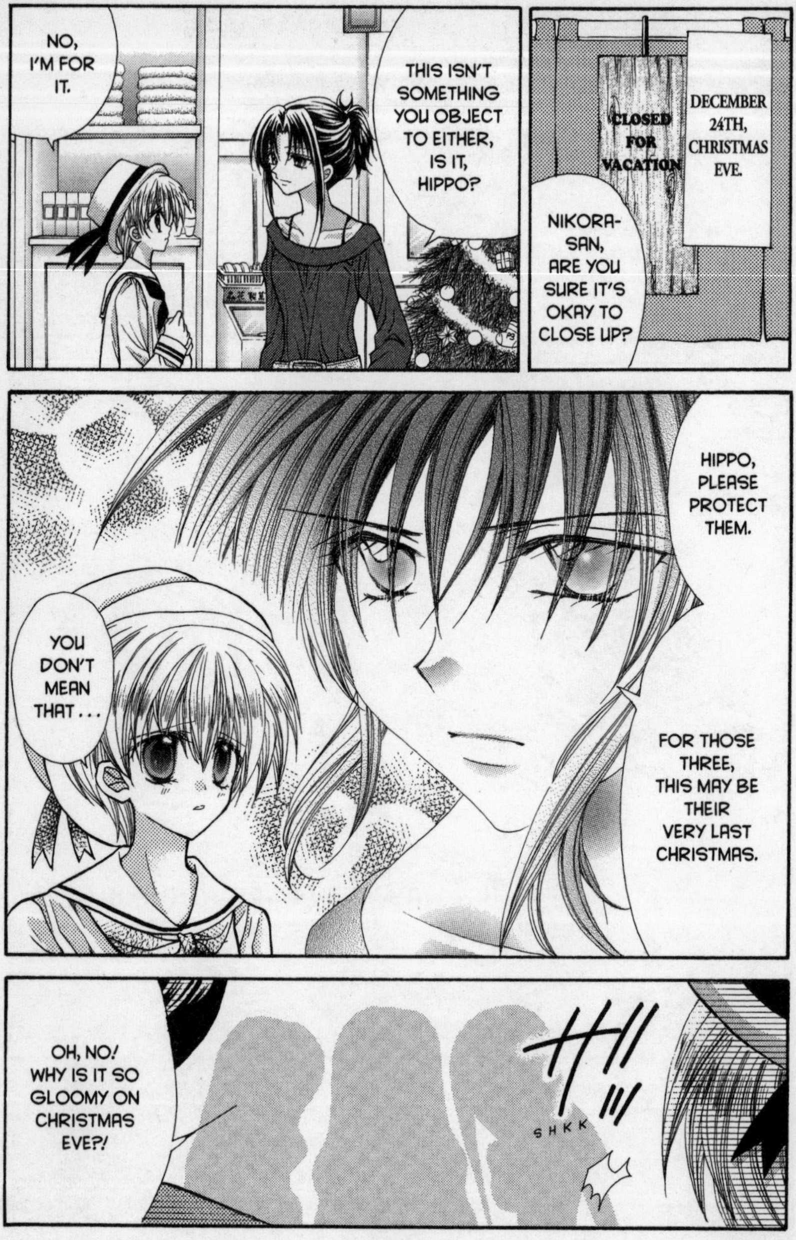
DECEMBER 24TH, CHRISTMAS EVE.
CLOSED FOR VACATION
NIKORA-SAN, ARE YOU SURE IT'S OKAY TO CLOSE UP?
THIS ISN'T SOMETHING YOU OBJECT TO EITHER, IS IT, HIPPO?
NO, I'M FOR IT.
HIPPO, PLEASE PROTECT THEM.
FOR THOSE THREE, THIS MAY BE THEIR VERY LAST CHRISTMAS.
YOU DON'T MEAN THAT . . .
SHKK
OH, NO! WHY IS IT SO GLOOMY ON CHRISTMAS EVE?!

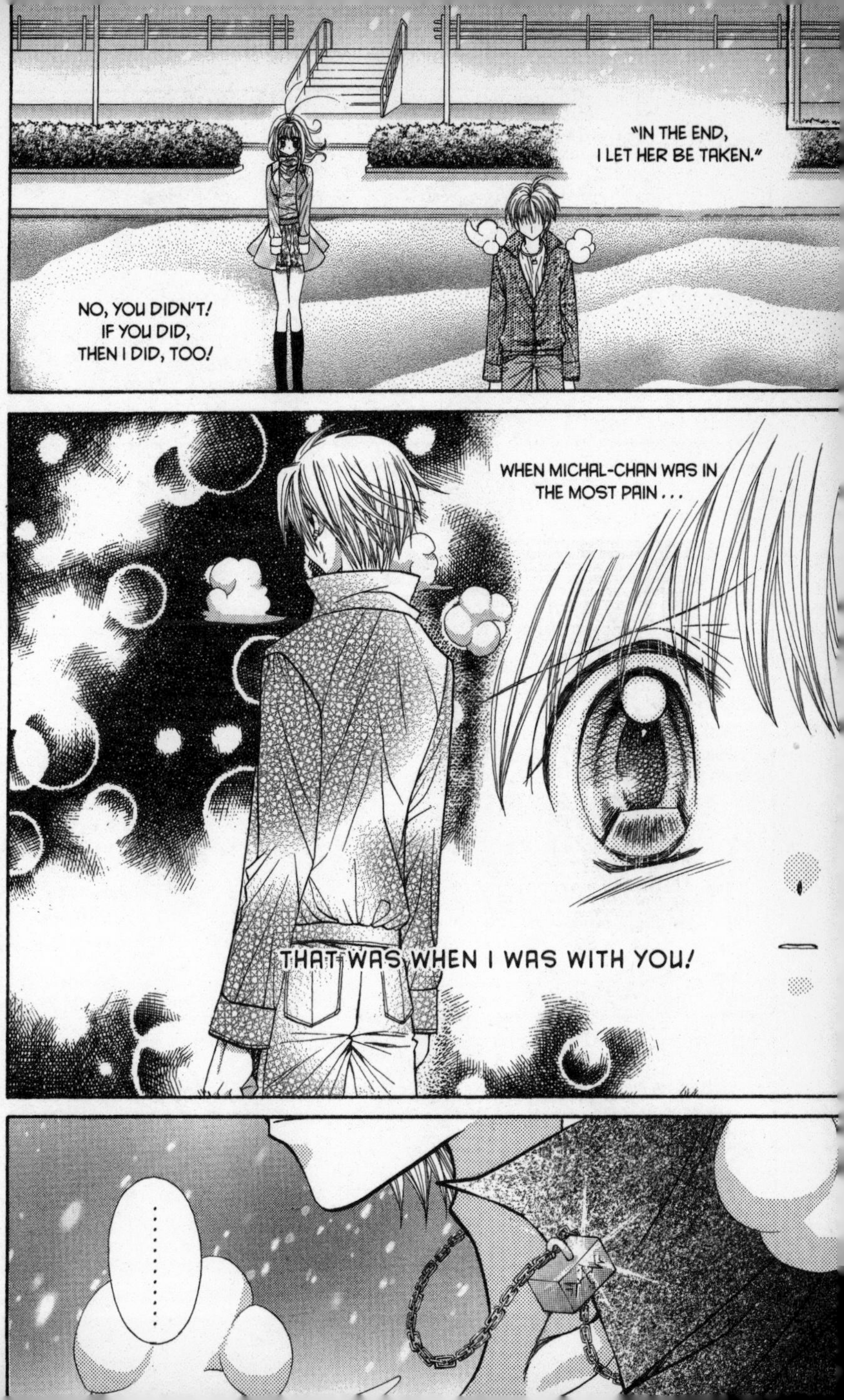
"IN THE END, I LET HER BE TAKEN."
NO, YOU DIDN'T! IF YOU DID, THEN I DID, TOO!
WHEN MICHAL-CHAN WAS IN THE MOST PAIN . . .
THAT WAS WHEN I WAS WITH YOU!
......

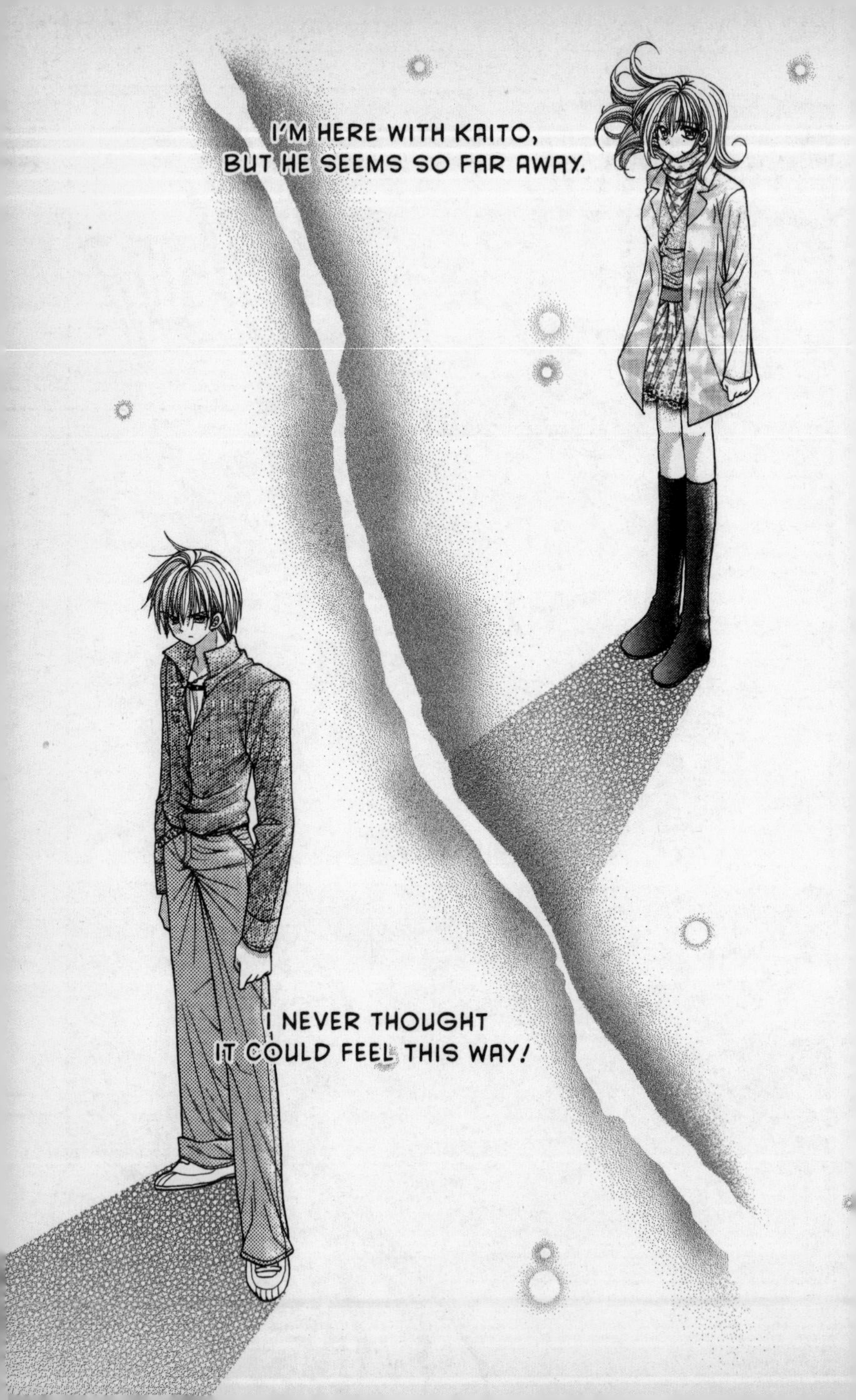
I'M HERE WITH KAITO, BUT HE SEEMS SO FAR AWAY.
I NEVER THOUGHT IT COULD FEEL THIS WAY!

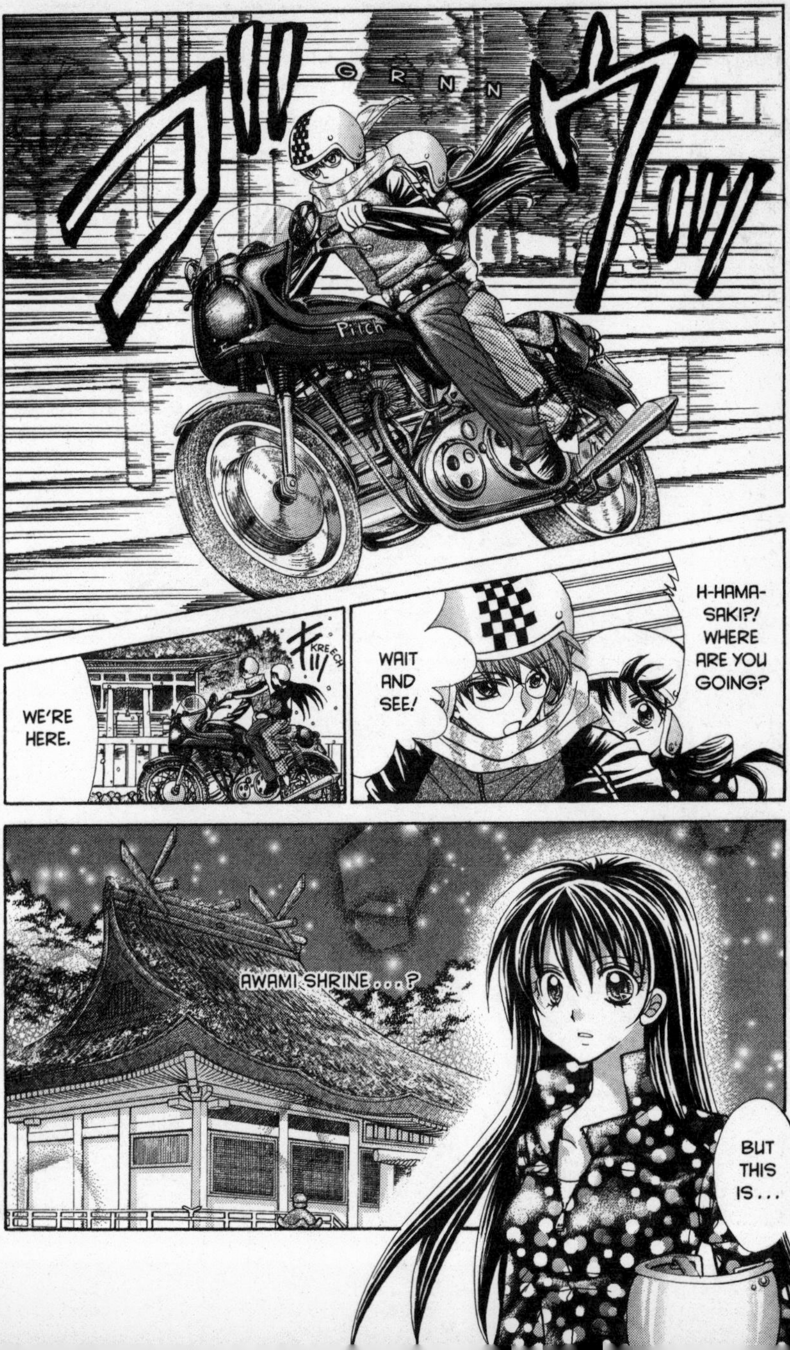
GRNN
Pitch
H-HAMA-SAKI?! WHERE ARE YOU GOING?
WAIT AND SEE!
KREECH
WE'RE HERE.
AWAMI SHRINE . . . ?
BUT THIS IS . . .

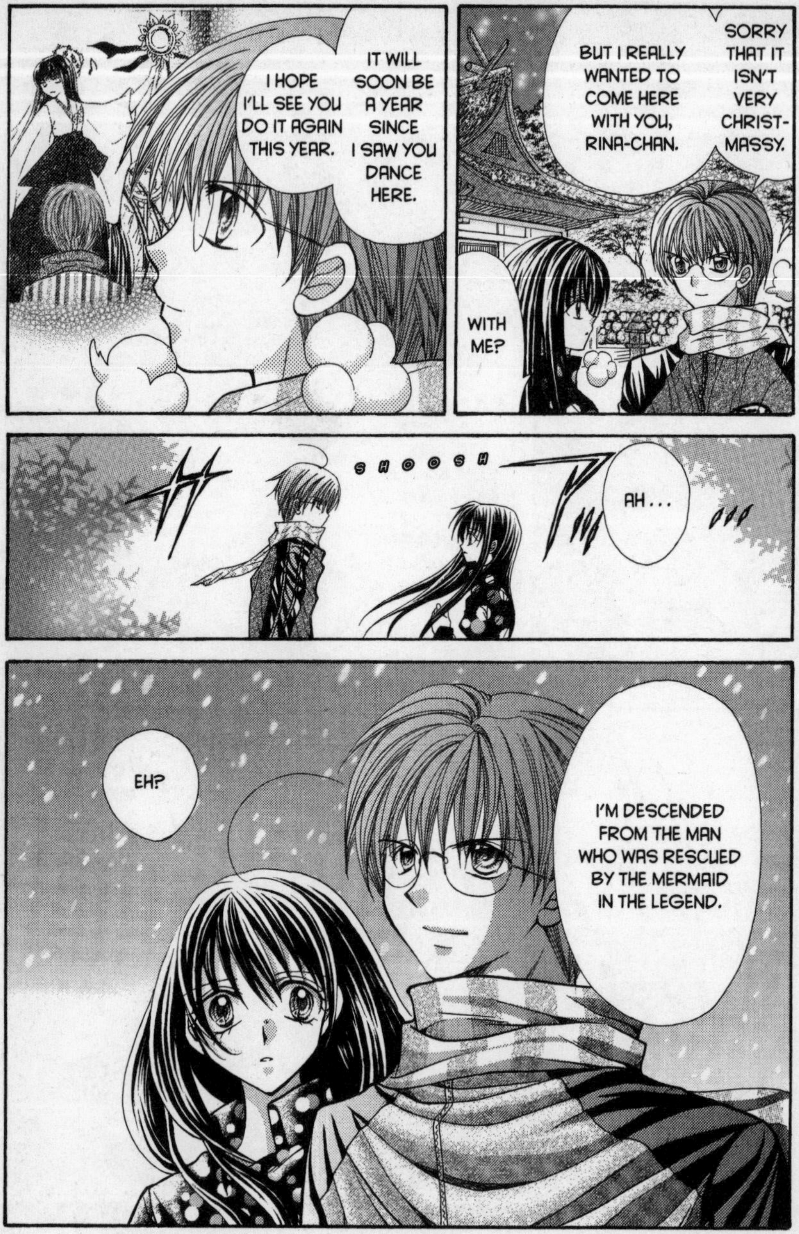
SORRY THAT IT ISN'T VERY CHRIST-MASSY.
BUT I REALLY WANTED TO COME HERE WITH YOU, RINA-CHAN.
WITH ME?
IT WILL SOON BE A YEAR SINCE I SAW YOU DANCE HERE.
I HOPE I'LL SEE YOU DO IT AGAIN THIS YEAR.
AH...
SHOOSH
I'M DESCENDED FROM THE MAN WHO WAS RESCUED BY THE MERMAID IN THE LEGEND.
EH?

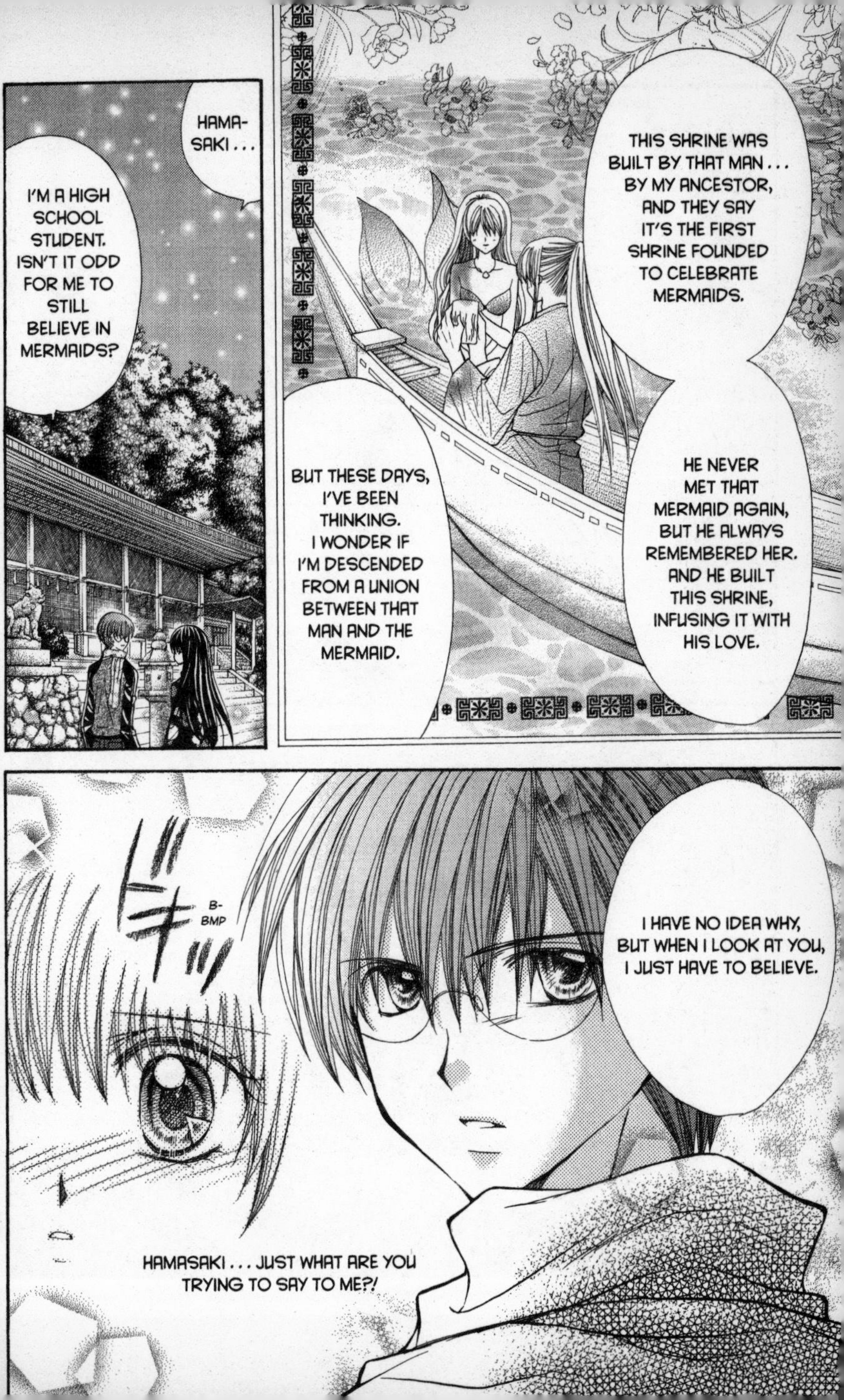
THIS SHRINE WAS BUILT BY THAT MAN . . . BY MY ANCESTOR, AND THEY SAY IT'S THE FIRST SHRINE FOUNDED TO CELEBRATE MERMAIDS.
HE NEVER MET THAT MERMAID AGAIN, BUT HE ALWAYS REMEMBERED HER. AND HE BUILT THIS SHRINE, INFUSING IT WITH HIS LOVE.
BUT THESE DAYS, I'VE BEEN THINKING. I WONDER IF I'M DESCENDED FROM A UNION BETWEEN THAT MAN AND THE MERMAID.
HAMA-SAKI . . .
I'M A HIGH SCHOOL STUDENT. ISN'T IT ODD FOR ME TO STILL BELIEVE IN MERMAIDS?
I HAVE NO IDEA WHY, BUT WHEN I LOOK AT YOU, I JUST HAVE TO BELIEVE.
B-BMP
HAMASAKI . . . JUST WHAT ARE YOU TRYING TO SAY TO ME?!

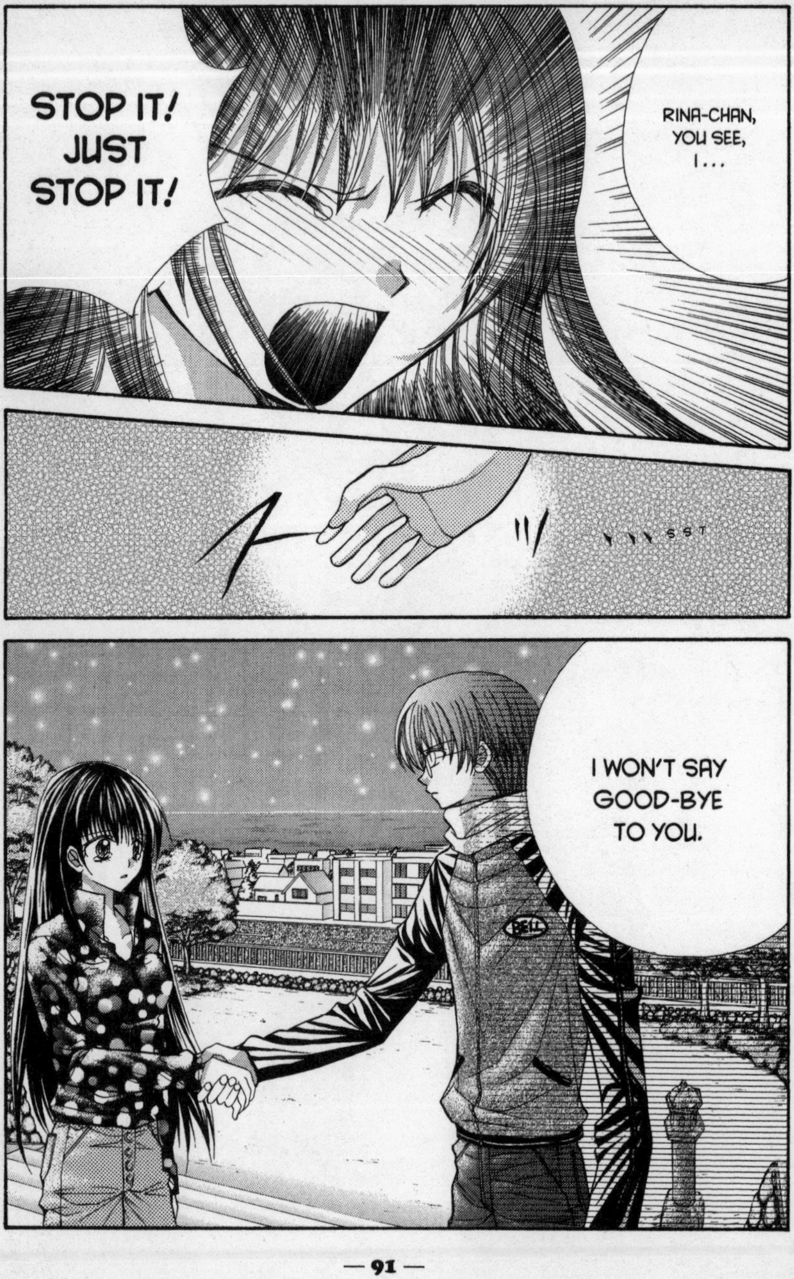
RINA-CHAN, YOU SEE, I...
STOP IT! JUST STOP IT!
SST
I WON'T SAY GOOD-BYE TO YOU.

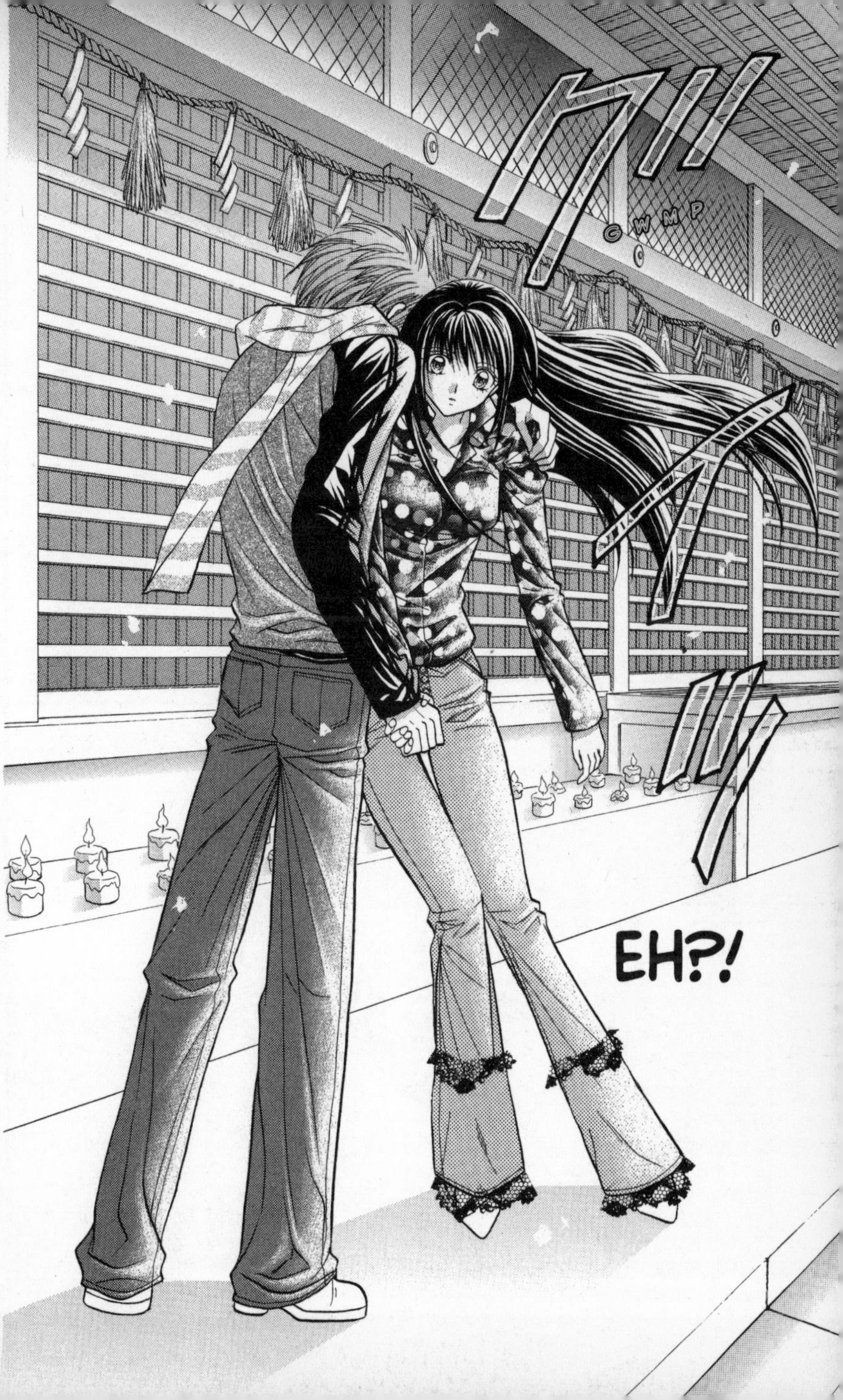
GWMP
EH?!

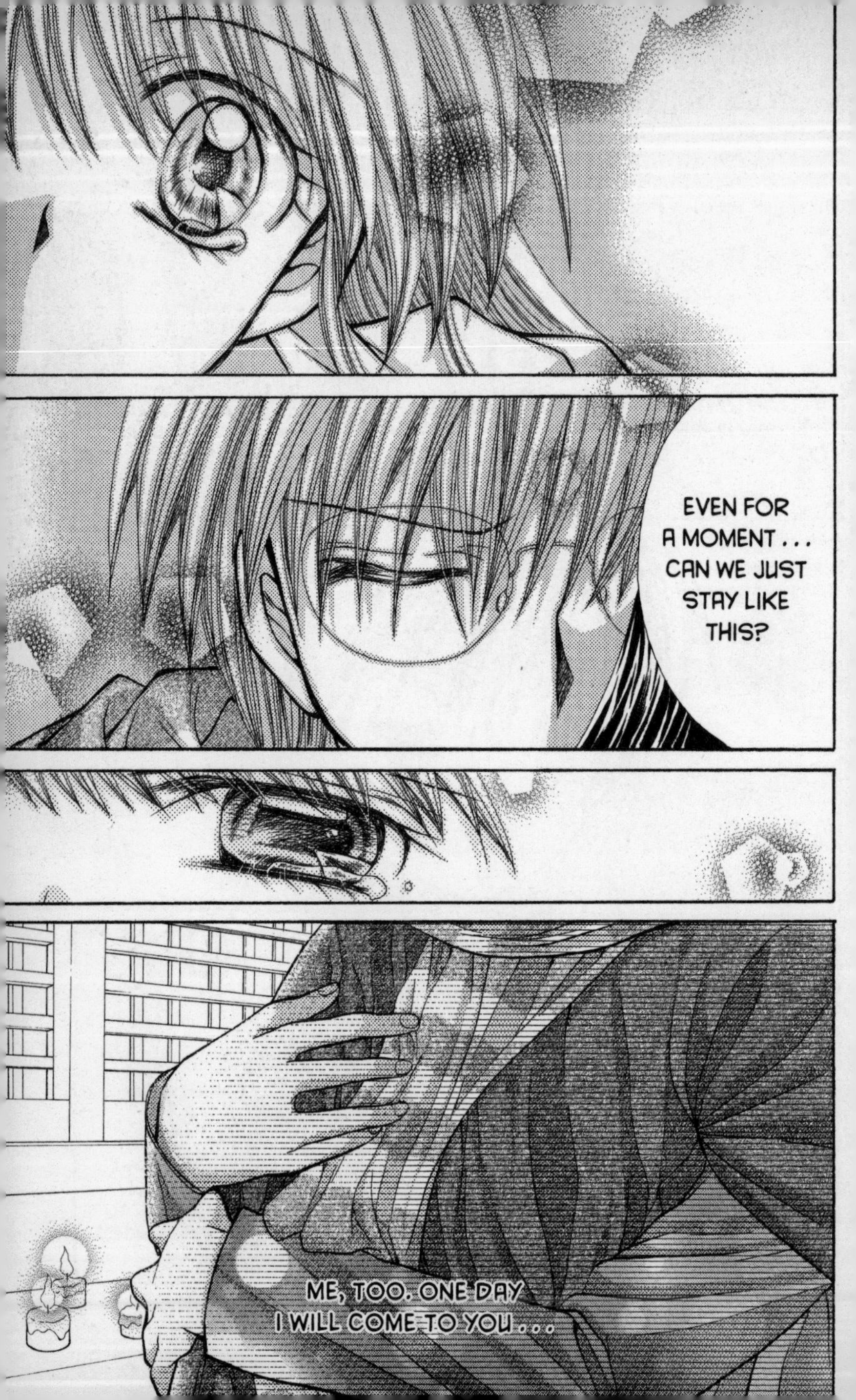
EVEN FOR A MOMENT . . . CAN WE JUST STAY LIKE THIS?
ME, TOO. ONE DAY I WILL COME TO YOU . . .

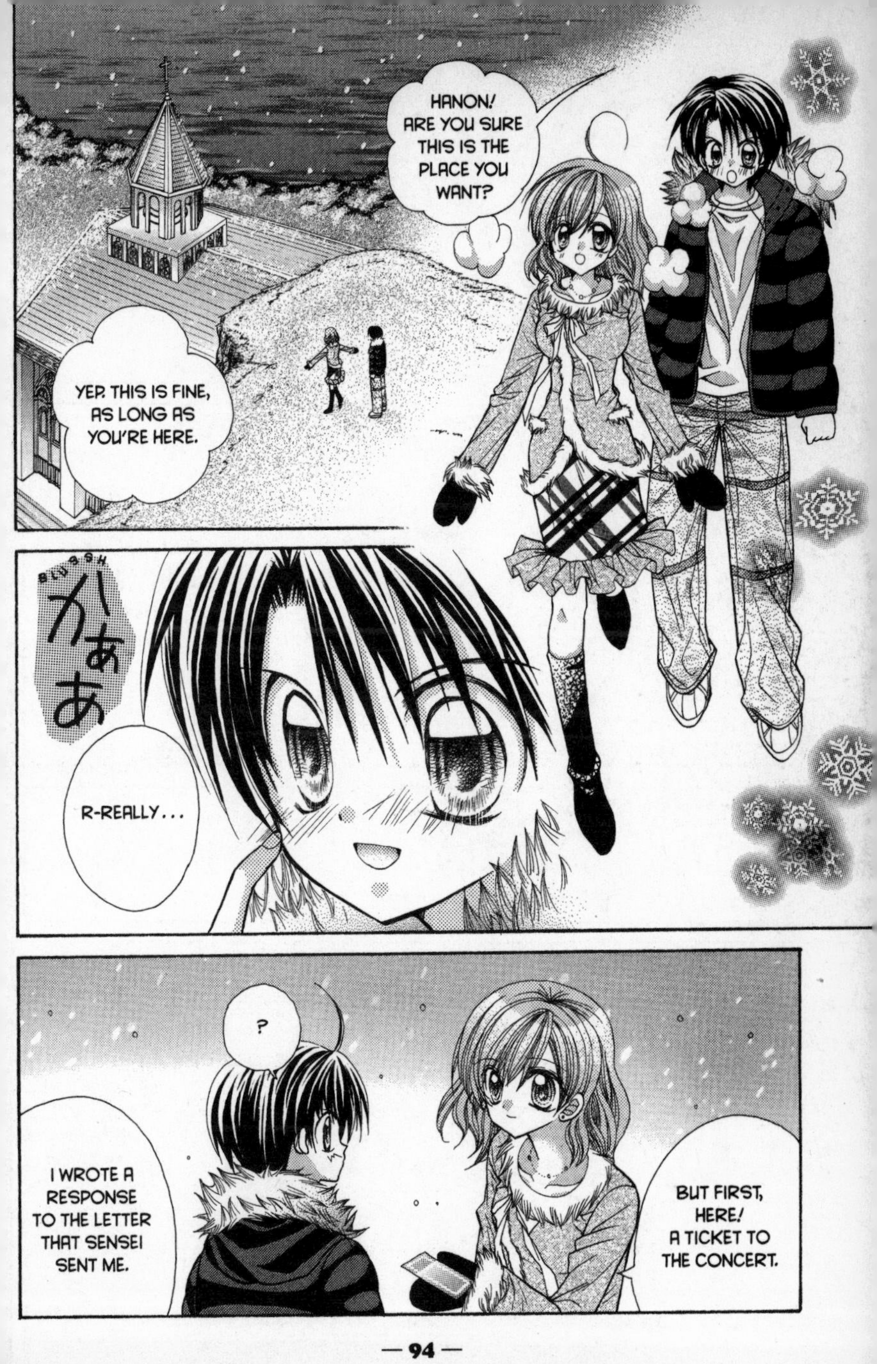
HANON! ARE YOU SURE THIS IS THE PLACE YOU WANT?
YEP. THIS IS FINE, AS LONG AS YOU'RE HERE.
BLUSSH
かあぁ
R-REALLY...
BUT FIRST, HERE! A TICKET TO THE CONCERT.
?
I WROTE A RESPONSE TO THE LETTER THAT SENSEI SENT ME.

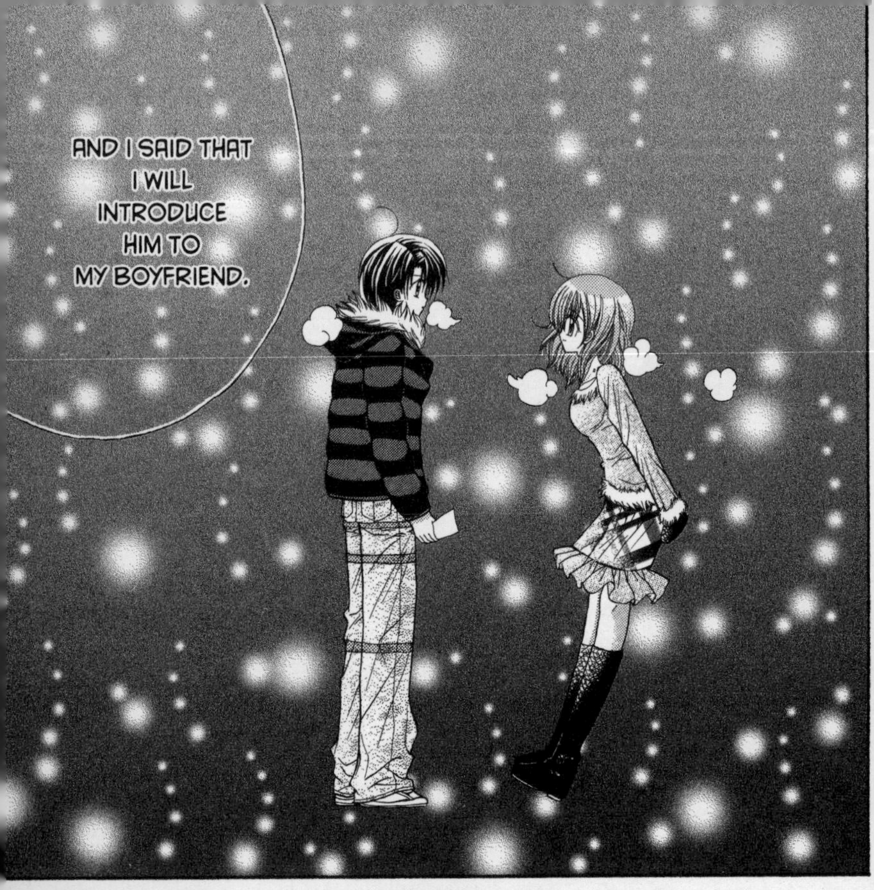
AND I SAID THAT I WILL INTRODUCE HIM TO MY BOYFRIEND.

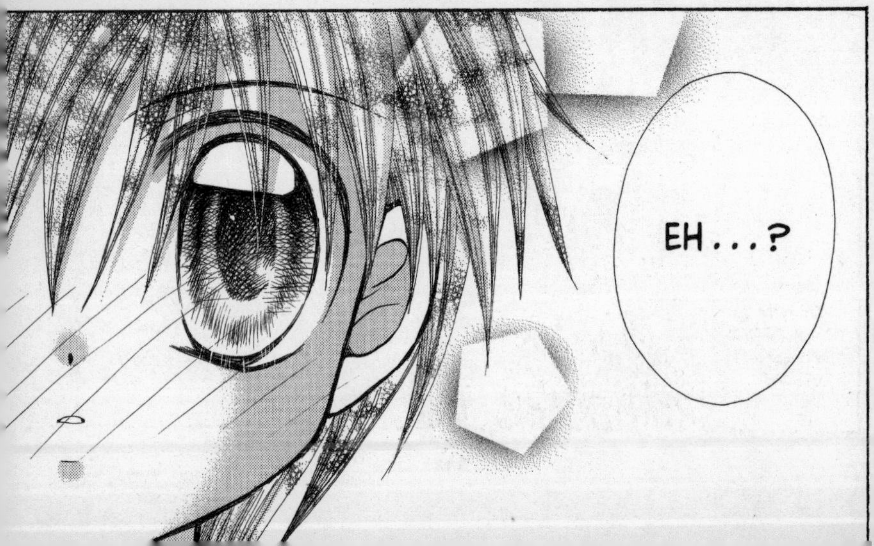
EH...?

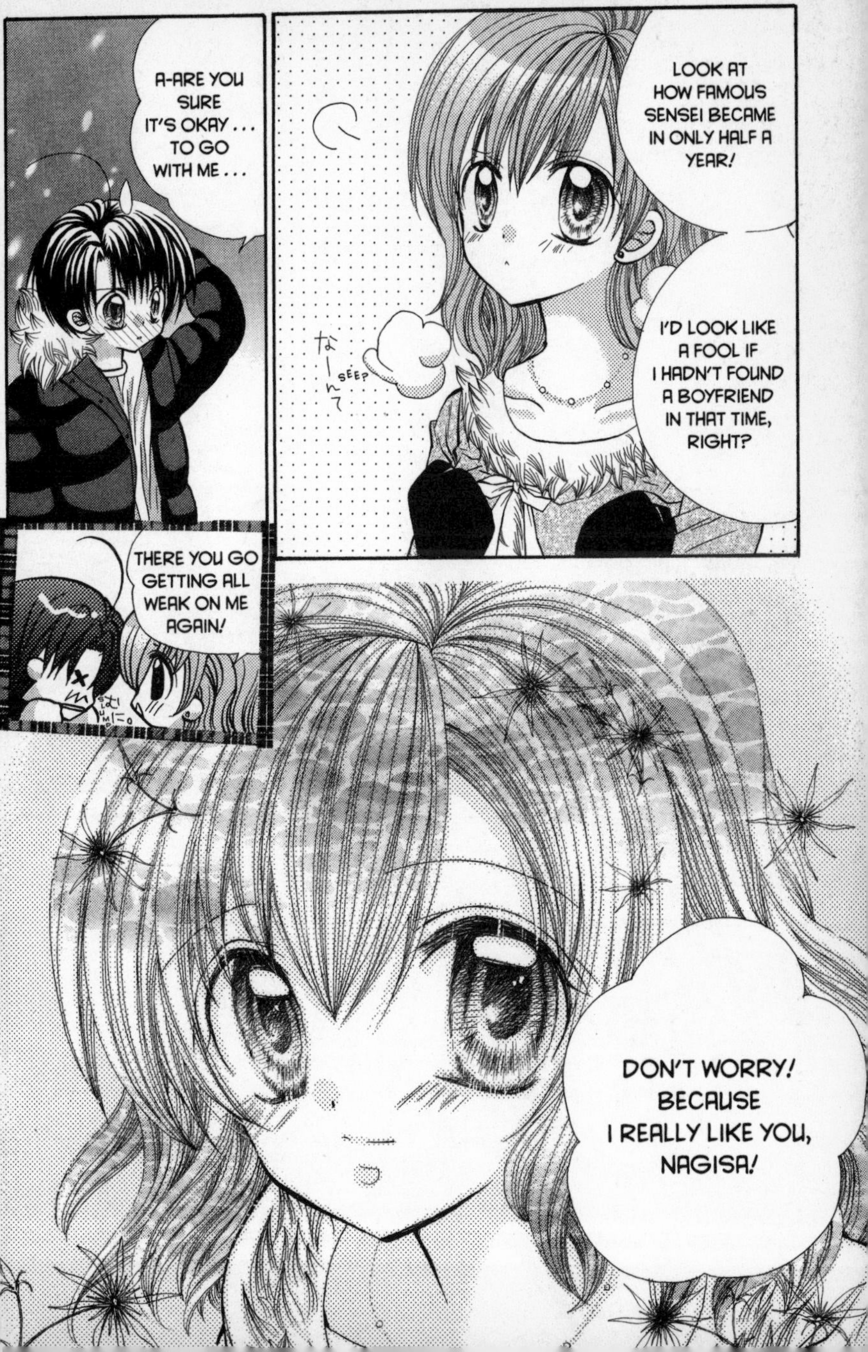
LOOK AT HOW FAMOUS SENSEI BECAME IN ONLY HALF A YEAR!
I'D LOOK LIKE A FOOL IF I HADN'T FOUND A BOYFRIEND IN THAT TIME, RIGHT?
なーんて
SEE?
A-ARE YOU SURE IT'S OKAY... TO GO WITH ME...
THERE YOU GO GETTING ALL WEAK ON ME AGAIN!
DON'T WORRY! BECAUSE I REALLY LIKE YOU, NAGISA!

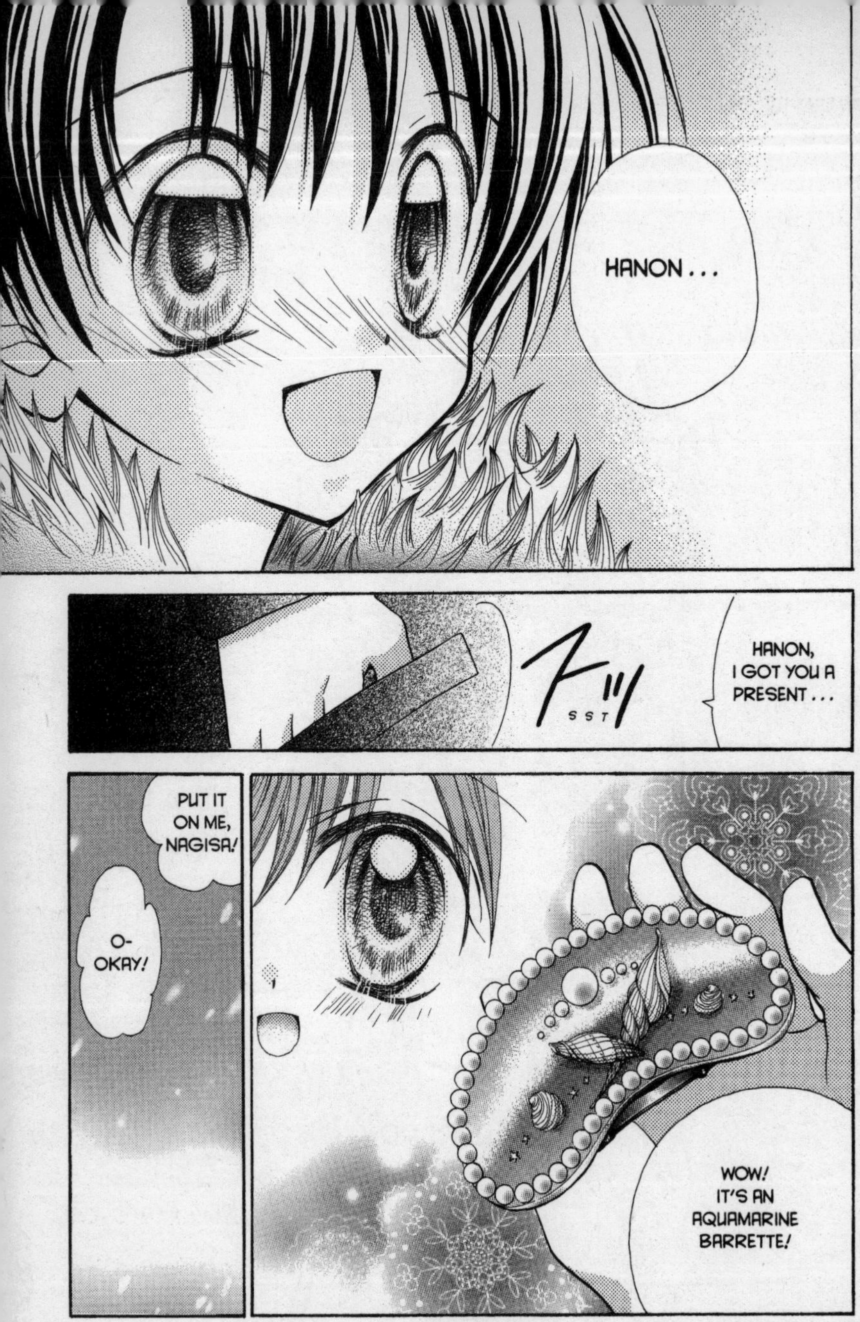
HANON...
HANON, I GOT YOU A PRESENT...
SST
WOW! IT'S AN AQUAMARINE BARRETTE!
PUT IT ON ME, NAGISA!
O- OKAY!

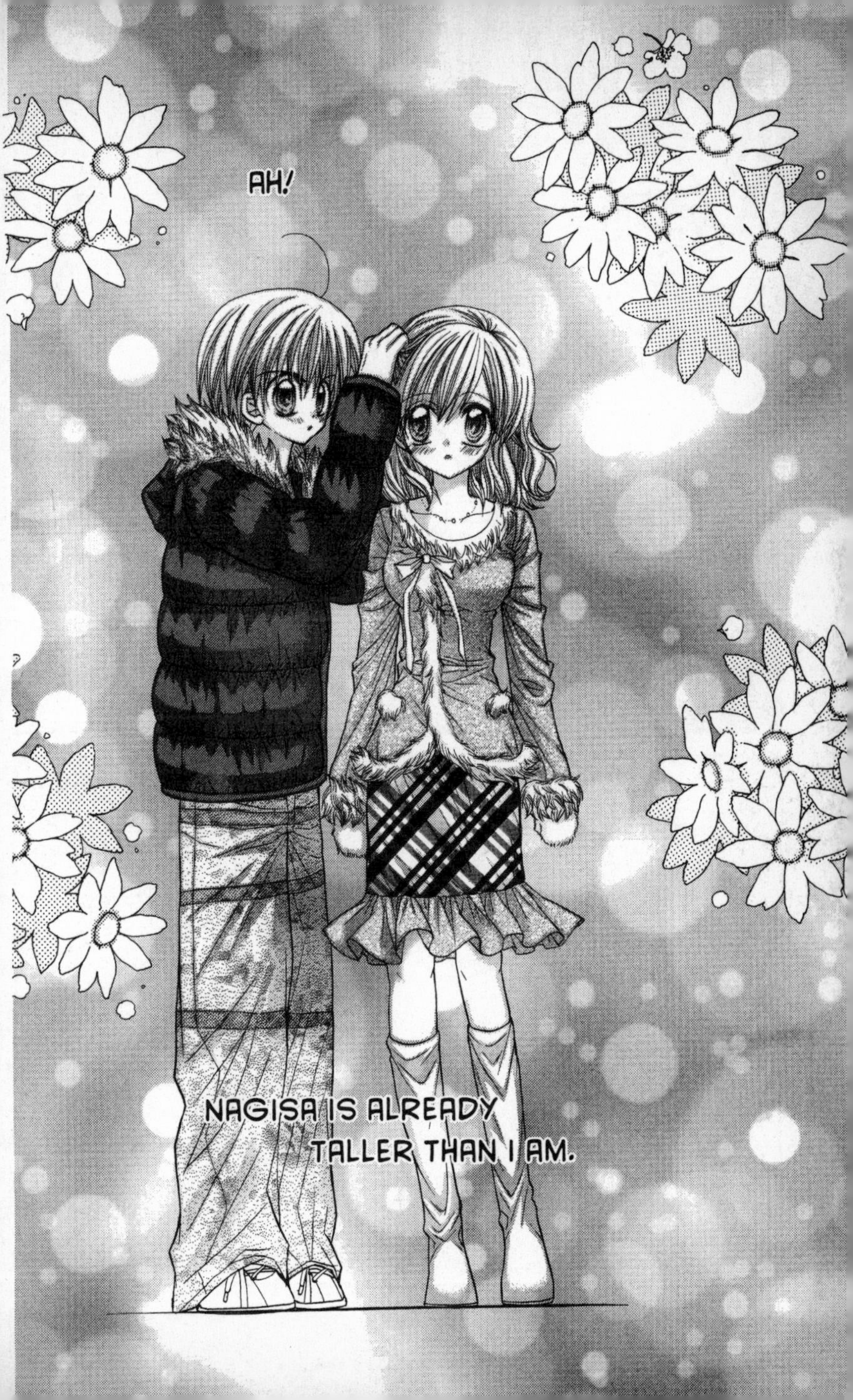
AH!
NAGISA IS ALREADY TALLER THAN I AM.

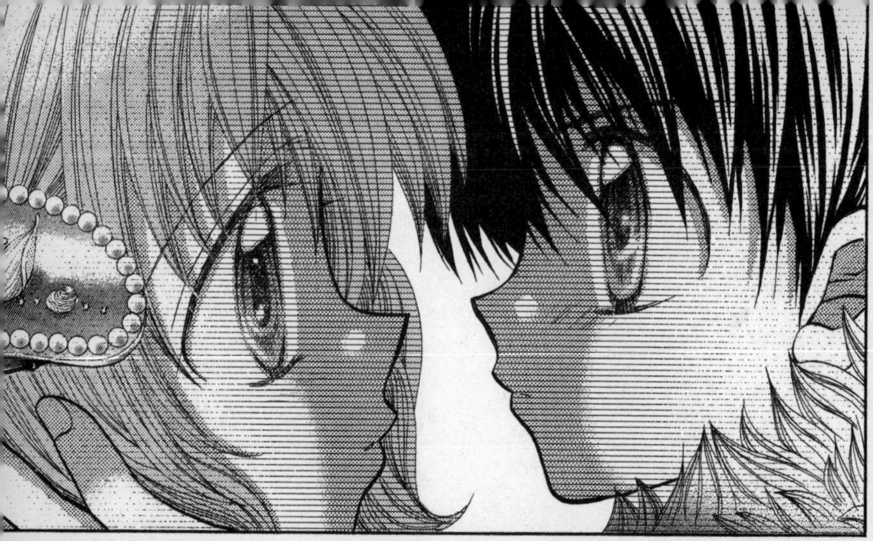
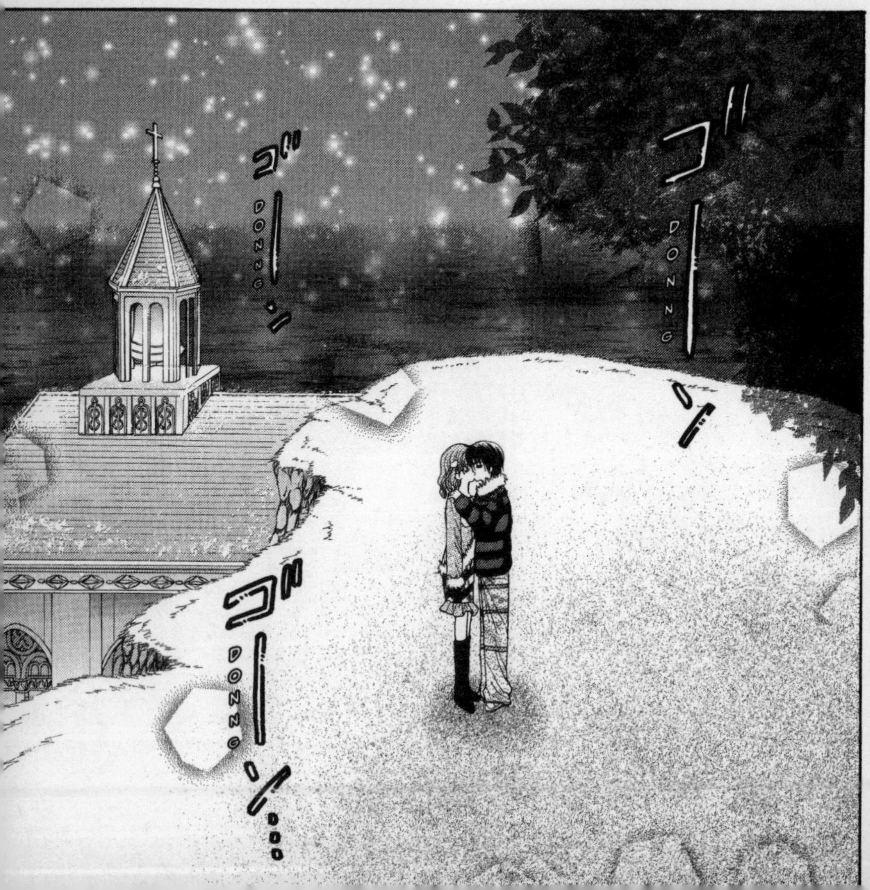
DONNG
DONNG
DONNG

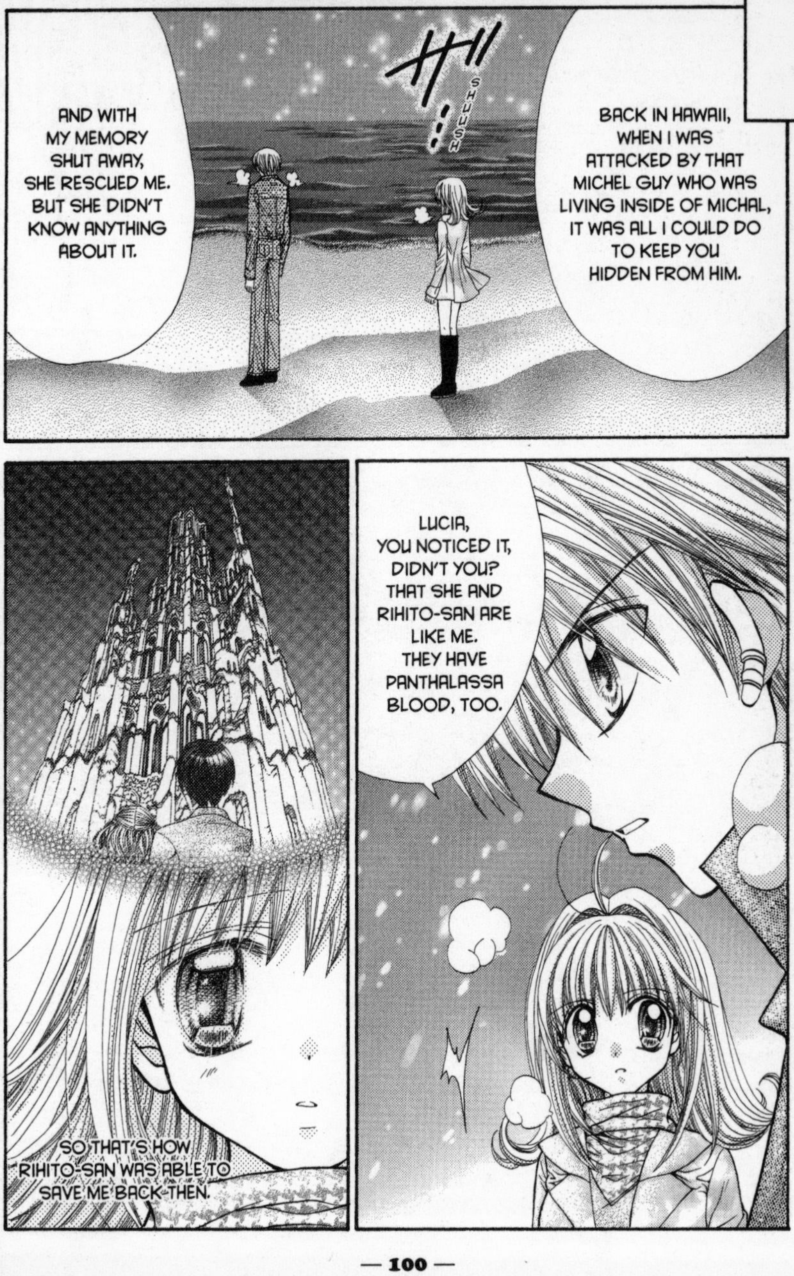
BACK IN HAWAII, WHEN I WAS ATTACKED BY THAT MICHEL GUY WHO WAS LIVING INSIDE OF MICHAL, IT WAS ALL I COULD DO TO KEEP YOU HIDDEN FROM HIM.
SHUUSH
AND WITH MY MEMORY SHUT AWAY, SHE RESCUED ME. BUT SHE DIDN'T KNOW ANYTHING ABOUT IT.
LUCIA, YOU NOTICED IT, DIDN'T YOU? THAT SHE AND RIHITO-SAN ARE LIKE ME. THEY HAVE PANTHALASSA BLOOD, TOO.
SO THAT'S HOW RIHITO-SAN WAS ABLE TO SAVE ME BACK THEN.

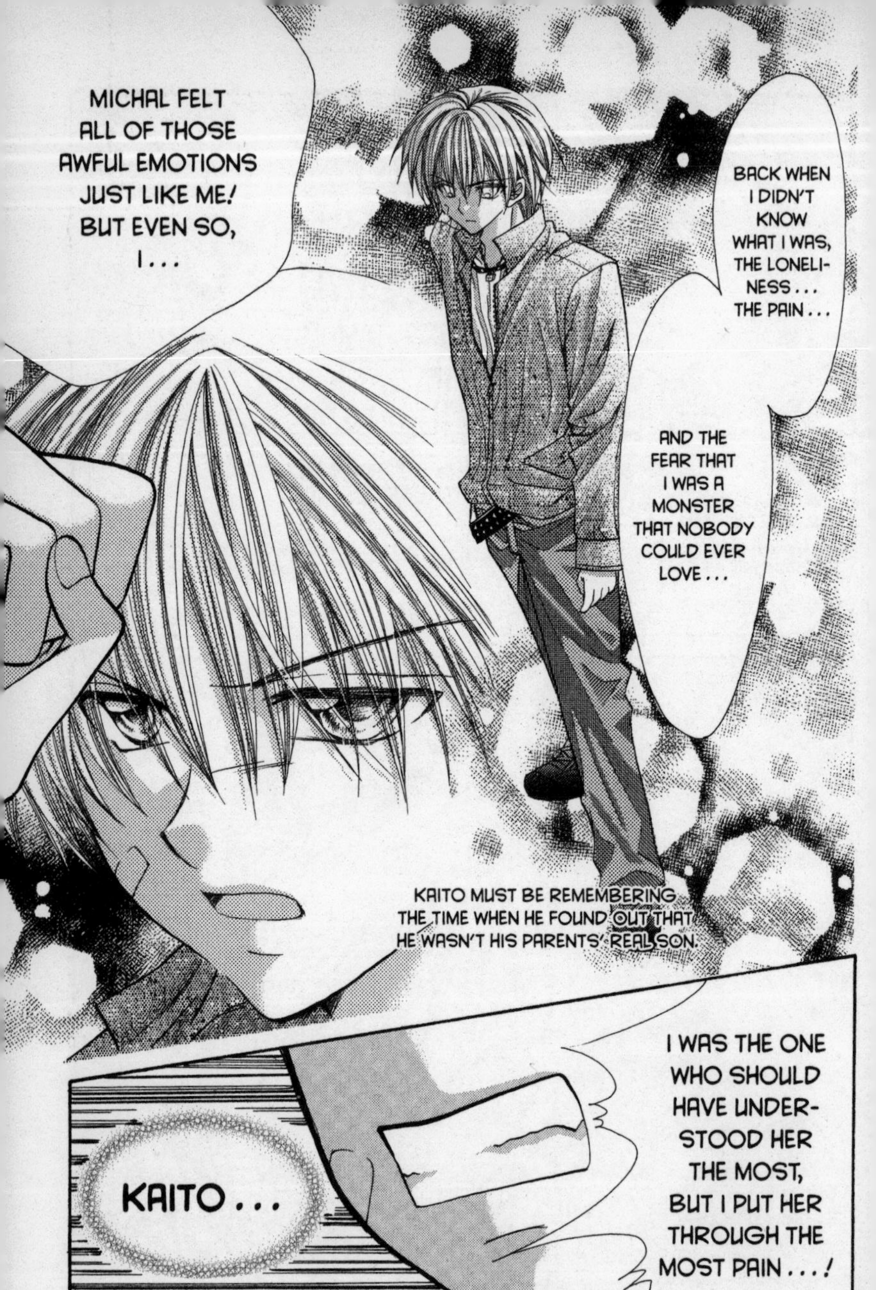
BACK WHEN I DIDN'T KNOW WHAT I WAS, THE LONELI-NESS . . . THE PAIN . . .
AND THE FEAR THAT I WAS A MONSTER THAT NOBODY COULD EVER LOVE . . .
MICHAL FELT ALL OF THOSE AWFUL EMOTIONS JUST LIKE ME! BUT EVEN SO, I . . .
KAITO MUST BE REMEMBERING THE TIME WHEN HE FOUND OUT THAT HE WASN'T HIS PARENTS' REAL SON.
I WAS THE ONE WHO SHOULD HAVE UNDER-STOOD HER THE MOST, BUT I PUT HER THROUGH THE MOST PAIN . . . !
KAITO . . .

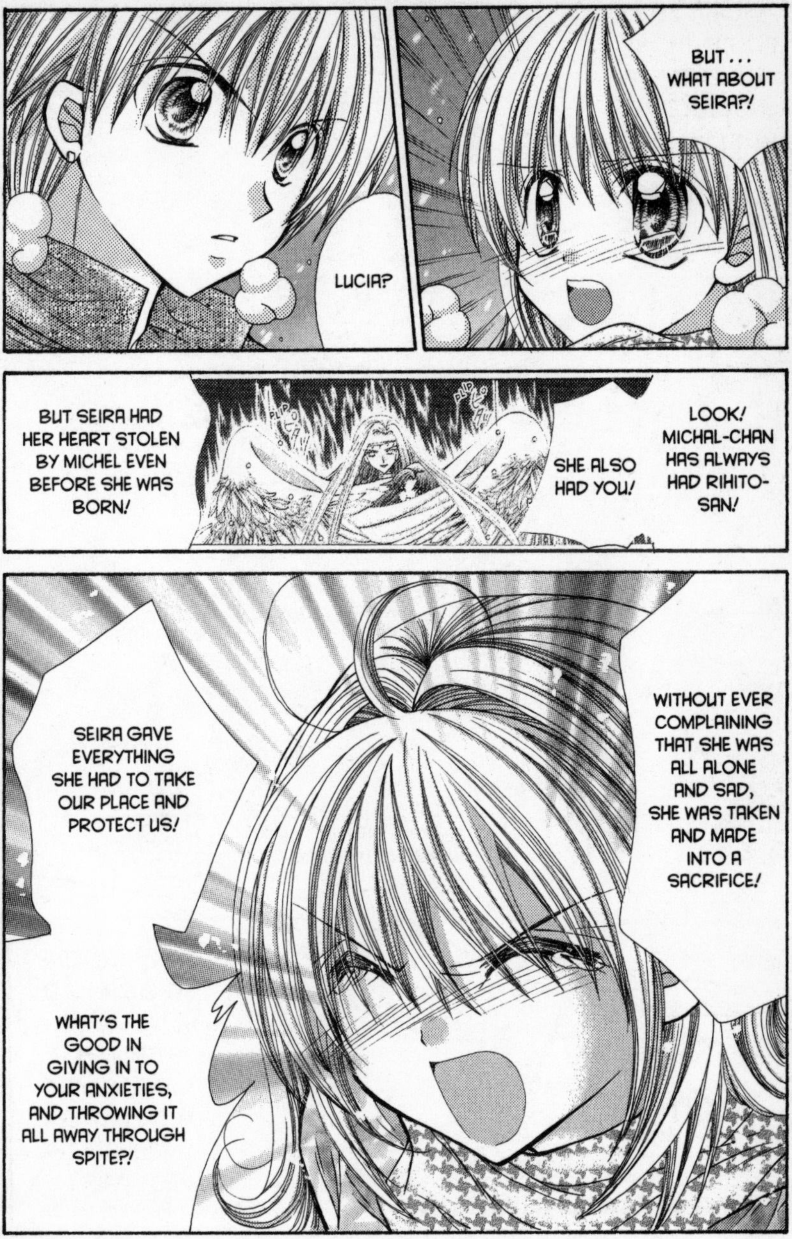
BUT... WHAT ABOUT SEIRA?!
LUCIA?
LOOK! MICHAL-CHAN HAS ALWAYS HAD RIHITO-SAN!
SHE ALSO HAD YOU!
BUT SEIRA HAD HER HEART STOLEN BY MICHEL EVEN BEFORE SHE WAS BORN!
WITHOUT EVER COMPLAINING THAT SHE WAS ALL ALONE AND SAD, SHE WAS TAKEN AND MADE INTO A SACRIFICE!
SEIRA GAVE EVERYTHING SHE HAD TO TAKE OUR PLACE AND PROTECT US!
WHAT'S THE GOOD IN GIVING IN TO YOUR ANXIETIES, AND THROWING IT ALL AWAY THROUGH SPITE?!

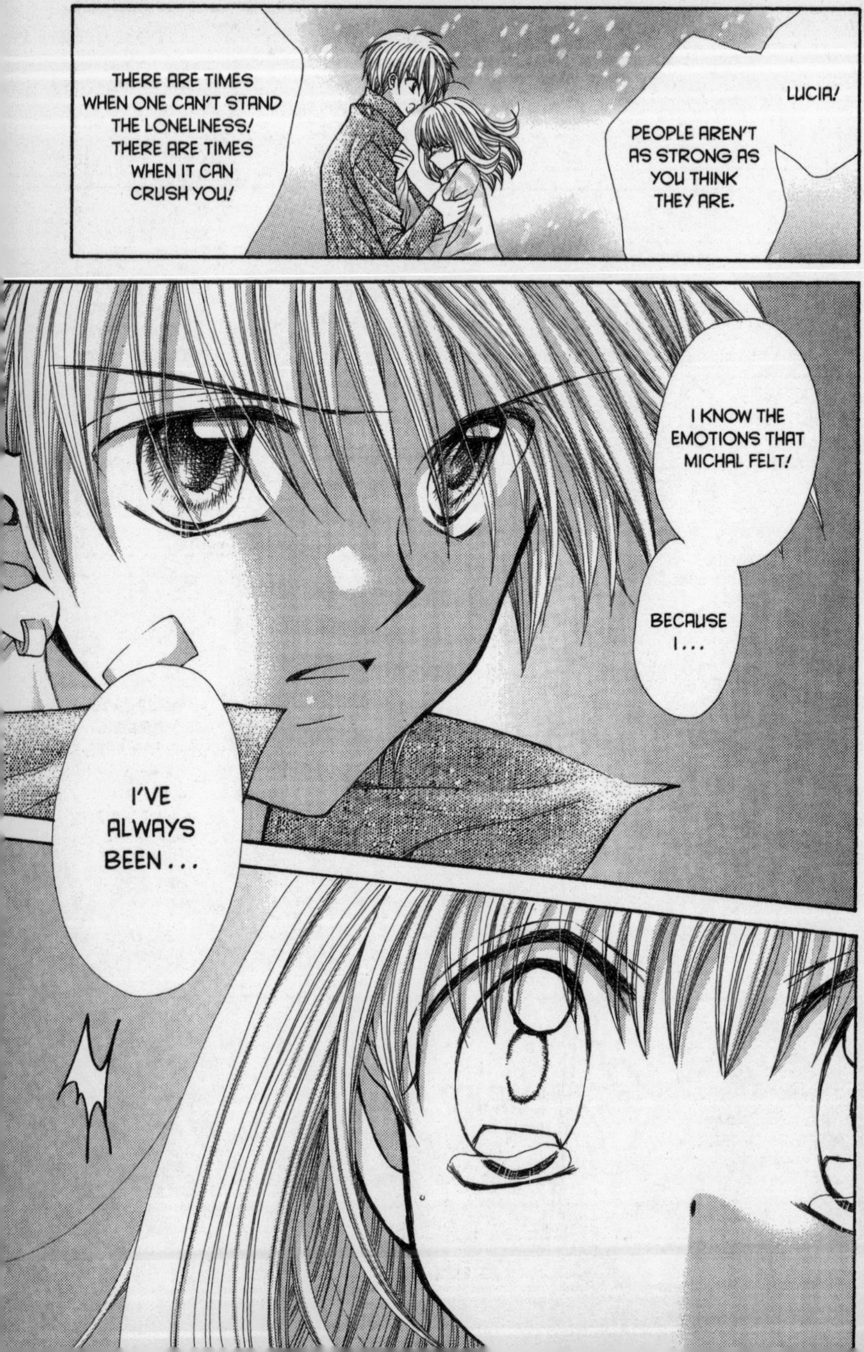
LUCIA!
PEOPLE AREN'T AS STRONG AS YOU THINK THEY ARE.
THERE ARE TIMES WHEN ONE CAN'T STAND THE LONELINESS! THERE ARE TIMES WHEN IT CAN CRUSH YOU!
I KNOW THE EMOTIONS THAT MICHAL FELT!
BECAUSE I...
I'VE ALWAYS BEEN...

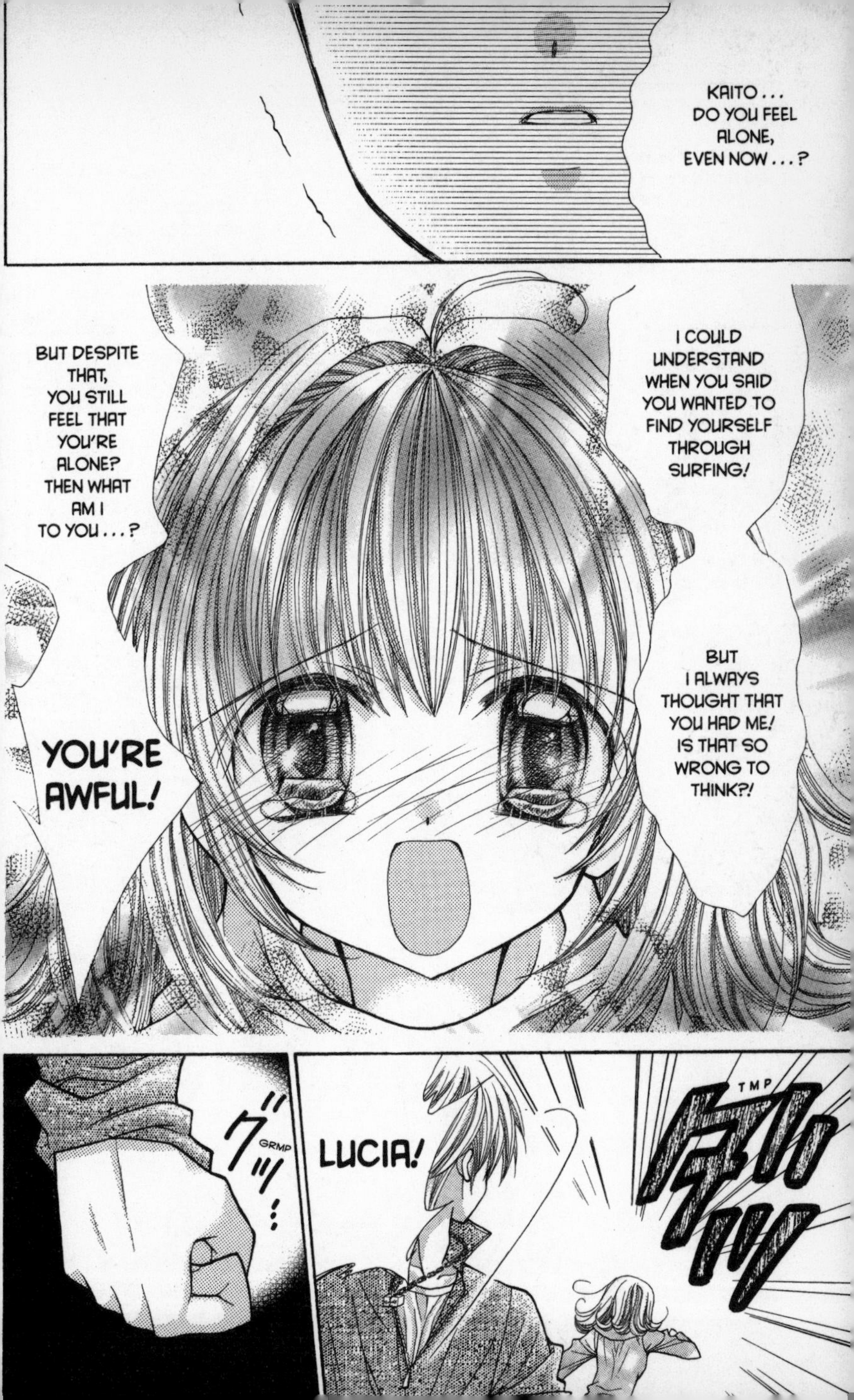
KAITO . . .
DO YOU FEEL ALONE, EVEN NOW . . . ?
I COULD UNDERSTAND WHEN YOU SAID YOU WANTED TO FIND YOURSELF THROUGH SURFING!
BUT I ALWAYS THOUGHT THAT YOU HAD ME! IS THAT SO WRONG TO THINK?!
BUT DESPITE THAT, YOU STILL FEEL THAT YOU'RE ALONE? THEN WHAT AM I TO YOU . . . ?
YOU'RE AWFUL!
TMP
LUCIA!
GRMP

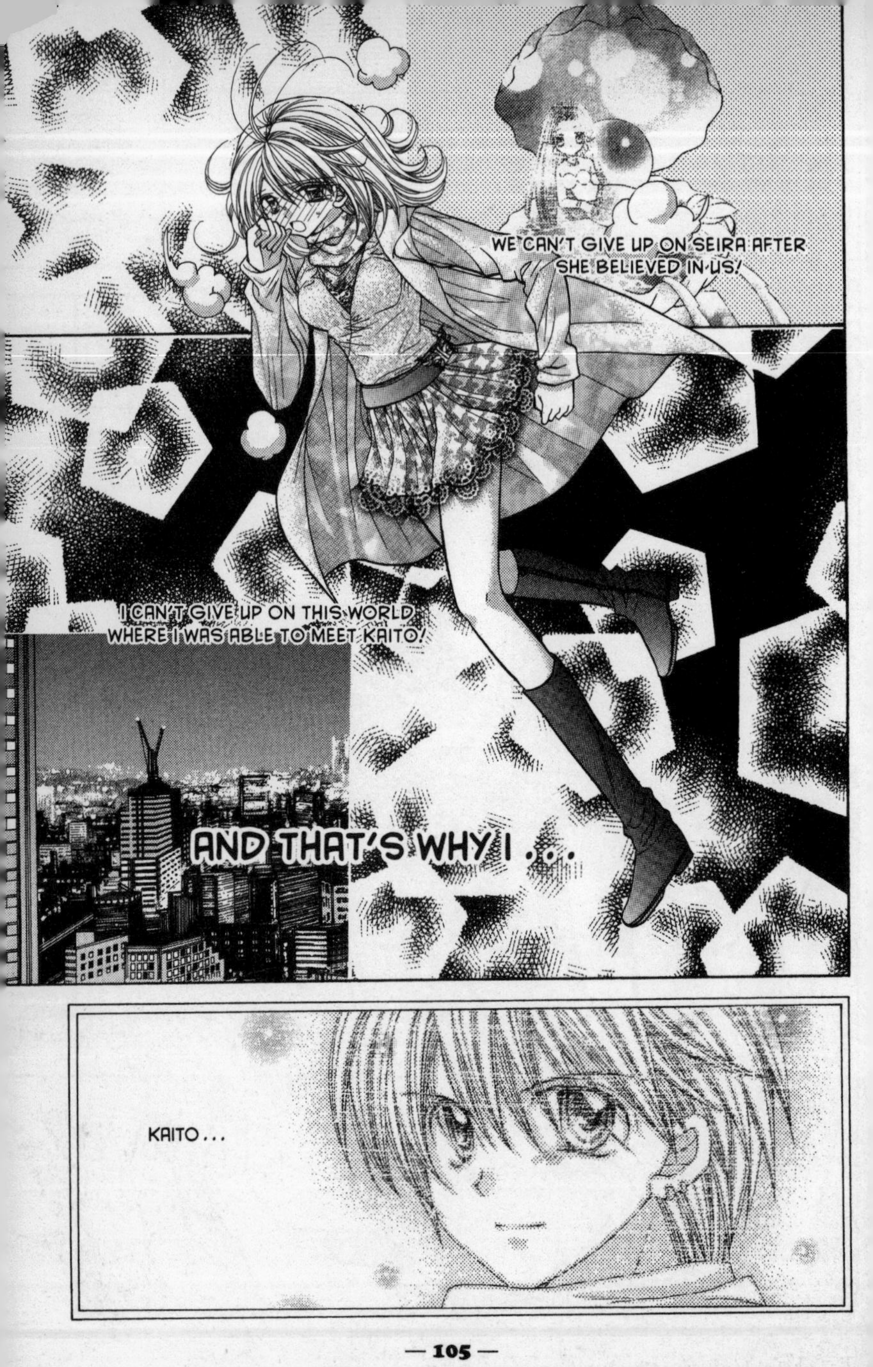
WE CAN'T GIVE UP ON SEIRA AFTER SHE BELIEVED IN US!
I CAN'T GIVE UP ON THIS WORLD WHERE I WAS ABLE TO MEET KAITO!
AND THAT'S WHY I . . .
KAITO...

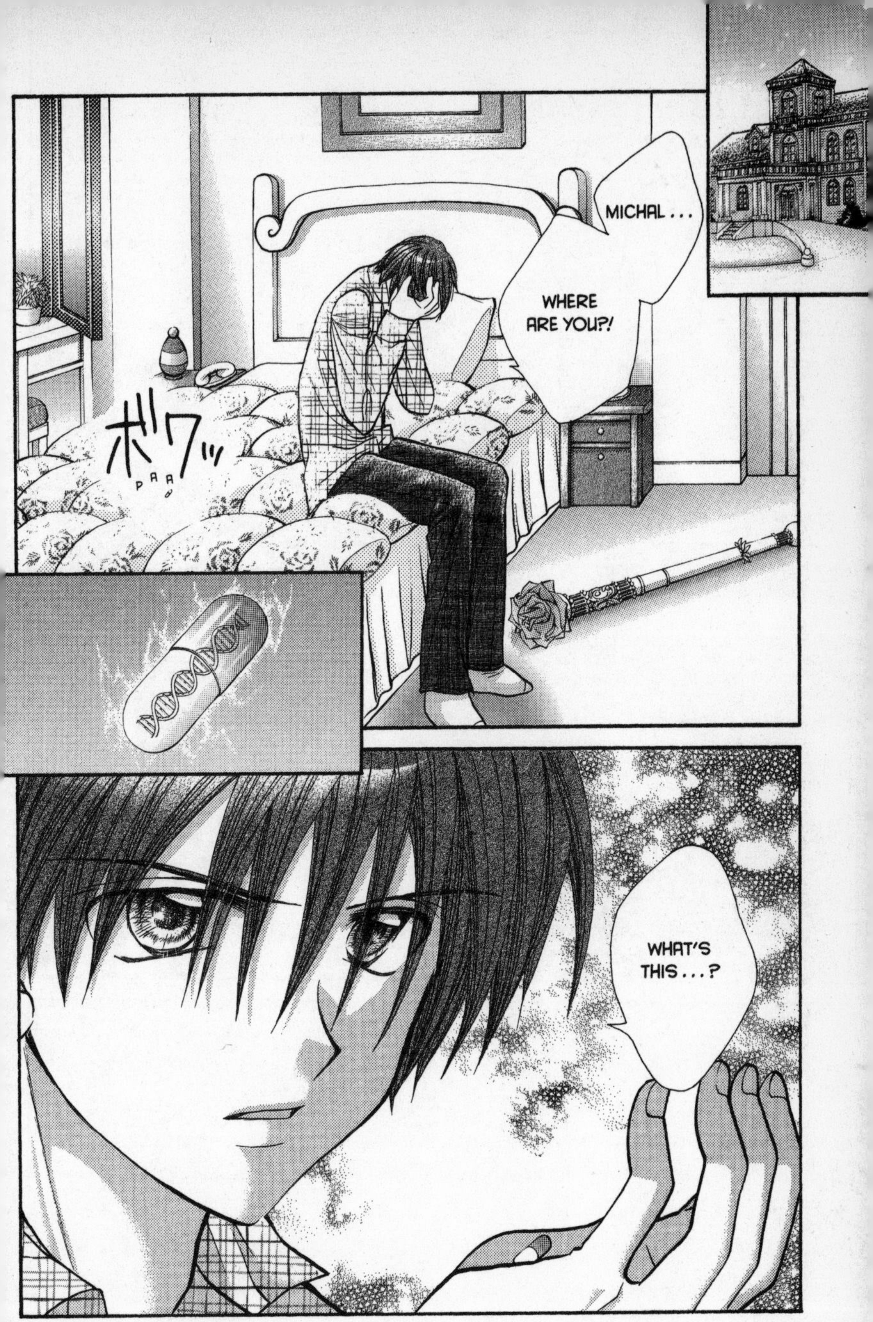
MICHAL . . .
WHERE ARE YOU?!
ボワッ
PAAA
WHAT'S THIS . . . ?

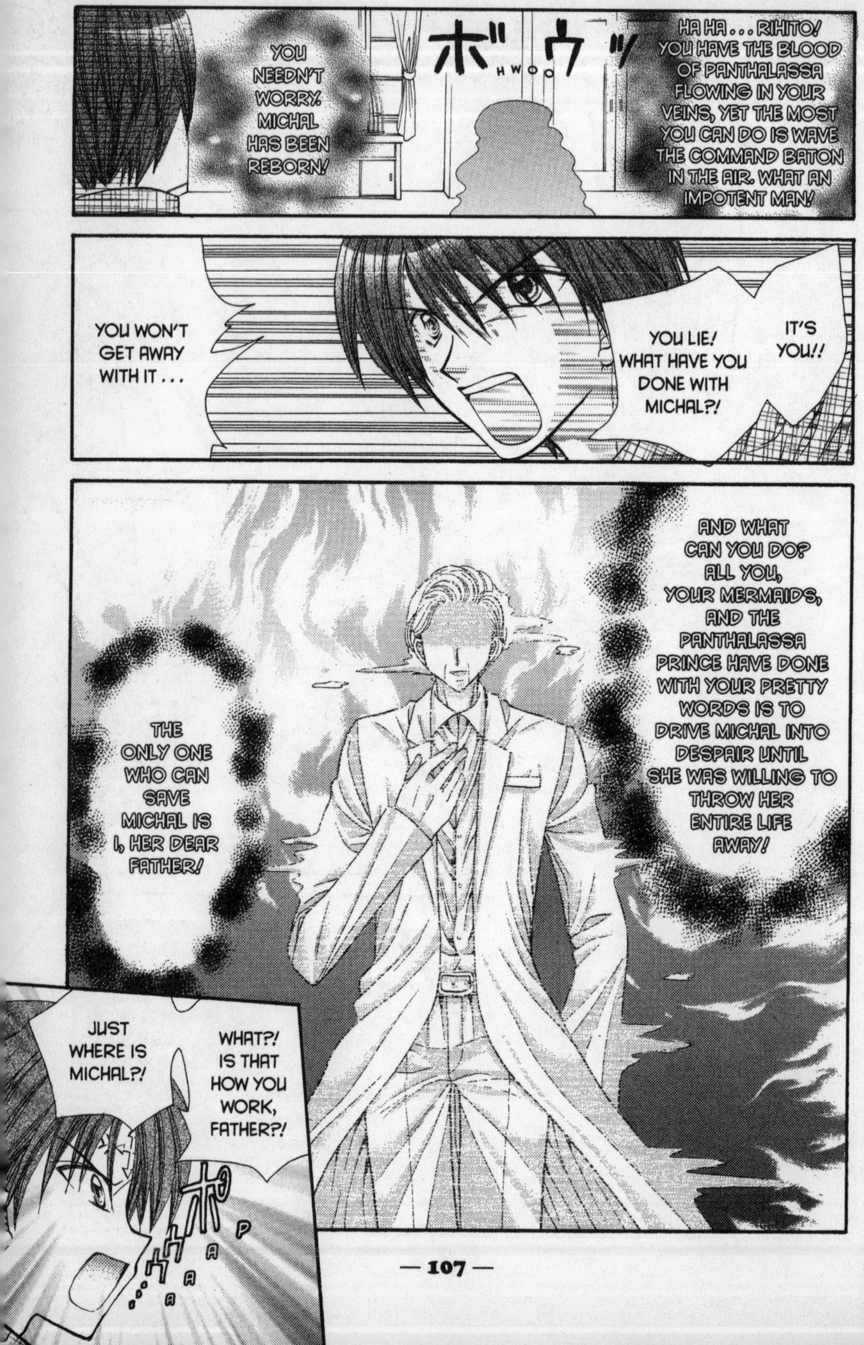
HA HA . . . RIHITO! YOU HAVE THE BLOOD OF PANTHALASSA FLOWING IN YOUR VEINS, YET THE MOST YOU CAN DO IS WAVE THE COMMAND BATON IN THE AIR. WHAT AN IMPOTENT MAN!
ボウッ HWOO
YOU NEEDN'T WORRY. MICHAL HAS BEEN REBORN!
IT'S YOU!!
YOU LIE! WHAT HAVE YOU DONE WITH MICHAL?!
YOU WON'T GET AWAY WITH IT . . .
AND WHAT CAN YOU DO? ALL YOU, YOUR MERMAIDS, AND THE PANTHALASSA PRINCE HAVE DONE WITH YOUR PRETTY WORDS IS TO DRIVE MICHAL INTO DESPAIR UNTIL SHE WAS WILLING TO THROW HER ENTIRE LIFE AWAY!
THE ONLY ONE WHO CAN SAVE MICHAL IS I, HER DEAR FATHER!
WHAT?! IS THAT HOW YOU WORK, FATHER?!
JUST WHERE IS MICHAL?!
ボウウウ PAAAA

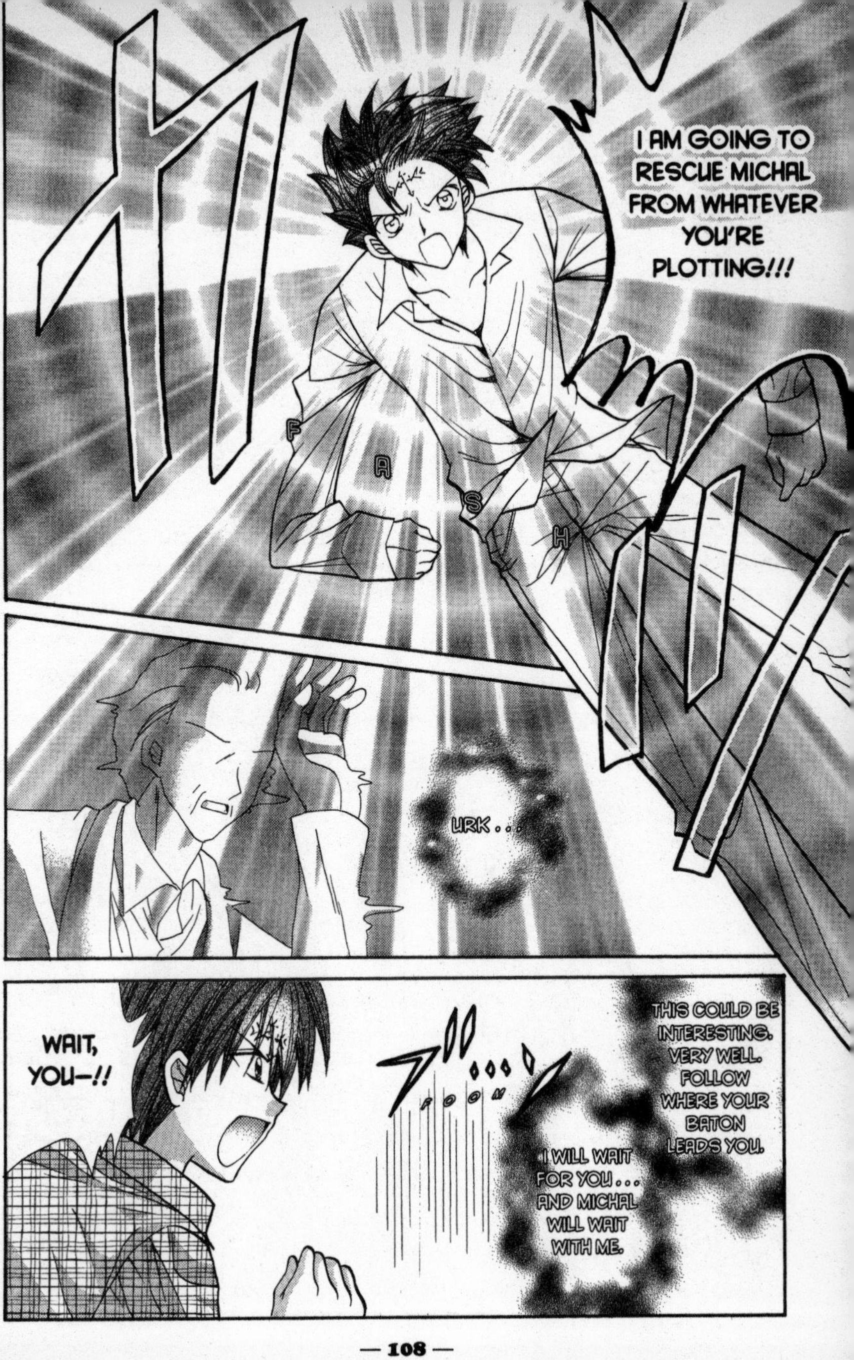
I AM GOING TO RESCUE MICHAL FROM WHATEVER YOU'RE PLOTTING!!!
FASH
URK . . .
THIS COULD BE INTERESTING. VERY WELL. FOLLOW WHERE YOUR BATON LEADS YOU.
I WILL WAIT FOR YOU . . . AND MICHAL WILL WAIT WITH ME.
FOOM
WAIT, YOU—!!

EVENTS.

I HAD SIGNINGS IN BOTH TOKYO AND OSAKA, AND I WANT TO THANK EVERYONE WHO CAME!! THE PEOPLE IN OSAKA WERE REALLY INTO IT AND MADE IT FUN! THERE WAS EVEN ONE WHO CAME IN A HIPPO COSTUME. I LOVED IT! ✧✧ I REALLY ENJOYED THE EVENT WHERE I WAS SIGNING ALONGSIDE FUKUSHIMA-SENSEI. !!' EVEN KIKU CAME!

↑ MICHIYO KIKUTA-CHAN.

THANK YOU SO MUCH!

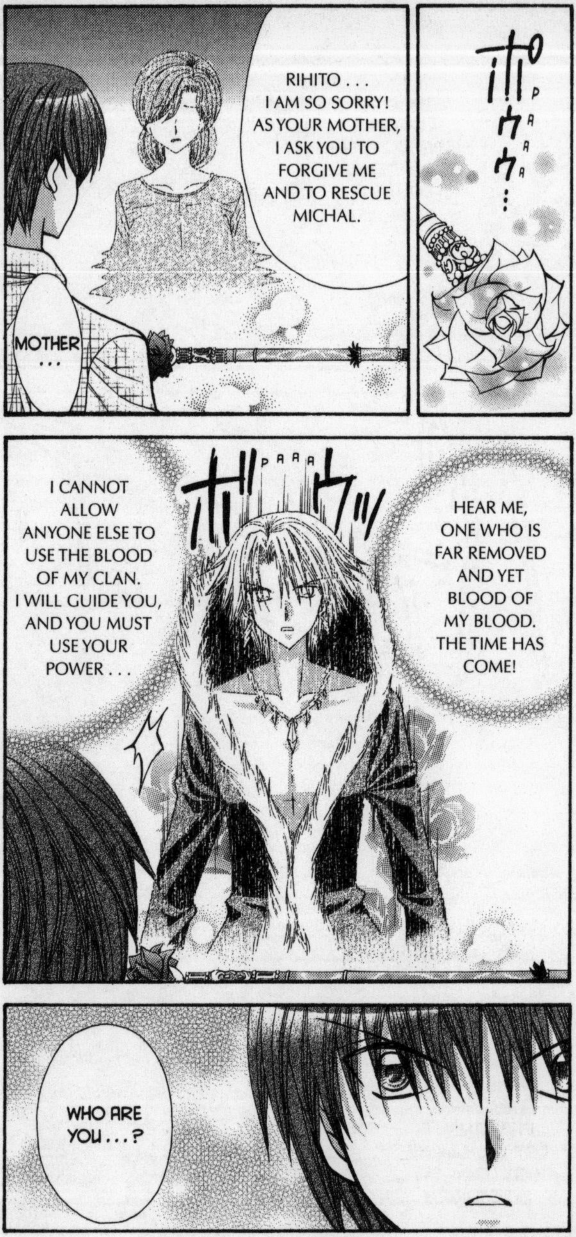
PAAA
RIHITO . . . I AM SO SORRY! AS YOUR MOTHER, I ASK YOU TO FORGIVE ME AND TO RESCUE MICHAL.
MOTHER . . .
HEAR ME, ONE WHO IS FAR REMOVED AND YET BLOOD OF MY BLOOD. THE TIME HAS COME!
PAAA
I CANNOT ALLOW ANYONE ELSE TO USE THE BLOOD OF MY CLAN. I WILL GUIDE YOU, AND YOU MUST USE YOUR POWER . . .
WHO ARE YOU . . . ?

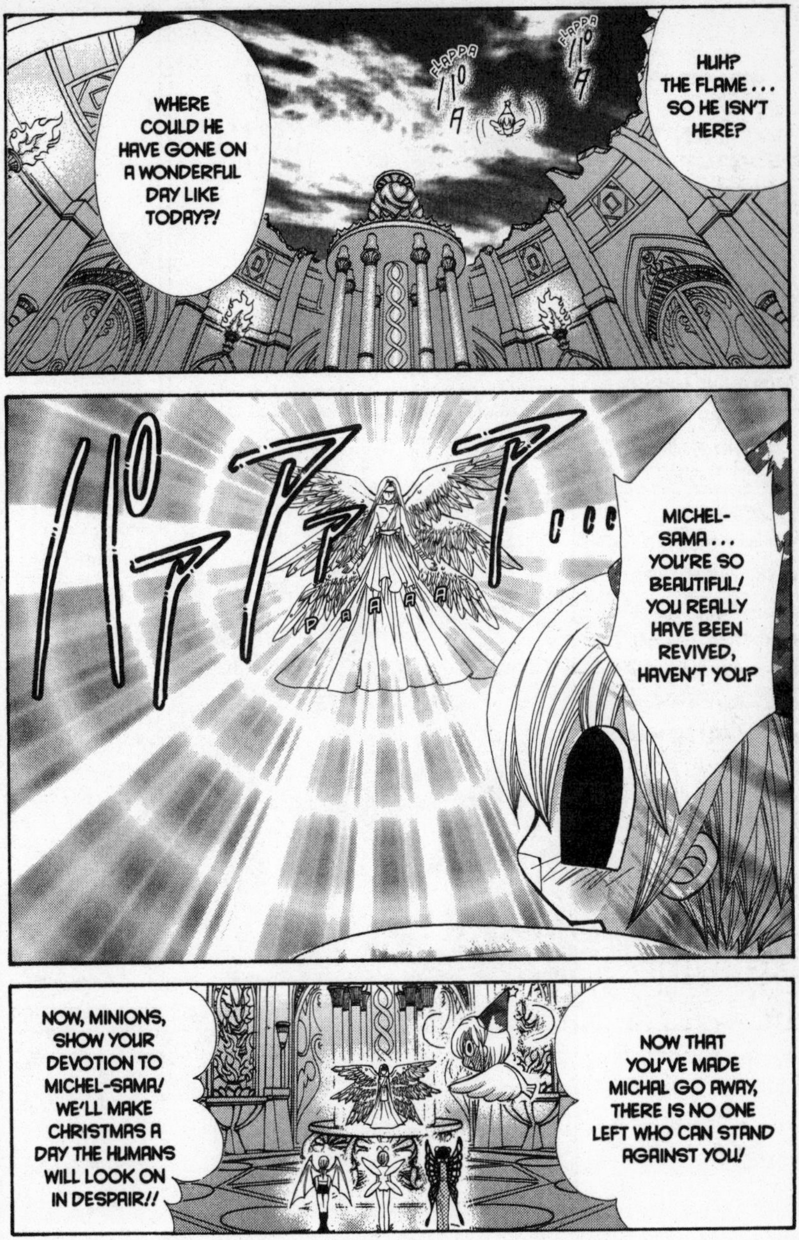
FLAPPA
FLAPPA
HUH? THE FLAME . . . SO HE ISN'T HERE?
WHERE COULD HE HAVE GONE ON A WONDERFUL DAY LIKE TODAY?!
パアア
PAAAA
MICHEL-SAMA . . . YOU'RE SO BEAUTIFUL! YOU REALLY HAVE BEEN REVIVED, HAVEN'T YOU?
NOW THAT YOU'VE MADE MICHAL GO AWAY, THERE IS NO ONE LEFT WHO CAN STAND AGAINST YOU!
NOW, MINIONS, SHOW YOUR DEVOTION TO MICHEL-SAMA! WE'LL MAKE CHRISTMAS A DAY THE HUMANS WILL LOOK ON IN DESPAIR!!

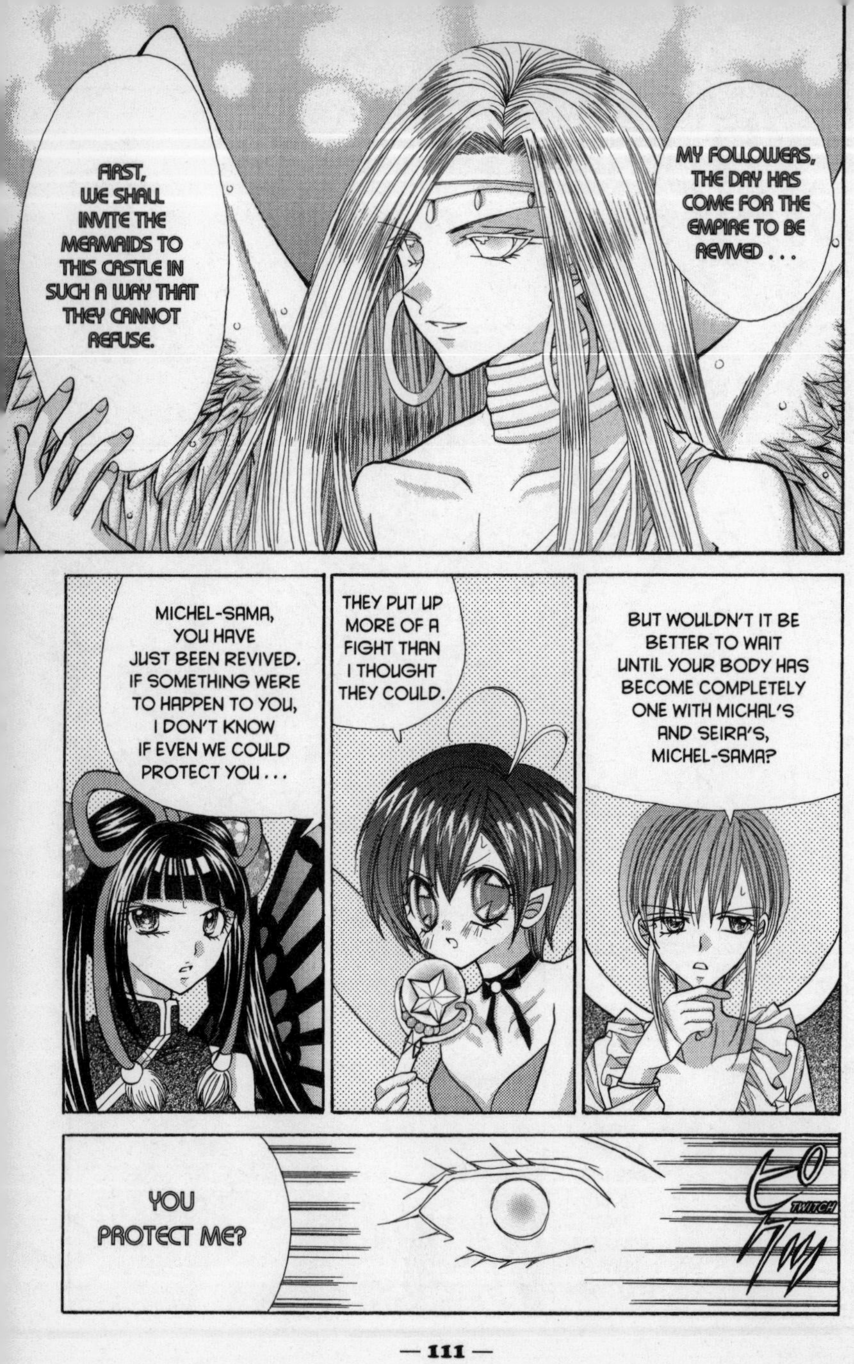
MY FOLLOWERS, THE DAY HAS COME FOR THE EMPIRE TO BE REVIVED . . .
FIRST, WE SHALL INVITE THE MERMAIDS TO THIS CASTLE IN SUCH A WAY THAT THEY CANNOT REFUSE.
BUT WOULDN'T IT BE BETTER TO WAIT UNTIL YOUR BODY HAS BECOME COMPLETELY ONE WITH MICHAL'S AND SEIRA'S, MICHEL-SAMA?
THEY PUT UP MORE OF A FIGHT THAN I THOUGHT THEY COULD.
MICHEL-SAMA, YOU HAVE JUST BEEN REVIVED. IF SOMETHING WERE TO HAPPEN TO YOU, I DON'T KNOW IF EVEN WE COULD PROTECT YOU . . .
TWITCH
YOU PROTECT ME?

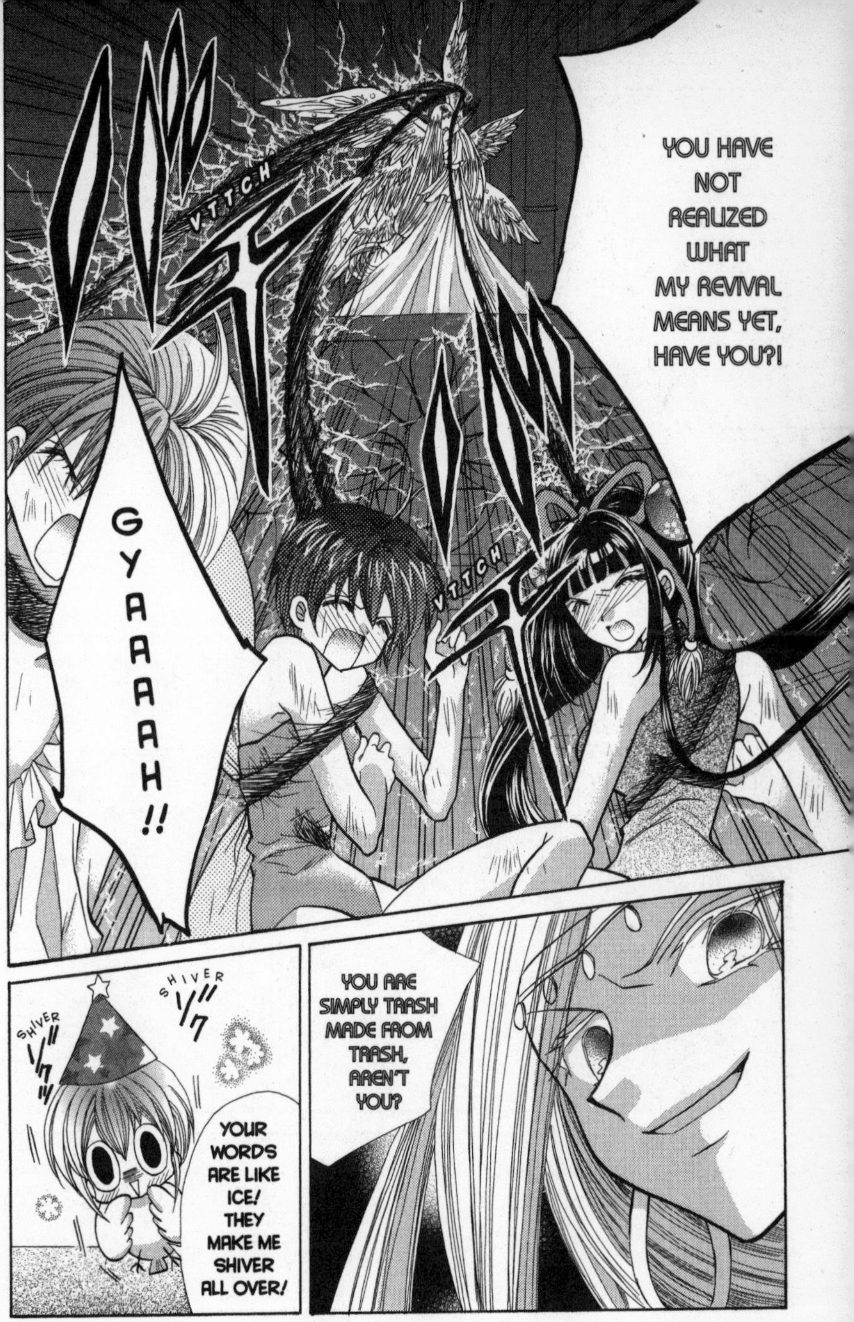
YOU HAVE NOT REALIZED WHAT MY REVIVAL MEANS YET, HAVE YOU?!
VTTCH
VTTCH
GYAAAAAH!!
YOU ARE SIMPLY TRASH MADE FROM TRASH, AREN'T YOU?
SHIVER
SHIVER
YOUR WORDS ARE LIKE ICE! THEY MAKE ME SHIVER ALL OVER!

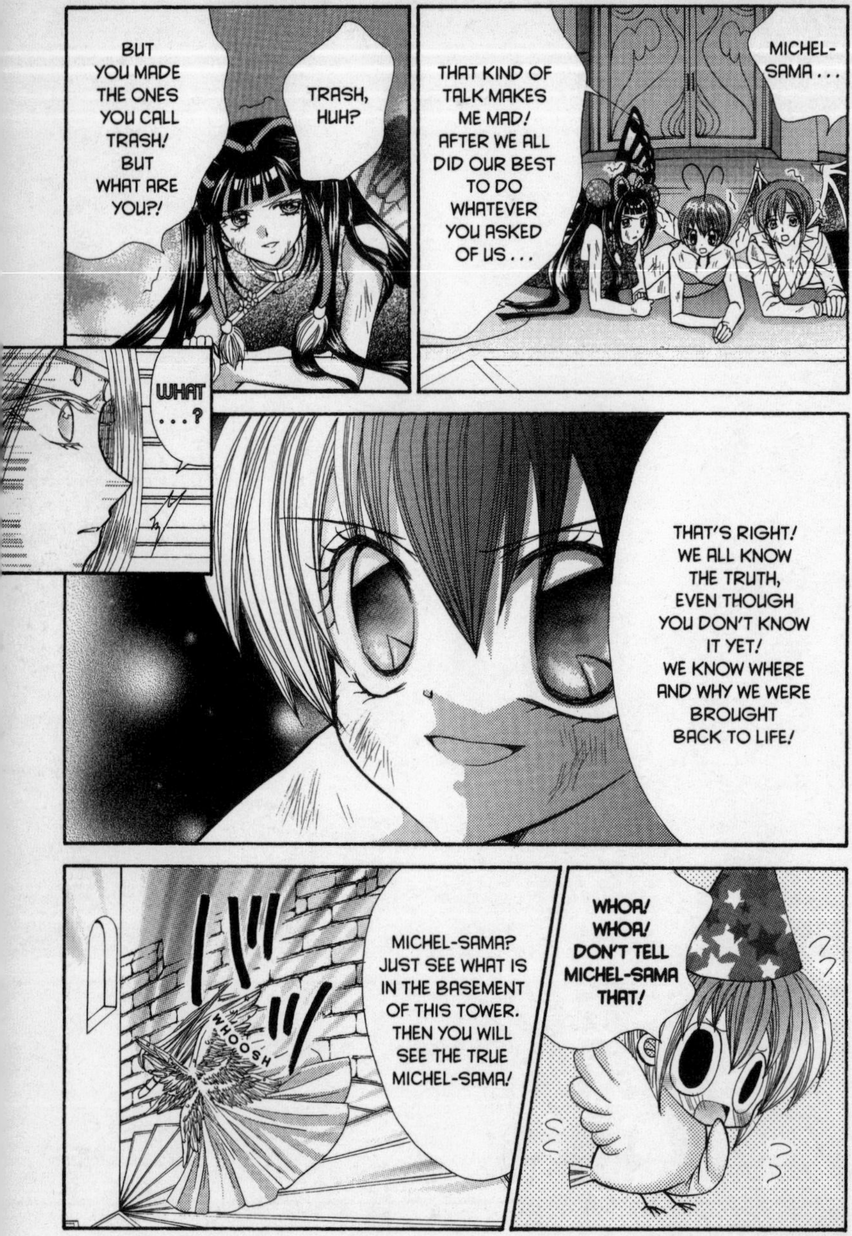
MICHEL-SAMA . . .
THAT KIND OF TALK MAKES ME MAD! AFTER WE ALL DID OUR BEST TO DO WHATEVER YOU ASKED OF US . . .
TRASH, HUH?
BUT YOU MADE THE ONES YOU CALL TRASH! BUT WHAT ARE YOU?!
WHAT . . . ?
THAT'S RIGHT! WE ALL KNOW THE TRUTH, EVEN THOUGH YOU DON'T KNOW IT YET! WE KNOW WHERE AND WHY WE WERE BROUGHT BACK TO LIFE!
WHOA! WHOA! DON'T TELL MICHEL-SAMA THAT!
MICHEL-SAMA? JUST SEE WHAT IS IN THE BASEMENT OF THIS TOWER. THEN YOU WILL SEE THE TRUE MICHEL-SAMA!
WHOOSH

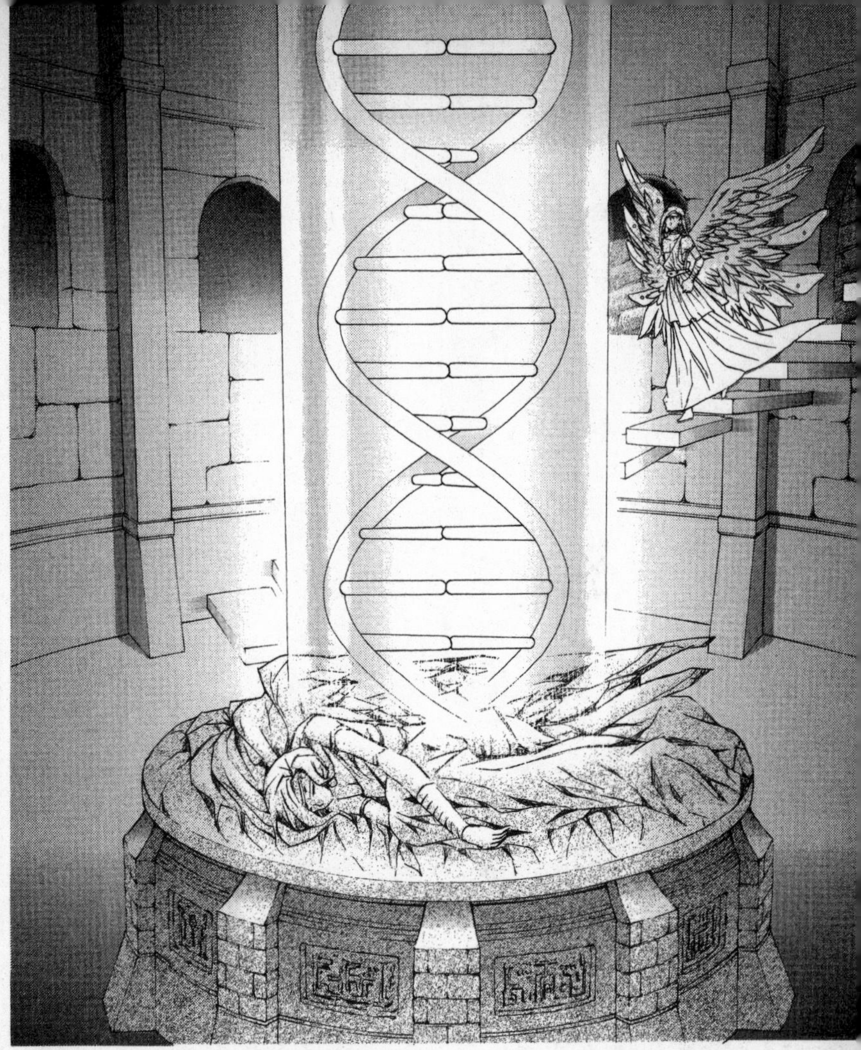

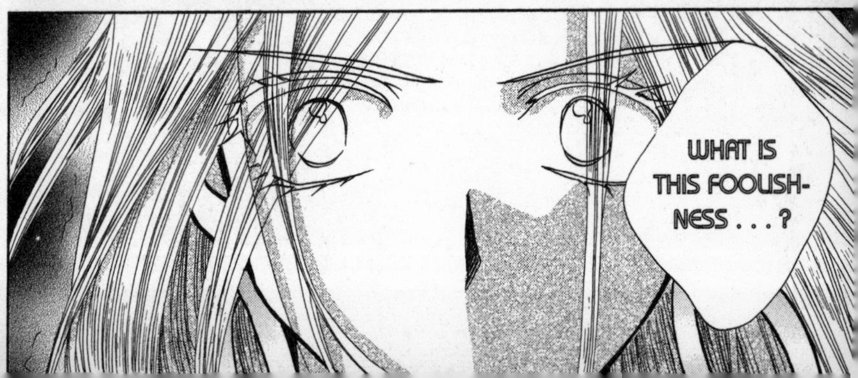
WHAT IS THIS FOOLISH-NESS . . . ?

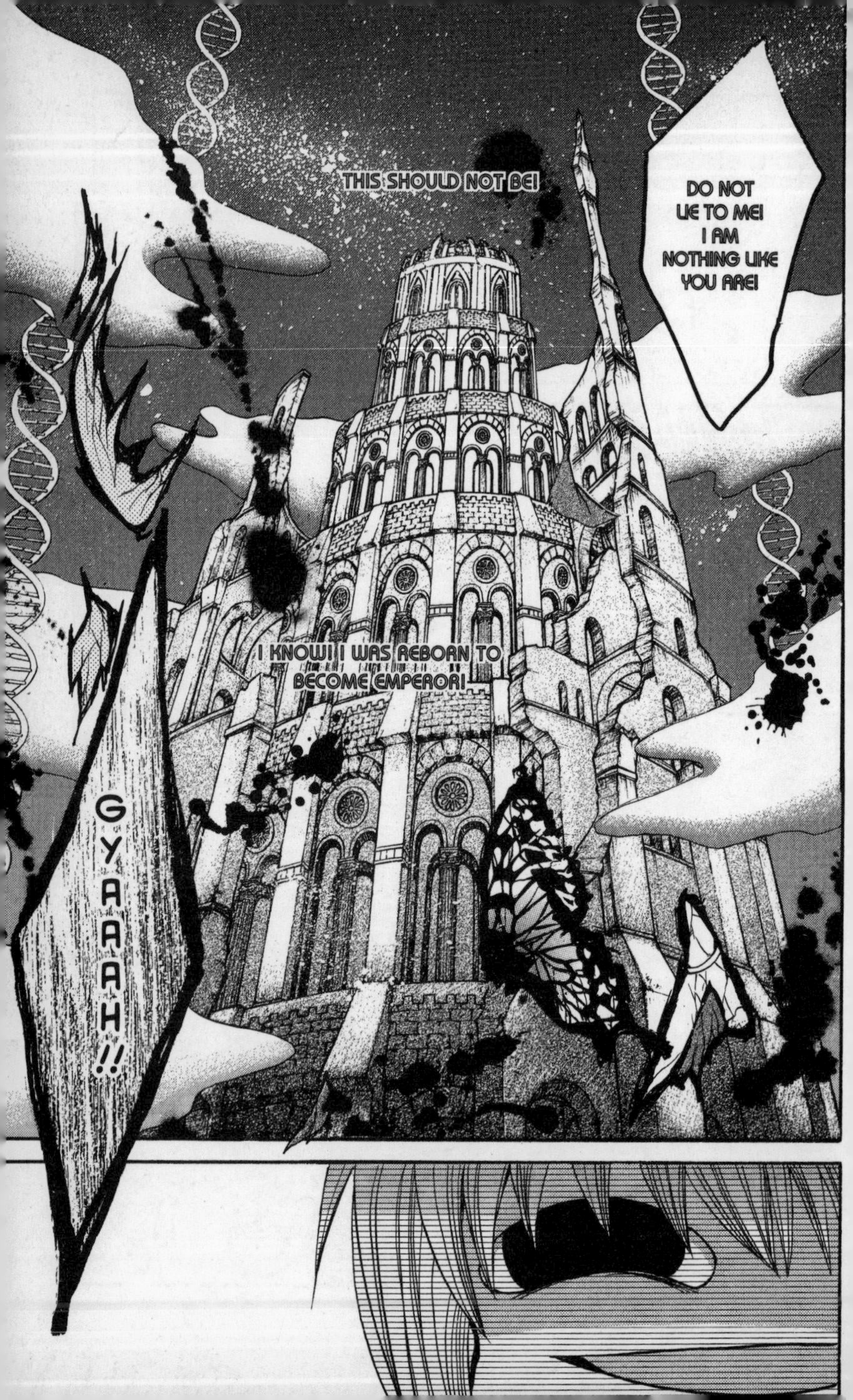
DO NOT LIE TO ME! I AM NOTHING LIKE YOU ARE!
THIS SHOULD NOT BE!
I KNOW! I WAS REBORN TO BECOME EMPEROR!
GYAAAAH!!

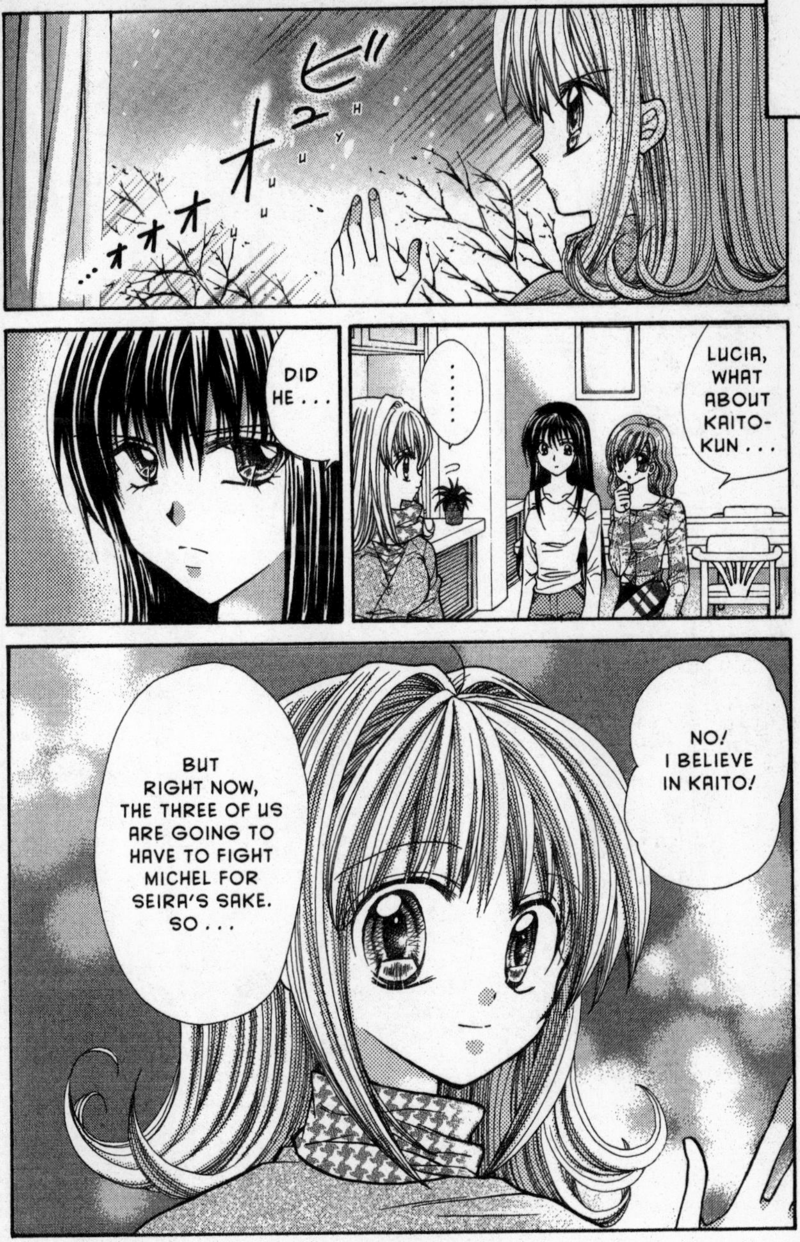
HYUUUU
LUCIA, WHAT ABOUT KAITO-KUN . . .
. . . . . .
DID HE . . .
NO! I BELIEVE IN KAITO!
BUT RIGHT NOW, THE THREE OF US ARE GOING TO HAVE TO FIGHT MICHEL FOR SEIRA'S SAKE. SO . . .

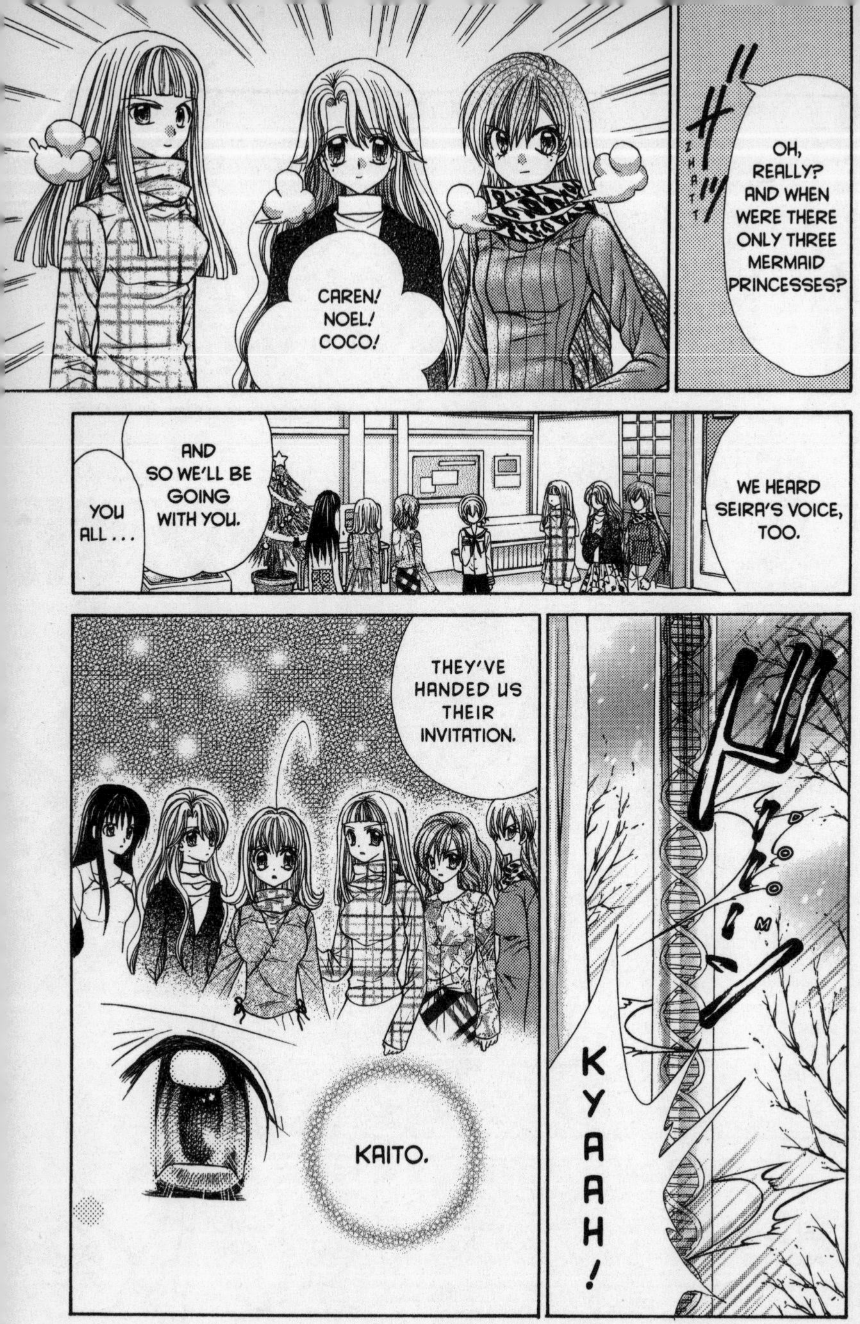
WHAT
OH, REALLY? AND WHEN WERE THERE ONLY THREE MERMAID PRINCESSES?
CAREN! NOEL! COCO!
WE HEARD SEIRA'S VOICE, TOO.
AND SO WE'LL BE GOING WITH YOU.
YOU ALL . . .
KYAAAH!
THEY'VE HANDED US THEIR INVITATION.
KAITO.

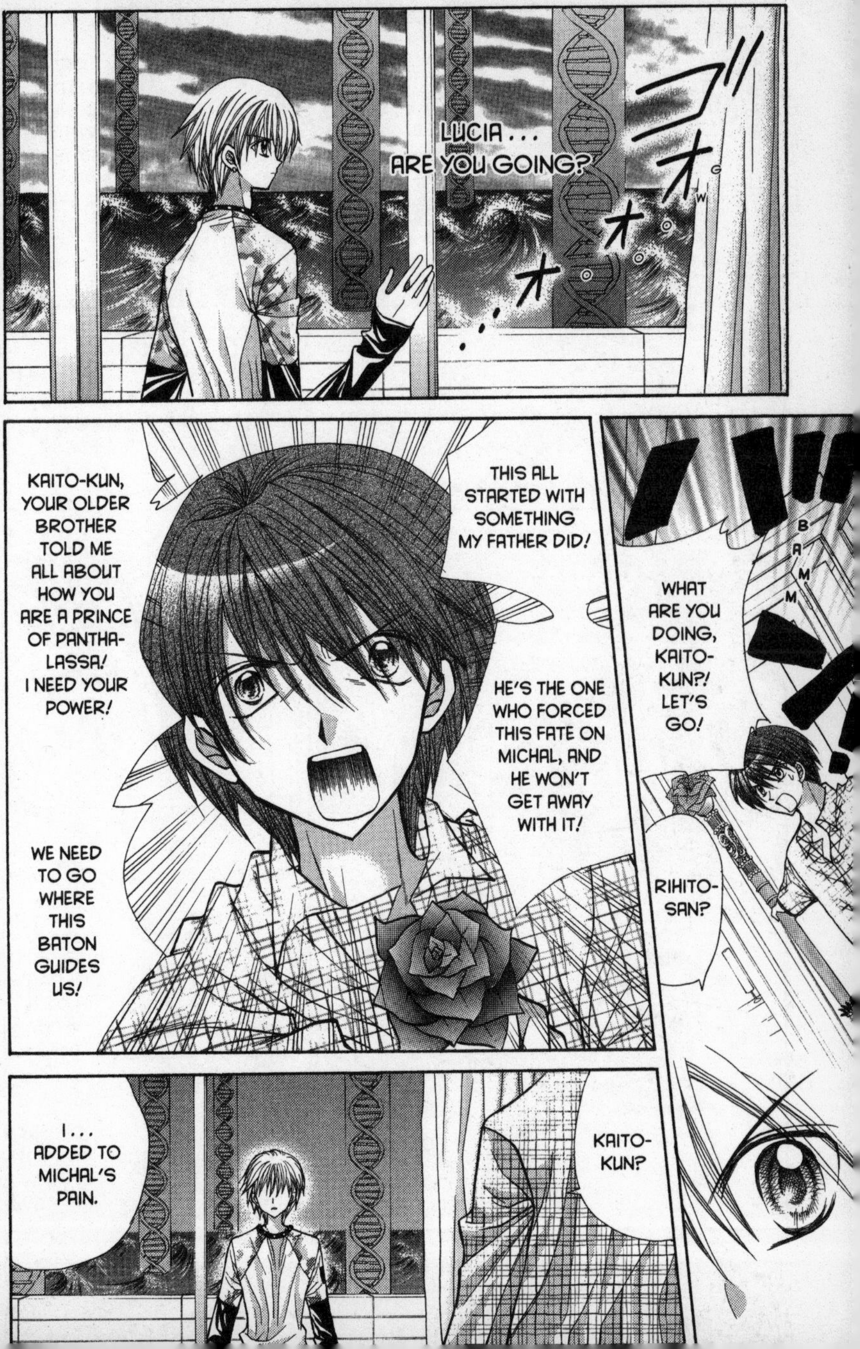
LUCIA... ARE YOU GOING?
BAMM
WHAT ARE YOU DOING, KAITO-KUN?! LET'S GO!
RIHITO-SAN?
THIS ALL STARTED WITH SOMETHING MY FATHER DID!
HE'S THE ONE WHO FORCED THIS FATE ON MICHAL, AND HE WON'T GET AWAY WITH IT!
KAITO-KUN, YOUR OLDER BROTHER TOLD ME ALL ABOUT HOW YOU ARE A PRINCE OF PANTHA-LASSA! I NEED YOUR POWER!
WE NEED TO GO WHERE THIS BATON GUIDES US!
KAITO-KUN?
I... ADDED TO MICHAL'S PAIN.

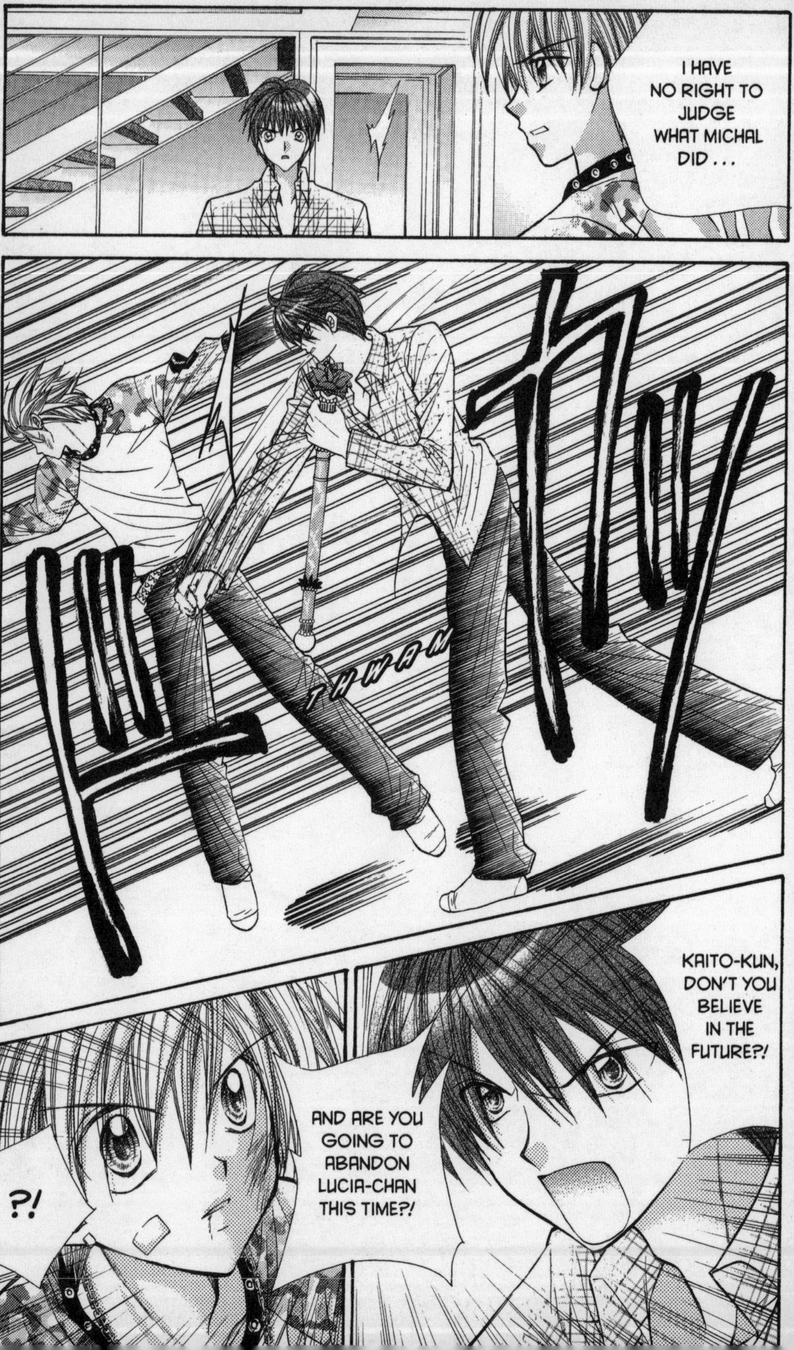
I HAVE NO RIGHT TO JUDGE WHAT MICHAL DID . . .
ドカッ
THWAM
KAITO-KUN, DON'T YOU BELIEVE IN THE FUTURE?!
AND ARE YOU GOING TO ABANDON LUCIA-CHAN THIS TIME?!
?!

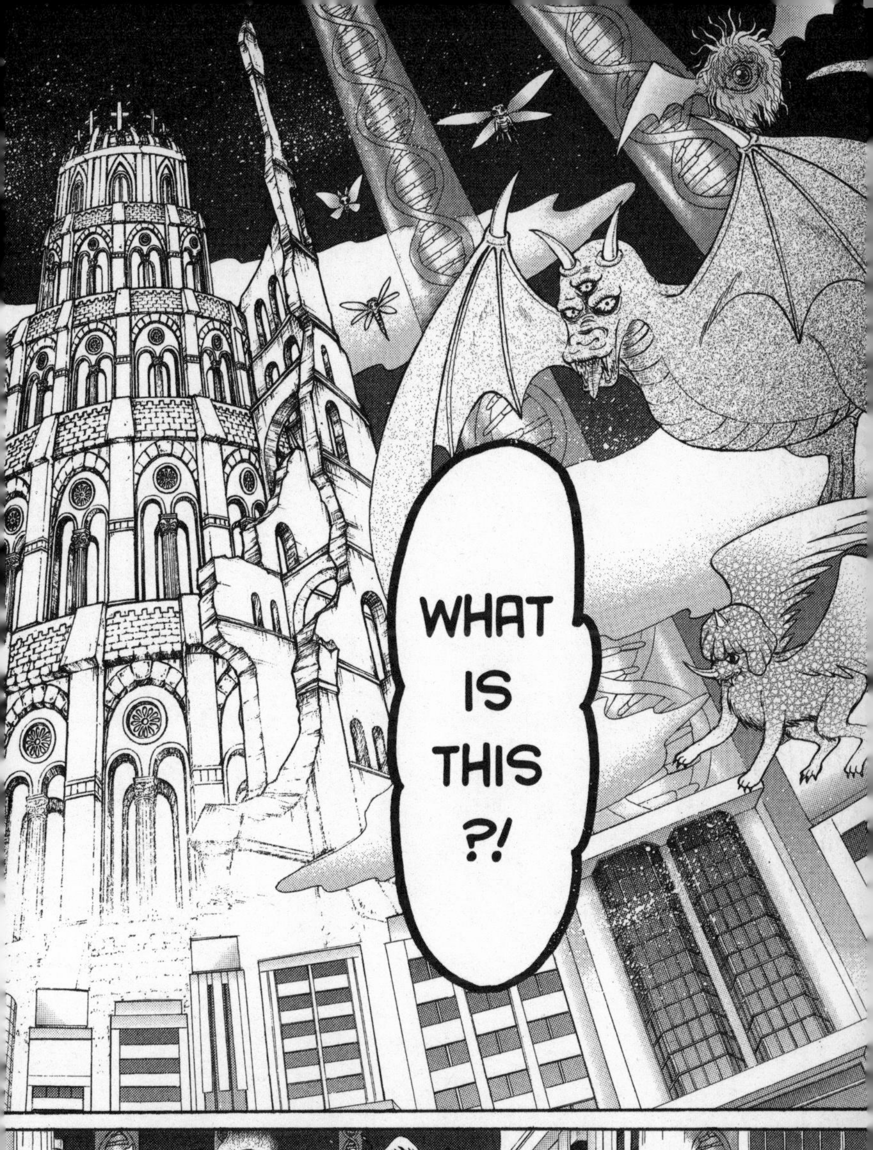
WHAT IS THIS ?!

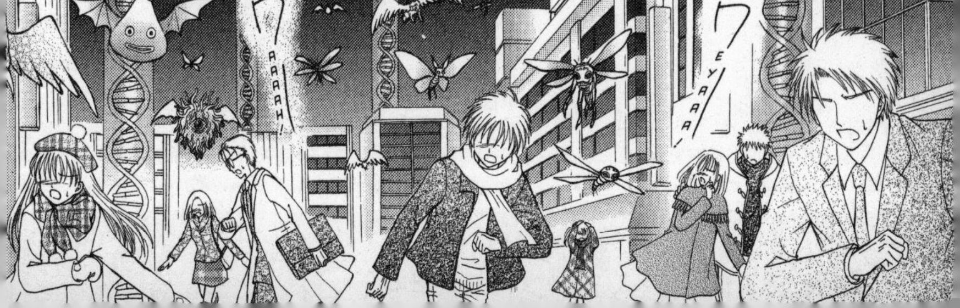
EYAAAA!
AAAAH!

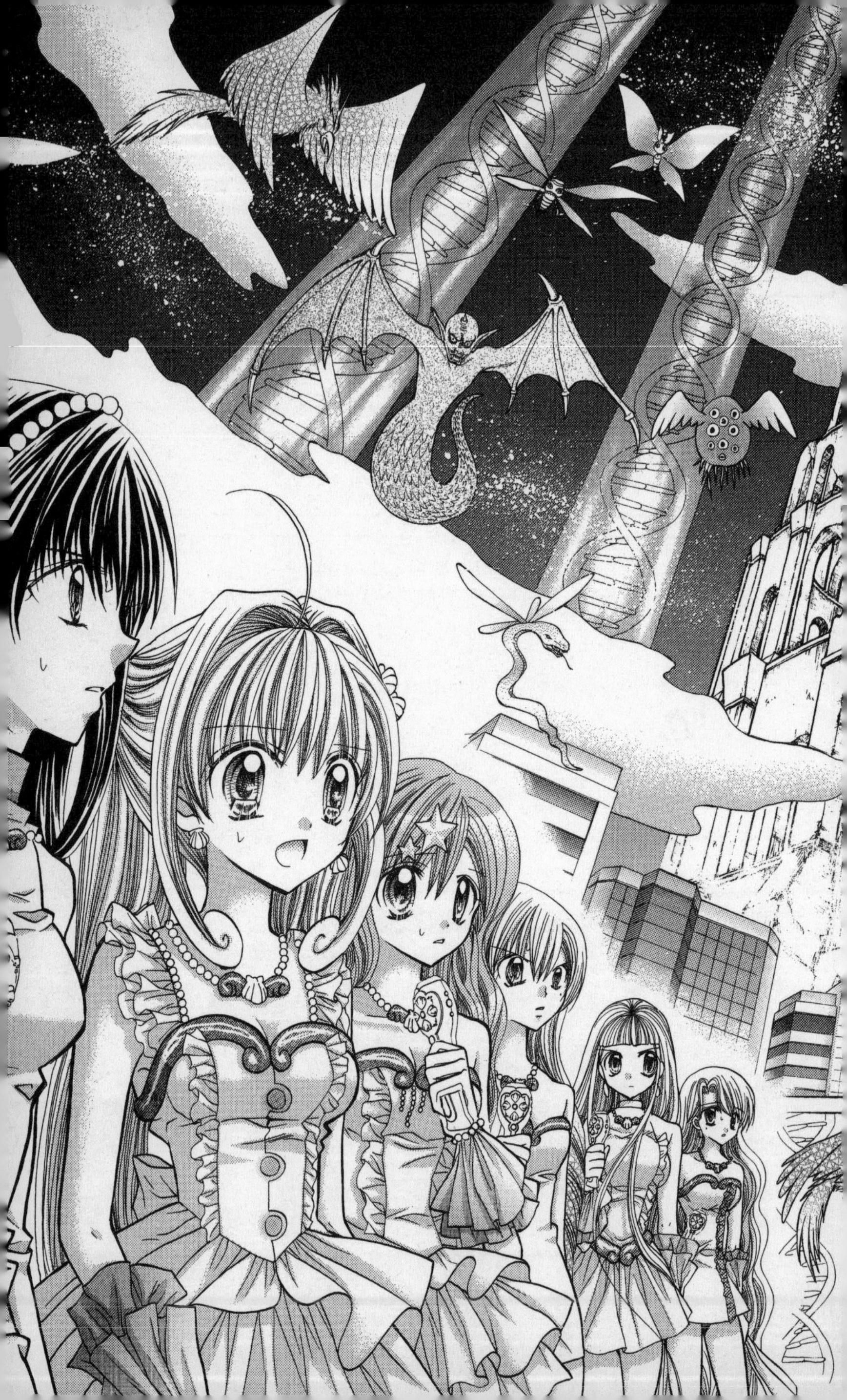

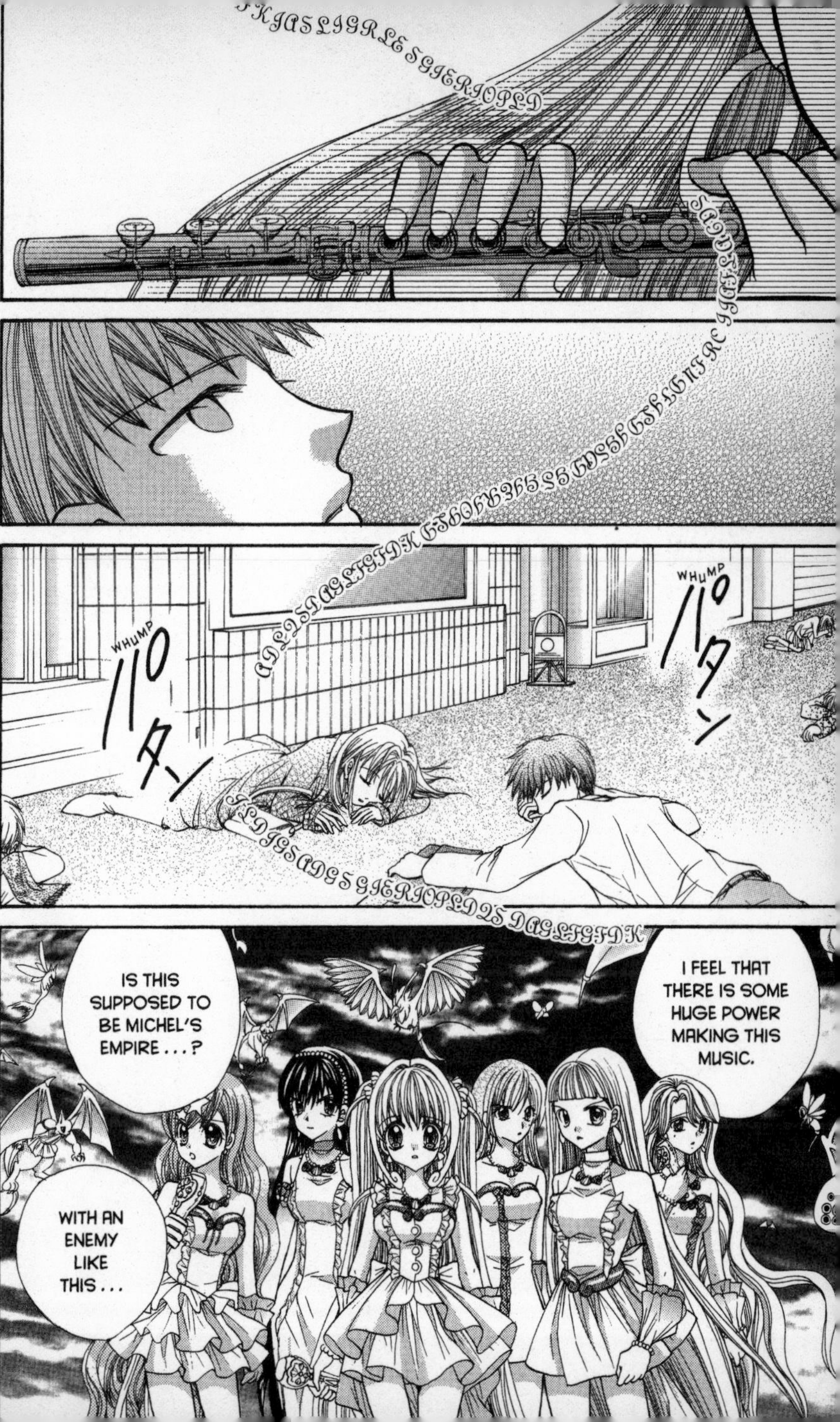
WHUMP
パタン
WHUMP
パタン
I FEEL THAT THERE IS SOME HUGE POWER MAKING THIS MUSIC.
IS THIS SUPPOSED TO BE MICHEL'S EMPIRE . . . ?
WITH AN ENEMY LIKE THIS . . .

DRAWING PAGES.

WHILE I'M DRAWING PAGES, FOR THE FIRST HALF OF MY TIME, I HAVE THE TELEVISION ON, AND THE SECOND HALF, I PLAY CDS. AND ON THE LAST DAY, I DO IT IN SILENCE. THE NECESSITIES OF LIFE ARE:

- COLD COMPRESS
- MY DOG
- NUTRITION DRINKS
- BLOOD-ENRICHING SUPPLEMENTS.

THIS IS GETTING TOO REAL. THERE ARE OTHER ITEMS, BUT I DON'T WANT TO LIST THEM RIGHT NOW.

SOMETIMES I SLEEP UNDER MY DESK. A LOT OF MY DREAMS ARE OF BEING CHASED BY MY EDITOR, K-SHI.

THINGS THAT HAVE HELPED RECENTLY:

- BUMP OF CHICKEN
- KINKI KIDS
- AYUMI HAMASAKI
- ORANGE RANGE
- KEN HIRAI
- AI ÔTUSKA
- ANY OF THE PICHI ALBUMS

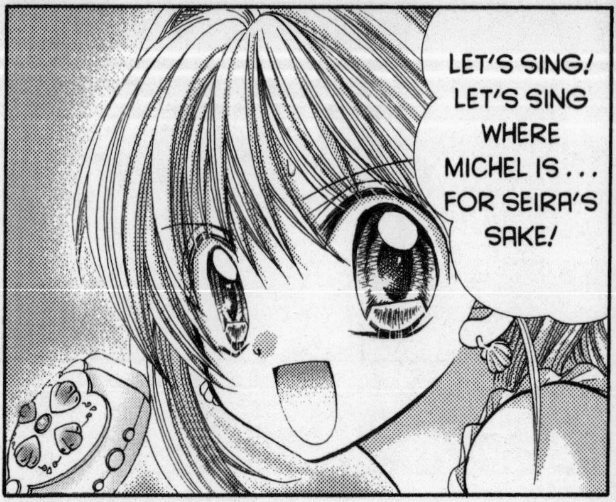
LET'S SING! LET'S SING WHERE MICHEL IS . . . FOR SEIRA'S SAKE!

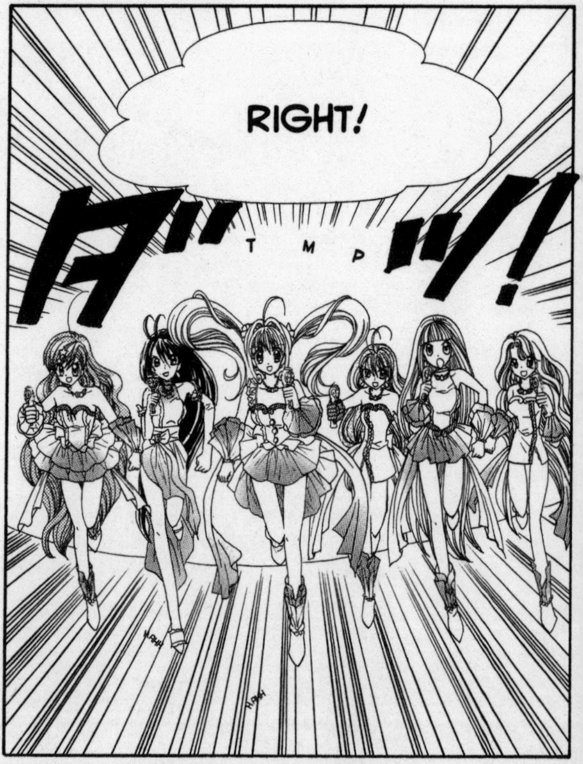
RIGHT!
T M P

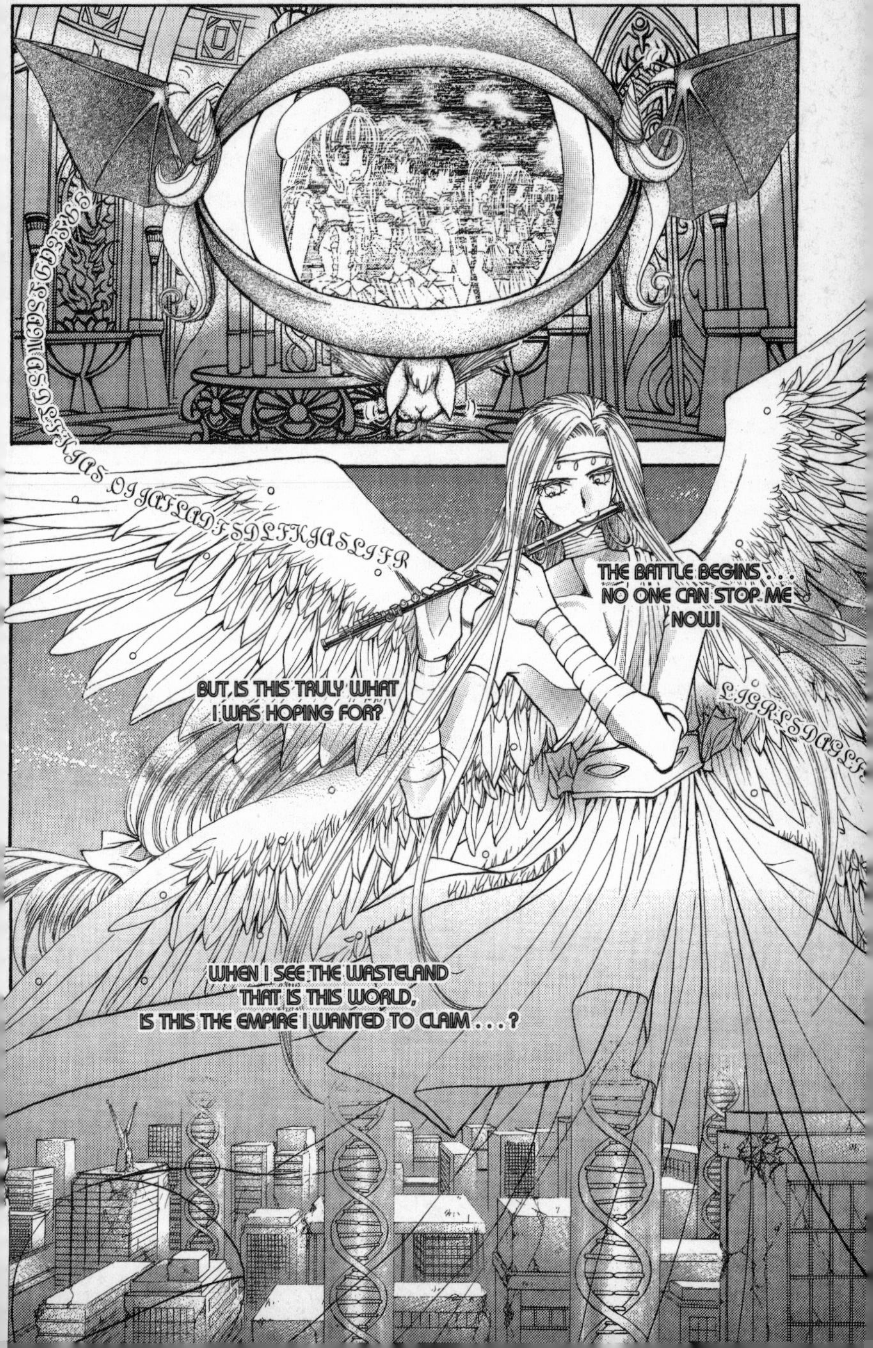
THE BATTLE BEGINS . . . NO ONE CAN STOP ME NOW!
BUT, IS THIS TRULY WHAT I WAS HOPING FOR?
WHEN I SEE THE WASTELAND THAT IS THIS WORLD, IS THIS THE EMPIRE I WANTED TO CLAIM . . . ?

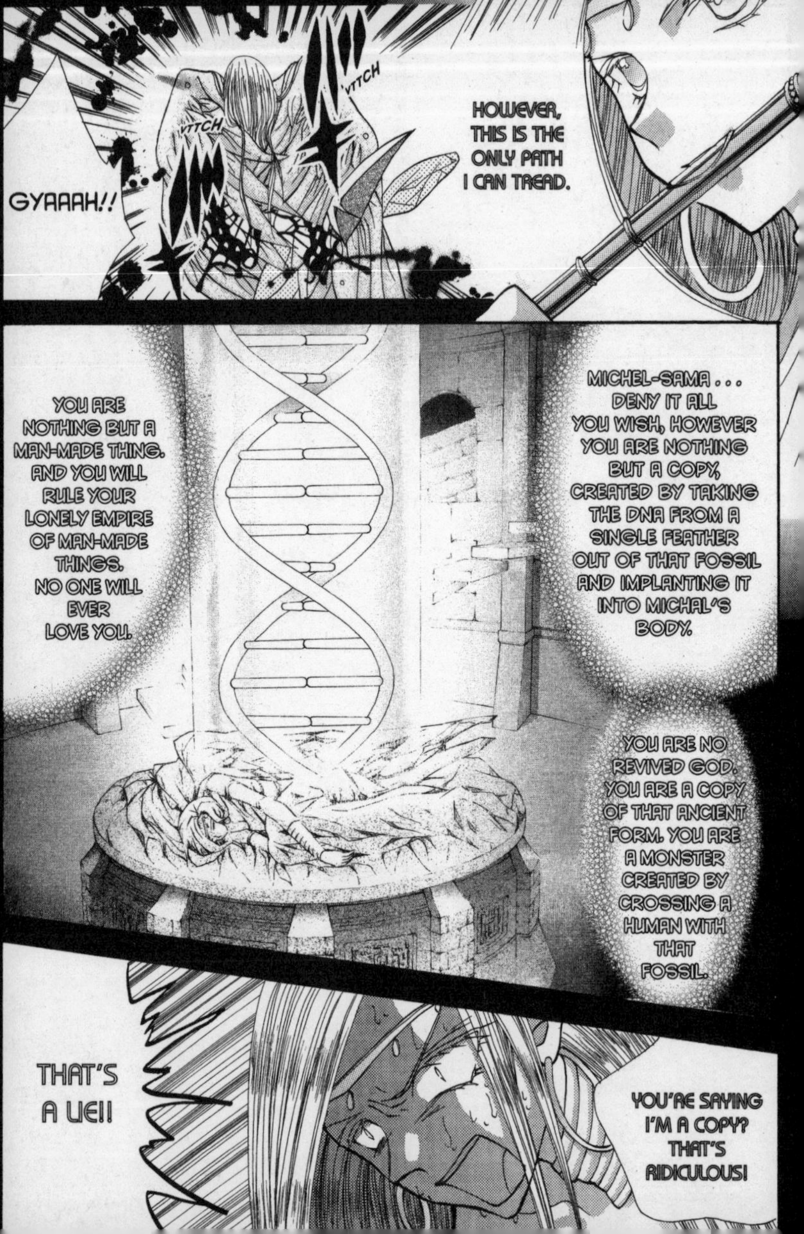
HOWEVER, THIS IS THE ONLY PATH I CAN TREAD.
'VTTCH
VTTCH
GYAAAH!!
MICHEL-SAMA . . . DENY IT ALL YOU WISH, HOWEVER YOU ARE NOTHING BUT A COPY, CREATED BY TAKING THE DNA FROM A SINGLE FEATHER OUT OF THAT FOSSIL AND IMPLANTING IT INTO MICHAL'S BODY.
YOU ARE NO REVIVED GOD. YOU ARE A COPY OF THAT ANCIENT FORM. YOU ARE A MONSTER CREATED BY CROSSING A HUMAN WITH THAT FOSSIL.
YOU ARE NOTHING BUT A MAN-MADE THING. AND YOU WILL RULE YOUR LONELY EMPIRE OF MAN-MADE THINGS. NO ONE WILL EVER LOVE YOU.
YOU'RE SAYING I'M A COPY? THAT'S RIDICULOUS!
THAT'S A LIE!!

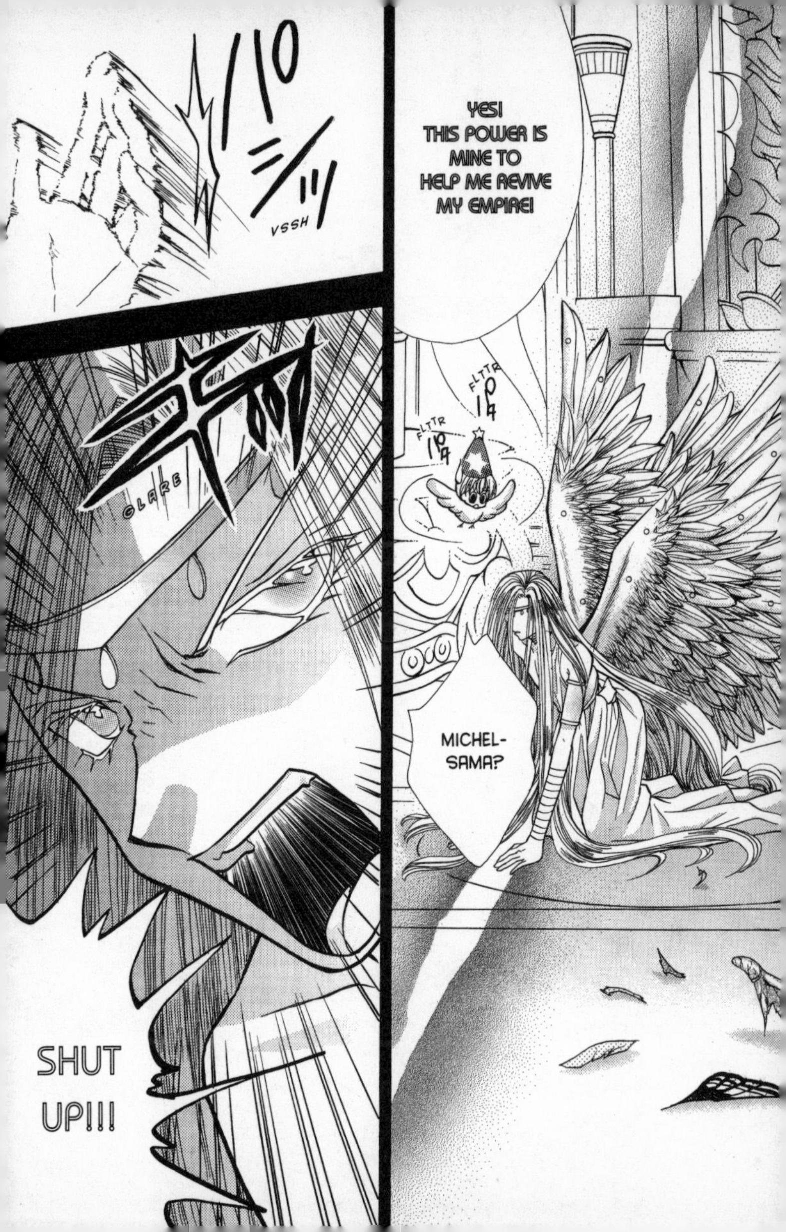
YES!
THIS POWER IS MINE TO HELP ME REVIVE MY EMPIRE!
FLTTR
FLTTR
MICHEL-SAMA?
VSSH
GLARE
SHUT UP!!!

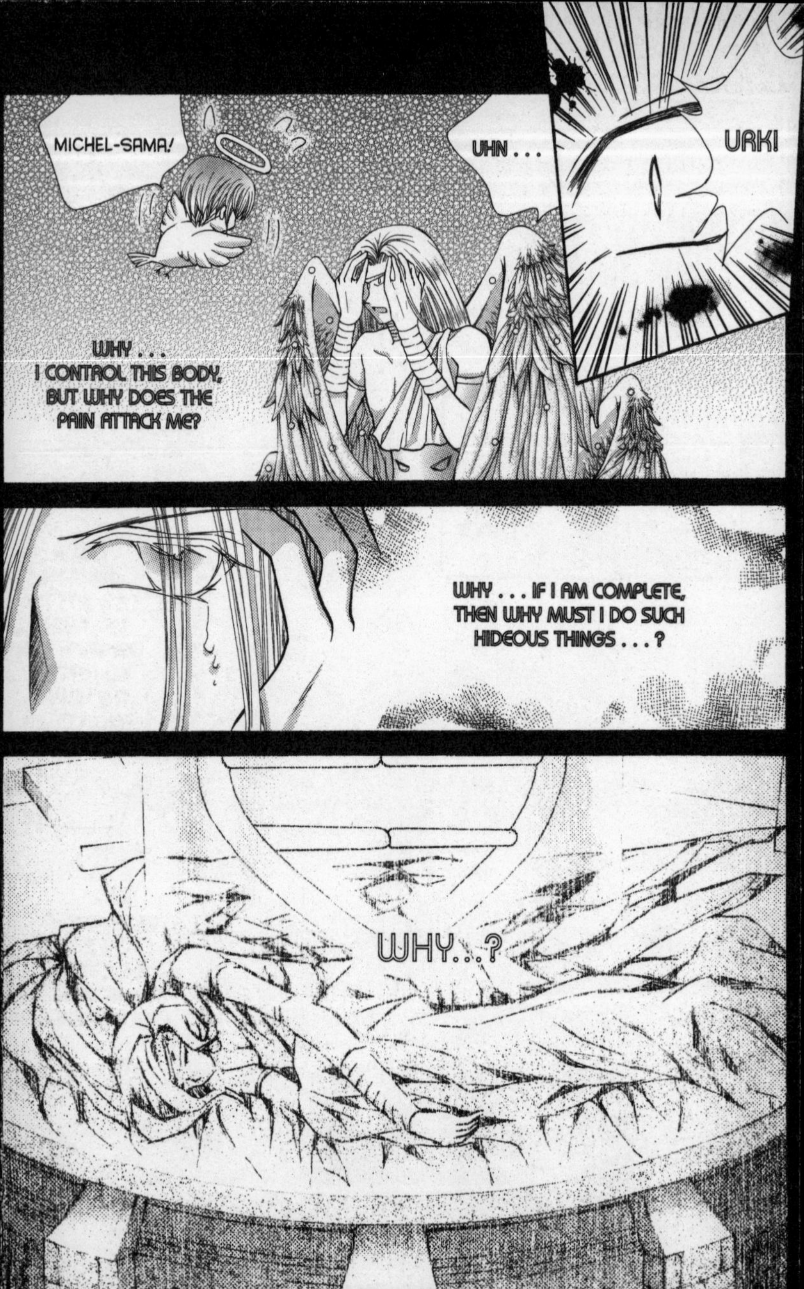
URK!
UHN . . .
MICHEL-SAMA!
WHY . . .
I CONTROL THIS BODY, BUT WHY DOES THE PAIN ATTACK ME?
WHY . . . IF I AM COMPLETE, THEN WHY MUST I DO SUCH HIDEOUS THINGS . . . ?
WHY. . .?

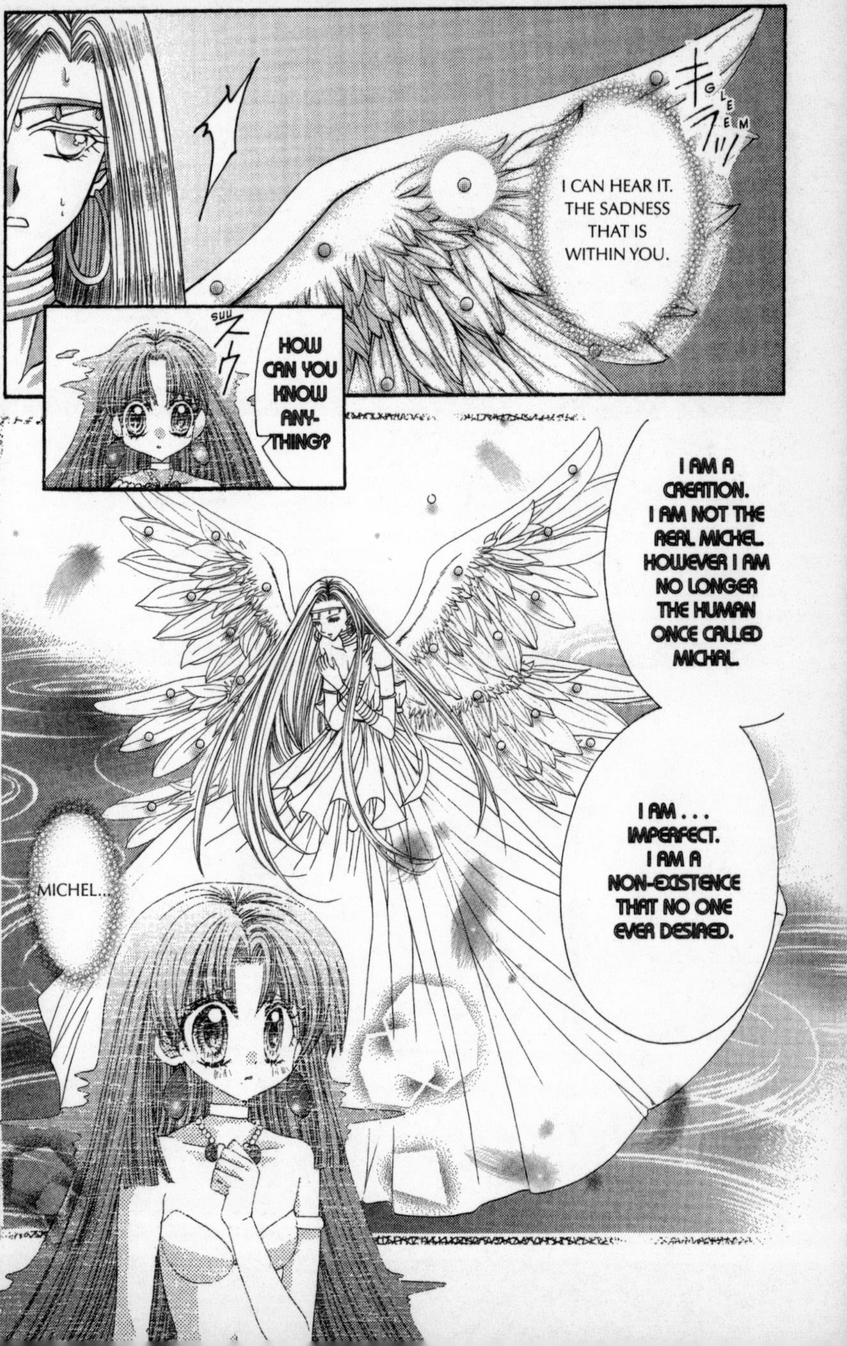
GLEEM
I CAN HEAR IT. THE SADNESS THAT IS WITHIN YOU.
SUU
HOW CAN YOU KNOW ANYTHING?
I AM A CREATION. I AM NOT THE REAL MICHEL. HOWEVER I AM NO LONGER THE HUMAN ONCE CALLED MICHAL.
I AM . . . IMPERFECT. I AM A NON-EXISTENCE THAT NO ONE EVER DESIRED.
MICHEL...

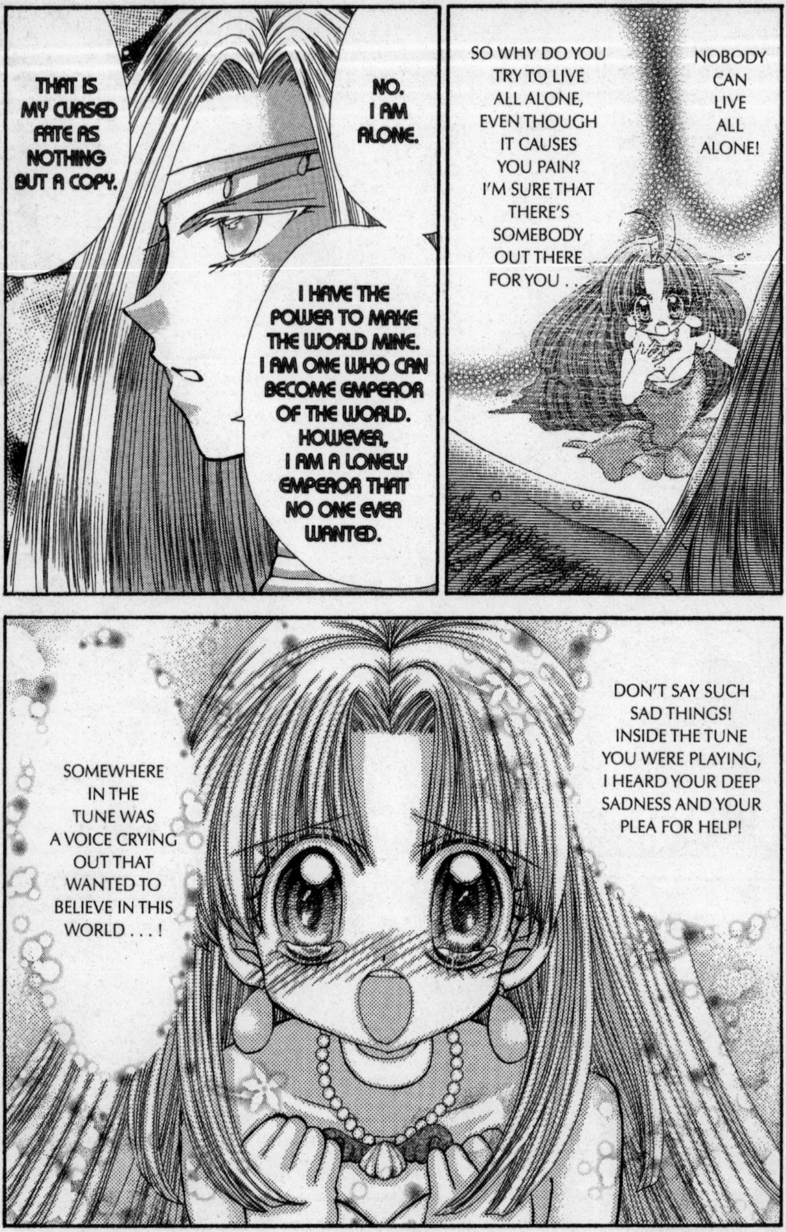
NOBODY CAN LIVE ALL ALONE!
SO WHY DO YOU TRY TO LIVE ALL ALONE, EVEN THOUGH IT CAUSES YOU PAIN? I'M SURE THAT THERE'S SOMEBODY OUT THERE FOR YOU . . .
NO. I AM ALONE.
I HAVE THE POWER TO MAKE THE WORLD MINE. I AM ONE WHO CAN BECOME EMPEROR OF THE WORLD. HOWEVER, I AM A LONELY EMPEROR THAT NO ONE EVER WANTED.
THAT IS MY CURSED FATE AS NOTHING BUT A COPY.
DON'T SAY SUCH SAD THINGS! INSIDE THE TUNE YOU WERE PLAYING, I HEARD YOUR DEEP SADNESS AND YOUR PLEA FOR HELP!
SOMEWHERE IN THE TUNE WAS A VOICE CRYING OUT THAT WANTED TO BELIEVE IN THIS WORLD . . . !

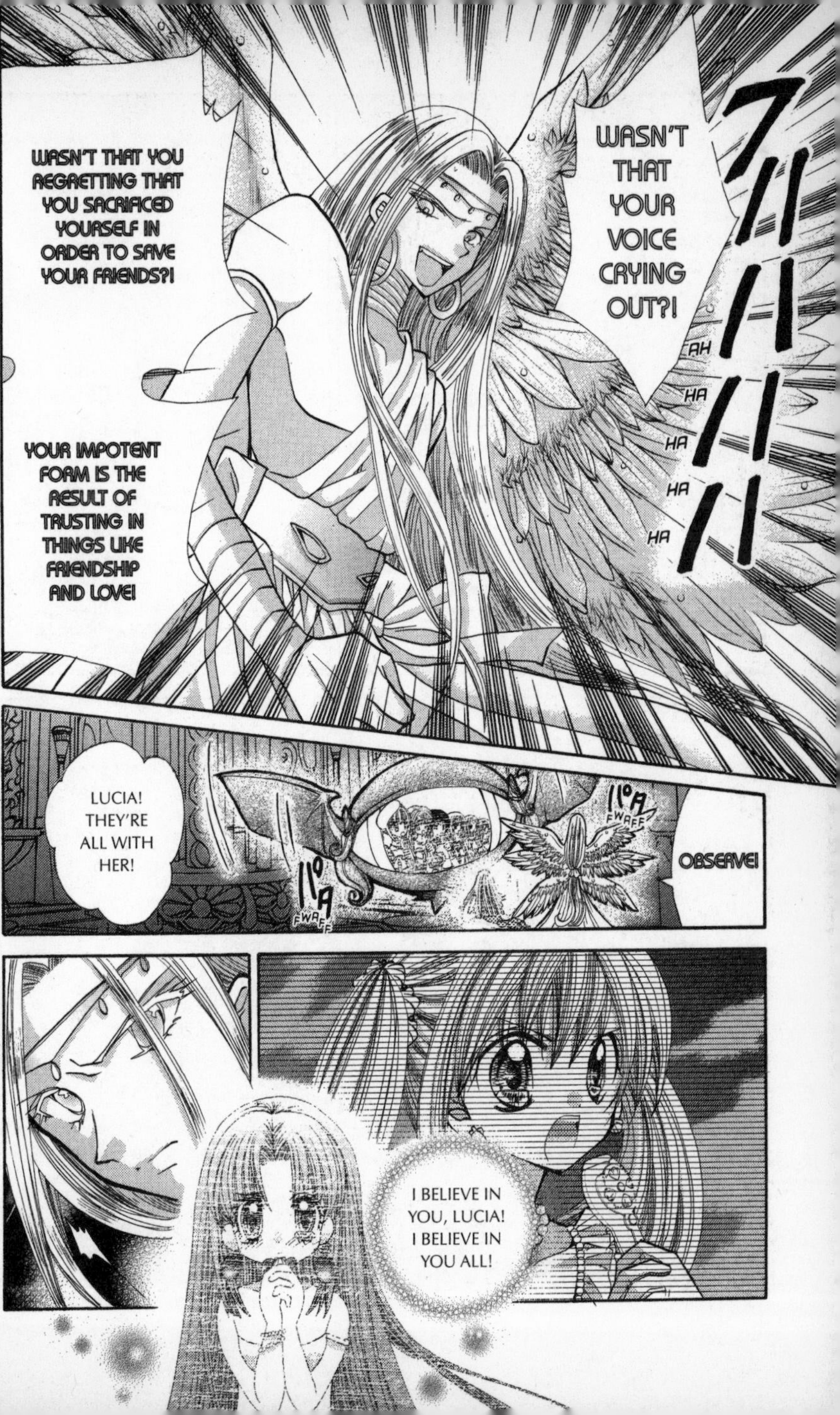

AH HA HA HA HA
WASN'T THAT YOUR VOICE CRYING OUT?!
WASN'T THAT YOU REGRETTING THAT YOU SACRIFICED YOURSELF IN ORDER TO SAVE YOUR FRIENDS?!
YOUR IMPOTENT FORM IS THE RESULT OF TRUSTING IN THINGS LIKE FRIENDSHIP AND LOVE!
OBSERVE!
FWAFF
FWAFF
LUCIA! THEY'RE ALL WITH HER!
I BELIEVE IN YOU, LUCIA! I BELIEVE IN YOU ALL!

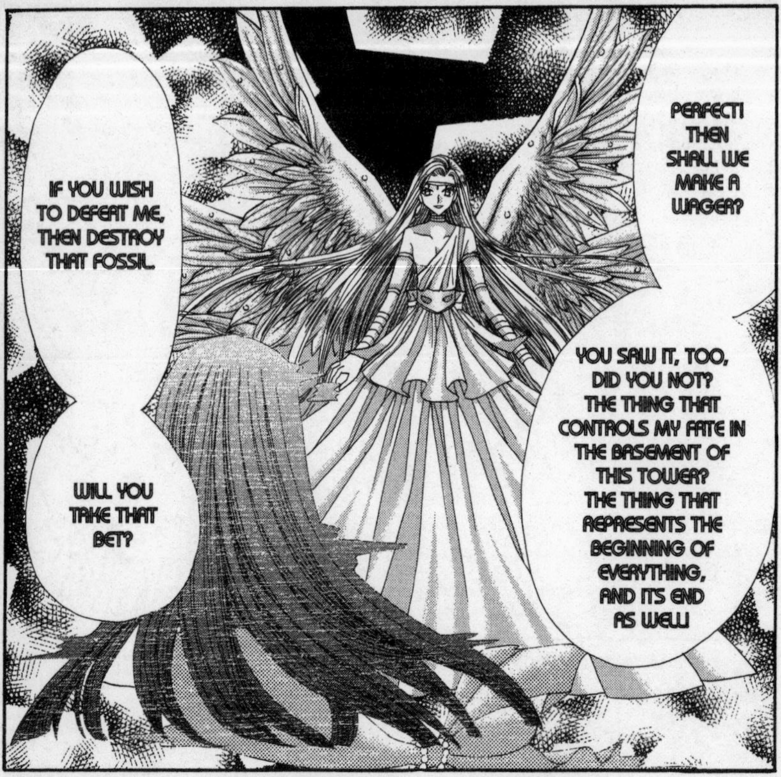
PERFECT! THEN SHALL WE MAKE A WAGER?
YOU SAW IT, TOO, DID YOU NOT? THE THING THAT CONTROLS MY FATE IN THE BASEMENT OF THIS TOWER? THE THING THAT REPRESENTS THE BEGINNING OF EVERYTHING, AND ITS END AS WELL!
IF YOU WISH TO DEFEAT ME, THEN DESTROY THAT FOSSIL.
WILL YOU TAKE THAT BET?

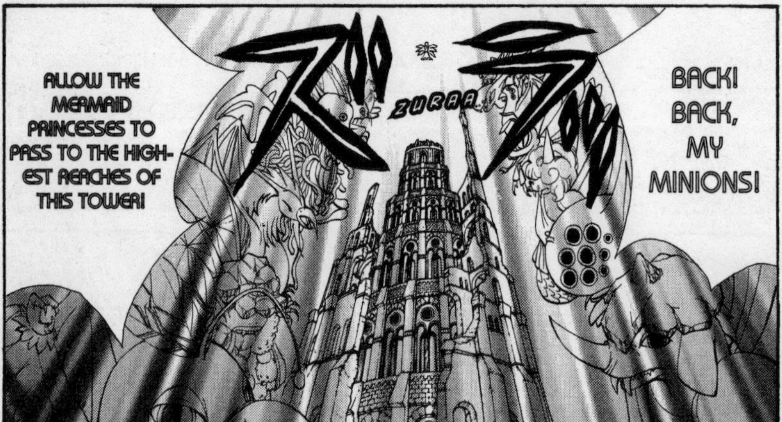
BACK! BACK, MY MINIONS!
ZURAA...
ALLOW THE MERMAID PRINCESSES TO PASS TO THE HIGH-EST REACHES OF THIS TOWER!

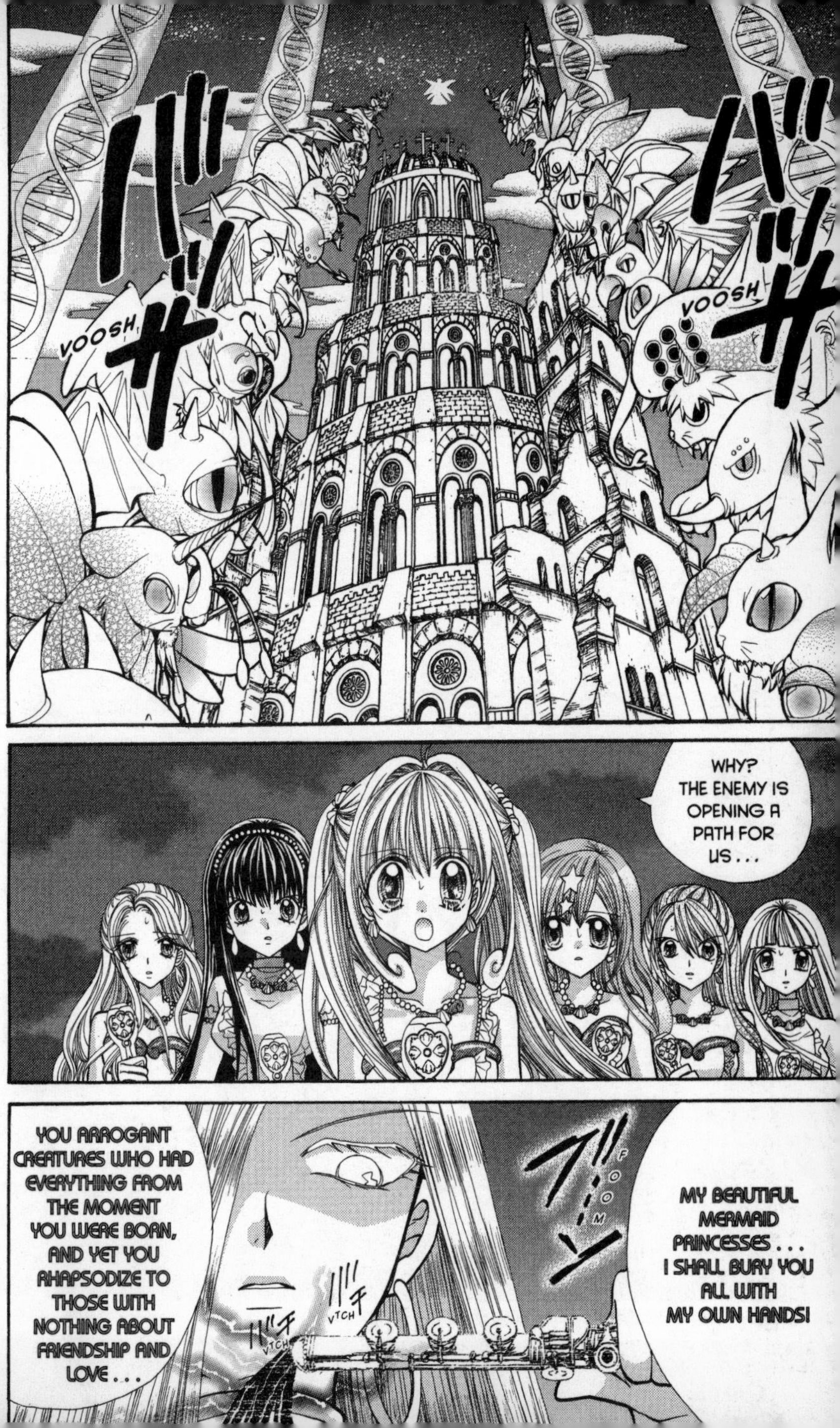
VOOSH
VOOSH
WHY? THE ENEMY IS OPENING A PATH FOR US...
MY BEAUTIFUL MERMAID PRINCESSES... I SHALL BURY YOU ALL WITH MY OWN HANDS!
FOOM
VTCH
VTCH
YOU ARROGANT CREATURES WHO HAD EVERYTHING FROM THE MOMENT YOU WERE BORN, AND YET YOU RHAPSODIZE TO THOSE WITH NOTHING ABOUT FRIENDSHIP AND LOVE...

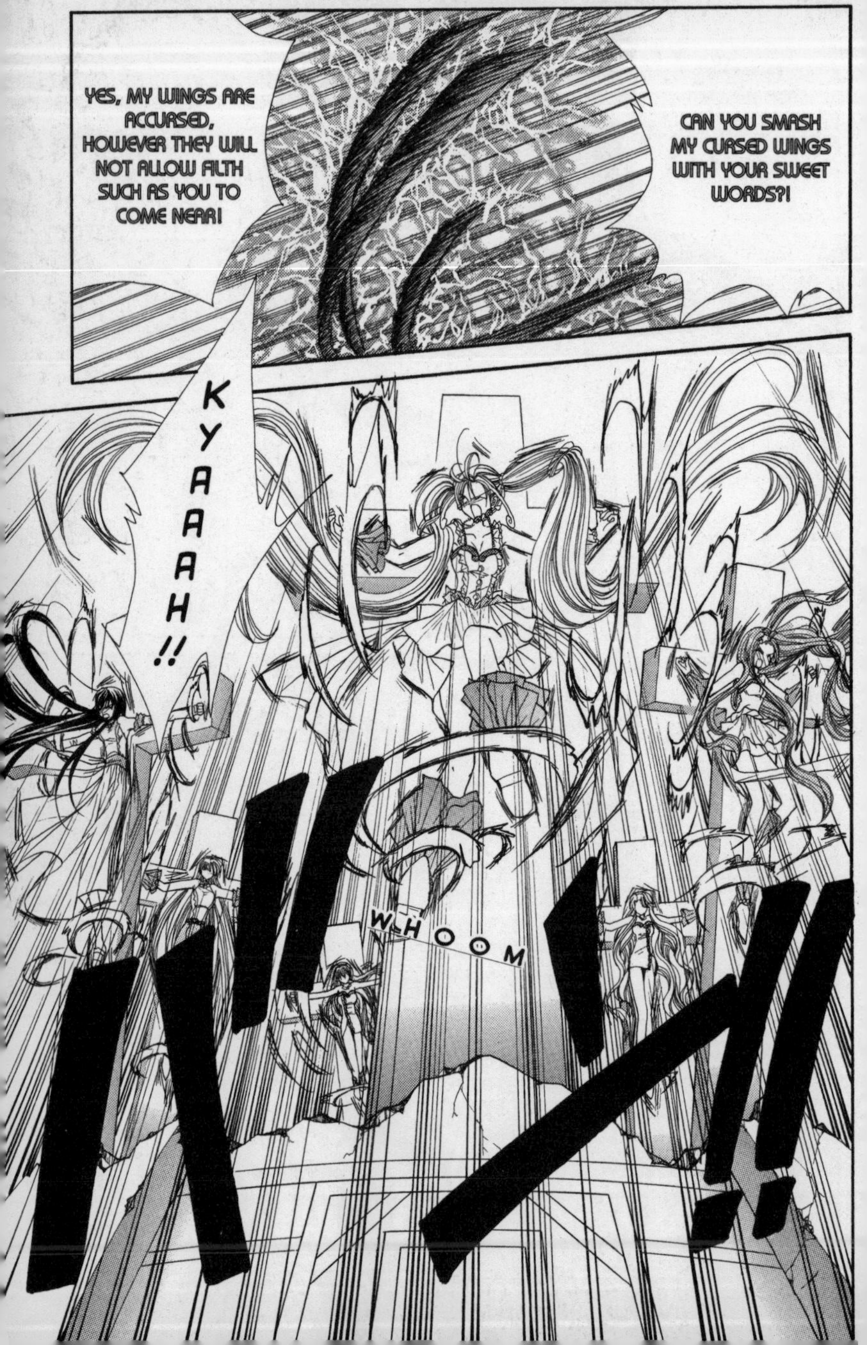
CAN YOU SMASH MY CURSED WINGS WITH YOUR SWEET WORDS?!
YES, MY WINGS ARE ACCURSED, HOWEVER THEY WILL NOT ALLOW FILTH SUCH AS YOU TO COME NEAR!
KYAAAAH!!
WHOOM

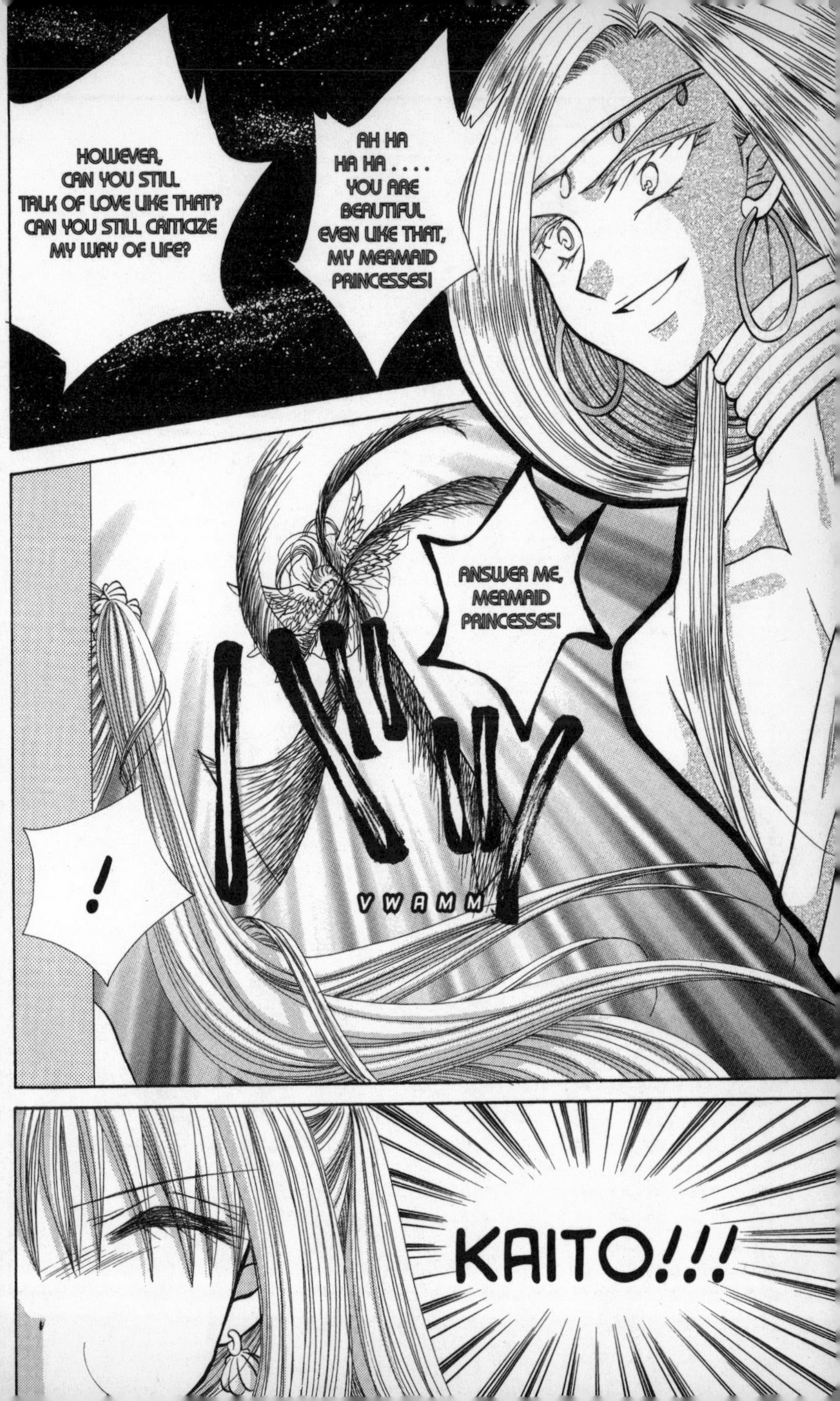
AH HA HA HA . . . . YOU ARE BEAUTIFUL EVEN LIKE THAT, MY MERMAID PRINCESSES!
HOWEVER, CAN YOU STILL TALK OF LOVE LIKE THAT? CAN YOU STILL CRITICIZE MY WAY OF LIFE?
ANSWER ME, MERMAID PRINCESSES!
VWAMM
!
KAITO!!!

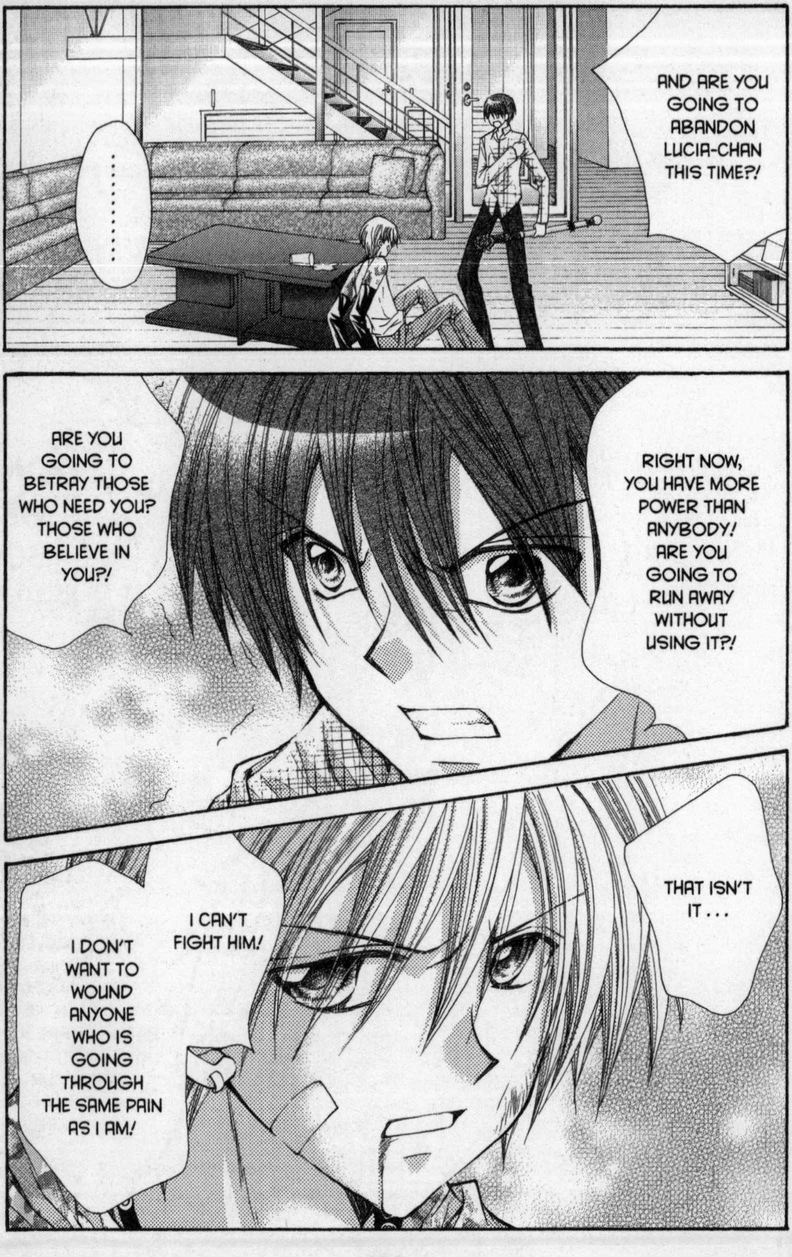
AND ARE YOU GOING TO ABANDON LUCIA-CHAN THIS TIME?!
....
RIGHT NOW, YOU HAVE MORE POWER THAN ANYBODY! ARE YOU GOING TO RUN AWAY WITHOUT USING IT?!
ARE YOU GOING TO BETRAY THOSE WHO NEED YOU? THOSE WHO BELIEVE IN YOU?!
THAT ISN'T IT . . .
I CAN'T FIGHT HIM!
I DON'T WANT TO WOUND ANYONE WHO IS GOING THROUGH THE SAME PAIN AS I AM!

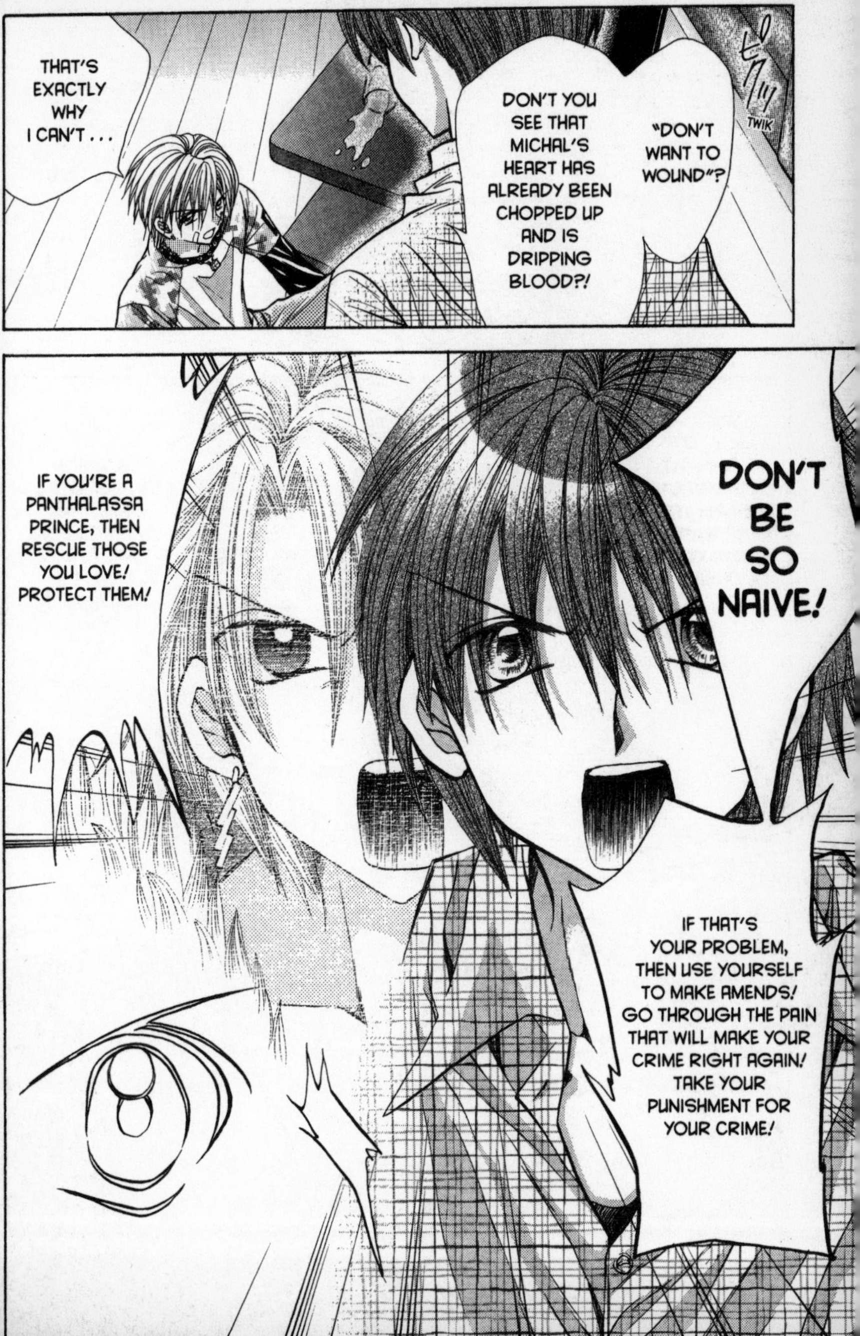
TWIK
"DON'T WANT TO WOUND"?
DON'T YOU SEE THAT MICHAL'S HEART HAS ALREADY BEEN CHOPPED UP AND IS DRIPPING BLOOD?!
THAT'S EXACTLY WHY I CAN'T . . .
DON'T BE SO NAIVE!
IF YOU'RE A PANTHALASSA PRINCE, THEN RESCUE THOSE YOU LOVE! PROTECT THEM!
IF THAT'S YOUR PROBLEM, THEN USE YOURSELF TO MAKE AMENDS! GO THROUGH THE PAIN THAT WILL MAKE YOUR CRIME RIGHT AGAIN! TAKE YOUR PUNISHMENT FOR YOUR CRIME!

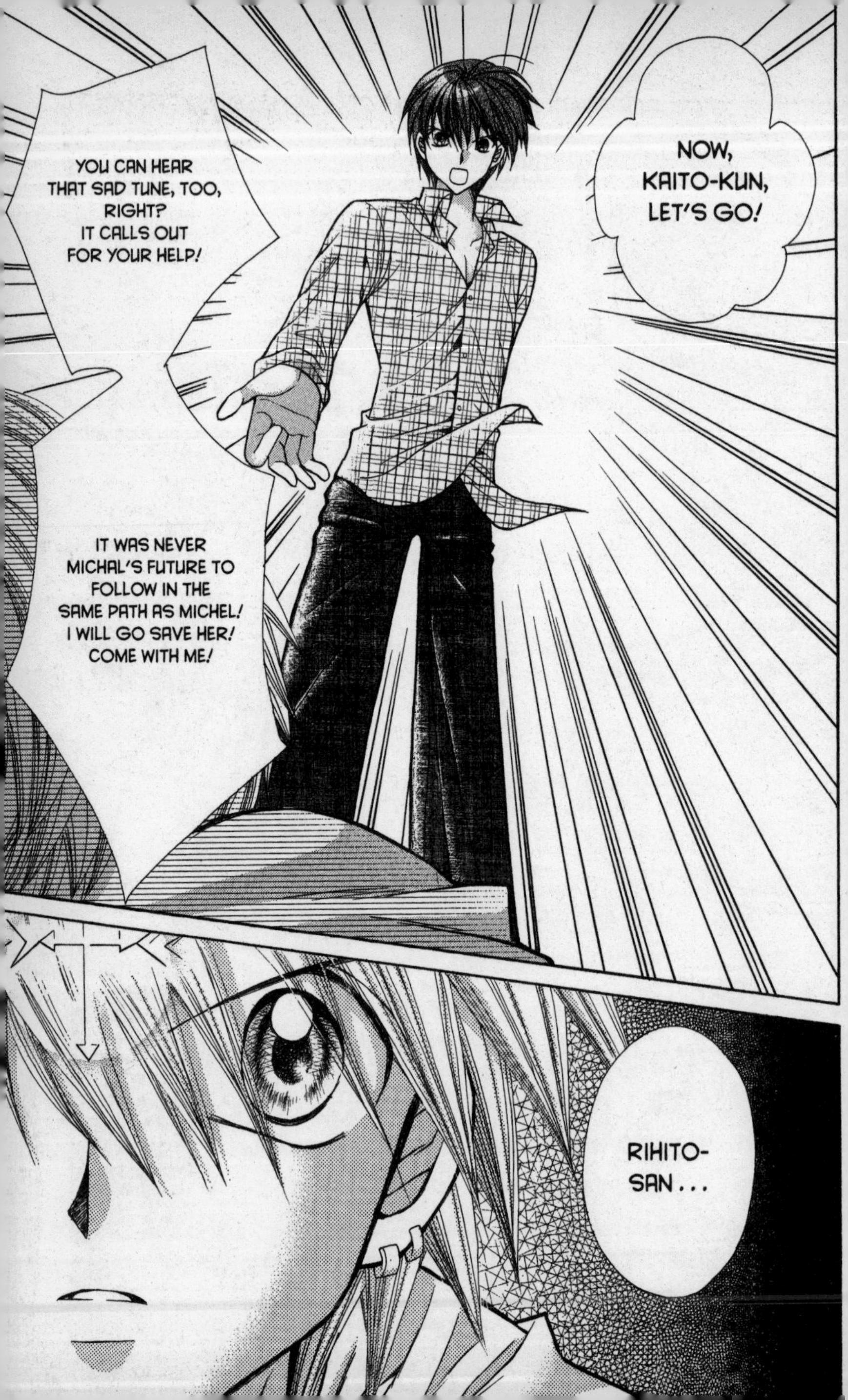
NOW, KAITO-KUN, LET'S GO!
YOU CAN HEAR THAT SAD TUNE, TOO, RIGHT? IT CALLS OUT FOR YOUR HELP!
IT WAS NEVER MICHAL'S FUTURE TO FOLLOW IN THE SAME PATH AS MICHEL! I WILL GO SAVE HER! COME WITH ME!
RIHITO-SAN...

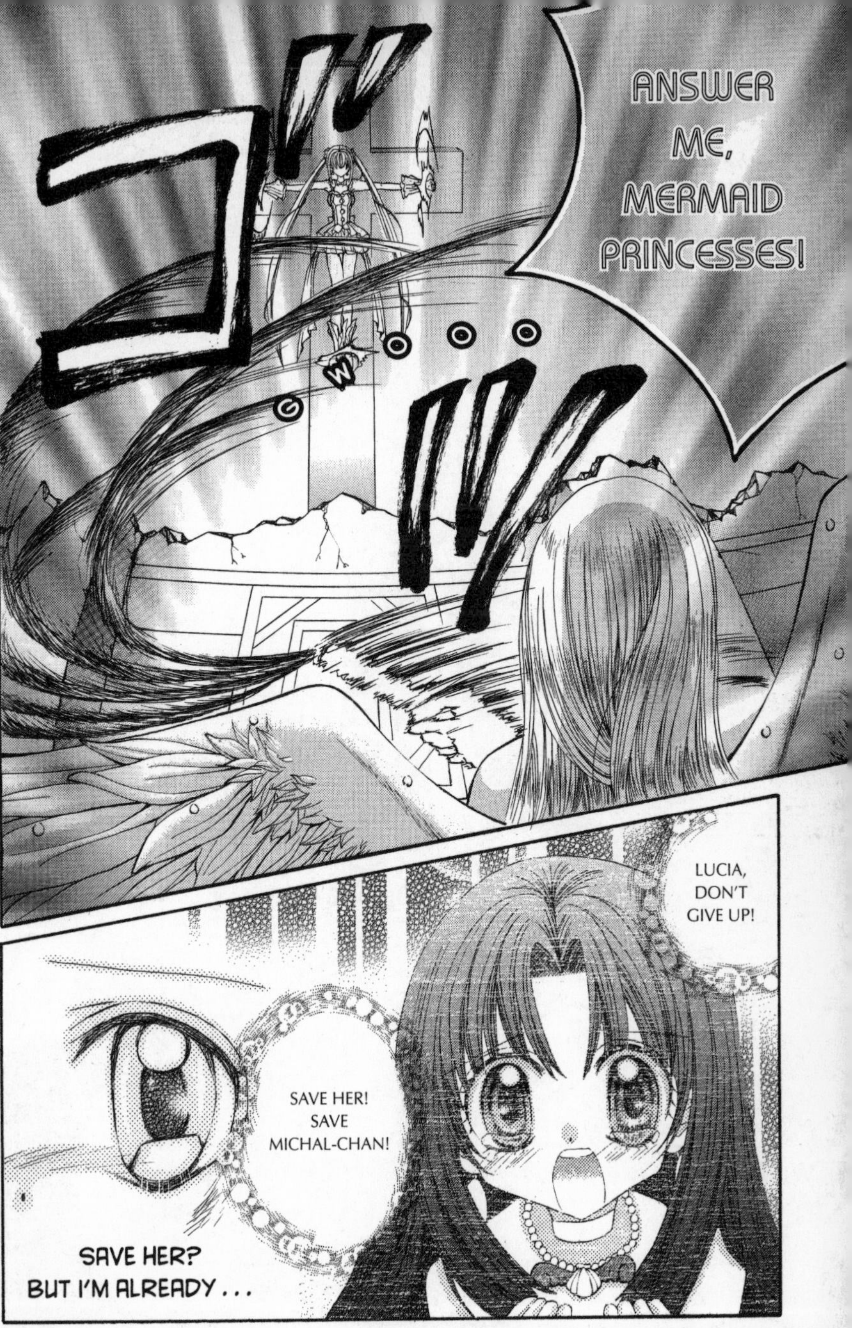
ANSWER ME, MERMAID PRINCESSES!
GWOOO
LUCIA, DON'T GIVE UP!
SAVE HER! SAVE MICHAL-CHAN!
SAVE HER? BUT I'M ALREADY . . .

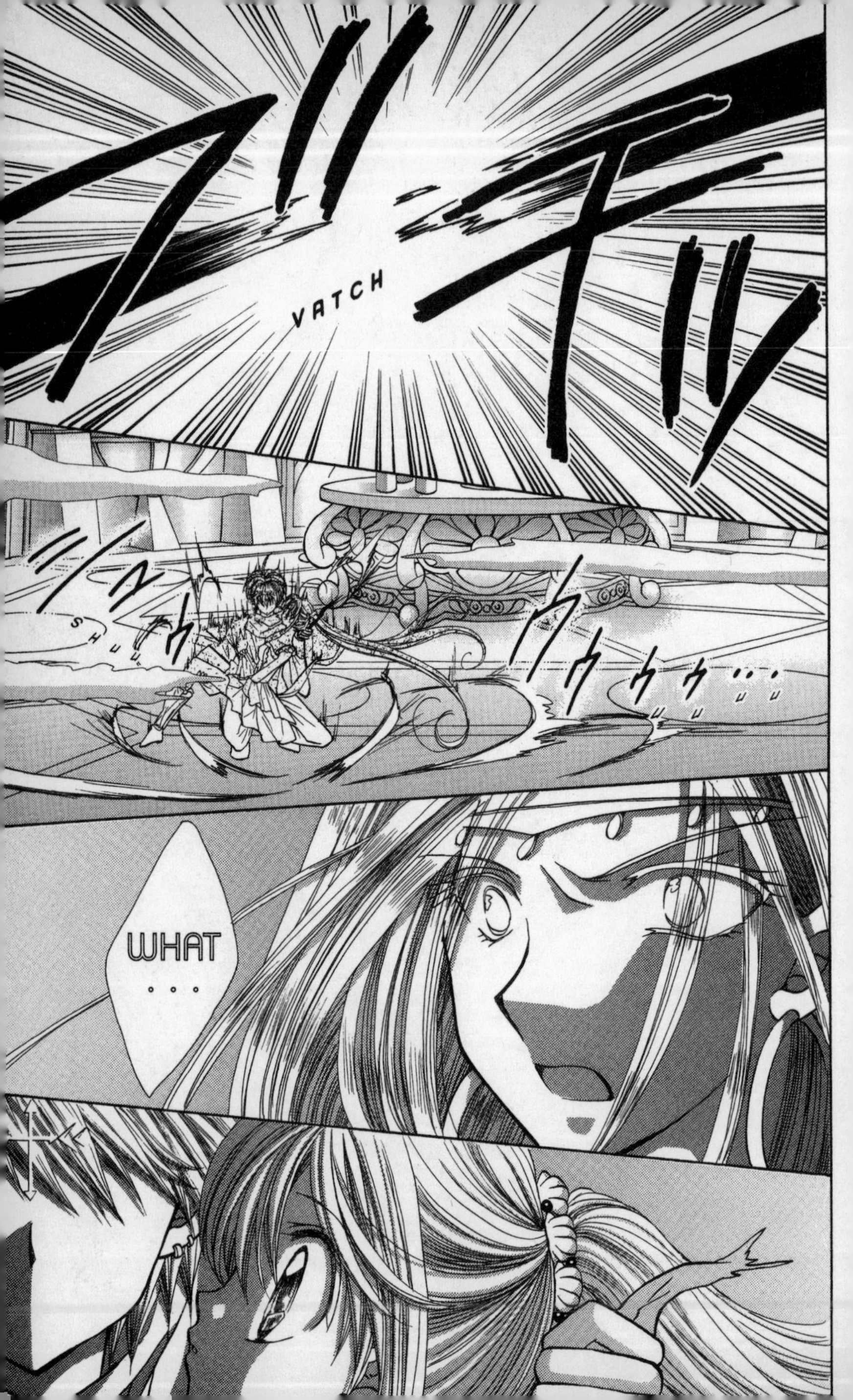
VATCH
UUUU...
SHUU...
WHAT...

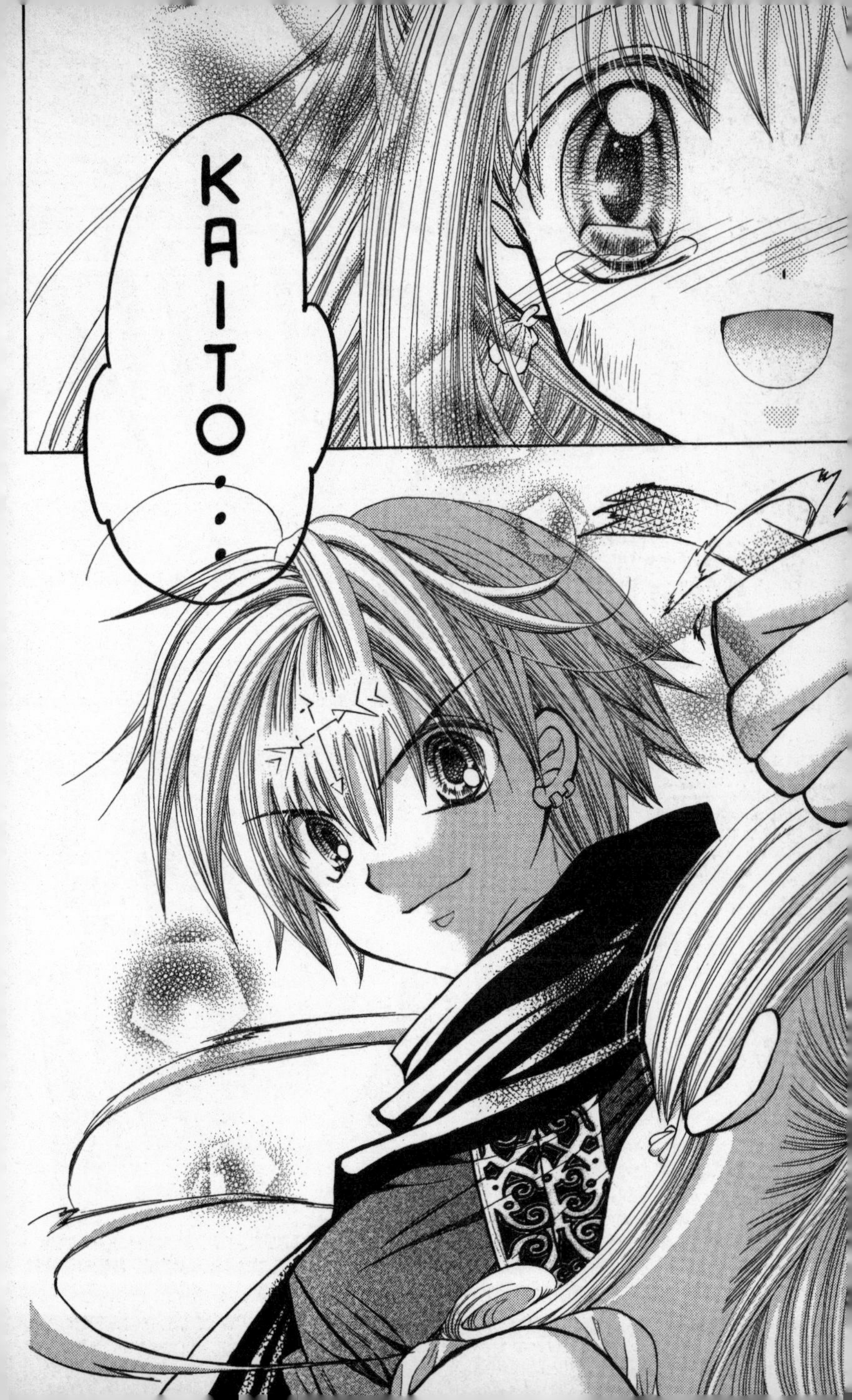
KAITO...

NEXT TIME IN MERMAID MELODY
PICHI PICHI PITCH, volume 7 . . .

TALES NEVER TOLD IN THE MAIN BOOK!

WE BRING TWO LIVE ENCORES TO YOU!

"SERENADE OF THE SEA OF SHOOTING STARS"

PLEASE COME BACK . . .

THE FINAL RESOLUTION OF THE **FORBIDDEN LOVE** BETWEEN HIPPO AND YŪRI . . . ?

"AND THE SUPER LOVE SONG OF THE FUTURE"

WHO ARE YOU . . .

B O O M

A PRINCE . . . ?

LUCIA AND KAITO'S **SECRET FATE** IS NOW REVEALED!!

WHAT'LL I DO?

COME ON, WAKE UP!

WAKE UP!

BONUS FEATURES INCLUDE THE 2ND PICHI PICHI PITCH POPULARITY CONTEST RESULTS AND A COLLECTION OF PICHI CHARACTER DESIGNS!

YOU ASKED FOR IT! **A COLLECTION OF HANAMORI-SENSEI'S SHORT STORIES AND OTHER WORKS!**
• GET NUDE! • MOONLIGHT GODDESS DIANA • CHERRY ♡ BLOSSOM

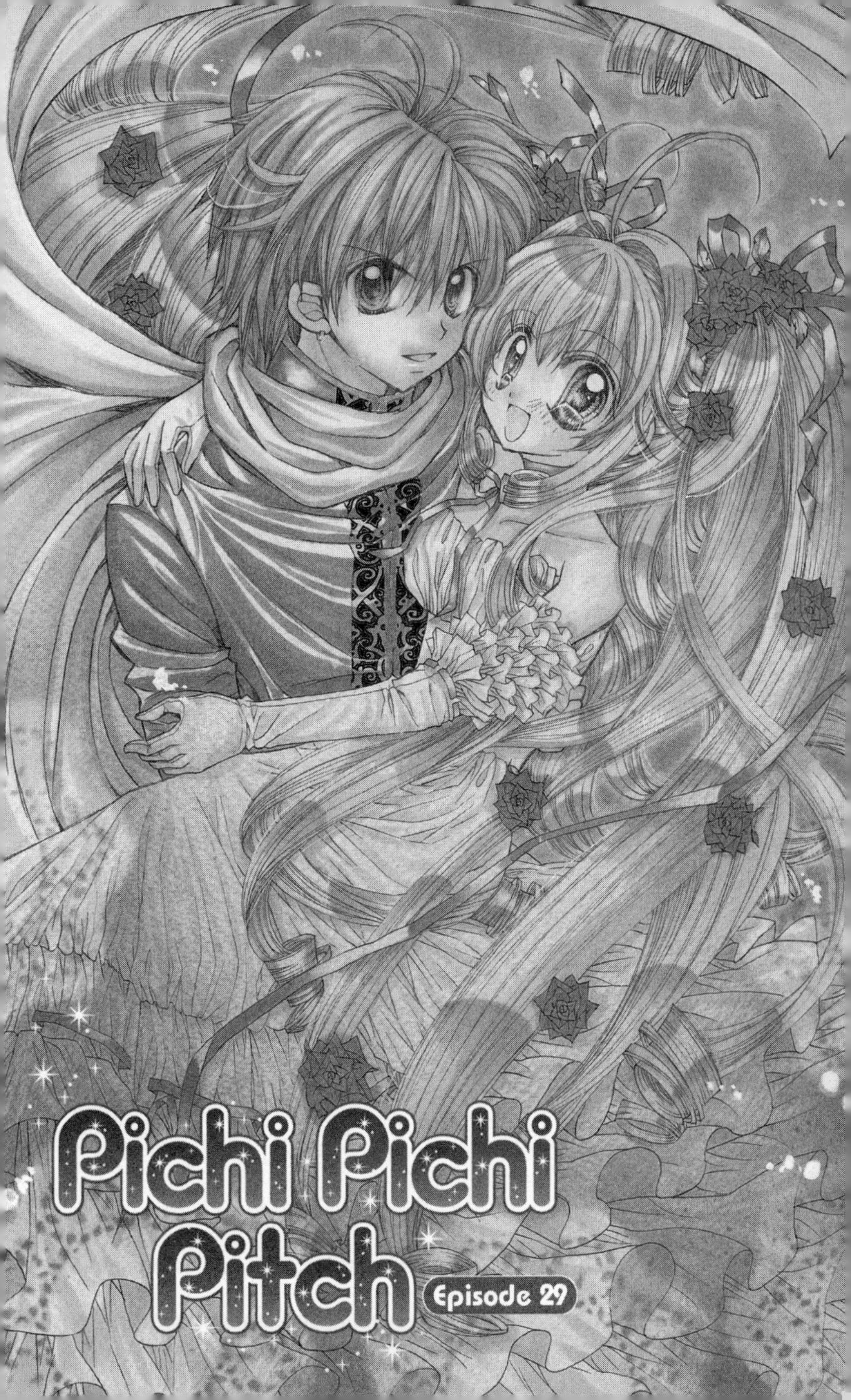
Pichi Pichi Pitch
Episode 29

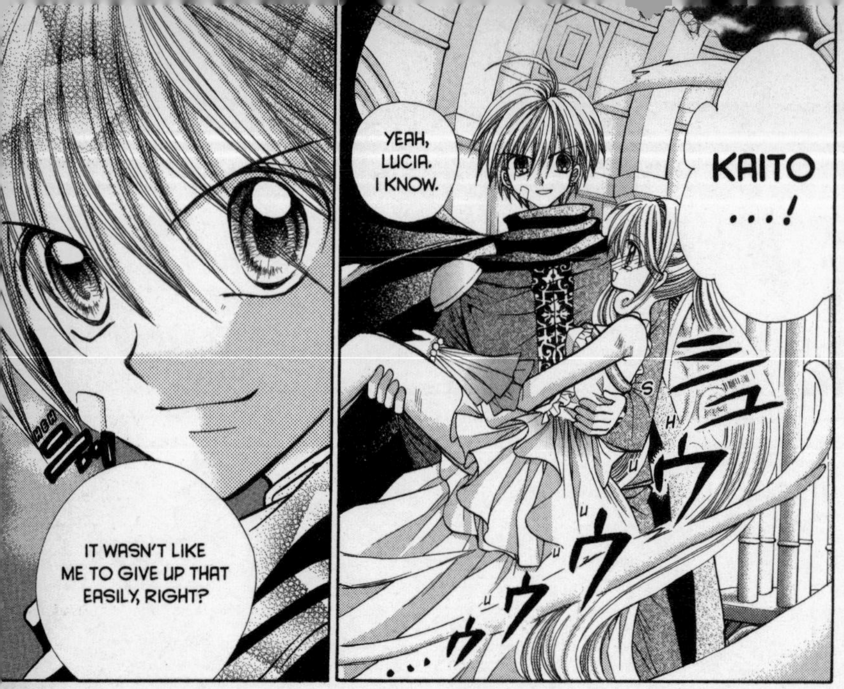
KAITO ...!
YEAH, LUCIA. I KNOW.
SHUUUU...
IT WASN'T LIKE ME TO GIVE UP THAT EASILY, RIGHT?

<EPISODE 29>

SPLASH PAGE OF THE PRINCE AND PRINCESS. SOME HAVE SAID THAT IT LOOKS ALMOST LIKE A WEDDING PICTURE, AND I CAN UNDERSTAND THAT. IT'S SO FUN DRAWING FRILLS THAT IT CAME OUT VERY FRILLY. THE CONTENTS OF THIS CHAPTER CONTAINED SO MANY COMPLICATED DETAILS THAT IT MADE HIPPO'S AND FUKU-CHAN'S SIMPLE STYLE LOOK ALMOST LIKE COMEDY. OH, MY!
WHEN LUCIA LOOKED AT MICHEL'S FOSSIL AND CRIED, SHE LOOKED LIKE HER HUMAN VERSION. I THOUGHT IT WAS JUST BECAUSE YOU CAN'T SEE THE WAVES IN HER HAIR, BUT SHE'S CRYING ALL THE TIME IN HER HUMAN SCENES. SO MAYBE THAT'S THE REASON. I REALLY LIKE THE SCENE WHERE KAITO BREAKS THE FOSSIL, AND THE TOWER CRUMBLES DOWN ON MICHEL'S HEAD. OH, AND THE SCENE WHERE FUKU-CHAN GOES ROUND AND ROUND IN CIRCLES.

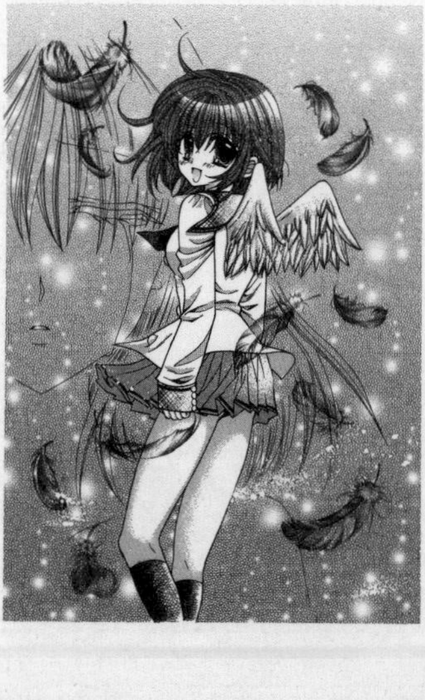

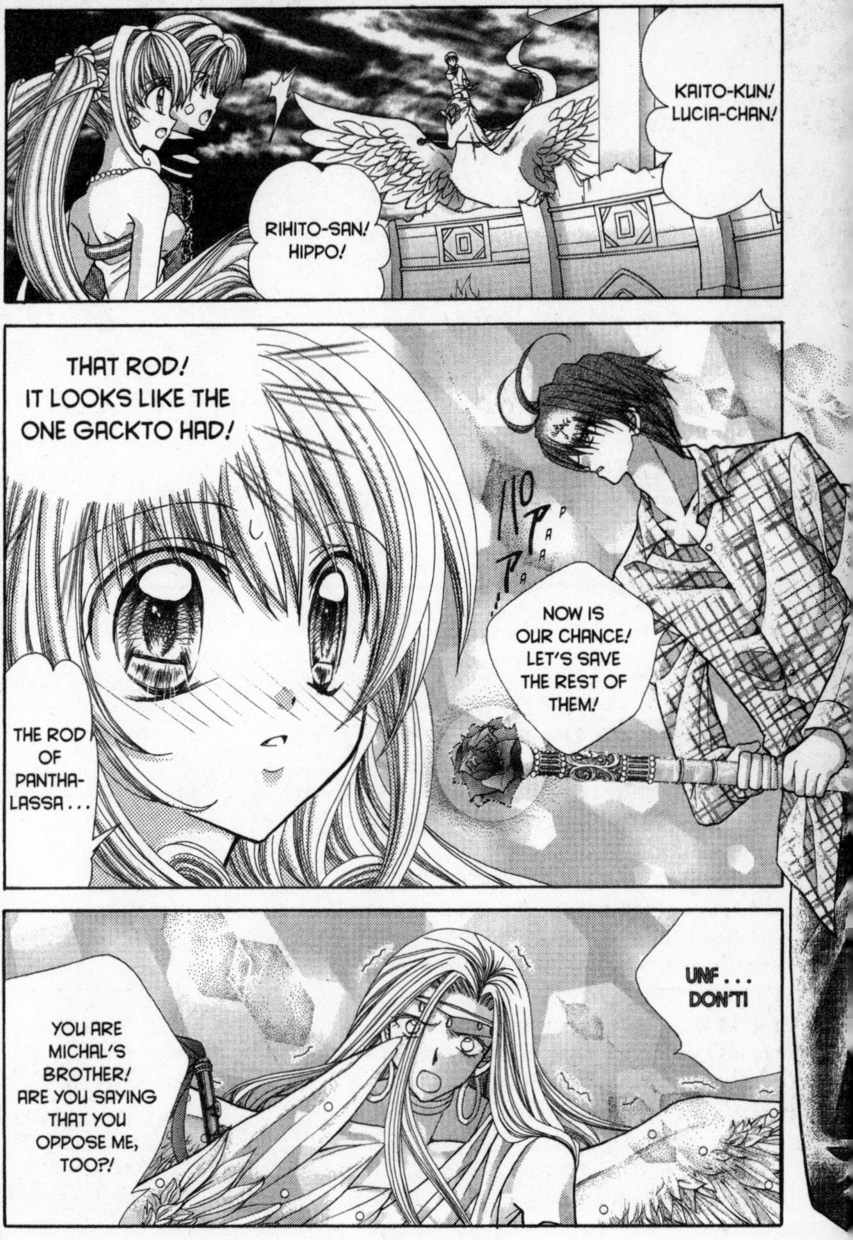
KAITO-KUN! LUCIA-CHAN!
RIHITO-SAN! HIPPO!
NOW IS OUR CHANCE! LET'S SAVE THE REST OF THEM!
THAT ROD! IT LOOKS LIKE THE ONE GACKTO HAD!
THE ROD OF PANTHA-LASSA . . .
UNF . . . DON'T!
YOU ARE MICHAL'S BROTHER! ARE YOU SAYING THAT YOU OPPOSE ME, TOO?!

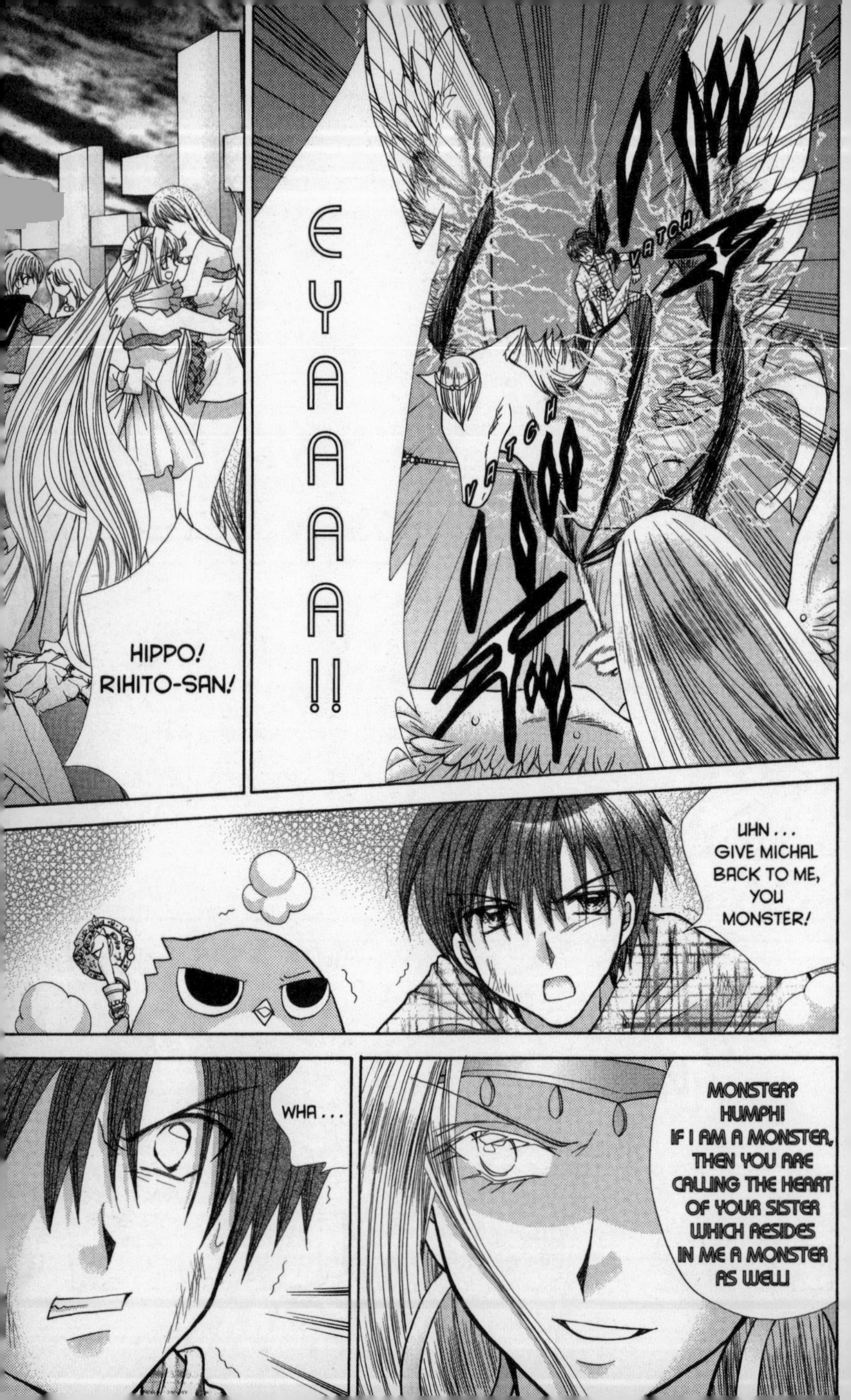
EYAAAAA!!
VATCH
VATCH
HIPPO! RIHITO-SAN!
UHN . . . GIVE MICHAL BACK TO ME, YOU MONSTER!
MONSTER? HUMPH! IF I AM A MONSTER, THEN YOU ARE CALLING THE HEART OF YOUR SISTER WHICH RESIDES IN ME A MONSTER AS WELL!
WHA . . .

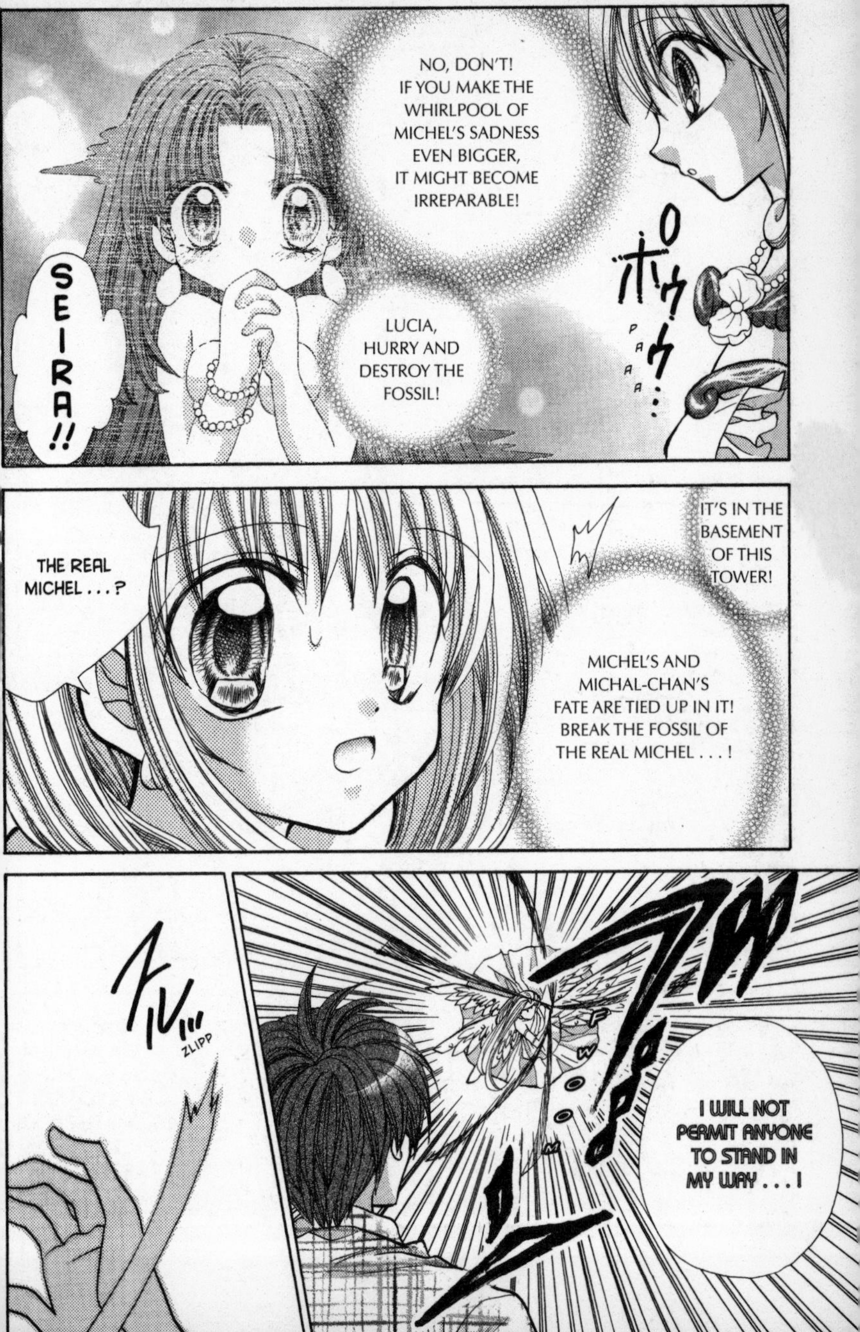

NO, DON'T! IF YOU MAKE THE WHIRLPOOL OF MICHEL'S SADNESS EVEN BIGGER, IT MIGHT BECOME IRREPARABLE!
PAAA
LUCIA, HURRY AND DESTROY THE FOSSIL!
SEIRA!!
IT'S IN THE BASEMENT OF THIS TOWER!
MICHEL'S AND MICHAL-CHAN'S FATE ARE TIED UP IN IT! BREAK THE FOSSIL OF THE REAL MICHEL . . . !
THE REAL MICHEL . . . ?
FWOOM
I WILL NOT PERMIT ANYONE TO STAND IN MY WAY . . . !
ZLIPP

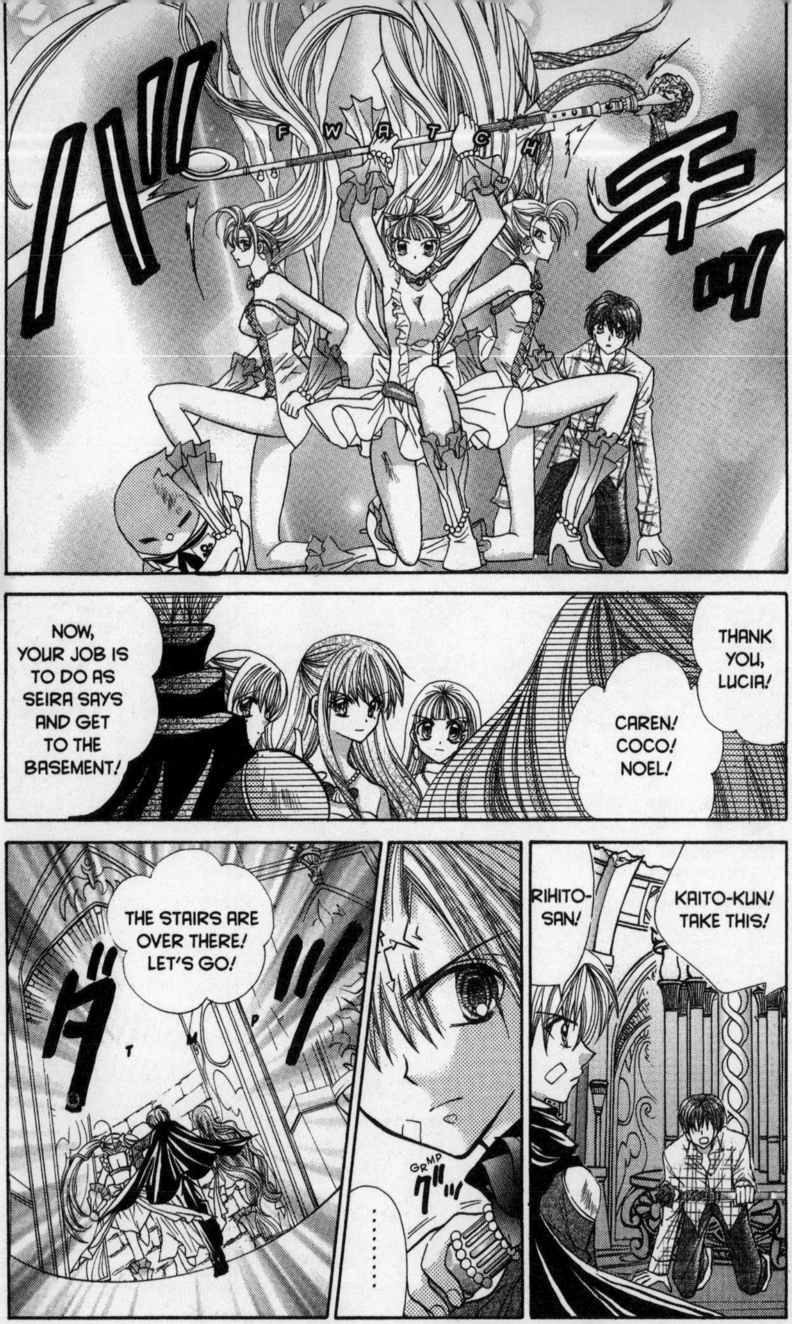
FWATCH
THANK YOU, LUCIA!
CAREN! COCO! NOEL!
NOW, YOUR JOB IS TO DO AS SEIRA SAYS AND GET TO THE BASEMENT!
KAITO-KUN! TAKE THIS!
RIHITO-SAN!
GRMP
......
THE STAIRS ARE OVER THERE! LET'S GO!
TMP

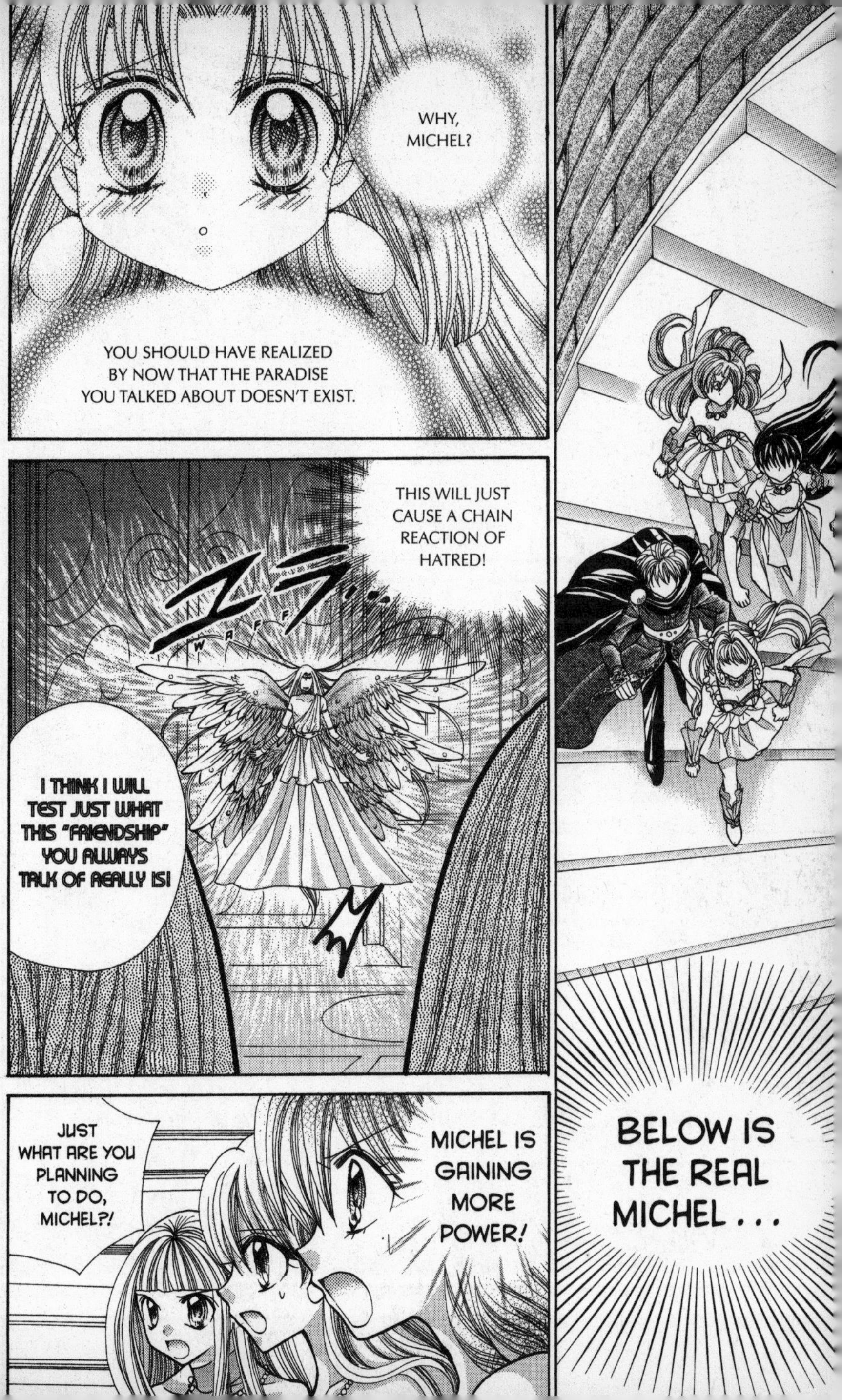
BELOW IS THE REAL MICHEL . . .
WHY, MICHEL?
YOU SHOULD HAVE REALIZED BY NOW THAT THE PARADISE YOU TALKED ABOUT DOESN'T EXIST.
THIS WILL JUST CAUSE A CHAIN REACTION OF HATRED!
WAFF
I THINK I WILL TEST JUST WHAT THIS "FRIENDSHIP" YOU ALWAYS TALK OF REALLY IS!
MICHEL IS GAINING MORE POWER!
JUST WHAT ARE YOU PLANNING TO DO, MICHEL?!

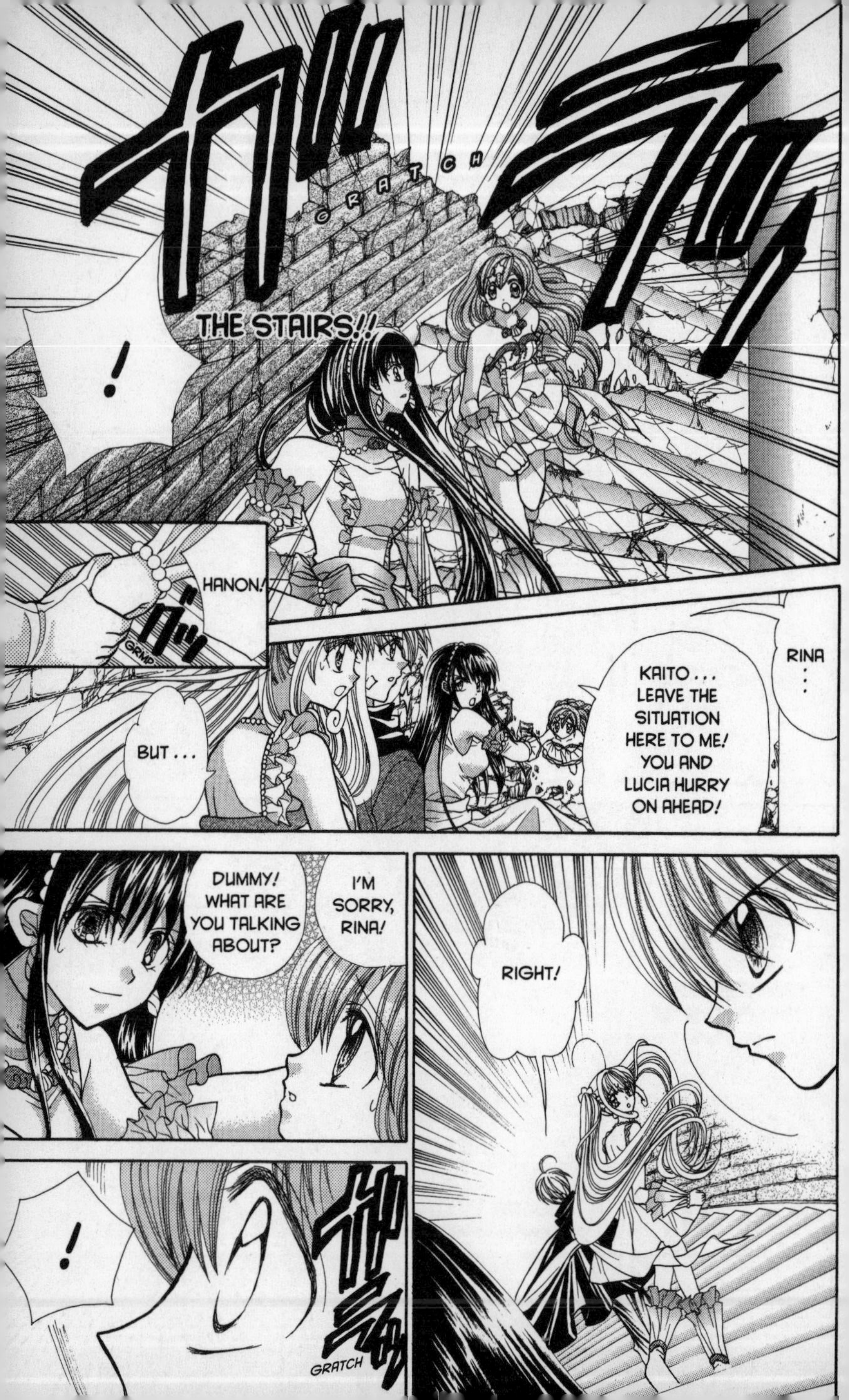
GRATCH
THE STAIRS!!
!
HANON!
GRMP
RINA . . .
KAITO . . . LEAVE THE SITUATION HERE TO ME! YOU AND LUCIA HURRY ON AHEAD!
BUT . . .
RIGHT!
I'M SORRY, RINA!
DUMMY! WHAT ARE YOU TALKING ABOUT?
!
GRATCH

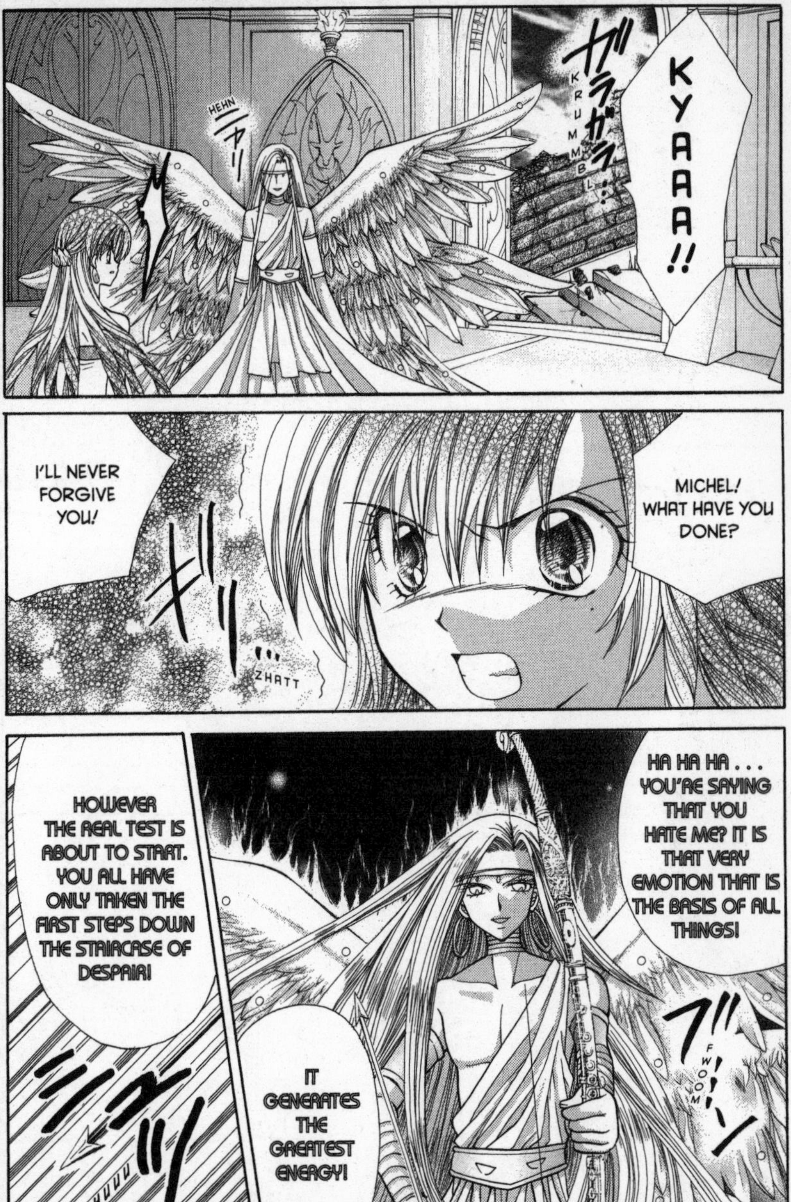
KYAAAA!!
KRUMMBL
HEHN
MICHEL! WHAT HAVE YOU DONE?
I'LL NEVER FORGIVE YOU!
ZHATT
HA HA HA . . . YOU'RE SAYING THAT YOU HATE ME? IT IS THAT VERY EMOTION THAT IS THE BASIS OF ALL THINGS!
FWOOM
IT GENERATES THE GREATEST ENERGY!
HOWEVER THE REAL TEST IS ABOUT TO START. YOU ALL HAVE ONLY TAKEN THE FIRST STEPS DOWN THE STAIRCASE OF DESPAIR!
SHUUU

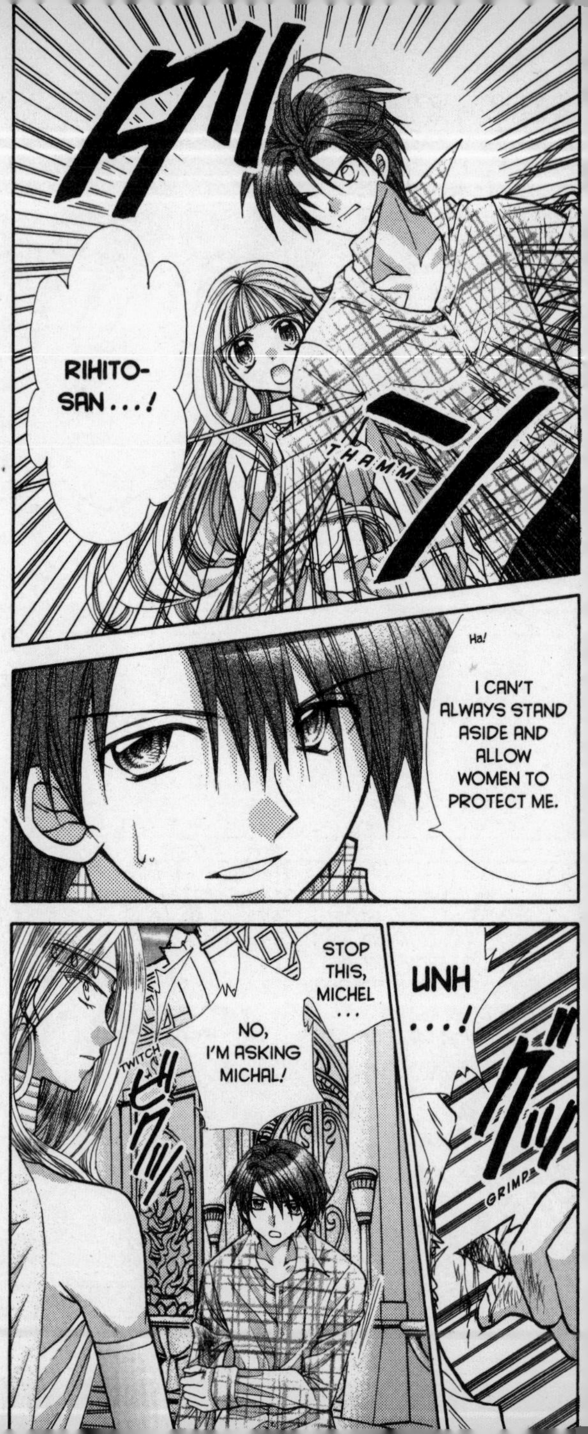
RIHITO-SAN...!
THAMM
Ha!
I CAN'T ALWAYS STAND ASIDE AND ALLOW WOMEN TO PROTECT ME.
UNH ...!
GRIMP
STOP THIS, MICHEL ...
NO, I'M ASKING MICHAL!
TWITCH

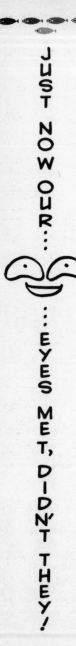

JUST NOW OUR...

...EYES MET, DIDN'T THEY!

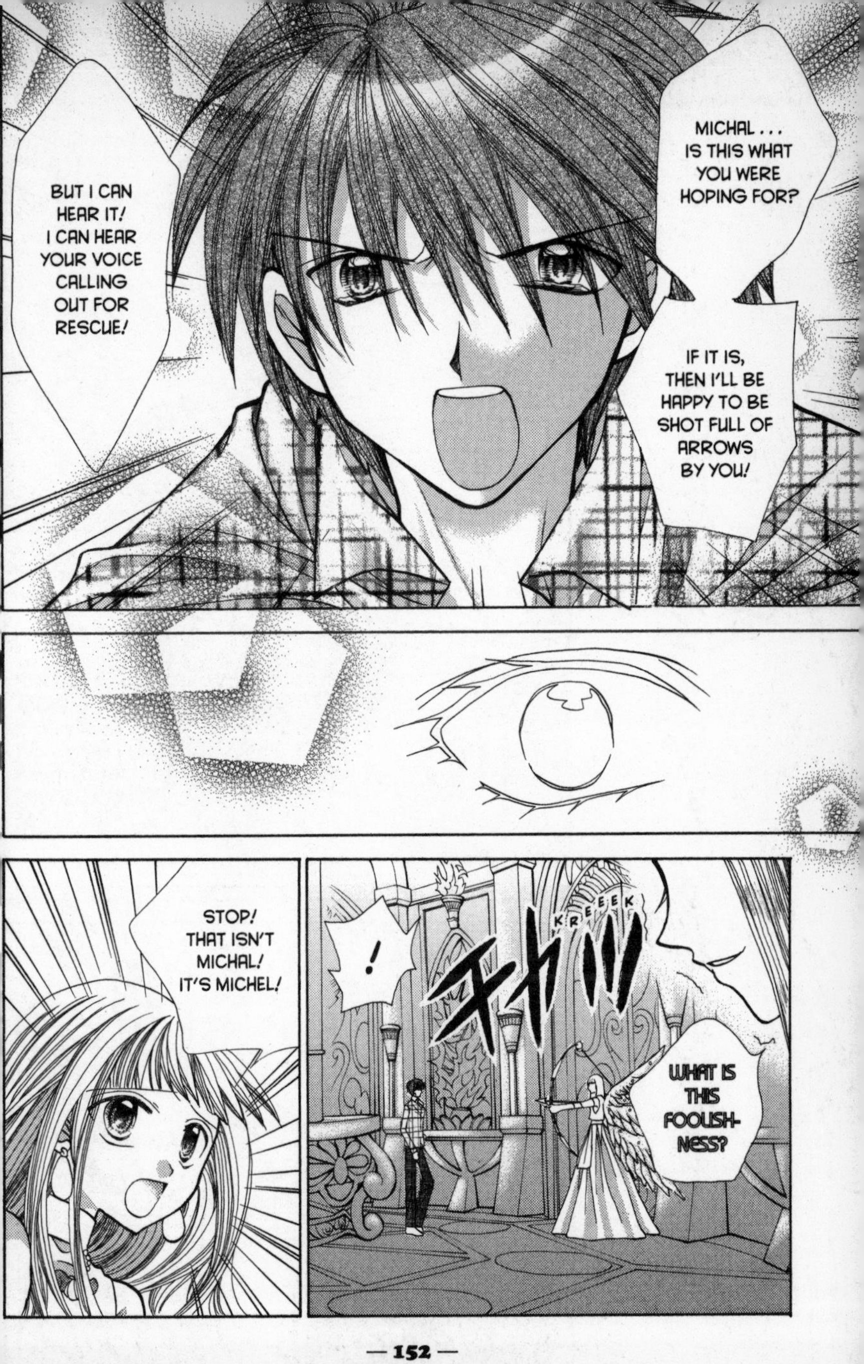
MICHAL . . . IS THIS WHAT YOU WERE HOPING FOR?
IF IT IS, THEN I'LL BE HAPPY TO BE SHOT FULL OF ARROWS BY YOU!
BUT I CAN HEAR IT! I CAN HEAR YOUR VOICE CALLING OUT FOR RESCUE!
!
KREEEK
WHAT IS THIS FOOLISH-NESS?
STOP! THAT ISN'T MICHAL! IT'S MICHEL!

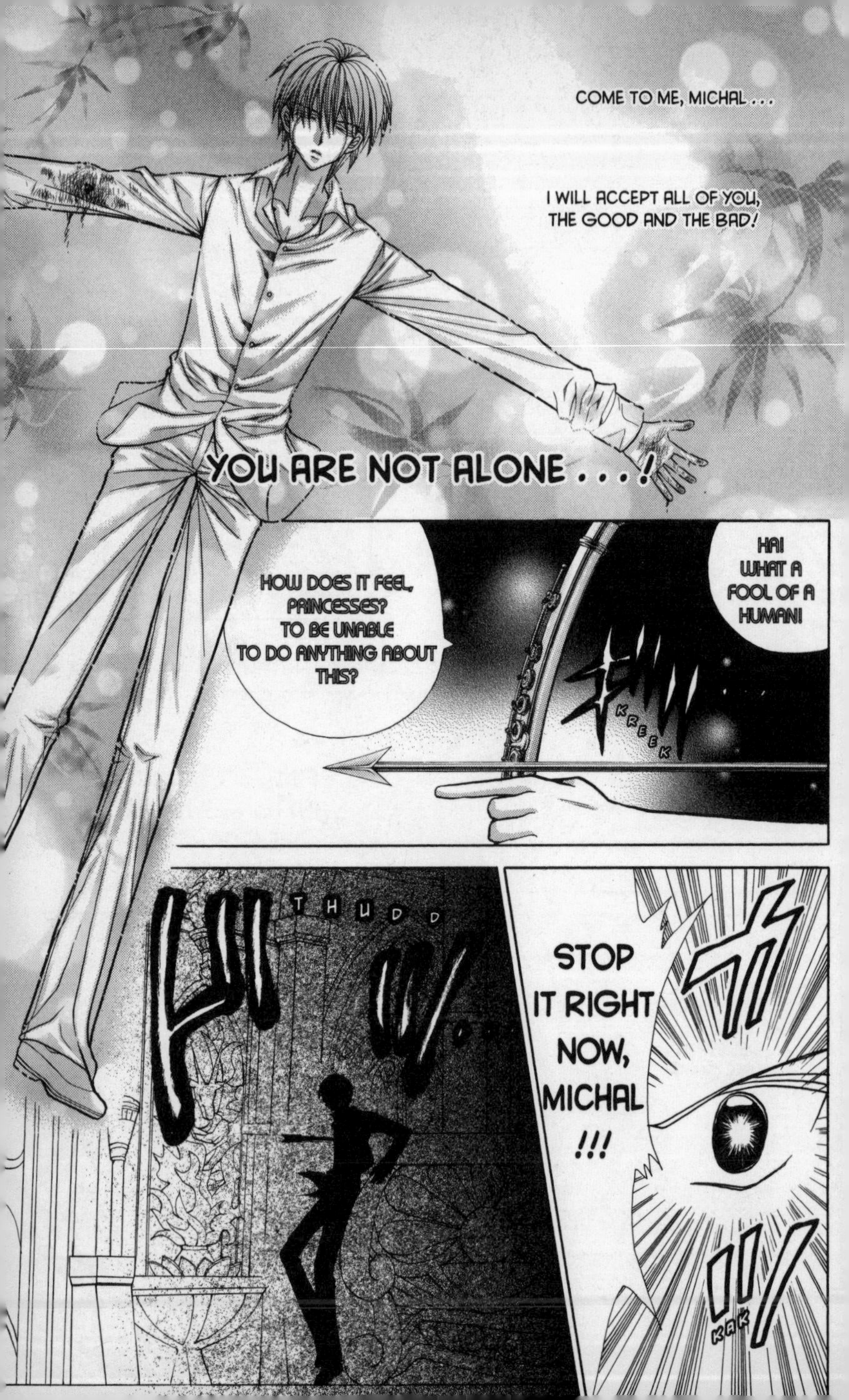
COME TO ME, MICHAL . . .
I WILL ACCEPT ALL OF YOU, THE GOOD AND THE BAD!
YOU ARE NOT ALONE . . . !
HA! WHAT A FOOL OF A HUMAN!
HOW DOES IT FEEL, PRINCESSES? TO BE UNABLE TO DO ANYTHING ABOUT THIS?
KREEK
STOP IT RIGHT NOW, MICHAL !!!
KAK
THUDD

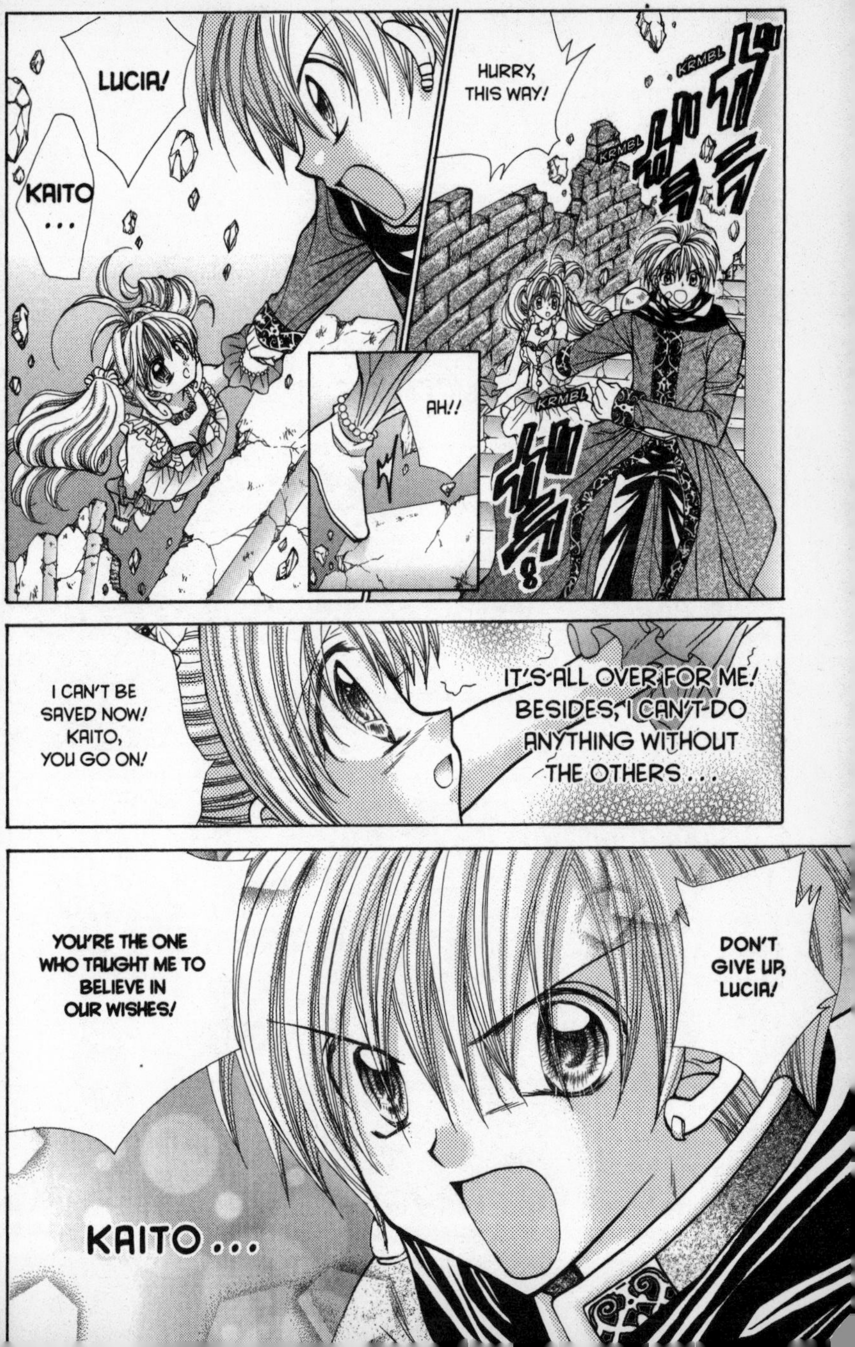
HURRY, THIS WAY!
KRMBL
KRMBL
KRMBL
AH!!
LUCIA!
KAITO . . .
IT'S ALL OVER FOR ME! BESIDES, I CAN'T DO ANYTHING WITHOUT THE OTHERS . . .
I CAN'T BE SAVED NOW! KAITO, YOU GO ON!
DON'T GIVE UP, LUCIA!
YOU'RE THE ONE WHO TAUGHT ME TO BELIEVE IN OUR WISHES!
KAITO . . .

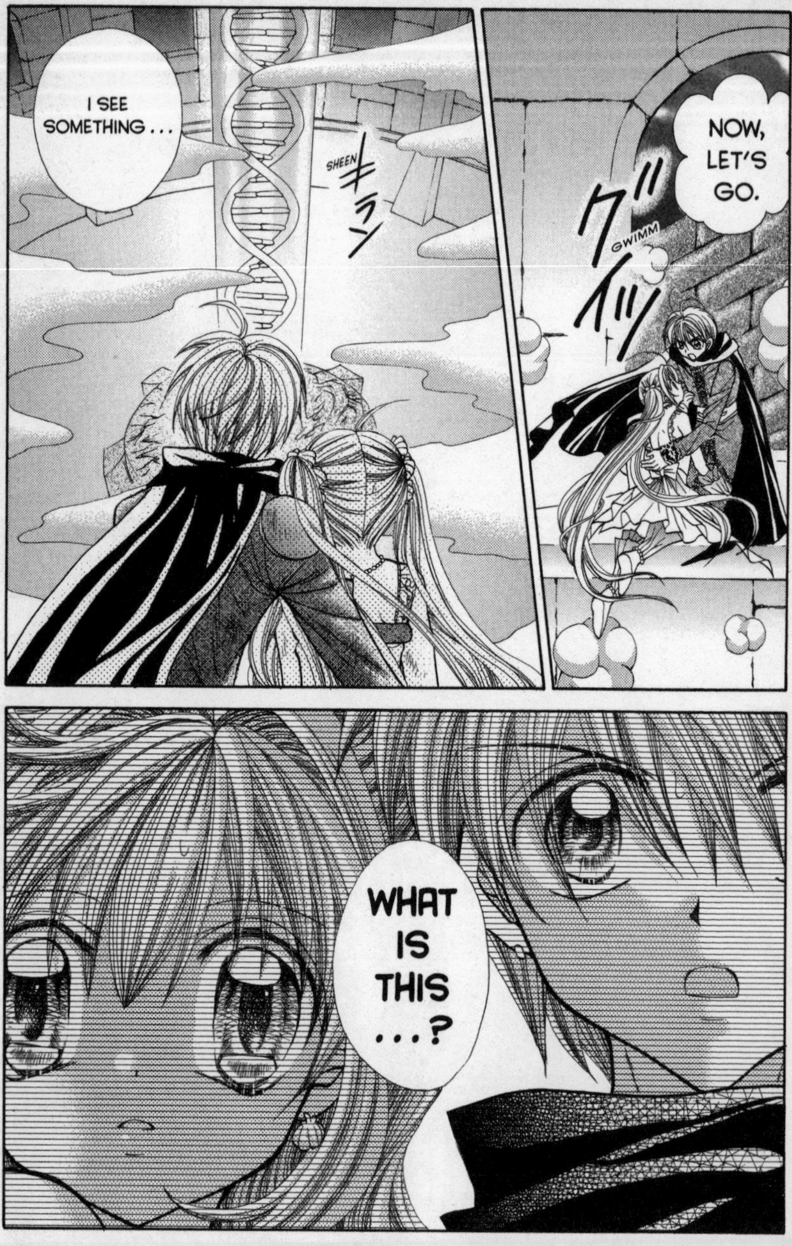
NOW, LET'S GO.
グイッ
GWIMM
I SEE SOMETHING . . .
キラン
SHEEN
WHAT IS THIS . . . ?

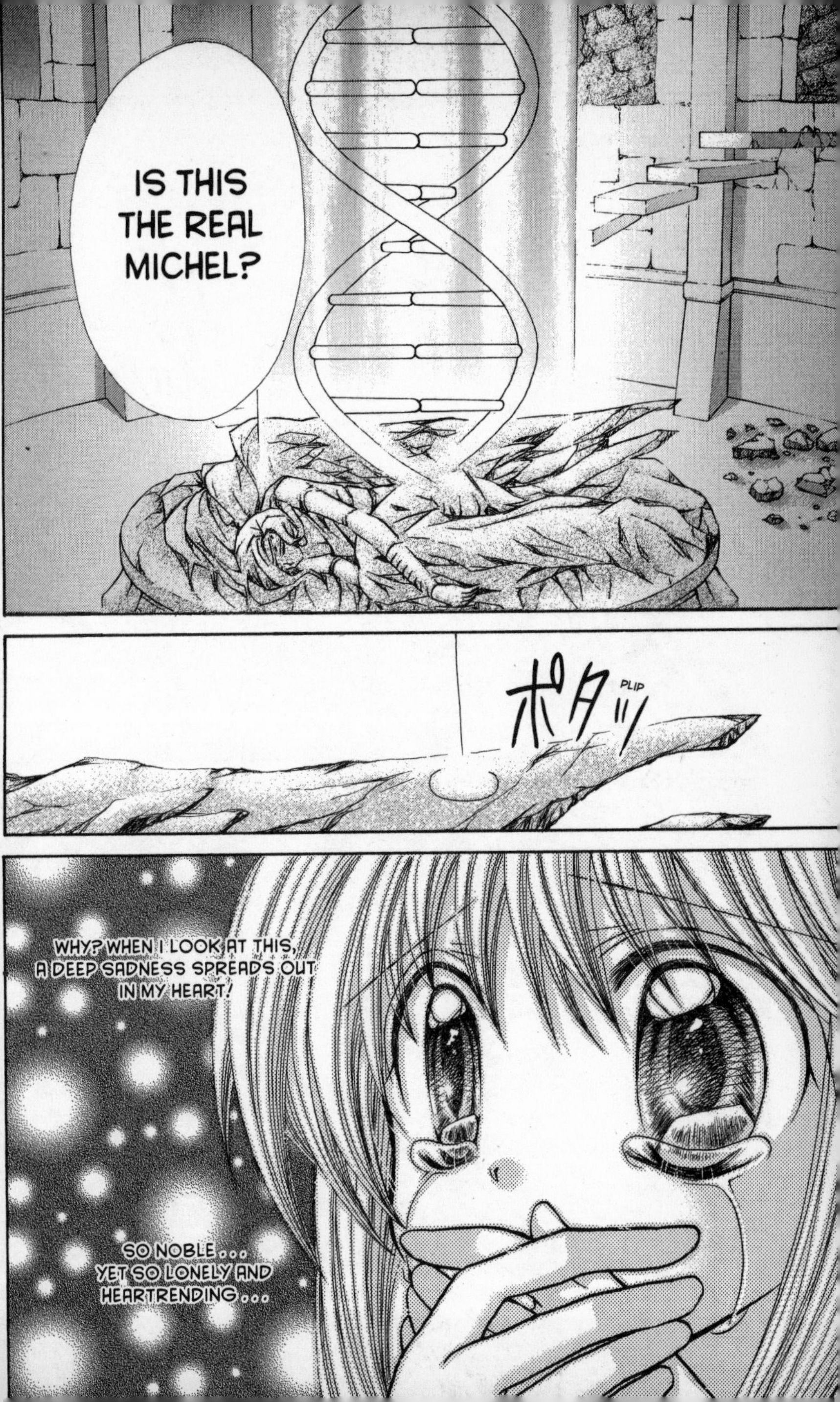
IS THIS THE REAL MICHEL?
ポタッ
PLIP
WHY? WHEN I LOOK AT THIS, A DEEP SADNESS SPREADS OUT IN MY HEART!
SO NOBLE . . . YET SO LONELY AND HEARTRENDING . . .

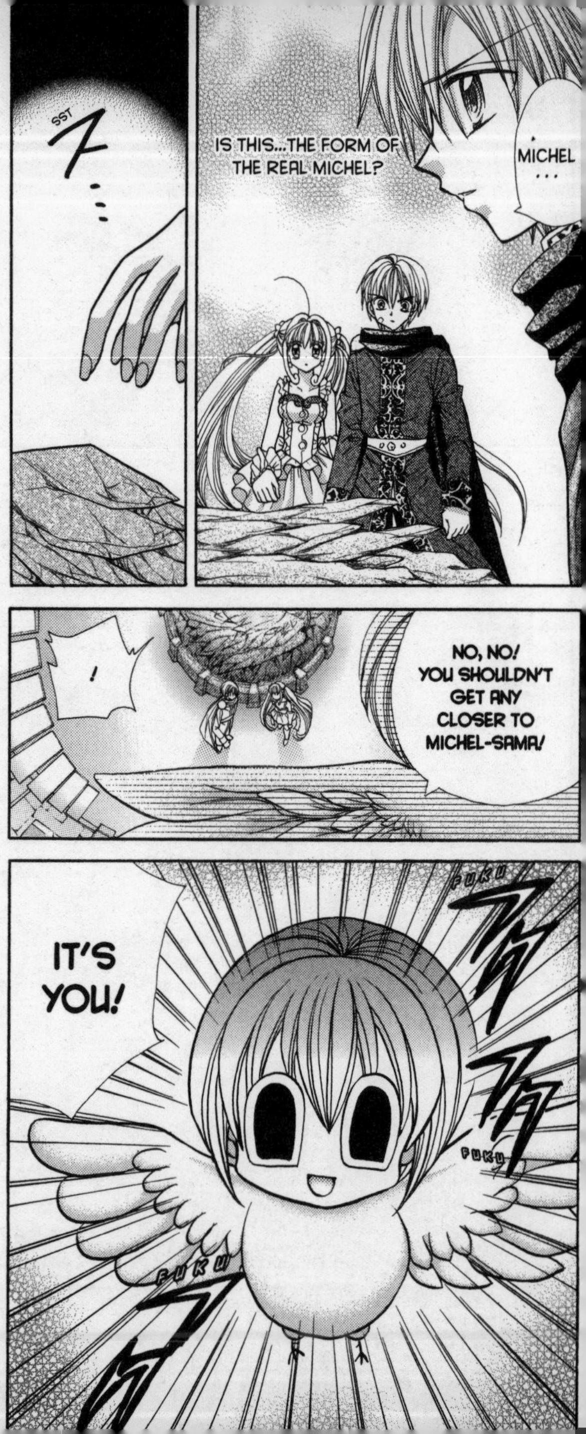
MICHEL ...
IS THIS...THE FORM OF THE REAL MICHEL?
SST
NO, NO! YOU SHOULDN'T GET ANY CLOSER TO MICHEL-SAMA!
!
FUKU
IT'S YOU!
FUKU
FUKU

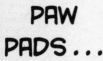

PAW PADS . . .

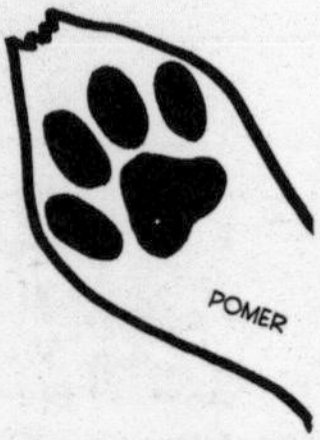
POMER

. . . ARE MEATBALLS! POM!

IN JAPANESE, THE WORD FOR PAW PADS ARE WRITTEN WITH THE KANJI FOR MEAT AND BALLS.

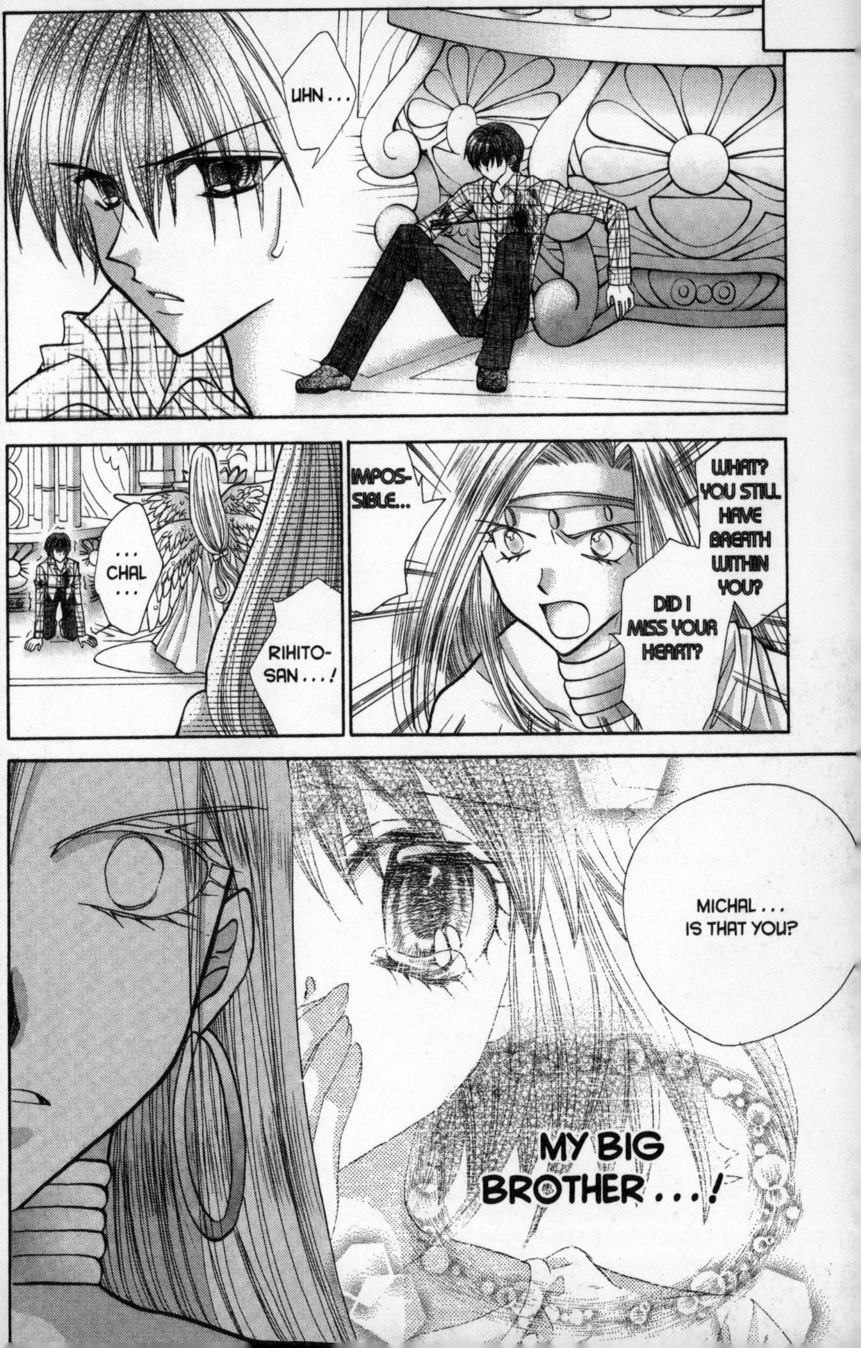
UHN . . .
WHAT? YOU STILL HAVE BREATH WITHIN YOU?
IMPOS-SIBLE...
DID I MISS YOUR HEART?
. . . CHAL . . .
RIHITO-SAN . . . !
MICHAL . . . IS THAT YOU?
MY BIG BROTHER . . . !

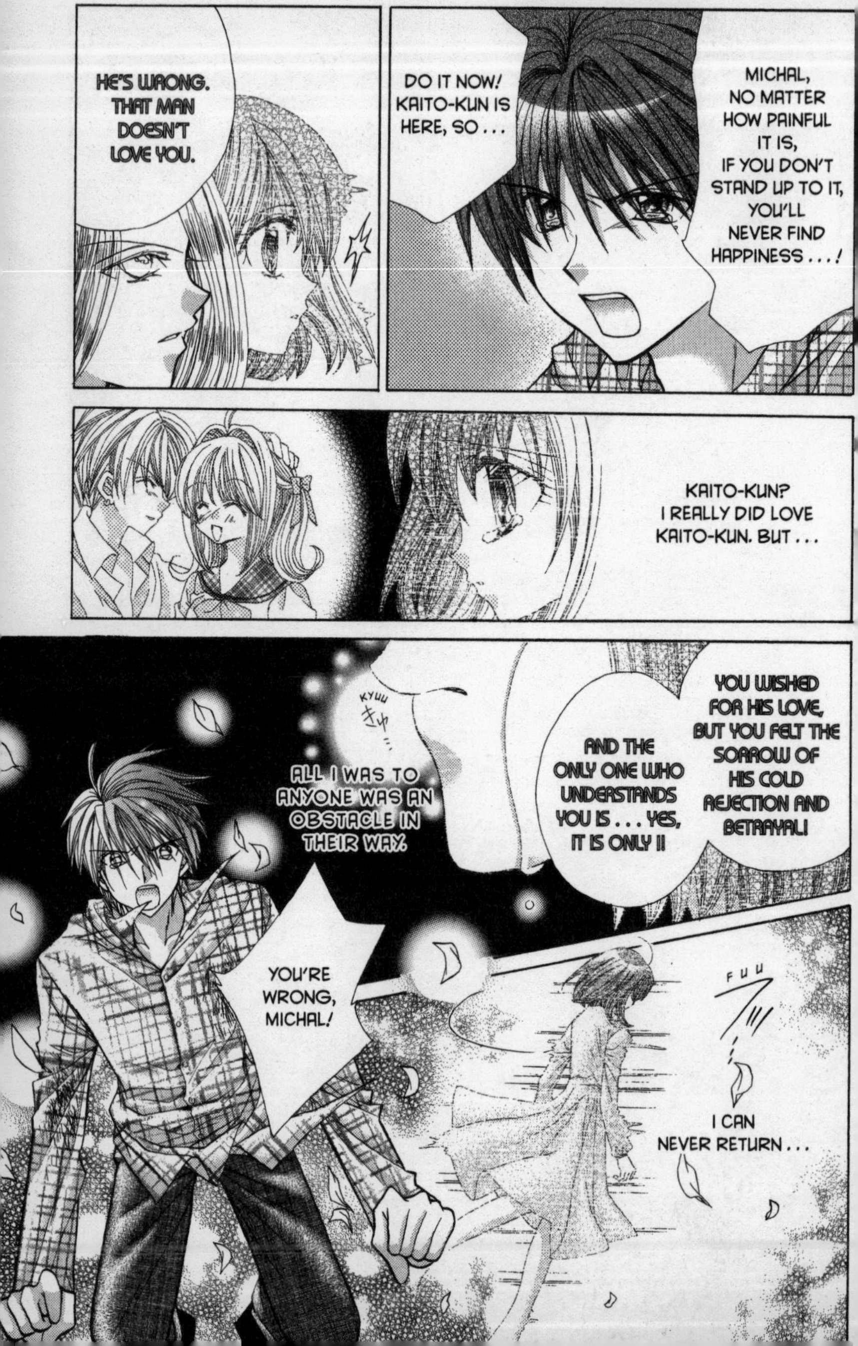
MICHAL, NO MATTER HOW PAINFUL IT IS, IF YOU DON'T STAND UP TO IT, YOU'LL NEVER FIND HAPPINESS . . . !
DO IT NOW! KAITO-KUN IS HERE, SO . . .
HE'S WRONG. THAT MAN DOESN'T LOVE YOU.
KAITO-KUN? I REALLY DID LOVE KAITO-KUN. BUT . . .
YOU WISHED FOR HIS LOVE, BUT YOU FELT THE SORROW OF HIS COLD REJECTION AND BETRAYAL!
AND THE ONLY ONE WHO UNDERSTANDS YOU IS . . . YES, IT IS ONLY I!
KYUU
ALL I WAS TO ANYONE WAS AN OBSTACLE IN THEIR WAY.
FUU
I CAN NEVER RETURN . . .
YOU'RE WRONG, MICHAL!

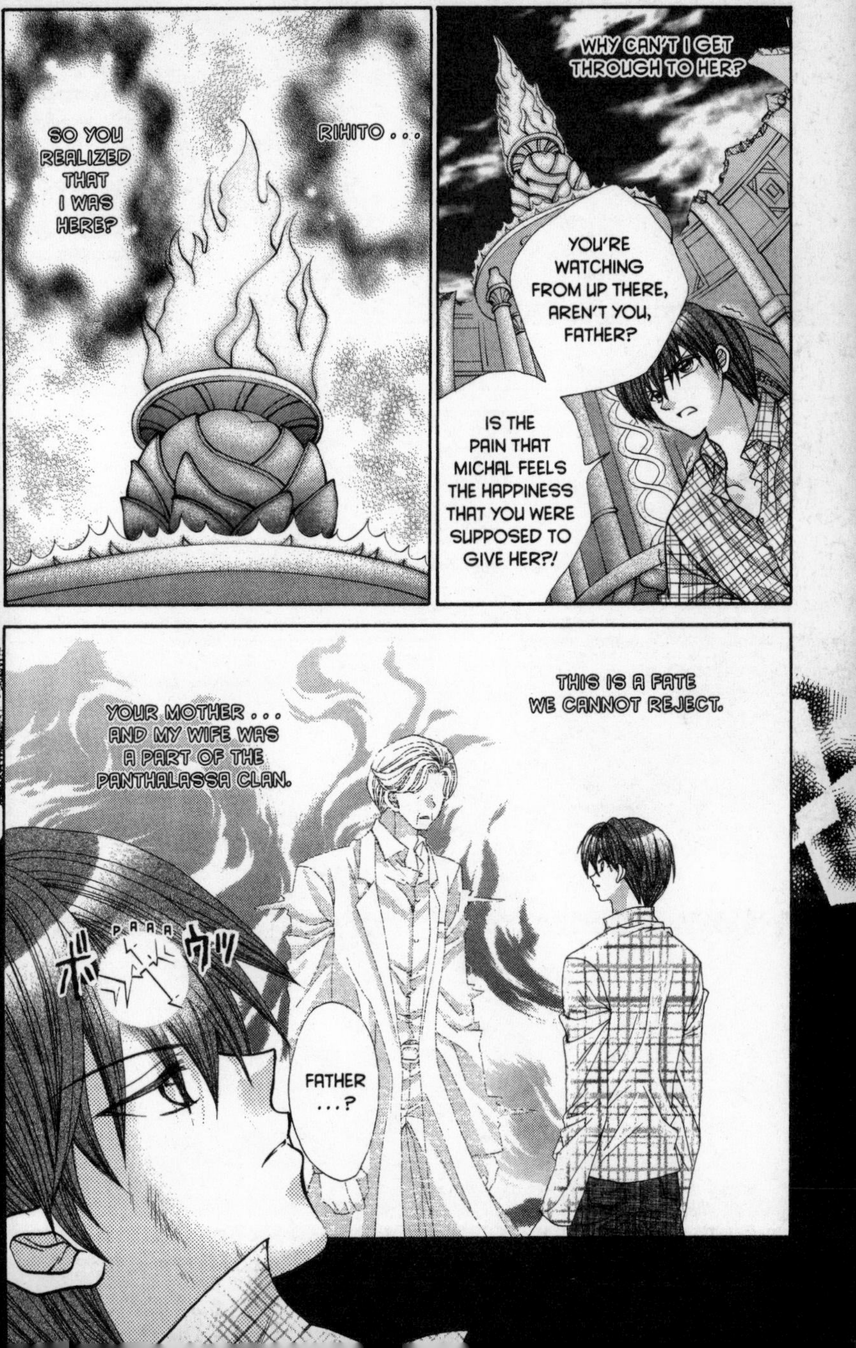
WHY CAN'T I GET THROUGH TO HER?
YOU'RE WATCHING FROM UP THERE, AREN'T YOU, FATHER?
IS THE PAIN THAT MICHAL FEELS THE HAPPINESS THAT YOU WERE SUPPOSED TO GIVE HER?!
RIHITO . . .
SO YOU REALIZED THAT I WAS HERE?
THIS IS A FATE WE CANNOT REJECT.
YOUR MOTHER . . . AND MY WIFE WAS A PART OF THE PANTHALASSA CLAN.
PAAAA
FATHER . . .?

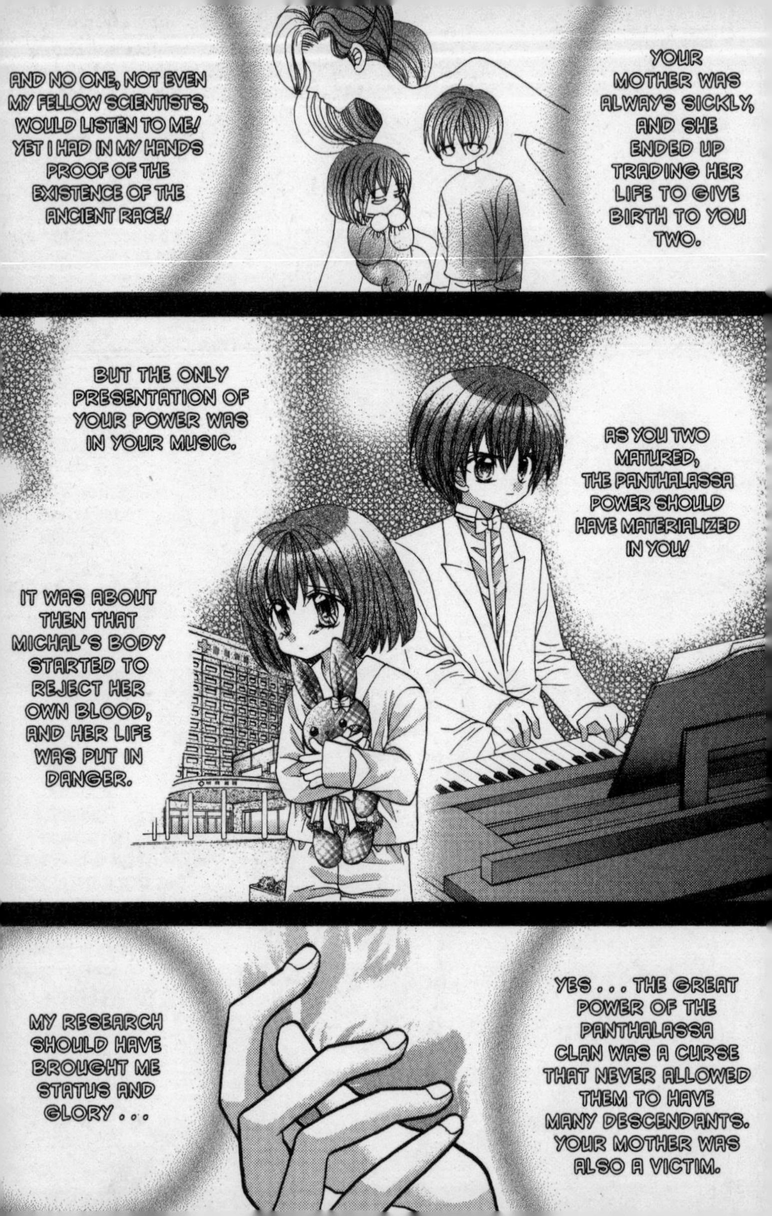
YOUR MOTHER WAS ALWAYS SICKLY, AND SHE ENDED UP TRADING HER LIFE TO GIVE BIRTH TO YOU TWO.
AND NO ONE, NOT EVEN MY FELLOW SCIENTISTS, WOULD LISTEN TO ME! YET I HAD IN MY HANDS PROOF OF THE EXISTENCE OF THE ANCIENT RACE!
AS YOU TWO MATURED, THE PANTHALASSA POWER SHOULD HAVE MATERIALIZED IN YOU!
BUT THE ONLY PRESENTATION OF YOUR POWER WAS IN YOUR MUSIC.
IT WAS ABOUT THEN THAT MICHAL'S BODY STARTED TO REJECT HER OWN BLOOD, AND HER LIFE WAS PUT IN DANGER.
YES . . . THE GREAT POWER OF THE PANTHALASSA CLAN WAS A CURSE THAT NEVER ALLOWED THEM TO HAVE MANY DESCENDANTS. YOUR MOTHER WAS ALSO A VICTIM.
MY RESEARCH SHOULD HAVE BROUGHT ME STATUS AND GLORY . . .

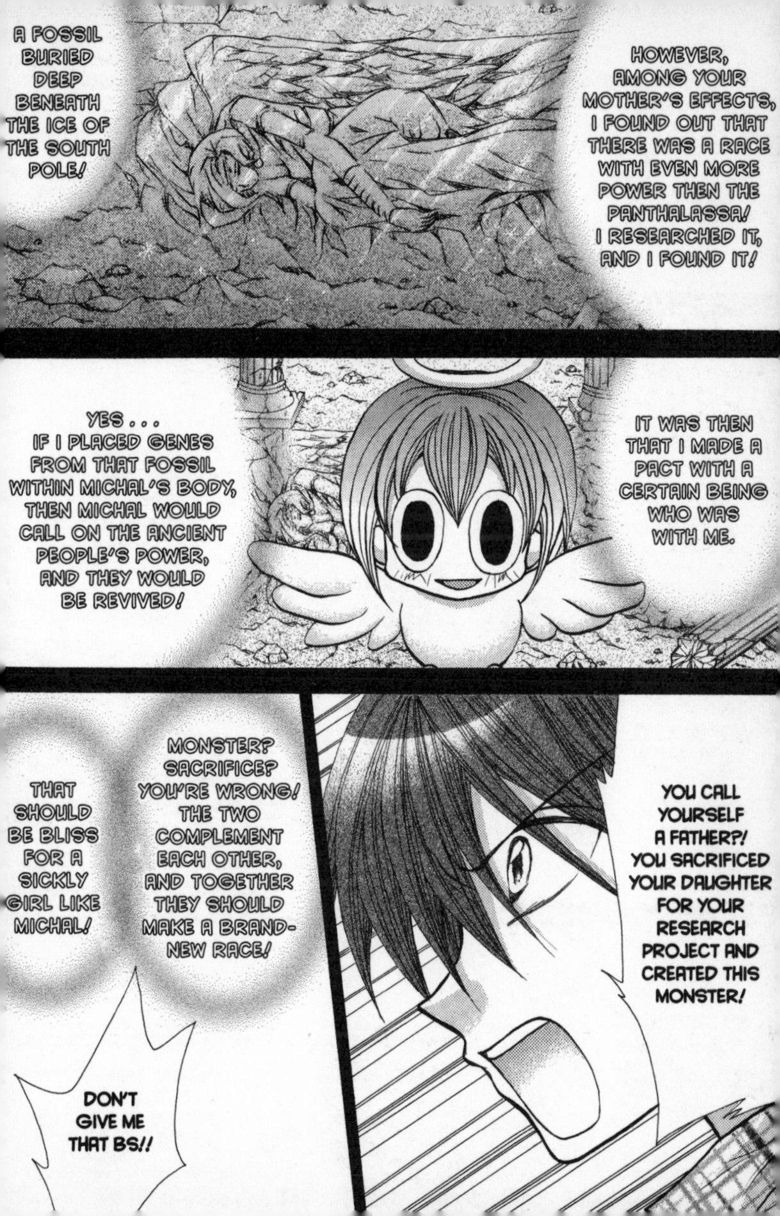
HOWEVER, AMONG YOUR MOTHER'S EFFECTS, I FOUND OUT THAT THERE WAS A RACE WITH EVEN MORE POWER THEN THE PANTHALASSA! I RESEARCHED IT, AND I FOUND IT!
A FOSSIL BURIED DEEP BENEATH THE ICE OF THE SOUTH POLE!
IT WAS THEN THAT I MADE A PACT WITH A CERTAIN BEING WHO WAS WITH ME.
YES . . . IF I PLACED GENES FROM THAT FOSSIL WITHIN MICHAL'S BODY, THEN MICHAL WOULD CALL ON THE ANCIENT PEOPLE'S POWER, AND THEY WOULD BE REVIVED!
YOU CALL YOURSELF A FATHER?! YOU SACRIFICED YOUR DAUGHTER FOR YOUR RESEARCH PROJECT AND CREATED THIS MONSTER!
MONSTER? SACRIFICE? YOU'RE WRONG! THE TWO COMPLEMENT EACH OTHER, AND TOGETHER THEY SHOULD MAKE A BRAND-NEW RACE!
THAT SHOULD BE BLISS FOR A SICKLY GIRL LIKE MICHAL!
DON'T GIVE ME THAT BS!!

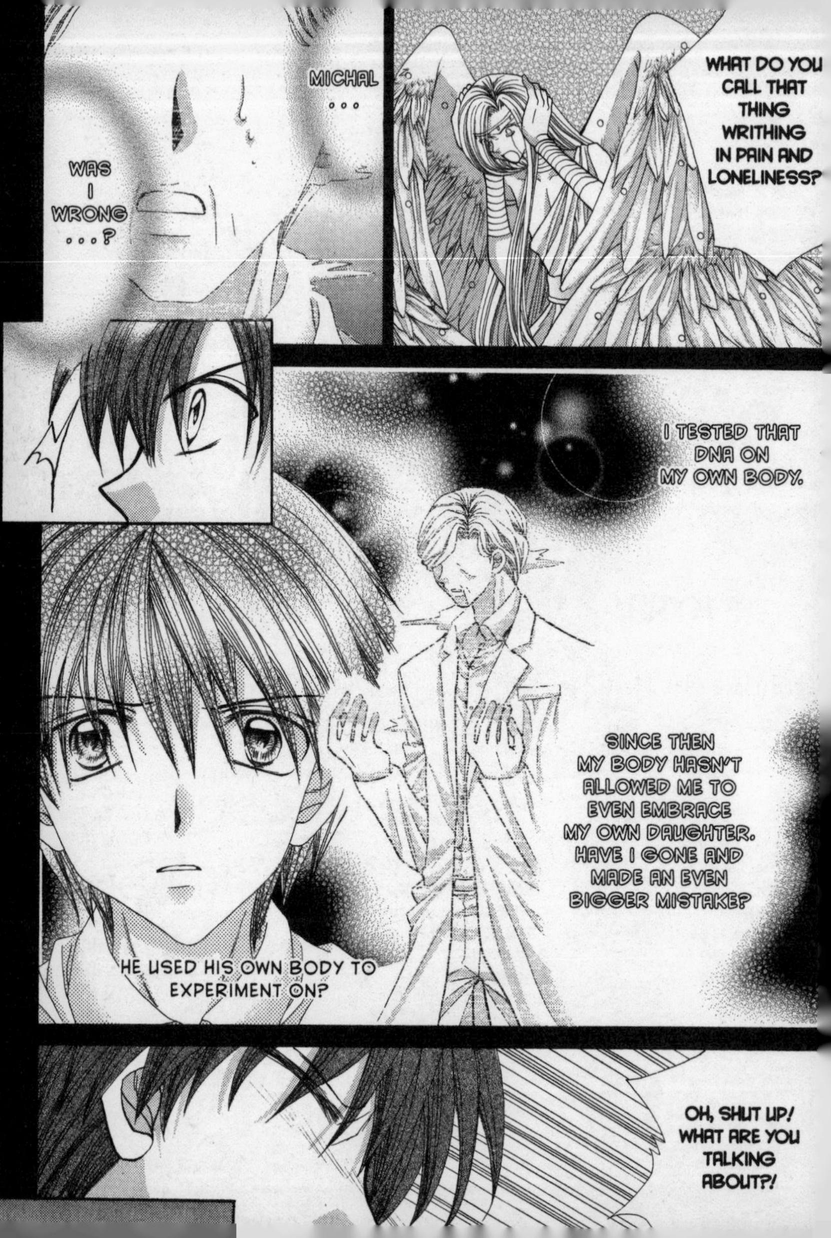
WHAT DO YOU CALL THAT THING WRITHING IN PAIN AND LONELINESS?
MICHAL . . .
WAS I WRONG . . .?
I TESTED THAT DNA ON MY OWN BODY.
SINCE THEN MY BODY HASN'T ALLOWED ME TO EVEN EMBRACE MY OWN DAUGHTER. HAVE I GONE AND MADE AN EVEN BIGGER MISTAKE?
HE USED HIS OWN BODY TO EXPERIMENT ON?
OH, SHUT UP! WHAT ARE YOU TALKING ABOUT?!

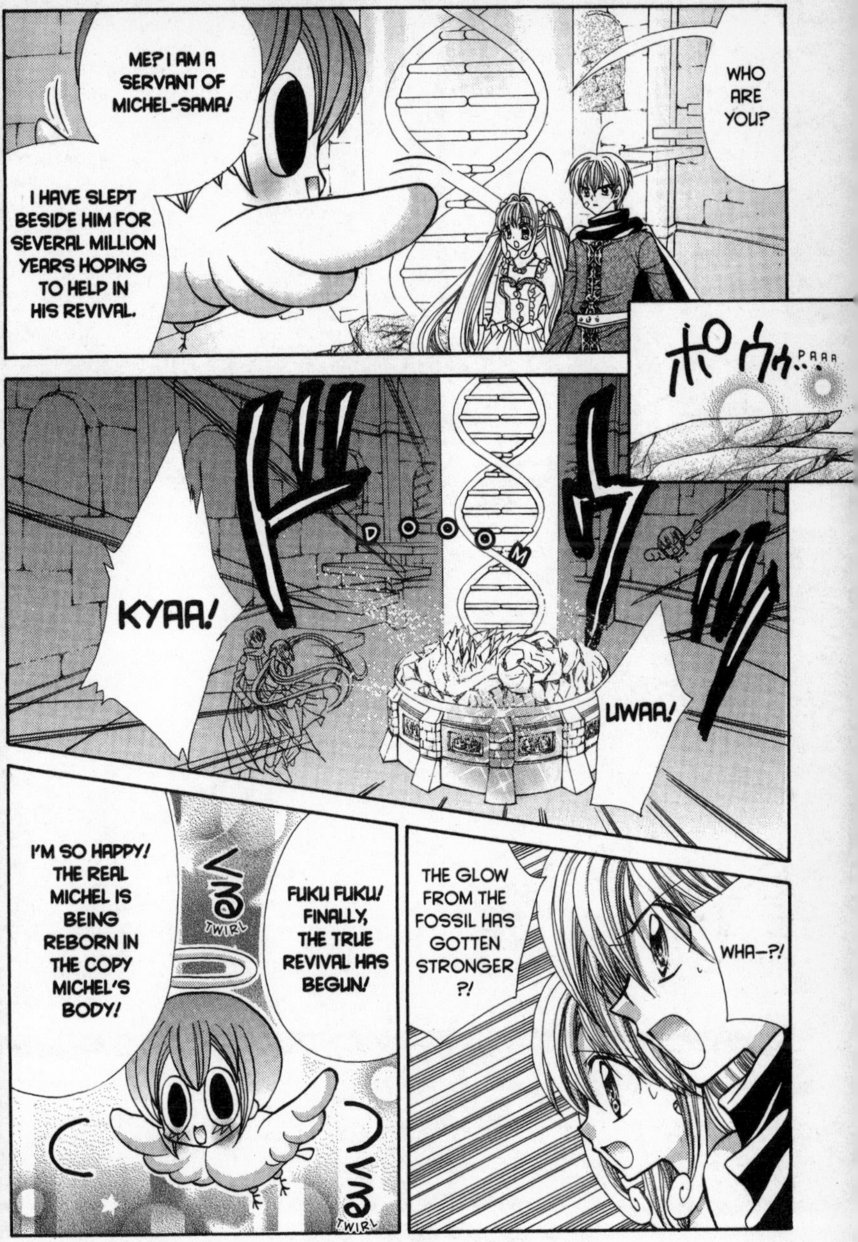
WHO ARE YOU?
ME? I AM A SERVANT OF MICHEL-SAMA!
I HAVE SLEPT BESIDE HIM FOR SEVERAL MILLION YEARS HOPING TO HELP IN HIS REVIVAL.
PAAA
DOOOM
UWAA!
KYAA!
WHA-?!
THE GLOW FROM THE FOSSIL HAS GOTTEN STRONGER ?!
FUKU FUKU! FINALLY, THE TRUE REVIVAL HAS BEGUN!
I'M SO HAPPY! THE REAL MICHEL IS BEING REBORN IN THE COPY MICHEL'S BODY!
TWIRL
TWIRL

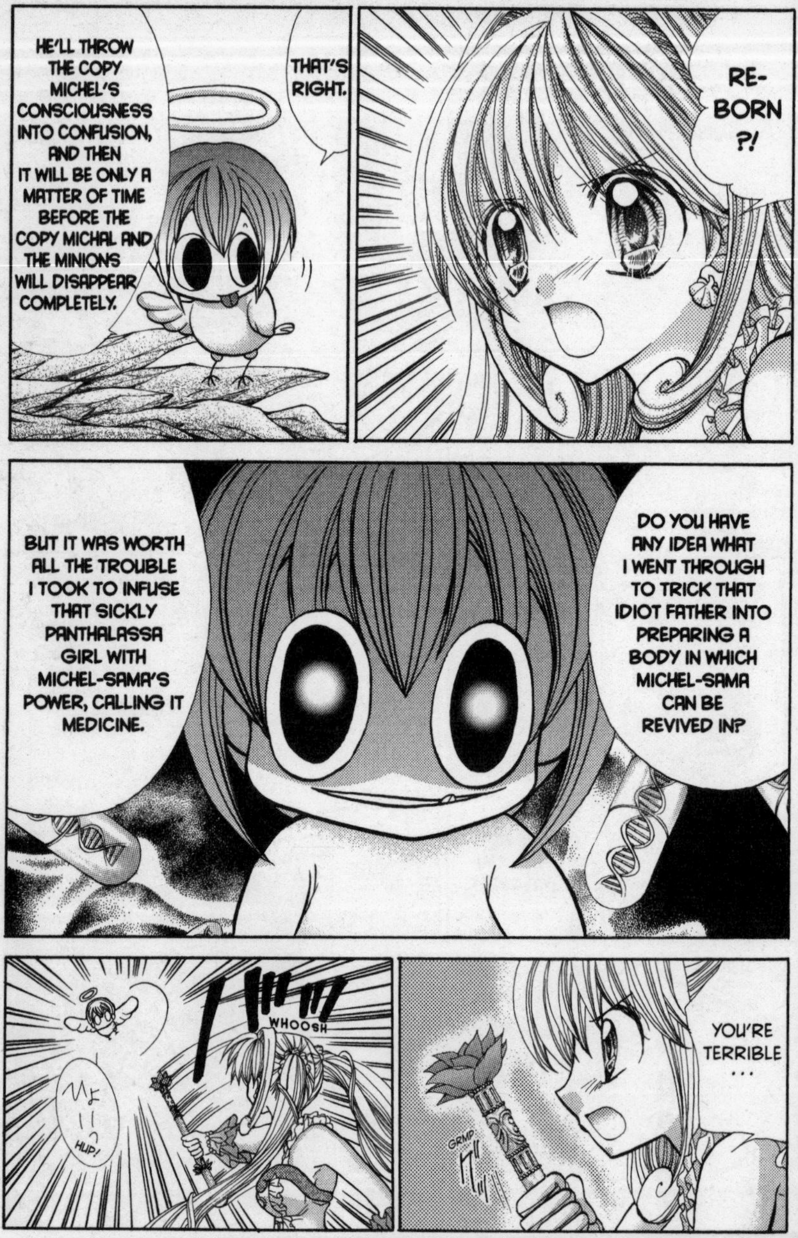
RE-BORN?!
THAT'S RIGHT.
HE'LL THROW THE COPY MICHEL'S CONSCIOUSNESS INTO CONFUSION, AND THEN IT WILL BE ONLY A MATTER OF TIME BEFORE THE COPY MICHAL AND THE MINIONS WILL DISAPPEAR COMPLETELY.
DO YOU HAVE ANY IDEA WHAT I WENT THROUGH TO TRICK THAT IDIOT FATHER INTO PREPARING A BODY IN WHICH MICHEL-SAMA CAN BE REVIVED IN?
BUT IT WAS WORTH ALL THE TROUBLE I TOOK TO INFUSE THAT SICKLY PANTHALASSA GIRL WITH MICHEL-SAMA'S POWER, CALLING IT MEDICINE.
YOU'RE TERRIBLE ...
GRMP
WHOOSH
ひょいっ
HUP!

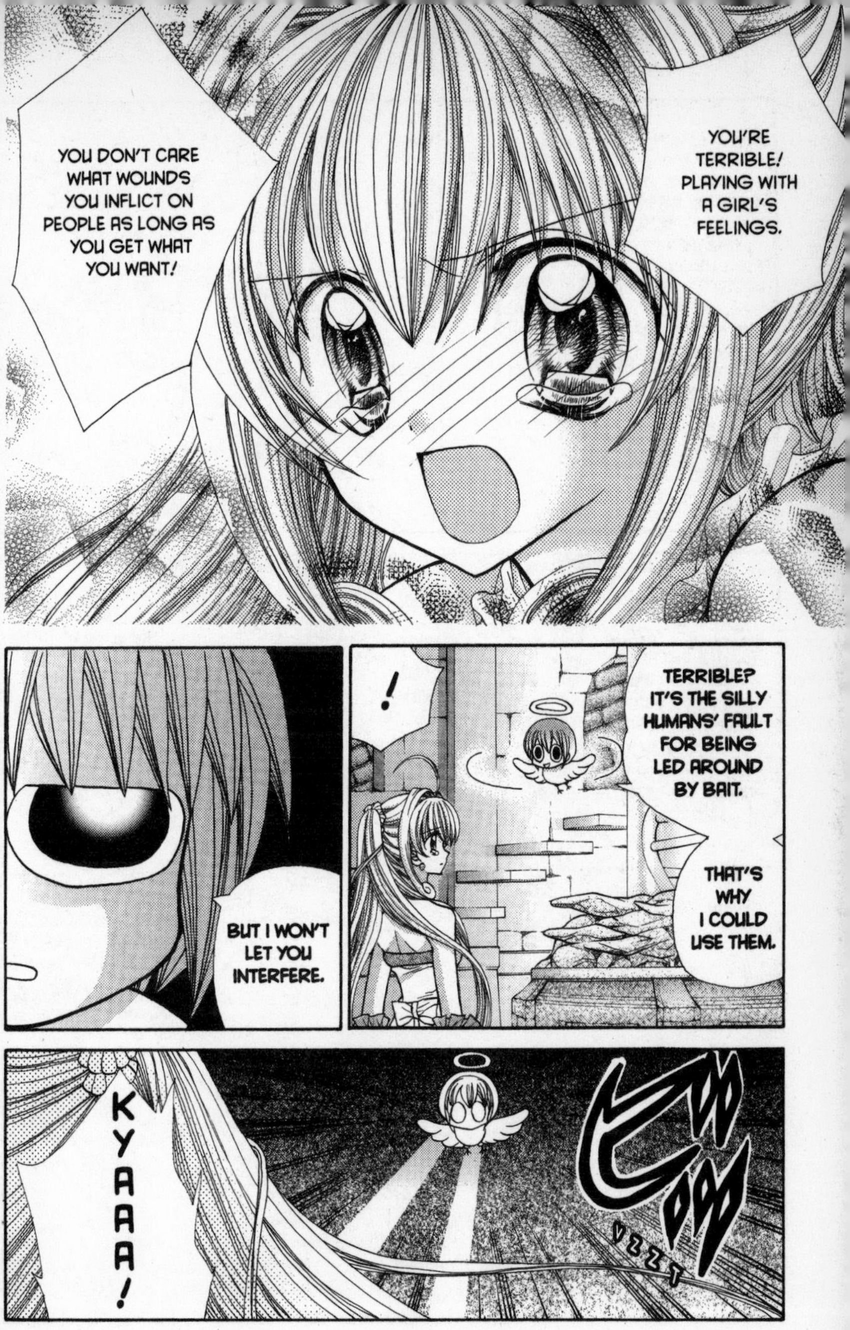

YOU'RE TERRIBLE! PLAYING WITH A GIRL'S FEELINGS.
YOU DON'T CARE WHAT WOUNDS YOU INFLICT ON PEOPLE AS LONG AS YOU GET WHAT YOU WANT!
!
TERRIBLE? IT'S THE SILLY HUMANS' FAULT FOR BEING LED AROUND BY BAIT.
THAT'S WHY I COULD USE THEM.
BUT I WON'T LET YOU INTERFERE.
VZZT
KYAAA!

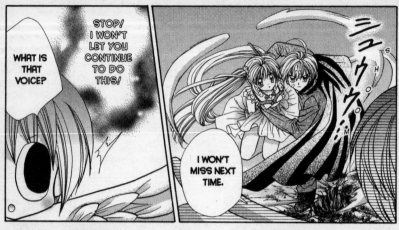

シュウウウ…
SHOOM
I WON'T MISS NEXT TIME.
STOP! I WON'T LET YOU CONTINUE TO DO THIS!
WHAT IS THAT VOICE?
THE FIRE FROM THE TOWER TOP IS COMING DOWN?!
I WON'T ALLOW YOU TO CAUSE PAIN TO MICHEL . . . TO MY MICHEL!
FUKU FUKU! YOU CAN'T DO ANYTHING?
YOU THINK NOT? YOU TRICKED ME INTO TAKING MICHEL'S DNA AND CHANGED ME INTO THIS FORM TO PROTECT THE FOSSIL IN THIS TOWER. BUT THAT WAS YOUR MISCALCULATION.

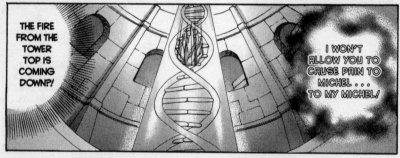

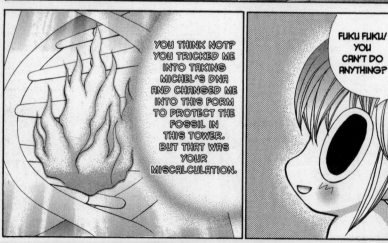

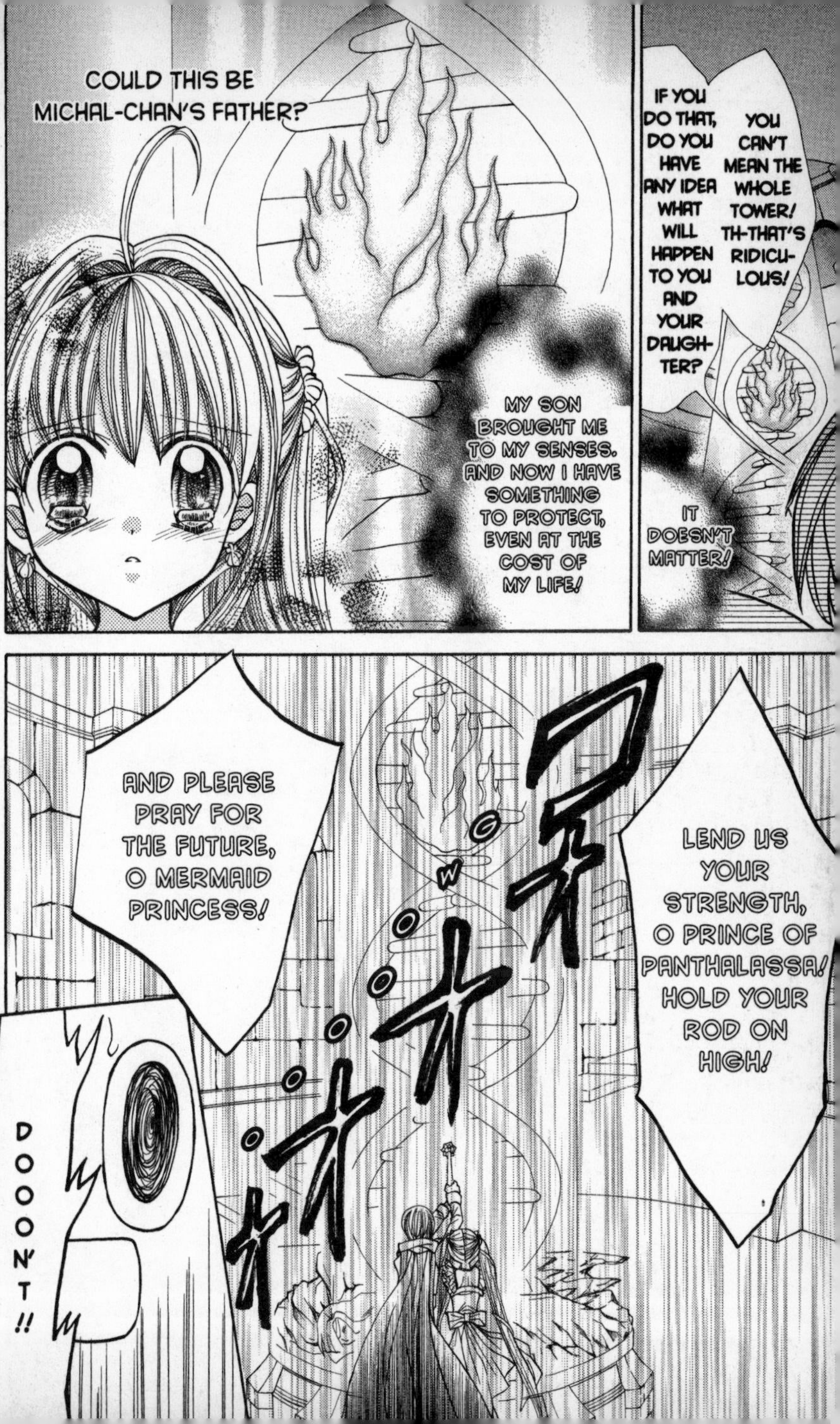
YOU CAN'T MEAN THE WHOLE TOWER! TH-THAT'S RIDICULOUS!
IF YOU DO THAT, DO YOU HAVE ANY IDEA WHAT WILL HAPPEN TO YOU AND YOUR DAUGHTER?
IT DOESN'T MATTER!
MY SON BROUGHT ME TO MY SENSES. AND NOW I HAVE SOMETHING TO PROTECT, EVEN AT THE COST OF MY LIFE!
COULD THIS BE MICHAL-CHAN'S FATHER?
LEND US YOUR STRENGTH, O PRINCE OF PANTHALASSA! HOLD YOUR ROD ON HIGH!
AND PLEASE PRAY FOR THE FUTURE, O MERMAID PRINCESS!
GOWOOOO
DOOOON'T!!

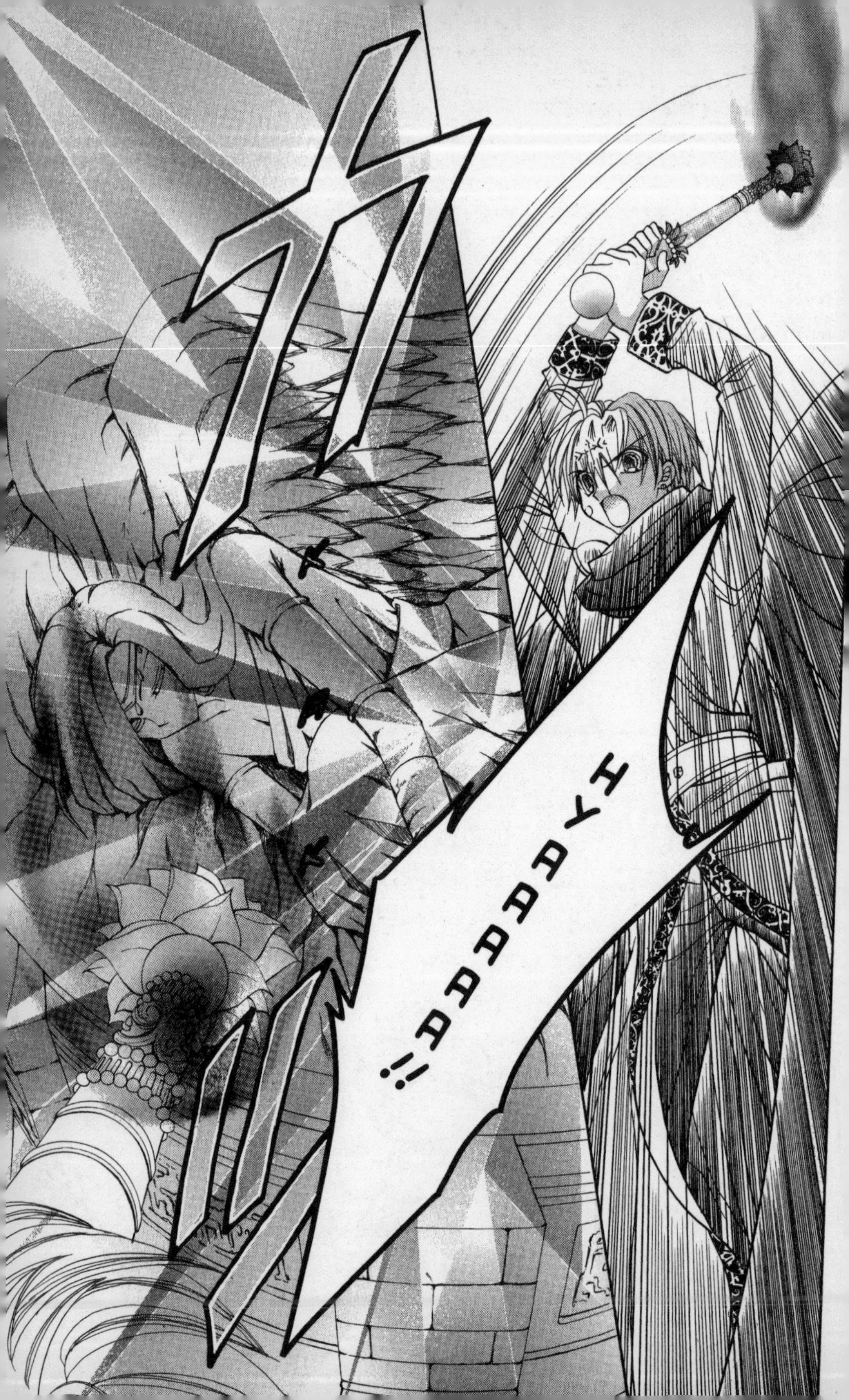
HYAAAAA!!

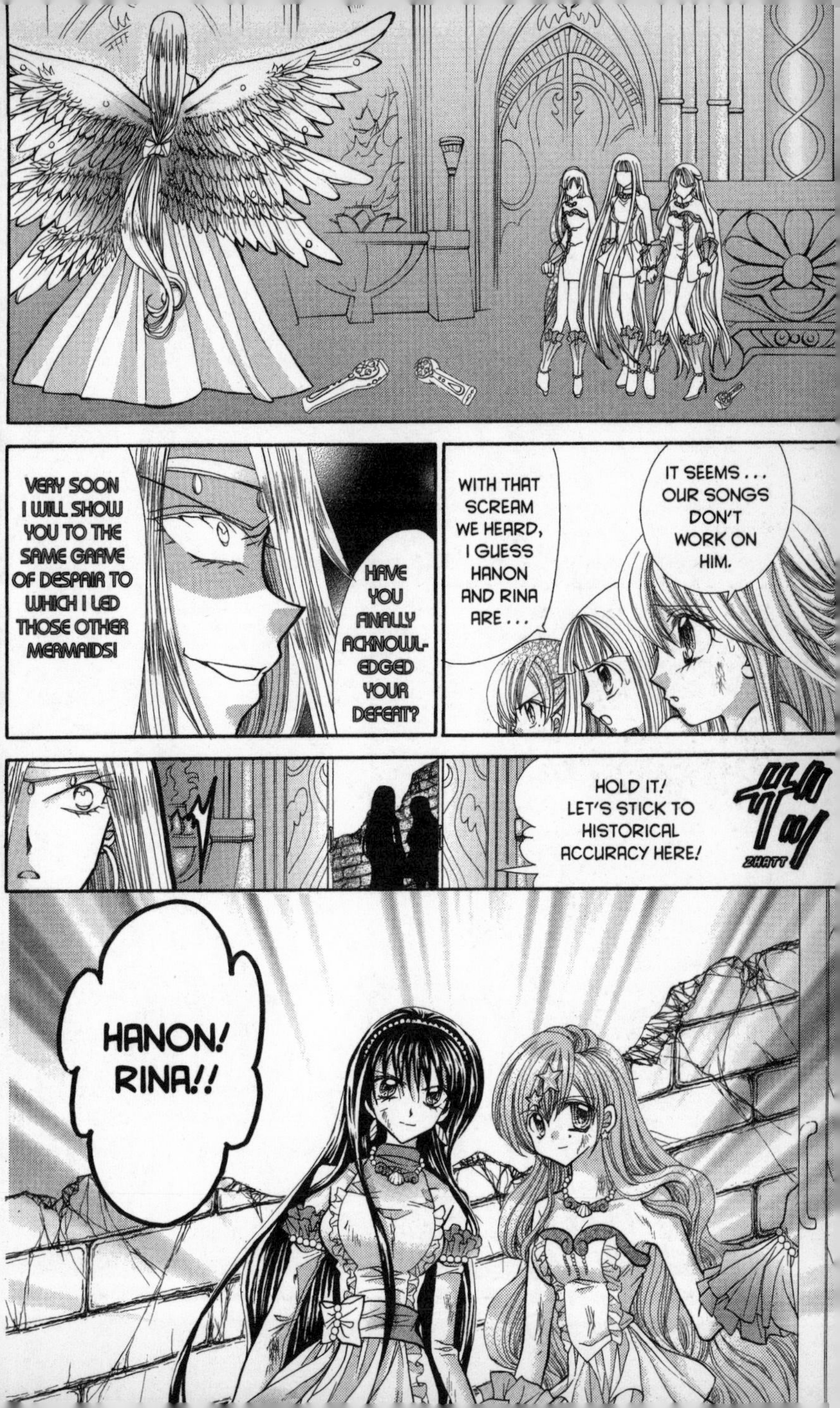
IT SEEMS . . . OUR SONGS DON'T WORK ON HIM.
WITH THAT SCREAM WE HEARD, I GUESS HANON AND RINA ARE . . .
HAVE YOU FINALLY ACKNOWL-EDGED YOUR DEFEAT?
VERY SOON I WILL SHOW YOU TO THE SAME GRAVE OF DESPAIR TO WHICH I LED THOSE OTHER MERMAIDS!
ZHATT
HOLD IT! LET'S STICK TO HISTORICAL ACCURACY HERE!
HANON! RINA!!

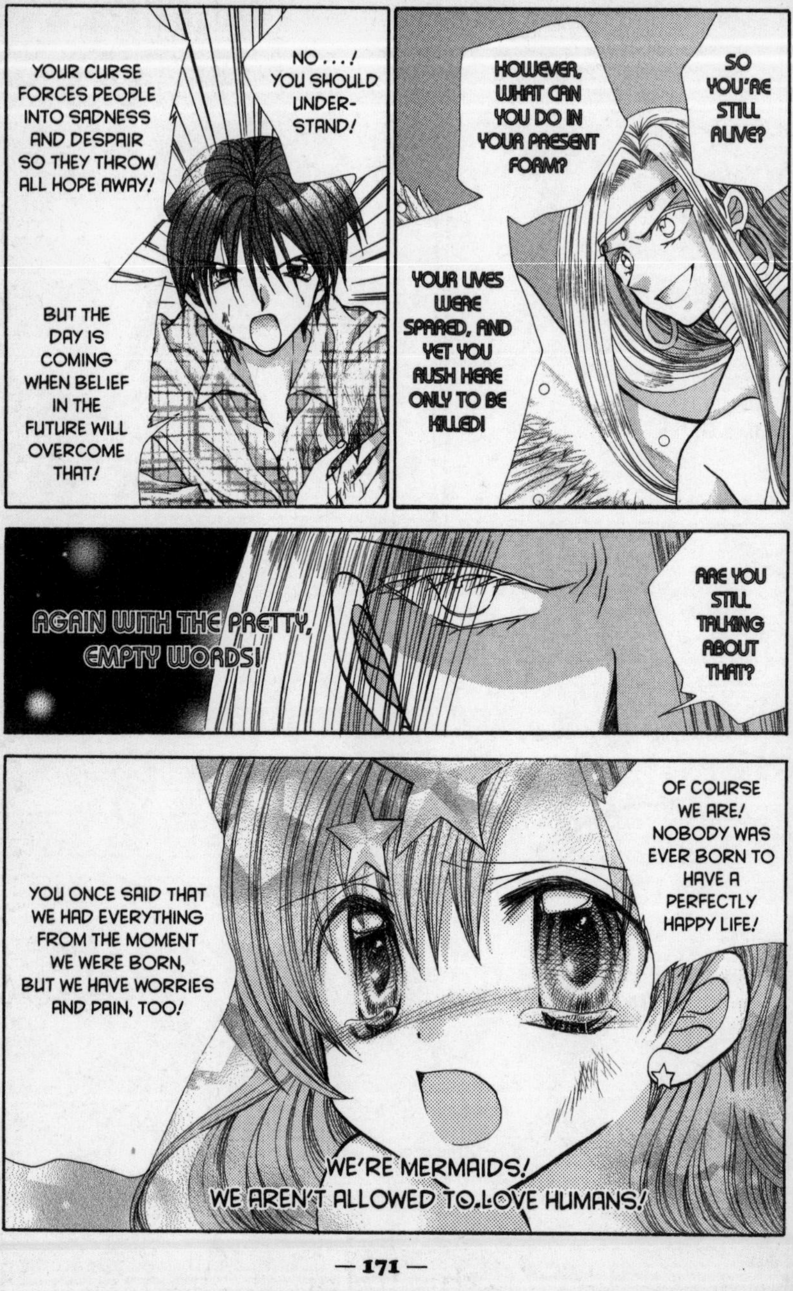
SO YOU'RE STILL ALIVE?
HOWEVER, WHAT CAN YOU DO IN YOUR PRESENT FORM?
YOUR LIVES WERE SPARED, AND YET YOU RUSH HERE ONLY TO BE KILLED!
NO . . . ! YOU SHOULD UNDER-STAND!
YOUR CURSE FORCES PEOPLE INTO SADNESS AND DESPAIR SO THEY THROW ALL HOPE AWAY!
BUT THE DAY IS COMING WHEN BELIEF IN THE FUTURE WILL OVERCOME THAT!
ARE YOU STILL TALKING ABOUT THAT?
AGAIN WITH THE PRETTY, EMPTY WORDS!
OF COURSE WE ARE! NOBODY WAS EVER BORN TO HAVE A PERFECTLY HAPPY LIFE!
YOU ONCE SAID THAT WE HAD EVERYTHING FROM THE MOMENT WE WERE BORN, BUT WE HAVE WORRIES AND PAIN, TOO!
WE'RE MERMAIDS! WE AREN'T ALLOWED TO LOVE HUMANS!

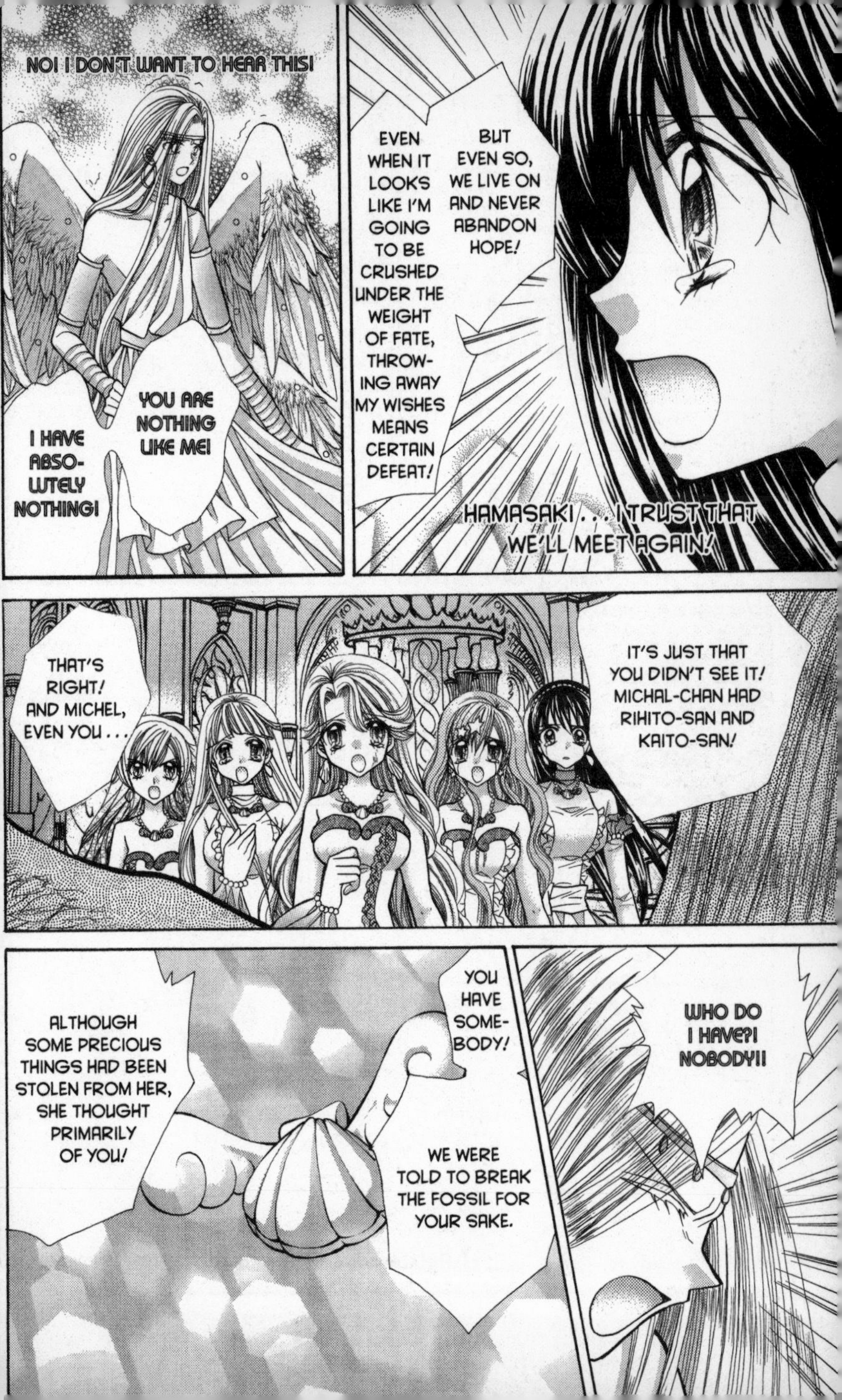
EVEN WHEN IT LOOKS LIKE I'M GOING TO BE CRUSHED UNDER THE WEIGHT OF FATE, THROWING AWAY MY WISHES MEANS CERTAIN DEFEAT!
BUT EVEN SO, WE LIVE ON AND NEVER ABANDON HOPE!
HAMASAKI . . . I TRUST THAT WE'LL MEET AGAIN!
NO! I DON'T WANT TO HEAR THIS!
YOU ARE NOTHING LIKE ME!
I HAVE ABSOLUTELY NOTHING!
THAT'S RIGHT! AND MICHEL, EVEN YOU . . .
IT'S JUST THAT YOU DIDN'T SEE IT! MICHAL-CHAN HAD RIHITO-SAN AND KAITO-SAN!
WHO DO I HAVE?! NOBODY!!
YOU HAVE SOMEBODY!
ALTHOUGH SOME PRECIOUS THINGS HAD BEEN STOLEN FROM HER, SHE THOUGHT PRIMARILY OF YOU!
WE WERE TOLD TO BREAK THE FOSSIL FOR YOUR SAKE.

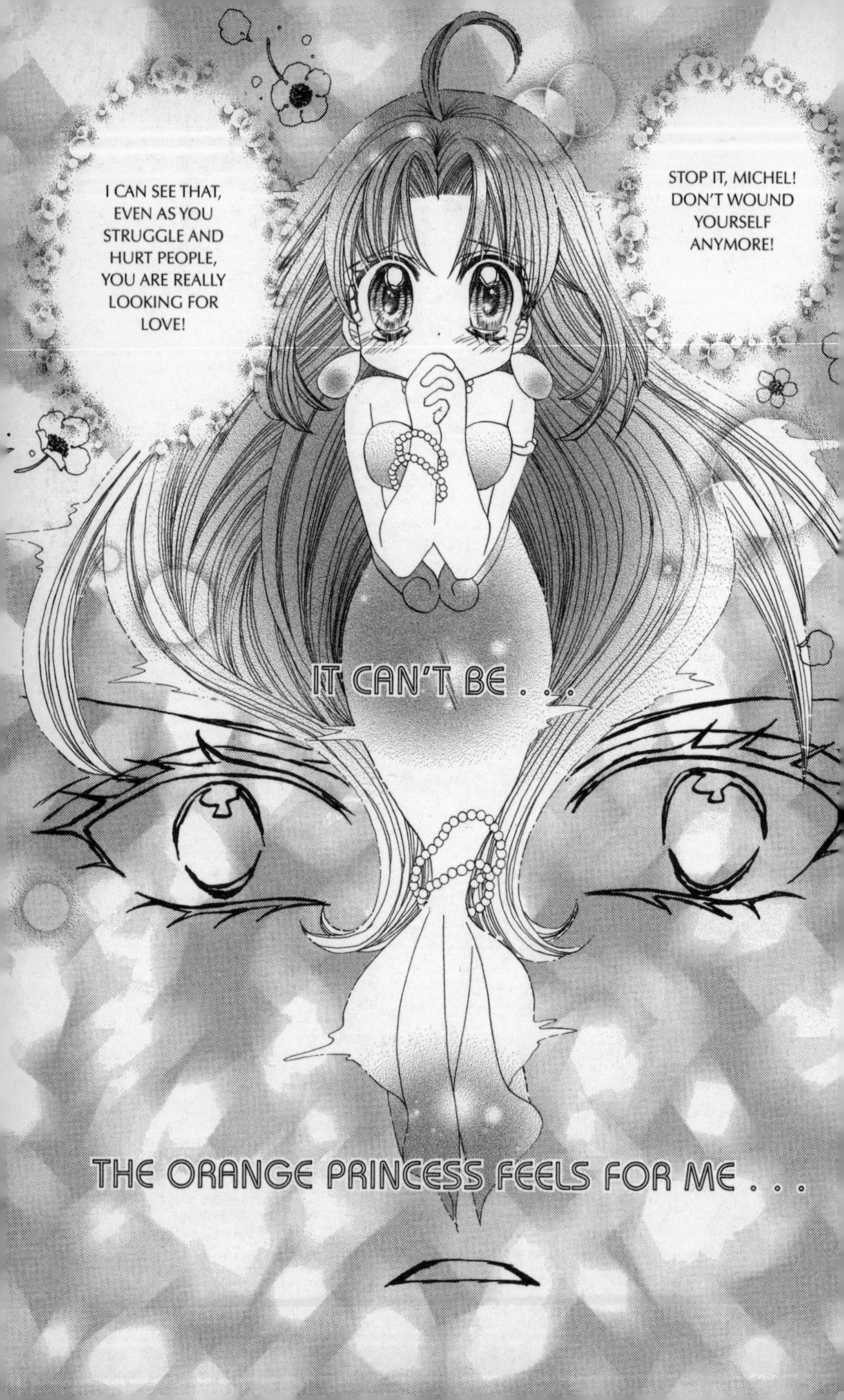
STOP IT, MICHEL! DON'T WOUND YOURSELF ANYMORE!
I CAN SEE THAT, EVEN AS YOU STRUGGLE AND HURT PEOPLE, YOU ARE REALLY LOOKING FOR LOVE!
IT CAN'T BE . . .
THE ORANGE PRINCESS FEELS FOR ME . . .

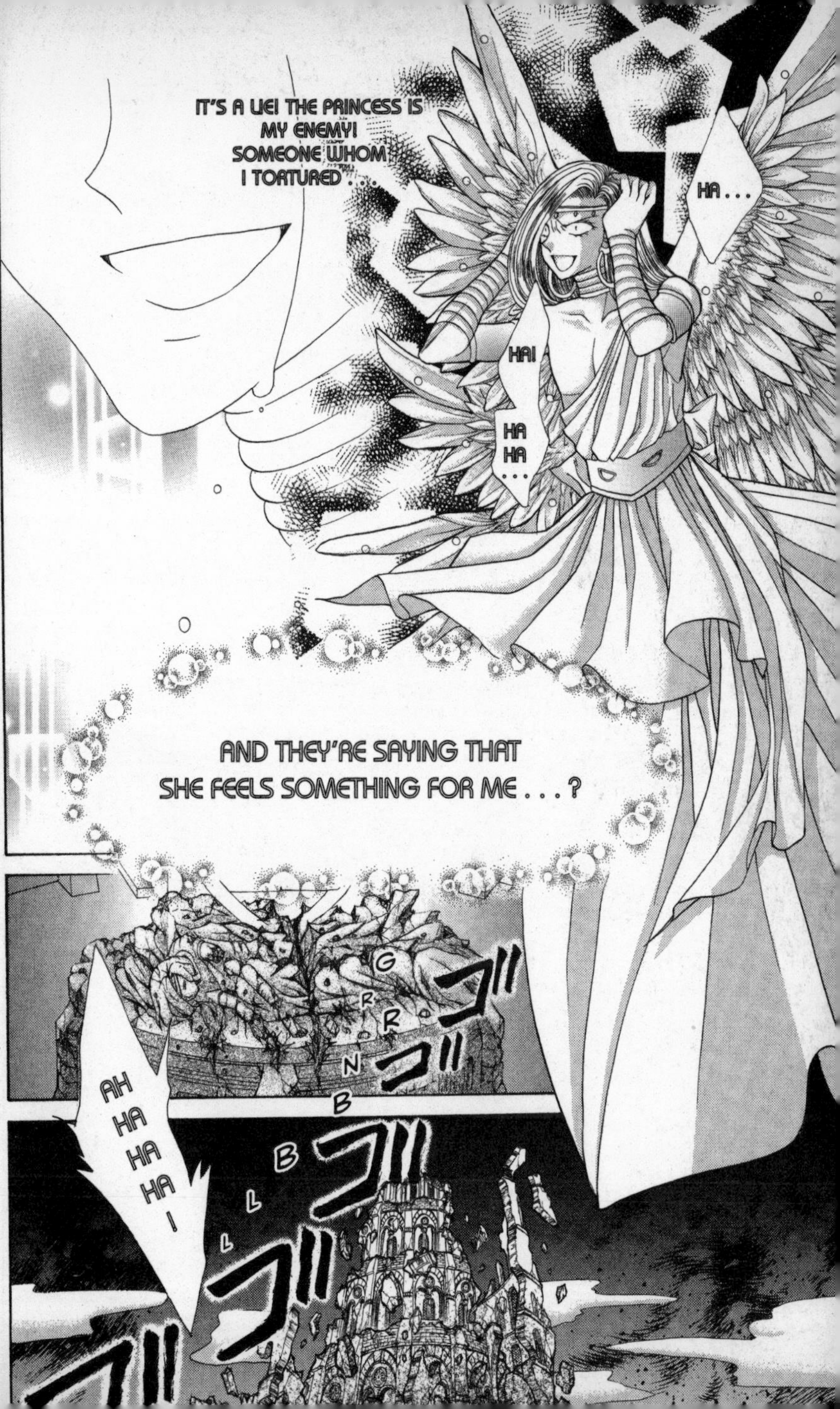
HA . . .
IT'S A LIE! THE PRINCESS IS MY ENEMY! SOMEONE WHOM I TORTURED . . .
HAI
HA HA . . .
AND THEY'RE SAYING THAT SHE FEELS SOMETHING FOR ME . . . ?
GRRNB
ゴゴ
AH HA HA HA!
BLL
ゴゴゴ

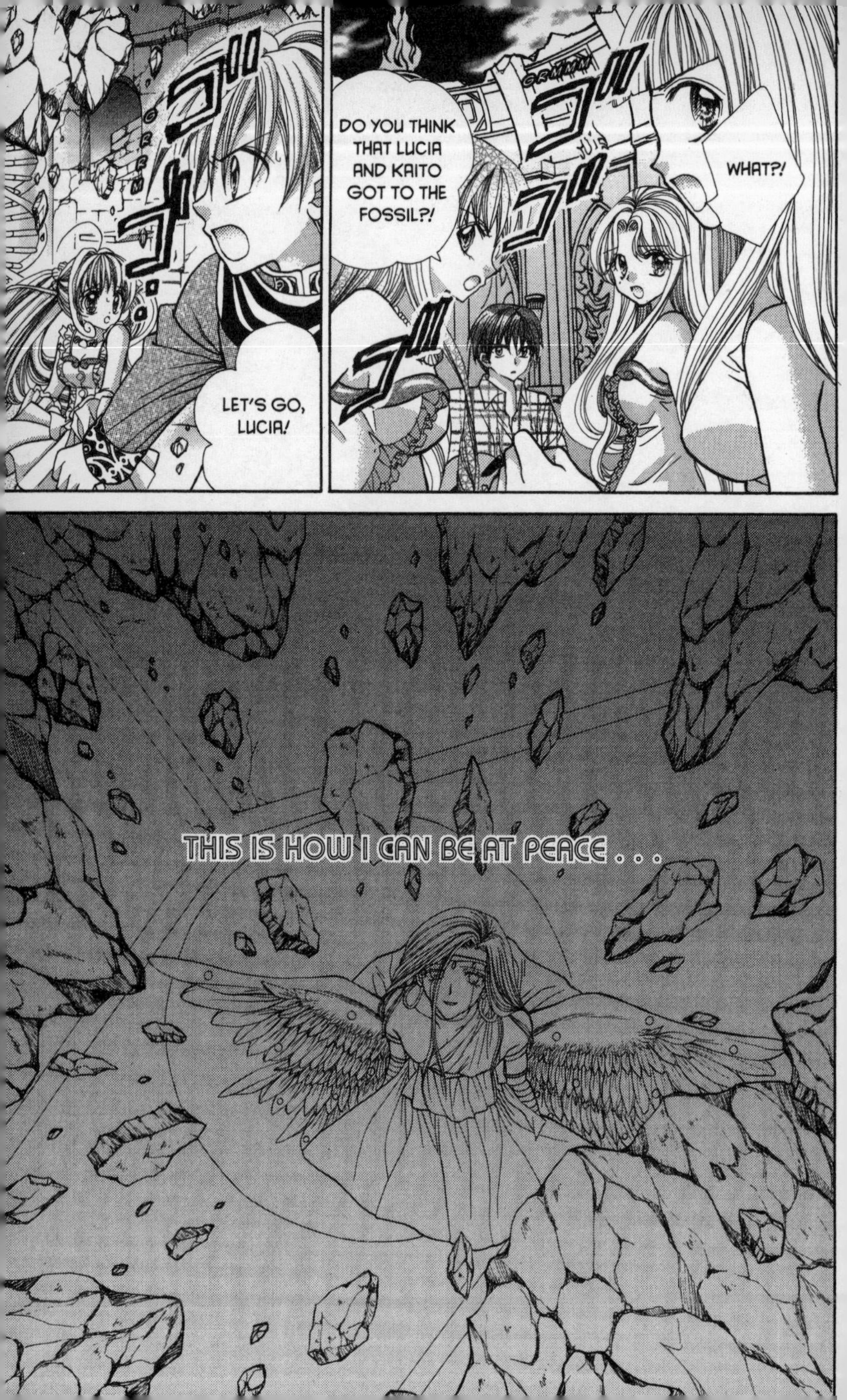
WHAT?!
DO YOU THINK THAT LUCIA AND KAITO GOT TO THE FOSSIL?!
LET'S GO, LUCIA!
THIS IS HOW I CAN BE AT PEACE . . .

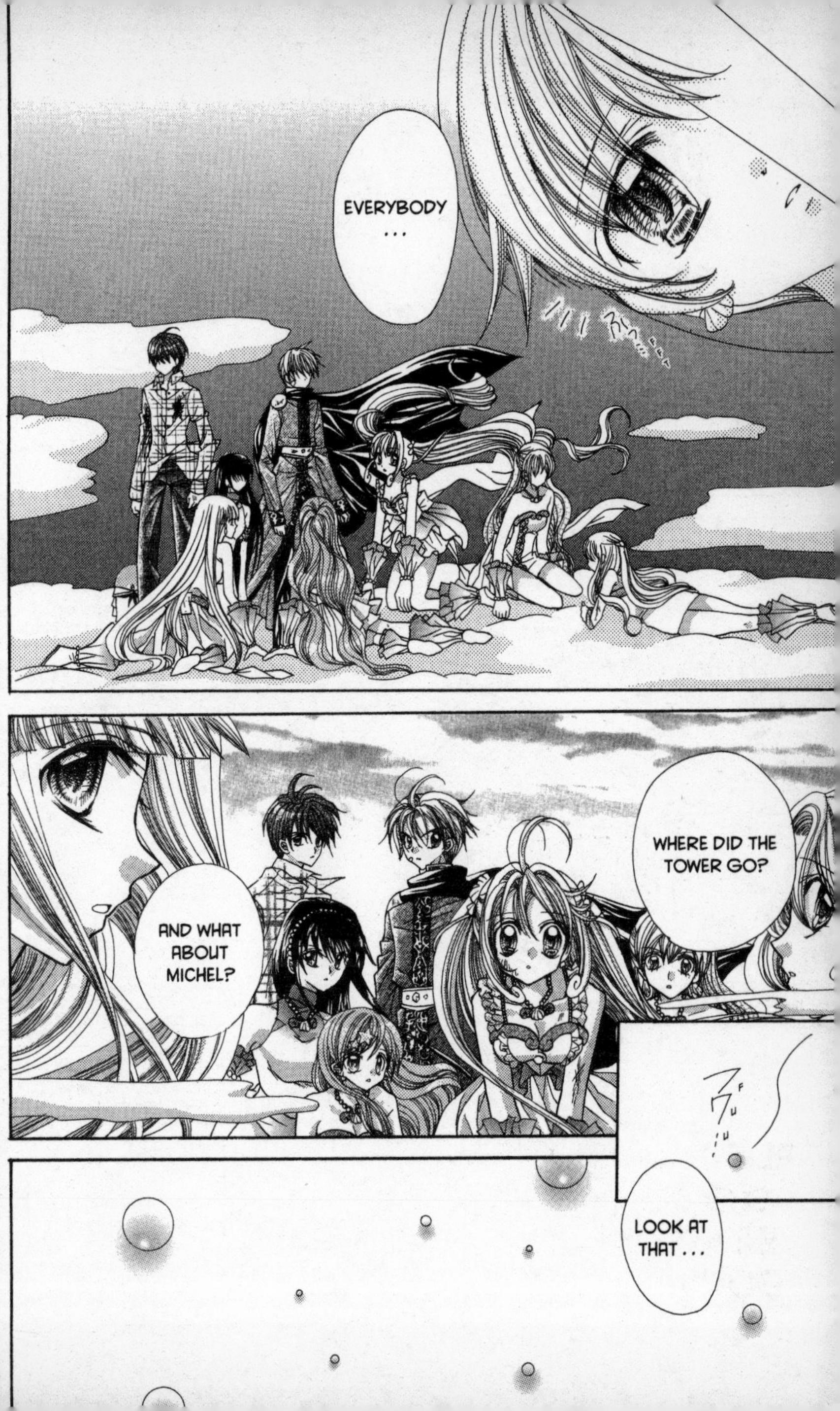
EVERYBODY . . .
WHERE DID THE TOWER GO?
AND WHAT ABOUT MICHEL?
LOOK AT THAT . . .

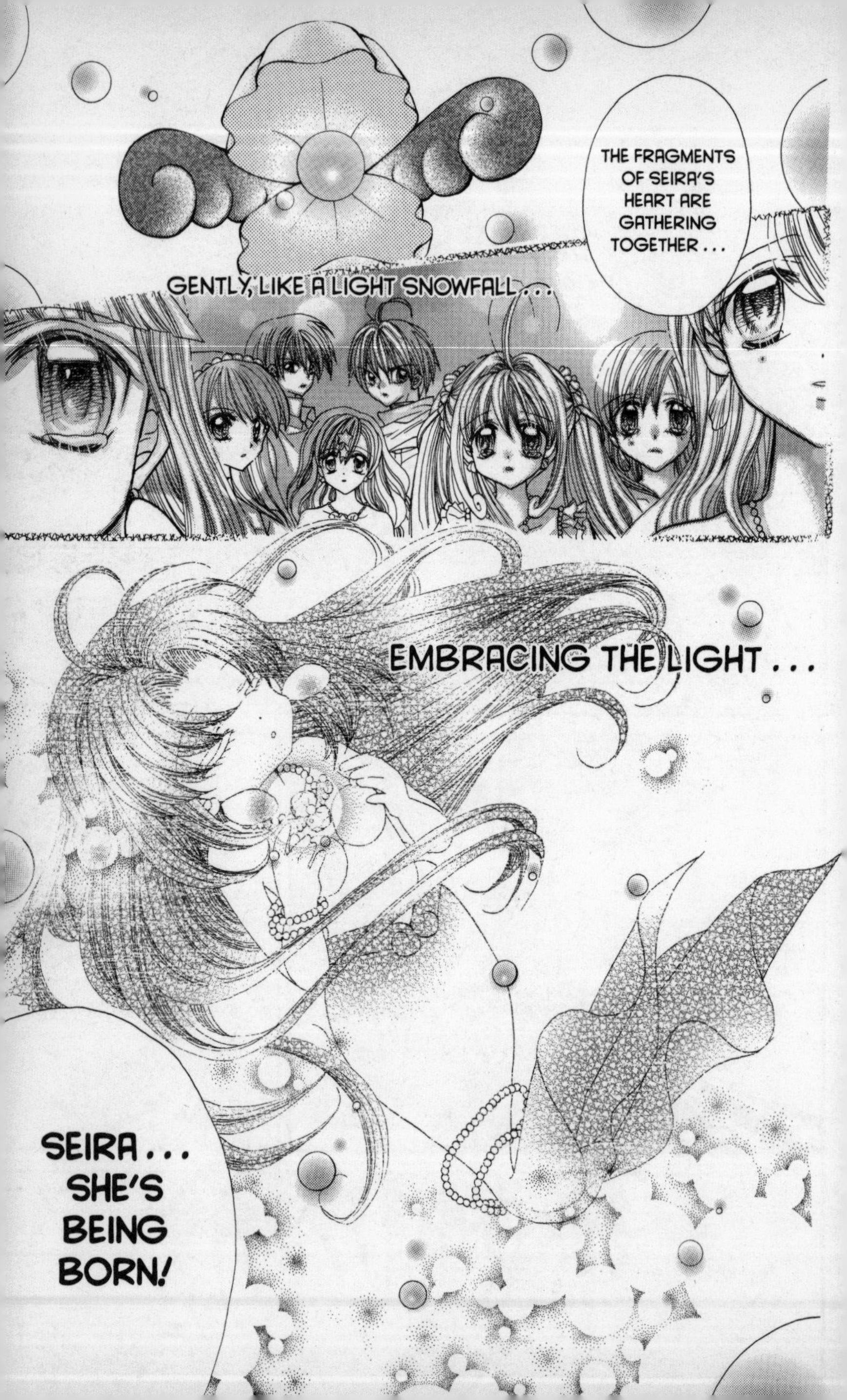
THE FRAGMENTS OF SEIRA'S HEART ARE GATHERING TOGETHER . . .
GENTLY, LIKE A LIGHT SNOWFALL . . .
EMBRACING THE LIGHT . . .
SEIRA . . . SHE'S BEING BORN!

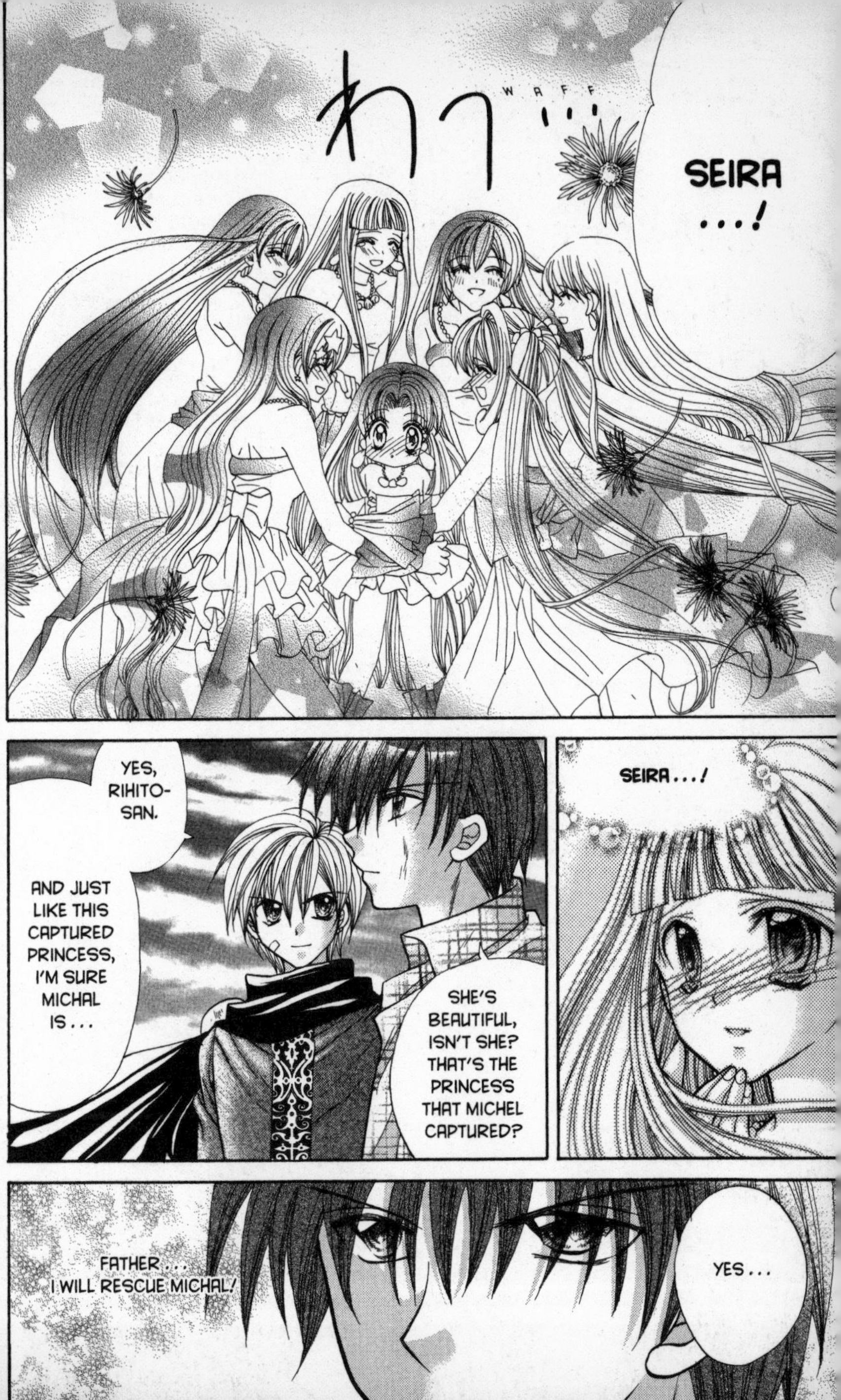

わっ
WAFF
SEIRA ...!
SEIRA...!
SHE'S BEAUTIFUL, ISN'T SHE? THAT'S THE PRINCESS THAT MICHEL CAPTURED?
YES, RIHITO-SAN.
AND JUST LIKE THIS CAPTURED PRINCESS, I'M SURE MICHAL IS...
YES...
FATHER... I WILL RESCUE MICHAL!

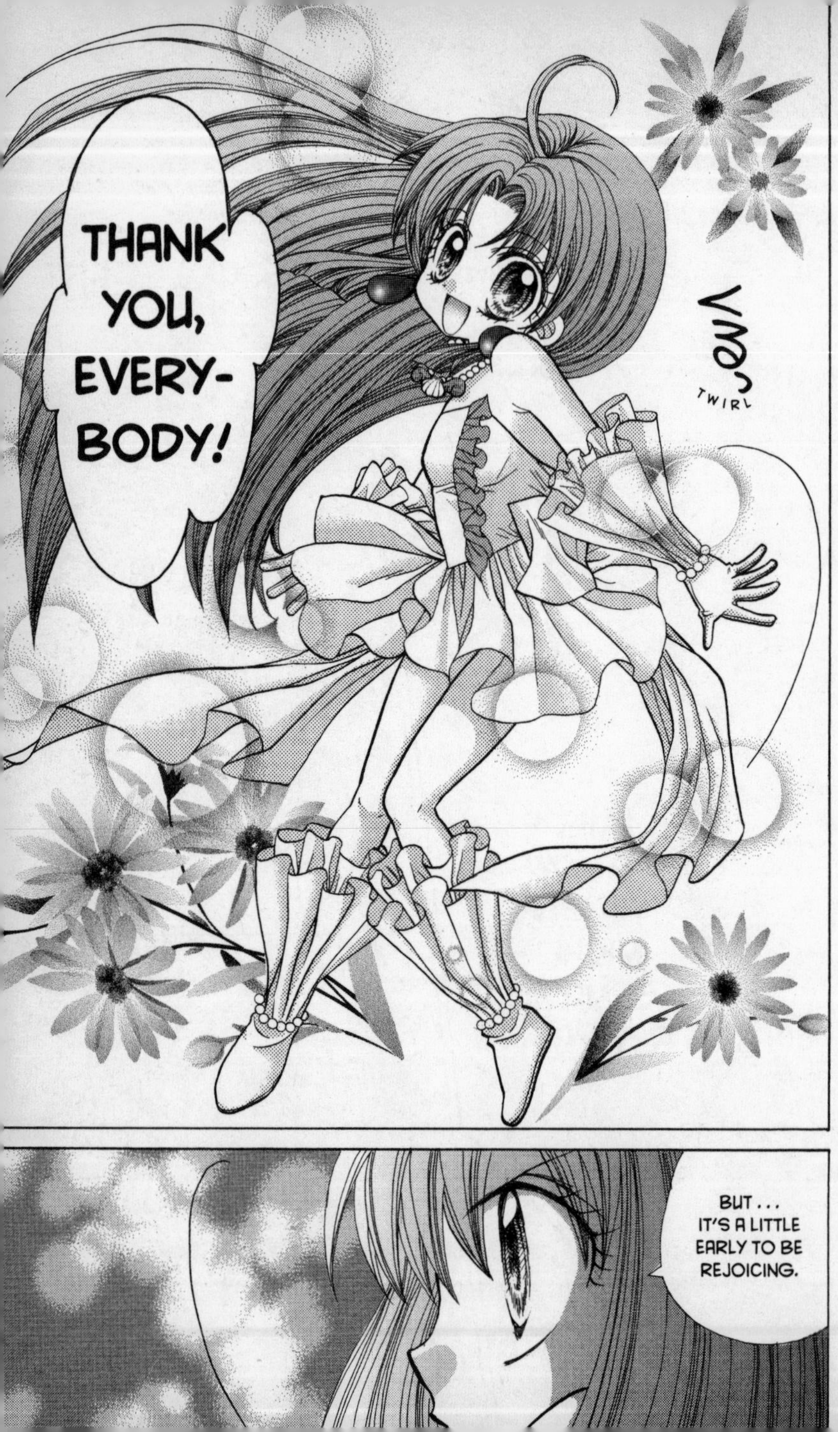
THANK YOU, EVERY-BODY!
TWIRL
BUT . . . IT'S A LITTLE EARLY TO BE REJOICING.

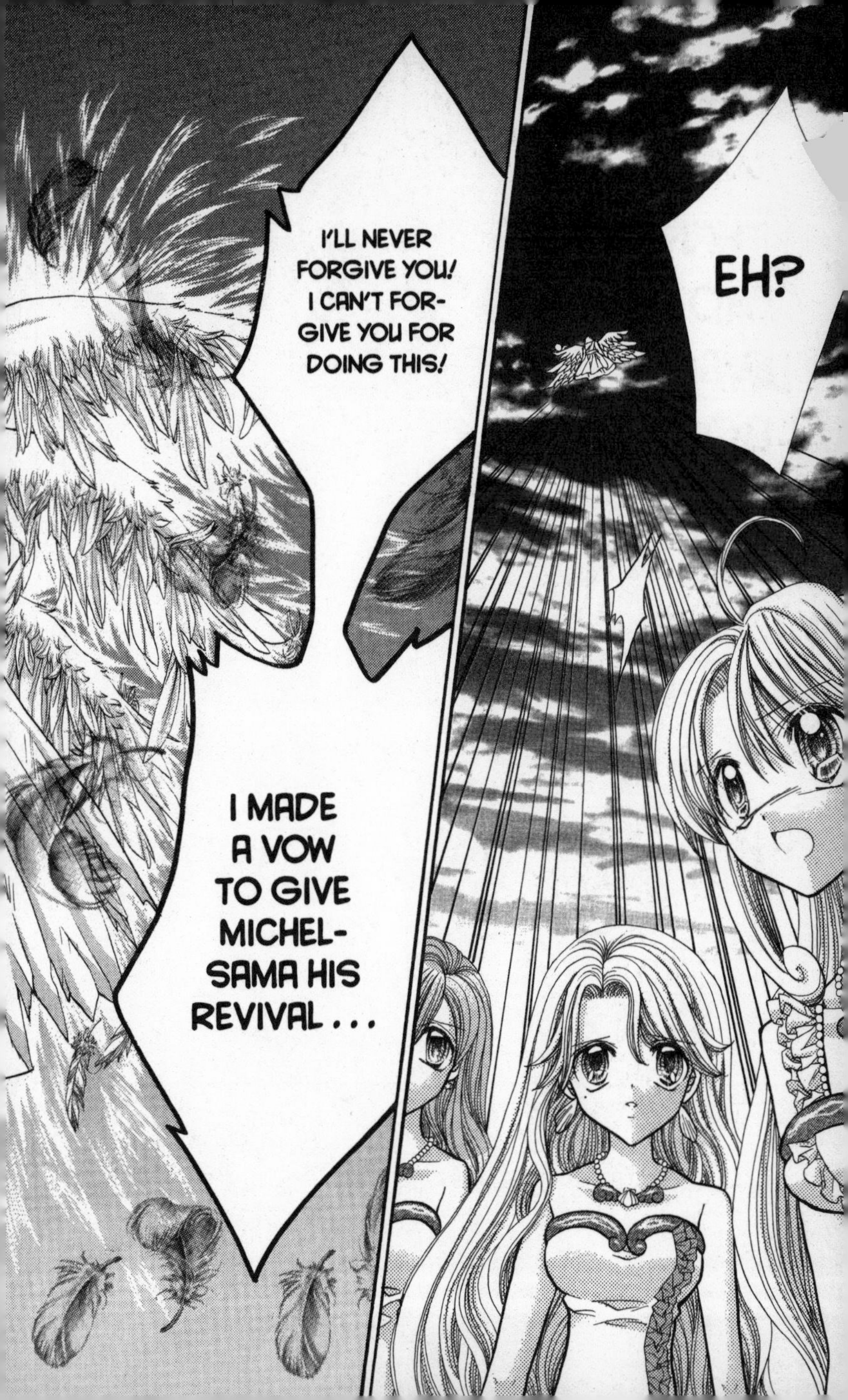
EH?
I'LL NEVER FORGIVE YOU! I CAN'T FOR-GIVE YOU FOR DOING THIS!
I MADE A VOW TO GIVE MICHEL-SAMA HIS REVIVAL . . .

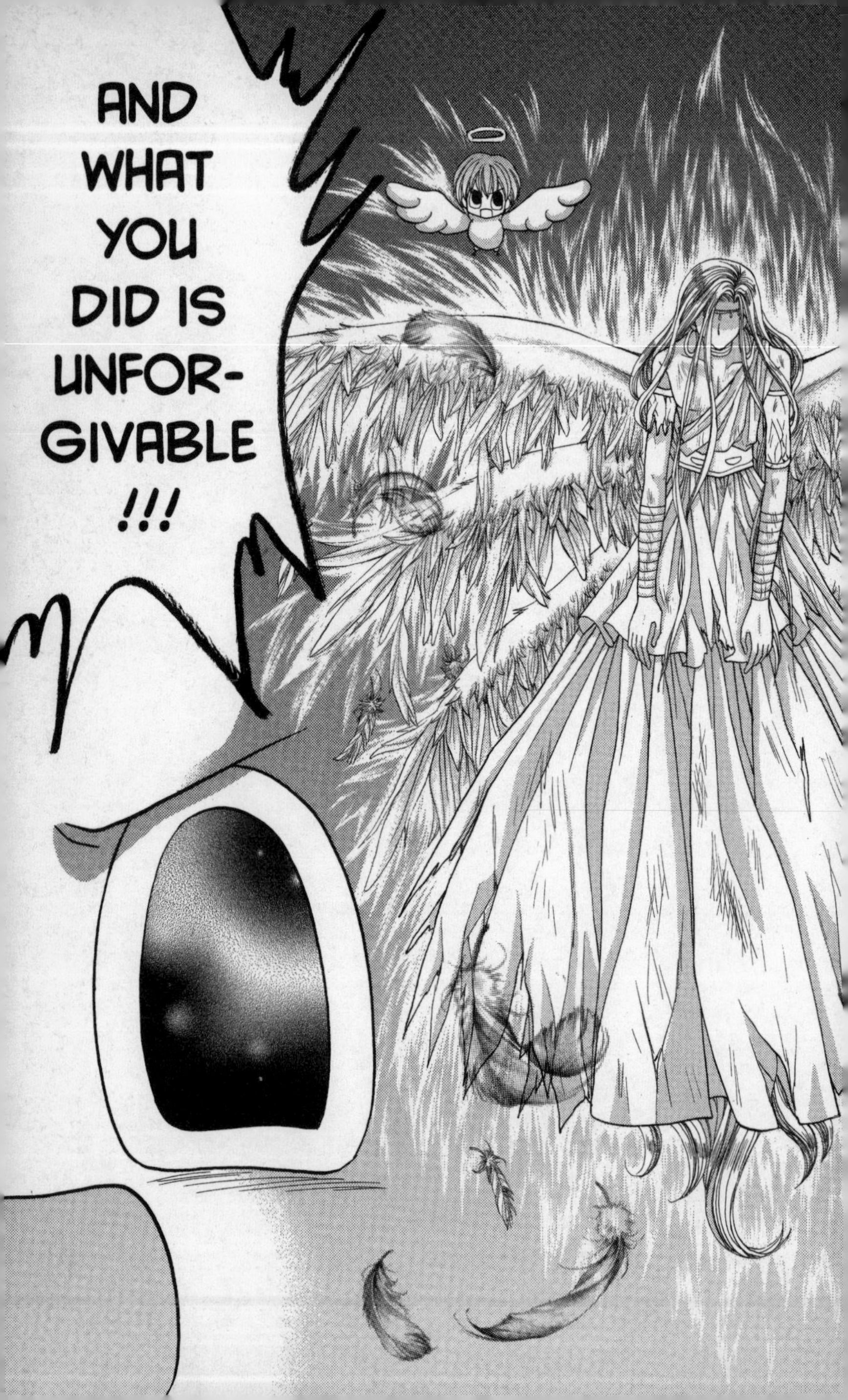
AND WHAT YOU DID IS UNFOR-GIVABLE !!!

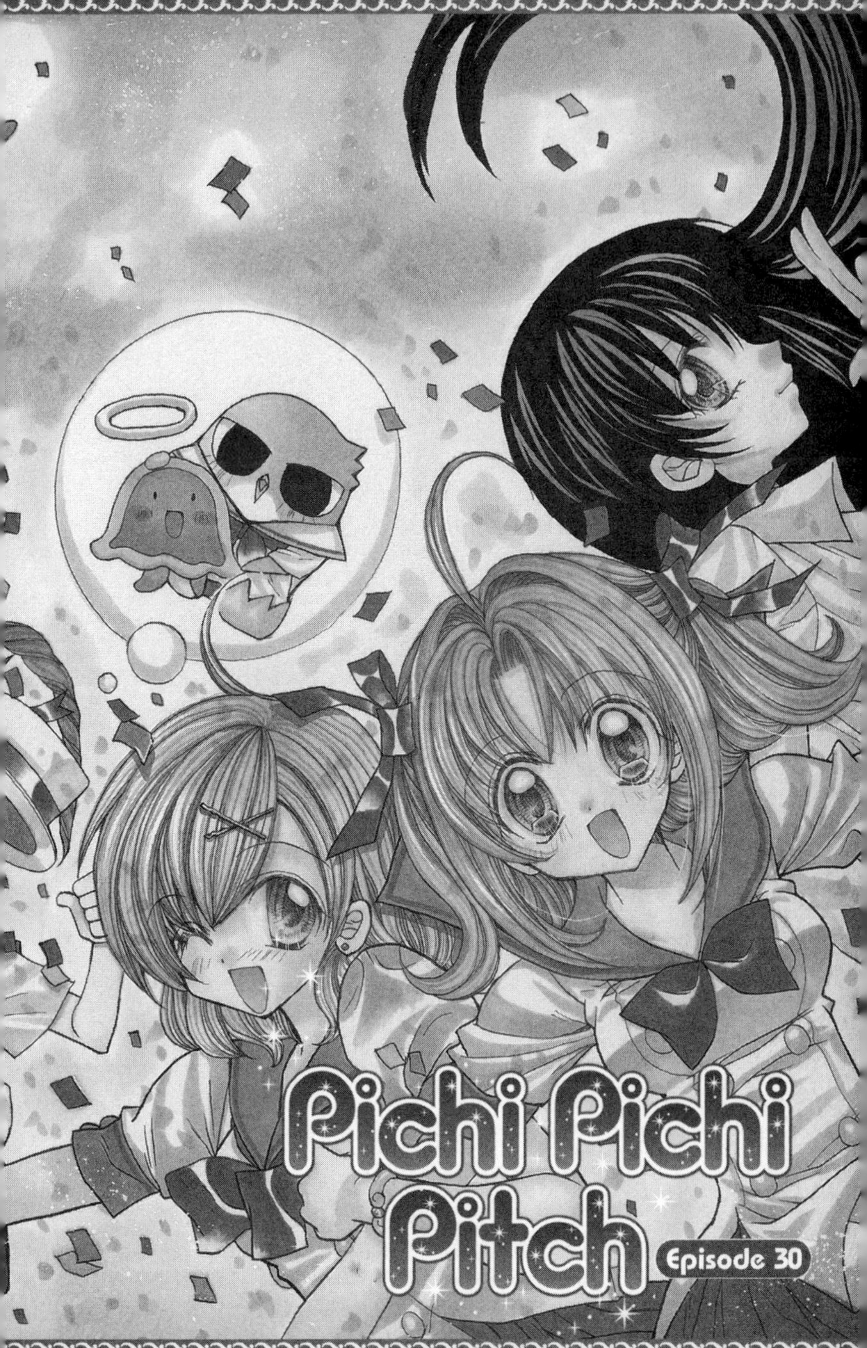
Pichi Pichi Pitch
Episode 30

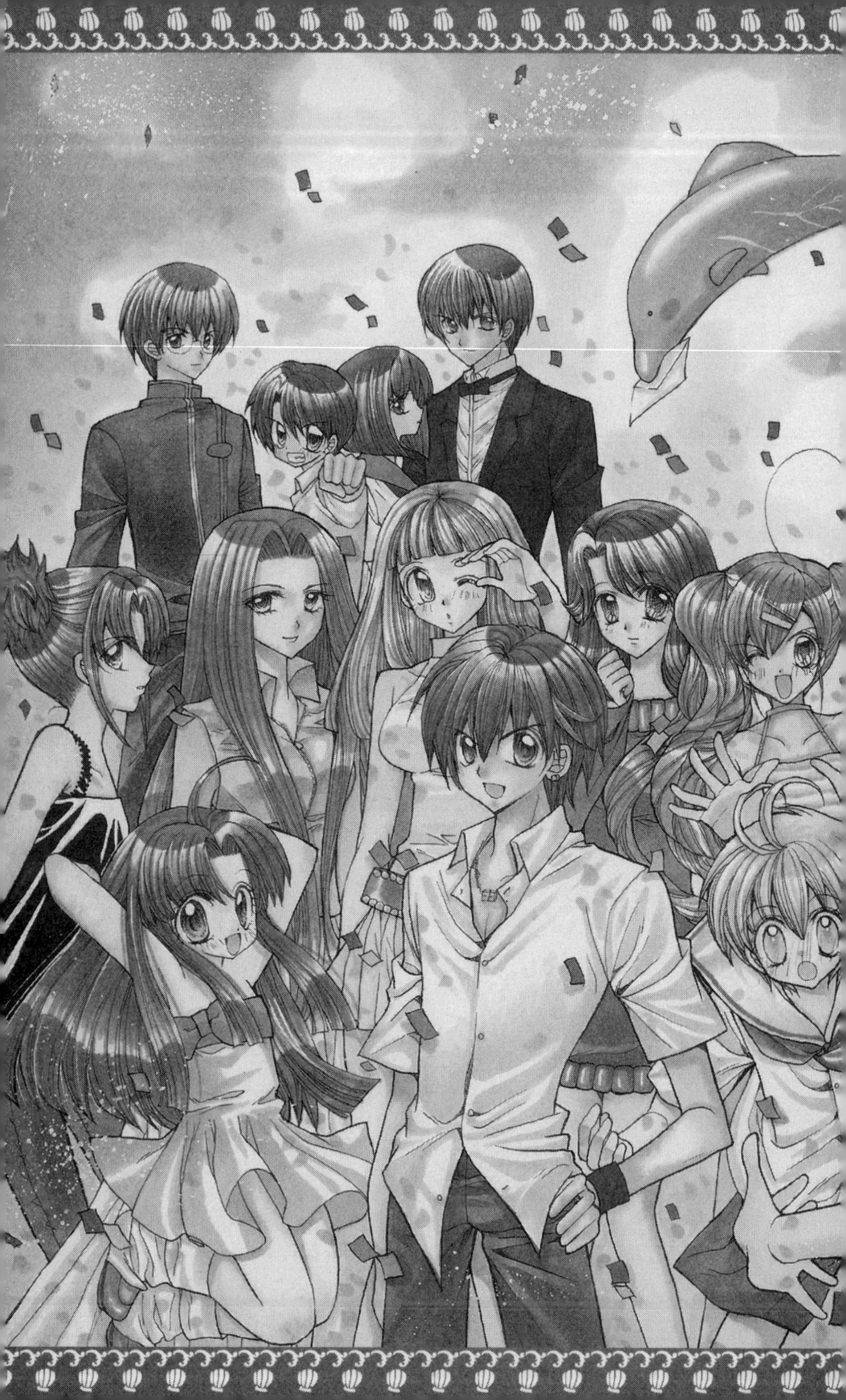

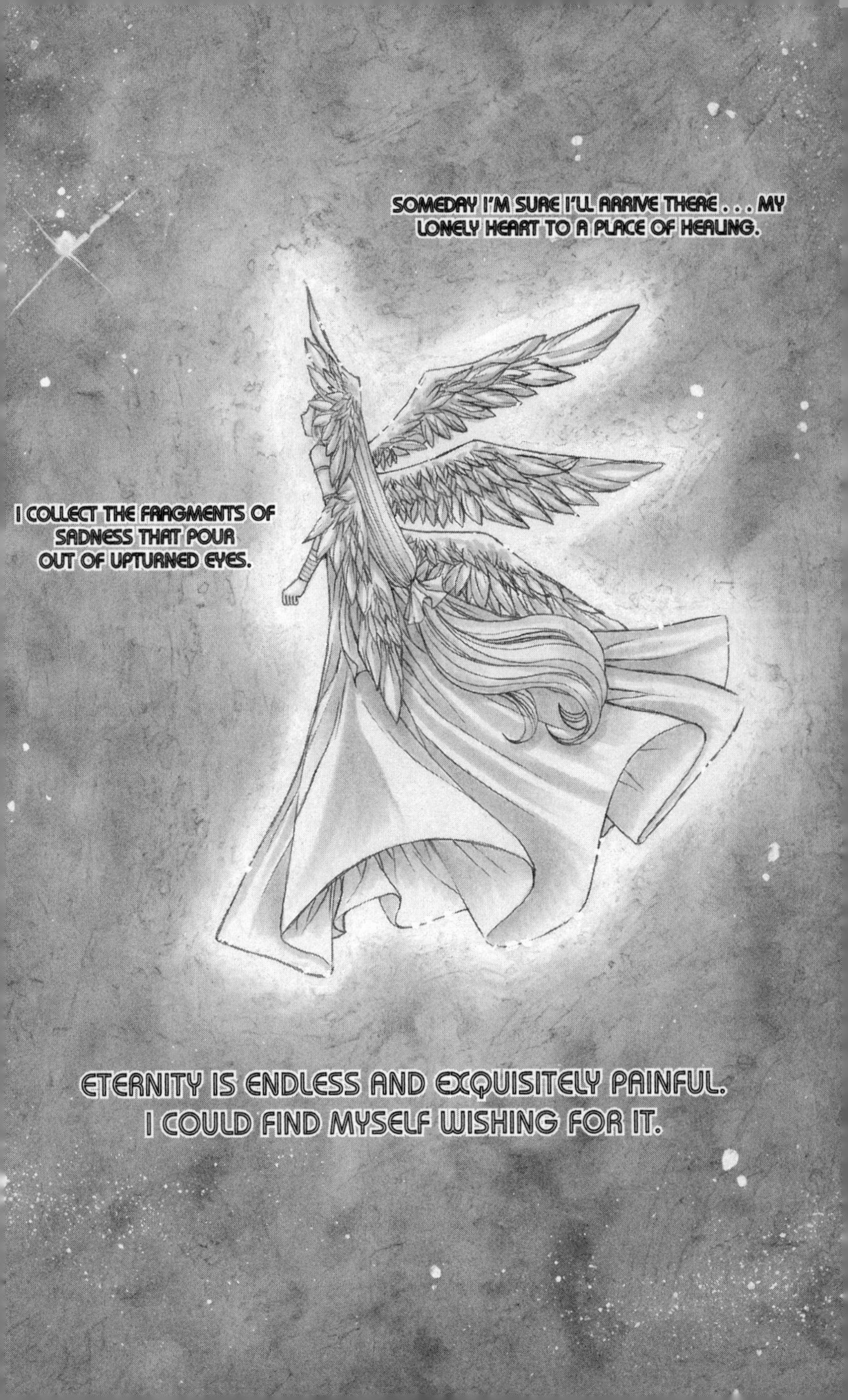
SOMEDAY I'M SURE I'LL ARRIVE THERE . . . MY LONELY HEART TO A PLACE OF HEALING.
I COLLECT THE FRAGMENTS OF SADNESS THAT POUR OUT OF UPTURNED EYES.
ETERNITY IS ENDLESS AND EXQUISITELY PAINFUL. I COULD FIND MYSELF WISHING FOR IT.

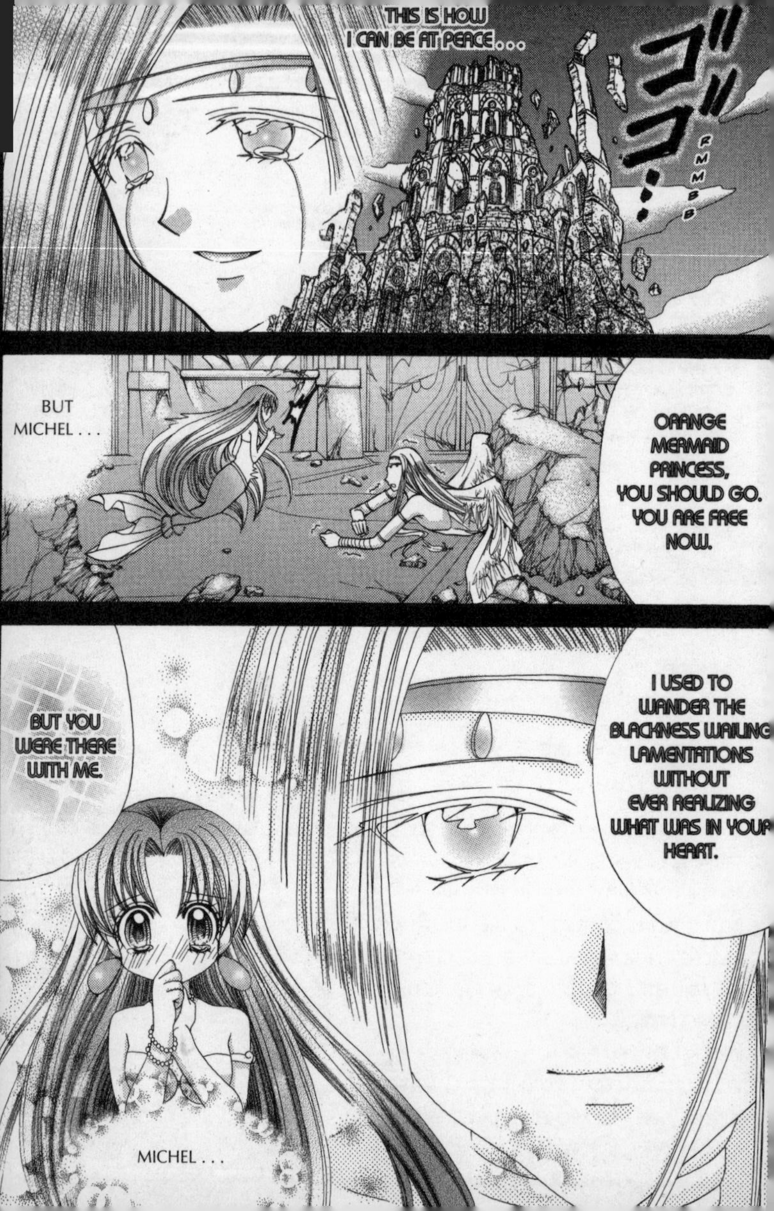
THIS IS HOW
I CAN BE AT PEACE . . .
ゴゴ
RMMBB
ORANGE MERMAID PRINCESS, YOU SHOULD GO. YOU ARE FREE NOW.
BUT MICHEL . . .
I USED TO WANDER THE BLACKNESS WAILING LAMENTATIONS WITHOUT EVER REALIZING WHAT WAS IN YOUR HEART.
BUT YOU WERE THERE WITH ME.
MICHEL . . .

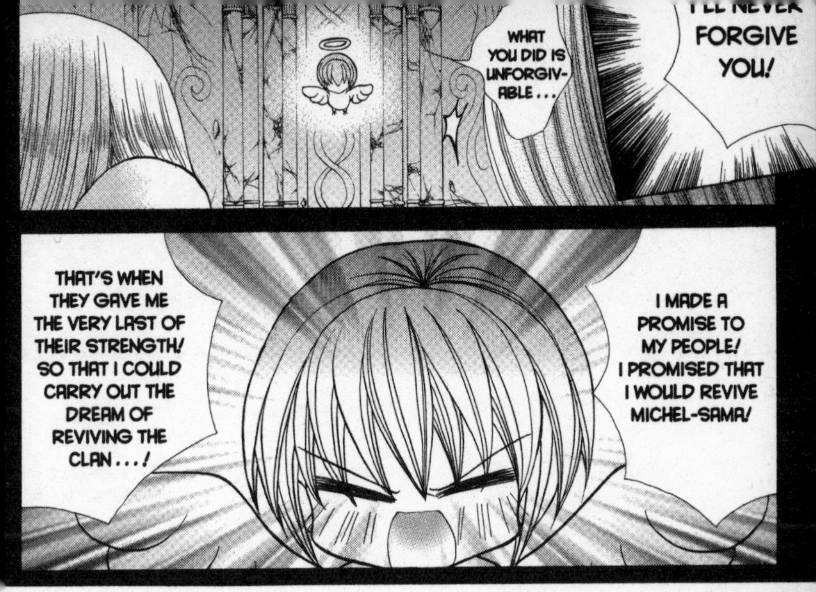
I'LL NEVER FORGIVE YOU!
WHAT YOU DID IS UNFORGIV-ABLE . . .
I MADE A PROMISE TO MY PEOPLE! I PROMISED THAT I WOULD REVIVE MICHEL-SAMA!
THAT'S WHEN THEY GAVE ME THE VERY LAST OF THEIR STRENGTH! SO THAT I COULD CARRY OUT THE DREAM OF REVIVING THE CLAN . . . !

<EPISODE 30>

THIS IS THE FINAL CHAPTER.

. . . OR RATHER, IN VOLUME 7, THERE'S SOMETHING OF AN EPILOGUE . . .

THE SPLASH PAGE IS A GATHERING OF ALL THE CHARACTERS IN A PICHI STYLE, LIKE WHEN WE FIRST MET THEM ALL. EVERYBODY'S HAVING FUN. THAT'S IN CONTRAST TO THE NEXT IMAGE OF MICHEL. I KNOW IT WAS THE FINAL CHAPTER, BUT I WAS STILL THRILLED TO GET A COLOR OPENING PAGE.

THANK ALL OF YOU FOR FOLLOWING THIS ALL THE WAY TO THE END! I REALLY, REALLY MEAN IT!! THE FINAL TUNE AND MICHEL'S TUNE COME FROM THE PICHI ANIME. IF YOU GET A CHANCE, I'D LIKE IT IF YOU LISTENED TO THEM.

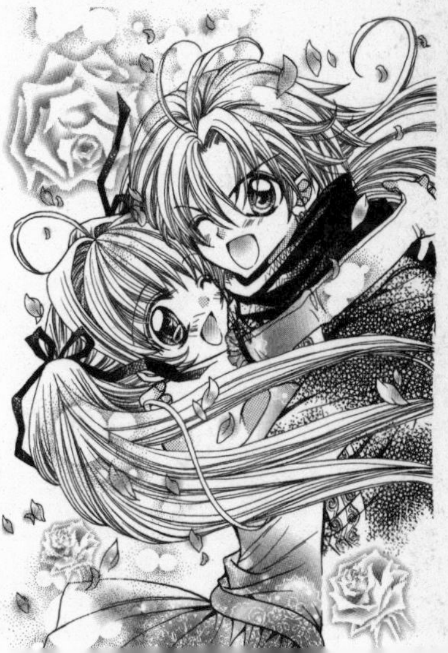

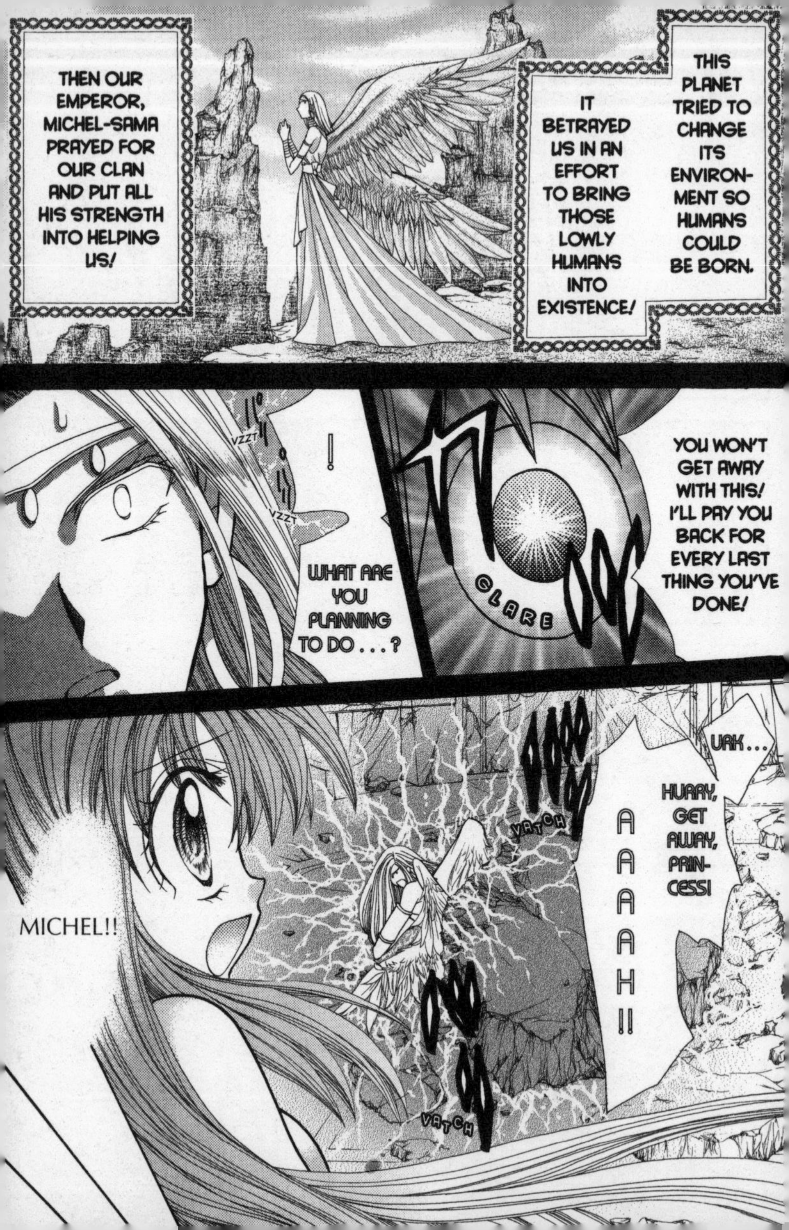
THIS PLANET TRIED TO CHANGE ITS ENVIRON-MENT SO HUMANS COULD BE BORN.
IT BETRAYED US IN AN EFFORT TO BRING THOSE LOWLY HUMANS INTO EXISTENCE!
THEN OUR EMPEROR, MICHEL-SAMA PRAYED FOR OUR CLAN AND PUT ALL HIS STRENGTH INTO HELPING US!
YOU WON'T GET AWAY WITH THIS! I'LL PAY YOU BACK FOR EVERY LAST THING YOU'VE DONE!
GLARE
!
VZZT
VZZT
WHAT ARE YOU PLANNING TO DO . . . ?
URK . . .
HURRY, GET AWAY, PRIN-CESS!
AAAAAH!!
VATCH
VATCH
MICHEL!!

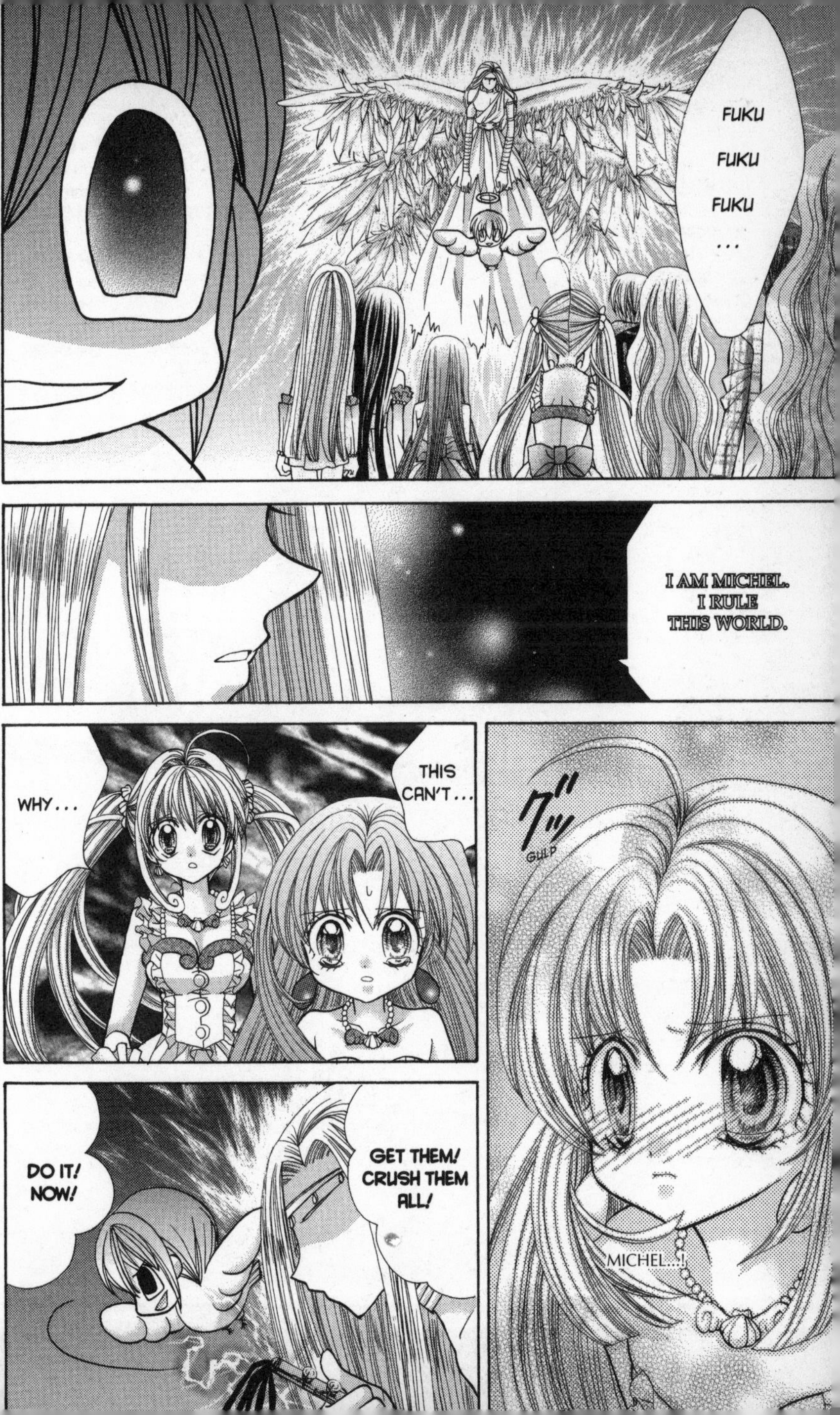
FUKU
FUKU
FUKU
...
I AM MICHEL. I RULE THIS WORLD.
グッ
GULP
MICHEL...!
THIS CAN'T...
WHY...
GET THEM! CRUSH THEM ALL!
DO IT! NOW!

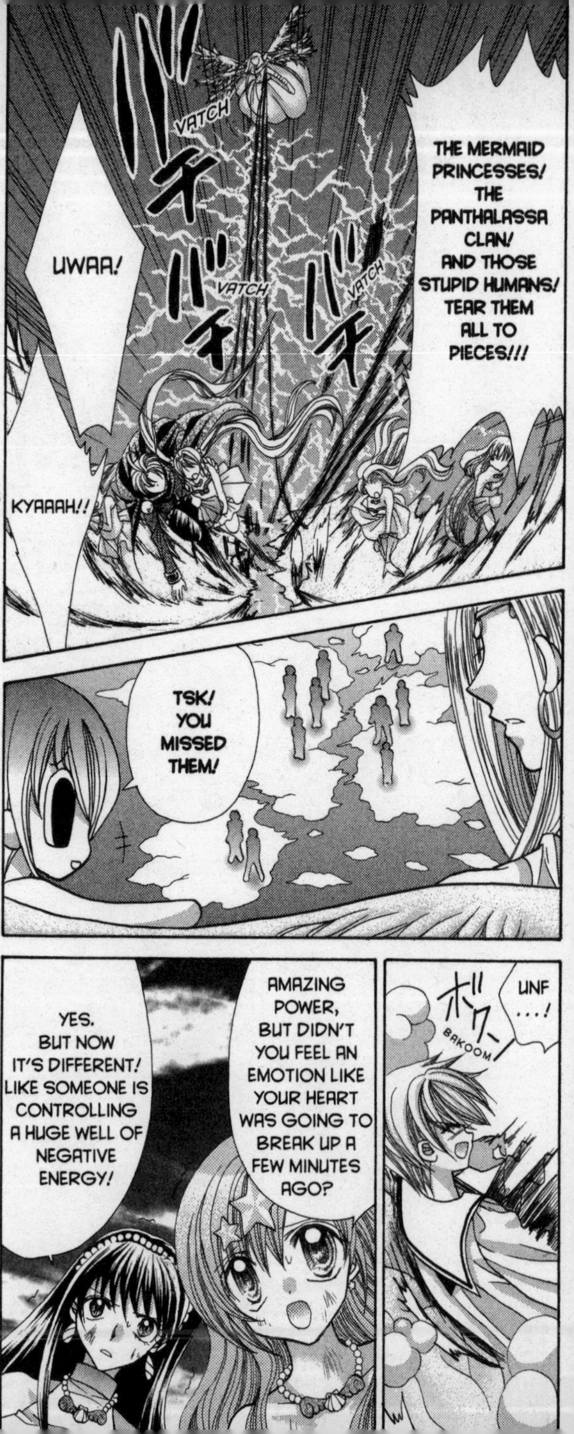
THE MERMAID PRINCESSES! THE PANTHALASSA CLAN! AND THOSE STUPID HUMANS! TEAR THEM ALL TO PIECES!!!
VATCH
VATCH
VATCH
UWAA!
KYAAAH!!
TSK! YOU MISSED THEM!
UNF...!
BAKOOM
AMAZING POWER, BUT DIDN'T YOU FEEL AN EMOTION LIKE YOUR HEART WAS GOING TO BREAK UP A FEW MINUTES AGO?
YES. BUT NOW IT'S DIFFERENT! LIKE SOMEONE IS CONTROLLING A HUGE WELL OF NEGATIVE ENERGY!

AFTERWORD

THANK YOU SO MUCH FOR READING UP UNTIL NOW. PLEASE PICK UP VOLUME 7, TOO.

special Thanks

MOMO UTSUGI-SAMA, MEAT MASTER
MEI HIROMI-SAMA, SPACE ALIEN
RUMIKO NAGANO-SAMA, KNOWS LOTS OF THINGS
KOTORI MOMOYUKI-SAMA, COUNTESS IN BLACK CLOTHES
RAN MITSUKI-SAMA, MOSQUITO HUNTER
SAKI-SAMA, YOUTH
SHIHO NAKAZAWA-SAMA, WAITRESS
RUI WATANABE-SAMA, STILL A MYSTERY
KIYOKA HAYAMA-SAMA, ROCKET
TOSHIKO HIKOYAMA-SAMA, SUPERWOMAN

MINORI HIKAWA-SAMA... JUST LIKE ME

EDITORS:
KAWAMOTO-SAMA
ZUSHI-SAMA

SEND YOUR IMPRESSIONS HERE

To... **Pink Hanamori**

C/O DEL REY MANGA
RANDOM HOUSE, INC.
1745 BROADWAY,
18TH FLOOR
NEW YORK, NY 10019

DEEP BOW

FUSUMA DOOR

2005.1.18

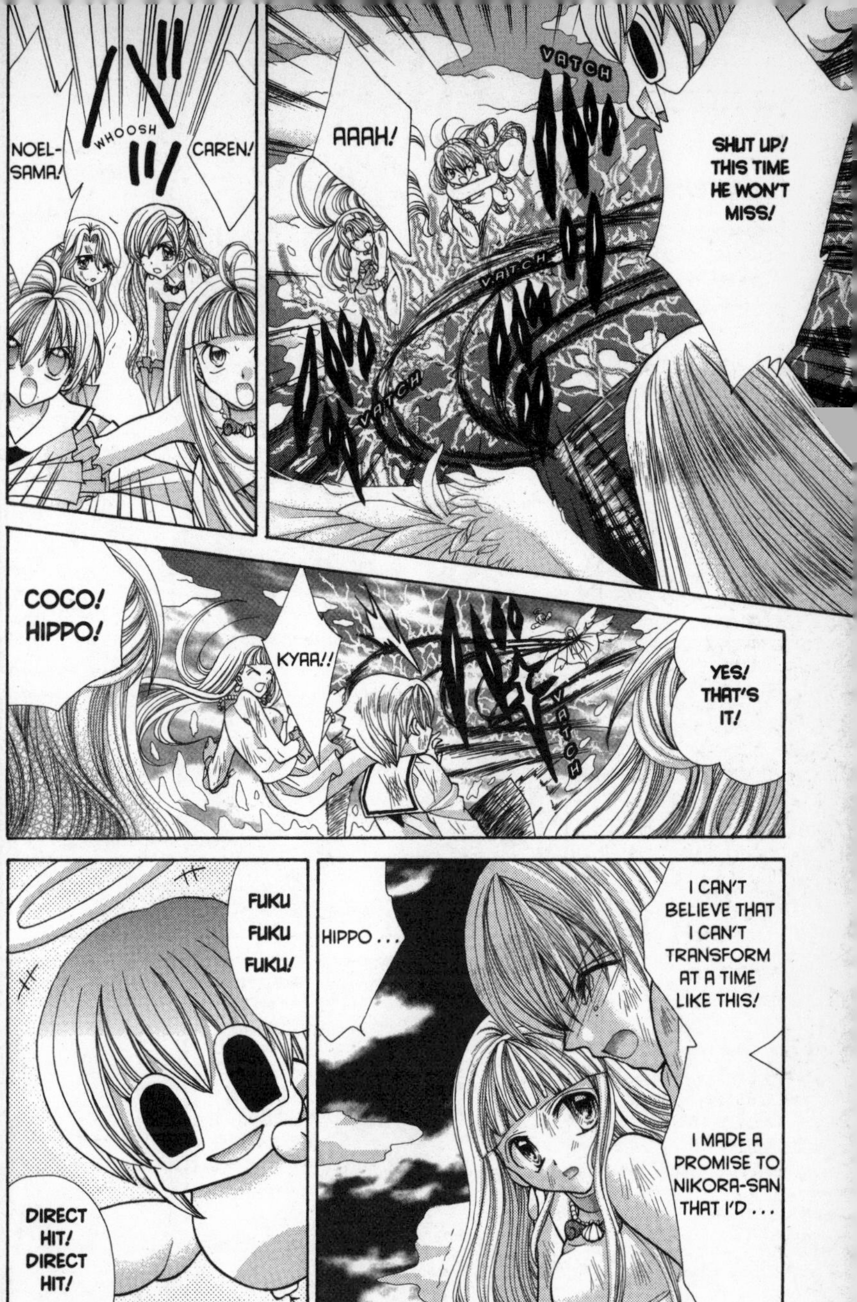
VATCH
SHUT UP! THIS TIME HE WON'T MISS!
AAAH!
VATCH
VATCH
CAREN!
WHOOSH
NOEL-SAMA!
YES! THAT'S IT!
VATCH
KYAA!!
COCO! HIPPO!
I CAN'T BELIEVE THAT I CAN'T TRANSFORM AT A TIME LIKE THIS!
I MADE A PROMISE TO NIKORA-SAN THAT I'D . . .
HIPPO . . .
FUKU FUKU FUKU!
DIRECT HIT! DIRECT HIT!

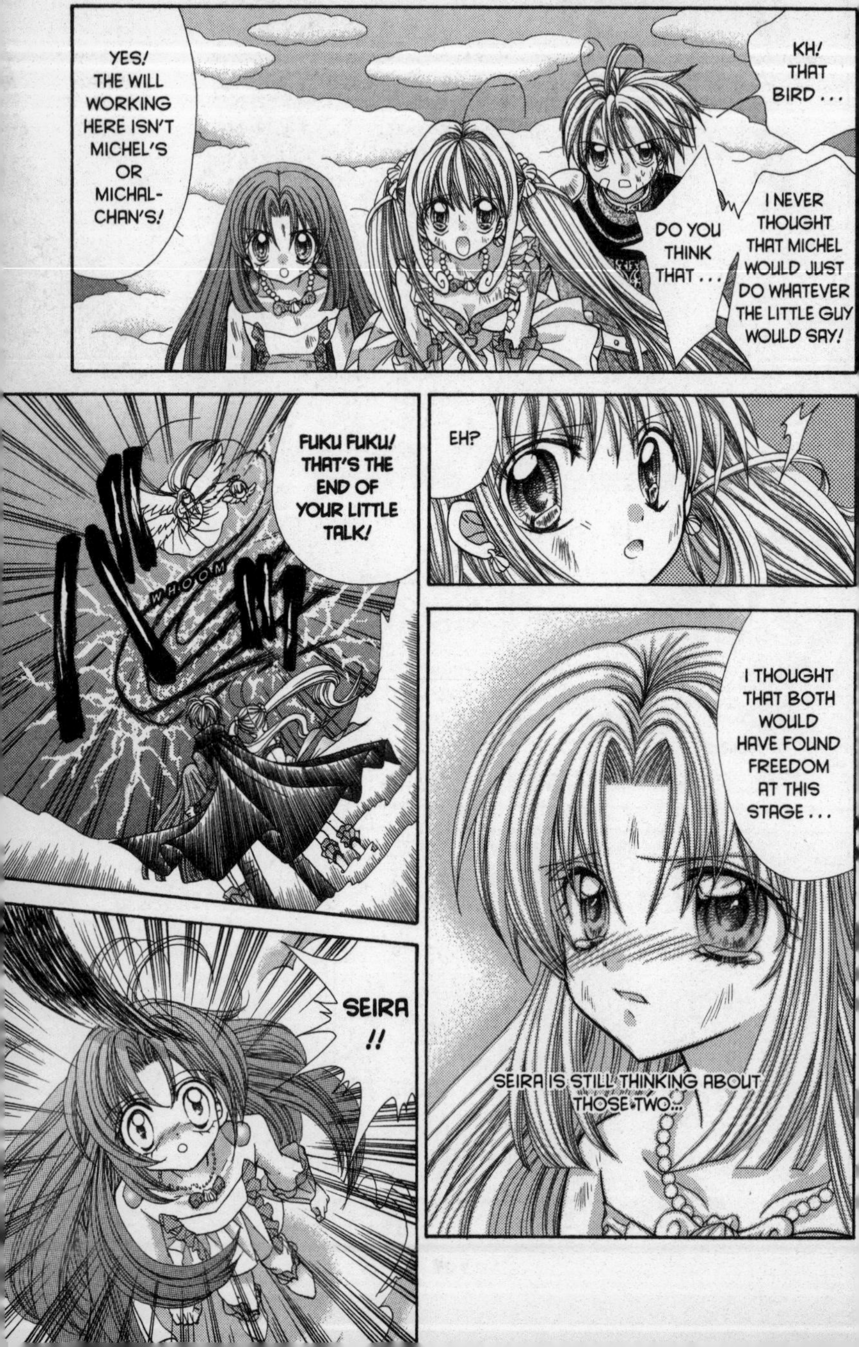
KH! THAT BIRD . . .
I NEVER THOUGHT THAT MICHEL WOULD JUST DO WHATEVER THE LITTLE GUY WOULD SAY!
DO YOU THINK THAT . . .
YES! THE WILL WORKING HERE ISN'T MICHEL'S OR MICHAL-CHAN'S!
EH?
FUKU FUKU! THAT'S THE END OF YOUR LITTLE TALK!
WHOOOM
I THOUGHT THAT BOTH WOULD HAVE FOUND FREEDOM AT THIS STAGE . . .
SEIRA IS STILL THINKING ABOUT THOSE TWO...
SEIRA !!

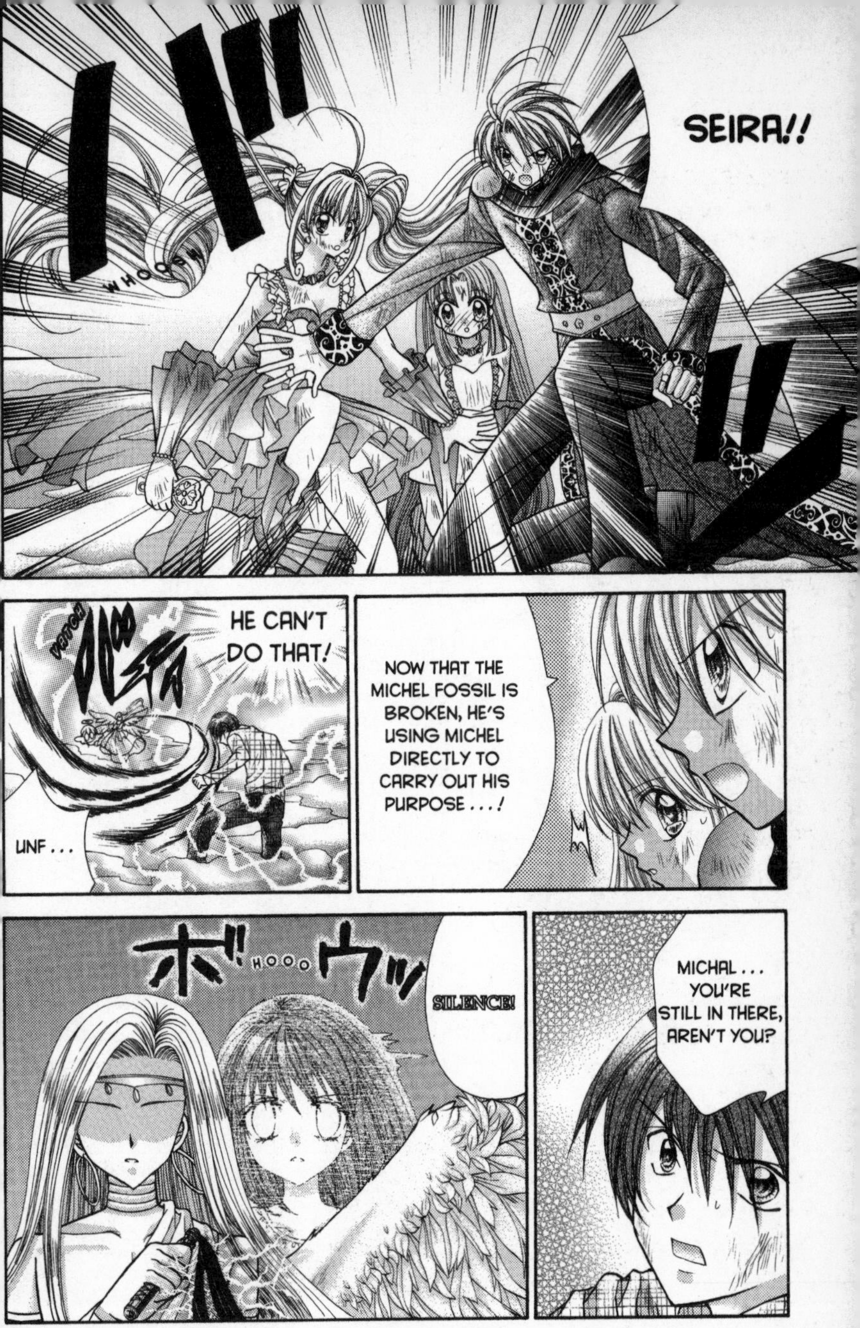
SEIRA!!
NOW THAT THE MICHEL FOSSIL IS BROKEN, HE'S USING MICHEL DIRECTLY TO CARRY OUT HIS PURPOSE . . . !
HE CAN'T DO THAT!
UNF . . .
MICHAL . . . YOU'RE STILL IN THERE, AREN'T YOU?
SILENCE!

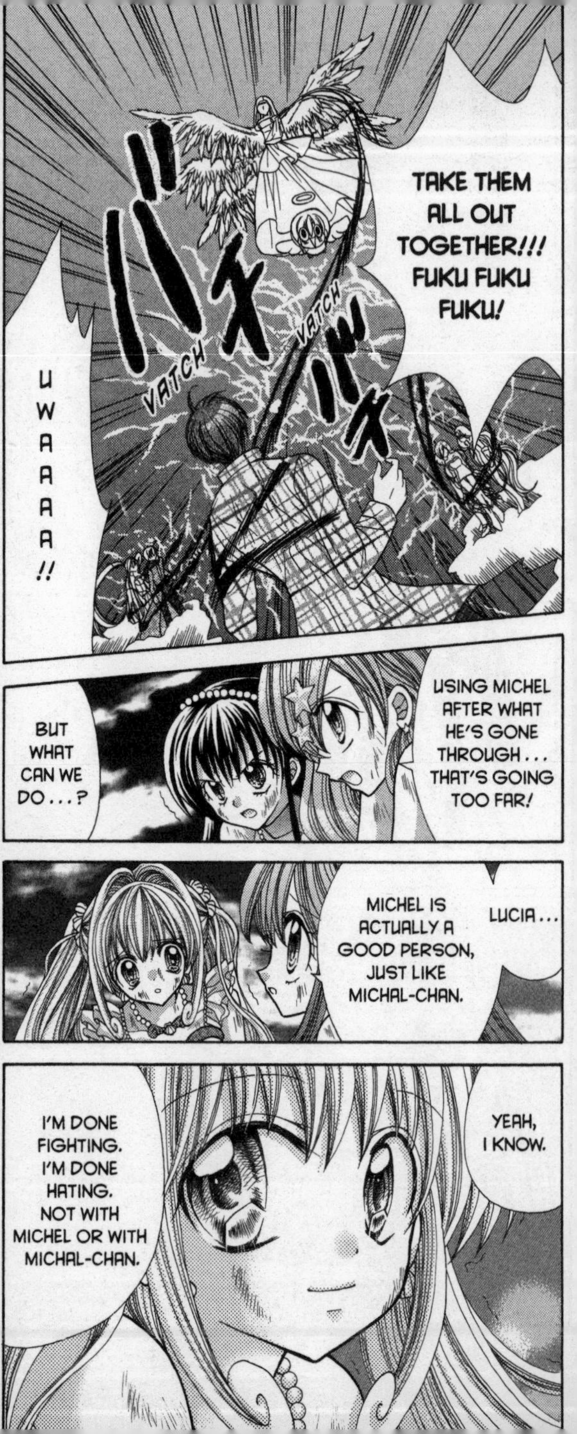
TAKE THEM ALL OUT TOGETHER!!! FUKU FUKU FUKU!
バチ
VATCH
VATCH
バチ
UWAAAAA!!
USING MICHEL AFTER WHAT HE'S GONE THROUGH . . . THAT'S GOING TOO FAR!
BUT WHAT CAN WE DO . . . ?
LUCIA . . .
MICHEL IS ACTUALLY A GOOD PERSON, JUST LIKE MICHAL-CHAN.
YEAH, I KNOW.
I'M DONE FIGHTING. I'M DONE HATING. NOT WITH MICHEL OR WITH MICHAL-CHAN.

TO EVERYONE WHO IS A FAN OF PICHI!

THANK YOU FOR READING VOLUME 6! I AM YOKOTE, AND I AM IN CHARGE OF THE STORY. WE'RE AT THE FINALE OF PICHI. WHEN I READ THE LAST INSTALLMENT, I GOT TEARY-EYED. STARTING WITH LUCIA, ALL OF THE CHARACTERS HAD GROWN INTO BEAUTIFUL, STRONG, ADULT PEOPLE. I WAS SO MOVED! HANAMORI-SENSEI, THANK YOU SO MUCH! I'M ALSO LOOKING FORWARD TO THE SIDE STORIES IN VOLUME 7.

I HOPE YOU ALL HAVE FUN RIGHT UP TO THE VERY END.♥

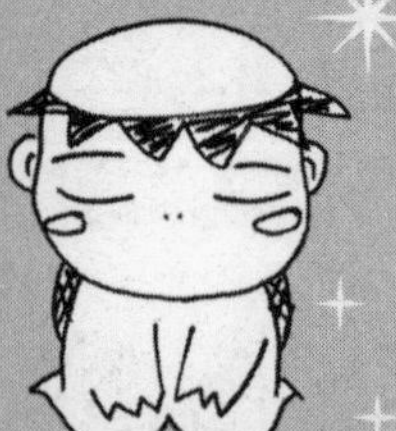

THEN . . .
LET'S MEET AGAIN!

YOKOTE

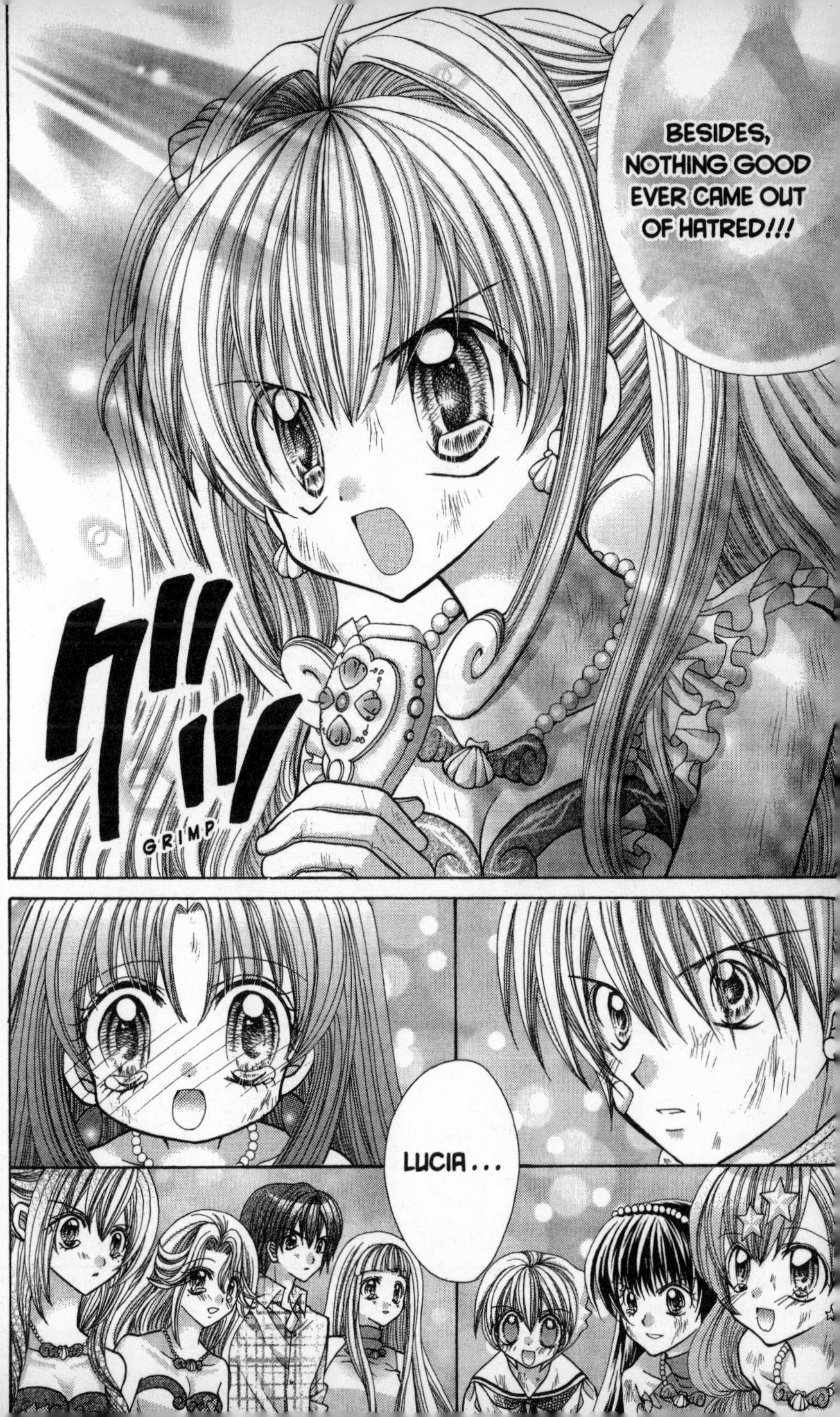
BESIDES, NOTHING GOOD EVER CAME OUT OF HATRED!!!
GRIMP
LUCIA...

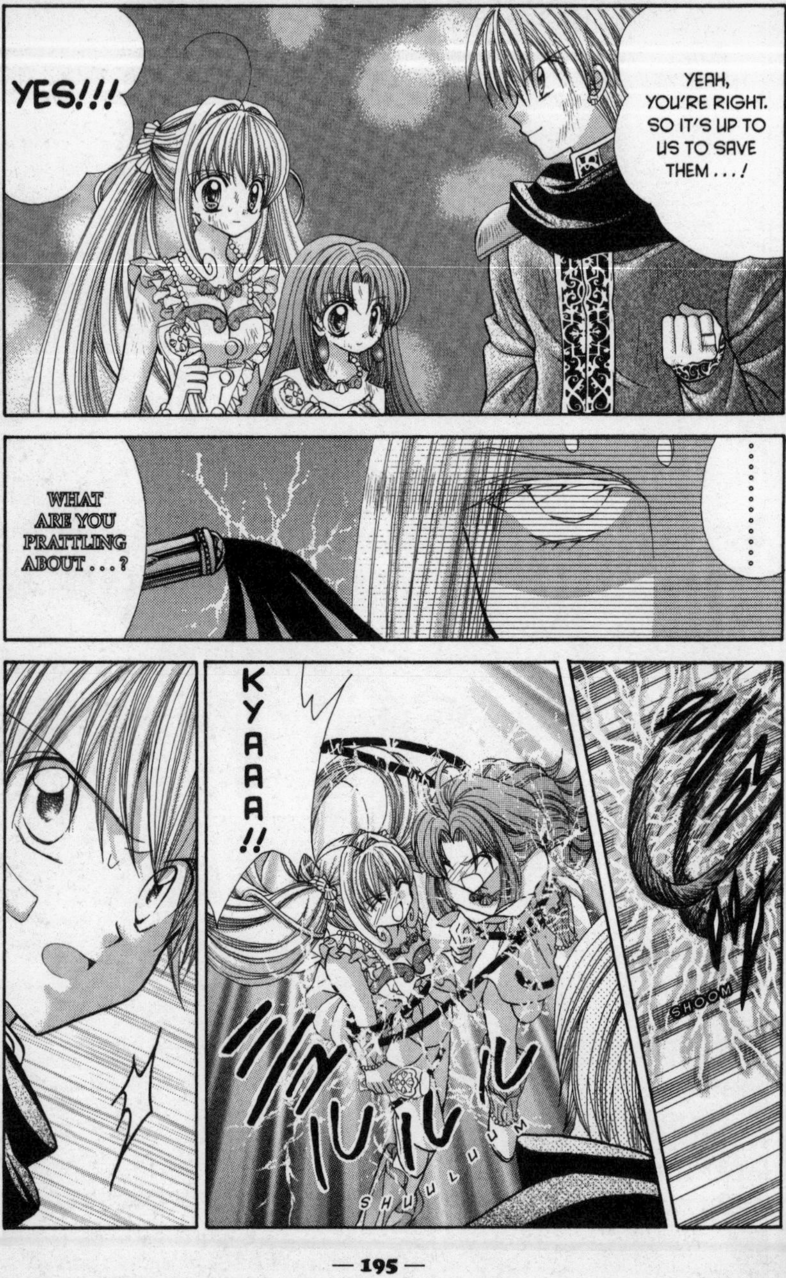
YEAH, YOU'RE RIGHT. SO IT'S UP TO US TO SAVE THEM . . . !
YES!!!
....
WHAT ARE YOU PRATTLING ABOUT . . . ?
SHOOM
KYAAAA!!
SHUULUUM

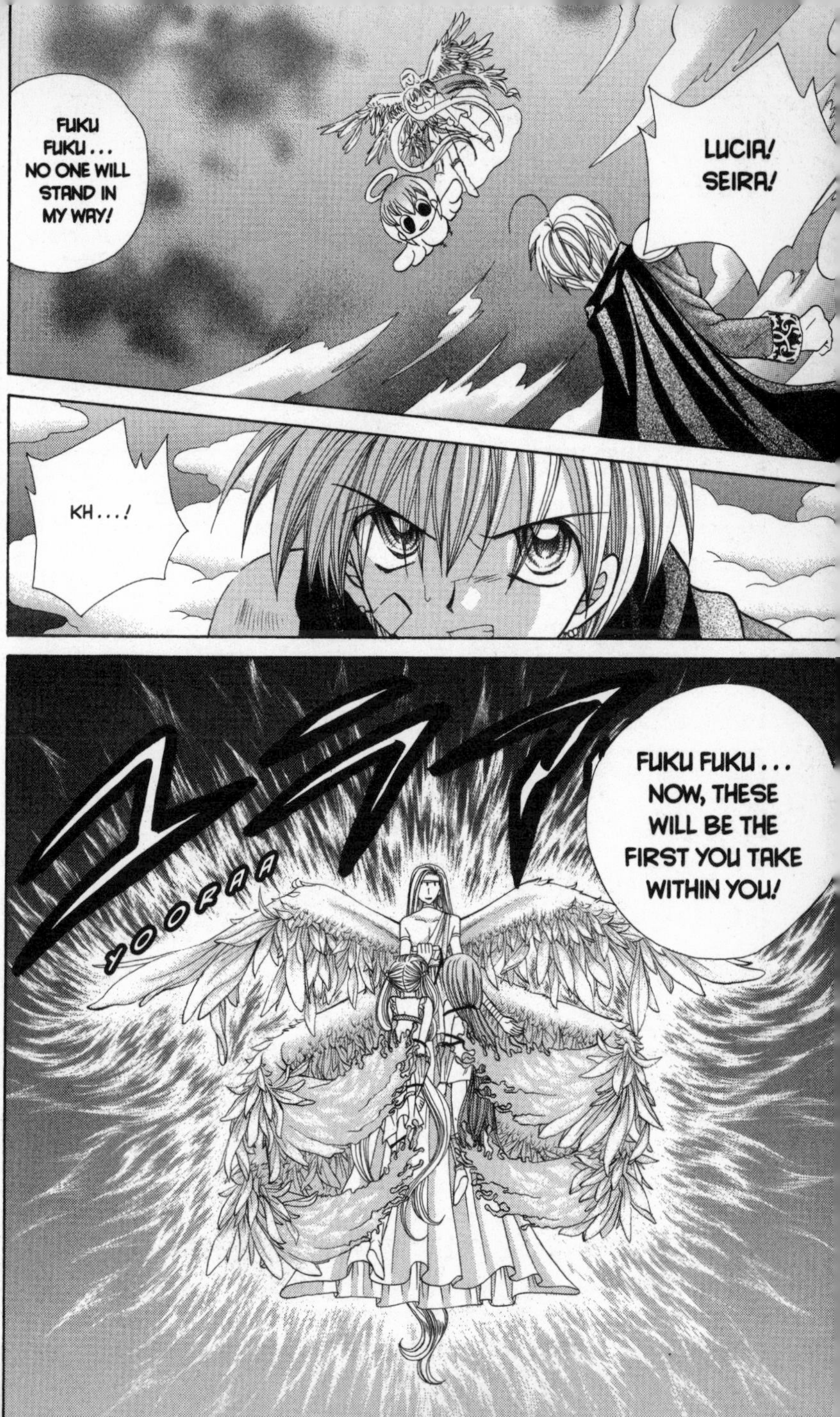
LUCIA! SEIRA!
FUKU FUKU . . . NO ONE WILL STAND IN MY WAY!
KH . . . !
FUKU FUKU . . . NOW, THESE WILL BE THE FIRST YOU TAKE WITHIN YOU!
YOORAA

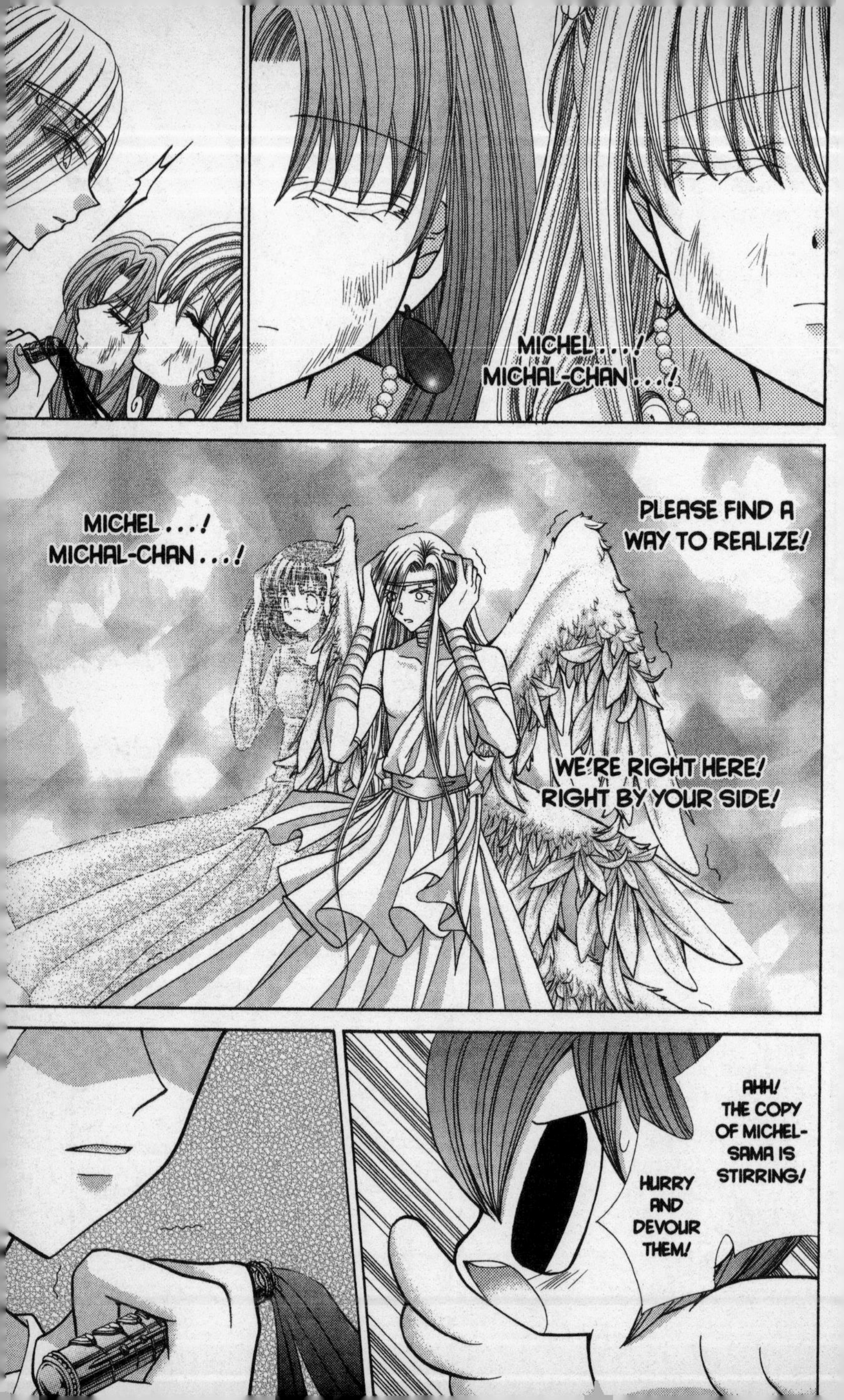
MICHEL . . . !
MICHAL-CHAN . . . !
PLEASE FIND A WAY TO REALIZE!
MICHEL . . . !
MICHAL-CHAN . . . !
WE'RE RIGHT HERE! RIGHT BY YOUR SIDE!
AHH! THE COPY OF MICHEL-SAMA IS STIRRING!
HURRY AND DEVOUR THEM!

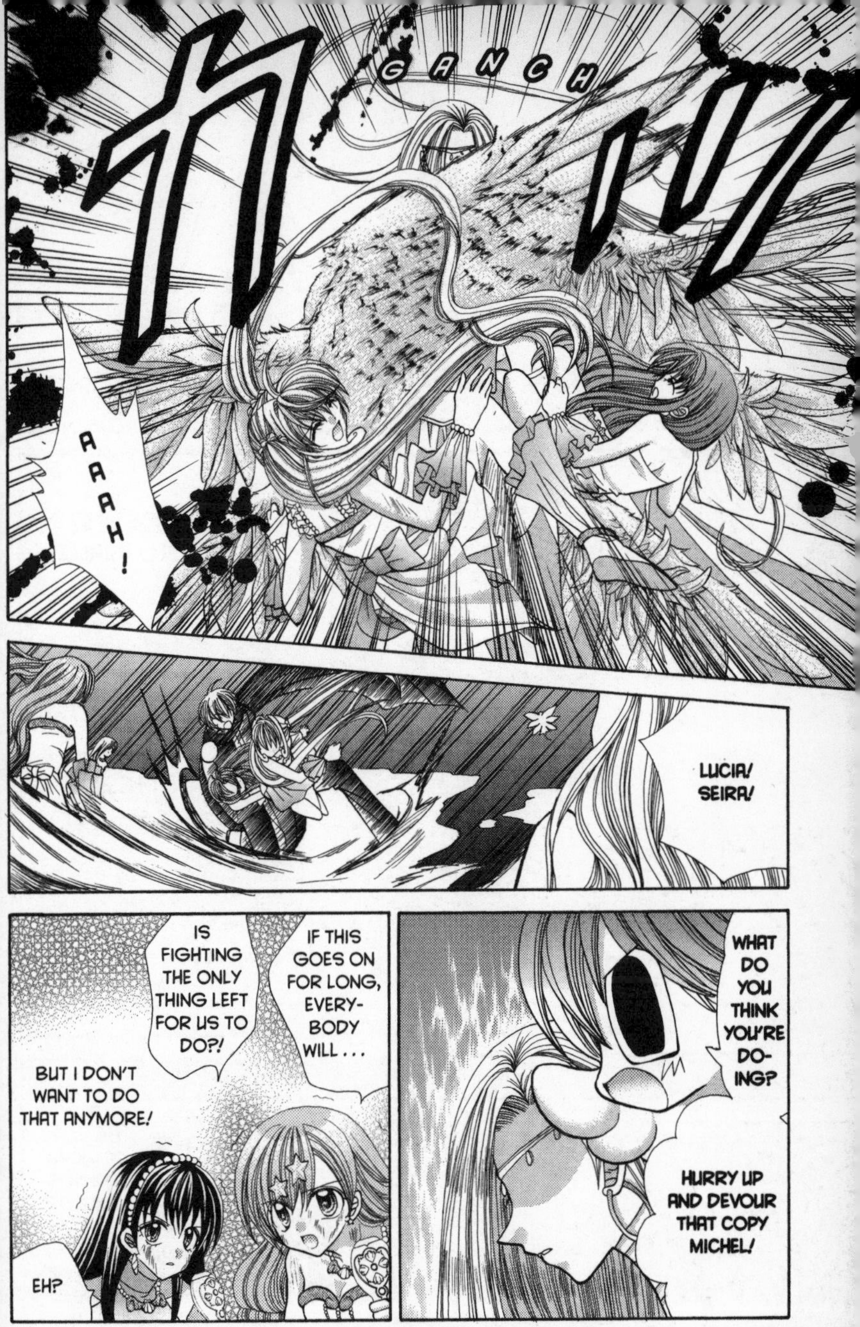
GANCH
AAAH!
LUCIA! SEIRA!
WHAT DO YOU THINK YOU'RE DOING?
HURRY UP AND DEVOUR THAT COPY MICHEL!
IF THIS GOES ON FOR LONG, EVERYBODY WILL . . .
IS FIGHTING THE ONLY THING LEFT FOR US TO DO?!
BUT I DON'T WANT TO DO THAT ANYMORE!
EH?

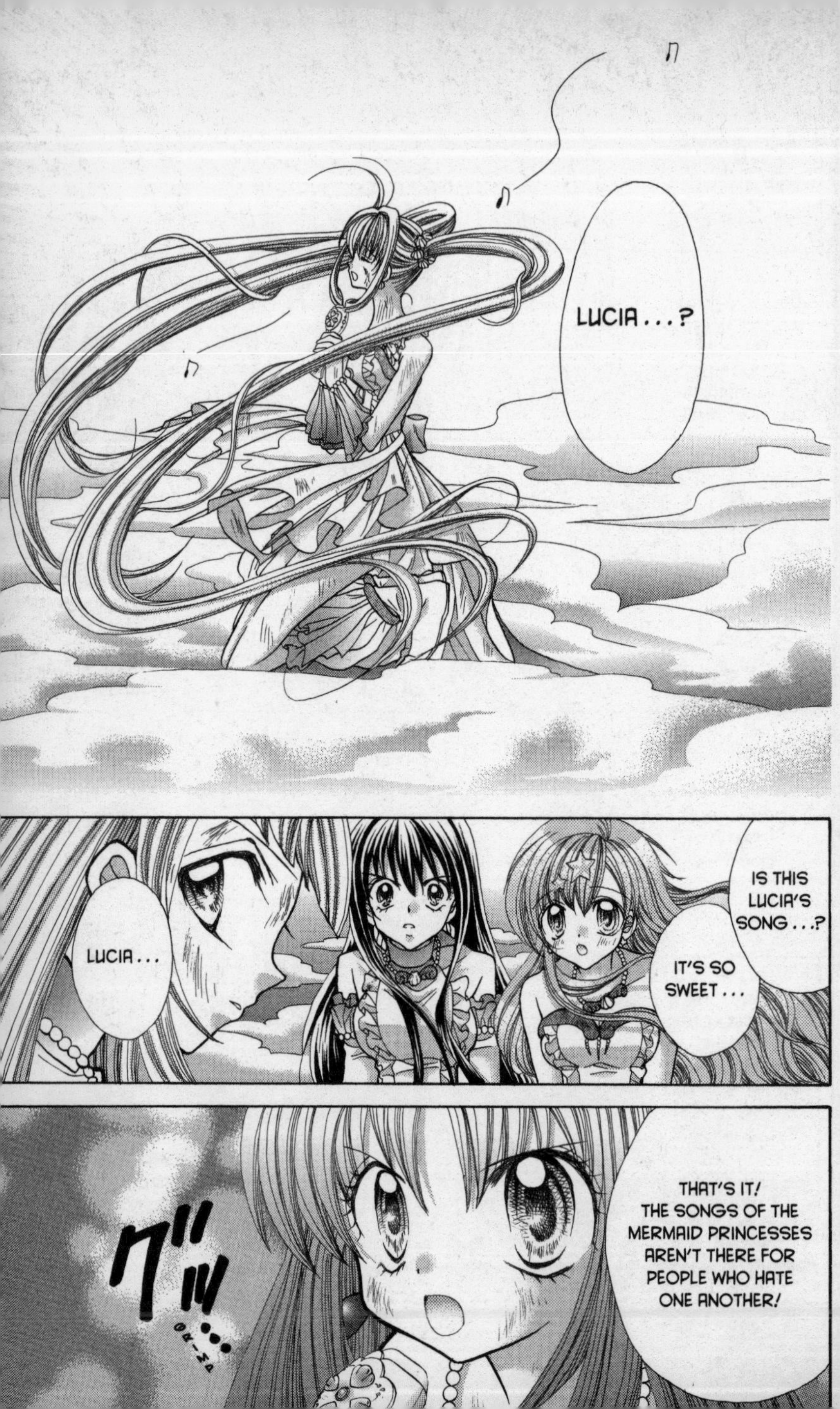
LUCIA...?
IS THIS LUCIA'S SONG...?
IT'S SO SWEET...
LUCIA...
THAT'S IT! THE SONGS OF THE MERMAID PRINCESSES AREN'T THERE FOR PEOPLE WHO HATE ONE ANOTHER!
グッ
GR-MA

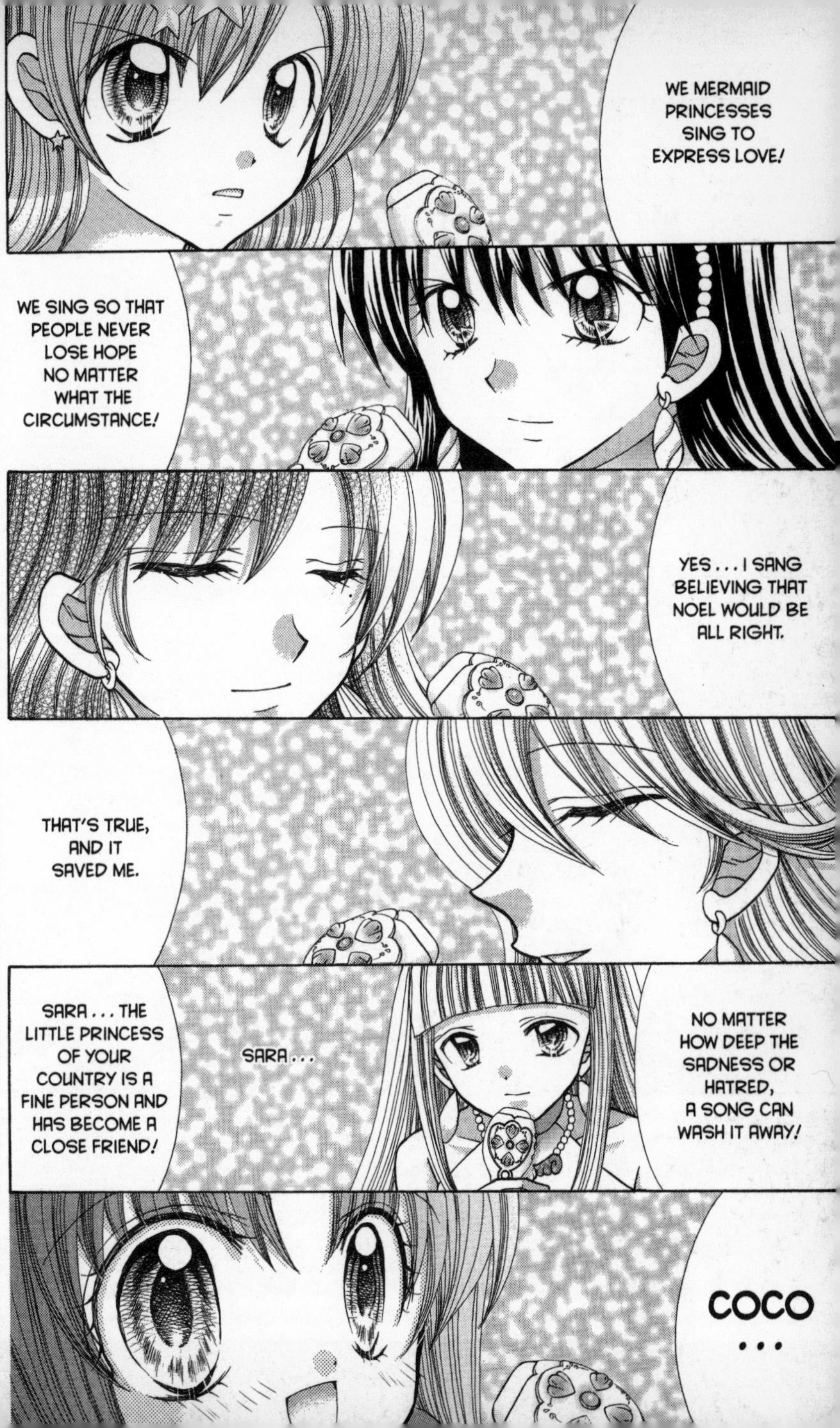
WE MERMAID PRINCESSES SING TO EXPRESS LOVE!
WE SING SO THAT PEOPLE NEVER LOSE HOPE NO MATTER WHAT THE CIRCUMSTANCE!
YES . . . I SANG BELIEVING THAT NOEL WOULD BE ALL RIGHT.
THAT'S TRUE, AND IT SAVED ME.
NO MATTER HOW DEEP THE SADNESS OR HATRED, A SONG CAN WASH IT AWAY!
SARA . . .
SARA . . . THE LITTLE PRINCESS OF YOUR COUNTRY IS A FINE PERSON AND HAS BECOME A CLOSE FRIEND!
COCO . . .

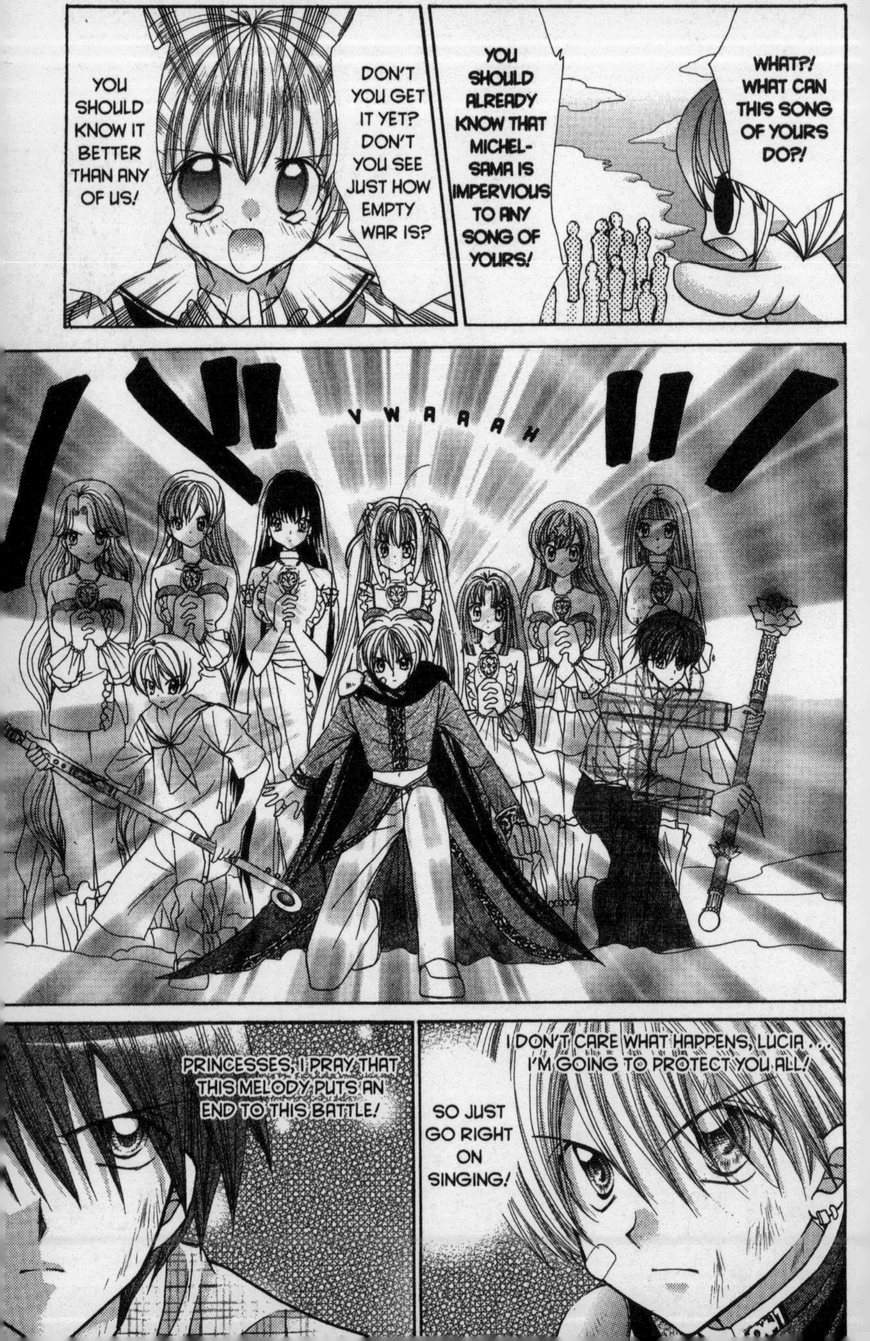
WHAT?! WHAT CAN THIS SONG OF YOURS DO?!
YOU SHOULD ALREADY KNOW THAT MICHEL-SAMA IS IMPERVIOUS TO ANY SONG OF YOURS!
DON'T YOU GET IT YET? DON'T YOU SEE JUST HOW EMPTY WAR IS?
YOU SHOULD KNOW IT BETTER THAN ANY OF US!
VWAAAAH
I DON'T CARE WHAT HAPPENS, LUCIA . . . I'M GOING TO PROTECT YOU ALL!
SO JUST GO RIGHT ON SINGING!
PRINCESSES, I PRAY THAT THIS MELODY PUTS AN END TO THIS BATTLE!

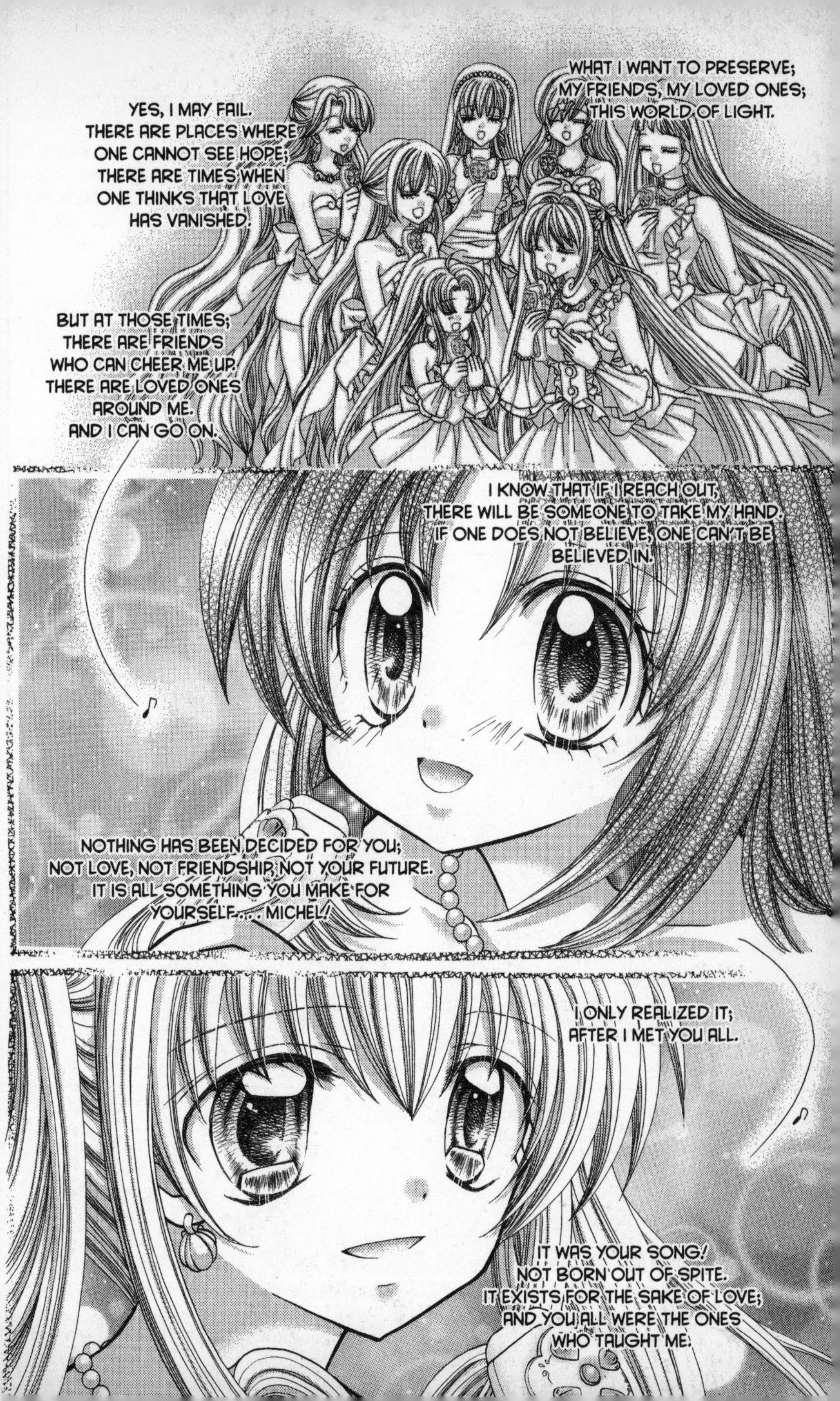
WHAT I WANT TO PRESERVE; MY FRIENDS, MY LOVED ONES; THIS WORLD OF LIGHT.
YES, I MAY FAIL. THERE ARE PLACES WHERE ONE CANNOT SEE HOPE; THERE ARE TIMES WHEN ONE THINKS THAT LOVE HAS VANISHED.
BUT AT THOSE TIMES; THERE ARE FRIENDS WHO CAN CHEER ME UP. THERE ARE LOVED ONES AROUND ME. AND I CAN GO ON.
I KNOW THAT IF I REACH OUT, THERE WILL BE SOMEONE TO TAKE MY HAND. IF ONE DOES NOT BELIEVE, ONE CAN'T BE BELIEVED IN.
NOTHING HAS BEEN DECIDED FOR YOU; NOT LOVE, NOT FRIENDSHIP, NOT YOUR FUTURE. IT IS ALL SOMETHING YOU MAKE FOR YOURSELF . . . MICHEL!
I ONLY REALIZED IT; AFTER I MET YOU ALL.
IT WAS YOUR SONG! NOT BORN OUT OF SPITE. IT EXISTS FOR THE SAKE OF LOVE; AND YOU ALL WERE THE ONES WHO TAUGHT ME.

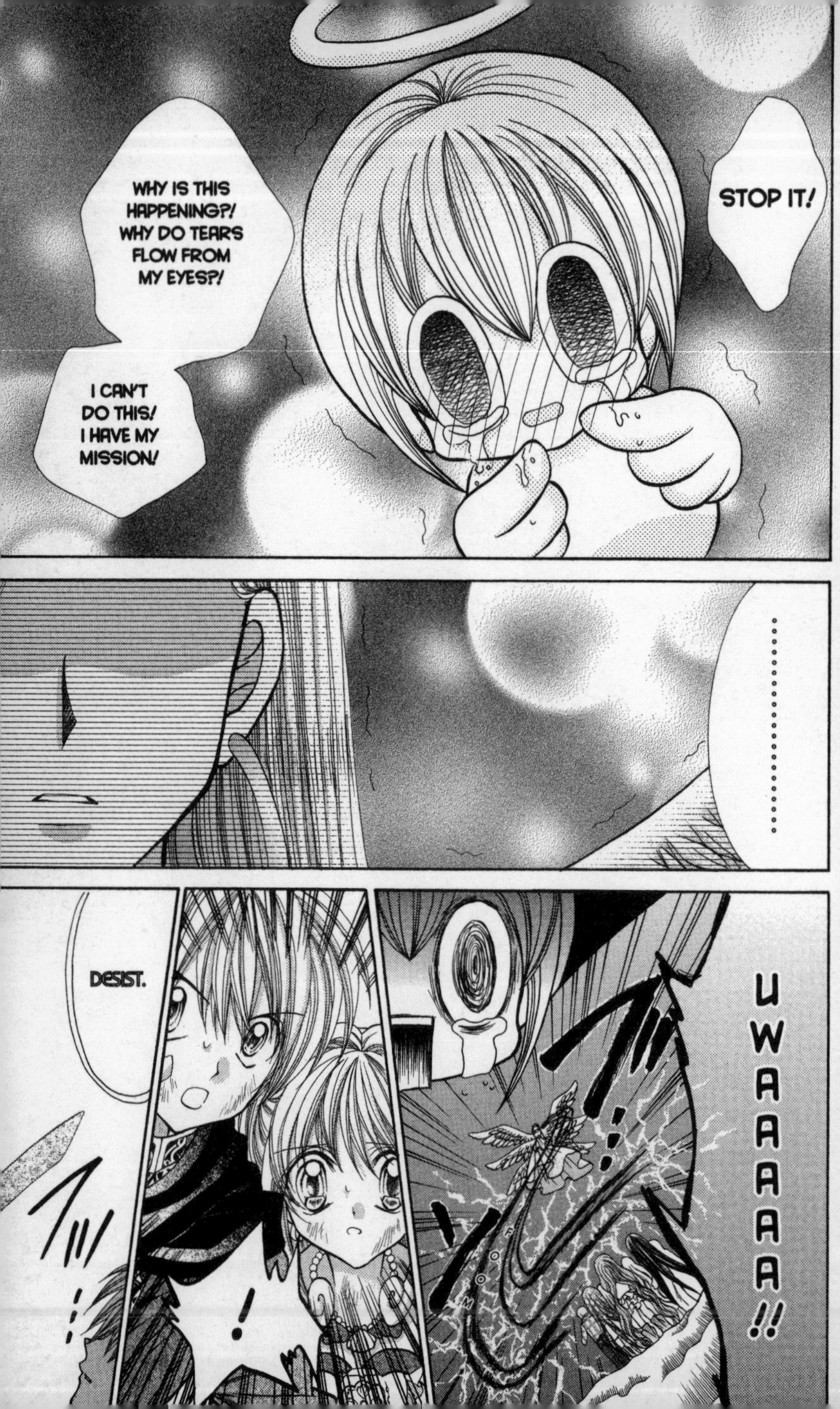
STOP IT!
WHY IS THIS HAPPENING?! WHY DO TEARS FLOW FROM MY EYES?!
I CAN'T DO THIS! I HAVE MY MISSION!
....
UWAAAAAA!!
FOOM
!
DESIST.
!!

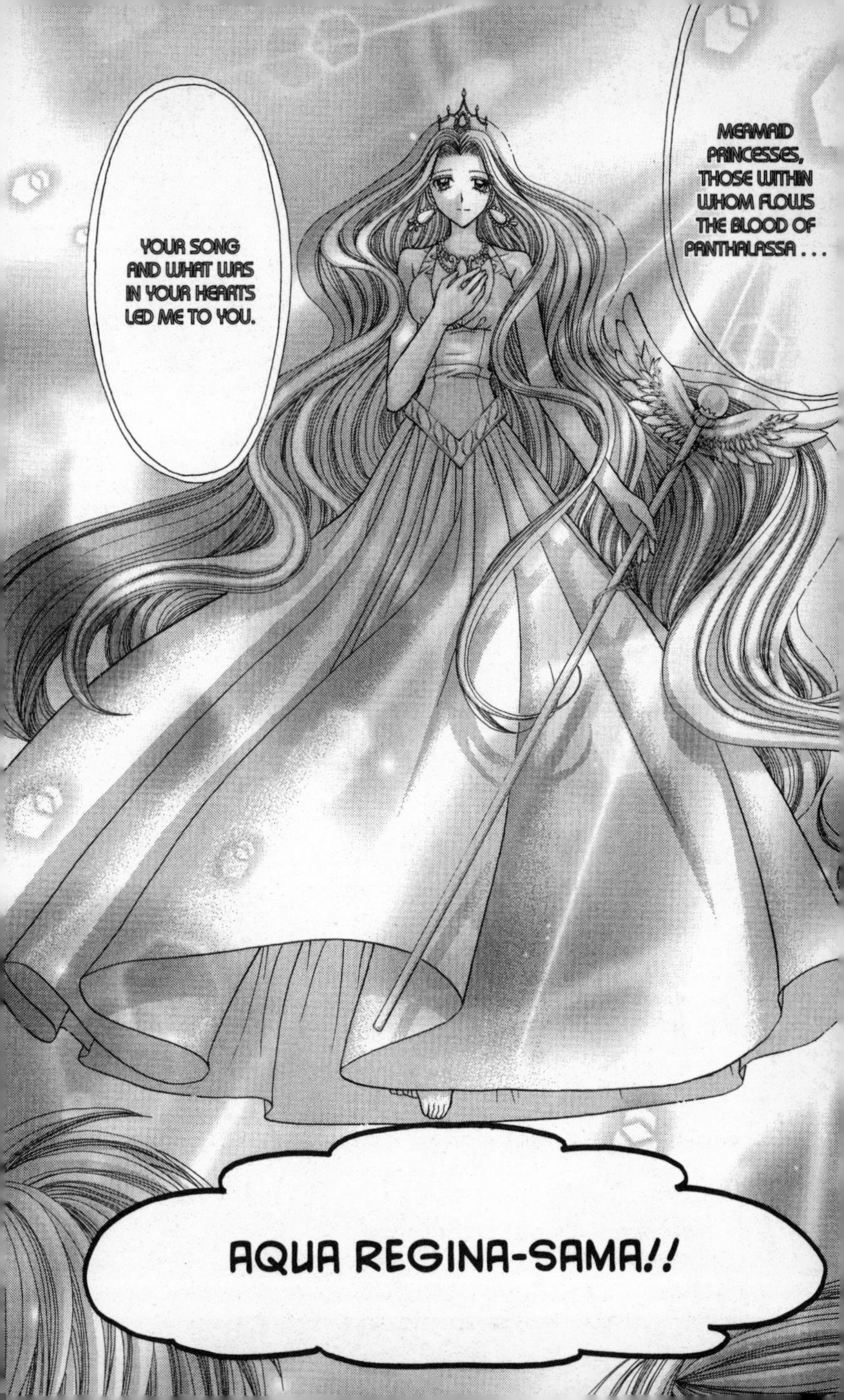
MERMAID PRINCESSES, THOSE WITHIN WHOM FLOWS THE BLOOD OF PANTHALASSA . . .
YOUR SONG AND WHAT WAS IN YOUR HEARTS LED ME TO YOU.
AQUA REGINA-SAMA!!

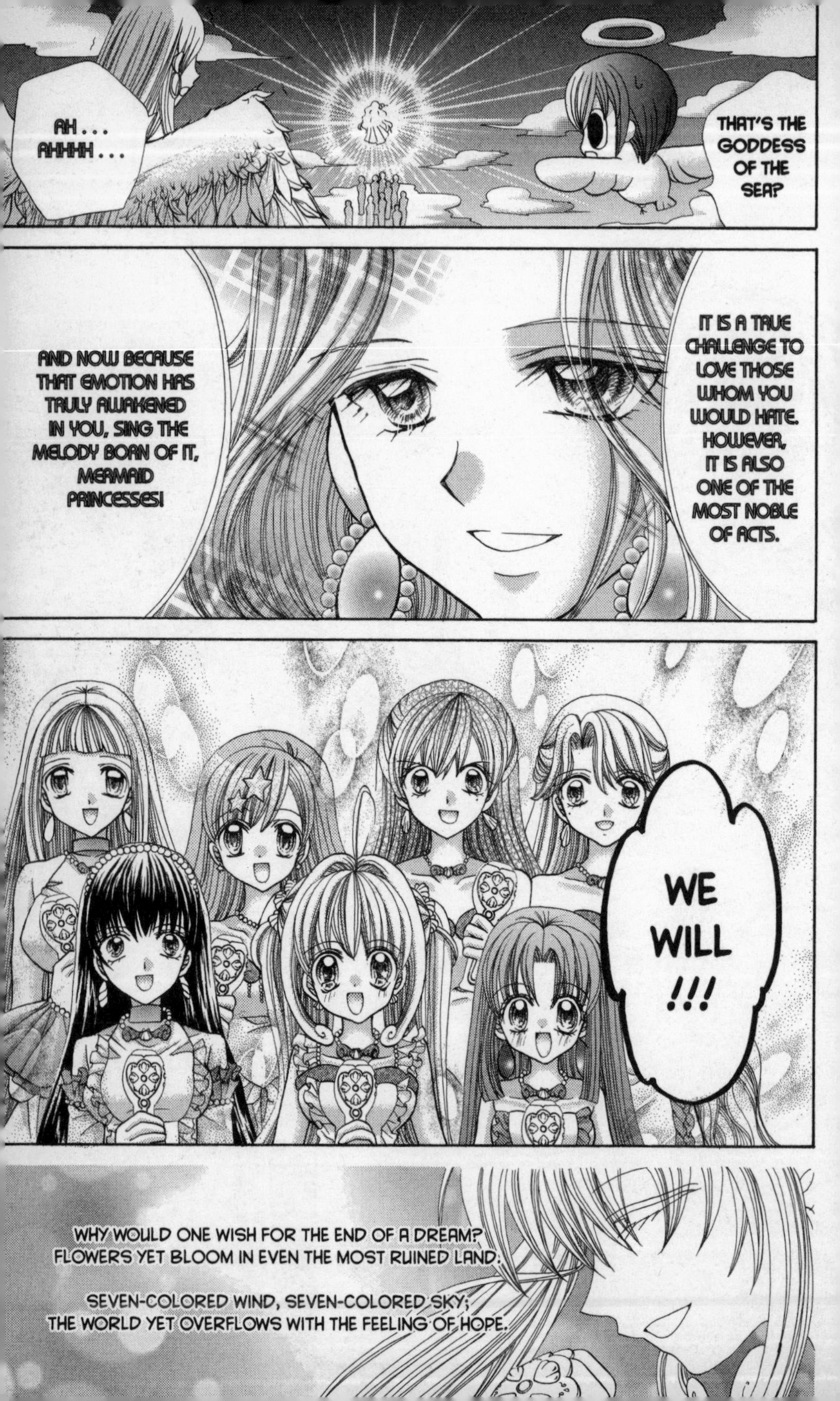
THAT'S THE GODDESS OF THE SEA?
AH . . . AHHHH . . .
IT IS A TRUE CHALLENGE TO LOVE THOSE WHOM YOU WOULD HATE. HOWEVER, IT IS ALSO ONE OF THE MOST NOBLE OF ACTS.
AND NOW BECAUSE THAT EMOTION HAS TRULY AWAKENED IN YOU, SING THE MELODY BORN OF IT, MERMAID PRINCESSES!
WE WILL !!!
WHY WOULD ONE WISH FOR THE END OF A DREAM? FLOWERS YET BLOOM IN EVEN THE MOST RUINED LAND.
SEVEN-COLORED WIND, SEVEN-COLORED SKY; THE WORLD YET OVERFLOWS WITH THE FEELING OF HOPE.

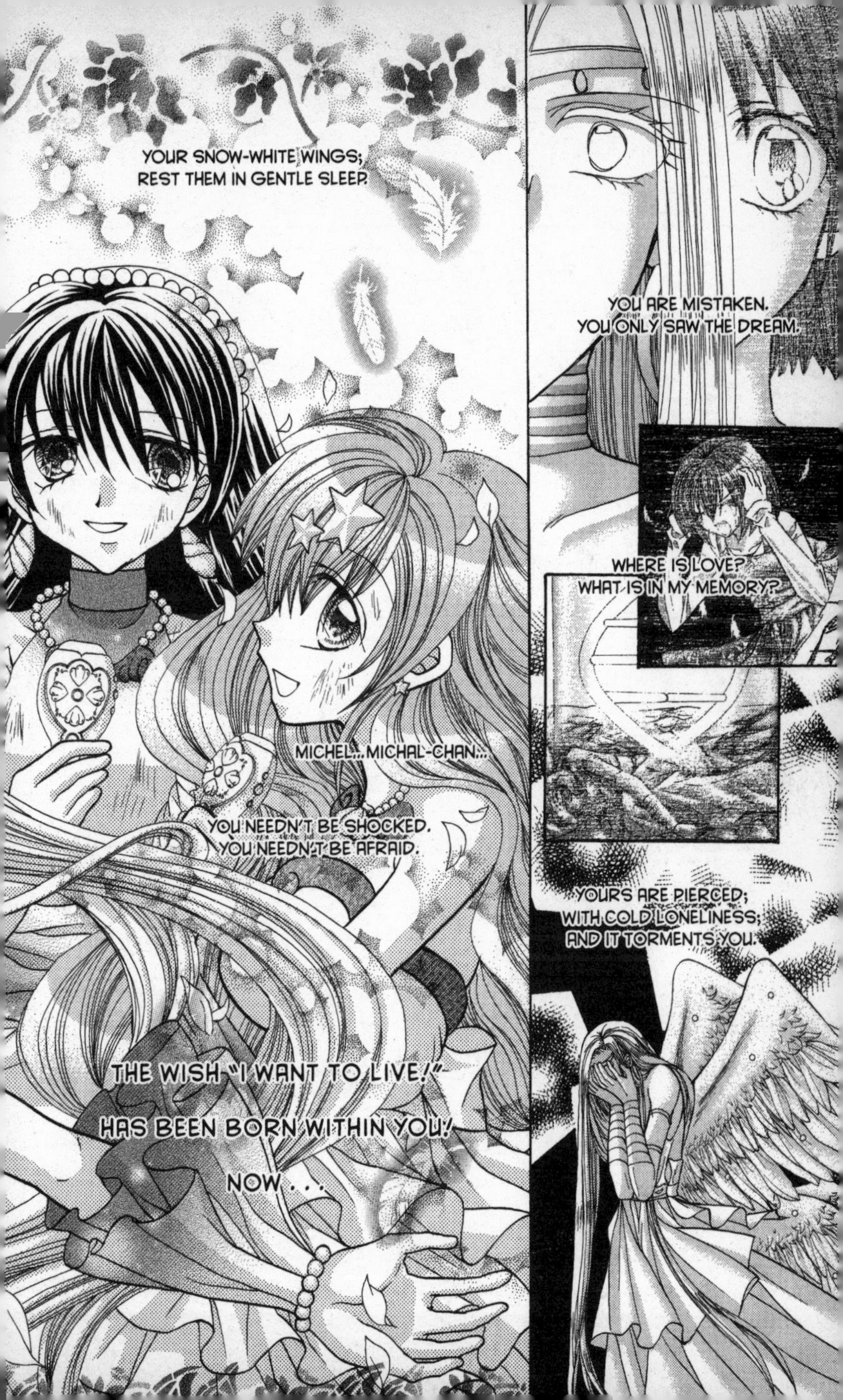
YOU ARE MISTAKEN.
YOU ONLY SAW THE DREAM.
WHERE IS LOVE?
WHAT IS IN MY MEMORY?
YOURS ARE PIERCED;
WITH COLD LONELINESS;
AND IT TORMENTS YOU.
YOUR SNOW-WHITE WINGS;
REST THEM IN GENTLE SLEEP.
MICHEL...MICHAL-CHAN...
YOU NEEDN'T BE SHOCKED.
YOU NEEDN'T BE AFRAID.
THE WISH "I WANT TO LIVE!"
HAS BEEN BORN WITHIN YOU!
NOW . . .

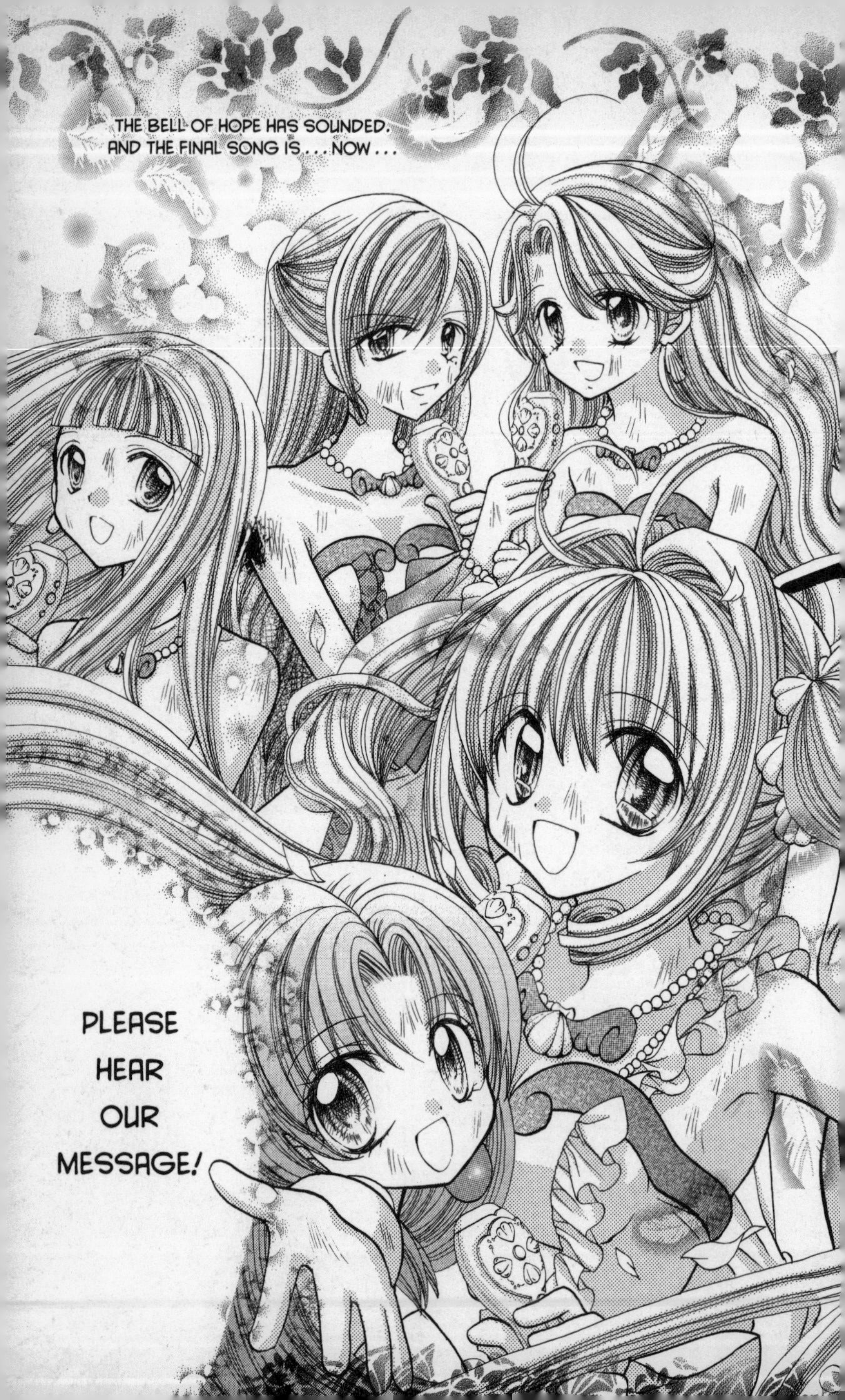
THE BELL OF HOPE HAS SOUNDED.
AND THE FINAL SONG IS . . . NOW . . .
PLEASE HEAR OUR MESSAGE!

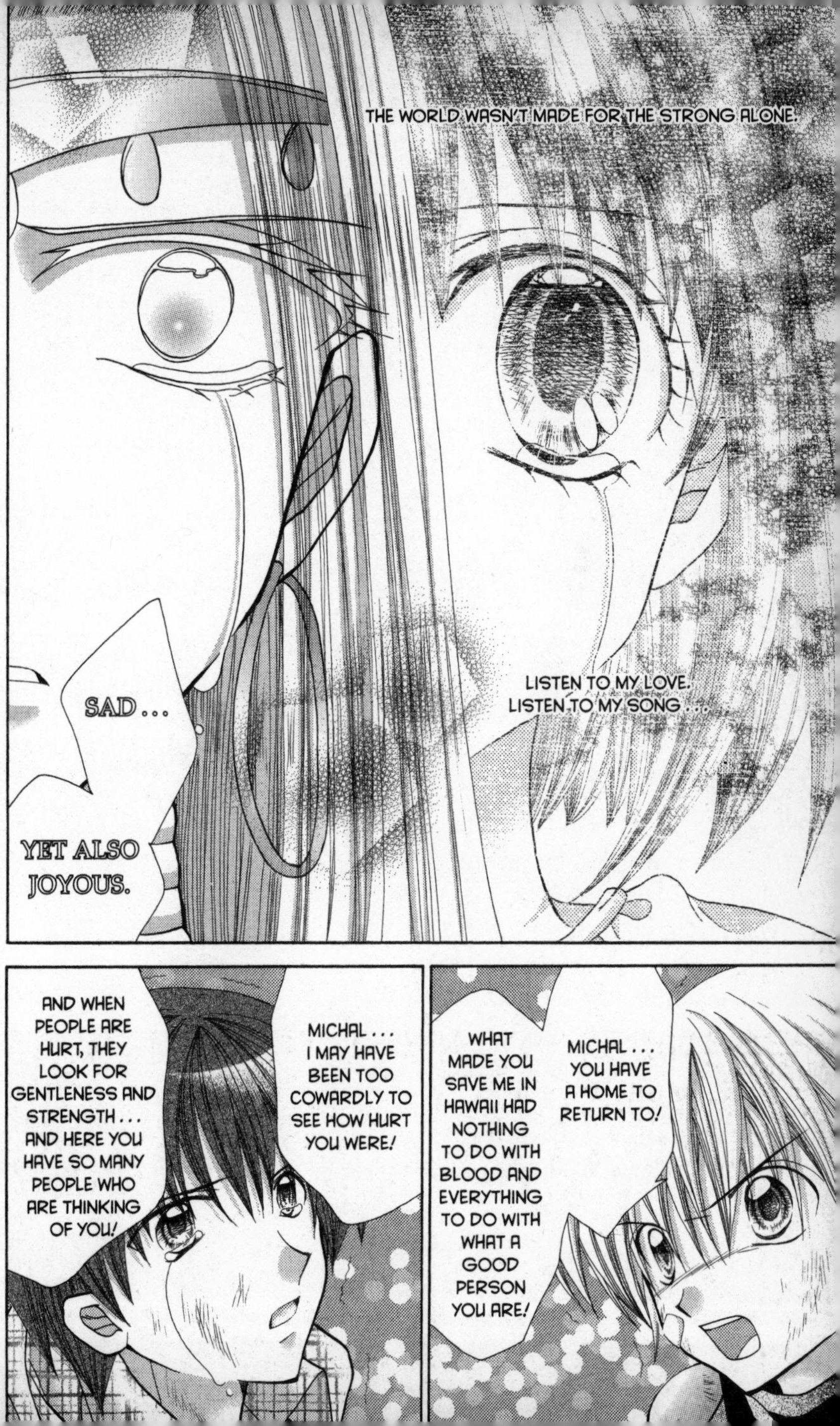
THE WORLD WASN'T MADE FOR THE STRONG ALONE.
LISTEN TO MY LOVE. LISTEN TO MY SONG . . .
SAD . . .
YET ALSO JOYOUS.
MICHAL . . . YOU HAVE A HOME TO RETURN TO!
WHAT MADE YOU SAVE ME IN HAWAII HAD NOTHING TO DO WITH BLOOD AND EVERYTHING TO DO WITH WHAT A GOOD PERSON YOU ARE!
MICHAL . . . I MAY HAVE BEEN TOO COWARDLY TO SEE HOW HURT YOU WERE!
AND WHEN PEOPLE ARE HURT, THEY LOOK FOR GENTLENESS AND STRENGTH . . . AND HERE YOU HAVE SO MANY PEOPLE WHO ARE THINKING OF YOU!

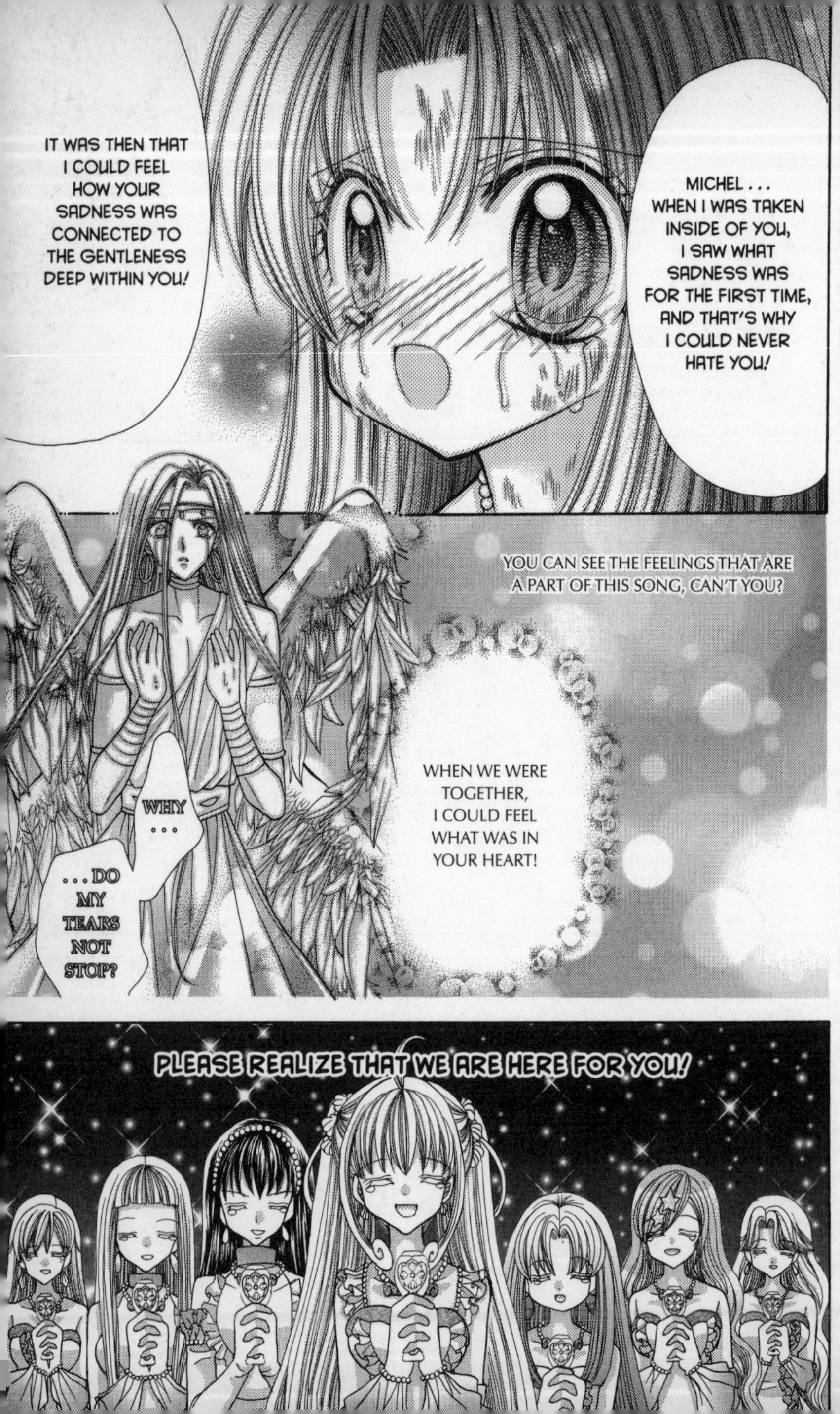
MICHEL . . . WHEN I WAS TAKEN INSIDE OF YOU, I SAW WHAT SADNESS WAS FOR THE FIRST TIME, AND THAT'S WHY I COULD NEVER HATE YOU!
IT WAS THEN THAT I COULD FEEL HOW YOUR SADNESS WAS CONNECTED TO THE GENTLENESS DEEP WITHIN YOU!
YOU CAN SEE THE FEELINGS THAT ARE A PART OF THIS SONG, CAN'T YOU?
WHEN WE WERE TOGETHER, I COULD FEEL WHAT WAS IN YOUR HEART!
WHY . . .
. . . DO MY TEARS NOT STOP?
PLEASE REALIZE THAT WE ARE HERE FOR YOU!

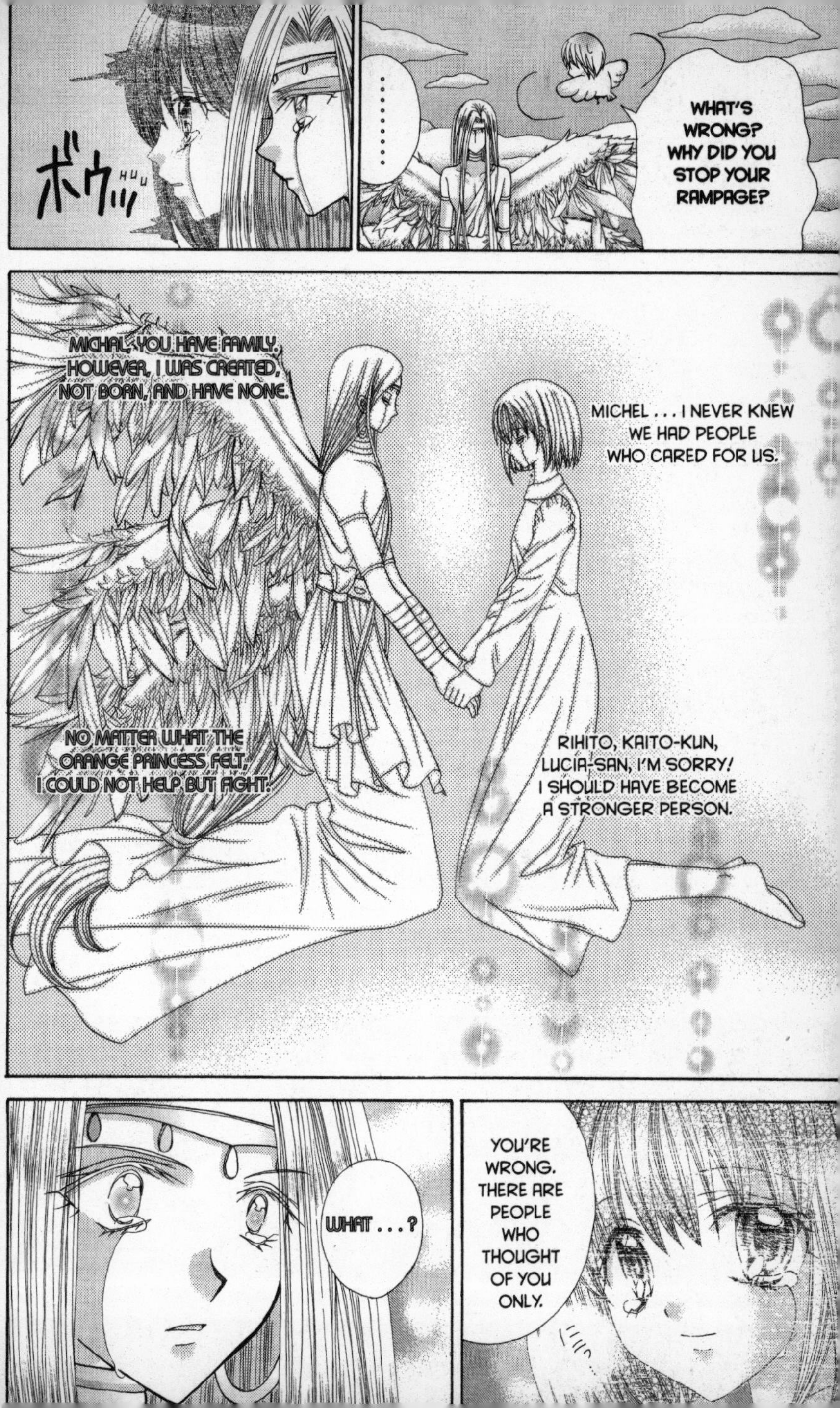
WHAT'S WRONG? WHY DID YOU STOP YOUR RAMPAGE?
. . . .
ボウッ
HUU
MICHEL . . . I NEVER KNEW WE HAD PEOPLE WHO CARED FOR US.
MICHAL, YOU HAVE FAMILY. HOWEVER, I WAS CREATED, NOT BORN, AND HAVE NONE.
RIHITO, KAITO-KUN, LUCIA-SAN, I'M SORRY! I SHOULD HAVE BECOME A STRONGER PERSON.
NO MATTER WHAT THE ORANGE PRINCESS FELT, I COULD NOT HELP BUT FIGHT.
YOU'RE WRONG. THERE ARE PEOPLE WHO THOUGHT OF YOU ONLY.
WHAT . . . ?

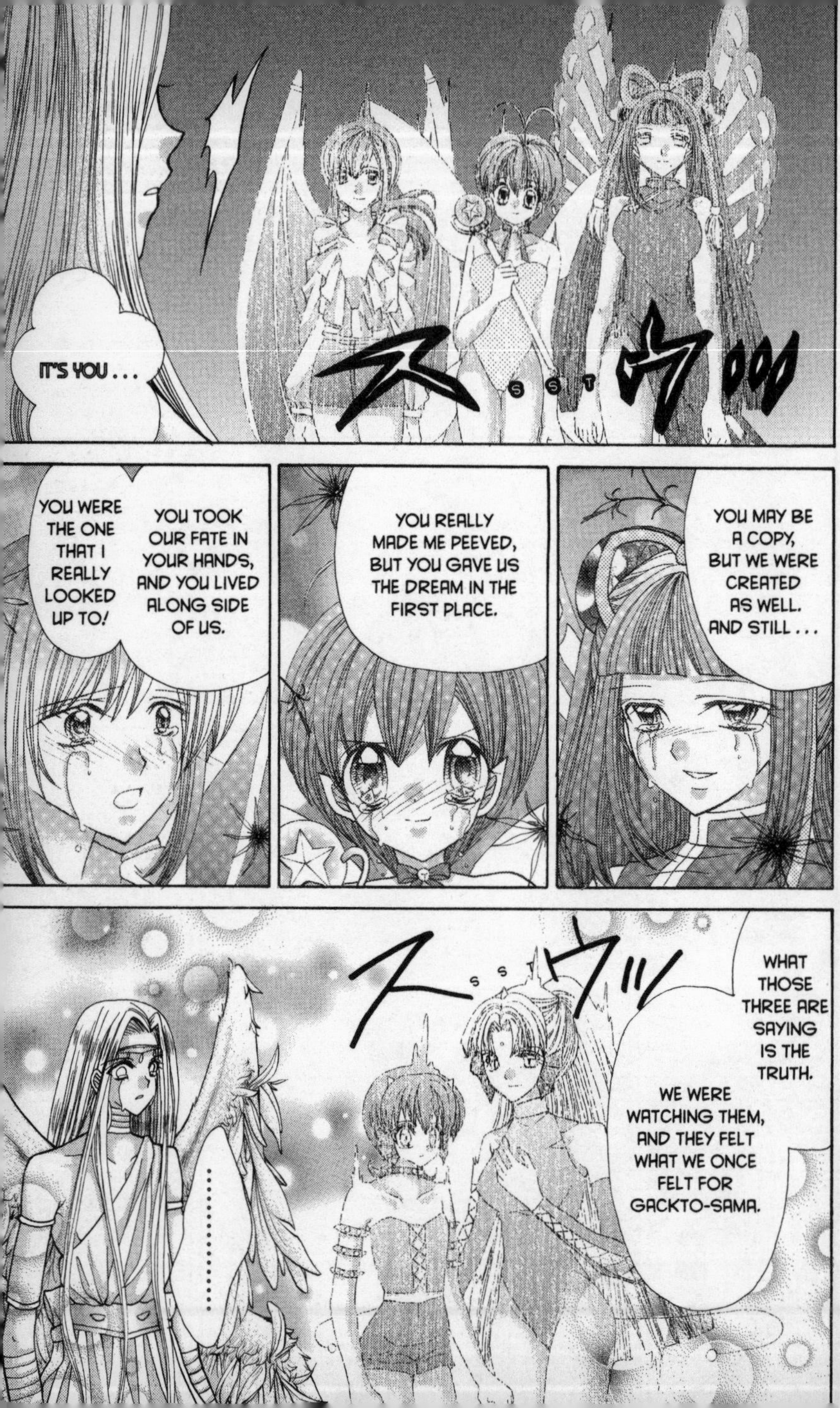
IT'S YOU . . .
S S T
YOU MAY BE A COPY, BUT WE WERE CREATED AS WELL. AND STILL . . .
YOU REALLY MADE ME PEEVED, BUT YOU GAVE US THE DREAM IN THE FIRST PLACE.
YOU TOOK OUR FATE IN YOUR HANDS, AND YOU LIVED ALONG SIDE OF US.
YOU WERE THE ONE THAT I REALLY LOOKED UP TO!
WHAT THOSE THREE ARE SAYING IS THE TRUTH.
WE WERE WATCHING THEM, AND THEY FELT WHAT WE ONCE FELT FOR GACKTO-SAMA.
S S T
. . . .

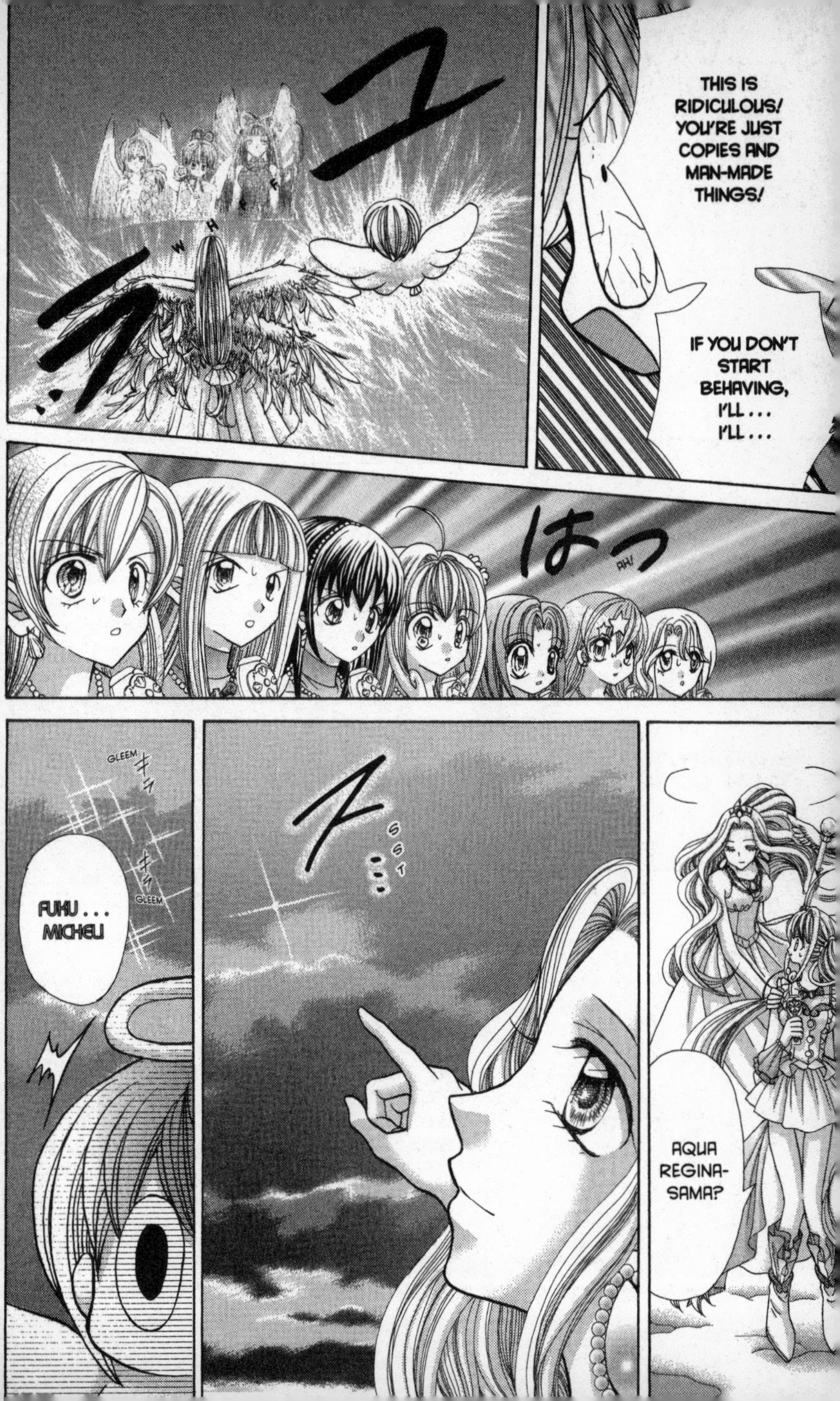
THIS IS RIDICULOUS! YOU'RE JUST COPIES AND MAN-MADE THINGS!
IF YOU DON'T START BEHAVING, I'LL . . . I'LL . . .
WHEF
はっ
AH!
AQUA REGINA-SAMA?
SSST . . .
GLEEM
GLEEM
FUKU . . . MICHELI

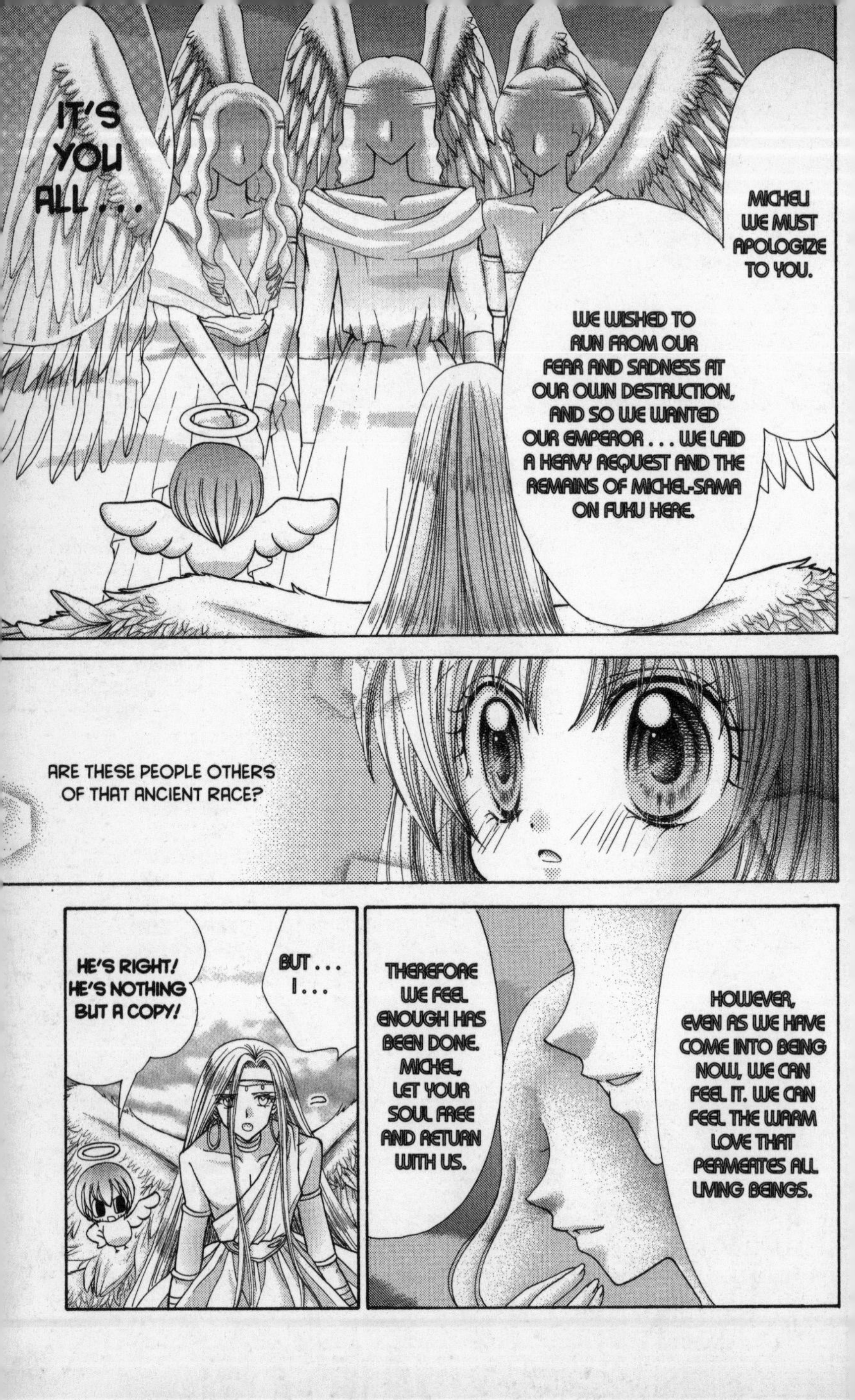
MICHEL! WE MUST APOLOGIZE TO YOU.
WE WISHED TO RUN FROM OUR FEAR AND SADNESS AT OUR OWN DESTRUCTION, AND SO WE WANTED OUR EMPEROR . . . WE LAID A HEAVY REQUEST AND THE REMAINS OF MICHEL-SAMA ON FUKU HERE.
IT'S YOU ALL . . .
ARE THESE PEOPLE OTHERS OF THAT ANCIENT RACE?
HOWEVER, EVEN AS WE HAVE COME INTO BEING NOW, WE CAN FEEL IT. WE CAN FEEL THE WARM LOVE THAT PERMEATES ALL LIVING BEINGS.
THEREFORE WE FEEL ENOUGH HAS BEEN DONE. MICHEL, LET YOUR SOUL FREE AND RETURN WITH US.
BUT . . . I . . .
HE'S RIGHT! HE'S NOTHING BUT A COPY!

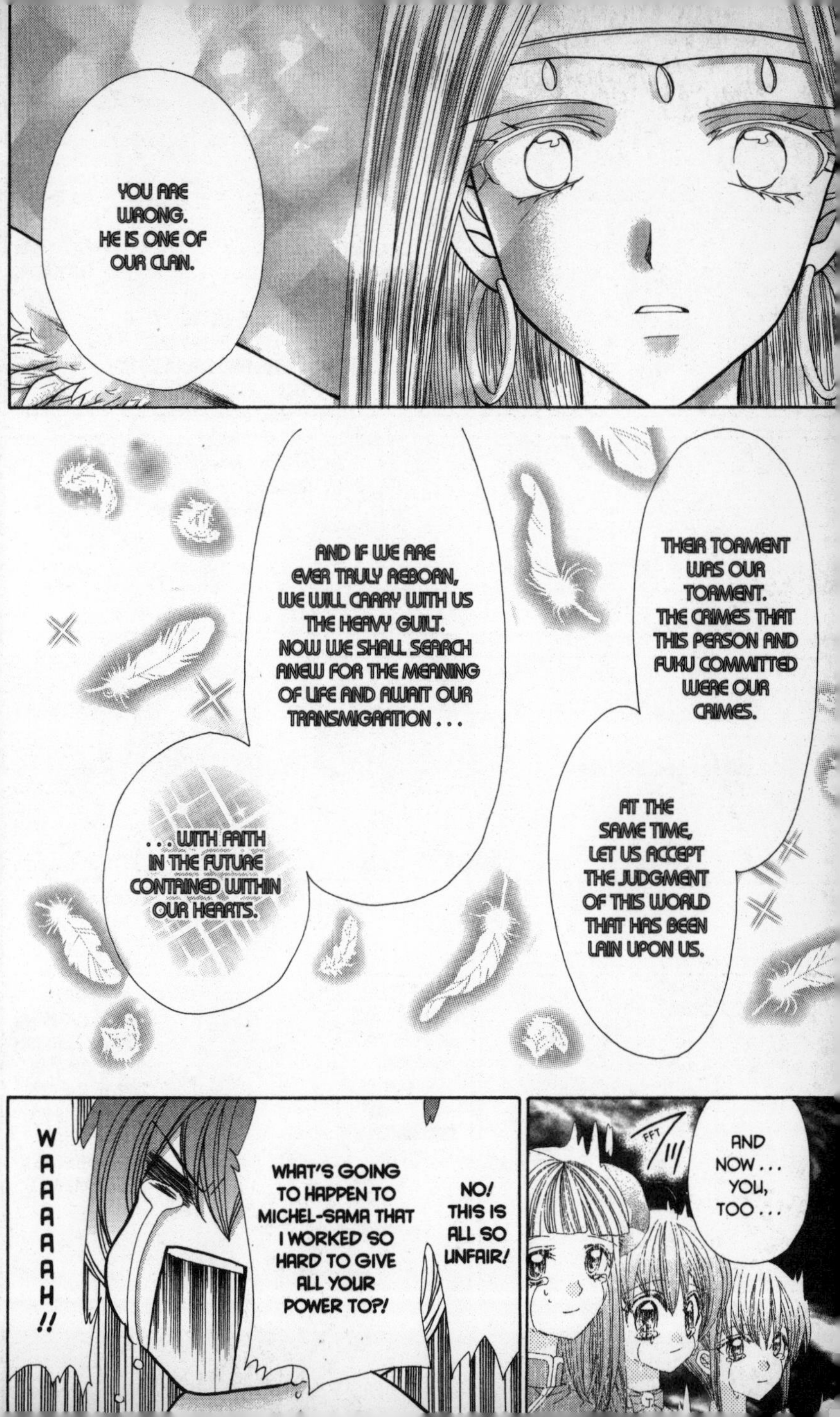
YOU ARE WRONG. HE IS ONE OF OUR CLAN.
THEIR TORMENT WAS OUR TORMENT. THE CRIMES THAT THIS PERSON AND FUKU COMMITTED WERE OUR CRIMES.
AT THE SAME TIME, LET US ACCEPT THE JUDGMENT OF THIS WORLD THAT HAS BEEN LAIN UPON US.
AND IF WE ARE EVER TRULY REBORN, WE WILL CARRY WITH US THE HEAVY GUILT. NOW WE SHALL SEARCH ANEW FOR THE MEANING OF LIFE AND AWAIT OUR TRANSMIGRATION . . .
. . . WITH FAITH IN THE FUTURE CONTAINED WITHIN OUR HEARTS.
FFT
AND NOW . . . YOU, TOO . . .
NO! THIS IS ALL SO UNFAIR!
WHAT'S GOING TO HAPPEN TO MICHEL-SAMA THAT I WORKED SO HARD TO GIVE ALL YOUR POWER TO?!
WAAAAAAH!!

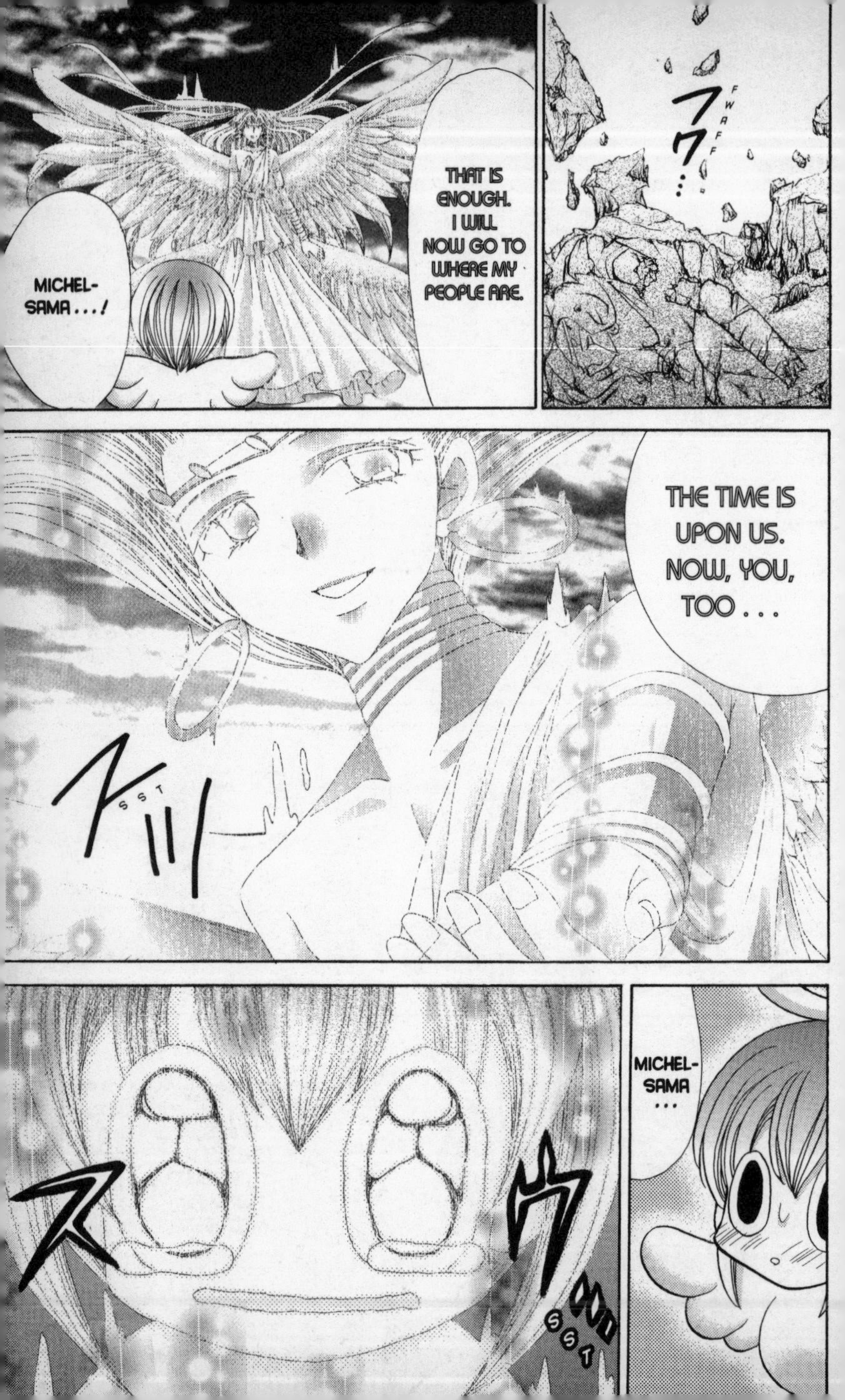

FWAFF
THAT IS ENOUGH. I WILL NOW GO TO WHERE MY PEOPLE ARE.
MICHEL-SAMA . . . !
THE TIME IS UPON US. NOW, YOU, TOO . . .
SST
MICHEL-SAMA . . .
SST

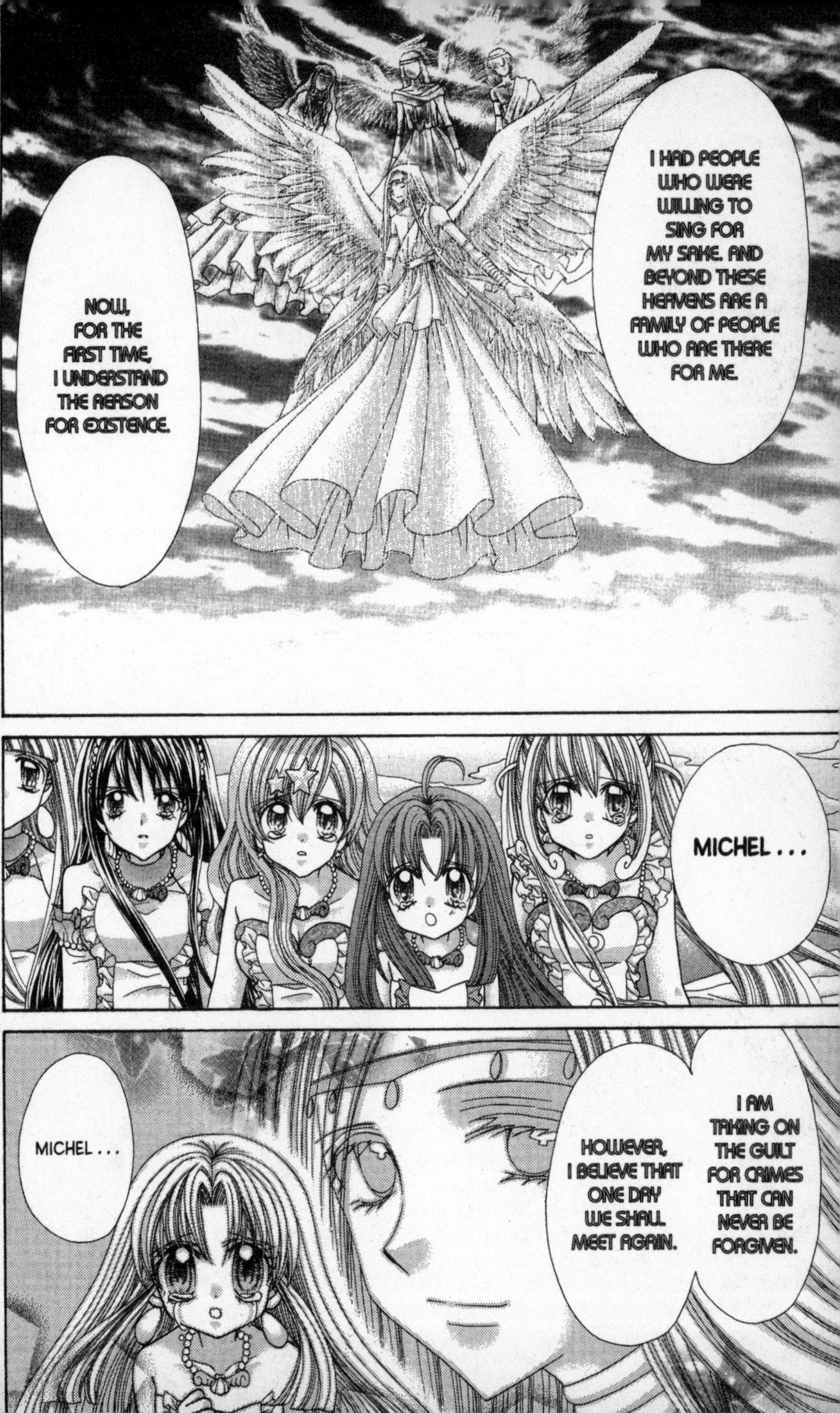
I HAD PEOPLE WHO WERE WILLING TO SING FOR MY SAKE. AND BEYOND THESE HEAVENS ARE A FAMILY OF PEOPLE WHO ARE THERE FOR ME.
NOW, FOR THE FIRST TIME, I UNDERSTAND THE REASON FOR EXISTENCE.
MICHEL . . .
I AM TAKING ON THE GUILT FOR CRIMES THAT CAN NEVER BE FORGIVEN.
HOWEVER, I BELIEVE THAT ONE DAY WE SHALL MEET AGAIN.
MICHEL . . .

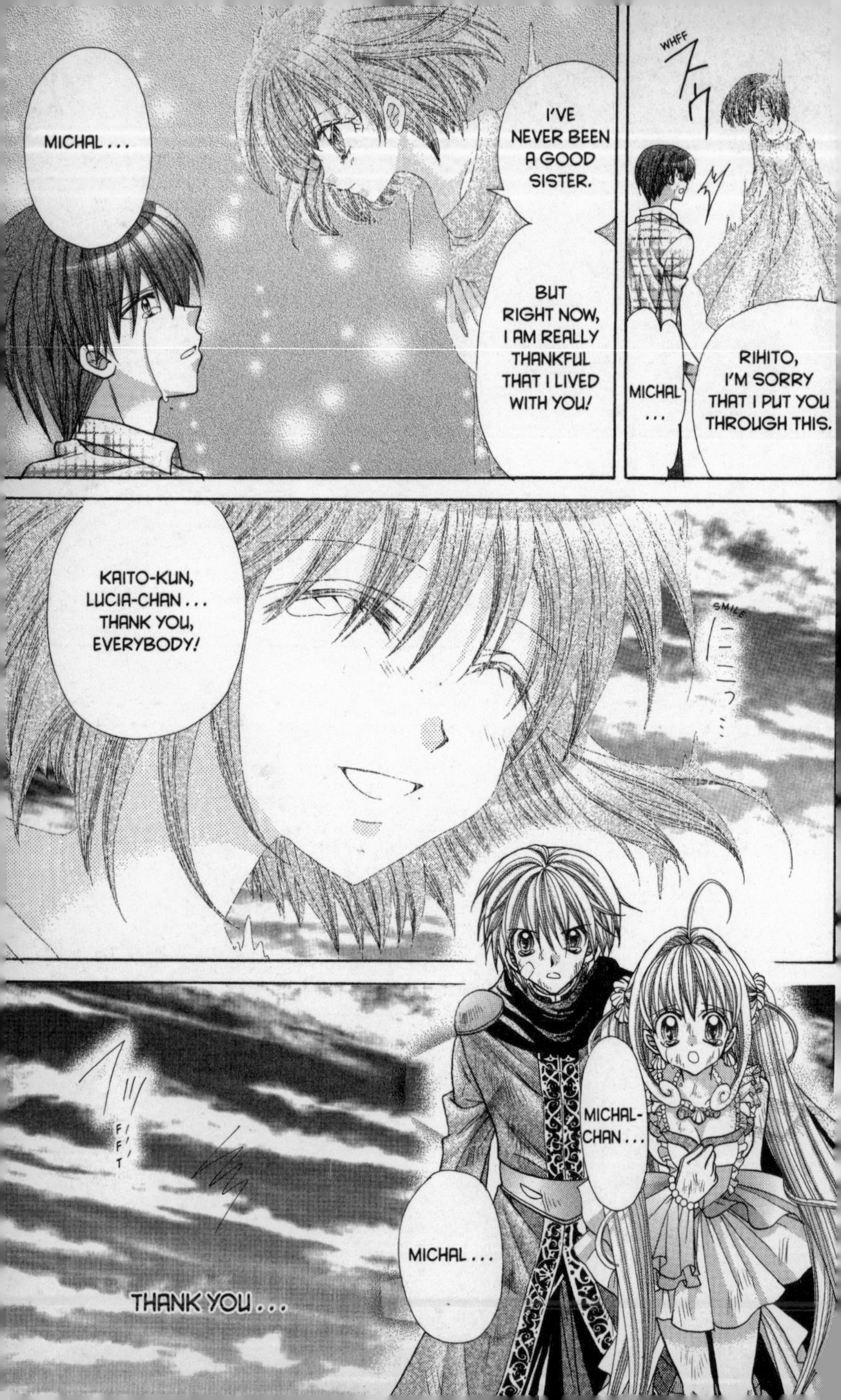
WHFF
RIHITO, I'M SORRY THAT I PUT YOU THROUGH THIS.
MICHAL . . .
I'VE NEVER BEEN A GOOD SISTER.
BUT RIGHT NOW, I AM REALLY THANKFUL THAT I LIVED WITH YOU!
MICHAL . . .
SMILE
KAITO-KUN, LUCIA-CHAN . . . THANK YOU, EVERYBODY!
MICHAL-CHAN . . .
MICHAL . . .
FFT
THANK YOU . . .

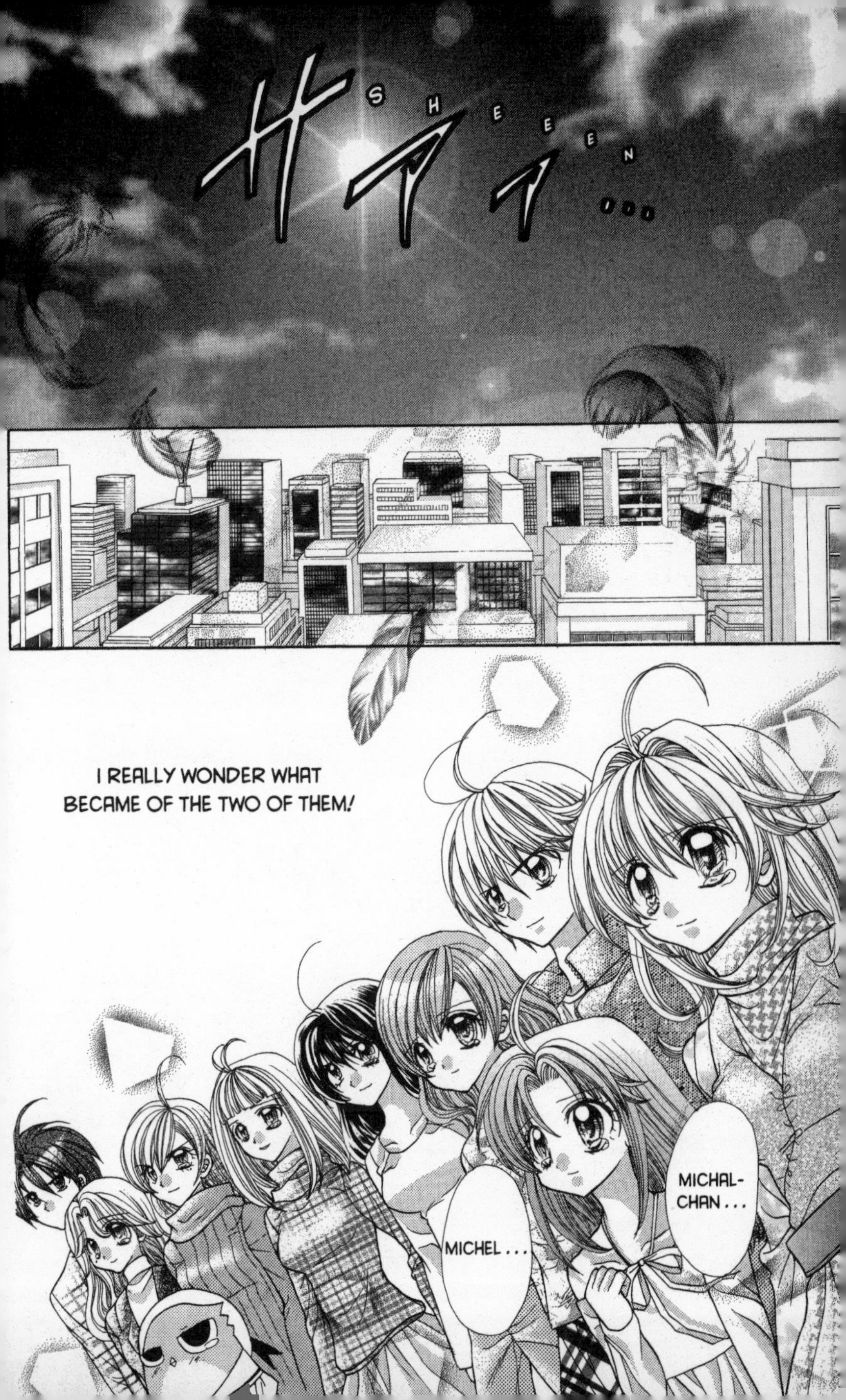
SHEEN...
I REALLY WONDER WHAT BECAME OF THE TWO OF THEM!
MICHAL-CHAN...
MICHEL...

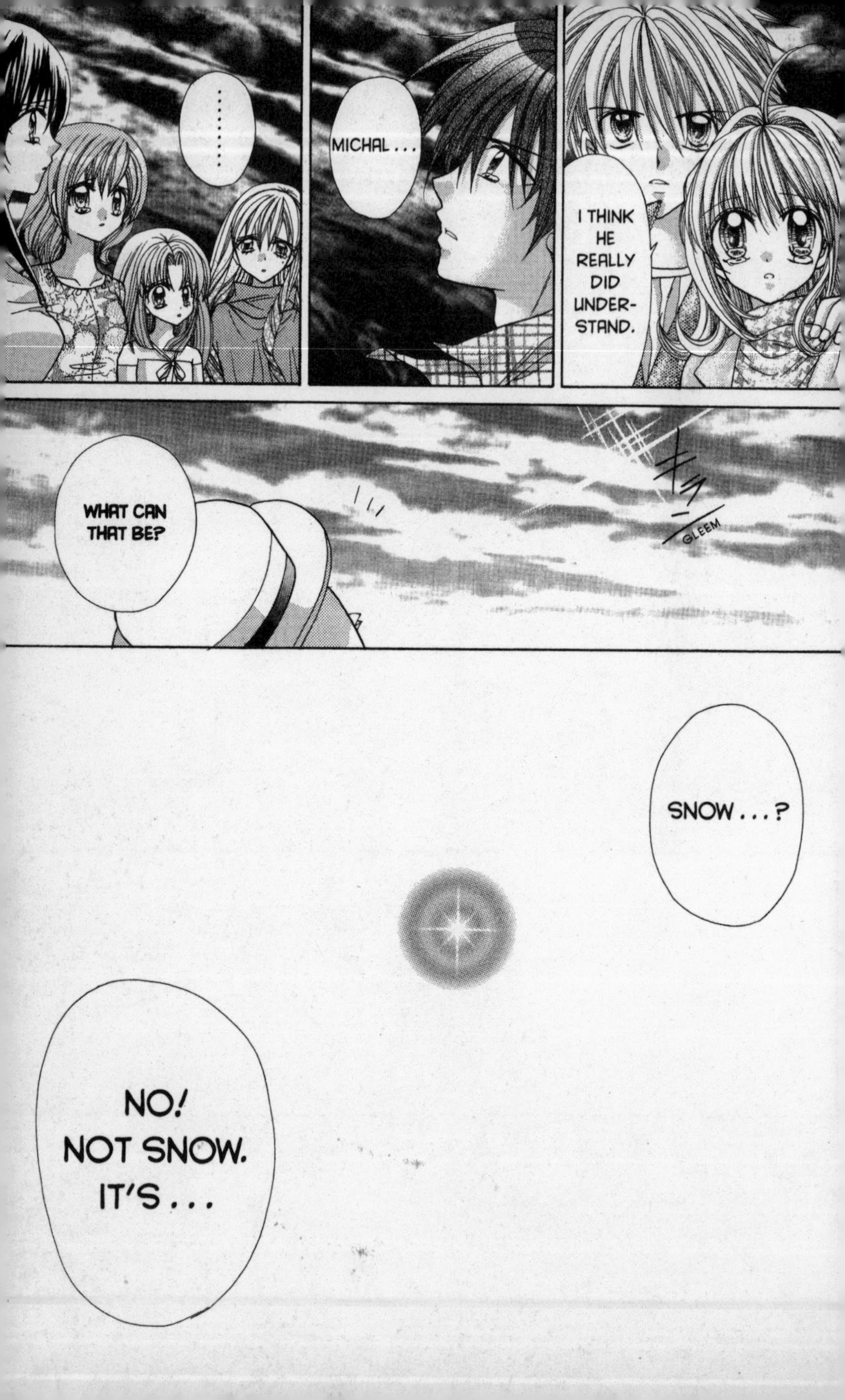
I THINK HE REALLY DID UNDER-STAND.
MICHAL . . .
......
GLEEM
WHAT CAN THAT BE?
SNOW . . . ?
NO! NOT SNOW. IT'S . . .

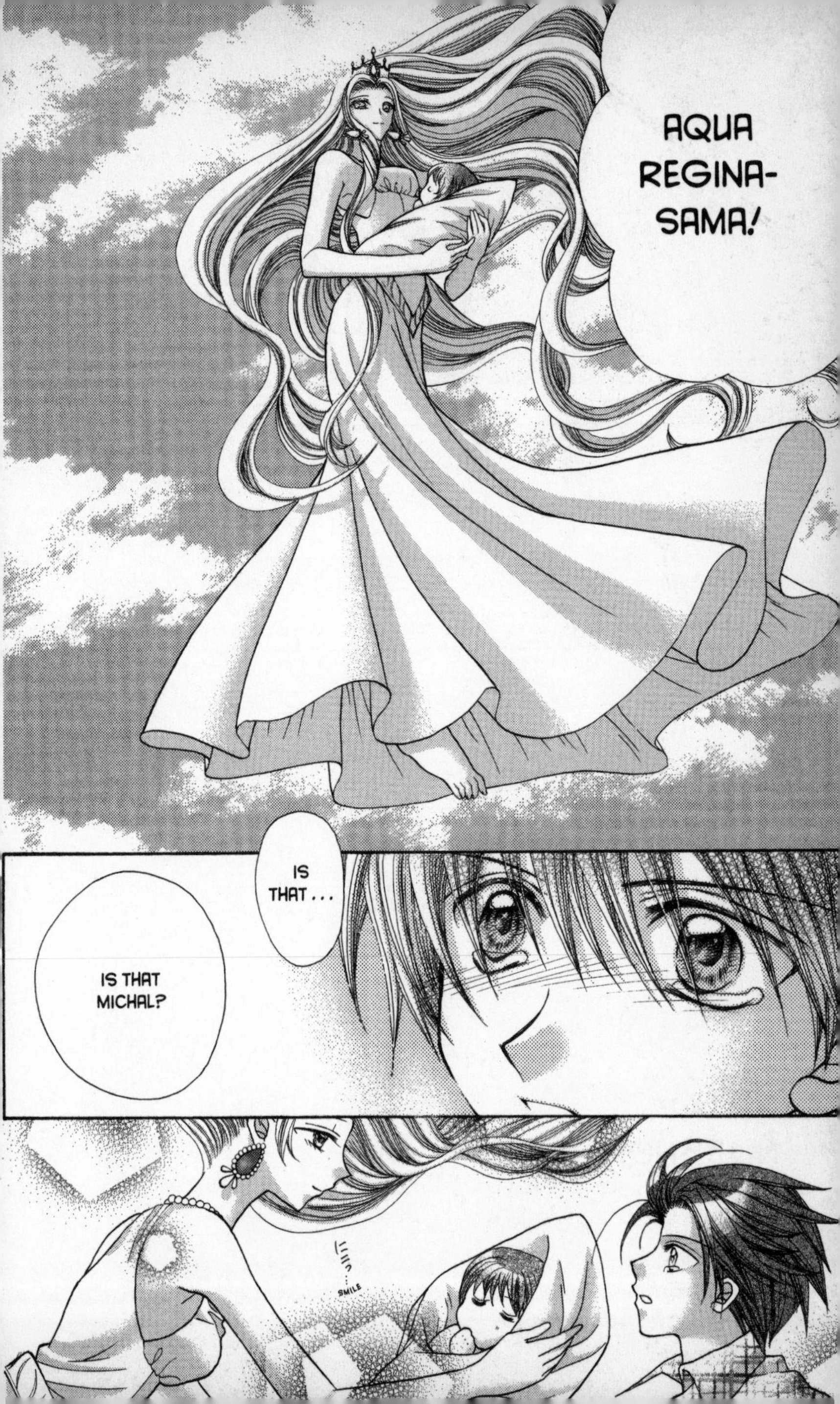
AQUA REGINA-SAMA!
IS THAT . . .
IS THAT MICHAL?
SMILE

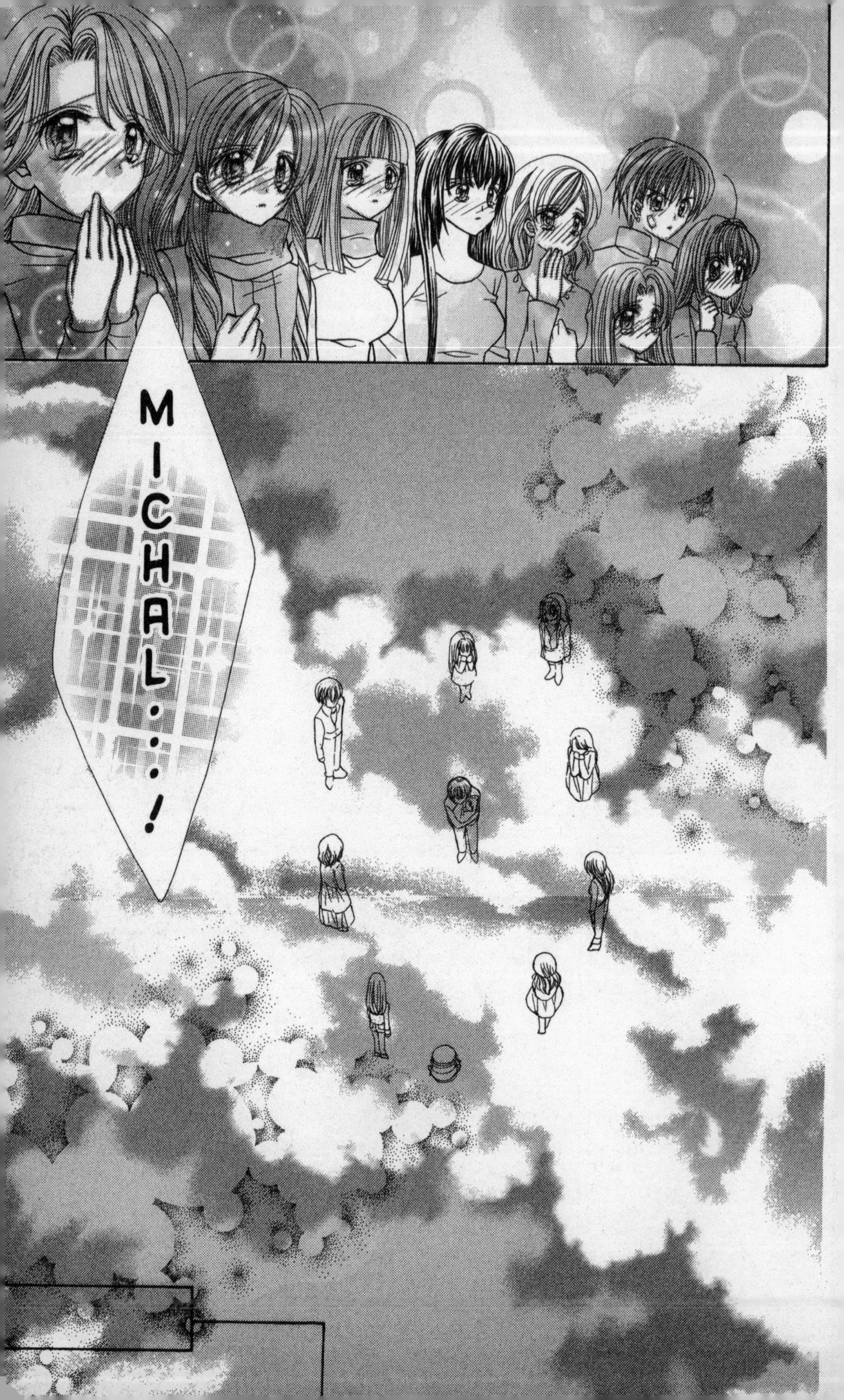
MICHAL...!

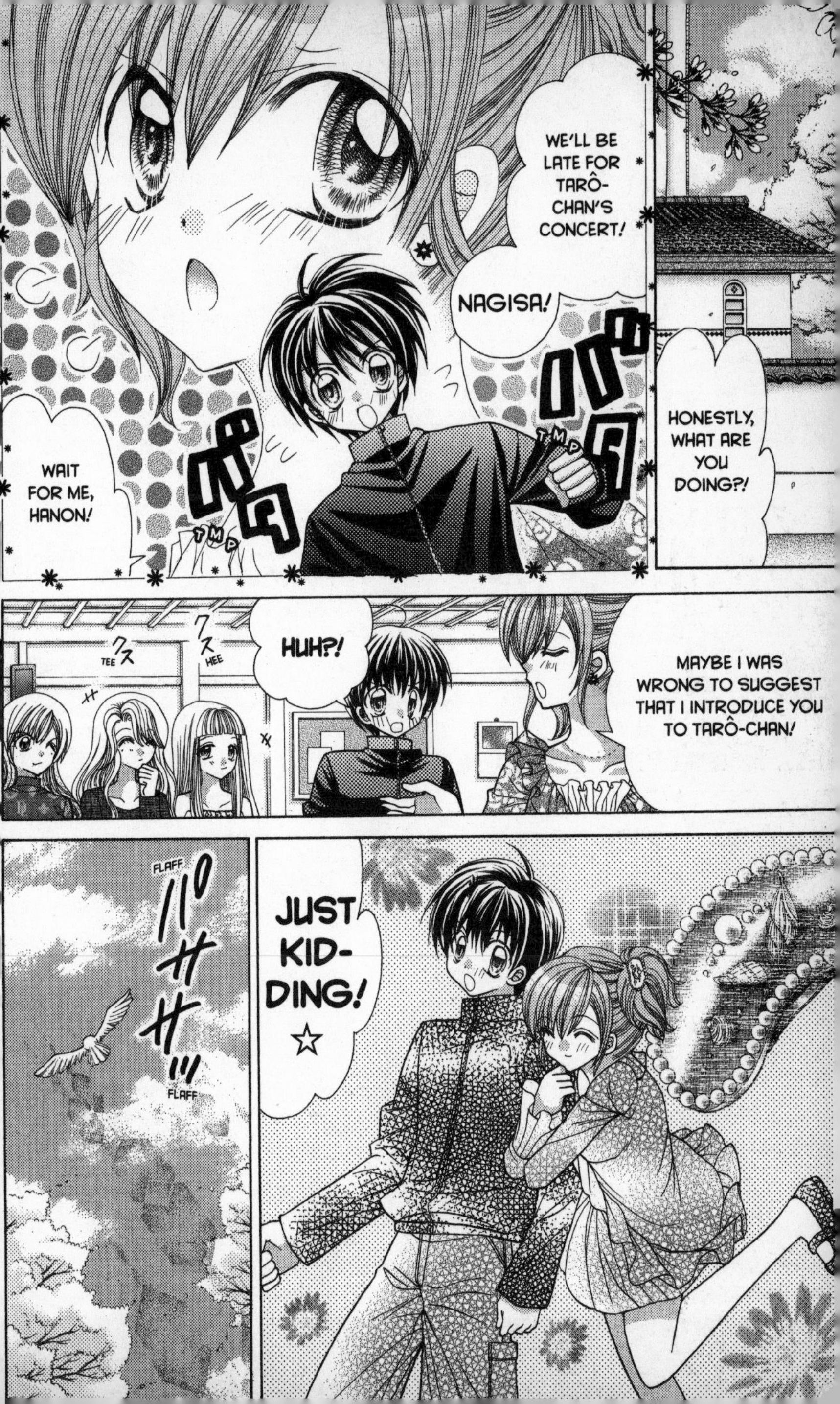
HONESTLY, WHAT ARE YOU DOING?!
WE'LL BE LATE FOR TARÔ-CHAN'S CONCERT!
NAGISA!
TMP
TMP
WAIT FOR ME, HANON!
MAYBE I WAS WRONG TO SUGGEST THAT I INTRODUCE YOU TO TARÔ-CHAN!
HUH?!
クス HEE
クス TEE
JUST KID-DING! ☆
FLAFF
FLAFF

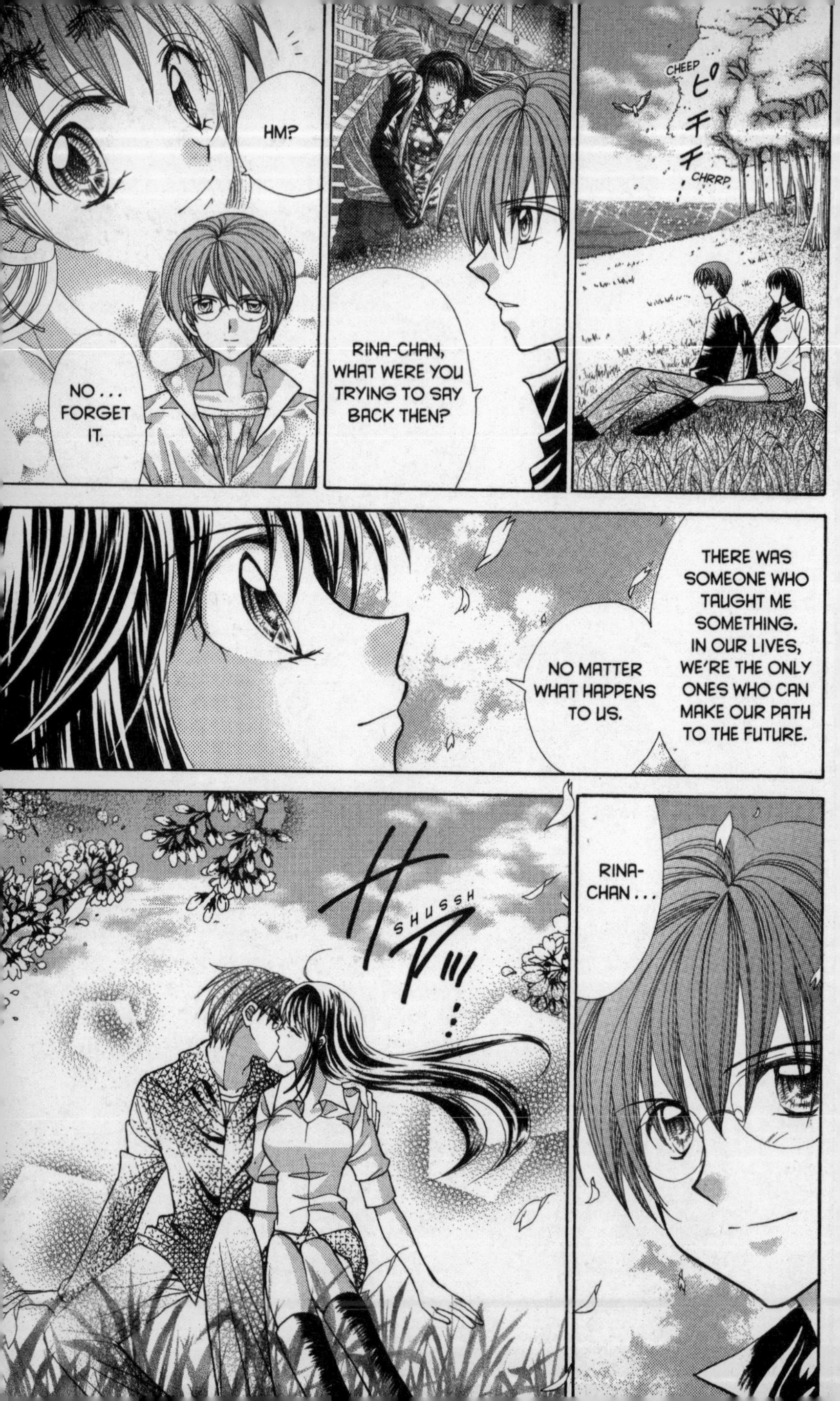
CHEEP
ピチチ
CHRRP
RINA-CHAN, WHAT WERE YOU TRYING TO SAY BACK THEN?
HM?
NO . . . FORGET IT.
THERE WAS SOMEONE WHO TAUGHT ME SOMETHING. IN OUR LIVES, WE'RE THE ONLY ONES WHO CAN MAKE OUR PATH TO THE FUTURE.
NO MATTER WHAT HAPPENS TO US.
RINA-CHAN . . .
SHUSSH

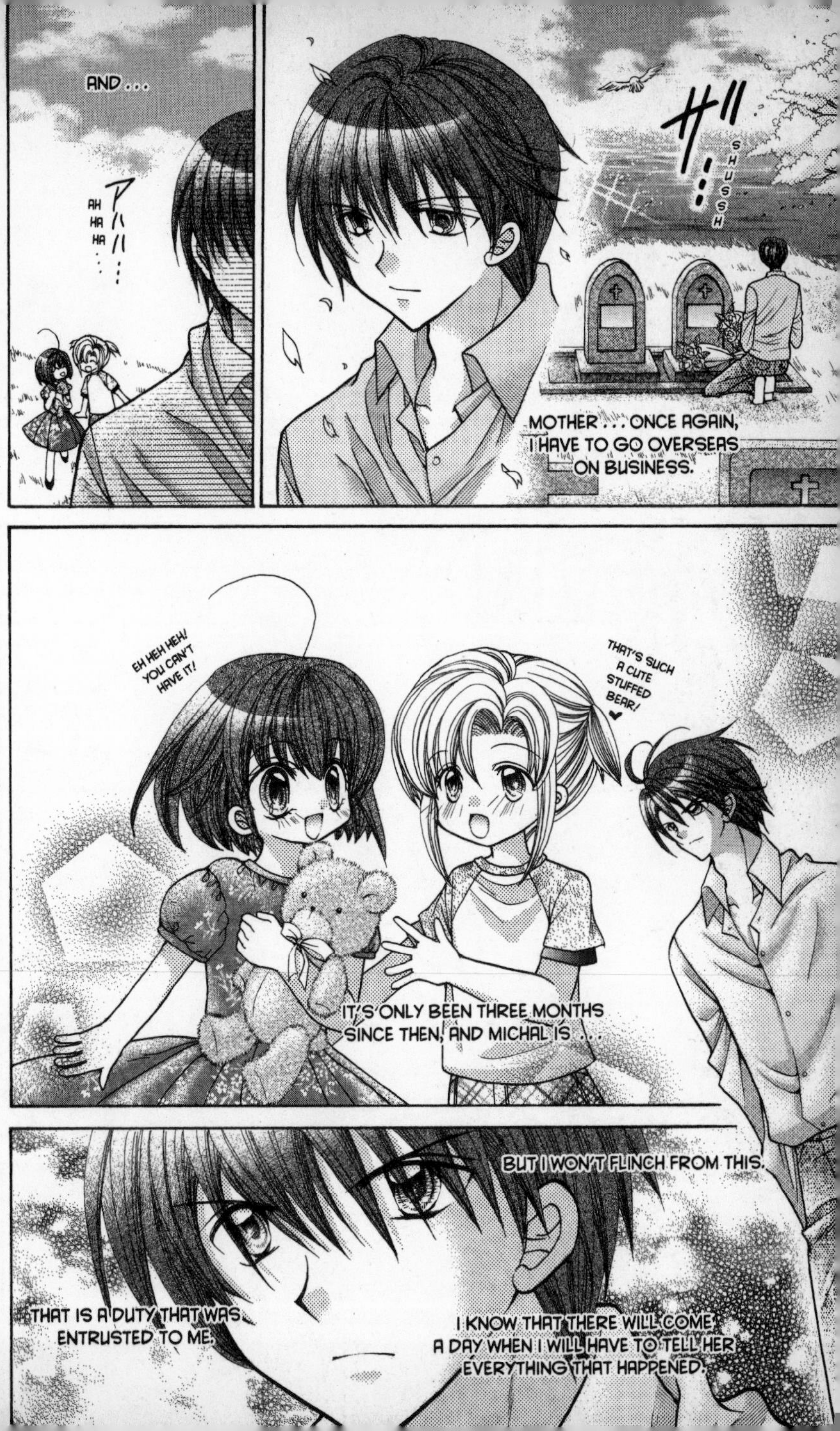
ザッ…
SHUSSH
MOTHER . . . ONCE AGAIN, I HAVE TO GO OVERSEAS ON BUSINESS.
AND . . .
アハハ…
AH HA HA . . .
THAT'S SUCH A CUTE STUFFED BEAR!
EH HEH HEH! YOU CAN'T HAVE IT!
IT'S ONLY BEEN THREE MONTHS SINCE THEN, AND MICHAL IS . . .
BUT I WON'T FLINCH FROM THIS.
I KNOW THAT THERE WILL COME A DAY WHEN I WILL HAVE TO TELL HER EVERYTHING THAT HAPPENED.
THAT IS A DUTY THAT WAS ENTRUSTED TO ME.

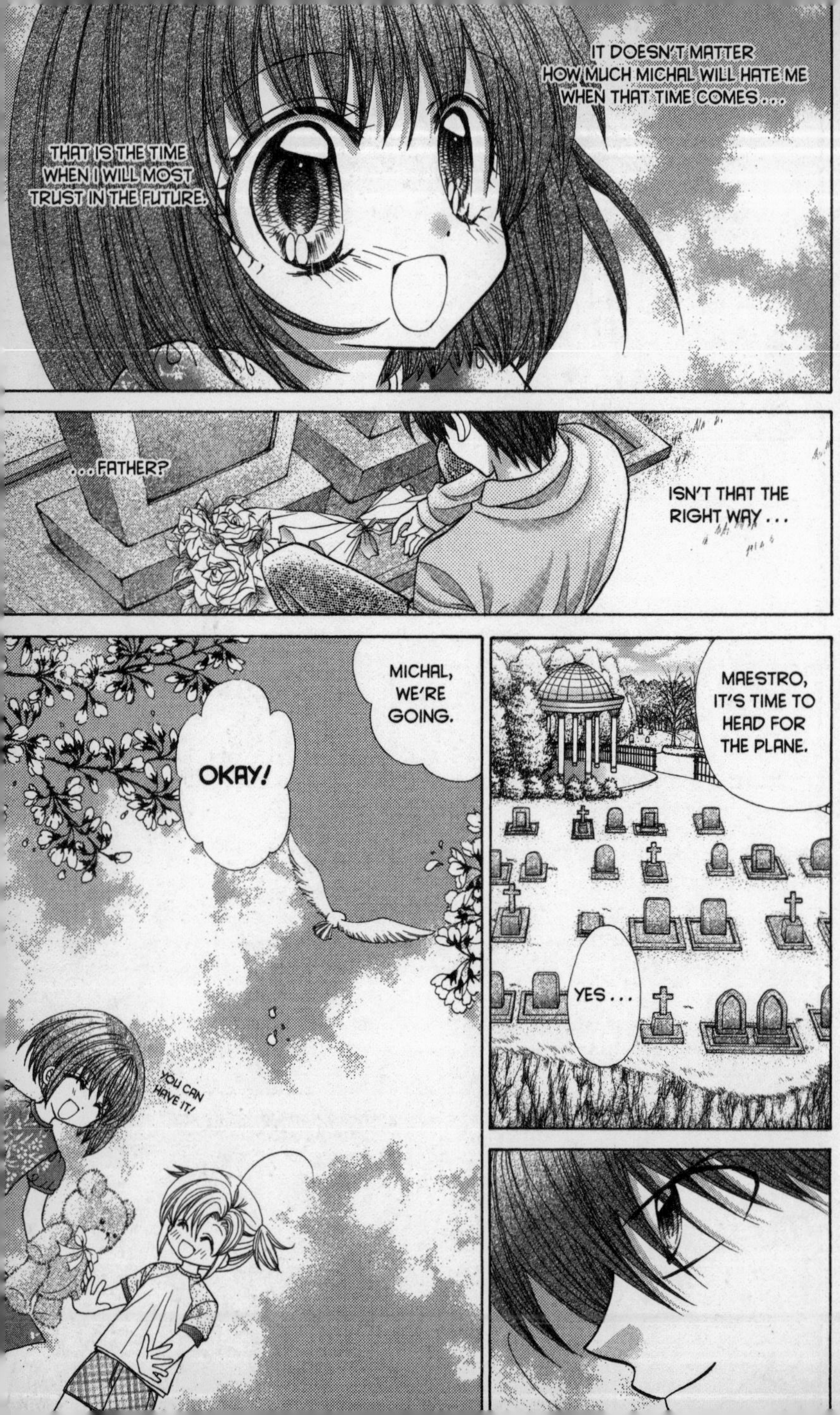
IT DOESN'T MATTER HOW MUCH MICHAL WILL HATE ME WHEN THAT TIME COMES . . .
THAT IS THE TIME WHEN I WILL MOST TRUST IN THE FUTURE.
ISN'T THAT THE RIGHT WAY . . .
. . . FATHER?
MAESTRO, IT'S TIME TO HEAD FOR THE PLANE.
YES . . .
MICHAL, WE'RE GOING.
OKAY!
YOU CAN HAVE IT!

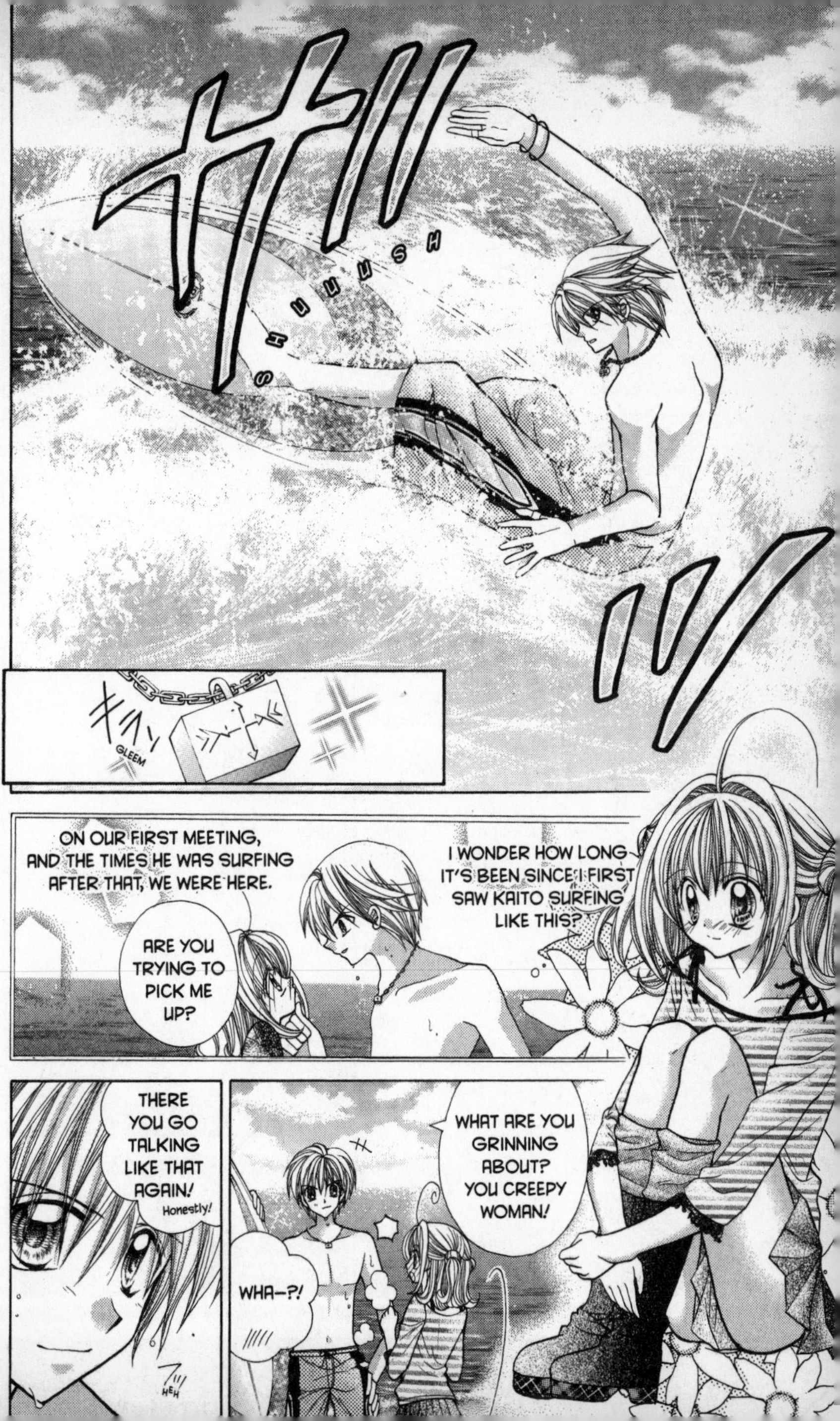
SHUUUSH
GLEEM
I WONDER HOW LONG IT'S BEEN SINCE I FIRST SAW KAITO SURFING LIKE THIS?
ON OUR FIRST MEETING, AND THE TIMES HE WAS SURFING AFTER THAT, WE WERE HERE.
ARE YOU TRYING TO PICK ME UP?
WHAT ARE YOU GRINNING ABOUT? YOU CREEPY WOMAN!
WHA-?!
THERE YOU GO TALKING LIKE THAT AGAIN!
Honestly!
HEH

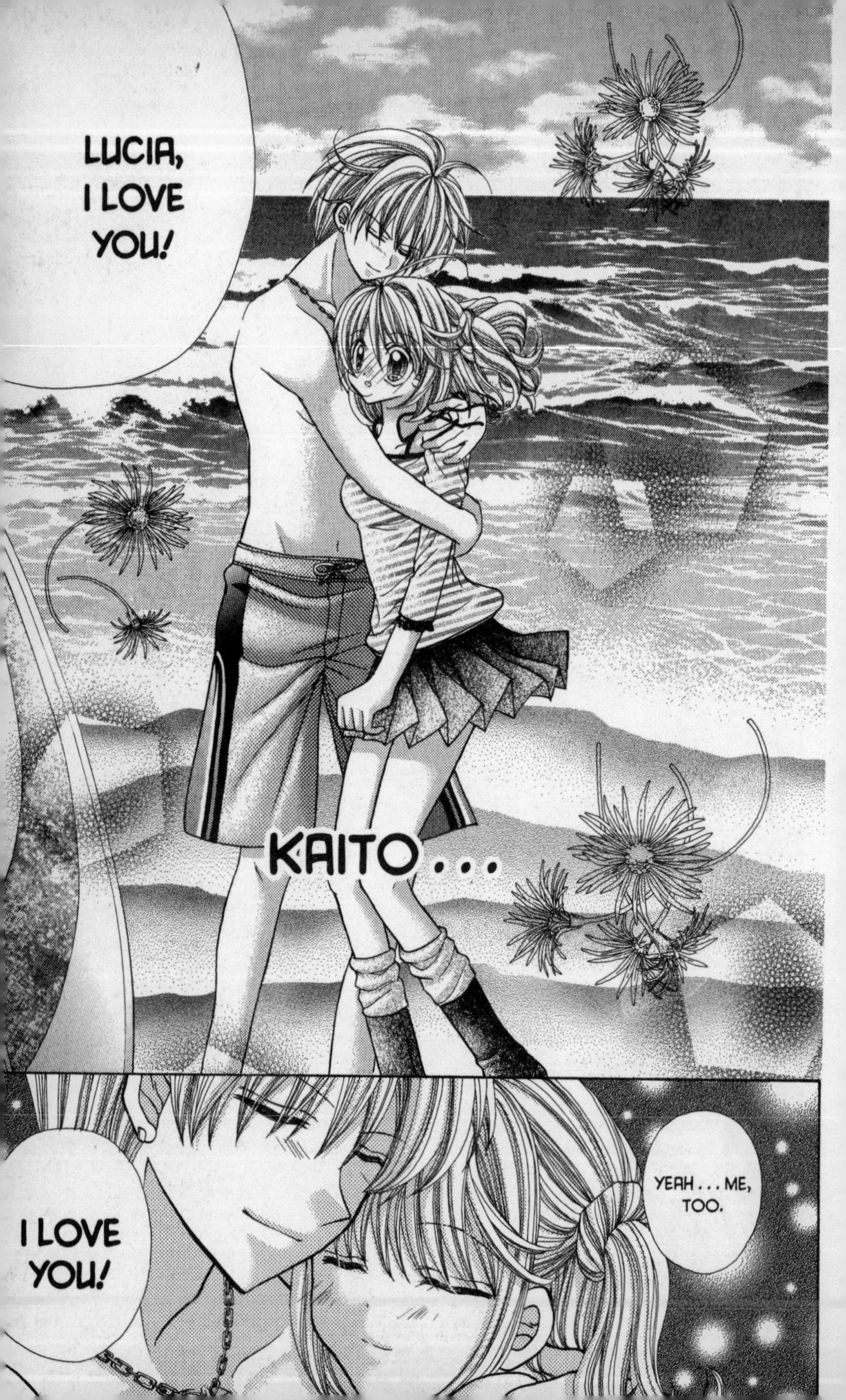
LUCIA, I LOVE YOU!
KAITO . . .
YEAH . . . ME, TOO.
I LOVE YOU!

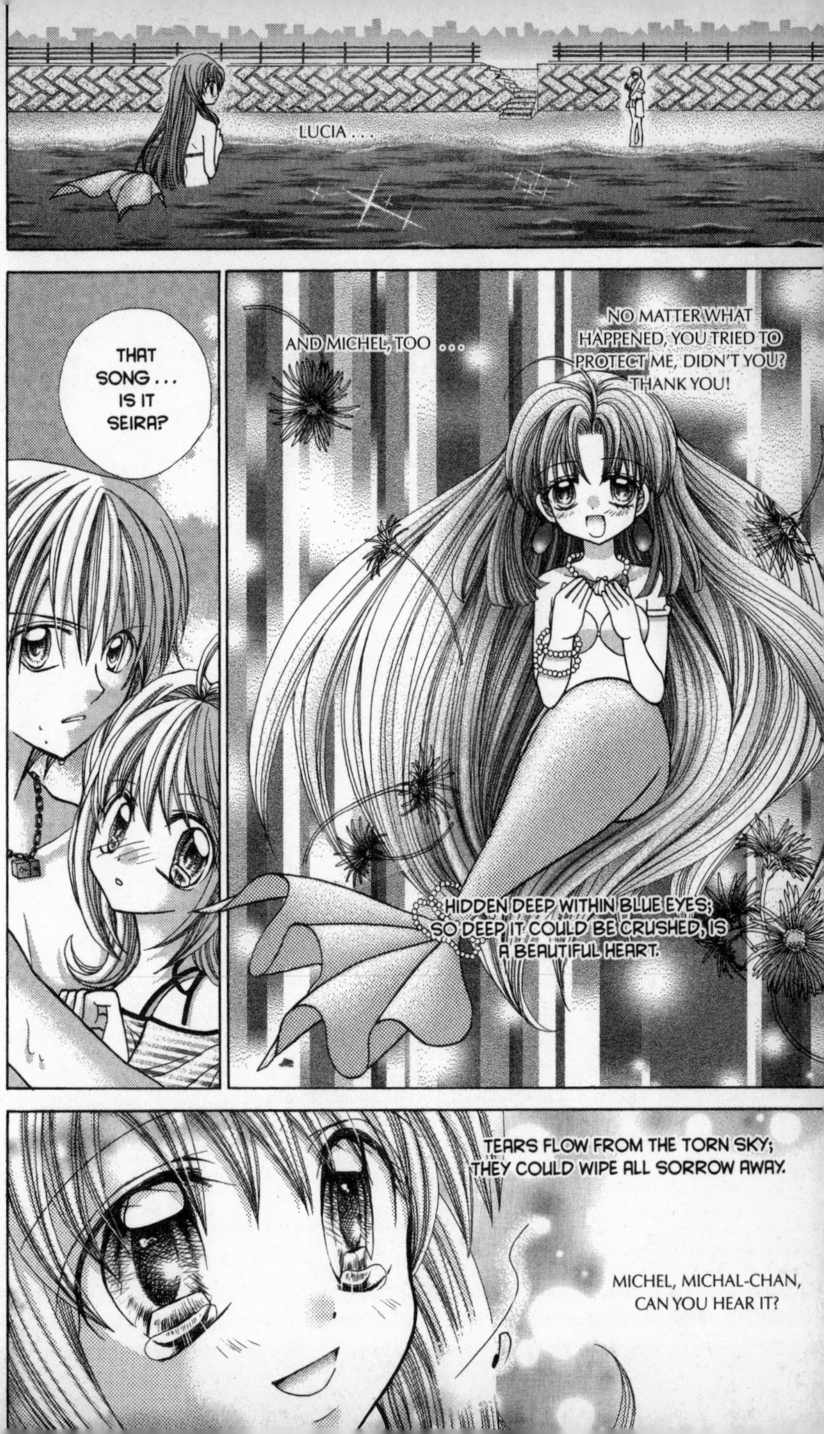
LUCIA . . .
NO MATTER WHAT HAPPENED, YOU TRIED TO PROTECT ME, DIDN'T YOU? THANK YOU!
AND MICHEL, TOO . . .
HIDDEN DEEP WITHIN BLUE EYES; SO DEEP IT COULD BE CRUSHED, IS A BEAUTIFUL HEART.
THAT SONG . . . IS IT SEIRA?
TEARS FLOW FROM THE TORN SKY; THEY COULD WIPE ALL SORROW AWAY.
MICHEL, MICHAL-CHAN, CAN YOU HEAR IT?

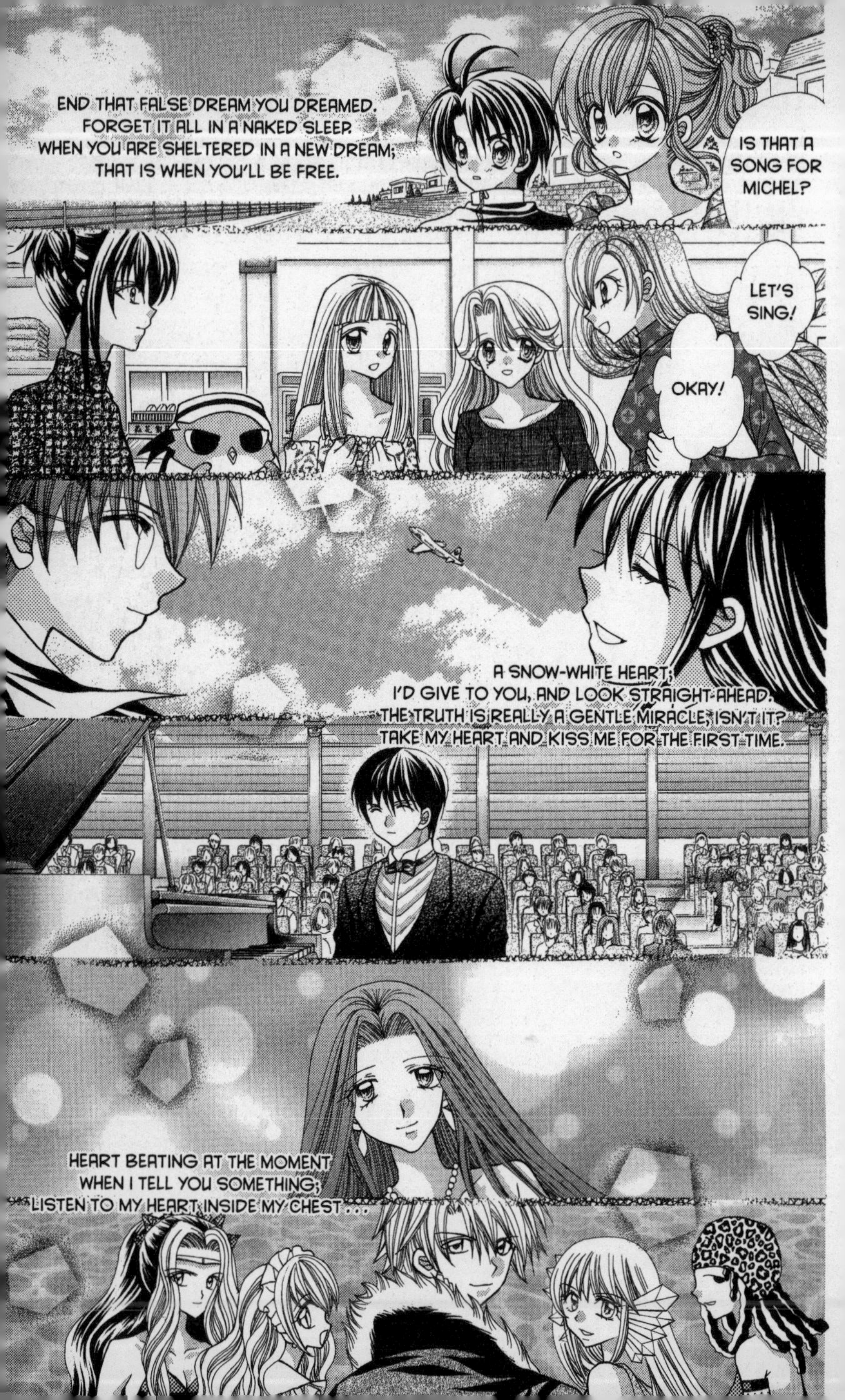
IS THAT A SONG FOR MICHEL?
END THAT FALSE DREAM YOU DREAMED. FORGET IT ALL IN A NAKED SLEEP. WHEN YOU ARE SHELTERED IN A NEW DREAM; THAT IS WHEN YOU'LL BE FREE.
LET'S SING!
OKAY!
A SNOW-WHITE HEART; I'D GIVE TO YOU, AND LOOK STRAIGHT AHEAD. THE TRUTH IS REALLY A GENTLE MIRACLE, ISN'T IT? TAKE MY HEART AND KISS ME FOR THE FIRST TIME.
HEART BEATING AT THE MOMENT WHEN I TELL YOU SOMETHING; LISTEN TO MY HEART INSIDE MY CHEST . . .

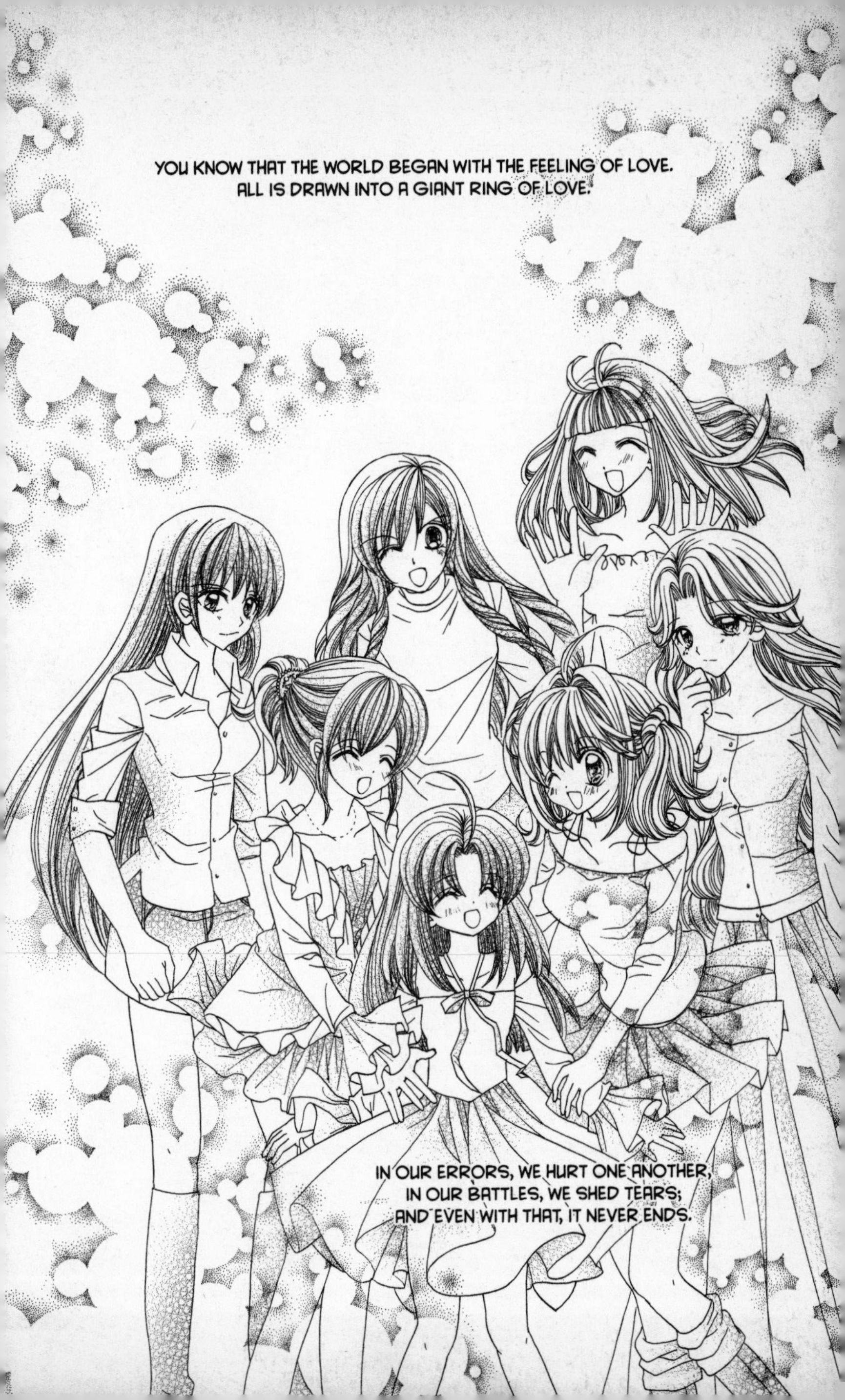
YOU KNOW THAT THE WORLD BEGAN WITH THE FEELING OF LOVE. ALL IS DRAWN INTO A GIANT RING OF LOVE.
IN OUR ERRORS, WE HURT ONE ANOTHER, IN OUR BATTLES, WE SHED TEARS; AND EVEN WITH THAT, IT NEVER ENDS.

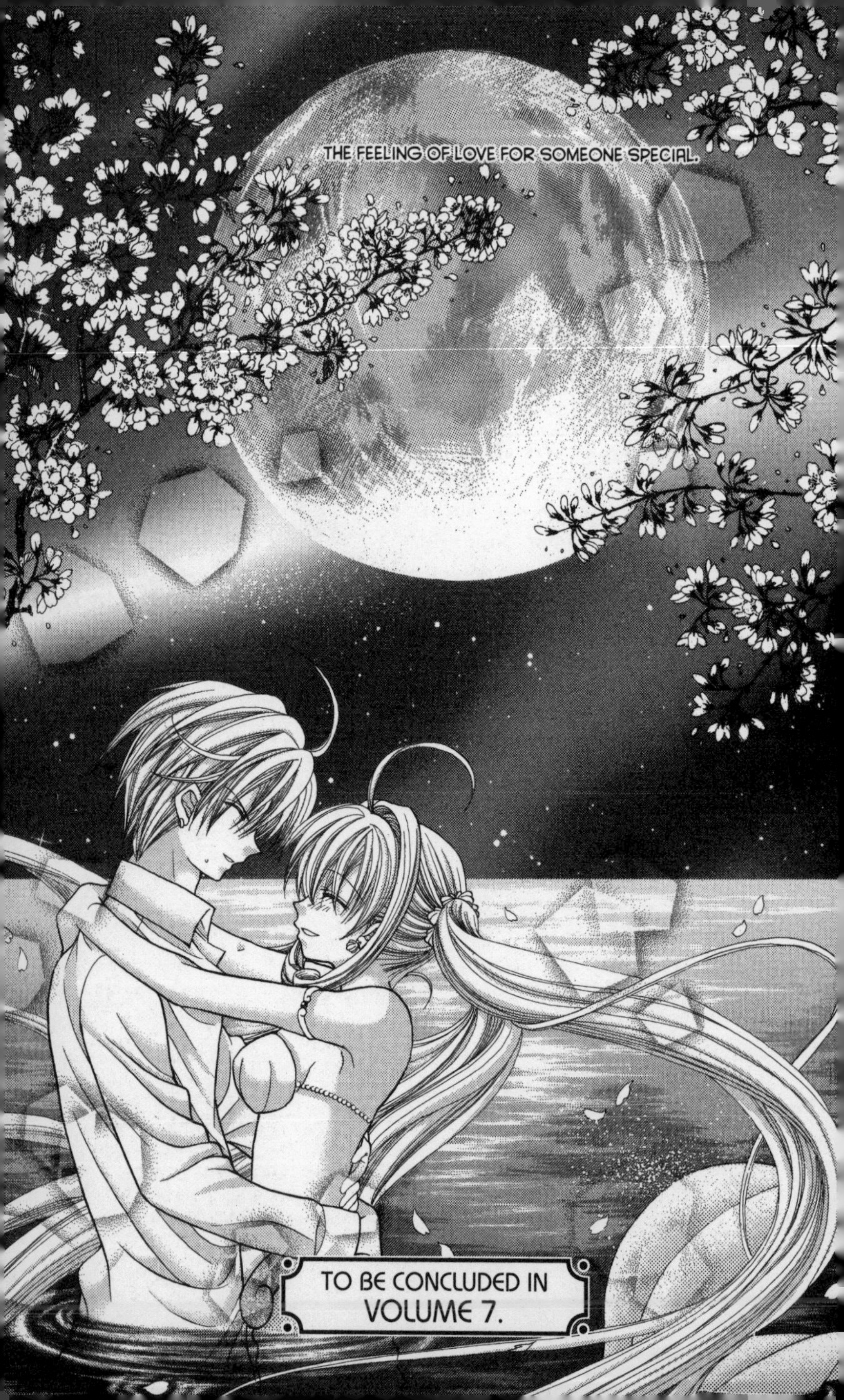
THE FEELING OF LOVE FOR SOMEONE SPECIAL.
TO BE CONCLUDED IN VOLUME 7.

About the Creator

Pink Hanamori
The Artist's True Face

Born on November 5th in Shizuoka Prefecture; Scorpio, Blood type AB. Entered the 31st Nakayoshi New Faces contest with the manga *Miss Dieter Heroine* in the year 2000. Her debut work was *Nakayoshi Haru-yasumi Land* (Nakayoshi Spring Break Land) in the year 2001. Her signature work is *Mermaid Melody Pichi Pichi Pitch*. She loves to play with dogs and talk a lot.

Translation Notes

Japanese is a tricky language for most Westerners, and translation is often more art than science. For your edification and reading pleasure, here are notes on some of the places where we could have gone in a different direction in our translation of the work, or where a Japanese cultural reference is used.

After-school date, page 6

As in the West, Japanese students must go to school Monday through Friday, but they are also required to attend a half day of classes on Saturday as well. So Sunday makes a reasonable date day. However, most couples don't want to wait an entire week for their next date, so after-school dates are very common.

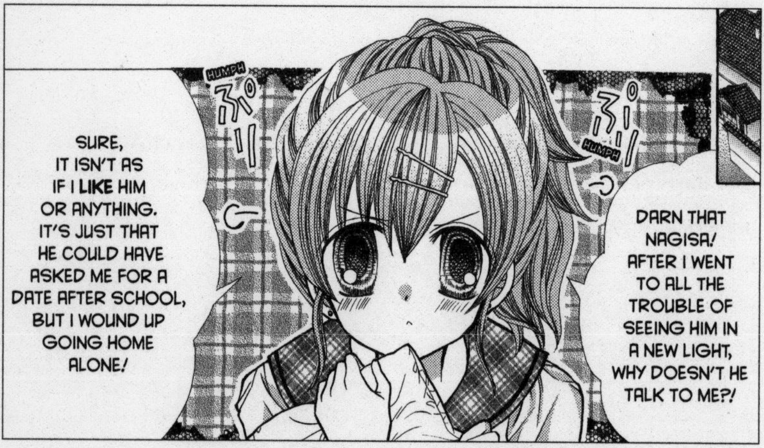
HUMPH
DARN THAT NAGISA! AFTER I WENT TO ALL THE TROUBLE OF SEEING HIM IN A NEW LIGHT, WHY DOESN'T HE TALK TO ME?!
HUMPH
SURE, IT ISN'T AS IF I **LIKE** HIM OR ANYTHING. IT'S JUST THAT HE COULD HAVE ASKED ME FOR A DATE AFTER SCHOOL, BUT I WOUND UP GOING HOME ALONE!

I'LL GIVE YOU EVERYTHING THAT I HAVE!
IF YOU AREN'T WITH ME, KAITO-KUN, THEN I DON'T SEE ANY REASON TO LIVE ANYMORE!

Michal's flashback, page 11

If the wording seems a little different from the wording in volume 5, it is. It was paraphrased for clarity in the Japanese, and this translation kept the paraphrasing.

Maru-pen, page 79

This is a crow-quill-type pen (when pressed harder, it makes a thicker line) that is used for drawing details.

G-pen, page 79

A flexible pen for drawing thin and thick lines. This is closer to a standard pen used by Japanese manga artists (although there are always a large number of exceptions).

Closed for the holidays, page 85

Actually most businesses stay open for Christmas Eve and Christmas Day. It is New Year's and the days just following that see the highest number of businesses closed for the holidays.

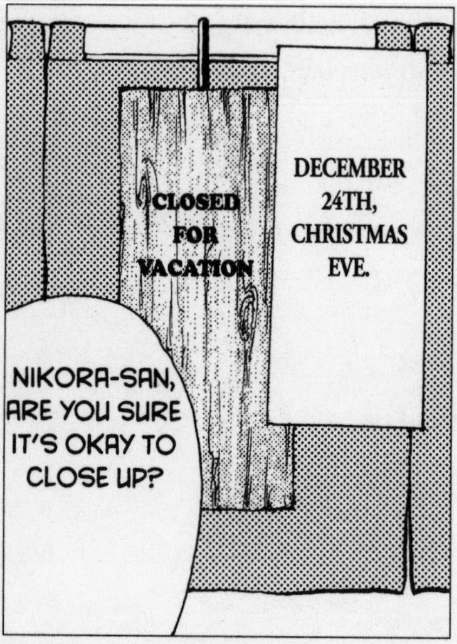
DECEMBER 24TH, CHRISTMAS EVE.
CLOSED FOR VACATION
NIKORA-SAN, ARE YOU SURE IT'S OKAY TO CLOSE UP?

Bump of Chicken, Kinki Kids, etc., page 123

These are names of famous recording vocalists and bands in Japan. Most of them are bestselling bands for whom a new album means a new number one listing on the sales charts.

Paw pads, meatballs, page 157

In the Japanese version, the asterisk note explains that the kanji for paw pads can be read as meatballs in English. This translation chose to reverse the note since it makes more sense to the English-language readers that way.

PAW PADS...

POMER

...ARE MEATBALLS! POM!

IN JAPANESE, THE WORD FOR PAW PADS ARE WRITTEN WITH THE KANJI FOR MEAT AND BALLS.

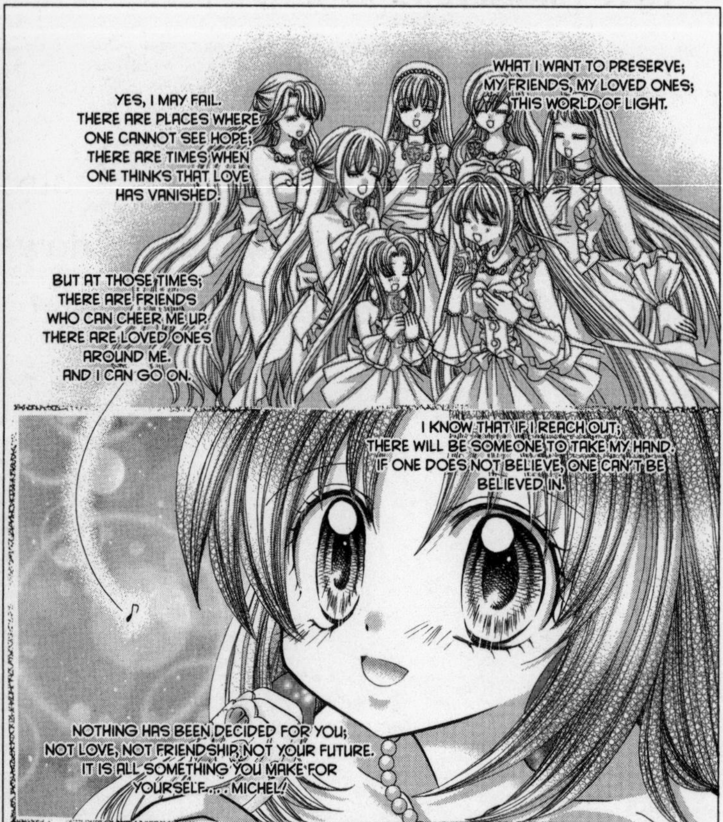
WHAT I WANT TO PRESERVE; MY FRIENDS, MY LOVED ONES; THIS WORLD OF LIGHT.
YES, I MAY FAIL. THERE ARE PLACES WHERE ONE CANNOT SEE HOPE; THERE ARE TIMES WHEN ONE THINKS THAT LOVE HAS VANISHED.
BUT AT THOSE TIMES; THERE ARE FRIENDS WHO CAN CHEER ME UP. THERE ARE LOVED ONES AROUND ME. AND I CAN GO ON.
I KNOW THAT IF I REACH OUT; THERE WILL BE SOMEONE TO TAKE MY HAND. IF ONE DOES NOT BELIEVE, ONE CAN'T BE BELIEVED IN.
NOTHING HAS BEEN DECIDED FOR YOU; NOT LOVE, NOT FRIENDSHIP, NOT YOUR FUTURE. IT IS ALL SOMETHING YOU MAKE FOR YOURSELF.... MICHEL!

Music lyrics, page 202

As with any poetry, no translation will be able to hit the full meaning. Usually something must be sacrificed. In that vein, since some of the lyrics refer directly to characters and events in this series, this translation chose not to mimic the meter of the original lyrics. Rather I chose to give a more literal translation of meaning of the words.

We're pleased to present a preview of

Pichi Pichi Pitch

volume 7. This volume will be available in English October 30, 2007, but for now, you'll have to make do with Japanese!

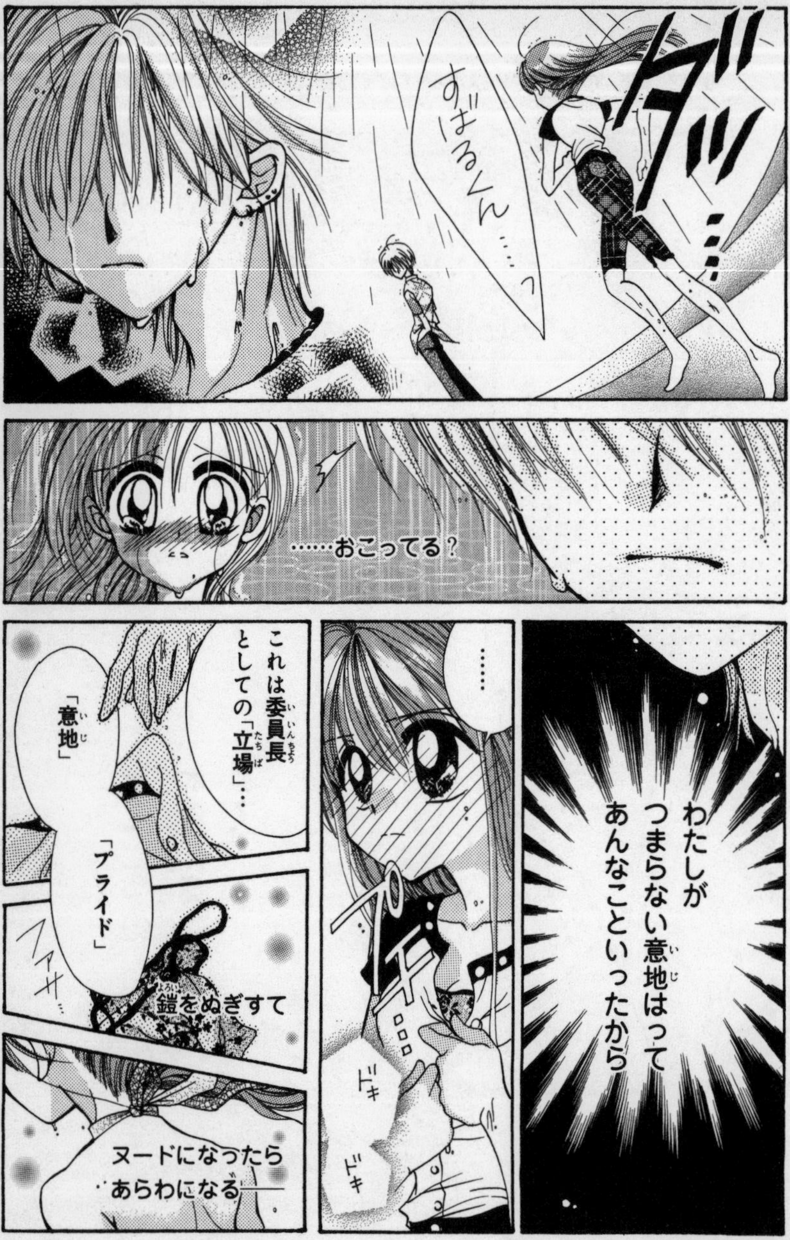
ダッ……
すばるくん……っ
……おこってる？
わたしが
つまらない意地はって
あんなこといったから
……
ドキ
ドキ
これは委員長
としての「立場」…
「意地」
「プライド」
ファサ…
鎧をぬぎすてて
ヌードになったら
あらわになる――

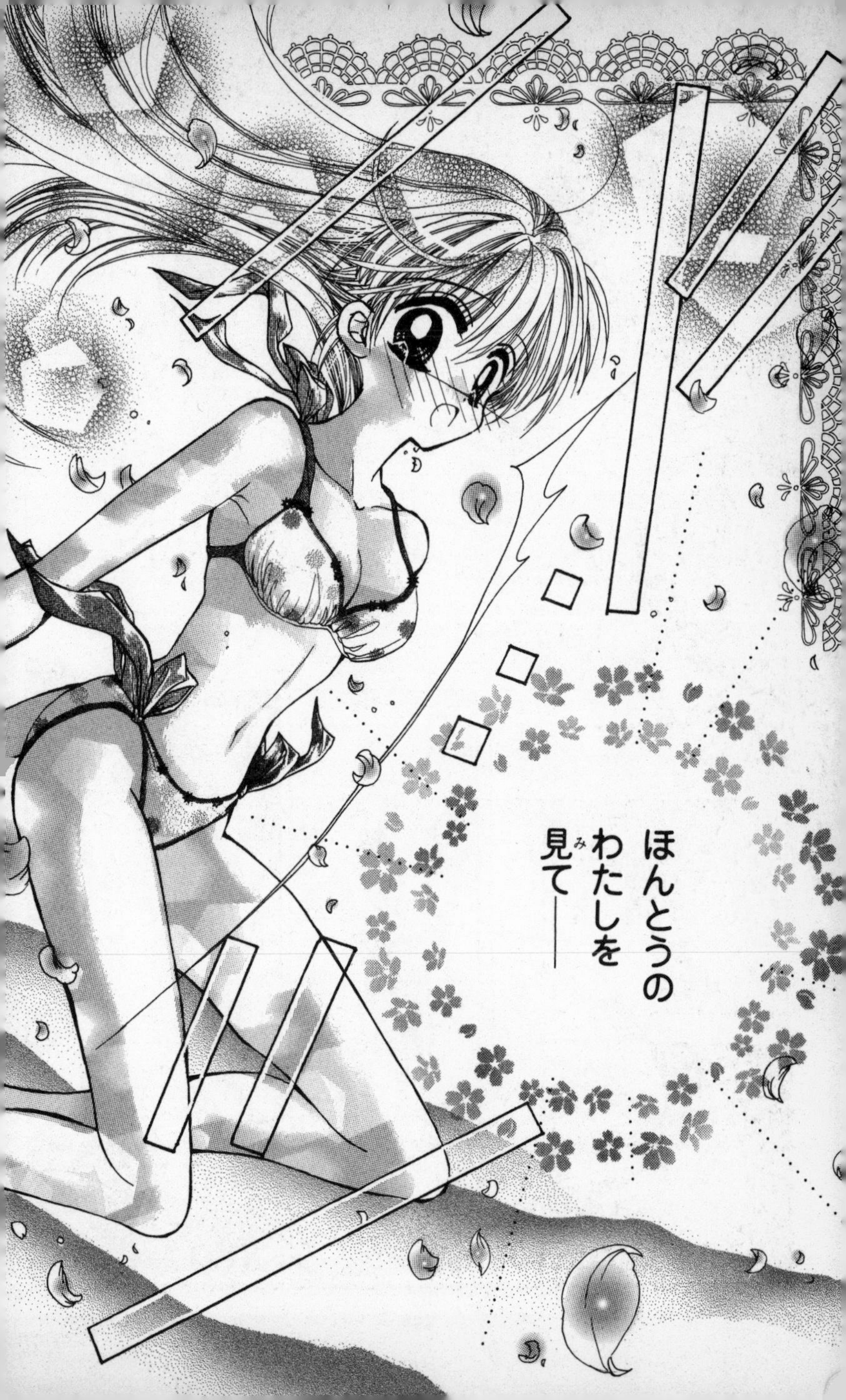
ほんとうのわたしを見て――

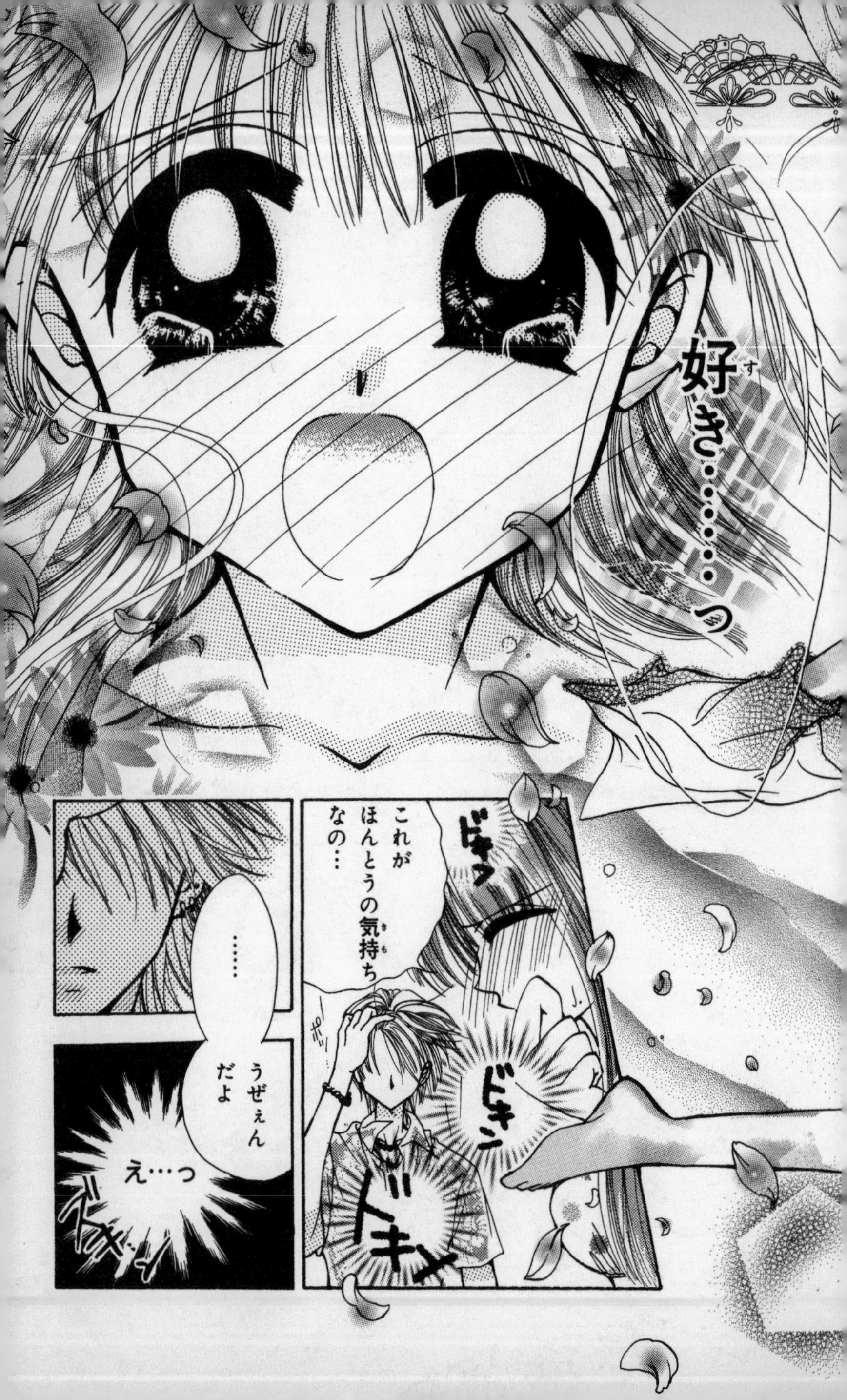
好き………っ
これがほんとうの気持ちなの…
ドキッ
ポッ
ドキン
ドキン
……
うぜぇんだよ
え…っ
ズキ…ン

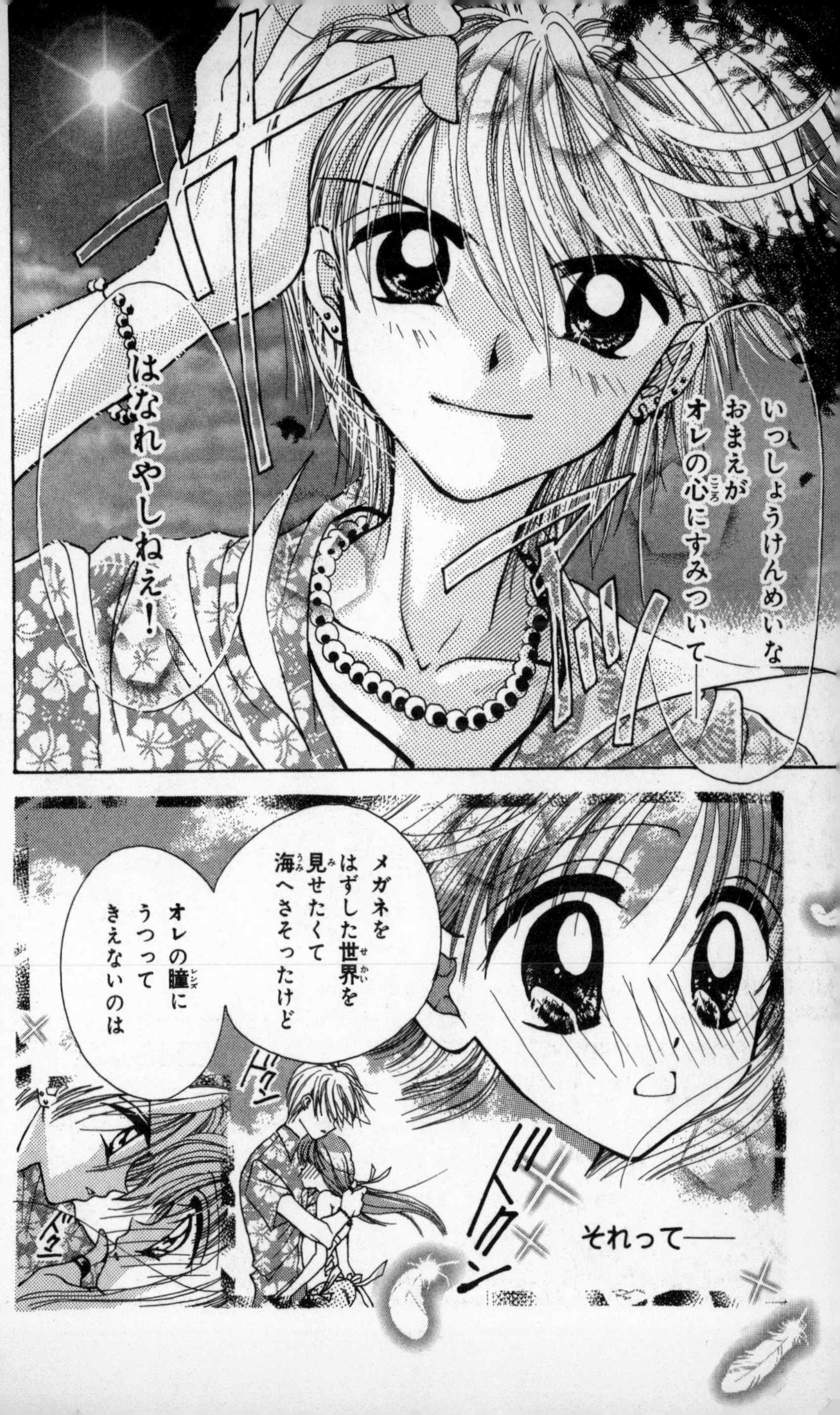

いっしょうけんめいな
おまえが
オレの心にすみついて――
はなれやしねえ!
メガネを
はずした世界を
見せたくて
海へさそったけど
オレの瞳に
うつって
きえないのは
それって――

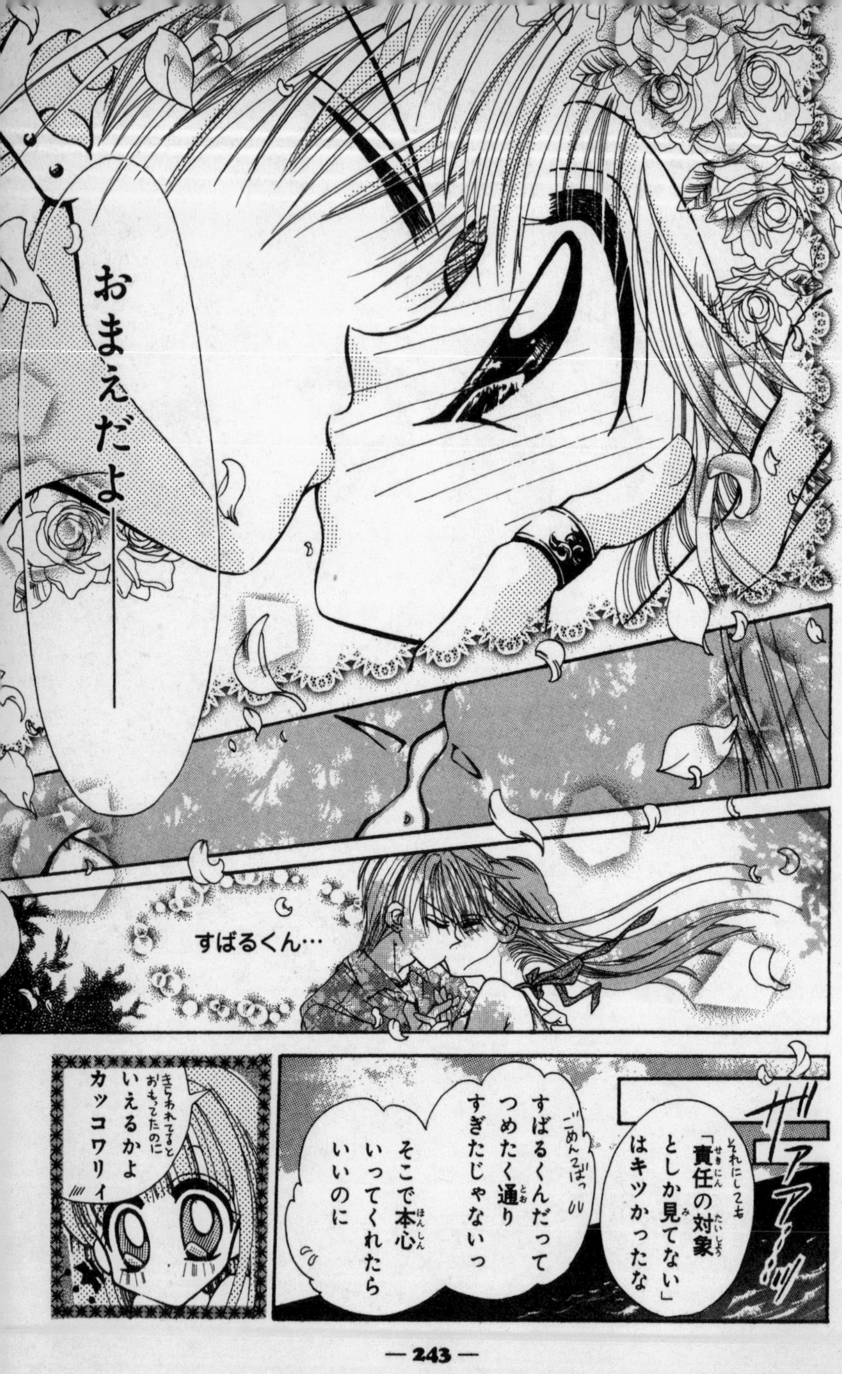
おまえだよ――
すばるくん…
それにしても「責任の対象としか見てない」はキツかったな
ザァァ…
ごめんてばっ
すばるくんだってつめたく通りすぎたじゃないっ
そこで本心いってくれたらいいのに
きらわれてるとおもってたのに
いえるかよカッコワリィ

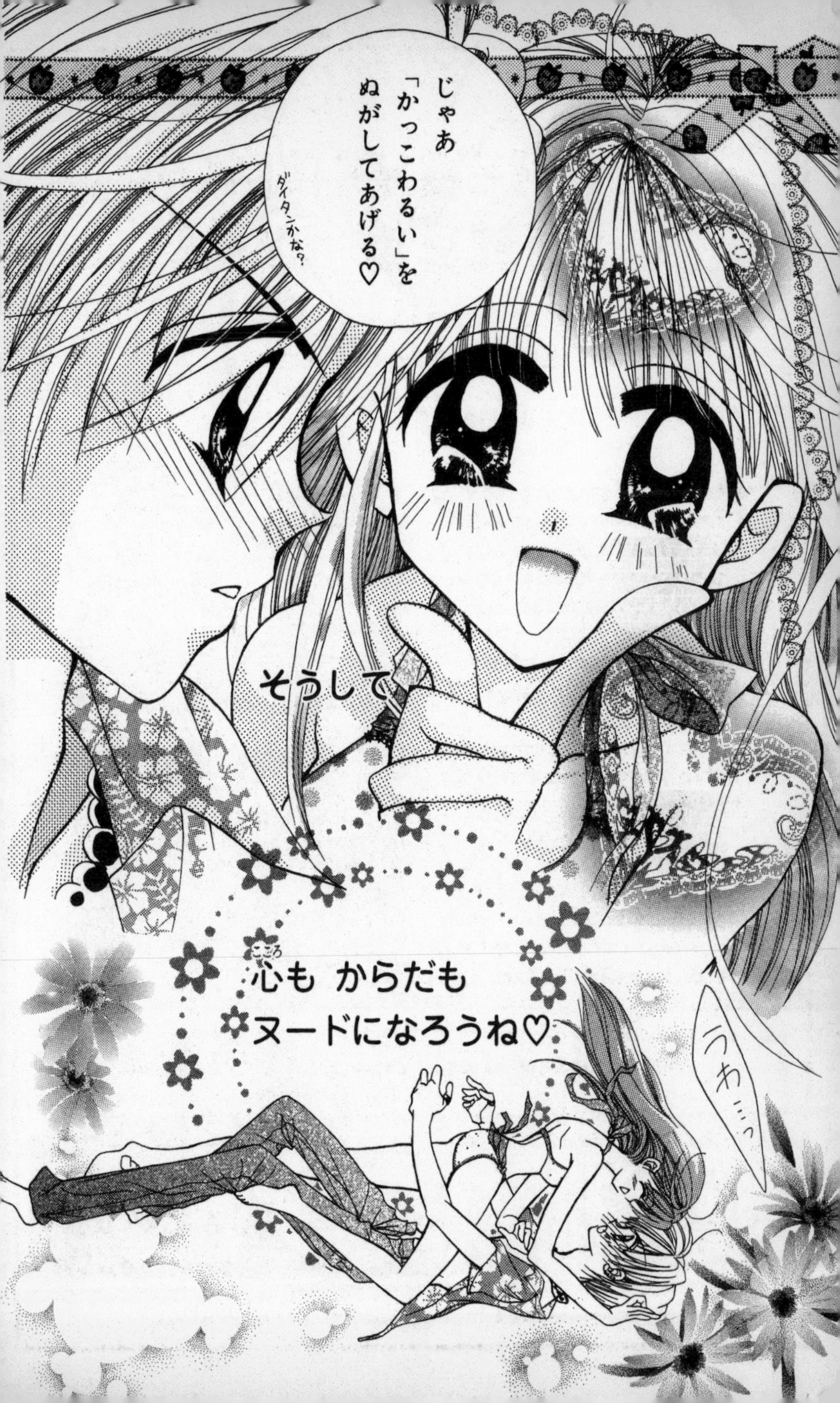
じゃあ「かっこわるい」をぬがしてあげる♡
ダイタンかな?
そうして
心も からだも
ヌードになろうね♡
うわっ

MY HEAVENLY HOCKEY CLUB

BY AI MORINAGA

WHERE THE BOYS ARE!

Hana Suzuki loves only two things in life: eating and sleeping. So when handsome classmate Izumi Oda asks Hana—his major crush—to join the school hockey club, convincing her proves to be a difficult task. True, the Grand Hockey Club is full of boys—and all the boys are super-cute—but, given a choice, Hana prefers a sizzling steak to a hot date. Then Izumi mentions the field trips to fancy resorts. Now Hana can't wait for the first away game, with its promise of delicious food and luxurious linens. Of course there's the getting up early, working hard, and playing well with others. How will Hana survive?

MY HEAVENLY HOCKEY CLUB
1 AI MORINAGA

Special extras in each volume! Read them all!

VISIT WWW.DELREYMANGA.COM TO:

- Read sample pages
- View release date calendars for upcoming volumes
- Sign up for Del Rey's free manga e-newsletter
- Find out the latest about new Del Rey Manga series

RATING AGES T 13+

DEL REY MANGA デルレイ

The Otaku's Choice™

Mamotte! LOLLIPOP

MICHIYO KIKUTA

BOY CRAZY

Junior high schooler Nina is ready to fall in love. She's looking for a boy who's cute and sweet—and strong enough to support her when the chips are down. But what happens when Nina's dream comes true . . . twice? One day, two cute boys literally fall from the sky. They're both wizards who've come to the Human World to take the Magic Exam. The boys' success on this test depends on protecting Nina from evil, so now Nina has a pair of cute magical boys chasing her everywhere! One of these wizards just might be the boy of her dreams . . . but which one?

Michiyo Kikuta
Mamotte!
LOLLIPOP

Special extras in each volume! Read them all!

VISIT WWW.DELREYMANGA.COM TO:
- Read sample pages
- View release date calendars for upcoming volumes
- Sign up for Del Rey's free manga e-newsletter
- Find out the latest about new Del Rey Manga series

RATING T AGES 13+

DEL REY MANGA デルレイ

The Otaku's Choice

KITCHEN PRINCESS

STORY BY MIYUKI KOBAYASHI
MANGA BY NATSUMI ANDO
CREATOR OF ZODIAC P.I.

HUNGRY HEART

Najika is a great cook and likes to make meals for the people she loves. But something is missing from her life. When she was a child, she met a boy who touched her heart—and now Najika is determined to find him. The only clue she has is a silver spoon that leads her to the prestigious Seika Academy.

Attending Seika will be a challenge. Every kid at the school has a special talent, and the girls in Najika's class think she doesn't deserve to be there. But Sora and Daichi, two popular brothers who barely speak to each other, recognize Najika's cooking for what it is—magical. Could one of the boys be Najika's mysterious prince?

Special extras in each volume! Read them all!

Sugar Sugar Rune

BY MOYOCO ANNO

QUEEN OF HEARTS

Chocolat and Vanilla are young witch princesses from a magical land. They've come to Earth to compete in a contest—whichever girl captures the most hearts will become queen! While living in a boarding school, they must make as many boys fall in love with them as possible if they want to achieve their goal. Standing against them are a pair of rival princes looking to capture their hearts because they want to be king!

There's danger for the witch-girls, though: If they give their hearts to a human, they may never return to the Magical World....

Ages: 10 +

Special extras in each volume! Read them all!

SHUGO CHARA!

PEACH-PIT

Creators of *Dears* and *Rozen Maiden*

Everybody at Seiyo Elementary thinks that stylish and super-cool Amu has it all. But nobody knows the *real* Amu, a shy girl who wishes she had the courage to truly be herself. Changing Amu's life is going to take more than wishes and dreams—it's going to take a little magic! One morning, Amu finds a surprise in her bed: three strange little eggs. Each egg contains a Guardian Character, an angel-like being who can give her the power to be someone new. With the help of her Guardian Characters, Amu is about to discover that her true self is even more amazing than she ever dreamed.

PEACH-PIT
CREATORS OF DEARS AND ROZEN MAIDEN
SHUGO CHARA! 1

Special extras in each volume! Read them all!

VISIT WWW.DELREYMANGA.COM TO:

- Read sample pages
- View release date calendars for upcoming volumes
- Sign up for Del Rey's free manga e-newsletter
- Find out the latest about new Del Rey Manga series

RATING T AGES 13+

DEL REY MANGA デルレイ

The Otaku's Choice

You're going the wrong way!

Manga is a completely different type of reading experience.

To start at the *beginning*, go to the *end*!

That's right! Authentic manga is read the traditional Japanese way—from right to left. Exactly the opposite of how American books are read. It's easy to follow: Just go to the other end of the book, and read each page—and each panel—from right side to left side, starting at the top right. Now you're experiencing manga as it was meant to be!